A HISTORY OF
AMERICAN LITERATURE,
1607-1765

one of its founders.

A HISTORY OF
American
Literature
1607-1765

Moses Coit Tyler

Cornell University Press

ITHACA, NEW YORK

Originally published 1878 by G. P. Putnam's Sons

Reissued 1949 by Cornell University Press

Second printing 1961
Third printing 1966

Printed in the United States of America by the
Vail-Ballou Press, Inc., Binghamton, New York

Foreword

OF A thousand histories of American literature published since Samuel L. Knapp brought out his lectures on the subject in 1829, almost all have perished. The one enduring writer, the author whom nobody has superseded, is Moses Coit Tyler, whose *A History of American Literature, 1607–1765* appeared in two volumes in 1878, to be followed by *The Literary History of the American Revolution, 1763–1783,* again in two volumes, in 1897. Despite differences in scale, the four books can be conveniently considered as a single work covering the literary history of the future United States down to the formal recognition of American independence.

American scholarship has not yet set aside the work of Tyler. As in the more magnificent case of Gibbon, later investigators have found new materials, unearthed new authors, corrected errors, and altered emphases, but Tyler remains the supreme master in his field. Nor is the comparison with Gibbon otiose. If Gibbon is in six stately volumes, Tyler is in four; and the care lavished by the historian of Rome upon source material was not, all things considered, proportionately greater than the labor of the American to assemble his. Tyler has, like Gibbon, solidity of information, a fine sense of order, a powerful personal style; he shares Gibbon's good sense and good judgment—that reference of historic fact to life and experience which bookish writers seldom make; and if Gibbon chronicles the decline of one empire, Tyler consciously records the beginnings of another. His great arc of time and the universal stage of his imperial tragedy give Gibbon an immense imaginative advantage, since, for all his insight into the nature of life amid the lonely spaces of the New World, Tyler, moving through a lesser

Foreword

gamut of time, is incapable of painting the vast and melancholy landscapes which Bryant, which Cooper, which Parkman could create to rival the majesty and breadth of Rome.

Of course Tyler was merely a literary historian. The affable condescension of this phrase reminds me of Jane Austen's outburst against those who, asked what they were reading, answered, "Only a novel." However vague the definition of literary history may be, for Tyler it did not begin and end in the library. "The American people, starting into life . . . ," he said at the beginning of his task,

have been busy . . . recording their intellectual history in laws, manners, institutions, in battles with man and beast and nature, in highways, excavations, edifices, in pictures, in statues, in written words. It is in written words that this people, from the very beginning, have made the most confidential and explicit record of their minds.

In the preface to *The Literary History of the American Revolution* he wrote:

Instead of fixing our eyes almost exclusively . . . upon statesmen and generals, upon party leaders, upon armies and navies, upon Congress, upon parliament, upon the ministerial agents of a brain-sick king, or even upon that brain-sick king himself, . . . we here for the most part turn our eyes away toward certain persons hitherto much neglected, in many cases wholly forgotten—toward persons who, as mere writers, . . . nourished the springs of great historic events by creating and shaping and directing public opinion during all that robust time; who, so far as we here regard them, wielded only spiritual weapons; who still illustrate . . . the majestic operation of ideas, the creative and decisive play of spiritual forces, in the development of history, in the rise and fall of nations, in the aggregation and the division of races.

Long before the founding of the *Journal of the History of Ideas,* it is evident, Tyler was practicing mature cultural history. He desired, he says, to present the soul of the American people through literature "as an instrument of humane and immediate utility"; he desired to create an "unbiased register" of the "very brain and heart" of the Americans, first as they struggled to maintain themselves as colonists, and afterward as they struggled to maintain themselves as an independent nation. Surely his is a great theme; and it is the

Foreword

failure of most literary historians thus greatly to conceive their subject that sets them below and apart from him.

Like every other historian who has endured, Tyler was emphatically the child of his age; and the stigmata of the nineteenth century are as visible on him as are the marks of the Enlightenment in Gibbon. Certain of these qualities are limitations. His is an Anglo-Saxon history; it is a New England history; it is a true-blue Protestant history; it is a history which records the moral triumph of a pure and virtuous patriotism over a "brain-sick" king, a corrupt parliament, and an invading army. He makes small reference to any literature in a modern foreign language, to any system of ideas outside the British Empire, to any Catholic, Latin, Celtic, or Mediterranean values. For him American writing is born out of an "Elizabethan" world which is, as it were, a piece of Victorian mythology; and when he tells us in the noble preface to *The Literary History of the American Revolution* that his "eirenic" purpose is to promote understanding, respect, and kindness "on both sides of the ocean," we understand that the Atlantic stretches only to the Solent and the Thames, not to the Seine or to what used to be called the German Ocean. And of course he could not know the discoveries of the twentieth century, like the finding of a New England poet to rival Mistress Bradstreet or the Pepysian diaries of "Col. William Byrd of Westover, in Virginia, Esq[u]."

But he had also the great lost virtues of the nineteenth century mind—that manliness, that civic gravity, that fullness of intellect for which we vainly search most literary criticism today. What he says of the style of Captain John Smith is true of himself: "As a writer his merits are really great—clearness, force, vividness, picturesque and dramatic energy, a diction racy and crisp." He really cared for the rhetorical structure of the English sentence; he has the rich modulation of the best Victorian prose; he drops apothegms by the way as if wisdom were as much a part of the duty of the literary historian as scholarship or aesthetic analysis. He is unashamedly of the opinion that literature has its full meaning in society, that it is written by men speaking to men, and that judgments to be passed upon it spring from its usefulness to the public weal. He has the enjoyment of persons, as Dickens had; he has humor, which once or

Foreword

twice betrays him into tediousness but more often leads him to savor more shrewdly the rich, belligerent personalities among whom he moves as if he were their contemporary and equal. He has the picture-making quality of Macaulay or Carlyle, evidenced, for example, in the brilliant introduction of Mather Byles to the reader. Because he writes with a large discourse, the chapter on "The Party of the Loyalists and Their Literature" is one of the noblest in the field of literary history; yet, four or five chapters earlier, he had been chuckling over Jonathan Trumbull. The range and variety of his sympathies are truly catholic; he lacks mainly an intuitive understanding of the mystics—otherwise he would be fully the correlative of his difficult, varied, and fascinating material. Others may know more about travel literature or New England theology or the development of philosophy in colonial America; no one, I think, has a more comprehensive grasp of the order, nature, and value of American writing from the founding of Jamestown to the Peace of Paris. In the true sense Tyler's work is classical—the discussion of a great theme by a great writer.

HOWARD MUMFORD JONES

Peacham, Vermont
June 28, 1949

Publisher's Note

IN this reissue of Tyler's *A History of American Literature*, the preface and text of the first edition of 1878 have been strictly followed except in the numbering of the footnotes. In the notes themselves titles and *ibid.*'s have been interchanged to conform to new paging. Changes made in the printings and editions of 1879, 1881, and 1897 are added in bracketed notes in the present edition, as are likewise most of the marginal notes that Tyler put in his correction set of the two volumes of the first edition. The changes made in 1879 and 1881 were chiefly corrections of errors, typographical and otherwise. A few substantial changes were made in 1897, when Tyler rewrote parts of the preface and several notes.

Unless otherwise indicated in the bracketed notes, it should be assumed that a correction appeared first in 1881. When Tyler's marginal notes are quoted as saying that a correction or addition was made in 1896 or in the "revised ed.," the edition meant is, of course, that of 1897.

Preface

IT is my purpose to write the history of American literature from the earliest English settlements in this country, down to the present time. I hope to accomplish the work within the space of three or four volumes. Each of these volumes will cover a distinct period in the intellectual life of the American people; and while between the several volumes there will exist the tie of mutual interpretation and of historical consecutiveness, it is intended that each shall be, with reference to the epoch which it portrays, a complete and independent work.

Such unity and completeness have been aimed at in the present volumes, which, together, may be described as a history of the rise of American literature at the several isolated colonial centres, where at first each had its peculiar literary accent; of the growth of this sporadic colonial literature in copiousness, range, flexibility, in elegance and force, and especially in tendency toward a common national accent; until, finally, in 1765, after all the years of our minority and of our filial obedience had been lived, the scattered voices of the thirteen colonies were for the first time brought together and blended in one great and resolute utterance:—an utterance expressive of criticism upon the parental control wielded over us by England, of dissent from that control, and at last of resistance to it; an utterance which meant, among other things, that the thirteen colonies were no longer thirteen colonies but a single nation only, with all its great hopes and great fears in common, with its ideas, its determinations, its literature, in common likewise. The real ending of our colonial epoch, the real beginning of our revolutionary epoch, coincided in that tremendous year of disenchantment, the year 1765. That year,

Preface

therefore, fixes the limit of the present volumes; for in these volumes I have tried to tell the story of American literary activity during the time of our contented subordination to the European commonwealth out of which we came.

It is possible that the scope of this work is well enough indicated in the words just written; yet to prevent misconception, I venture to state my plan a little more explicitly. I have not undertaken to give an indiscriminate dictionary of all Americans who ever wrote anything, or a complete bibliographical account of all American books that were ever written. It is our literary history only, that I have undertaken to give;—that is, the history of those writings, in the English language, produced by Americans, which have some noteworthy value as literature, and some real significance in the literary unfolding of the American mind. But within the barriers fixed by the nature of this scheme, my work does aspire to be exhaustive. I have endeavored to examine the entire mass of American writings, during the colonial time, so far as they now exist in the public and private libraries of this country; and in the exercise of a most anxious judgment, and of a desire for completeness that has not grown weary even under physical fatigue, I have tried in these volumes to make an appropriate mention of every one of our early authors whose writings, whether many or few, have any appreciable literary merit, or throw any helpful light upon the evolution of thought and of style in America, during those flourishing and indispensable days.*

In the composition of a work of this kind, it is a very grave judicial

---

[* A note on the first page of the preface in Tyler's corrected copy of the 1878 edition reads: "Re-write first two paragraphs." Actually, in the 1897 edition the first three paragraphs were replaced by a single paragraph, as follows:

"In the two volumes here devoted to the History of American Literature prior to the American Revolution, I have not undertaken to give either a dictionary of all Colonial Americans who ever wrote anything, or a bibliographical list of all American writings that have survived to us from the Colonial Time. It is our early literary history that I here endeavor to set forth;—that is, the history of those writings produced by Americans during the period of our undisturbed subordination to England, which have some noteworthy value as literature, and some real significance in the literary unfolding of the American mind. But within the barriers fixed by the nature of this scheme, my work does aspire to be exhaustive. I have tried to examine the entire mass of American writings, during the Colonial Time, so far as they now exist in the public and private libraries of this country; and in the exercise of a most anxious judgment, and

Preface

responsibility that the author is forced to assume; it is also a very sacred responsibility. With reference to every name presented to him, there arises the debate, first, over its admission into the history at all; and, secondly, if admitted, over the amount of prominence to be given to it. Upon these two questions, scarcely any two persons can ever exactly agree. As to my own solution of these questions, I can only say that I have studied, as I believe, every American writer of the colonial time, in his extant writings; I have included him within this history or have excluded him from it, after fair inspection of his claims; and I have given to every writer whom I have admitted, just so much room as was demanded by my own sense of his relative literary importance, and by my own view of the necessary adjustment of historical proportions in this book. Upon no topic of literary estimation have I formed an opinion at second hand. In every instance, I have examined for myself the work under consideration. Wherever, upon any subject, I have consciously used the opinion of another, I have made specific acknowledgment of my indebtedness; and by constant reference in the foot-notes to the sources of my information, I have tried to help others in testing my own statements, and in prosecuting similar studies for themselves. Having, after the utmost painstaking, reached my own conclusions, I have endeavored to utter them frankly, accepting the responsibility of them; and yet, so various are human judgments that I may not dare to hope that any other student of the subject will in all particulars agree with me.

Some difference of opinion, also, is likely to exist over the question of weaving into the text of a history of literature, passages from the authors who are described in it. First of all, let it be mentioned that to do this skilfully is by no means a saving of labor for the literary historian: indeed, after the great matters of construction have been settled, no part of his task is more difficult than this; none requires a daintier touch, a more sensitive judgment, or a literary sense more delicate and alert. It would be far easier to write a history of litera-

---

of a desire for completeness that has not grown weary even under physical fatigue, I have aimed in these volumes to make an appropriate mention of every one of our early authors whose writings, whether many or few, have any appreciable literary merit, or throw any helpful light upon the evolution of thought and of style in America, during those flourishing and indispensable days."]

Preface

ture without illustrative quotations than with them. But in the service of his art, the true literary man can never think of his own ease as an offset to the pleasure of doing his work well; and for one, I do not see how a history of literature can be well done, or be of much use, without the frequent verification and illustration of its statements by expertly chosen examples from the authors under study. Unless such examples are given, the most precise, clear, and even vivid delineations of literary characteristics must, for those who have not read the authors spoken of, fade away into pallor and vagueness, and after a time become wearisome; while the whole work, as a presentation of literature, will seem, as Motley once wittily said to George Ticknor, "a kind of Barmecide's feast, in which the reader has to play the part of Shacabac, and believe in the excellence of the lamb stuffed with pistachio nuts, the flavor of the wines, and the perfume of the roses, upon the assertion of the entertainer, and without assistance from his own perceptions." [1] On the general theory, therefore, which I hold of this department of the historical art, I should certainly have introduced into my history specimens of the literature concerning which I write; but there is an additional reason why I ought to do so in the present case. The literature of which I have here given an account, is a neglected literature, and probably must always remain neglected: the most of the books of which it is composed have not been read and cannot be read by many people now living; since those books exist in but few copies, and lurk as rare and costly literary treasures in a small number of libraries. To give only abstract descriptions of such a literature, and to assume that my readers can verify my statements, by their own recollections of it, or by immediate and easy references to it, would be mere trifling. The only course left to me, if I would render my labors of any real benefit to those for whom I write, is to give freely, and with as much discrimination as I possess, such portions of our early literature as may form a sort of terse anthology of it, and as may enable my own readers to feel for themselves something of what I have felt in my direct and prolonged researches in it.

It is my duty, likewise, to state here just what method I have

[1] "Life, Letters, and Journals of George Ticknor," II. 257.

Preface

adopted in the reproduction of the literary specimens that are given in this book. Obviously, their value for the purpose now in view would be destroyed, if they should be tampered with; if the historian of this body of literature should undertake to improve it by his own emendations of it,—correcting its syntax, chastising its vocabulary, or recomposing the structure of its sentences. This I have never knowingly done. I have tried to reproduce my illustrative passages precisely as they stand in the original texts, excepting in three particulars relating to mere mechanical form. The seventeenth century and the first half of the eighteenth, were times of extreme inaccuracy in proof-reading, and of extreme confusion in punctuation and spelling; and I have thought it no violation of the integrity of quotation for me to spell and punctuate any sentence of those times according to present usage, and occasionally to correct a palpable error of the press. It will be understood, also, that whenever, in citing a passage, long or short, the purpose of my citation would be satisfied by giving only a fragment of it, I have given only the fragment; and that in such cases I have indicated, in the usual manner, the presence of an ellipsis.

The studies upon which this book is founded have been for several years my principal occupation; and it is my purpose to continue those studies, till I shall have gone over the remainder of the field. The result will be given to the public as soon as practicable; and I shall think it a good fortune if, by the publication of the present work, I may be brought into communication with the possessors of rare materials relating to the periods that I have yet to survey, and may thus be enabled to prosecute my further labors with some generous assistance which otherwise I might not have.*

[* The last three paragraphs, beginning with this one, and the place and date lines of the original preface were replaced in 1897 by the following:

"In the eighteen years and more that have passed since the first publication of this work, I have been constantly on the watch for errors in its text, and in my own efforts to improve its accuracy, I have been aided by criticisms from many quarters, both public and private. For such kindness I owe an expression of thanks particularly to John A. Doyle, Fellow of All Souls College, Oxford; to Justin Winsor, of the library of Harvard University; to Samuel Abbot Green, of the library of the Massachusetts Historical Society; and to two friends who are no longer within the reach of my thanks, Robert C. Winthrop and Henry Martyn

Preface

The years which I have given to the preparation of this book would not be regretted by me, were it for no other reason than that the prosecution of my researches has made me acquainted with the noble spirit of mutual helpfulness prevailing among men of letters. I have not found them the irritable race that they have been named, but rather brethren, and friends, and benefactors. In all my explorations of public and private libraries, in all the conversation and correspondence that I have had to seek in my hunt after the sources of our literature, I have not one instance of unkindness to remember, or even of aid doled out reluctantly; but, on the contrary, more instances than I am able to remember of considerate and most bountiful help even from strangers, who, recognizing me as a working-brother in the guild of letters, have freely bestowed their kindness upon me. First of all, I must thank my Alma Mater, Yale College, and her accomplished librarian, Mr. Addison Van Name, for the loan of needed books sent to me in my distant home. For several months together, I was at work in the Astor Library, and had there every courtesy from the late Dr. Edward R. Straznicky, from Mr. Frederick Saunders, and from my kinsman, Mr. Arthur W. Tyler, now the librarian of the Johns Hopkins University. For a still longer time, have I pursued my studies at the library of the New York Historical Society, where Dr. George H. Moore, now of the Lenox Library, Mr. John Austin Stevens, and especially Mr. William Kelby, have given me every facility. I must add that my indebtedness to the first of the three gentlemen just named, is much greater than is implied in official assistance, however generous; since, for a number of years, I have had the privilege of consulting him personally upon any difficult problem that I encountered in my studies, and of receiving the benefit that could come only from such prolonged, minute, and accurate acquaintance as he possesses with American history and bibliography. While upon my researches in the Prince Library, which is in the good keeping of the Public Library of Boston, I was constantly aided by Mr. Arthur Mason Knapp, by my college-mate,

---

Dexter. No criticism, whether valid or otherwise, which has come under my eye, has been disregarded; and the work, as now offered to the public, is as free from errors of detail as I am at present able to make it.   M. C. T.
CORNELL UNIVERSITY, 21 January, 1897."]

Preface

Mr. James L. Whitney, and by Mr. Justin Winsor; from the latter of whom I have also had kind assistance since his appointment to the superintendence of the library of Harvard College. I hardly know in what terms to thank the officers of the Massachusetts Historical Society, particularly Mr. Charles Deane and Dr. Samuel Abbott Green, for the cordiality and fulness of my welcome to the privileges of their library, and for innumerable acts of courtesy and of real help on their part. Mr. Charles * Ward Dean, the librarian of the New England Historic-Genealogical Society, has been most friendly in his efforts to serve me. I also had willing help from the officers of the Boston Athenæum, upon my visit to that institution. In Providence, through the polite intervention of Mr. John Russell Bartlett, I experienced that generosity which may now be called hereditary, and which throws open to students the treasures of the superb library founded by the late John Carter Brown; while Mr. C. Fiske Harris, of the same city, gave me not only cordial hospitality but his personal assistance, when he permitted me to explore his unique collection of American poetry,—the most extensive, I suppose, in the world. My studies in Philadelphia were promoted to the utmost by the kind offices of Mr. William F. Ford, one of the editors of "The Times" newspaper in that city; of Mr. Lloyd P. Smith, the librarian of the Library Company; of Mr. John William Wallace, the president of the Historical Society of Pennsylvania, and of Mr. Frederick D. Stone, its librarian. In pursuing my researches in the Library of Congress, I had the most efficient and affable help from Mr. Ainsworth R. Spofford, under whose enlightened and energetic direction the national library is becoming not only an honor to the country, but a blessing to every citizen.

In conclusion, I take pleasure in offering here my hearty thanks, for help of various kinds, to the Reverend Henry Martyn Dexter, of Boston; to Mr. John Langdon Sibley, of Cambridge; to Mr. John Bigelow, of New York; to Mr. Henry A. Homes, of the State Library at Albany; to the Reverend O. S. St. John, of Brooklyn, N. Y.; to the Reverend Edward D. Neill, of Macalister * College, Minnesota; to Mr. Samuel F. Haven, of Worcester, Mass.; to Mr. Henry A. Chaney

[* Changed to "John."]
[* Corrected to "Macalester."]

Preface

and Mr. C. Endicott, of Detroit; and to my friends and associates in the University of Michigan,—Professors Thomas M. Cooley, Henry S. Frieze, Elisha Jones, Edward L. Walter, and Isaac N. Demmon. The critical help that Professor Demmon has given in the revision of the proof-sheets, has been to me invaluable, as on his part it has been without stint of courtesy or toil.

University of Michigan, Ann Arbor,
October 5, 1878.

Contents

FIRST COLONIAL PERIOD: 1607–1676

CHAPTER I

THE BEGINNING

I. The Procession of the first English-speaking colonies from the old world to the new—Our first literary period that of the planting of the American nation—Our first American writers immigrant Americans—True Fathers of American Literature—The literary traits they brought with them 6

II. Why those first Americans wrote books—True classification of early American writings—Tidings sent back—Controversial appeals—Defences against calumny—Descriptions of the new lands—And of the new life there—Books of religion—Poetry—Histories—Miscellaneous prose. 7

III. Birth year of American literature—State of English literature when American literature was born—Interest of Englishmen then in their barbaric American empire—Departure from England of the first English Americans—Michael Drayton's farewell ode to them 10

CHAPTER II

VIRGINIA: THE FIRST WRITER

I. The arrival in America of the first Americans—A fortunate blunder—Satisfaction with their new home 15

II. The sort of men they were—Their leaders—Captain John Smith—His previous career—His character—His important relation to early American settlements—The first writer in American literature 16

III. His first book—Its publication in London in 1608—A literary synchronism—American literature and John Milton—Synopsis of the book—Notable passages—The fable of his rescue by Pocahontas—The place of the book at the head of American literature—Summary of its literary traits 19

Contents

IV. His second American writing—A bold letter to his London patrons—His knowledge refusing to be commanded by their ignorance—The kind of men to make good colonists of—Early symptoms of American recalcitrance.. 25
V. His third American work—Vivid pictures of Virginia—The climate—The country—The productions—The Indians—His fine statement of the utility of the Virginian enterprise............................ 27
VI. Captain John Smith's return to England—His subsequent career—A baffled explorer—His pride in the American colonies—Utilized by the playwrights—Thomas Fuller's sarcastic account of him—His champions—Final estimate.. 31

CHAPTER III

VIRGINIA: OTHER EARLY WRITERS

I. George Percy of Northumberland—His worthiness—His graphic sketches of the brightness and gloom of their first year in America.... 35
II. William Strachey—His terrible voyage and wreck with Sir Thomas Gates—His book descriptive of it and of the state of the colony in Virginia—Some germs of Shakespeare's Tempest—Strachey's wonderful picture of a storm at sea.. 37
III. Alexander Whitaker, the devoted Christian missionary—His life and death and memory in Virginia—His appeal to England in "Good News from Virginia".. 41
IV. John Pory—His coming to Virginia—His previous career—A cosmopolite in a colony—His return to England—His amusing sketches of Indian character—The humors and consolations of pioneer life along the James River.. 43
V. George Sandys—His high personal qualities and his fine genius—His literary services before coming to America—Michael Drayton's exhortation to entice the Muses to Virginia—Sandys's fidelity to his literary vocation amid calamity and fatigue—His translation of Ovid—Its relation to poetry and scholarship in the new world—Passages from it—The story of Philomela—His poetic renown.................................... 45

CHAPTER IV

VIRGINIA: ITS LITERATURE DURING THE REMAINDER OF THE FIRST PERIOD

I. The establishment of Maryland upon the territory of Virginia—Maryland's slight literary record for this period blended with that of Virginia—Father Andrew White and his Latin narrative—John Hammond, the Anglo-American, studying the social problems of England—His solution of them in the word America—His book, "Leah and Rachel," and its original American flavor............................ 53

Contents

II. George Alsop—His life in Maryland—His droll book about Maryland—Comic descriptions of the effects of his voyage—Vivid accounts of the country, of its productions................................. 57

III. Sketch of Bacon's rebellion in 1676—The heroic and capable qualities of Bacon—The anonymous manuscripts relating to the rebellion—Literary indications furnished by these writings—Descriptions of a beleaguered Indian fort—Of Bacon's conflicts with Berkeley—Of Bacon's military stratagem—Bacon's death—Noble poem upon his death...... 61

IV. Review of the literary record of Virginia during this period—Its comparative barrenness—Explanation found in the personal traits of the founders of Virginia—And in their peculiar social organization—Resulting in inferior public prosperity—Especially in lack of schools and of intellectual stimulus—Sir William Berkeley's baneful influence—Printing prohibited in Virginia by the English government—Religious freedom prohibited by the people of Virginia—Literary development impossible under such conditions................................. 70

CHAPTER V

NEW ENGLAND TRAITS IN THE SEVENTEENTH CENTURY

I. Transition from Virginia to New England—The race-qualities of the first New-Englanders—The period of their coming—Their numbers, and the multitude of their posterity..................................... 81

II. Two classes of Englishmen in the seventeenth century; those resting upon the world's attainments, those demanding a new departure—From the second class came the New-Englanders—The purpose of their coming an ideal one... 83

III. Their intellectuality—The large number of their learned men—Their esteem for learning... 86

IV. Their earnestness of character—Religion the master-thought—Their conceptions of providence and of prayer—Their religious intensity leading to moroseness, to spiritual pedantry, to a jurisprudence based on theology, and to persecution..................................... 87

V. The outward forms of New England life—Its prosperity—Literature in early New England—A literary class from the first—Circumstances favorable to literary action—The limits of their literary studies—Restraints upon the liberty of printing—Other disadvantages—The quality in them which gave assurance of literary development............ 95

CHAPTER VI

NEW ENGLAND: HISTORICAL WRITERS

I. Early development of the historic consciousness in New England.... 100

II. William Bradford—His career in England, Holland, and America—

Contents

His History of Plymouth—Singular fate of the manuscript—His fitness for historical writing—Outline of the work—Condition and feelings of the Pilgrims when first ashore at Plymouth—Portrait of a clerical mountebank—The skins needed by the founders of colonies—Unfamiliar personal aspects of the Pilgrims—Their predominant nobility—Summary of this historian's traits..................................... 101

III. Nathaniel Morton—His life—His "Memorial," and how he made it—Lack of originality in it and in him.............................. 109

IV. The sailing of the Winthrop fleet—John Winthrop himself—His "Model of Christian Charity"—His "History of New England"—An historical diary—Its minute fidelity and graphic power—Examples—His famous speech.. 112

V. Edward Johnson—His "Wonder-Working Providence"—How he came to write it—Reflects the greatness and pettiness of the New England Puritans—Examples—Its literary peculiarities................. 118

VI. The literature of the Pequot War—John Mason its hero and historian—His book—His story of the Mystic fight......................... 127

VII. The high worth of Daniel Gookin—An American sage, patriot, and philanthropist—The trials and triumphs of his life—His two historical works relating to the Indians..................................... 130

CHAPTER VII

NEW ENGLAND: DESCRIPTIONS OF NATURE AND PEOPLE IN AMERICA

I. Sensitiveness of the first Americans to the peculiar phenomena of the new world... 137

II. "Journal" of Bradford and Winslow—First contact of the Pilgrims with America—Gropings—American thunder—Indian visits—An Indian king at home—Winslow's letter—His "Good News from New England"—History as cultivated by the Indians—Men who are not called to be colonists... 138

III. Francis Higginson, churchman, dissenter, immigrant—His "True Relation"—His "New England's Plantation"—Pictures of sea and land—The bright side of things in America............................... 144

IV. William Wood—His "New England's Prospect"—His uncommon literary ability—Analysis of his book—His defence of the honesty of travellers—His powers of description—Merit of his verses—Mirthfulness—Wolves, humming-birds, fishes—Eloquent and playful sketches of Indians 147

V. John Josselyn—His kindred—No lover of the New England Puritans—His habits in America—A seventeenth century naturalist in our woods—His "New England's Rarities Discovered"—His "Two Voyages to New England"—The White Hills—His true value as a reporter of natural

Contents

history—Generous gifts to the credulous reader—His friendly attitude toward the unknown.. 156

CHAPTER VIII

NEW ENGLAND: THEOLOGICAL AND RELIGIOUS WRITERS

I. The supremacy of the clergy in early New England—Their worthiness—Their public manifestations—How they studied and preached—The quality and vastness of the work they did.................... 162

II. Thomas Hooker one of the three greatest—His career in England—Comes to Massachusetts—Founds Hartford—A prolific writer—His commanding traits as a man and an orator—His published writings—Literary characteristics—His frankness in damnatory preaching—Total depravity—Formalism—Need of Christ—The versatility and pathos of his appeals... 167

III. New England's debt to Archbishop Laud—Thomas Shepard's animated interview with him, and its consequences—Shepard's settlement in America—Personal peculiarities—Illustrations of his theology and method of discourse.. 177

IV. John Cotton—His brave sermon in St. Mary's Church, Cambridge—Becomes rector of St. Botolph's, Boston—His great fame in England—His ascendency in New England—Correspondence with Cromwell—His death announced by a comet—As a student and writer............... 181

V. A group of minor prophets—Peter Bulkley founder of Concord—The man—His "Gospel Covenant"—John Norton—Succeeds John Cotton—His style as a writer—William Hooke—His life—His "New England's Tears for Old England's Fears"—Charles Chauncey's career in England and America—Becomes president of Harvard—Great usefulness as an educator—His scholarship, industry, old age—His "Plain Doctrine of Justification"—His unpublished writings made useful.............. 187

CHAPTER IX

NEW ENGLAND: MISCELLANEOUS PROSE WRITERS

I. Nathaniel Ward and his collisions with Laud—His position in early American literature—His large experience before coming to America—A reminiscence of Prince Rupert................................. 196

II. Career of Nathaniel Ward in New England—His "Simple Cobbler of Agawam"—Summary of the book—The author's mental traits—His attitude toward his age—Vindicates New England from the calumny that it tolerates variety of opinions—His satire upon fashionable dames in the colony and upon long-haired men—His discussion of the troubles in England—Literary traits of the book......................... 198

xxiii

Contents

III. Roger Williams as revealed in his own writings—His exceptional attractiveness as an early New-Englander—What he stood for in his time in New England—A troublesome personage to his contemporaries and why—His special sympathy with Indians and with all other unfortunate folk... 208

IV. First visit of Roger Williams to England—His first book—His interest in the great struggle in England—His reply to John Cotton's justification of his banishment from Massachusetts—His book against a national church—His "Bloody Tenet of Persecution"—John Cotton's reply—Williams's powerful rejoinder—Other writings—His letters—Personal traits shown in them—His famous letter against lawlessness and tyranny.. 213

CHAPTER X

NEW ENGLAND: THE VERSE-WRITERS

I. The attitude of Puritanism toward Art—Especially toward Poetry—The unextinguished poetry in Puritanism......................... 227

II. The Puritans of New England universally addicted to versification—The mirth of their elegies and epitaphs—The poetical expertness of Pastor John Wilson.. 229

III. The pleasant legend of William Morrell—His poem in Latin and English on New England... 234

IV. The prodigy of "The Bay Psalm Book"—Its Reverend fabricators—Their conscientious mode of proceeding—A book fearfully and wonderfully made.. 236

V. Anne Bradstreet the earliest professional poet of New England—First appearance of her book—Her career—Her prose writings—Her training for poetry—Her guides and masters the later euphuists in English verse—List of her poetical works—Analysis of "The Four Elements"—"The Four Monarchies"—The fundamental error in her poetry—Her "Contemplations"—The first poet of the Merrimac—Her devout poems—Her allusions to contemporary politics—Her championship of women—Final estimate... 239

SECOND COLONIAL PERIOD: 1676–1765

CHAPTER XI

NEW ENGLAND: THE VERSE-WRITERS

I. The two literary periods in our colonial age—Their points of distinction—The times and the men—Our intended line of march through the second period.. 260

xxiv

Contents

II. John Norton—His poem on the death of Anne Bradstreet—John Rogers—His poetic praise of Anne Bradstreet........................ 263
III. Urian Oakes—His high literary gifts—His elegy on the death of Thomas Shepard... 268
IV. Peter Folger, the ballad-writer—Benjamin Tompson, the satirist.... 272
V. Michael Wigglesworth, the sturdy rhymer of New England Calvinism—His great popularity—Puts into verse the glooms and the comforts of the prevailing faith—The realistic poet of hell-fire—"God's Controversy with New England"—"Meat out of the Eater"—"The Day of Doom"—Synopsis of the latter poem—Its wide diffusion and influence—His son, Samuel Wigglesworth, a true poet—"A Funeral Song" by the latter... 276
VI. Nicholas Noyes, the last and greatest of our Fantastics—His fine personal career—The monstrosities of his muse—Prefatory poem on the "Magnalia"—Lines on John Higginson—Elegy on Joseph Green—Verses on the painful malady of a Reverend friend......................... 291
VII. Strong influence in America of the contemporary English poets, especially Pope, Blackmore, Watts, Thomson, Young—Echoes of them in Francis Knapp, Benjamin Colman, Jane Turell, Mather Byles—The career and poetry of Roger Wolcott—His Connecticut epic—His "Poetical Meditations".. 296
VIII. Humorous poetry—John Seccomb and his burlesque verses—The facetiousness of Joseph Green—His impromptus—His "Entertainment for a Winter Evening"... 299
IX. War-verses—Popular ballads—"Lovewell's Fight"—Tilden's "Miscellaneous Poems"—John Maylem, Philo-Bellum—His "Conquest of Louisburg"—His "Gallic Perfidy".. 304
X. A group of serious singers—John Adams—His accomplishments and poetry—"Poems by Several Hands"—Peter Oliver, the literary politician—His poem in honor of Josiah Willard......................... 307
XI. "Pietas et Gratulatio"—Its occasion—Its authors—A burst of American loyalty to the English monarchs—Its Greek and Latin verses—Its English verses—Apotheosis of George the Second—Salutation to George the Third... 309

CHAPTER XII

NEW ENGLAND: THE DYNASTY OF THE MATHERS

I. The founder of the dynasty, Richard Mather—His flight from England and career in America—His traits—His writings—An ecclesiastical politician—His love of study.................................. 316
II. Increase Mather—His American birth and breeding—His residence in Ireland and England—Returns to New England—His great influence

xxv

Contents

there—Pulpit-orator, statesman, courtier, college president—His learning—His laboriousness in study—His manner in the pulpit—The literary qualities of his writings—Specimens—Number and range of his published works—His "Illustrious Providences"—Origin of the book—Its value 318

III. Cotton Mather—His preëminence—The adulation received by him—His endowments—His precocity—The development of his career—His religious character and discipline—His intellectual accomplishments—His habits as a reader—The brilliancy of his talk—Contemporaneous admiration—The watchword of his life—The multitude of his books—Characteristic titles—The fame of his "Magnalia"—His anxieties respecting its publication—Its scope—His advantages and disadvantages for historical writing—Estimate of the historical character of the "Magnalia"—The best of his subsequent writings—"Bonifacius"—"Psalterium Americanum"—"Manuductio ad Ministerium"—Its counsels to a young prophet—Study of Hebrew, of history, of natural philosophy—Assault on Aristotle—The place of Cotton Mather in American literature—The last of the Fantastics in prose—Traits of his style—Pedantry—His style not agreeable to his later contemporaries—His theory of style—Defence of his own style against his critics 323

IV. Samuel Mather—His days and deeds—A stanch patriot—The end of the dynasty 337

CHAPTER XIII

NEW ENGLAND: TOPICS OF POPULAR DISCUSSION

I. Early literary prominence of the clergy—Growth of the laity in intellectual influence—The range of the people's thought and talk during the second colonial period 340

II. The mournful reminiscences of Joshua Scottow—The witchcraft spasm—Robert Calef and "More Wonders of the Invisible World" 341

III. The diary in literature—Sarah Kemble Knight—Her "Journal"—Pictures of travel and of rustic manners early in the eighteenth century 343

IV. Samuel Sewall—His brave life—The man—His attitude toward witchcraft and slavery—His "Selling of Joseph"—Among the prophets—"A Description of the New Heaven"—The New Jerusalem to be in America—A gallant champion of the immortality of the souls of women 345

V. John Wise—His inadequate fame—His genius as a writer—His career as preacher, muscular Christian, and opponent of despotism—The first great American expounder of democracy in church and state—His victorious assault upon a scheme for clerical aggrandizement—"The Churches' Quarrel Espoused"—The logic, wit, and eloquence of the book—His "Vindication of the Government of New England Churches"—Analysis of the book—Traits of his mind and style 349

Contents

VI. Jeremiah Dummer—His early fame—Short career as a preacher—Goes to London and becomes courtier, barrister, and colonial agent—A faithful American always—His "Letter to a Noble Lord"—His "Defence of the New England Charters"—The elegance and strength of his style.. 360

VII. The almanac in modern literature—Its early prominence in America—Its function—Wit and wisdom in almanacs not originated by Franklin—Nathaniel Ames, the greatest of our colonial almanac-makers—His "Astronomical Diary and Almanac," an annual miscellany of information and amusement—Its great popularity and utility—Its predictions—Its shrewd and earnest appeals to the common mind—Its suggestions concerning health—Its original verses—Predicts the Day of Judgment—A noble prophecy of universal peace—Vision of the coming greatness of America—A friendly address to posterity.................................. 363

CHAPTER XIV

NEW ENGLAND: HISTORY AND BIOGRAPHY

I. Further development of the historic spirit in New England—Biography and biographers—Ebenezer Turell—His biographies of Jane Turell and of Benjamin Colman 374

II. William Hubbard—Picture of him by John Dunton—His literary culture and aptitude—Qualities of his style—His "General History of New England"—His "Indian Wars"—Celebrity of the latter—Its faults and merits—Represents the wrath of the people against the Indians—Portrait of a noble savage.. 375

III. Other literary memorials of the long conflict with the Indians—Mary Rowlandson and her thrilling "Narrative" of Indian captivity—"The Redeemed Captive," by John Williams of Deerfield—Benjamin Church—His history of King Philip's War and of other struggles with the Indians—Interest of his narratives—Samuel Penhallow—His history of Indian wars—Pictures of heroism and cruelty—His reminiscences of classical study—Samuel Niles—His "History of the Indian and French Wars".. 379

IV. Thomas Prince—His eminent career—His special taste and training for history—Has the cardinal virtues of an historian—His "Chronological History of New England"—Thoroughness of his methods—Salient features of the book—Its worthiness........................... 384

V. John Callender—His careful sketch of the first century of Rhode Island's history.. 389

VI. William Douglass—The life and the singularities of the man—A literary Ishmaelite—His ability and self-confidence—His sarcastic account of the medical profession in America—His "Summary"—A pas-

Contents

sionate, heterogeneous, able book—Its style and scope—Its drolleries—His dislike of the Indians, of the French, of Whitefield, of Bishop Berkeley, and of paper-money—General estimate of his book.......... 390

CHAPTER XV

NEW ENGLAND: THE PULPIT IN LITERATURE

I. Continued ascendency of the clergy—Their full maintenance of the grand traits of their predecessors,—manliness, scholarship, thoughtfulness, eloquence—Their improvement upon their predecessors in breadth, and in social and literary urbanity......................... 398

II. John Higginson—Sketch of him by John Dunton—The power of his character and of his long life—His election-sermon—His "Attestation" to the "Magnalia".. 399

III. William Stoughton, preacher and statesman—His "Narrative of the Proceedings of Andros"—His discourse on "New England's True Interest, not to Lie"—Its literary ability—Its courage..................... 400

IV. Urian Oakes—His greatness in prose as well as in verse—Contemporaneous estimates of him—His first artillery-sermon—Its great eloquence—Its delineation of the Christian soldier—His election-sermon—His second artillery-sermon... 402

V. Samuel Willard—His "Complete Body of Divinity"—His career—His theological lectures—Their great influence—Their publication in 1726 in the first American folio—Strong qualities of the book.......... 405

VI. Solomon Stoddard—His activity as a writer—His special reputation for soundness of judgment—His "Answer to Some Cases of Conscience respecting the Country"—The sinfulness of long hair and of periwigs—Condemnation of other frivolities................................. 407

VII. Benjamin Colman—His great contemporaneous influence in church and state—His fine culture—His residence in England—His particular friendships there—His return to Boston—His long and prosperous public career—His discourses—Their literary polish—His charitable spirit.. 408

VIII. John Barnard of Marblehead—His versatile culture—His eminence—His intellectual traits—His volumes of sermons—His gentlemanly treatment of sinners... 412

IX. Jonathan Edwards—Outline of his life—His qualities, spiritual and intellectual—His precocity in metaphysics, and in physics—His juvenile writings—His more mature studies in science—His spiritual self-discipline—His resolutions—The sorrows of his life—Habits as a student and thinker—His power as a preacher—Analysis of his method in discourse—"Sinners in the Hands of an Angry God"—His literary characteristics... 414

X. Mather Byles—A scene in Hollis Street Church early in the Revolution—His brilliant career before the Revolution—His versatility—The

Contents

misfortune of his later reputation as a jester—A great pulpit-orator—His literary qualities—His exposition of the preacher's character—His favorite themes—Passages from his sermons 426

XI. Jonathan Mayhew—The lines of his influence—Estimate of him by John Adams—Charles Chauncey—His traits—His hatred of inaccurate and emotional utterance—His contempt for Whitefield—His discourse on "Enthusiasm"—His "Seasonable Thoughts"—His portrait of the enthusiast 432

CHAPTER XVI
LITERATURE IN THE MIDDLE COLONIES

1. NEW YORK AND NEW JERSEY

I. Traits of life in New York before it became English—After it became English—A many-tongued community—Metropolitan indications—Education neglected—Literary effort only in spasms 439

II. Daniel Denton, a pioneer of American literature there—His "Brief Description of New York"—His pictures of nature and of social felicity—Thomas Budd, of New Jersey, another pioneer writer—His "Good Order established in Pennsylvania and New Jersey"—William Leeds, a refugee from Philadelphia—His "News of a Trumpet sounding in the Wilderness" 441

III. Lewis Morris of Morrisania—His vivacious boyhood—Turns vagabond—Settlement into steady courses—A powerful politician—His literary inclinations—His letters from London—Provincial loyalty disenchanted by going to the metropolis 442

IV. Cadwallader Colden—His long career—Manifold activity—Extraordinary range of his studies and of his writings—His "History of the Five Indian Nations"—Its characteristics—Its descriptions of the savage virtues 445

V. Daniel Coxe of New Jersey—His "Description of the English Province of Carolana"—His statesmanly view of colonial affairs—Anticipates Franklin's plan of a union of the colonies 447

VI. Jonathan Dickinson, pulpit-orator, physician, teacher, author—First president of the College of New Jersey—His personal traits—His eminence as a theological debater—His "Familiar Letters" 448

VII. William Livingston—His "Philosophic Solitude"—Manner and spirit of the poem—Antithesis between his ideal life and his real one—His strong character—Outward engagements—His activity as a pamphleteer and as a writer in the journals—His burlesque definition of his own creed—His "Review of the Military Operations in North America"—His "Verses to Eliza" 450

xxix

Contents

VIII. William Smith—The course of his life—His special interest in the history of his native province—His "History of New York"—Criticisms upon it—Samuel Smith and his "History of the Colony of Nova Cæsarea, or New Jersey" 455

2. PENNSYLVANIA

I. The founders of Pennsylvania—The high motives of their work—Their social severity—Intellectual greatness of William Penn—Justice and liberality imparted by him to the constitution of his province—Education provided for—First impulses to literary production in Pennsylvania—The development of a literary spirit in Philadelphia 456

II. Gabriel Thomas—A brisk Quaker—His "Account" of Pennsylvania and of West New Jersey—His enthusiasm for his province—Its freedom from lawyers and doctors—Its proffer of relief to the distressed in the old world—Richard Frame—His "Short Description of Pennsylvania"—John Holme—His "True Relation of the Flourishing State of Pennsylvania"—Jonathan Dickenson—His "God's Protecting Providence Man's Surest Help" 458

III. James Logan—Penn invites him to America and trusts to him his affairs there—His fidelity to the Penns and to the people—Difficulties of his position—His great intellectual attainments—His writings, published and unpublished 461

IV. William Smith—His influence upon intellectual culture in the middle colonies—Arrival at New York—His "General Idea of the College of Mirania"—Is invited to Philadelphia—His useful career as educator, preacher, and writer 463

V. A succession of small writers—Jacob Taylor—Henry Brooke—Samuel Keimer—Aquila Rose—James Ralph—George Webb and his "Bachelors' Hall"—Joseph Breintnal—A poem from "Titan's Almanac" for 1730—Joseph Shippen—John Webbe—Lewis Evans 464

VI. Samuel Davies—Born and educated in Pennsylvania—Acquires in Virginia great fame as a pulpit-orator—His mission to England—Becomes president of the College of New Jersey—His death—Great popularity of his published sermons down to the present time—His traits as a preacher—Passage from his sermon on "The General Resurrection" 470

VII. Thomas Godfrey, the poet—Connection of his father's family with Franklin—His early life and death—Publication of his "Juvenile Poems" —His "Prince of Parthia," the first American drama—A study of it 473

VIII. Benjamin Franklin, the first man of letters in America to achieve cosmopolitan fame—His writings during our present period—His great career during the subsequent period 479

Contents

CHAPTER XVII

LITERATURE IN MARYLAND, VIRGINIA, AND THE SOUTH

1. MARYLAND

I. Ebenezer Cook, Gentleman—A rough satirist—His "Sot-Weed Factor"—Outline of the poem—Lively sketches of early Maryland life—Hospitality—Manners—Indians—A court-scene—Encounter with a Quaker and a lawyer—Swindled by both—His curse upon Maryland—His "Sot-Weed Redivivus".. 483

2. VIRGINIA

I. James Blair, the true founder of literary culture in Virginia—His coming to Virginia—Forcible qualities of the man—His zeal for education—Founds the College of William and Mary—First president of it—The Commencement celebration in 1700—His writings—"The Present state of Virginia and the College"—His published discourses on the Sermon on the Mount—His literary qualities—Passages from his sermons... 488

II. Robert Beverley—Parentage—Education in England—His study of the history of Virginia—How he came to write it—The blunders of Oldmixon—Reception of Beverley's book—The author himself seen in it—A noble Virginian—A friend of the Indians—His love of nature—His style—Humor—Hatred of indolence—Virginia hospitality and comfort—Calumnies upon its climate............................ 491

III. Hugh Jones, clergyman, teacher, and school-book maker—His "Present State of Virginia"—Objects of the book—Its range—Its sarcasms upon the other colonies—Its criticisms upon Virginia—Suggestions for improvement... 495

IV. William Byrd of Westover—His princely fortune and ways—His culture—Foreign travel—Public spirit—His writings—"History of the Dividing Line"—The humor and literary grace of the book—Amusing sketch of early history of Virginia—The Christian duty of marrying Indian women—Sarcasms upon North Carolina—Notices of plants, animals, and forest-life—The praise of ginseng—His "Progress to the Mines"—His "Journey to the Land of Eden"....................... 497

V. William Stith—Various utilities of his life—His "History of Virginia"—Defects of the work—Its good qualities—Bitter description of James the First.. 504

3. NORTH CAROLINA

I. John Lawson—His picture of Charleston in 1700—His journey to North Carolina—What he saw and heard by the way—Becomes surveyor-

xxxi

Contents

general of North Carolina—His descriptions of that province—Its coast—Sir Walter Raleigh's ship—A land of Arcadian delight—The playful alligator—A study of Indians—Amiability and beauty of their women—An ancient squaw—A conjuror—Indian self-possession—The author's fate—His "History of North Carolina".............................. 507

4. South Carolina

I. Alexander Garden, rector of Saint Philip's, Charleston—The force of his character—Greatness of his influence—His abhorrence of Whitefield—His sermons and letters against Whitefield—Their bitterness and their literary merit.. 513

5. Georgia

I. Georgia's entrance into our literature—A conflict with Oglethorpe—The expert and witty book of Patrick Tailfer and others—"A True and Historical Narrative of the Colony of Georgia"—Outline of it—A masterly specimen of satire—Its mock dedication to Oglethorpe.......... 515

CHAPTER XVIII

GENERAL LITERARY FORCES IN THE COLONIAL TIME

I. Tendency in each colony toward isolation—Local peculiarities in thought and language—Distribution of personal and literary types 522
II. General tendencies toward colonial fellowship, founded on kinship, religion, commerce, subjection to the same sovereign, peril from the same enemies—Special intellectual tendencies toward colonial fellowship, founded on the rise of journalism, the establishment of colleges, and the study of physical science.................................... 524
III. The rise of American journalism—"Public Occurrences," in 1690—"The Boston News-Letter," in 1704—Dates of the founding of the first newspapers in the several colonies—Whole number founded in each colony before 1765—Description of the colonial newspapers—Their effect on intercolonial acquaintance—The growth of literary skill in them—Early literary magazines—First one founded by Franklin, in 1741—"The American Magazine," at Boston—"The Independent Reflector," at New York—"The American Magazine," at Philadelphia............. 526
IV. Early American colleges—Seven founded before 1765—Harvard, William and Mary, Yale, New Jersey, King's, Philadelphia, Rhode Island—Grade and extent of instruction in them—Predominant study of the ancient classics—Requirements for admission at Harvard and Yale—Latin in ordinary use in the colleges—Range of studies—Expertness in the use of the ancient languages—How the early colleges led to colonial union—Their vast influence on literary culture—Their promotion of

Contents

the spiritual conditions on which the growth of literature depends—One effect of their work seen in the state papers of the Revolutionary period—Lord Chatham's tribute................................... 529

V. Study of physical science in America—Begun by the earliest Americans—Eminence of John Winthrop of Connecticut—His connections with the Royal Society—Fitz John Winthrop—Stimulus given to study of nature in New England—Increase Mather—John Williams—Cotton Mather—Jared Eliot—Joseph Dudley—Paul Dudley—Study of science in Virginia—John Banister—William Byrd—Mark Catesby—John Clayton—John Mitchell—John Bartram of Pennsylvania—John Winthrop of Harvard College—The intercolonial correspondence of scientific men—Culmination of scientific research between 1740 and 1765—The brilliant services of Franklin—America instructing Europe in electricity—Leading scientific men in the several colonies—Scientific fellowship a preparation for political fellowship—Impulse given by science to literature... 532

VI. Great change in the character of American literature after 1765...... 538

Index 539

FIRST COLONIAL PERIOD: 1607–1676

AMERICAN LITERATURE — FIRST COLONIAL PERIOD: 1607–1676

- **Writers of Narration and Description, including American Apologetics**
  - Captain John Smith
  - George Percy
  - William Strachey
  - Alexander Whitaker
  - John Pory
  - Edward Winslow
  - Francis Higginson
  - William Wood
  - John Hammond
  - John Josselyn
  - George Alsop

- **Historical Writers**
  - William Bradford
  - John Winthrop
  - Nathaniel Morton
  - John Mason
  - Edward Johnson
  - Daniel Gookin
  - Author of Burwell Papers

- **Theological and Religious Writers**
  - Thomas Hooker
  - Thomas Shepard
  - John Cotton
  - Peter Bulkley
  - John Norton
  - William Hooke
  - Charles Chauncey

- **Miscellaneous Prose Writers**
  - Nathaniel Ward
  - Roger Williams

- **Writers of Verse**
  - George Sandys
  - William Morrell
  - Anne Bradstreet

Chapter I

The Beginning

I.   The Procession of the first English-speaking colonies from the old world to the new—Our first literary period that of the planting of the American nation—Our first American writers immigrant Americans—True Fathers of American Literature—The literary traits they brought with them.
II. Why those first Americans wrote books—True classification of early American writings—Tidings sent back—Controversial appeals—Defences against calumny—Descriptions of the new lands—And of the new life there—Books of religion—Poetry—Histories—Miscellaneous prose.
III. Birth year of American literature—State of English literature when American literature was born—Interest of Englishmen then in their barbaric American empire—Departure from England of the first English Americans—Michael Drayton's farewell ode to them.

THERE is but one thing more interesting than the intellectual history of a man, and that is the intellectual history of a nation. The American people, starting into life in the early part of the seventeenth century, have been busy ever since in recording their intellectual history in laws, manners, institutions, in battles with man and beast and nature, in highways, excavations, edifices, in pictures, in statues, in written words. It is in written words that this people, from the very beginning, have made the most confidential and explicit record of their minds. It is in these written words, therefore, that we shall now search for that record.

History of American Literature

I

We need to picture to ourselves the outgoing of the several English colonies which made their way hither in our earliest time, joining that long, grim, many-tongued procession which during all that era pushed westward from Europe toward this hemisphere. Between the year 1607, when Virginia, the first of these colonies, set its timid foot safely down on the American shores, and the year 1682, when the last of them, Pennsylvania, arrived here, we are able to count no less than ten other local communities, of English blood and English speech, that began to find food and lodging and some sense of home-comfort in this land. Their names will never be too despicable to deserve repetition by us: they are, in the order of their establishment, Plymouth, New Hampshire, Massachusetts Bay, Maryland, Connecticut, Rhode Island, North Carolina, New York, New Jersey, South Carolina. These English colonies of the seventeenth century, which Francis Bacon nobly heralded as "amongst ancient, primitive, and heroical works," [1] were not accidental things: they formed parts of a grand series of popular migrations from the old world to the new, all stimulated by an impulse acting on many nations, and over the space of many years. And so far as it concerned England and that portion of the new world which we now mean by the word America, the impulse just spoken of spent itself in that brave group of colonial enterprises which began with Virginia and ended with Pennsylvania.[2] The present race of Americans who are of English lineage—that is, the most numerous and decidedly the dominant portion of the American people of to-day—are the direct descendants of the crowds of Englishmen who came to America in the seventeenth century. Our first literary period, therefore, fills the larger part of that century in which American civilization had its planting; even as its training into some maturity and power has been the business of the eighteenth and

[1] "Essays," XXXIII.—Of Plantations. This essay contains several passages evidently founded upon the author's observation of Virginian affairs as reported in England. In one sentence he expressly mentions Virginia.

[2] Within the territory which afterward became the United States was established before the revolution one other English colony, Georgia. Its establishment, however, was in the eighteenth century, and was an isolated event, due to the philanthropy of one good man, who sought to provide in America a refuge for the debtors and paupers of Europe.

The Beginning

the nineteenth centuries. Of course, also, the most of the men who produced American literature during that period were immigrant authors of English birth and English culture; while the most of those who have produced American literature in the subsequent periods have been authors of American birth and of American culture. Notwithstanding their English birth, these first writers in America were Americans: we may not exclude them from our story of American literature. They founded that literature; they are its Fathers; they stamped their spiritual lineaments upon it; and we shall never deeply enter into the meanings of American literature in its later forms without tracing it back, affectionately, to its beginning with them. At the same time, our first literary epoch cannot fail to bear traces of the fact that nearly all the men who made it were Englishmen who had become Americans merely by removing to America. American life, indeed, at once reacted upon their minds, and began to give its tone and hue to their words; and for every reason, what they wrote here, we rightfully claim as a part of American literature; but England has a right to claim it likewise as a part of English literature. Indeed England and America are joint proprietors of this first tract of the great literary territory which we have undertaken to survey. Ought any one to wonder, however, if in the American literature of the seventeenth century he shall find the distinctive traits, good and bad, which during the same period characterized English literature? How could it be otherwise? Is it likely that an Englishman undergoes a literary revolution by sitting down to write in America instead of in England; or that he will write either much better or much worse only for having sailed across a thousand leagues of brine?

II

Undoubtedly literature for its own sake was not much thought of, or lived for, in those days. The men and women of force were putting their force into the strong and most urgent tasks pertaining to this world and the next. There was an abundance of intellectual vitality among them; and the nation grew

"strong thru shifts, an' wants, an' pains,
Nussed by stern men with empires in their brains." [3]

[3] James Russell Lowell, "The Biglow Papers," Second Series, 68.

Literature as a fine art, literature as the voice and the ministress of æsthetic delight, they had perhaps little skill in and little regard for; but literature as an instrument of humane and immediate utility, they honored, and at this they wrought with all the earnestness that was born in their blood. They wrote books not because they cared to write books, but because by writing books they could accomplish certain other things which they did care for.

And what were those other things? If we can discover them we shall at once grasp the clue to the right classification and the right interpretation of that still chaotic heap of writings which make up American literature in the colonial age.

1. The task to which those men and women gave themselves—the colonization of America—was, under all the circumstances of the time, a very hard one, slow, wearisome, menaced by nearly every form of danger, full of awe even for stout hearts. Their earliest motive for writing books was bound up in a natural and even pathetic desire to send back news of themselves to the old world—that safe, regulated, populous world—which they had left behind them when they sailed out toward the risks and mysteries of the great ocean and of the still greater wilderness which lay hidden in the shadow beyond it. This gives us our first group of American writings, and explains for us a multitude of titles in that primal period—the books written upon the instant of arrival, and at intervals afterward, with the purpose of sending home tidings of welfare or of ill fare.

2. Close to this was the fact that for all of them the supreme legal authority, and for some of them also the source of pecuniary supply, were at home; and thither they occasionally made appeal from the hot controversies into which at times they fell, pleading their causes before a tribunal across the sea, in eager and rough-hewn narratives, which still throb with the passions that prompted them, and are authentic pictures of the thought and the life of those rugged days.

3. It was of the utmost importance that the new settlements in America should be reënforced in population by steady accessions from the dense multitudes of the old world, especially of the motherland; and this obviously depended on the maintenance there of their good repute. But their good repute in England was assailed from time to time by certain ill-conditioned persons, who, having come

The Beginning

to America, and having left it again either in discontent or under compulsion, sought vengeance in the publication of injurious accounts of the country, the climate, and the people. Curiously enough, also, there were in England certain other persons—old Crashawe [4] quaintly classified them at the time as "the papists, the players, and the devil"—who manifested a dislike toward the American settlements not now easy to be accounted for, and who were very busy in swelling the chorus of bad words concerning them. The necessity of repelling these charges prompted in part the composition of some of the books included in the first two groups, and also developed a distinct class of writings—that of American Apologetics.

4. Furthermore, those uncouth dusky creatures, the savage proprietors of the continent, whom, both in friendship and in hostility, the colonists at once came in contact with, for a long time seemed to our ancestors to be most mysterious beings, and were the objects of an unspeakable interest in England as well as here. What were those creatures? Were they indeed human beings? But if human beings, they must of course be descended from Adam; and if descended from Adam, how did they get to America? And when did they come? And what had they been doing in America all this time? What, moreover, were their forms of government, their laws, their languages, their creeds, their domestic usages, their means of livelihood, the extent of their intellectual development? Above all things, if they indeed had souls, could they not be reached by the Christian message which would save their souls? To us, of course, the American Indian is no longer a mysterious or even an interesting personage—he is simply a fierce dull biped standing in our way; and it is only by a strong effort of the imagination that we can in any degree reproduce for ourselves the zest of ineffable curiosity with which, during the most of the seventeenth century, he was regarded by the English on both sides of the ocean. Scarcely a book was written here on any subject into which he was not somehow introduced; and there remains to us a large class of writings—our fourth group—particularly devoted to him, and to the rather melancholy experiences of the white people in trying to live in his neighborhood.

[4] "A New Year's Gift to Virginia," by W. Crashawe. B.D., London, 1610. This tract is without paging.

5. Neither must it be forgotten that there was in the seventeenth century, both for those who came to America and for those who remained in England, the enchantment of utter novelty in the wild, magnificent, tender, or terrifying aspects of nature, which a voyage over the Atlantic and a residence in the new world would present—the new heavens and the new earth which they then beheld for the first time, the stupendous empire of unexplored wildernesses, the unwonted wrath of earthquakes, thunders, and winds, the new vegetation, the new specimens of beast and bird and fish, and whatever vision they had of majesty or loveliness in the American landscapes. Thus we have as our fifth group of writings the books descriptive of nature in America.

6. There was still another realm of novelty in America that the people of England desired to look into—the new organization of society which the altered conditions of life in the new world compelled the English colonists to develop, their gradual innovations in politics, laws, creeds, in religious and domestic usages, the new crystallization of church and state slowly working itself clear in the English kingdom of America.

7. The several groups of writings which have been mentioned thus far, sprang in considerable measure from motives looking toward the love, or the interest, or the authority of the people of England, from whom those earliest Americans had but recently withdrawn themselves. These groups of writings, however, by no means constitute a moiety of American literature even in our first period. By far the larger portion of our writings were composed for our own people alone, and with reference to our own interests, inspirations, and needs. These include, first, sermons and other religious treatises; second, histories; and third, poetry and some examples of miscellaneous prose.

III

Since the earliest English colonists upon these shores began to make a literature as soon as they arrived here, it follows that we can fix the exact date of the birth of American literature. It is that year 1607, when Englishmen, by transplanting themselves to America,

The Beginning

first began to be Americans. Thus may the history of our literature be traced back from the present hour, as it recedes along the track of our national life, through the early days of the republic, through five generations of colonial existence, until, in the first decade of the seventeenth century, it is merged in its splendid parentage—the written speech of England. And the birth-epoch of American literature was a fortunate one: it was amid the full magnificence of the Elizabethan period, whose creative vitality, whose superb fruitage, reached forward and cast their glory across the entire generation succeeding the death of Elizabeth herself. The first lispings of American literature were heard along the sands of the Chesapeake and near the gurgling tides of the James River, at the very time when the firmament of English literature was all ablaze with the light of her full-orbed and most wonderful writers, the wits, the dramatists, scholars, orators, singers, philosophers, who formed that incomparable group of titanic men gathered in London during the earlier years of the seventeenth century; when the very air of London must have been electric with the daily words of those immortals, whose casual talk upon the pavement by the street-side was a coinage of speech richer, more virile, more expressive, than has been known on this planet since the great days of Athenian poetry, eloquence, and mirth.

I find it hard to hasten past this event—the dawn upon the world of American literature and of American civilization. It is pleasant to trace in contemporaneous English literature some tokens of the interest which the English people of that day took in the romantic and perilous enterprise of laying the foundations of a new English commonwealth beyond the ocean, and of extending the domain of their own speech into lands remote and illimitable. All along during the latter half of the reign of Elizabeth attempt after attempt had been made by her indomitable subjects to get a foothold in that portion of America which she claimed as hers and which in her honor was named Virginia. All these attempts had failed, some of them tragically. In the very last year of her reign, however, a glorious old English sailor had come back to England with the great tidings that he had found it possible to make the voyage to Virginia by shooting his ships straight to the west, thus avoiding the tedious, costly, sickly route thither by way of the West Indies. This bit of news sent a

History of American Literature

thrill of excitement through England; it was talked over at innumerable firesides; it caused a great buzz and fluttering among the merchants and bankers on the London Exchange; it was caught up and tossed about on the stage of the London theatres, which then had the function now filled by daily newspapers for the public discussion of current events.[5] From that moment a fresh impulse was given to the interest of Englishmen in Virginia—their own vast, unpossessed, barbaric empire, now made more accessible to them, and supposed by them to be fat with gold and precious stones and all sorts of unimaginable treasures.[6] Multitudes of Englishmen became eager to go to Virginia, even as in our own time, from the same quenchless passion for swiftly gotten wealth, we have seen men eager to go to the gold fields of California and Australia. And year by year during the early portion of the reign of James the First, the desire for a new attempt to get possession of Virginia crept up among the highest classes, and down among the lowest; and in April of the year 1606 a royal patent was conferred on certain "firm and hearty lovers" of colonization, giving them power to conduct a colony thither. Then once more the good work went forward with vigor and glee. All the summer and all the autumn of that year were spent in making ready the intended expedition. For several weeks before setting sail, the three vessels that were to carry the colonists had waited in the Thames while the managers were completing their preparations. During that time the eyes of all London were upon them; prayers for their safety were offered in the churches; and one of the mighty poets of England, Michael Drayton, poured into a noble ode the high hope, the anxiety, the ambition, the eager sympathy, with which all ranks of thoughtful and watchful Englishmen were sending the travellers out upon their great quest.

> "You brave heroic minds,
> Worthy your country's name,
> That honor still pursue,
> Whilst loit'ring hinds
> Lurk here at home with shame,
> Go and subdue.

[5] E. D. Neill, "Hist. of Va. Co. of London," vi.
[6] John Marston's Works, Halliwell's ed., 1856, Vol. III., play of "Eastward Ho."

The Beginning

Britons, you stay too long:
Quickly aboard bestow you;
    And with a merry gale
    Swell your stretch'd sail
With vows as strong
As the winds that blow you.

   . . .

And cheerfully at sea,
Success you still entice,
    To get the pearl and gold;
    And ours to hold;
Virginia,
Earth's only paradise.

   . . .

In kenning of the shore,
Thanks to God first given,
    O you the happiest men,
    Be frolic then;
Let cannons roar,
Frighting the wide heaven.

And in regions far
Such heroes bring ye forth,
    As those from whom we came;
    And plant our name
Under that star
Not known unto our north."

Thus far in his ode, the poet gives voice merely to the sturdy joy which by nature every Englishman has in daring adventure, in the victories of heroism, in the hope of a vast enlargement of his country's wealth and imperial sway. But this grand old Elizabethan singer could not stifle another ambition—the ambition that England might win for herself in America even nobler trophies than those of political dominion and material wealth. With the pride of an English poet and of an English man of letters, he utters in a single stanza the superb prediction of a new English literature to spring up in that far-off land. In poetic vision he then foresaw, and he hailed and greeted from afar, the unborn poets that were to rise beyond the

Atlantic, and, under new constellations as he supposed, were to create a new empire of English letters:

> "And as there plenty grows
> Of laurel everywhere,—
>   Apollo's sacred tree,
>   You, it may see,
> A poet's brows
> To crown, that may sing there." [7]

[7] Works of Drayton, Anderson's ed., 583.

Chapter II

Virginia: The First Writer

I. The arrival in America of the first Americans—A fortunate blunder—Satisfaction with their new home.
II. The sort of men they were—Their leaders—Captain John Smith—His previous career—His character—His important relation to early American settlements—The first writer in American literature.
III. His first book—Its publication in London in 1608—A literary synchronism—American literature and John Milton—Synopsis of the book—Notable passages—The fable of his rescue by Pocahontas—The place of the book at the head of American literature—Summary of its literary traits.
IV. His second American writing—A bold letter to his London patrons—His knowledge refusing to be commanded by their ignorance—The kind of men to make good colonists of—Early symptoms of American recalcitrance.
V. His third American work—Vivid pictures of Virginia—The climate—The country—The productions—The Indians—His fine statement of the utility of the Virginian enterprise.
VI. Captain John Smith's return to England—His subsequent career—A baffled explorer—His pride in the American colonies—Utilized by the playwrights—Thomas Fuller's sarcastic account of him—His champions—Final estimate.

I

THE three little ships which bore so many hopes, dropping from London down the Thames on the 20th of December,[1] 1606, were vexed by opposing winds and were kept shivering within sight of the

[1] George Percy, in Purchas, IV. 1685.

History of American Literature

English coast for several weeks; then, instead of pursuing the straightforward westerly course to America, they curved southward, meandering foolishly by the Canaries, Dominica, Guadeloupe and elsewhere, to the great loss of time, food, health, and patience; and did not reach their journey's end until the 26th of April, 1607—a journey's end to which they were at last blown by the providence of a rough storm, after "the mariners had three days passed their reckoning and found no land." [2] No blunder in man's performance could have been more happily condoned by Heaven's pity; for these poor little ships, groping along the coast of America in great geographic darkness, and seeking only "to find out a safe port in the entrance of some navigable river," [3] were guided by the finger of Him who points out the tracks of the winds and the courses of national destiny, into the noblest bay along the whole coast, and upon a land of balm and verdure. They had come to Virginia at the happy moment when nature in that region wears her sweetest smile and sings her loveliest notes. They were amazed, as one [4] of them tells us, at the opulence of life visible all about them; at the oysters "which lay on the ground as thick as stones," many with pearls in them; at the earth "all flowing over with fair flowers of sundry colors and kinds, as though it had been in any garden or orchard in England;" at "the woods full of cedar and cypress trees, with other trees which issue out sweet gums, like to balsam." "Heaven and earth," exclaimed another [5] of that delighted company, "never agreed better to frame a place for man's habitation."

II

Thus began our American civilization; and among those first Englishmen huddled together behind palisadoes in Jamestown in 1607, were some who laid the foundations of American literature. There were about a hundred of them all. As we look over the ancient list of their names and designations, we alight upon some facts which bode little good to an enterprise in which there is no safe room for

[2] Capt. J. Smith, "Gen. Hist." I. 150.
[3] From their Instructions, given in Neill, "Hist. Va. Co. Lond." 9.
[4] George Percy, in Purchas, IV. 1688.   [5] Capt. J. Smith, "Gen. Hist." I. 114.

Virginia: The First Writer

persons afflicted with constitutional objections to hard work. The earliest formal History of Virginia [6] contains testimony that herein lay the worst peril of the enterprise; that besides one carpenter, two blacksmiths, two sailors, and a few others named "laborers," "all the rest were poor gentlemen, tradesmen, serving-men, libertines, and such like, ten times more fit to spoil a commonwealth than either begin one, or but help to maintain one." But in this heterogeneous party of forcible Feebles, were a few men of some grip and note, such as brave old Bartholomew Gosnold, Edward Maria Wingfield, John Martin, Gabriel Archer, Robert Hunt their saintly chaplain, and George Percy a brother of the Earl of Northumberland. And there was one other man in that little group of adventurers who still has a considerable name in the world. In that year 1607, when he first set foot in Virginia, Captain John Smith was only twenty-seven years old; but even then he had made himself somewhat famous in England as a daring traveller in Southern Europe, in Turkey and the East. He was perhaps the last professional knight-errant that the world saw; a free lance, who could not hear of a fight going on anywhere in the world without hastening to have a hand in it; a sworn champion of the ladies also, all of whom he loved too ardently to be guilty of the invidious offence of marrying any one of them; a restless, vain, ambitious, overbearing, blustering fellow, who made all men either his hot friends or his hot enemies; a man who down to the present hour has his celebrity in the world chiefly on account of alleged exploits among Turks, Tartars, and Indians, of which exploits he alone has furnished the history—never failing to celebrate himself in them all as the one resplendent and invincible hero.

This extremely vivid and resolute man comes before us now for particular study, not because he was the most conspicuous person in the first successful American colony, but because he was the writer of the first book in American literature. It is impossible to doubt that as a storyteller he fell into the traveller's habit of drawing a long bow. In the narration of incidents that had occurred in his own wild life he had an aptitude for being intensely interesting; and it seemed to be his theory that if the original facts were not in themselves quite so interesting as they should have been, so much the

[6] Capt. J. Smith, "Gen. Hist." I. 241.

worse for the original facts. Yet in spite of this habit, Captain John Smith had many great and magnanimous qualities; and we surely cannot help being drawn to him with affectionate admiration, when we remember his large services in the work of colonizing both Virginia and New England, his sufferings in that cause, and his unquenchable love for it until death. In his later life, after he had been baffled in many of his plans and hopes, he wrote, in London, of the American colonies these words: "By that acquaintance I have with them, I call them my children; for they have been my wife, my hawks, hounds, my cards, my dice, and in total my best content, as indifferent to my heart as my left hand to my right." [7]

Then, too, as students of literature we shall be drawn to Captain John Smith as belonging to that noble type of manhood of which the Elizabethan period produced so many examples—the man of action who was also a man of letters, the man of letters who was also a man of action: the wholesomest type of manhood anywhere to be found; body and brain both active, both cultivated; the mind not made fastidious and morbid by too much bookishness, nor coarse and dull by too little; not a doer who is dumb, not a speech-maker who cannot do; the knowledge that comes of books widened and freshened by the knowledge that comes of experience; the literary sense fortified by common sense; the bashfulness and delicacy of the scholar hovering as a finer presence above the forceful audacity of the man of the world; at once bookman, penman, swordsman, diplomat, sailor, courtier, orator. Of this type of manhood, spacious, strong, refined, and sane, were the best men of the Elizabethan time, George Gascoigne, Sir Philip Sidney, Sir Walter Raleigh, and in a modified sense Hakluyt, Bacon, Sackville, Shakespeare, Ben Jonson, and nearly all the rest. To this type of manhood Captain John Smith aspired to belong. "Many of the most eminent warriors," said he, "what their swords did, their pens writ. Though I be never so much their inferior, yet I hold it no great error to follow good examples." [8] In another book,[9] he expanded the thought in a way that shows it to

---

[7] Smith's "Gen. Hist." in Pinkerton, XIII. 245. He adds, in the plain English of the period: "for all their discoveries I have yet heard of are but pigs of my own sow."

[8] Dedication of "True Travels."   [9] "General History," I. 57.

Virginia: The First Writer

have been a pleasant one to him: "This history . . . might and ought to have been clad in better robes than my rude military hand can cut out in paper ornaments; but because of the most things therein I am no compiler by hearsay but have been a real actor, I take myself to have a property in them, and therefore have been bold to challenge them to come under the reach of my own rough pen." And that he had achieved his ambition for this spherical form of excellence was the belief of many of his contemporaries, one of whom wrote thus of him and of his book on the history of Virginia and New England:

> "Like Cæsar now thou writ'st what thou hast done,
> These acts, this book, will live while there's a sun." [10]

III

Captain John Smith became a somewhat prolific author;[11] but while nearly all of his books have a leading reference to America, only three of them were written during the period of his residence as a colonist in America. Only these three, therefore, can be claimed by us as belonging to the literature of our country.

The first of these books, "A True Relation of Virginia,"[12] is of deep interest to us, not only on account of its graphic style and the strong light it throws upon the very beginning of our national history, but as being unquestionably the earliest book in American literature. It was written during the first thirteen months of the life of the first American colony, and gives a simple and picturesque account of the stirring events which took place there during that time, under his own eye. It was probably carried to London by Captain Nelson of the good ship Phœnix, which sailed from Jamestown on the second of June, 1608; and it was published in London and sold "at the Grey-hound in Paul's Church-Yard," in the latter part of the same year—not far from the very day when the child John Milton was born, and in a house only three streets distant. Perhaps

---

[10] Capt. J. Smith's "General History," I. 65.

[11] For a complete list of his writings, see Charles Deane's ed. of Smith's "True Relation," Preface, xlvi.

[12] Reprinted, Boston, 1866, and edited in his own admirable manner, with fulness of learning and great accuracy, by Charles Deane.

19

History of American Literature

I may be pardoned for indulging what will seem to some a mere literary caprice, by placing these two events side by side in this history, even as they were placed side by side in the happenings of actual fact. John Milton was born into life, and the first American book was born into print, in the same year, and in the same part of the year, and almost on the same spot. The child born on that ninth of December, 1608, in Bread Street, a few steps from the book-shop where the earliest of American writings was first placed on sale—the child around whose cradle may have been repeated by his father some of the wild and exciting incidents related in that book—was to grow up into a colossal literary figure not only in that century but in all centuries: he was to be in an eminent degree the exponent of the great ideas of * religious and political freedom that were to form the basis of American civilization, which, like himself, was then beginning to live; and the moral peculiarities of his genius, austere earnestness, a devout ethical force, an obstinate habit of judging of life and even of art and letters from the throne of moral laws and of moral tendencies, were to be likewise the most marked spiritual qualities of that remote and unfriended national literature which began its career almost at the very same moment when he began his, and almost on the very same spot.

The title-pages of the seventeenth century are not the least expressive or amusing portions of the books of that century; and if ever an old title-page shall deserve full quotation at our hands, this does so. It is as follows: "A True Relation of such occurrences and accidents of note as hath happened in Virginia since the first planting of that colony, which is now resident in the South part thereof, till the last return from thence. Written by Captain Smith, Coronel of the said colony, to a worshipful friend of his in England. London: Printed for John Tappe, and are to be sold at the Grey-hound in Paul's Church-Yard, by W. W.   1608."

Barely hinting at the length and tediousness of the sea-voyage, the author plunges with epic promptitude into the midst of the action by describing their arrival in Virginia, their first ungentle passages with

[* The corrected copy of 1878 has a line in the right-hand margin extending from "not far from the very day when" to "exponent of the great ideas of," which ended the text page. In the margin is the notation, "See Macaulay Essays, I. 233."]

Virginia: The First Writer

the Indians, their selection of a place of settlement, their first civil organization, their first expedition for discovery toward the upper waters of the James River, the first formidable Indian attack upon their village, and the first return for England, two months after their arrival, of the ships that had brought them to Virginia. Upon the departure of these ships, bitter quarrels broke out among the colonists; "things were neither carried with that discretion nor any business effected in such good sort as wisdom would; . . . through which disorder, God being angry with us plagued us with such famine and sickness that the living were scarce able to bury the dead. . . . As yet we had no houses to cover us; our tents were rotten, and our cabins worse than nought. . . . The president and Captain Martin's sickness compelled me to be cape-merchant,[13] and yet to spare no pains in making houses for the company, who, notwithstanding our misery, little ceased their malice, grudging, and muttering . . . being in such despair as they would rather starve and rot with idleness than be persuaded to do anything for their own relief without constraint."[14] But the energetic Captain had an eager passion for making tours of exploration along the coast and up the rivers; and after telling how he procured corn from the Indians and thus supplied the instant necessities of the starving colonists, he proceeds to relate the history of a tour of discovery made by him up the Chickahominy, on which tour happened the famous incident of his falling into captivity among the Indians. The reader will not fail to notice that in this earliest book of his, written before Powhatan's daughter, the princess Pocahontas, had become celebrated in England, and before Captain Smith had that enticing motive for representing himself as specially favored by her, he speaks of Powhatan as full of friendliness to him; he expressly states that his own life was in no danger at the hands of that Indian potentate; and of course he has no situation on which to hang the romantic incident of his rescue by Pocahontas from impending death.[15] Having ascended the Chickahominy about sixty miles, he took with him a single Indian guide and pushed into the woods. Within a quarter of an hour he "heard a loud cry and a hallooing of

---

[13] Treasurer.   [14] "True Relation," Deane's ed., 12-15.

[15] This pretty story has now lost historical credit, and is generally given up by critical students of our early history.

Indians;" and almost immediately he was assaulted by two hundred of them, led by Opechancanough, an under-king to the emperor Powhatan. The valiant Captain, in a contest so unequal, certainly was entitled to a shield; and this he rather ungenerously extemporized by seizing his Indian guide and with his garters binding the Indian's arm to his own hand, thus, as he coolly expresses it, making "my hind" "my barricado." As the Indians still pressed toward him, Captain Smith discharged his pistol, which wounded some of his assailants and taught them all a wholesome respect by the terror of its sound; then, after much parley, he surrendered to them, and was carried off prisoner to a place about six miles distant. There he expected to be at once put to death, but was agreeably surprised by being treated with the utmost kindness. For supper that night they gave him "a quarter of venison and some ten pound of bread;" and each morning thereafter three women presented him with "three great platters of fine bread," and "more venison than ten men could devour." "Though eight ordinarily guarded me, I wanted not what they could devise to content me; and still our larger acquaintance increased our better affection." [16] After many days spent in travelling hither and yon with his captors, he was at last, by his own request, delivered up to Powhatan, the over-lord of all that region. He gives a picturesque description of the barbaric state in which he was received by this potent chieftain, whom he found "proudly lying upon a bedstead a foot high, upon ten or twelve mats," the emperor himself being "richly hung with many chains of great pearls about his neck, and covered with a great covering of raccoon skins. At head sat a woman; at his feet, another; on each side, sitting upon a mat upon the ground were ranged his chief men on each side the fire, ten in a rank; and behind them, as many young women, each a great chain of white beads over their shoulders, their heads painted in red; and with such a grave and majestical countenance as drave me into admiration to see such state in a naked salvage. He kindly welcomed me with good words, and great platters of sundry victuals, assuring me his friendship and my liberty within four days." Thus day by day passed in pleasant discourse with his imperial host, who asked him about "the manner of our ships, and sailing the seas, the

[16] "True Relation of Va." 22–33.

Virginia: The First Writer

earth and skies, and of our God," and who feasted him not only with continual "platters of sundry victuals," but with glowing descriptions of his own vast dominions stretching away beyond the rivers and the mountains to the land of the setting sun. "Seeing what pride he had in his great and spacious dominions, . . . I requited his discourse in describing to him the territories of Europe which was subject to our great king, . . . the innumerable multitude of his ships. I gave him to understand the noise of trumpets and terrible manner of fighting were under Captain Newport my father. . . . Thus having with all the kindness he could devise sought to content me, he sent me home with four men, one that usually carried my gown and knapsack after me, two other loaded with bread, and one to accompany me." [17] The author then gives a description of his journey back to Jamestown, where "each man with truest signs of joy" welcomed him; of his second visit to Powhatan; of various encounters with hostile and thievish Indians; and of the arrival from England of Captain Nelson in the Phœnix, April the twentieth, 1608—an event which "did ravish" them "with exceeding joy." Late in the narrative he makes his first reference to Pocahontas, whom he speaks of as "a child of ten years old, which not only for feature, countenance and proportion much exceedeth any of the rest of his people, but for wit and spirit the only nonpareil of his country." [18] After mentioning some further dealings with the Indians, he concludes the book with an account of the preparations for the return to England of Captain Nelson and his ship; and describes those remaining as "being in good health, all our men well contented, free from mutinies, in love one with another, and as we hope in a continual peace with the Indians, where we doubt not but by God's gracious assistance and the adventurers' willing minds and speedy furtherance to so honorable an action in after times, to see our nation to enjoy a country, not only exceeding pleasant for habitation, but also very profitable for commerce in general, no doubt pleasing to Almighty God, honorable to our gracious sovereign, and commodious generally to the whole kingdom." [19]

Thus, with words of happy omen, ends the first book in American literature. It is a book that was written, not in lettered ease, nor in

[17] "True Relation of Va." 33–38.   [18] Ibid. 72–73.   [19] Ibid. 76–77.

23

History of American Literature

"the still air of delightful studies," but under a rotten tent in the wilderness, perhaps by the flickering blaze of a pine knot, in the midst of tree-stumps and the filth and clamor of a pioneer's camp, and within the fragile palisades which alone shielded the little band of colonists from the ever-hovering peril of an Indian massacre. It was not composed as a literary effort. It was meant to be merely a budget of information for the public at home, and especially for the London stockholders of the Virginia Company. Hastily, apparently without revision, it was wrought vehemently by the rough hand of a soldier and an explorer, in the pauses of a toil that was both fatiguing and dangerous, and while the incidents which he records were fresh and clinging in his memory. Probably he thought little of any rules of literary art as he wrote this book: probably he did not think of writing a book at all. Out of the abundance of his materials, glowing with pride over what he had done in the great enterprise, eager to inspire the home-keeping patrons of the colony with his own resolute cheer, and accustomed for years to portray in pithy English the adventures of which his life was fated to be full, the bluff Captain just stabbed his paper with inken words; he composed not a book but a big letter; he folded it up, and tossed it upon the deck of Captain Nelson's departing ship. But though he may have had no expectation of doing such a thing, he wrote a book that is not unworthy to be the beginning of the new English literature in America. It has faults enough, without doubt. Had it not these, it would have been too good for the place it occupies. The composition was extemporaneous; there appears in it some chronic misunderstanding between the nominatives and their verbs; now and then the words and clauses of a sentence are jumbled together in blinding heaps; but in spite of all its crudities, here is racy English, pure English, the sinewy, picturesque and throbbing diction of the navigators and soldiers of the Elizabethan time. And although the materials of this book are not moulded in nice proportion, the story is well told. The man has an eye and a hand for that thing. He sees the essential facts of a situation, and throws the rest away; and the business moves straight forward.

Virginia: The First Writer

IV

About three months after the departure for England of the ship which carried to the printing-press the book of which an extended account has just been given, there arrived from England another ship, bringing a new supply of colonists, and bringing likewise a letter of fantastic instructions and of querulous complaints from the London stockholders of the company. It fell to Captain John Smith, as the new president of the colony, to make reply to this document; and he did it in the production which forms the second title in our list of his American writings. This production is brief; but it is a most vigorous, trenchant, and characteristic piece of writing, a transcript of the intense spirit of the man who wrote it, all ablaze with the light it casts into that primal hot-bed of wrangling, indolence, and misery, the village of Jamestown. Let us reproduce some parts of this letter, the sentences of which seem to fly as straight and hard as bullets:—"I received your letter wherein you write that our minds are so set upon faction and idle conceits in dividing the country without your consents; and that we feed you but with if's and and's, hopes, and some few proofs, as if we would keep the mystery of the business to ourselves; and that we must expressly follow your instructions sent by Captain Newport, the charge of whose voyage amounts to near two thousand pounds,—the which if we cannot defray by the ship's return, we are alike to remain as banished men. To these particulars, I humbly entreat your pardons if I offend you with my rude answer. For our factions, . . . I cannot prevent them. . . . For the idle letter sent to my Lord of Salisbury by the president and his confederates for dividing the country and so forth, what it was I know not; for you saw no hand of mine to it, nor ever dreamt I of any such matter. That we feed you with hopes and so forth, though I be no scholar, I am past a school-boy; and I desire but to know what either you and these here do know, but that I have learned to tell you by the continual hazard of my life. I have not concealed from you anything I know. . . . Expressly to follow your instructions by Captain Newport, though they be performed, I was directly against it; but . . . I was content to be overruled by the major part of the council, I fear to the hazard of us all; which now is generally confessed, when it is too late. . . . For the charge of this voyage of two or three thousand pounds, we have not received the value of an hundred pounds. . . . From your ship we had not provision in victuals worth twenty pound; and we are more than two hundred to live upon this,—the one half sick, the other little better. For the sailors, I confess they daily make good cheer; but our diet is a little meal and water, and not sufficient of that. Though there be fish in the sea, fowls in the air, and beasts in the woods, their bounds are so large, they so wild, and we so weak and ignorant, we cannot much trouble them. . . . Captain Ratcliffe is now called Sicklemore. . . . I have sent you him home, lest the company should cut his throat. . . . When you send again, I entreat you rather send but thirty carpenters, husbandmen, gardeners, fishermen, blacksmiths, masons, and diggers up of trees' roots, well provided, than a thousand of such as we have; for except we be able both to lodge them and feed them, the most will consume with want of necessaries, before they can be made good for anything. . . . These are the causes that have kept us in Virginia from laying such a foundation that ere this might have given much better content and satisfaction; but as yet you must not look for any profitable returns. So I humbly rest." [20]

Such are the principal portions of Captain John Smith's letter of explanation to the London proprietors of the company whose affairs in Virginia he was just then conducting. Certainly this writing is racy, terse, fearless; a style of sentence carved out by a sword; the incisive speech of a man of action; Hotspur rhetoric, jerking with impatience, truculence, and noble wrath. And it is not without an under-meaning in many ways, that this production, among the very earliest in American literature, should communicate to England a foretaste of what proved to be the incurable American habit of talking back to her. From the beginning, it was hard for England to see the just limits of her interference with her own colonial children in America; and though three thousand miles away from them, she could not stay her motherly tongue from advising and commanding them concerning the details of their life in the wilderness about which they inevitably knew more than she did. One can easily imagine what a shock this epistolary retort of Captain John Smith

[20] Printed in Capt. J. Smith's "Gen. Hist." I. 200–203.

must have given to the dignified nerves of those kindly and lordly patrons in London; how its saucy sentences must have made them gasp and stare. Almost the earliest note, then, of American literature is a note of unsubmissiveness. Captain John Smith's letter, in the first decade of the seventeenth century, is a premonitory symptom of the Declaration of Independence.

V

In the same parcel with this remarkable letter of Captain Smith's was enclosed by him to the adventurers in London another document —a proof of his irrepressible activity and of his versatile talent—a "Map of the Bay and the Rivers, with an annexed Relation of the countries, and nations that inhabit them." [21] This document did not get into print until 1612, when it was published at Oxford, and constitutes the third work in the list of the author's American writings. It deals with the climate and topography of Virginia, with its fauna and flora, and particularly with the characteristics of its earlier inhabitants, the Indians. As a whole the work is uncommonly picturesque and even amusing; for though devoted to climatic and topographic descriptions, to matters of natural history, and to the coarse features of savage existence, the genius of the writer quickens and brightens it all, strewing his pages with easy and delightful strokes of imagery, quaint humor, shrewdness, and a sort of rough unconscious grace. His introductory chapter is full of the joy which the first visitors to this country felt in the sweet air, the rich soil, the waters, the mountains, in all the large and majestic framework of nature in the new world: "The temperature of this country doth agree well with English constitutions. . . . The summer is hot as in Spain; the winter cold as in France or England. . . . The winds here are variable; but the like thunder and lightning to purify the air, I have seldom either seen or heard in Europe. . . . There is but one entrance by sea into this country, and that is at the mouth of a very goodly bay, eighteen or twenty miles broad. . . . Within is a country that may have the prerogative over the most pleasant places known,

---

[21] Reprinted with some alterations of text in Capt. J. Smith's "Gen. Hist." I. 113–148.

for large and pleasant navigable rivers. . . . Here are mountains, hills, plains, valleys, rivers and brooks all running most pleasantly into a fair bay, compassed, but for the mouth, with fruitful and delightsome land. In the bay and rivers are many isles, both great and small. . . . The mountains are of divers natures; for at the head of the bay the rocks are of a composition like mill-stones, some of marble and so forth. And many pieces like crystal we found, as thrown down by water from those mountains. . . . These waters wash from the rocks such glistering tinctures that the ground in some places seemeth as gilded; where both the rocks and the earth are so splendent to behold that better judgments than ours might have been persuaded they contained more than probabilities. The vesture of the earth in most places doth manifestly prove the nature of the soil to be lusty and very rich." [22]

This charming passage, pregnant with adroit hints, must have proved very seductive when it came to be read in England; it must have made many an eye sparkle with the expectation of golden returns from this mysterious new realm of theirs, all bulging and variegated with precious metals and precious stones. And the passage just quoted contains, likewise, not a few of the best traits of the author's descriptive manner, which is vital with the breath of imagination, and tinted with the very hues of nature. One has not to go far along the sentences elsewhere in this book without finding all the dull and hard details of his subject made delightful by felicities of phrase that seem to spring up as easily as wild flowers in the woods of his own Virginia. He speaks of "an infinite number of small rundels and pleasant springs that disperse themselves for the best service as do the veins of a man's body;" [23] of "a bay wherein falleth three or four pretty brooks and creeks that half intrench the inhabitants of Warraskoyac;" [24] of the river Pamaunkee that "divideth itself into two gallant branches;" [25] of the river Patawomeke "fed . . . with many sweet rivers and springs which fall from the bordering hills." [26] There is often a quaint flavor in his words—that racy and piquant simplicity which so much charms us in the English descrip-

[22] From the reprint in Capt. J. Smith's "Gen. Hist." I. 113–115.
[23] Ibid. I. 116. [24] Ibid. I. 116.
[25] Ibid. I. 117. [26] Ibid. I. 118.

Virginia: The First Writer

tive prose of the sixteenth century, and the first third of the seventeenth. He speaks of a plum called Putchamins, which when unripe "will draw a man's mouth awry with much torment;" [27] of the Indian men of Virginia who "wear half their beards shaven, the other half long; for barbers they use their women, who with two shells will grate away the hair of any fashion they please." [28] Referring to the personal ornaments of the Indians, he mentions that "in each ear commonly they have three great holes, whereat they hang chains, bracelets, or copper. Some of their men wear in those holes a small green and yellow colored snake, near half a yard in length, which crawling and lapping herself about his neck oftentimes familiarly would kiss his lips. Others wear a dead rat tied by the tail." [29] "The men bestow their times in fishing, hunting, wars, and such man-like exercises, scorning to be seen in any woman-like exercise, which is the cause that the women be very painful, and the men often idle." [30] He says that "for their music they use a thick cane, on which they pipe as on a recorder. . . . But their chief instruments are rattles made of small gourds or pumpions' shells. . . . These mingled with their voices sometimes twenty or thirty together, make such a terrible noise as would rather affright than delight any man." [31] He describes their orators as making speeches of welcome to a public guest, "testifying their love . . . with such vehemency, and so great passions that they sweat till they drop, and are so out of breath that they can scarce speak; so that a man would take them to be exceeding angry or stark mad." [32] He tells of a certain Indian king who "did believe that our God as much exceeded theirs as our guns did their bows and arrows; and many times did send to me to Jamestown, entreating me to pray to my God for rain, for their gods would not send them any." [33] Remembering those tender-fingered drones calling themselves "gentlemen" who constituted so large and so useless a portion of the first colonists in Virginia, one cannot help relishing the frequent sarcasms with which this impetuous and indomitable man spices his references to them; in one place characterizing them as persons who never "did anything but devour the fruits of other men's labor;" and who, "be-

---

[27] Capt. J. Smith's "Gen. Hist." I. 122.
[28] Ibid. I. 129.
[29] Ibid. I. 130.
[30] Ibid. I. 131.
[31] Ibid. I. 136.
[32] Ibid. I. 136, 137.
[33] Ibid. I. 141.

cause they found not English cities, nor such fair houses, nor at their own wishes any of their accustomed dainties, with feather beds and down pillows, taverns and alehouses in every breathing place, neither such plenty of gold and silver and dissolute liberty as they expected, had little or no care of anything but to pamper their bellies, to fly away with our pinnaces, or procure their means to return for England; for the country was to them a misery, a ruin, a death, a hell." [34]

There are in this book some specimens of portrait-painting that show no slight power. Let us take, for example, his description of the appearance and state of the famous Indian king, Powhatan: "He is of personage a tall well-proportioned man, with a sour look, his head somewhat gray, his beard so thin that it seemeth none at all, his age near sixty; of a very able and hardy body to endure any labor. About his person ordinarily attendeth a guard of forty or fifty of the tallest men his country doth afford. Every night upon the four quarters of his house are four sentinels, each from other a slight shoot, and at every half hour one from the *corps de garde* doth halloo, shaking his lips with his finger between them; unto whom every sentinel doth answer round from his stand. If any fail, they presently send forth an officer that beateth him extremely." [35] Here, likewise, is some effective description in his account of the Susquehanna Indians, whom he encountered on one of his tours of discovery, and whose huge shapes and strange costumes appear to have impressed him greatly: "But to proceed, sixty of those Susquehannocks came to us with skins, bows, arrows, targets, beads, swords, and tobacco pipes for presents. Such great and well proportioned men are seldom seen; for they seemed like giants to the English, yea and to the neighbors, yet seemed of an honest and simple disposition, with much ado restrained from adoring us as gods. Those are the strangest people of all those countries, both in language and attire. For their language, it may well beseem their proportions, sounding from them as a voice in a vault. Their attire is the skins of bears and wolves. . . . One had the head of a wolf hanging in a chain for a jewel, his tobacco pipe three quarters of a yard long . . . sufficient to beat out one's brains; with bows, arrows, and clubs suitable to their greatness. . . . The picture of the greatest of them is signified in the map; the calf of

---

[34] Capt. J. Smith's "Gen. Hist." I. 145.   [35] Ibid. I. 142, 143.

whose leg was three quarters of a yard about, and all the rest of his limbs so answerable to that proportion that he seemed the goodliest man we ever saw." [36]

Near the end of this little book occurs one sentence in which the author has admirably compacted a statement of all the nobler utilities of the young colony of Virginia: "So, then, here is a place, a nurse for soldiers, a practice for mariners, a trade for merchants, a reward for the good; and that which is most of all, a business, most acceptable to God, to bring such poor infidels to the knowledge of God and his holy gospel." [37]

We may be well content to let this strong and beautiful sentence linger in our memories as the last one we shall draw from Captain John Smith's American writings, and as an honorable token of his broad and clear grasp of the meaning of that great national impulse which stirred the heart of England in his time, for the founding of a new English empire in America.

VI

The book which we have just inspected is the third work written by Captain John Smith in America; and as students of American literature, we must here end our study of his writings. He remained in Virginia about twelve months after the time to which the latest of these writings refers, returning to England in the fall of 1609. It is not improbable that he was recalled to England by the displeasure of the London proprietors of the Virginia company. Dropped from their service, he remained in England until 1614, when with two ships he made a voyage of trade and exploration to New England, and came back the same year with a map, drawn by himself, of the country between the Penobscot and Cape Cod. In the year 1615 he sailed again for New England, taking with him a colony for settlement there; but on the voyage out he was captured by a French pirate and carried prisoner to Rochelle, whence he soon escaped and made his way back to England. From that time until his death in 1631 he probably never left England again. His career of daring adventure was over. Though he continued to take the most passionate interest

---

[36] Capt. J. Smith's "Gen. Hist." I. 119, 120.   [37] Ibid. I. 128.

in American colonization, and to agitate and plot and strive for it, he had to appease his restless spirit with the tame joys of authorship. He appears to have been looked upon henceforward as the veteran explorer, and to have been consulted and quoted as an authority in the practical details of colonization. The marvellous tales of his exploits which he told in his books furnished welcome materials for Ben Jonson and other playwrights; so that he himself said, half in pride, half in complaint, "they have acted my fatal tragedies upon the stage and racked my relations at their pleasure." [38] Even then there were not wanting those who suspected the fidelity of his narratives, and who accused him of adorning his heroic anecdotes with exploits which he had wrought only in imagination. "Envy hath taxed me," he says, "to have writ too much and done too little." [39] Thomas Fuller, in his "Worthies of England," [40] first published thirty-one years after Captain Smith's death, gives perhaps the cool afterthought of many of the Captain's contemporaries, in these contemptuous and delicately cutting words: "From the Turks in Europe he passed to the pagans in America, where . . . such his perils, preservations, dangers, deliverances, they seem to most men above belief, to some beyond truth. Yet have we two witnesses to attest them, the prose and the pictures, both in his own book; and it soundeth much to the diminution of his deeds, that he alone is the herald to publish and proclaim them." Probably it was this base incredulity of his contemporaries, this hard historical Sadduceeism, that Captain Smith and his immediate champions meant to designate by the words "envy," and "detraction," which meet us in their allusions to the reception then given to his writings. A namesake of the author, one N. Smith, thus bravely steps forward as his defender:

> "Sith thou, the man deserving of these ages,
>   Much pain hast ta'en for this our kingdom's good,
> In climes unknown, 'mongst Turkës and salvages,
>   T' enlarge our bounds, though with thy loss of blood,
> Hence damn'd Detraction—stand not in our way!
> Envy itself will not the truth gainsay." [41]

[38] "Epistle Dedicatory" in "True Travels."   [39] Ibid.
[40] Edition of 1840, I. 275, 276.   [41] Capt. J. Smith's "Gen. Hist." I. 246.

Virginia: The First Writer

It is quite plain that while the weak spot in Captain Smith's character, his love of telling large stories, was suspected by many of his contemporaries, he nevertheless had among the best of them stanch and admiring friends. Sir Robert Cotton, the Earls of Pembroke, of Lindsay, and of Dover, the Duchess of Lenox, and Lord Hunsdon, were those in the upper spheres of society whom he could publicly name as his patrons and friends. Among the writers of commendatory verses prefixed and affixed to his books, are such eminent persons as Samuel Purchas, George Wither, and John Donne; and nearly all of these writers, whether now famous or obscure, apply to him terms of homage and endearment. Donne calls him "brave Smith;" Richard James calls him "dear noble Captain;" Ed. Jordan exclaims:

> "Good men will yield thee praise; then slight the rest;
> 'Tis best, praise-worthy, to have pleased the best;" [42]

while an anonymous writer, after reciting the names of the great explorers, Columbus, Cabot, Frobisher, Humphrey Gilbert, Drake, Gosnold, and others, says:

> "Though these be gone and left behind a name,
>   Yet Smith is here to anvil out a piece
> To after ages and eternal fame,
>   That we may have the golden Jason's fleece.
> He, Vulcan-like, did forge a true plantation,
>   And chained their kings to his immortal glory,
> Restoring peace and plenty to the nation,
>   Regaining honor to this worthy story." [43]

After all the abatements which a fair criticism must make from the praise of Captain John Smith either as a doer or as a narrator, his writings still make upon us the impression of a certain personal largeness in him, magnanimity, affluence, sense, and executive force. Over all his personal associates in American adventure he seems to tower, by the natural loftiness and reach of the perception with which he grasped the significance of their vast enterprise, and the means to its success. As a writer his merits are really great—clearness, force, vividness, picturesque and dramatic energy, a diction racy and crisp.

[42] In Capt. J. Smith's "Gen. Hist."   [43] Ibid. 61.

He had the faults of an impulsive, irascible, egotistic, and imaginative nature; he sometimes bought human praise at too high a price; but he had great abilities in word and deed; his nature was upon the whole generous and noble; and during the first two decades of the seventeenth century he did more than any other Englishman to make an American nation and an American literature possible.

Chapter III

Virginia: Other Early Writers

I. George Percy of Northumberland—His worthiness—His graphic sketches of the brightness and gloom of their first year in America.
II. William Strachey—His terrible voyage and wreck with Sir Thomas Gates—His book descriptive of it and of the state of the colony in Virginia—Some germs of Shakespeare's Tempest—Strachey's wonderful picture of a storm at sea.
III. Alexander Whitaker, the devoted Christian missionary—His life and death and memory in Virginia—His appeal to England in "Good News from Virginia."
IV. John Pory—His coming to Virginia—His previous career—A cosmopolite in a colony—His return to England—His amusing sketches of Indian character—The humors and consolations of pioneer life along the James River.
V. George Sandys—His high personal qualities and his fine genius—His literary services before coming to America—Michael Drayton's exhortation to entice the Muses to Virginia—Sandys's fidelity to his literary vocation amid calamity and fatigue—His translation of Ovid—Its relation to poetry and scholarship in the new world—Passages from it—The story of Philomela—His poetic renown.

I

IN that little colony of earliest Americans, seated at Jamestown, and for more than twenty years struggling against almost every menace of destruction from without and within, were several other writers who have some claim to our notice. One of these was George Percy. Every slight glimpse we get of him through the chinks of contemporary reference tends to convince us that the uncommon respect in which he was held by his associates was rendered to him quite as much because he was a modest, brave, and honorable man, as because he was a brother of the great Earl of Northumberland. He composed a "Discourse of the Plantations of the Southern Colony in Virginia by the English," of which, however, only a fragment is preserved—the fragment occupying six folio pages in Purchas's "Pilgrims." The portion of his book thus preserved relates the history of the colony from its departure out of England down to September, 1607; and is written in that style of idiomatic and nervous English prose which seems to have been the birthright of so many active Englishmen in the Elizabethan age. His descriptions of the beauty and fertility of Virginia as it appeared to the sea-sad eyes of the colonists in that happy month of their arrival, throw by contrast a deeper gloom upon the picture which he soon has to paint of the miseries besetting their first summer in Virginia—a summer which dragged over them slowly its horrible trail of homesickness, discord, starvation, pestilence, and Indian hostility. "Our men were destroyed with cruel diseases, as swellings, flixes, burning fevers, and by wars; and some departed suddenly. But for the most part they died of mere famine. There were never Englishmen left in a foreign country in such misery as we were, in this new discovered Virginia. We watched every three nights lying on the bare cold ground, what weather soever came; warded all the next day which brought our men to be most feeble wretches. Our food was but a small can of barley sod in water to five men a day; our drink cold water taken out of the river, which was at a flood very salt, at a low tide full of slime and filth, which was the destruction of many of our men. Thus we lived for the space of five months in this miserable distress, not having five able men to man our bulwarks upon any occasion. If it had not pleased God to put a terror in the savages' hearts, we had all perished by those wild and cruel pagans, being in that weak estate as we were; our men night and day groaning in every corner of the fort most pitiful to hear. If there were any conscience in men, it would make their hearts to bleed to hear the pitiful murmurings and outcries of our sick men, without relief every night and day for the space of six weeks; some departing out of the world, many times three or four in a night,

Virginia: Other Early Writers

in the morning their bodies trailed out of their cabins like dogs to be buried." [1]

II

During the first decade of American literature a little book was written in Virginia, which, as is believed by some authors, soon rendered an illustrious service to English literature by suggesting to Shakespeare the idea of one of his noblest masterpieces, "The Tempest." It was in May of the year 1610 that sixty tattered and forlorn colonists—the last remnants of five hundred who were alive there six months before—crawled out from the block-house at Jamestown, and moved toward the river-bank to greet with a sickly welcome the unexpected arrival of Sir Thomas Gates. This brave commander with two small vessels and a hundred and fifty companions, had at last found his way into the James River after a voyage of almost incredible difficulty and peril. Just eleven months before, he had set sail from England for Virginia, with a fleet of nine ships and in charge of five hundred emigrants. On their passage, when they had been seven weeks at sea and were drawing near to the Virginia coast, they encountered a frightful tempest in which the fleet was scattered; and the admiral's ship, the Sea-Adventure, containing Sir Thomas Gates, Sir George Somers, and other distinguished and undistinguished company, was driven ashore upon one of the Bermudas. Not being heard from for many months, that ship with all on board was given up for lost. Indeed the ship itself was lost, battered to pieces upon the rocks; but out of its fragments the passengers constructed the two clumsy pinnaces in which, as just related, they at last completed their voyage to Jamestown. Among those who had

[1] Purchas, IV. 1690. Among the manuscripts of the English State Paper Office are three anonymous tracts relating to the same period as that covered by the American writings of Captain John Smith and of George Percy. These tracts were evidently written by one of their companions. They are the rough jottings of an inexpert diarist, and are too crude in expression to attract us on account of any literary merit. From copies made for George Bancroft, the American Antiquarian Society printed them in Vol. IV. of its Transactions. They were edited by Edward Everett Hale. They do contain one rather graphic and amusing passage, a description of the sturdy Indian Queen Apumatec.

borne a part in this ghastly and almost miraculous expedition was William Strachey, of whom but little is known except what is revealed in his own writings. He was a man of decided literary aptitude. Soon after his arrival here he was made secretary of Virginia, and, as he tells us, he "held it a service of duty . . . to be remembrancer of all accidents, occurrences, and undertakings"[2] connected with the colony during the time of his residence in it. Accordingly in July, 1610, when he had been in Virginia less than three months, he wrote at Jamestown and sent off to England "A True Reportory of the Wrack and Redemption of Sir Thomas Gates, Kt., upon and from the islands of the Bermudas; his coming to Virginia; and the estate of that colony then and after under the government of the Lord La Ware."[3] Whoever reads this little book will be quite ready to believe that it may have brought suggestion and inspiration even to the genius of William Shakespeare. It is a book of marvellous power. Its account of Virginia is well done; but its most striking merit is its delineation of his dreadful sea-voyage, and particularly of the tempest which, after the terror and anguish of a thousand deaths, drove them upon the rocks of the Bermudas. Here his style becomes magnificent; it has some sentences which for imaginative and pathetic beauty, for vivid implications of appalling danger and disaster, can hardly be surpassed in the whole range of English prose. It was upon St. James's day, July the twenty-fourth, 1609, "the clouds gathering thick upon us, and the winds singing and whistling most unusually," that "a dreadful storm and hideous began to blow from out the north-east, which, swelling and roaring as it were by fits, some hours with more violence than others, at length did beat all light from heaven, which, like an hell of darkness, turned black upon us, so much the more fuller of horror as in such cases horror and fear use to overrun the troubled and overmastered senses of all. . . . For surely, . . . as death comes not so sudden nor apparent, so he comes not so elvish and painful to men . . . as at sea. . . . For four and twenty hours the storm, in a restless tumult, had blown so exceedingly as we could not apprehend in our imaginations any possibility of greater violence; yet did we still find it, not only more terrible but

[2] Preface to "Laws, Divine, Moral, and Martial," in Force, Hist. Tracts, III. 2.
[3] Reprinted in Purchas, IV. 1734-1758.

more constant, fury added to fury; and one storm, urging a second more outrageous than the former . . . sometimes strikes in our ship amongst women and passengers not used to such hurly and discomforts, made us look one upon the other with troubled hearts and panting bosoms, our clamors drowned in the winds, and the winds in thunder. Prayers might well be in the heart and lips, but drowned in the outcries of officers; nothing heard that could give comfort, nothing seen that might encourage hope. It is impossible for me, had I the voice of Stentor, and expression of as many tongues as his throat of voices, to express the outcries and miseries, not languishing, but wasting our spirits. . . . Our sails wound up lay without their use; . . . the sea swelled above the clouds and gave battle unto heaven. It could not be said to rain: the waters like whole rivers did flood in the air. And this I did still observe that, whereas upon the land, when a storm hath poured itself forth once in drifts of rain, the wind, as beaten down and vanquished therewith, not long after endureth; here the glut of water . . . was no sooner a little emptied and qualified, but instantly the winds, as having gotten their mouths now free and at liberty, spake more loud, and grew more tumultuous and malignant. What shall I say? Winds and seas were as mad as fury and rage could make them. . . . There was not a moment in which the sudden splitting or instant oversetting of the ship was not expected. Howbeit, this was not all. It pleased God to bring a greater affliction upon us; for in the beginning of the storm we had received likewise a mighty leak; and the ship, in every joint almost having spewed out her oakum, . . . was grown five foot suddenly deep with water above her ballast, and we almost drowned within whilst we sat looking when to perish from above. This, imparting no less terror than danger, ran through the whole ship with much fright and amazement, startled and turned the blood, and took down the braves of the most hardy mariner of them all, insomuch as he that before happily felt not the sorrow of others, now began to sorrow for himself. . . . Once so huge a sea brake . . . upon us, as it covered our ship from stern to stem, like a garment or vast cloud; it filled her brimful . . . from the hatches up to the spar-deck. . . . During all this time the heavens looked so black upon us that it was not possible the elevation of the Pole might be observed; nor a star by night, nor sun-beam by day, was to be seen. Only upon the Thursday night, Sir George Somers being upon the watch, had an apparition of a little round light, like a faint star, trembling and streaming along with a sparkling blaze, half the height upon the main mast, and shooting sometimes from shroud to shroud, tempting to settle as it were upon any of the four shrouds; and for three or four hours together, or rather more, half the night, it kept with us, running sometimes along the main-yard to the very end and then returning. . . . But it did not light us any whit the more to our known way, who ran now, as do hoodwinked men, at all adventures. . . . East and by south we steered away as much as we could to bear upright, . . . albeit we much unrigged our ship, threw overboard much luggage, many a trunk and chest, . . . and staved many a butt of beer, hogsheads of oil, cider, wine, and vinegar, and heaved away all our ordnance on the starboard side, and had now purposed to cut down the main mast. . . . For we were much spent, and our men so weary as their strengths together failed them with their hearts, having travailed now from Tuesday till Friday morning, day and night, without either sleep or food. . . . And it being now Friday, the fourth morning, it wanted little but that there had been a general determination to have shut up hatches, and, commending our sinful souls to God, committed the ship to the mercy of the sea. . . . But see the goodness and sweet introduction of better hope, by our merciful God given unto us. Sir George Somers, when no man had dreamed of such happiness, had discovered and cried land. Indeed the morning, now three quarters gone, had won a little clearness from the days before; and it being better surveyed, the very trees were seen to move with the wind upon the shore-side. . . . By the mercy of God unto us, making out our boats, we had ere night brought all our men, women, and children . . . safe into the island. We found it to be the dangerous and dreaded island, or rather islands, of the Bermudas. . . . They be so terrible to all that ever touched on them, and such tempests, thunders, and other fearful objects are seen and heard about them, that they be called commonly the Devil's Islands, and are feared and avoided of all travellers alive, above any other place in the world; . . . it being counted of most that they can be no habitation for men, but rather given over to devils and wicked spirits."

Virginia: Other Early Writers

III

At the very time when William Strachey, in some rude cabin near the banks of the James River, was writing his most eloquent and thrilling book about Virginia and the awful voyage thither, there lived, in a comfortable parish in the north of England, a noble-minded clergyman, Alexander Whitaker, a man of apostolic zeal for the gospel, and of apostolic sorrow for all men who were still beyond the reach of the gospel; a man to whom his creed was so vivid and tremendous a fact that he stood ready to be a missionary for it, and a martyr, even at the world's end. His father was the celebrated divine, William Whitaker, master of Saint John's College, Cambridge; he himself had taken his degrees at that university; and he was happily settled, in full parochial composure, a man of property, usefulness, and good repute. But to him, such appeals from Virginia as those of William Strachey, came as a wailing cry of his own brethren for help,—all the more persuasive for the fascinating doom of danger and pain for Christ's sake, to which those appeals invited him. Accordingly in the following year, 1611, in the company of Sir Thomas Dale, this prosperous priest "did voluntarily leave his warm nest, and to the wonder of his kindred and amazement of them that knew him, undertook this . . . heroical resolution to go to Virginia, and help to bear the name of God unto the heathen."[4] Thenceforward, and for more than three years, even until his death by drowning sometime before the year 1617, Alexander Whitaker lived in Virginia a brave and blameless life, a true missionary for Christ,—the pure and beautiful light of his message going with him everywhere, across plantation and through wilderness, into the colonist's hut and the wigwam of the savage; and when at last he was seen no more of men, the tradition of him lingered there as a hallowing influence, and his name still lives in our early history under the tender and sacred title of "the Apostle of Virginia."[5] After he had been in America two years, and had made himself master of his subject, he put his experience, and his benign hopes, and his passionate sense of Christian duty, into a book which furnishes the next event

---

[4] Wm. Crashawe, in "Epistle Dedicatory," prefixed to Whitaker's "Good News from Va." London, 1613.   [5] F. L. Hawks, "Eccl. Hist. Va." 29.

to be mentioned in our literary annals, "Good News from Virginia," published in London, in 1613. The habits of the pulpit clung to him at his writing-table; and the book which he wrote for the enlightenment of England concerning Virginia, has the form and tone of a hortatory sermon; a "pithy and godly exhortation," as old Crashawe called it, [6] "interlaced with narratives of many particulars touching the country, climate, and commodities." He prefixes to it a biblical text; he expounds from that text the Christian doctrine of trying to do good to others even by a sacrifice of ourselves; and he points out the great opportunity which England has of illustrating this doctrine in the case of her forlorn colony in the new world,—a colony which he compares "to the growth of an infant which hath been afflicted from his birth with some grievous sickness, that many times no hope of life hath remained, and yet it liveth still." [7] In presenting to the mother-land the claims of Virginia upon her interest and pity, he gives a clear and well-wrought sketch of the country, the climate, and the Indians, expressing himself throughout the whole book in the diction of an earnest, simple-minded, scholarly man, although without any shining superiorities in thought or style. His own heart is full of grief for the Indians, to whose blighted and desolate natures he would bring the comfort of heavenly truth; and he sees not why other Christian Englishmen should not feel as he does: "Let the miserable condition of these naked slaves of the devil move you to compassion toward them. They acknowledge that there is a great God, but know him not; . . . wherefore they serve the devil for fear, after a most base manner. . . . They live naked in body, as if the shame of their sin deserved no covering. . . . They esteem it a virtue to lie, deceive, and steal, as their master teacheth them. . . . If this be their life, what think you shall become of them after death, but to be partakers with the devil and his angels in hell for evermore?" [8] Having in this book tried to induce England to bring only her noblest moods to her consideration of the affairs of Virginia, having appealed to piety, compassion, magnanimity, even the love of gain, at last, like a true-born Englishman, from the wilderness of America where his English heart still beat within him, he stretched his hand homeward and touched the chord of national pride: "Shall

[6] In "Epistle Dedicatory."   [7] "Good News from Va." 22.   [8] Ibid. 23, 24.

our nation, hitherto famous for noble attempts, and the honorable finishing of what they have undertaken, be now taxed for inconstancy? . . . Yea, shall we be a scorn among our neighbor princes, for basely leaving what we honorably began? . . . Awake, you true-hearted Englishmen: . . . remember that the plantation is God's, and the reward your country's." [9]

IV

On the nineteenth of April, 1619, there arrived at Jamestown a ship from England having on board a new governor for Virginia, Sir George Yeardley, and in his train as secretary for the colony a man of considerable distinction at that time in Europe, Master John Pory. This man was then about forty-nine years of age. He had received his education at Cambridge, and had started out in life with bright tokens of coming usefulness and renown. He had many accomplishments; he was, besides, a wit and a boon companion; his style of writing was facile and sparkling; and he had the gift of making friends in high places, who conceived great hopes of him and were glad to help him to realize them. He became a member of Parliament; for several years he was much employed abroad in the diplomatic service of his country; but before middle life there had become manifest in him certain traits of moral infirmity which, while they did not end his career, cast a shadow across it and dwarfed it in efficiency and honor. Evidently, his convivial habits came to predominate over his resolution for work; he developed a restlessness of temper, an uneasy curiosity, a fickle will, a scorn of plodding tasks, which turned him into a sort of genteel vagabond, sent him wandering over Europe and the East, and threw him into rather frequent familiarity with the pawnbroker and the sponging-house. More unfortunate than all, as was gently said of him by one of his acquaintances, he "followed the custom of strong potations." He never altogether lost his hold upon his influential friends; and doubtless it was in the hope of giving him a fresh start in life that they procured for him the fine appointment of secretary of Virginia and sent him over with Sir George Yeardley to work out a better career for himself in the new

[9] "Good News from Va." 33.

world. His attractive manners, his vivacity of speech, his various learning, his great political experience, his manifold knowledge of the world, rendered him an important personage in the new settlements along the James River. He was at once added to the colonial council; and on the meeting of the general assembly he was given the speakership—an office which his brisk talent and his parliamentary experience enabled him to fill with unusual acceptance. But he ceased from all his offices in 1621, and in 1622 he left the colony for England, on his way dropping in upon the staid young community of Pilgrims at Plymouth and paying them a visit which proved to be mutually agreeable. During his residence in Virginia he had made three excursions among the Indians, of which he has left a very lively account,[10] spicing it with anecdotes that reveal the author's alertness for the grotesque and amusing aspects of the savage character. For example, he introduces us to a certain Namenacus, the king of Pawtuxent, a crafty, complimentary, and murderous potentate, who, hoping to have the pleasure of assassinating Pory and his companions, very characteristically began his acquaintance with them by dramatic assurances of his guileless friendship. "He led us into a thicket where, all sitting down, he showed us his naked breast, asking if we saw any deformity upon it. We told him, 'No.' 'No more,' said he, 'is the inside, but as sincere and pure. Therefore come freely to my country and welcome.'" Upon a subsequent interview, the king "much wondered at our Bible, but much more to hear it was the law of our God; and the first chapter of Genesis, expounded of Adam and Eve, and simple marriage. To which he replied, 'He was like Adam in one thing, for he never had but one wife at once.'"

The most sprightly specimen of Pory's writings is a letter which he sent from Virginia to the celebrated English diplomatist and statesman, Sir Dudley Carleton, and which may be accepted likewise as a pleasant example of the best epistolary style of the period—colloquial, gossiping, playful, just a little stiff here and there with the embroidery of seventeenth century formalism; deeply interesting also for its life-like sketches of the wilderness, the Indians, and the daily life of the infant colony.[11] He is in raptures over the fertility of the

[10] Published in Capt. J. Smith's "Gen. Hist." II. 61–64.
[11] This letter is printed in 4 Mass. Hist. Soc. Coll. IX. 4–30.

country. "Vines here are in such abundance, as wheresoever a man treads they are ready to embrace his foot. I have tasted here of a great black grape as big as a Damascene, that hath a true Muscatel taste; the vine whereof, now spending itself to the tops of high trees, if it were reduced into a vineyard and there domesticated, would yield incomparable fruit." Animals brought from Europe, he discovers, do not degenerate in America. "For cattle, they do mightily increase here, both kine, hogs, and goats, and are much greater in stature than the race of them first brought out of England." But Pory had the eye of a humorist, and he amused himself in watching the germs of a jubilant and lusty social display in this raw community of pioneers: "Now that your lordship may know that we are not the veriest beggars in the world, our cow-keeper here of James City on Sundays goes accoutred all in fresh flaming silk; and a wife of one that in England had professed the black art, not of a scholar, but of a collier of Croydon, wears her rough beaver hat, with a fair pearl hat-band and a silken suit thereto correspondent." And it is pleasant to hear him tell how he contrived to adapt himself to such a life and to get rid of his time in a dull place like this: "At my first coming hither, the solitary uncouthness of this place, compared with those parts of Christendom or Turkey where I had been, and likewise my being sequestered from all occurrents and passages which are so rife there, did not a little vex me. And yet in these five months of my continuance here, there have come at one time or another eleven sail of ships into this river; but freighted more with ignorance than with any other merchandise. At length being hardened to this custom of abstinence from curiosity, I am resolved wholly to mind my business here, and next after my pen to have some good book always in store, being in solitude the best and choicest company. Besides among these crystal rivers and odoriferous woods I do escape much expense, envy, contempt, vanity, and vexation of mind."

V

We now come to the last one of this group of early writers—Argonauts of the first two decades of Virginia—who, achieving more than they knew, laid in America the foundations of the new English literature. The writer whom we are about to study, George Sandys, was perhaps the only one of all his fellow-craftsmen here who was a professed man of letters. Like William Strachey and John Pory before him, he held an official appointment in the colony, where he arrived in the autumn of 1621, in the company of Sir Francis Wyat, who at that time began his administration as governor. In personal character George Sandys was a man very different from his literary predecessor, the jocular and bibulous Bohemian, John Pory. His social connections in England were high; his father being the celebrated Edwin Sandys, archbishop of York; and an elder brother being the noble-natured politician Sir Edwin Sandys, who was the friend of Richard Hooker, and was so dreaded by James the First that the latter once objected to his election as treasurer of the Virginia Company in these vigorous words:—"Choose the devil if you will, but not Sir Edwin Sandys." At the time of his arrival in America George Sandys was forty-four years old, and was then well known as a traveller in Eastern lands, as a scholar, as an admirable prose-writer, but especially as a poet. His claim to the title of poet then rested chiefly on his fine metrical translation of the first five books of Ovid's Metamorphoses, the second edition of which came from the press in that very year 1621 in which the poet sailed away to America in the retinue of Sir Francis Wyat. This fragment was a specimen of literary workmanship in many ways creditable. The rendering of the original is faithful; and though in some places the version labors under the burden of Latin idioms and of unmusical proper names, it often rises into freedom and velocity of movement, and into genuine sweetness, ease, and power. 'How great a pity,' perhaps some of his readers thought in 1621, 'that a man of such gifts and accomplishments should banish himself to the savagery of the Virginia wilderness, when by staying at home he might give us, in a version so pure and masterful, the remaining ten books of the Metamorphoses.' But there was one great poet then in England, Michael Drayton, who did not take so melancholy a view of the departure of George Sandys for Virginia. He, too, wished the translation of Ovid completed by that same deft and scholarly hand; but he saw no reason why the lamp of letters should not burn on the banks of the James River, as well as on those of the Thames. Therefore he addressed to his dear friend a

Virginia: Other Early Writers

poetic epistle in which he exhorts him to keep up his literary occupations, even in the rough desert to which he has gone:

> "And, worthy George, by industry and use,
> Let's see what lines Virginia will produce.
> Go on with Ovid, as you have begun
> With the first five books; let your numbers run
> Glib as the former; so shall it live long
> And do much honor to the English tongue.
> Entice the Muses thither to repair;
> Entreat them gently; train them to that air;
> For they from hence may thither hap to fly." [12]

These exhortations were not wasted on the gentle poet. His vocation to the high service of letters was too distinct to be set aside even by the privations of pioneer life in Virginia and by the oppressive tasks of his official position there. And yet those privations and those tasks proved to be greater, as it chanced, than any human eye had foreseen; for, only a few months after his arrival, namely in March, 1622, came that frightful Indian massacre of the white settlers along the James River, which nearly annihilated the colony; which drove in panic into Jamestown the survivors from the outlying settlements; which turned the peaceful plantation, just beginning to be prosperous, into an overcrowded camp of half-fed but frenzied hunters, hunting only for red men with rifle and bloodhound, and henceforward for several years living only to exterminate them from the earth. It was under these circumstances—the chief village thronged with panic-struck and helpless people; all industry stopped; suspicions, fears, complaints, filling the air; his high official position entailing upon him special cares and responsibilities; without many books, without a lettered atmosphere or the cheer of lettered men—that the poet was to pursue his great task, if he was to pursue it at all. It is not much to say that ordinary men would have surrendered to circumstances such as these. George Sandys did not surrender to them; and that he was able, during the next few years, robbing sleep of its rights, to complete his noble translation of the fifteen books of Ovid's Metamorphoses, is worthy of being chronicled among the

[12] Drayton, Works, Anderson's ed. 542.

heroisms of authorship. It is probable that Sandys returned to England in 1625; at any rate, in the year 1626 he brought out in London, in a folio volume, the first edition of his finished work; and in his dedication of it to King Charles, he made a touching reference to the disasters in Virginia from which he had only just escaped, and to the great difficulties he had overcome in the composition of the book that he thus laid at his sovereign's feet. He speaks of his translation as "this . . . piece limned by that unperfect light which was snatched from the hours of night and repose. For the day was not mine, but dedicated to the service of your great father and yourself; which, had it proved as fortunate as faithful in me, and others more worthy, we had hoped, ere many years had turned about, to have presented you with a rich and well peopled kingdom; from whence now, with myself, I only bring this composure:

Inter victrices hederam tibi serpere laurus.

It needeth more than a single denization, being a double stranger; sprung from the stock of the ancient Romans, but bred in the new world, of the rudeness whereof it cannot but participate, especially having wars and tumults to bring it to light instead of the Muses."

This production, handed down to us in stately form through two centuries and a half, is the very first expression of elaborate poetry, it is the first utterance of the conscious literary spirit, articulated in America. The writings which precede this book in our literary history—the writings of Captain John Smith, of Percy, of Strachey, of Whitaker, of Pory—were all produced for some immediate practical purpose, and not with any avowed literary intentions. This book may well have for us a sort of sacredness, as being the first monument of English poetry, of classical scholarship, and of deliberate literary art, reared on these shores. And when we open the book, and examine it with reference to its merits, first, as a faithful rendering of the Latin text, and second, as a specimen of fluent, idiomatic, and musical English poetry, we find that in both particulars it is a work that we may be proud to claim as in some sense our own, and to honor as the morning-star at once of poetry and of scholarship in the new world. For an illustration of the vigor and melody of his verse, we may select a brief passage from the sixth book, relating the woful story of Philomela. King Tereus has perpetrated an ineffable crime of cruelty and lust upon Philomela, who is the sister of his wife Procne; and the latter, having at last discovered the horrid fact, passes into a rage against her husband which stimulates all her faculties to the invention of some form of revenge that may be worthy, in its exquisite torment and in its annihilating doom, of the monster whom she intends to punish:

>   ——"her bosom hardly bears
> So vast a rage."

Her innocent sister, the terror-smitten and passive victim of the appalling crime, she sees weeping, and gently chides her for so doing:

> "No tears, said she, our lost condition needs,
> But steel; or, if thou hast what steel exceeds,
> I for all horrid practices am fit—
> To wrap this roof in flame, and him in it;
> His eyes, his tongue, . . .
> T' extirp; or, with a thousand wounds divorce
> His guilty soul. The deed I intend is great,
> But what, as yet I know not."

In the terrible calm of her white wrath, while she is thus waiting for some device of perfect retribution with which to overwhelm her husband, suddenly enters her own beloved son Itys. But Itys is his son, likewise; the one object in all the world most dear to him. In the instant there flames through her soul the most fierce and hideous inspiration that ever possessed a mother's mind: by a bloody sacrifice of that son she can thrust the knife of anguish deepest into the heart of her husband. The whole plan evolves itself before her in a flash; and even the warmth of her own love for her darling child is frozen well-nigh dead in comparison with the intolerable heat of her purpose of vengeance. And yet

> "when her son saluted her, and clung
> Unto her neck; mixed kisses, as he hung,
> With childish blandishments; her high-wrought blood
> Began to calm, and rage distracted stood:
> Tears trickled from her eyes by strong constraint."

But, in a moment, the sight of her sister once more, standing in the woe of her speechless shame and pain, recalls her to her unpitying purpose, and she breaks out into a renewed cry of vengeance against her husband through the sacrifice of their son. Him she now clutches with a maniacal fury,

> "as when by Ganges' floods
> A tigress drags a fawn through silent woods.
> Retiring to the most sequestered room,
> While he, with hands upheaved, foresees his doom,
> Clings to her bosom; mother! mother! cried;
> She stabs him, nor once turned her face aside.
>
> . . .
>
> His yet quick limbs, ere all his soul could pass,
> She piecemeal tears. Some boil in hollow brass,
> Some hiss on spits. The pavements blushed with blood.
> Procne invites her husband to this food,
> And feigns her country's rite, which would afford
> No servant, nor companion, but her lord."

The king unwittingly accepts her invitation; he comes to the feast; and seated on his grandsire's throne, devours, unknowingly, the tender flesh of his own son. Then, when exhilarated by the feast, he

> "bids her—so soul-blinded!—call his boy.
> Procne could not disguise her cruel joy.
> In full fruition of her horrid ire,
> Thou hast, said she, within thee thy desire.
> He looks about, asks where; and while again
> He asks and calls, all bloody with the slain,
> Forth like a Fury, Philomela flew
> And at his face the head of Itys threw;
> Nor ever more than now desired a tongue
> To express the joy of her revengëd wrong.
> He with loud outcries doth the board repel,
> And calls the Furies from the depths of hell;
> Now tears his breast, and strives from thence in vain
> To pull the abhorrëd food; now weeps amain,
> And calls himself his son's unhappy tomb;
> Then draws his sword, and through the guilty room

Virginia: Other Early Writers

> Pursues the sisters, who appear with wings
> To cut the air; and so they did.   One [13] sings
> In woods; the other [14] near the house remains,
> And on her breast yet bears her murder's stains.
> He, swift with grief and fury, in that space
> His person changed.   Long tufts of feathers grace
> His shining crown; his sword a bill became;
> His face all armed; whom we a lapwing name." [15]

Immediately upon its publication the work attained in England a great celebrity, and during the seventeenth century passed through at least eight editions. The author lived on to a good old age, devoting himself not only to original poetry but to the translation of the Psalms and of other poetical books of the Bible; and at last died, beloved and honored, at Bexley Abbey, in Kent, in 1644. His fame did not pass away with his earthly life. Eighteen years afterward Thomas Fuller, in terms of affectionate praise, enrolled him among the worthies of England: "He most elegantly translated Ovid's Metamorphoses into English verse; so that as the soul of Aristotle was said to have transmigrated into Thomas Aquinas, . . . Ovid's genius may seem to have passed into Master Sandys." He "was altogether as dexterous at inventing as translating; and his own poems as sprightful, vigorous, and masculine." [16] John Dryden spoke of Sandys as "the best versifier of the former age," [17] and is said to have declared that had Sandys finished the translation of Virgil which he had begun, he himself would not have attempted it after him. Pope, whose critical ear for verse was most exacting, and whose praise was never easily won, said that he "liked extremely" [18] Sandys's translation of Ovid.

[13] Philomela, the nightingale. [14] Procne, the swallow.
[15] Sandys's Ovid, 214, 215.
[16] Thomas Fuller, "Worthies of Eng." ed. 1840, III. 434.
[17] Works of Dryden, ed. 1779, XV. 14. [18] Spence, "Anecdotes," ed. 1820, 276.

Chapter IV

Virginia: Its Literature During the Remainder of the First Period

I. The establishment of Maryland upon the territory of Virginia—Maryland's slight literary record for this period blended with that of Virginia—Father Andrew White and his Latin narrative—John Hammond, the Anglo-American, studying the social problems of England—His solution of them in the word America—His book, "Leah and Rachel," and its original American flavor.

II. George Alsop—His life in Maryland—His droll book about Maryland—Comic descriptions of the effects of his voyage—Vivid accounts of the country, of its productions.

III. Sketch of Bacon's rebellion in 1676—The heroic and capable qualities of Bacon—The anonymous manuscripts relating to the rebellion—Literary indications furnished by these writings—Descriptions of a beleaguered Indian fort—Of Bacon's conflicts with Berkeley—Of Bacon's military stratagem—Bacon's death—Noble poem upon his death.

IV. Review of the literary record of Virginia during this period—Its comparative barrenness—Explanation found in the personal traits of the founders of Virginia—And in their peculiar social organization—Resulting in inferior public prosperity—Especially in lack of schools and of intellectual stimulus—Sir William Berkeley's baneful influence—Printing prohibited in Virginia by the English government—Religious freedom prohibited by the people of Virginia—Literary development impossible under such conditions.

THE brilliant fact in the first period of the literary history of Virginia, contributed to it by the services of George Sandys, may awaken within us the expectation of finding there, as we pass onward in our

Virginia: Its Literature

researches, other facts of the same kind. But we shall scarcely find them. During the remaining years of the period that we are now studying, the intellectual life of the great colony found vent, if at all, chiefly in some other way than that of literature.

I

It was but a few years after the departure of George Sandys from Virginia that the Roman Catholic nobleman, Lord Baltimore, a favorite of King Charles, paying a visit to Virginia, and being fascinated by the loveliness and the opulence of nature there, obtained for his intended colony that choice portion of Virginia which lies north of the Potomac, and which Virginia parted with only after a jealous and reluctant pang that did not cease to ache for many a year afterward. Had the colony of Maryland, for the period now under view, any story of literary achievement for us to tell, it would be fitting to tell it in this place, in immediate connection with the early literary history of Virginia. The most of what was written during those years on either side of the Potomac, was in the form of angry pamphlets relating to their local feuds,[1] or of homely histories of pioneer experience,[2] or of mere letters about business,—all being too crude and elemental to be of any interest to us in our present studies. The Jesuit priest, Father Andrew White, an accomplished man and a devout servant of his order, wrote in Latin an elegant account[3] of the voyage of the first colonists to Maryland, and of "the manifold advantages and riches" of the new land to which he dedicated his life, and in which he hoped would "be sown not so much the seeds of grain and fruit trees as of religion and piety."[4]

In exploring this raw and savage time, we encounter one man, John Hammond, who became, in a small way, an author in spite of himself, an Englishman transformed by his long residence here into

---
[1] See documents in "Virginia and Maryland," Force, Hist. Tracts, II. No. 12.
[2] As Henry Fleet's "Journal," in Neill's "Founders of Md." 19–37; or, "A Relation of Md.," in Sabin's Reprints, No. 2.
[3] "Relatio Itineris in Marylandum;" discovered in Rome in 1832; translated into Eng. and printed in Force, Hist. Tracts, IV. No. 12. Better ed. in Maryland Hist. Soc. Collections, 1874.
[4] White's "Relation," 4.

a stanch and emphatic American, and belonging equally to Virginia and to Maryland. To the former colony he came in 1635; after living there nineteen years he removed to Maryland, whence at the end of two years, namely, in 1656, he went temporarily to England. Though back in the old home, he was at once homesick for the new one: "It is not long since I came from thence, . . . nor do I intend, by God's assistance, to be long out of it again;"[5] "it is that country in which I desire to spend the remnant of my days, in which I covet to make my grave."[6] As he went about England, two things greatly grieved him: one was, that he found England full of poor people, who were borne down in the press and rush for existence there, ragged, half-fed, crushed mortals, without any hope of ever rising out of their misery so long as they stayed in the old world; the second thing was, that while the most of these hapless people might escape from such troubles by going to the new world—where were room and chance enough for all—they were frightened from the attempt by certain wild and rank calumnies against America which then pervaded England. It seemed, therefore, to be his duty as an American abroad to sit down immediately and write a little book, giving the testimony of his own experience in America for "upward of one and twenty years," and by the truth putting to flight those clouds of lies that had "blinded and kept off many from going thither whose miseries and misfortunes by staying in England are much to be lamented, and much to be pitied."[7]

Thus was produced in London, and published there, in 1656, an extremely vigorous and sprightly tract, which the author quaintly named "Leah and Rachel,"[8] these words representing "the two fruitful sisters, Virginia and Maryland." Evidently John Hammond had but little practice in the use of a pen; even to himself his sentences looked "so harsh and disordered" that he was rather sorry to fix his name to them. But he was a man of strong sense; he was very much in earnest; and he spoke his mind in a language so manly, frank, and vital, that even its uncouthness cannot take away the interest with which we stop and listen to him. The charges made against Virginia and Maryland, he bluntly repeats, not softening them: "The

[5] "Leah and Rachel," 7.   [6] Ibid. 26, 27.
[7] Ibid. 7.   [8] Printed in Force, Hist. Tracts, No. 14.

country is reported to be an unhealthy place; a nest of rogues, . . . dissolute and rooking persons." As regards Virginia, he admits that "at the first settling and many years after, it deserved those aspersions; nor were they then aspersions, but truths." For then in England "were jails emptied, youth seduced, and infamous women drilled in" and sent to Virginia; where were "no civil courts of justice but under a martial law, no redress of grievances; complaints were repaid with stripes, moneys with scoffs, tortures made delights, and in a word all and the worst that tyranny could inflict. . . . Yet was not Virginia all this while without divers honest and virtuous inhabitants," who at last rallied, put down their white barbarians, and brought about the beginning of a better state, causing good laws to be made, encouraging industry, and even sending to England for preachers. Unfortunately not many of the preachers who came in response to this appeal were of the kind to benefit the Virginians or any one else; for "very few of good conversation would adventure thither; . . . yet many came, such as wore black coats, and could babble in a pulpit, roar in a tavern, exact from their parishioners, and rather by their dissoluteness destroy than feed their flocks."[9] But in spite of all disadvantages, Virginia had done much to redeem itself; had "become a place of pleasure and plenty," and "a model on which industry may as much improve itself as in any habitable part of the world;" and both Virginia and Maryland offered an almost boundless opportunity to those who in England had no opportunity at all. This was the burden of his valiant and hearty speech. He could not get over his astonishment at "the dull stupidity of people necessitated in England, who . . . live here a base, slavish, penurious life; . . . choosing rather than they will forsake England to stuff Newgate, Bridewell, and other jails with their carcasses, nay, cleave to Tyburn itself. . . . Others itch out their wearisome lives in reliance of other men's charities, an uncertain and unmanly expectation. Some, more abhorring such courses, betake themselves to almost perpetual and restless toil and drudgeries, out of which . . . they make hard shift to subsist from hand to mouth, until age or sickness takes them off from labor, and directs them the way to beggary."[10] One can almost see now the droll mixture of pity and impatience with which this clear-headed

[9] "Leah and Rachel," 7–9.   [10] Ibid. 17, 18.

History of American Literature

and forceful American, fresh from the ample elbow-room and the easy subsistence of his own country, must have stalked about the streets of London and stared at the paltry and painful devices that poor men and women had to resort to there for keeping soul and body together. How grim is the unintended satire of this picture! "I have seriously considered when I have (passing the streets) heard the several cries, and noting the commodities and the worth of them they have carried and cried up and down, how possibly a livelihood could be exacted out of them, as to cry 'matches,' 'small-coal,' 'blacking,' 'pen and ink,' 'thread laces,' and a hundred more such kind of trifling merchandises. Then looking on the nastiness of their linen habits and bodies, I conclude if gain sufficient could be raised out of them for subsistence, yet their manner of living was degenerate and base, and their condition . . . far below the meanest servant in Virginia." [11] One day this determined student of social science got his eye fastened upon an individual specimen of wretchedness in the London streets, a poor fagot-pedler, whom our author thereupon followed up and investigated thoroughly hour by hour. "I saw a man heavily loaden with a burden of fagots on his back, crying, 'dry fagots,' 'dry fagots.' He travelled much ground, bawled frequently, and sweat with his burden; but I saw none buy. Near three hours I followed him, in which time he rested. I entered into discourse with him; offered him drink, which he thankfully accepted of. . . . I inquired what he got by each burden when sold: he answered me, 'three pence.' I further asked him what he usually got a day: he replied, 'some days nothing, some days sixpence; sometimes more, but seldom.' Methought it was a pitiful life, and I admired how he could live on it!" [12] Therefore he would speak out the truth about Virginia and Maryland, and thus "stop those black-mouthed babblers," who, abusing "God's great blessing in adding to England so flourishing a branch," wickedly persuaded "many souls rather to follow desperate and miserable courses in England than to engage in so honorable an undertaking as to travel . . . there." [13]

This, indeed, is genuine American talk. Here, certainly, in these brusque sentences, do we find a literature smacking of American soil and smelling of American air. Here, thus early in our studies, do

[11] "Leah and Rachel," 18.   [12] Ibid. 18.   [13] Ibid. 20.

Virginia: Its Literature

we catch in American writings that new note of hope and of help for humanity in distress, and of a rugged personal independence, which, almost from the hour of our first settlements in this land, America began to send back, with unveiled exultation, to Europe. Henceforward, for myriads of men and women in the ancient nations, to whom life had always been a hard battle and a losing one, this single word America blossomed into a whole vocabulary of words, all testifying plainly to them of a better time coming, of a reasonable chance, somewhere, even in this world, of getting a fresh start in life, and of winning the victory over poverty, nastiness, and fear; nourishing within them a manly might and pride, a resolute discontent with failure, a rightful ambition to get on in the race, a healthy disdain of doing in this life anything less than one's best. For the first time, perhaps, in the long experience of mankind on this planet, was then proclaimed this strong and jocund creed; and it was proclaimed first, as it has been since proclaimed continually, in American literature. Of that literature it still constitutes a most original, racy, and characteristic trait.

II

Whatsoever distinction may be derived from the little book that has been just spoken of, Maryland and Virginia may divide it between them. We have now to mention a book the distinction of which belongs to Maryland alone. In 1666, just ten years after John Hammond's fearless and dashing brochure started out to tilt with English misapprehensions of America, there appeared in London another brochure on a somewhat similar errand,—an errand explained in the work itself in some lines addressed to the author:

> "Thou held'st it noble to maintain the truth
> 'Gainst all the rabble-rout that yelping stand
> To cast aspersions on thy Maryland." [14]

This book, altogether a jovial, vivacious, and most amusing production, was entitled "A Character of the Province of Maryland." [15]

---
[14] "H. W." to his friend George Alsop.
[15] New ed. by John Gilmary Shea, N. Y. 1869.

Of its author, George Alsop, little is known. He was born in 1638; and he had served in London a two years' apprenticeship to something—probably to the profession of solicitor—when, in 1658, being just twenty years old, and breathing out threatenings and slaughter against Oliver Cromwell, he embarked for Maryland, so poor that he bound himself, as is supposed, to repay the price of his transportation by laboring as a servant for four years after his arrival in the colony. He had the good fortune to fall into the hands of a generous master; and with his unique gift of cheerfulness he even found in his four years of servitude "a commanding and undeniable enjoyment." [16] The restoration of King Charles brought a perfect tempest of pleasure to this original Mark Tapley; and he celebrated in verse the satisfaction with which, in his distant abiding-place, he reflected on

> "Noll's old brazen head,
> Which on the top of Westminster's high lead
> Stands on a pole, erected to the sky,
> As a grand trophy to his memory." [17]

As soon as he could do so, he seems to have gone back to England. Whether he remained there, or returned to Maryland, is not known. At any rate, for Maryland he cherished only kind recollections; he was willing, probably for a consideration, to be her literary champion; and in the year already named, he huddled together and printed that medley of frolicsome papers, which appear to have been written mostly in Maryland, and which set forth from various droll points of view a description of that province. There was but one other American book [18] produced in the seventeenth century that for mirthful, grotesque, and slashing energy, can compare with this. Alsop's book is written both in prose and in verse, and is a heterogeneous mixture of fact and fiction, of description and speculation, of wild fun and wild nonsense. "If I have . . . composed anything," says this literary merry-andrew, in his dedication of the book to Lord Baltimore, "that's wild and confused, it is because I am so myself; and the world, as far as I can perceive, is not much out of the same trim."

[16] Dedication.   [17] "A Character of the Province of Md." 102, 103.
[18] "The Simple Cobbler of Agawam."

Virginia: Its Literature

Then turning to "the merchant adventurers for Maryland," he tells them pertly: "This dish of discourse was intended for you at first, but it was manners to let my Lord have the first cut, the pie being his." From the beginning to the end of his book, nearly everything is jocular, much of it coarse, some of it indelicate and even obscene. His good humor is of the loud-laughing kind. He is a scaramouch with pen in hand, and he pokes fun at himself as at everybody else. "I have ventured to come abroad in print, and if I should be laughed at for my good meaning, it would so break the credit of my understanding that I should never dare to show my face upon the Exchange of conceited wits again." [19] His own praises, likewise, he sounds in lusty fashion; yet he hopes that no one will think this unjustifiable: "For I dwell so far from my neighbors, that if I do not praise myself, nobody else will." [20] After the frequent manner of authors in those days, he has, besides prefatory addresses to patrons, readers, and friends in general, a prefatory address to the book itself:

> "Farewell, poor brat! thou in a monstrous world,
> In swaddling clothes, thus up and down art hurled;
> There to receive what destiny doth contrive,
> Either to perish or be saved alive.
> Good Fate protect thee from a critic's power;
> . . .
> For if they once but wring and screw their mouth,
> Cock up their hats, and set the point due-south,
> Arms all akimbo, and with belly strut
> As if they had Parnassus in their gut,
> These are the symptoms of the murthering fall
> Of my poor infant, and his burial." [21]

His direct account of Maryland he presents in four parts: first, the country; second, its inhabitants; third, the arrangements for carrying poor people thither; fourth, traffic and agriculture. He then gives a description of "the wild and naked Indians of Maryland, their customs, manners, absurdities, and religion." Finally, he inserts some of the letters—piquant and ridiculous they are—which he wrote while in Maryland to his friends at home.

[19] Address to the Merchant Adventurers.   [20] Preface.
[21] "A Character of the Province of Md." 28.

Even his rough voyage over the sea, and the disagreeable effects of it upon himself, he cannot speak of seriously. "We had a blowing and dangerous passage of it," he says; "and for some days after I arrived I was an absolute Copernicus, it being one point of my moral creed to believe the world had a pair of long legs, and walked with the burthen of creation upon her back. For, to tell you the very truth of it, for some days upon land, after so long and tossing a passage, I was so giddy that I could hardly tread an even step; so that all things, both above and below, . . . appeared to me like the Kentish Britons to William the Conqueror—in a moving posture." [22] Undertaking to give some idea of the topography of the province, he accomplishes it, but under a rather bold anatomical image: "Maryland is a province situated upon the large extending bowels of America;" [23] and the country itself is "pleasant in respect of the multitude of navigable rivers and creeks that conveniently and most profitably lodge within the arms of her green-spreading and delightful woods." [24] He is captivated by the beauty of this magnificent and merry new world: "He who out of curiosity desires to see the landskip of the creation drawn to the life, or to read nature's universal herbal without book, may, with the optics of a discreet discerning, view Maryland dressed in her green and fragrant mantle of the Spring," [25] where the trees, plants, and flowers "by their dumb vegetable oratory each hour speak to the inhabitants in silent acts, that they need not look for any other terrestrial paradise to suspend or tire their curiosity upon while she is extant." [26] He is delighted also at the multitude and the physical thrift of the animals wandering in these illimitable forests; and he expresses his peculiar enthusiasm in his own comic and obstreperous style: "Herds of deer are as numerous in this province of Maryland as cuckolds can be in London, only their horns are not so well dressed and tipped with silver;" [27] "the park they traverse their ranging and unmeasured walks in, is bounded and impanelled in with no other pales than the rough and billowed ocean." [28] "Here, if the devil had such a vagary in his head as he had once among the Gadarenes, he might drown a thousand head of hogs, and

---

[22] "A Character of the Province of Md." 93. [23] Ibid. 35.
[24] Ibid. 35. [25] Ibid. 36. [26] Ibid. 37.
[27] Ibid. 94. [28] Ibid. 39.

Virginia: Its Literature

they'd ne'er be missed; for the very woods of this province swarm with them."[29]

III

In the year 1676 there occurred in Virginia an outburst of popular excitement which, for a hundred and fifty years afterward, was grotesquely misrepresented by the historians, and which only within recent years has begun to work itself clear of the traditional perversion. This excitement is still indicated by the sinister name that was at first applied to it, Bacon's rebellion. With this remarkable event the literary history of Virginia now becomes curiously involved; and it is necessary to our purposes that we should give here at least an outline of it.

Upon the restoration of Charles the Second in 1660, the Old Dominion of Virginia, which is accurately described by its latest historian as having been "the most Anglican . . . and most loyal of the colonies," [30] was treated with characteristic ingratitude by the Stuart king, whose accession to power, it was wittily said, signified indemnity to his enemies and oblivion to his friends. There was long a tradition in this country that at his coronation the restored monarch wore a robe of silk sent to him by his cavalier subjects in Virginia. "But this," bitterly remarks the old Virginia historian, Beverley,[31] "was all the reward the country had for their loyalty." Even this reward, however, the country did not have; for the agreeable tradition relating to the coronation-robe has now been exploded.[32] The first parliament under King Charles passed a series of navigation acts so selfish and so pitiless as nearly to annihilate every agricultural and commercial interest of Virginia, to lead to a general paralysis of industry there, and to excite a universal discontent and alarm. Moreover, in disregard of all valid land-titles and of all valuable improvements upon the lands, the king kept giving away to his favorites large tracts of the most populous territory in Virginia, ignoring the real owners of the soil, or transferring them with it, as if they had been but herds of cattle or gangs of serfs. These acts of parliamentary and regal

---

[29] "A Character of the Province of Md." 94. [30] C. Campbell, "Hist. Va." 282.
[31] "Hist. Va." I. 53. [32] C. Campbell, "Hist. Va." 256.

injustice, continued recklessly from 1660 to 1676, were enough to destroy all public and private prosperity in Virginia, and to give to them, instead of their old loyal serenity and submissiveness, hearts burning with exasperation or sullen with a sort of lawless despair. But even this was not all. Just on the tangled western verge of the narrow territory occupied by the white settlements in Virginia, began the wilderness—the still immense and impenetrable lair of the red men. Twice before in the life of the colony, first in 1622 and again in 1639, Virginia had tasted the horrors of an Indian massacre. And now once more, in the spring of 1676, at the very moment when the minds of men were torn by anxieties at the lawless interference of the king and parliament with their most valuable rights, and were in anguish over the next possible development in this tragedy of despotism from beyond the ocean, suddenly, from the opposite quarter, out of the abysses of the woods, there swept toward them the heart-shaking terror of an aggressive Indian war. In a tumult and thicket of miseries like this, the people called earnestly upon the royal governor, Sir William Berkeley, as their military and civil chief, to take the necessary measures for repelling these horrid assaults—to organize the people into an army and to lead them against the foe, so that a thousand scattered homes might be protected from the peril that was moving swiftly toward them. For reasons that cannot here be described in detail—the basest reasons of jealousy, indolence, selfishness, and especially avarice—this renowned governor gave to the people promises of help, and promises only. But something was to be done at once by somebody. Nearer and nearer came the great danger, and still bloodier and more frequent became the onslaughts of the Indians. Then the people arose in their anger, and since their governor would not lead them to the war, with unanimous voice they called upon one of their own number to be their leader, Nathaniel Bacon, a man only thirty years of age, of considerable landed wealth, of high social connections, a lawyer trained in the Inns of Court in London, an orator of commanding eloquence, a man who by his endowments of brain and eye and hand was a natural leader and king of men. He, already exasperated against the Indians by injuries inflicted on his own family, obeyed the call of the people. He led them against the Indians, whom he drove back with tremen-

Virginia: Its Literature

dous punishment. But by the jealous and haughty despot in the governor's chair, he was at once proclaimed a rebel, a price was set upon his head; and the people who followed him were put under ban for the crime of doing the duty which the governor himself would not do —the crime of defending their own homes from butchery and flame. Then followed a series of swift conflicts, military and political, between Bacon and the governor; and at last, in that same year, Bacon himself died, suddenly and mysteriously, leaving no competent successor to carry on the struggle; sadder than all, leaving no barrier between his devoted and now forlorn followers, and the heated vengeance of Sir William Berkeley. Twenty-five persons were hung or shot to soothe that vengeance,—an atrocious fact, which, when reported in England, drew from Charles the Second the indolent sneer that "the old fool had taken away more lives in that naked country, than himself had taken for the murder of his father.[33] *

It would have been strange indeed if a great popular movement like this—so deep, passionate, so full of tragic and picturesque incident, and concentrated about a hero who had every personal attribute to inthrall the imaginations of the people—had not found expression in some contemporaneous literary form. And yet for more than a hundred years afterward it was not known that there had been any such expression. Shortly after our Revolutionary War, however, it was discovered that in an old and honorable family in the Northern Neck of Virginia, some manuscripts had been preserved, evidently belonging to the seventeenth century, evidently written by one or more of the adherents of Nathaniel Bacon, and casting much new light upon Bacon's character, and upon the tumultuous events with which his name is connected.[34]

In studying these writings, produced in Virginia in the last quarter of the seventeenth century, every one will be likely to notice the total transformation in the spirit and form of prose style which they represent, when compared with the writings produced in Virginia dur-

---

[33] Williamson, "Hist. North Carolina," I. 229.

[34] These manuscripts were first printed in 2 Mass. Hist. Soc. Coll. I. 27–80, and are sometimes called the Burwell Papers from the name of a family in King William County by whom they were first given to the public.

[* Quotation marks were omitted in both the 1878 and 1897 editions.]

ing the first quarter of the seventeenth century. In the more modern compositions we find no longer the childlike unconsciousness, the idiomatic ease, the simple, fluent, brave picturesqueness that attracted our notice and excited our pleasure in the earlier ones. Evidently between these two groups of writings have passed fifty years of intellectual change, during which, at the metropolis of English speech and of English literature, fantastic poetry and literary quibbling have come into vogue. Evidently in this interval the strength of writers in our tongue has been given to the chase after conceits and surprises in style; the reign of French mannerisms has come in with the reign of the second Charles, and with it the ambition for smartness of phrase, for epigram, antithesis, and pun. The author of the prose portions of these manuscripts reflects, on this side of the ocean, the literary foibles that were in fashion on the other side of the ocean. He composes his sentences as if he were writing for a club of jaded London wits, and were conscious of being unable, by the inward worth of his ideas, to hold their flabby attention, and of having to do so by continually fluttering in their faces the ribbons and tassels of his brisk phrases. But apart from the disagreeable air of verbal affectation and of effort in these writings, they are undeniably spirited; they produce before us departed scenes with no little energy and life; and the flavor of mirth which seasons them is not unpleasant.

The writer gives, in the first place, an account of the preliminary troubles with the Indians; then of the invocation to Bacon to lead the people, who had no other leader; then of prominent events, political and military, during Bacon's brief but most magnanimous and most efficient public career; finally of his death, and of the futile efforts of a worthless fellow named Ingram to catch the hero's mantle, and to play out the remainder of the hero's part. The introductory sentences of the narrative have perished; and the story opens in a broken way with a description of a band of Indians besieged in some rude, extemporized fortification of theirs, by a half-organized army of white men. The Indians "found that their store was too short to endure a long siege without making empty bellies; and that empty bellies make weak hearts, which always makes an unfit serving man to wait upon the god of war. Therefore, they were resolved, before that their spirits were down, to do what they could to keep their stores up, as opportunities should befriend them; and although they were by the law of arms, as the case now stood, prohibited the hunting of wild deer, they resolved to see what good might be done by hunting tame horses; which trade became their sport so long that those [white men] who came on horse-back to the siege began to fear they should be compelled to trot home afoot, and glad if they scaped so too. For these beleaguered blades made so many sallies, and the besiegers kept such negligent guards, that there was very few days passed without some remarkable mischief. But what can hold out always? Even stone walls yields to the not-to-be-gainsaid summons of time." The narrative goes on to relate how, driven by hunger, the besieged Indians at last sent out six of their chief men as commissioners to negotiate a peace with the English; and how the latter, instead of negotiating a peace with the commissioners, knocked out their brains. This unpleasant reception was somewhat discouraging to the Indians in the fort, who resolved "to forsake their station, and not to expostulate the cause any further. Having made this resolution, and destroyed all things in the fort that might be serviceable to the English, they boldly, undiscovered, slip through the leaguer, leaving the English to prosecute the siege, as Schogin's wife brooded the eggs that the fox had sucked." Thus the Indians broke out of the pen in which they had been rather carelessly cooped up, and fled away to their forests; but they fled away only to return again at their pleasure, and in larger force, and to swoop down with unsparing havoc upon every white settlement that they could find unprotected. In this hour of extreme danger, the people called Nathaniel Bacon to be their leader, a man endeared to them not so much for what "he had yet done as the cause of their affections," as for "what they expected he would do to deserve their devotion; while with no common zeal they send up their reiterated prayers, first to himself and next to heaven, that he may become their guardian angel, to protect them from the cruelties of the Indians, against whom this gentleman had a perfect antipathy."

An account is then given at some length of the energetic measures taken by Bacon against the Indians, of the anger of the governor against him, and of the adroitness with which the parasites of the governor devised means to inflame his anger more and more. "They began . . . to have Bacon's merits in mistrust, as a luminary that threatened an eclipse to their rising glories; for though he was but a young man, yet they found that he was master and owner of those induements which constitute a complete man." Meanwhile Bacon himself fell upon the Indians "with abundance of resolution and gallantry . . . in their fastness, killing a great many and blowing up their magazine of arms and powder;" though proclaimed a rebel he then returned home; was elected member of the colonial assembly; was taken prisoner by the governor, and brought to trial upon the charge of rebellion. He was, however, "not only acquitted and pardoned all misdemeanors, but restored to the council-table," and was likewise promised a commission "as general for the Indian war to the universal satisfaction of the people who passionately desired the same. . . . And here who can do less than wonder at the mutable and impermanent deportments of that blind goddess, Fortune, who in the morning loads man with disgraces and ere night crowns him with honors, sometimes depressing and again elevating, as her fickle humor is to smile or frown. . . . For in the morning, before his trial, he was in his enemies' hopes and his friends' fears, judged for to receive the guerdon due to a rebel; . . . and ere night, crowned the darling of the people's hopes and desires, as the only man fit in Virginia to put a stop unto the bloody resolutions of the heathen. And yet again, as a fuller manifestation of Fortune's inconstancy, within two or three days the people's hopes and his desires were both frustrated by the governor's refusing to sign the promised commission." Upon this, Bacon determined no longer to be trifled with, and hurried once more to the capital at the head of five hundred men in arms. His demand for a commission, backed up by such logic, could not be refused; but he had no sooner got it and got out of sight with it, on his way to fight the Indians, than this fine old governor mustered up courage still again to proclaim the young hero a rebel. "The noise of which proclamation . . . soon reached the general's ears not yet stopped up from listening to apparent dangers. This strange and unexpected news put him and some with him shrewdly to their trumps. . . . It vexed him to the heart, as he was heard to say, for to think that while he was a-hunting wolves, tigers, and foxes, which daily destroyed our harmless sheep and lambs, he and those with him should be pursued in the rear with a full cry, as a more savage or no less ravenous beast." The story is then told of the difficult part that Bacon had to play, with one arm keeping back the Indians from murdering the people, and with the other keeping back the governor from murdering him. His white enemies never dared to confront him upon the open field; and even in a campaign of stratagem, they found him more than a match for them. Of his ability to cope with them in craft as well as in force, one amusing incident is given. On learning that he had once more been treated with perfidy by the governor and had been proclaimed a rebel in spite of his commission, Bacon, "with a marvellous celerity, outstripping the swift wings of fame," pushed back to Jamestown, and in a trice blocked up the governor there, "to the general astonishment of the whole country, especially when that Bacon's numbers was known, which at this time did not exceed above a hundred and fifty. . . . Yet not knowing but that the paucity of his numbers being once known to those in town, it might raise their hearts to a degree of courage, having so much the odds, . . . he thought it not amiss, since the lion's strength was too weak, to strengthen the same with the fox's brains. . . . For immediately he despatcheth two or three parties of horse, . . . to bring into the camp some of the prime gentlewomen whose husbands were in town; where, when arrived, he sends one of them to inform her own and the others' husbands, for what purposes he had brought them into the camp, namely, to be placed in the forefront of his men, at such time as those in town should sally forth upon him. The poor gentlewomen were mightily astonished at this project, neither were their husbands void of amazements at this subtle invention. If Mr. Fuller thought it strange that the Devil's black guard should be enrolled God's soldiers, they made it no less wonderful that their innocent and harmless wives should thus be entered a white guard to the Devil. This action was a method in war that they were not well acquainted with, . . . that before they could come to pierce their enemies' sides, they must be obliged to dart their weapons through their wives' breast. . . . Whether it was these considerations or some others, I do not know, that kept their swords in their scabbards; but this is manifest, that Bacon knit more knots by his own head in one day than all the hands in town was able to untie in a whole week; while these ladies' white aprons became of greater force to keep the besieged from sallying out than his works—a pitiful trench—had strength to repel the weakest shot that should have been sent into his leaguer, had he not made use of this invention."

But through all that terrible summer of 1676, events trod upon one another's heels; and by the first of October the chief actor in them suddenly died—broken down, as many believed, by exposure, anxiety, and fatigue; or, as others suspected, taken off by poison. The old manuscript tells of the event in characteristic military metaphor: "Bacon having for some time been besieged by sickness, and now not able to hold out any longer, all his strength and provisions being spent, surrendered up that fort he was no longer able to keep, into the hands of that grim and all-conquering captain, Death."

As the cause of his death was a mystery, so a mystery covered even the place of his burial; for his friends, desiring to save his lifeless body from violation at the hands of the victorious party, placed it secretly in the earth; "but where deposited," says the old manuscript, "till the General Day, not known only to those who are resolutely silent in that particular." And the love of Bacon's followers, which in his lifetime had shown itself in services of passionate devotion, and which, after his death, thus hovered as a protecting silence over his hidden grave, found expression also in some sorrowing verses that, upon the whole, are of astonishing poetic merit. Who may have been the author of these verses, it is perhaps now impossible to discover. They are prefaced by the quaint remark that after Bacon "was dead, he was bemoaned in these following lines, drawn by the man that waited upon his person as it is said, and who attended his corpse to their burial place." Of course this statement is but a blind: the author of such a eulogy of the dead rebel could not safely avow himself. But certainly no menial of Bacon's, no mere "man that waited upon his person," could have written this noble dirge, which has a stateliness, a compressed energy, and a mournful eloquence, reminding one of the commemorative verse of Ben Jonson.

> "Death, why so cruel? What! no other way
> To manifest thy spleen, but thus to slay
> Our hopes of safety, liberty, our all,

Virginia: Its Literature

Which, through thy tyranny, with him must fall
To its late chaos? Had thy rigid force
Been dealt by retail, and not thus in gross,
Grief had been silent. Now, we must complain,
Since thou in him hast more than thousands slain;
Whose lives and safeties did so much depend
On him their life, with him their lives must end.
If 't be a sin to think Death bribed can be,
We must be guilty; say 't was bribery
Guided the fatal shaft. Virginia's foes,
To whom for secret crimes just vengeance owes
Deservëd plagues, dreading their just desert,
Corrupted Death by Paracelsian art
Him to destroy; whose well-tried courage such,
Their heartless hearts, nor arms, nor strength could touch.
Who now must heal those wounds, or stop that blood
The heathen made, and drew into a flood?
Who is 't must plead our cause? Nor trump, nor drum,
Nor deputations; these, alas, are dumb,
And cannot speak. Our arms—though ne'er so strong—
Will want the aid of his commanding tongue,
Which conquered more than Cæsar: he o'erthrew
Only the outward frame; this could subdue
The rugged works of nature. Souls replete
With dull chill cold, he'd animate with heat
Drawn forth of reason's lymbic. In a word
Mars and Minerva both in him concurred
For arts, for arms, whose pen and sword alike,
As Cato's did, may admiration strike
Into his foes; while they confess withal,
It was their guilt styled him a criminal.
Only this difference doth from truth proceed,
They in the guilt, he in the name, must bleed;
While none shall dare his obsequies to sing
In deservëd measures, until Time shall bring
Truth crowned with freedom, and from danger free;
To sound his praises to posterity.

Here let him rest; while we this truth report,
He's gone from hence unto a higher court,

To plead his cause, where he by this doth know
Whether to Cæsar he was friend or foe." [35]

Who was there in Virginia two hundred years ago with the genius and the literary practice to write these masterly verses? They alone shed splendor upon the intellectual annals of Virginia for the seventeenth century. If much of that century was for her a literary desert, these verses form a delightful oasis in it.

IV

During the first epoch in the history of American literature, there were but two localities which produced in the English language anything that can be called literature,—Virginia and New England. We have now inspected whatever literature sprang up in Virginia in the course of that period; and before passing to the investigation of the literature of New England for the same time, we need to stop and review the ground we have already traversed, and gather, if we may, the choicest fruit to be had from studies like these.

As we have seen, there were in Virginia, during the first twenty years of its existence, as many as six authors who there produced writings that live yet and deserve to live. But at the end of that period and for the remainder of the century, nearly all literary activity in Virginia ceased; the only exception to this statement being the brief anonymous literary memorials which have come down to us from the wrathful and calamitous uprising of the people under Nathaniel Bacon. Even of those six writers of the first two decades, all excepting one, Alexander Whitaker, flitted back to England after a brief residence in Virginia: so that besides Whitaker, the colony had during all that period no writer who gave his name to her as being willing to identify himself permanently with her fate, and to

[35] This poem and all the foregoing prose quotations relating to Bacon, are cited from the printed copy of them given in 2 Mass. Hist. Soc. Coll. I. 27–62; but as that copy was very inaccurately made, I have corrected my quotations by collating them with the perfect copy subsequently printed by the same society. See their "Proceedings" for 1866–1867. The authorship of these interesting manuscripts is still a matter of conjecture. My own opinion is that they were written by one Cotton, of Acquia Creek, husband of Ann Cotton, and author of a letter written from Jamestown, June 9, 1676, printed in Force, Hist. Tracts, I. No. 9. For this opinion, which I suppose to be new, the reasons cannot be given here.

Virginia: Its Literature

live and die in her immediate service. This, as we shall see in our further studies, is in startling contrast to the contemporaneous record of New England, which, even in that early period, had a great throng of writers, nearly all of whom took root in her soil.

These, then, are the salient facts in the early literary history of Virginia. They are certainly very remarkable facts. How do we account for them?

First of all, we need to ask, who were the people who during that great epoch founded the Old Dominion of Virginia? What sort of people were they? Of what texture of body and brain and spirit? What were they as regards industry, enterprise, thrift? What were their predominant notions concerning church and state? Especially, what did they come to America for? And what were they living for, principally, whether in America or anywhere else? If we can work out for ourselves the true answers to these questions, we shall be able to see why we might expect to get out of the people of Virginia, during the seventeenth century and afterward, no great amount of literature: hospitality, courtly manners, military leadership, political acumen, statesmanship, but not many books.

A foolish boast still floats on the current of talk, to the effect that Virginia was originally populated to a large extent by families of wealth and of aristocratic rank in England. On the other hand a cruel taunt is sometimes heard in response to this boast, to the effect that the first families of Virginia have really sprung from the loins of bastards, bankrupts, fugitives, transported criminals, and other equivocal Englishmen, who in the seventeenth century left their country for their country's good. The truth seems to lie in neither of these statements alone, but in both of them mixed together and mutually modified. For the first forty years the larger portion of the settlers in Virginia were of inferior quality, personally and socially: many of them were tramps from the pavements of London; vagrants who wandered to Virginia because they had to wander somewhere; gentlemen of fashion who were out at the elbow; aristocrats gone to seed; " 'broken men,' adventurers, bankrupts, criminals." [36] Indeed, for some time after the first few ship-loads had gone out to Virginia, and the news had come back to England of the perils and

[36] J. R. Green, "A Short Hist. of the English People," Harper's ed. 498.

distresses that the colonists were fallen into, not even paupers and knaves would any longer go there of their own accord, and the company in London became "humble suitors to his Majesty" to compel "vagabonds and condemned men to go thither. Nay, . . . some did choose to be hanged before they would go thither, and were." [37] In the year 1611, Sir Thomas Dale sailed out to Virginia with three hundred emigrants, whom, to use his own words, he gathered "in riotous, lazy, and infected places: such disordered persons, so profane, so riotous, so full of mutiny and treasonable intendments, that in a parcel of three hundred not many gave testimony, beside their names, that they were Christians; and besides, were of such diseased and crazed bodies that the sea-voyage hither and the climate here, but a little scratching them, render them so unable, faint, and desperate of recovery, that . . . not three score may be employed upon any labor or service." [38] But by the year 1617, and thenceforward for many years, the cultivation of tobacco in Virginia became so profitable that the labor even of English convicts was welcome; and they were accordingly transported thither in large numbers and became gradually merged in the general population of the country. In 1619, the first negro slaves were imported into the colony; and thereafter their presence contributed a new element of prosperity and of woe to Virginia. From about the year 1640 to the year 1660, that is during the period of the civil war and of the commonwealth in England, many persons of much finer and stronger quality emigrated to Virginia; men of force and weight in England, churchmen, cavaliers, who, especially when the cause of the king became hopeless, very naturally moved away to Virginia to find there a permanent home, and a refuge from the odious ascendency of Cromwell and his Puritans. At the restoration in 1660, still another class of emigrants, also forceful and worthy, passed over to Virginia, men of the Cromwellian party, a few even of his iron-sided troopers, who did not care to abide in sight of the jubilant cavaliers, and who chose Virginia in preference to New England, on account of its more genial climate. Moreover, long before the close of the seventeenth century, Virginia had placed severe restrictions upon the importation of malefactors

[37] Capt. J. Smith, "Gen. Hist." in Pinkerton, XIII. 240.
[38] Aspinwall Papers, 4 Mass. Hist. Coll. IX. 1, note.

into the colony. Of course, from the first these colonists, whether of weak type or strong, were mostly of the party of the English church, and of royalist views in politics. Unlike the first colonists in New England, they had no dispute with the established order of things in old England; and made Virginia, not a digression from English society, but, as George Bancroft happily describes it, "a continuation of English society."[39] As compared with the people of New England, they of Virginia were less austere, less enterprising, less industrious, more worldly, more self-indulgent; they were impatient of asceticism, of cant, of long faces, of long prayers; they rejoiced in games, sports, dances, merry music, and in a free, jovial, roistering life.

In close connection with this study of the people who in our earliest age came to Virginia, we need to observe the most characteristic features of the social organization that they formed after they got there. Though they were of the same stock and speech as the founders of New England, in ideas they were very different; and at once proceeding to incarnate their ideas in the visible frame of society, they erected in Virginia a fabric of church and state which was of course a veracious expression of themselves, and which presents an almost perfect antithesis to the fabric of church and state which at about the same time began to be erected in New England. The germ of the whole difference between them lay in their different notions concerning the value of vicinity among the units of society. The founders of New England were inclined to settle in groups of families forming neighborhoods, villages, and at last cities; from which it resulted that among them there was a constant play of mind upon mind; mutual stimulation, mutual forbearance also; likewise an easier and more frequent reciprocation of the social forces and benefits; facility in conducting the various industries and trades; facility in maintaining churches, schools, and higher literary organizations; facility in the interchange of books, letters, and the like. The course chosen by the founders of Virginia was precisely the opposite of this: they were inclined to settle not in groups of families forming neighborhoods, but in detached establishments forming individualized domestic centres. They brought with them, as a type of the highest human felicity, the memory of the English territorial lord, seated

[39] Bancroft, "Hist. U. S." II. 190.

proudly in his own castle, breasting back all human interference by miles and miles of his own land, which lay outspread in all directions from the view of his castle-windows. Their ambition was to become territorial lords in Virginia; to own vast tracts of land, even though unimproved; to set up imitations—crude and cheap imitations they necessarily were—of the vast and superb baronial establishments which they had gazed at in the mother-country. And many things united to favor them in this wish. It was extremely easy to get large tracts of land in Virginia. Every settler received at the outset a king's grant of fifty acres for himself and for each person transported by him to Virginia; and in addition to this, by a fee of a few shillings to a clerk in the secretary's office, grants could be accumulated upon grants.[40] Moreover Virginia is veined by a multitude of navigable rivers; so that every man who wished to segregate himself in his own mansion, amid a vast territorial solitude, needed not to wait for the construction of a public road to enable him to get to it, and occasionally to get from it; but by erecting his house near to a river bank, he could find almost at his door a convenient shipping-point for the productions of his farm, and a convenient means of ingress and egress for himself and his friends. Thus, from the first, while the social structure of New England was that of concentration, the social structure of Virginia was that of dispersion. The one sought personal community, the other domestic isolation: the one developed coöperation in civil affairs, in mechanism, in trade, in culture, in religion; the other developed solitary action in all these, and consequently made but little progress in any of them: the one tended to mitigate individualism by a thousand social compromises; the other tended to stimulate individualism through an indulgence of it untempered by any adequate colliding personal force. Let any one cast his eye on a map of Virginia for the seventeenth century. He will find local names on that map; but those local names do not indicate cities, or even villages, but merely theoretic organizations of church and state —parishes, over which the inhabitants were so widely scattered that no man could have seen his neighbor without looking though a telescope, or be heard by him without firing off a gun. George Ban-

---

[40] C. Campbell, "Hist. Va." 350. Also "Virginia's Cure," 1662, in Force Hist. Tracts, III. No. 15, 8.

Virginia: Its Literature

croft does not exaggerate when, in speaking of Virginia for the latter part of the seventeenth century, he says, "There was hardly such a sight as a cluster of three dwellings." [41] Even Jamestown, the capital, had but a state-house, one church, and eighteen private houses.

Since the units of this dispersed community inclined thus to isolation rather than to close fellowship, it followed that all those public tasks which depend on coöperation were ill done, or not done at all: the making of high roads, bridges; the erection of court-houses, school-houses, churches; the promotion of commercial and manufacturing establishments; postal communication; literary interchanges, the involuntary traffic of ideas. In short, the tendency of the social structure in Virginia was from the first toward a sort of rough extemporaneous feudalism, toward the grandeur and the weakness of the patriarchal state, rather than toward those complex, elaborate, and refined results which are the achievements of an advanced modern civilization, and which can be procured only by the units of society pulling together, instead of pulling apart. There was considerable individual property: * there was no public thrift. Manual labor was of course scorned by the man who owned slaves, and was the master of a baronial hall with its far-stretching empire of wild lands. From him likewise descended to his inferiors the sentiment of contempt for labor,—the notion that labor was not any man's glory, but his shame. Their earliest historian born in Virginia, Robert Beverley, himself of a distinguished Virginian family, writing just at the dawn of the eighteenth century, fills his book with sarcasms at the indolence and shiftlessness of his fellow-countrymen. Naming Virginia, he says: "I confess I am ashamed to say anything of its improvements, because I must at the same time reproach my countrymen with a laziness that is unpardonable." [42] "They are such abominable ill-husbands,[43] that though their country be overrun with wood, yet they have all their wooden ware from England—their cabinets, chairs, tables, stools, chests, boxes, cart-wheels, and all other things, even so much as their bowls and birchen brooms, to the eternal reproach of their laziness." [44] "Thus they depend altogether

[41] Bancroft, "Hist. U. S." II. 212.
[43] *i. e.*, bad economists.
[42] Beverley, "Hist. Va." Book IV. 59.
[44] Beverley, "Hist. Va." Book IV. 58.

[* Changed to "prosperity."]

upon the liberality of nature, without endeavoring to improve its gifts by art or industry. They sponge upon the blessings of a warm sun and a fruitful soil, and almost grutch the pains of gathering in the bounties of the earth." [45]

The dispersed social organization of Virginia had effects as evil in the direction of religious institutions, as in the direction of material enterprise and thrift. "The Virginia parishes," says Charles Campbell, "were so extensive that parishioners sometimes lived at the distance of fifty miles from the parish church;" hence, "paganism, atheism, or sectaries." [46]

But the result which immediately concerns us in our present studies has to do with the intellectual development of the people. First of all, then, in those highly rarefied communities, where almost nothing was in common, how could there be common schools? [47] To have included within a school-district a sufficient number of families to constitute a school, the distances for many of the pupils would have been so great as to render attendance impracticable. For the first three generations there were almost no schools at all in Virginia. The historian Burk says that "until the year 1688 no mention is anywhere made in the records, of schools or of any provision for the instruction of youth." [48] Who can wonder that under such circumstances the children in most cases grew up in ignorance; and that the historian Campbell should be obliged to testify that the first and second generations of those born in Virginia were inferior in knowledge to their ancestors? [49]

If primary education was so grossly neglected in Virginia during the seventeenth century, we hardly need to ask what could have been the condition of higher education there during the same period. Near the end of this century, when all English-speaking communities were finally delivered from the Stuart incubus, and when all those communities on both sides of the ocean seemed to take a fresh

[45] Beverley, "Hist. Va." Book IV. 83.
[46] "Hist. Va." 382. Also "Va.'s Cure," in Force, III. No. 15, 4, 5.
[47] "Va.'s Cure," in Force, Hist. Tracts, III. No. 15, 6.
[48] "Hist. Va." II. Appendix, xxxi. But the author of "A Perfect Descrip. of Va.," A. D. 1648, mentions "a free school and other petty schools." Force, Hist. Tracts, II. No. 8, 13.
[49] "Hist. Va." 352.

start toward nobler things in civilization, we find traces of an educational awakening in Virginia. Among other traces of this awakening was the suggestion of a college, which in 1692 took tangible form in the establishment of the institution named in honor of the monarchs, William and Mary. In the eighteenth century this college did much to stimulate and guide the intellectual life of the colony; but we must not be misled by its imposing name. It was called a college; but during its earlier years it was only a boarding-school for very young boys in very rudimental studies.

Thus it must be seen that Virginia in the seventeenth century was entitled to the description which Sir Philip Sidney gave to Ireland in the sixteenth century,—a place "where truly learning goeth very bare." [50] Indeed, so late as the year 1715, Governor Spotswood dissolved the colonial assembly of Virginia with this taunt upon the educational defects of a body composed of their principal gentry: "I observe that the grand ruling party in your house has not furnished chairmen of two of your standing committees who can spell English or write common sense, as the grievances under their own handwriting will manifest." [51]

It must not be supposed that the people of Virginia were generally indifferent to the intellectual disadvantages accruing to them from their peculiar social organization. Especially did they grieve over the lack of educational privileges for their children; and from time to time they suggested methods for the establishment of accessible public schools. But they were in the gripe of hostile circumstances, and all their efforts were for that day vain. Besides, during a large portion of the seventeenth century, they had the affliction of a royal governor, Sir William Berkeley, who threw the whole weight of his office and the whole energy of his despotic will in favor of the fine old conservative policy of keeping subjects ignorant in order to keep them submissive. This policy, which he most consistently maintained throughout his entire administration, from 1641 to 1677, was frankly avowed by him in his celebrated reply to the English commissioners who in 1670 questioned him concerning the condition of Virginia: "I thank God there are no free schools, nor printing; and I hope we shall not have, these hundred years; for learning has

[50] "Apologie for Poetrie," Arber's ed. 22.   [51] C. Campbell, "Hist. Va." 395.

brought disobedience, and heresy, and sects into the world, and printing has divulged them, and libels against the best government. God keep us from both." [52] We owe to Sir William the meed of our cordial acknowledgment that at least in this article of his creed he never failed to show his faith by his works, and that he did his best while governor of Virginia to secure the answer of his own dark prayer. And unfortunately when he was recalled from Virginia, his policy for the encouragement of popular ignorance was not recalled with him: on the contrary it was continued by the government at home, and was prescribed in the official instructions laid upon his successors. There is no record of a printing-press in Virginia earlier than 1681; and soon after a printing-press was set up, the printer was summoned before Lord Culpepper and required to enter into bonds "not to print anything hereafter, until his majesty's pleasure shall be known," [53]—a gracious way of intimating a perpetual prohibition. In 1683, when Lord Effingham came out as governor of Virginia, he received from the ministry instructions "to allow no person to use a printing-press on any occasion whatsoever." [54] From that date onward till about the year 1729, no printing was done in Virginia; and from 1729 until ten years before the Declaration of Independence, Virginia had but one printing-house, and even that "was thought to be too much under the control of the governor." [55] What a base extremity of intolerance! And how base the popular listlessness which could permit it! In other countries it has been thought hard enough to have the printing-press clogged by the interference of official licensers and spies; in Virginia the printing-press was forbidden to work at all. There, even the first thrust of the press-man's lever was a crime.

The whole truth with reference to the intellectual condition of Virginia in the seventeenth century will not become manifest to us, unless we rest our eyes on still another trait. Thought was not free in Virginia; religion was not free in Virginia; and this by the explicit and reiterated choice of the people of Virginia. The Puritan zealots of New England have for a hundred years borne the just censure of

[52] Hening, II. 511. [53] Thomas, "Hist. Printing in Am." I. 331.
[54] Chalmers, "Political Annals," I. 345.
[55] Thomas, "Hist. Printing in Am." I. 332.

Virginia: Its Literature

mankind for their religious intolerance,—their ungentle treatment of Baptists, Quakers, and witches. These pages are not to be stained by any apology for religious intolerance in New England. But in simple fairness we may not close our eyes to the fact—seldom mentioned and little known—that the jovial fox-hunters of Virginia, the cant-despising cavaliers of the Old Dominion, were not a whit less guilty of religious intolerance. We are informed by Burk [56] of the burning of witches in Virginia; and as to the molestation of men for their religious opinions, we are told by Campbell that so early as the year 1632 an act of the assembly of Virginia laid upon all who dissented from the Episcopal Church as there established "the penalty of the pains and forfeitures in that case appointed." [57] Just thirty years later, the same assembly imposed a fine of two thousand pounds of tobacco on "schismatical persons" that would not have their children baptized; and on persons who attended other religious meetings than those of the established church, a penalty of two hundred pounds of tobacco for the first offence, of five hundred pounds of tobacco for the second offence, and of banishment for the third offence.[58] Marriage was not tolerated under any other form than that of the Prayer Book. No one, unless a member of the established church, might instruct the young, even in a private family. Any shipmaster who should convey non-conformist passengers to Virginia was to be punished. Against Quakers as well as Baptists the severest laws were passed; and in 1664 large numbers of the former were prosecuted. Indeed, religious persecution remained rampant and flourishing in Virginia long after it had died of its own shame in New England. As late as 1741 penal laws were enacted in Virginia against Presbyterians and all other dissenters.[59] As late as 1746 the most savage penalties were denounced there against Moravians, New Lights, and Methodists.[60] In the presence of this array of facts relating to the people of Virginia in its primal days, and to the social

---

[56] "Hist. Va." II. Appendix, xxxi.   [57] "Hist. Va." 185.
[58] Ibid. 258.   [59] Ibid. 442.
[60] Burk, "Hist. Va." III. 125. For other authorities upon early religious intolerance in Va., see Bancroft, "Hist. U. S." II. 190, 192, 201, 202; Beverley, "Hist. Va." ed. of 1855, 210, 212; R. R. Howison, "Hist. Va." I. 317–321; Hildreth, "Hist. U. S." I. 126, 336; W. C. Rives, "Life of Madison," I. 41–55; Writings of Washington, II. 481; Works of Jefferson, I. 38, 39, 174, VIII. 398–402.

organization that they created there, is not the phenomenon of the comparative literary barrenness of Virginia fully explained? How could literature have sprouted and thriven amid such conditions? Had much literature been produced there, would it not have been a miracle? The units of the community isolated; little chance for mind to kindle mind; no schools; no literary institutions high or low; no public libraries; no printing-press; no intellectual freedom; no religious freedom; the forces of society tending to create two great classes,—a class of vast land-owners, haughty, hospitable, indolent, passionate, given to field-sports and politics, and a class of impoverished white plebeians and black serfs;—these constitute a situation out of which may be evolved country-gentlemen, loud-lunged and jolly fox-hunters, militia heroes, men of boundless domestic heartiness and social grace, astute and imperious politicians, fiery orators, and by and by, here and there, some men of elegant literary culture, mostly acquired abroad; here and there, perhaps, after a while, a few amateur literary men; but no literary class, and almost no literature.

Chapter V

New England Traits in the Seventeenth Century

I. Transition from Virginia to New England—The race-qualities of the first New-Englanders—The period of their coming—Their numbers, and the multitude of their posterity.

II. Two classes of Englishmen in the seventeenth century; those resting upon the world's attainments, those demanding a new departure—From the second class came the New-Englanders—The purpose of their coming an ideal one.

III. Their intellectuality—The large number of their learned men—Their esteem for learning.

IV. Their earnestness of character—Religion the master-thought—Their conceptions of providence and of prayer—Their religious intensity leading to moroseness, to spiritual pedantry, to a jurisprudence based on theology, and to persecution.

V. The outward forms of New England life—Its prosperity—Literature in early New England—A literary class from the first—Circumstances favorable to literary action—The limits of their literary studies—Restraints upon the liberty of printing—Other disadvantages—The quality in them which gave assurance of literary development.

I

JUST thirteen years after American civilization had established its first secure outpost upon the soil of Virginia, it succeeded in establishing a second outpost, four hundred miles northward, in that bleaker and more rugged portion of the continent which bears a

History of American Literature

name suggestive of tender and loyal memories—the name of New England. Thus, within so brief a period, were the beginnings made in the task of planting those two great colonial communities of English blood and speech, Virginia and New England, which, with many things in common, had still more things in contrast, and which have been the "two great distributing centres of the English race"[1] in America.

But who, and of what sort, were these people who in the seventeenth century took possession of New England, and who through their descendants hold possession of it still? At the first glance we see that they were a prolific race, marrying early, and if opportunity presented, marrying often; never declining to rejoice in having their houses "edified and beautified with many children."[2] The first English settlers began to come to New England in 1620; during the subsequent ten years their immigration was slow and slight; but between 1630 and 1640 they came in multitudes, thronging every ship that pointed its prow hitherward. With the latter year, suddenly, all immigration stopped; for the opening of the Long Parliament, by giving to the English Puritans the hope of curing the ills in church and state which they had suffered at home, took from them the impulse to escape from those ills by going abroad. Since the year 1640, the New England race has not received any notable addition to its original stock; and to-day their Anglican blood is as genuine and as unmixed as that of any county in England. In the year 1640 there were in New England twelve independent groups of colonists, fifty towns, a total population of about twenty-one thousand souls.[3] During the one hundred and twenty-five years following that date, more persons, it is supposed, went back from the New to the Old England than came from the Old England to the New.[4] Yet so thrifty and teeming have been these New-Englanders, that from that primal community of twenty-one thousand persons have descended the three and a half millions who compose the present population of New England; while of the entire population now spread over the United

[1] James Russell Lowell, "Among My Books," 1st series, 239.
[2] C. Mather, "Magnalia," I. 498.
[3] Francis A. Walker, in "First Century of the Republic," 215, who here adopts the opinions of Bancroft and Hildreth.
[4] T. Hutchinson, "Hist. Mass. Bay," I. Pref. iii.

States, probably every third person can read in the history of the first settlement of New England the history of his own progenitors.[5] It hardly needs to be mentioned, after this, that the conditions of life there were not at all those for which Malthus subsequently invented his theory of inhospitality to infants. Population was sparse; work was plentiful; food was plentiful; and the arrival in the household of a new child was not the arrival of a new appetite among a brood of children already half fed,—it was rather the arrival of a new helper where help was scarcer than food; it was in fact a fresh installment from heaven of what they called, on Biblical authority, the very "heritage of the Lord." The typical household of New England was one of patriarchal populousness. Of all the sayings of the Hebrew Psalmist—except perhaps the damnatory ones—it is likely that they rejoiced most in those which expressed the Davidic appreciation of multitudinous children: "As arrows are in the hand of a mighty man, so are children of the youth. Happy is the man that hath his quiver full of them: they shall not be ashamed, but they shall speak with the enemies in the gate." The New-Englanders had for many years quite a number of enemies in the gate, whom they wished to be able to speak with, in the unabashed manner intimated by the devout warrior of Israel.[6]

II

The personal traits of the original New-Englanders were in many ways remarkable. To know these people we need to know the people from whom they came. The English race has been described as one

---

[5] J. G. Palfrey, "Hist. N. E." I. Pref. ix.

[6] Pleasant examples of the early New England family meet one at almost every turn in the field of New England biography. The sturdy patriot, Roger Clap of Dorchester, was happy in the possession of fourteen children, among whom were Experience, Waitstill, Preserved, Hopestill, Wait, Thanks, Desire, Unite, and Supply. Cotton Mather was not so abundant in children as he was in books, since of the former he had only fifteen. Benjamin Franklin was one of seventeen children; and in his autobiography he recalls the cheerful picture of thirteen of them seated all at once at his father's table, "who all arrived to years of maturity and were married." William Phips, who attained the honor of knighthood, and became a royal governor of Massachusetts, was the son of a poor gunsmith of Pemaquid, and belonged to a flock of twenty-six children, all of them of the same father and mother, and twenty-one of them sons.

having practical sagacity rather than ideas; as being weighted by grossness of fibre, sluggishness, animal instincts, earthly preferences; as caring more for dull precedents than for brilliant intuitions; as making whatever progress it achieves by feeling its way safely step by step, rather than by projecting its way boldly from the beginning with the easy infallibility of abstract reasoners. There is some truth in this description; but it is far from being the whole truth. Especially far is it from being the whole truth if applied to the English people as they were in the first half of the seventeenth century. At that time, though they were apparently divided into many classes, they were really divided into only two:—first, the disciples of things as they are; second, the disciples of things as they ought to be.[7] Without doubt, in the first of these two classes were included vast numbers of thoughtful and noble natures, who with intelligent deliberation accepted things as established notwithstanding their faults, rather than encounter the frightful risk of having all things unsettled, and of making them worse in the very attempt to make them better; but in this class, likewise, were included the still larger number of those whose natures were neither noble nor thoughtful, and whose conservatism was only the expression of their intellectual torpor, their frivolity, their sensualism, their narrowness, or their cowardice. As to the second class, it certainly included many base persons also, many crackbrained and shallow persons, multitudes who shouted and wrangled for change, impelled to it by all sorts of contemptible motives,—aimless discontent, curiosity, lust, lawlessness, folly, cruelty, ambition, hope of pillage amid the wreck of other people's possessions. Nevertheless in this class, if anywhere, were to be found those men, whether many or few, in whom at that time centred for the English-speaking race the possibility of any further progress in human society; the men who not only dared to have ideas, but dared to put them together and to face the logical results of them; who regarded their own souls, and truth, more than they did gold, or re-

[7] Of course this distinction is to be seen among any people who have begun to think; but it is particularly to be seen among the English people at the period just mentioned. At that time they were especially given to thinking, and their thinking was turned in an uncommon degree to this particular dispute between what is and what ought to be,—in which dispute, indeed, they were then taking sides openly, with dangerous weapons in their hands.

New England Traits

spectability, or bodily comfort, or life; who had a high and stout confidence that as God in wisdom had made the world, so man by increasing in wisdom might improve his own condition in the world; and who proposed then and there, if possible, to bring all things in religion and in politics to some genuine test, in which nothing foolish should be retained because it was old, and nothing wise rejected because it was new. At no other time, probably, has there been in England a greater activity of brain directed toward researches into the very roots of things, than there was during that time; and never in England has the class of persons just described been larger in numbers, wider in the range of its individual peculiarities, more heterogeneous, more resolute, or more hopeful.

It was principally out of this second class, this vast, loosely connected, and deeply excited class of Englishmen in the seventeenth century—the Englishmen who were not sluggish, were not living for physical comfort, were not ruled by animal instincts, were not tied to precedents, were not afraid of ideas—that the twenty-one thousand people came who between 1620 and 1640 populated New England. Primarily, then, these first New-Englanders were thinkers in some fashion; they assumed the right to think, the utility of thinking, and the duty of standing by the fair conclusions of their thinking, even at very considerable cost. Of course among them were representatives of all degrees of intellectual radicalism, from the wealthy, reputable, and moderate non-conformists of Massachusetts Bay, down to the lowly and discreet separatists of Plymouth, and still further down to that inspired concourse of crotchety and purehearted enthusiasts, the Anabaptists, Antinomians, Quakers, Ranters, and Seekers, who found their first earthly paradise in Rhode Island. But the one grand distinction between the English colonists in New England and nearly all other English colonists in America was this, that while the latter came here chiefly for some material benefit, the former came chiefly for an ideal benefit. In its inception New England was not an agricultural community, nor a manufacturing community, nor a trading community: it was a thinking community; an arena and mart for ideas; its characteristic organ being not the hand, nor the heart, nor the pocket, but the brain.

III

The proportion of learned men among them in those early days was extraordinary. It is probable that between the years 1630 and 1690 there were in New England as many graduates of Cambridge and Oxford as could be found in any population of similar size in the mother-country. At one time, during the first part of that period, there was in Massachusetts and Connecticut a Cambridge graduate for every two hundred and fifty inhabitants, besides sons of Oxford not a few.[8] Among the clergy in particular were some men of a scholarship accounted great even by the heroic standard of the seventeenth century,—John Cotton, John Davenport, Richard Mather, Eliot, Norton, Hooker, Roger Williams, Stone, Bulkley, Nathaniel Ward, Thomas Shepard, Dunster, Chauncey; while the laity had among them several men of no inconsiderable learning,—the elder and the younger Winthrop, Thomas Dudley, Simon Bradstreet, William Brewster, William Bradford, Pynchon, Daniel Gookin, John Haynes. Probably no other community of pioneers ever so honored study, so reverenced the symbols and instruments of learning. Theirs was a social structure with its corner-stone resting on a book. Universal education seemed to them to be a universal necessity; and they promptly provided for it in all its grades. By the year 1649 every colony in New England, except Rhode Island, had made public instruction compulsory; requiring that in each town of fifty householders there should be a school for reading and writing, and in each town of a hundred householders, a grammar school with a teacher competent "to fit youths for the University;" and they did this, as their old law frankly stated it, in order that "learning may not be buried in the grave of our fathers,"[9] and especially in order to baffle "that old deluder Sathan," "one chief project" of whose dark ambition it is "to keep men from the knowledge of the Scriptures" by persuading them "from the use of tongues."[10] Only six years after John Winthrop's arrival in Salem harbor the people of Massachusetts took from their own treasury the funds with which to found a university; so that while the tree-stumps

---

[8] James Savage, in Winthrop, "Hist. N. E." I. 173, 318.
[9] Hildreth, "Hist. U. S." I. 370, 371.   [10] Ibid.

were as yet scarcely weather-browned in their earliest harvest-fields, and before the nightly howl of the wolf had ceased from the outskirts of their villages, they had made arrangements by which even in that wilderness their young men could at once enter upon the study of Aristotle and Thucydides, of Horace and Tacitus, and the Hebrew Bible. Sixty-three years later, a representative of the king of England, the Earl of Bellomont, congratulated the people of New England on this superb achievement, by which, as he said, their "youth were not put to travel for learning, but had the Muses at their doors." The learned class were indeed an order of nobility among them. "Child," said a high-spirited New England matron to her little boy, "if God make thee a good Christian and a good scholar, thou hast all that thy mother ever asked for thee." The praise of studiousness was a eulogium warm enough even for the rhetoric of an epitaph. "The ashes of an hard student, a good scholar, and a great Christian:" this was the inscription consecrating the tomb-stone of a young preacher snatched away to another and a better world, at the age of nineteen. The life of a learned man, as it seemed to them to be full of human distinction, so they thought it full of human beneficence; and the fantastic biographer of many of those early scholars has described one of them as "a tree of knowledge, but so laden with fruit that he stooped for the very children to pick off the apples ready to drop into their mouths." [11] A book of learning was a treasure almost rising to the dignity of real estate. In 1649 a sturdy merchant of Boston conveyed to Harvard College a copy of Stephens's "Thesaurus," but upon the written condition that the book should be returned to him should he ever have a child studious of Greek and desirous of that book. He subsequently had such a child, and actually got back his book.[12]

IV

Closely connected with this great trait of intellectuality in them was their earnestness, which, indeed, seems to have been not so much a separate trait of character, as an all-pervading moral atmosphere,

[11] C. Mather, "Magnalia," I. 411.
[12] Josiah Quincy, "Hist. Harv. Univ." I. 512, note.

in which every function of their natures breathed and wrought. This intensity of theirs went with them into everything—piety, politics, education, work, play. It was an earnestness that could well be called terrible. It lifted them above human weakness; it made them victorious and sad. They were not acquainted with indolence; they forgot fatigue; they were stopped by no difficulties; they knew that they could do all things that could be done. Life to them was a serious business—they meant to attend to it; a grim battle—they resolved not to lose it; a sacred opportunity—they hoped not to throw it away:

> "All is, if I have grace to use it so,
> As ever in my great Task-Master's eye."

Above all, it was toward religion, as the one supreme thing in life and in the universe, that all this intellectuality of theirs and all this earnestness, were directed. The result was tremendous. Perhaps not since the time of the apostles had there been in the world a faith so literal, a zeal so passionate: not even in the time of the apostles was there connected with these an intelligence so keen and so robust. For the first time, it may be, in the history of the world, these people brought together the subtle brain of the metaphysician and the glowing heart of the fanatic; and they flung both vehemently into the service of religion. Never were men more logical or self-consistent, in theory and in practice. Religion, they said, was the chief thing; they meant it; they acted upon it. They did not attempt to combine the sacred and the secular; they simply abolished the secular, and left only the sacred. The state became the church; the king, a priest; politics, a department of theology; citizenship, the privilege of those only who had received baptism and the Lord's Supper.

The literalness and the logic, which they applied to everything, they applied particularly to the doctrines of providence and of prayer. They believed that God was always near at hand, and more than willing to interpose in their smallest affairs. Those Biblical texts about the divine observation of the sparrow that falls to the ground, and of the number of the hairs growing on our heads, they took exactly as the words stood. A certain man named Anthony Thacher, being shipwrecked along the coast, was thrown upon a rock. "As

I was sliding off the rock into the sea," he says, "the Lord directed my toes into a joint in the rock's side, as also the tops of some of my fingers, . . . by means whereof, the wave leaving me, I remained so, hanging on the rock, only my head above the water."[13] Holding this faith, they looked for a precise providential meaning in every small incident in their lives; and it was the mark of a holy and a wise man to be able to solve the various pantomimic riddles with which God was all the time trying to communicate his thoughts to them. Thus, in the village of Watertown there occurred one day in the view of many witnesses, "a great combat between a mouse and a snake; and after a long fight the mouse prevailed, and killed the snake. The pastor of Boston, Mr. Wilson, a very sincere, holy man, hearing of it, gave this interpretation: that the snake was the devil; the mouse was a poor contemptible people which God had brought hither, which should overcome Satan here, and dispossess him of his kingdom."[14] About 1640, John Winthrop, the younger, had in a chamber a large number of books; and, as his father relates, among them was "one wherein the Greek Testament, the Psalms, and the Common Prayer were bound together. He found the Common Prayer eaten with mice, every leaf of it, and not any of the two other touched, nor any other of his books, though there were above a thousand."[15] This extraordinary proceeding on the part of the mice in singling out the Prayer-Book for destruction was indeed an ominous fact. The venerable historian has forborne to intrude upon us his own interpretation of it; yet his manner of telling the story intimates that in his own mind there was not much doubt that the ravages of those little animals upon the Episcopal Prayer-Book were expressly directed by the Almighty, and contained a strong hint of the divine disapprobation of the very objectionable book that was devoured by them.[16] With this belief in minute providential interventions there was united a corresponding conception of prayer. To

---

[13] Young, "Chron. Mass. Bay," 490.   [14] J. Winthrop, "Hist. N. E." I. 97.
[15] Ibid. II. 24.

[16] A modern and a very learned commentator upon this passage in Winthrop has ingeniously suggested that the conduct of the mice is susceptible of another interpretation, and one quite inoffensive to the Church that still cherishes the Prayer-Book; namely, that "the mice, not liking psalmody, and not understanding Greek, took their food from another part of the volume." James Savage, ibid.

them prayer was something more than a devout soliloquy, or an exercise in spiritual gymnastics valuable only for its reactionary effects. When they prayed they thought that they moved the hand that moved the world. They spoke of direct answers to prayer as one of the common and indubitable facts of almost daily experience. Thus, one season, their crops were imperilled by caterpillars. What was to be done? The people got together in their churches and asked the Lord to drive off the caterpillars: "and presently after," says the old historian, "the caterpillars vanished away." [17] Once, being at sea along that coast, some of them were "carried by a violent storm among the rocks, where they could find no place to get out. So they went to prayer; and presently there came a great sea and heaved their vessel over into the open sea, in a place between two rocks." [18] At another time, when they had to go upon a dangerous and momentous military expedition, they who went and they who stayed at home "kept the wheel of prayer in a continual motion," [19] —not without some effect, they believed, upon the results of the expedition. One of the celebrated pastors of Cambridge relates this incident of his life as a student:—"When I could not take notes of the sermon, . . . I was troubled at it, and prayed the Lord earnestly that he would help me to note sermons; and . . . as soon as ever I had prayed . . . him for it, I presently the next Sabbath was able to take notes, who the precedent Sabbath could do nothing at all that way." [20] On one occasion a certain Mr. Adams being on a journey with the saintly Boston minister, John Wilson, received tidings of the dangerous illness of his daughter. "Mr. Wilson, looking up to heaven, began mightily to wrestle with God for the life of the young woman: . . . then turning himself about unto Mr. Adams, 'Brother,' said he, 'I trust your daughter shall live; I believe in God she shall recover of this sickness.' And so it marvellously came to pass, and she is now the fruitful mother of several desirable children." [21]

[17] J. Winthrop, "Hist. N. E." II. 327.   [18] Ibid. 411.
[19] C. Mather, "Magnalia," I. 192.
[20] Thomas Shepard, Autobiography, in Young, "Chron. Mass. Bay," 502, 503.*
[21] "Magnalia," I. 314.

[* Below this note is Tyler's comment: "This Autobiography was first printed in 1832, & was copied by Young."]

New England Traits

So intense a light could but cast some deep shadows: suppressing sweetness and gaiety in the human heart; stiffening conscientiousness into scrupulosity, rectitude into asceticism; making punishment a species of retributive vengeance; so stimulating zeal for their own creed that this zeal should become intolerance and even violence toward those who held a creed that was different. At Plymouth a maid-servant of Samuel Gorton "was threatened with banishment from the colony as a common vagabond." Her crime was that she had smiled in church. We read of a truly excellent minister, one Thomas Parker, who, hearing some young persons laughing very freely in a room below, came down from his chamber and thus smote them with his sanctity: "Cousins, I wonder you can be so merry, unless you are sure of your salvation." [22] The wife of one minister, being rich in her own right, had somewhat costlier apparel than ministers' wives were wont to have; and several unenvious dames in the parish expressed deep horror at her carnal-mindedness in wearing whalebone in the bodice and sleeves of her gown, corked shoes, and other like things. One aged and feminine saint, likewise, was painfully affected because a certain "godly man" had his band "something stiffened with starch." [23] The taking of the creature called tobacco seemed to many to be a heinous sin. In their legislatures they passed laws against it; in their discourses they compared the smoke of it to the smoke ascending from the bottomless pit. In common with their brethren in England they suffered great distress of mind over the abomination of long hair. Grave divines thundered against it in their anniversary sermons; and potent statesmen solemnly put their own cropped heads together in order to devise some scheme for compelling all other heads to be as well shorn as theirs were. In 1649 John Endicott became by renewed election governor of Massachusetts Bay; and one of the first acts of his administration for that year was "to institute a solemn association against long hair." [24] A distinguished divine, about the year 1660, in a writing composed in his old age, poured out an indignant wail over the degeneracy of the times:

[22] "Magnalia," I. 487.
[23] These two incidents occurred among the brethren in England and Holland, as related by Bradford. Young, "Chron. Pilgrims," 446, 447.
[24] Morton, "N. E. Memorial," 316, note by Davis.

"I do also protest against all the evil fashions and devices of this age, both in apparel and that general disguisement of long, ruffianlike hair, a custom most generally taken up at that time when the grave and modest wearing of hair was a part of the reproach of Christ." [25] President Chauncey raised his eloquent voice against the capillary enormity. The apostle Eliot, a most saintly, wise, and sweet spirit, spoke out his deep grief against the thing, believing that it was indeed a "luxurious feminine prolixity for men to wear their hair long," and that it was peculiarly shameful for ministers to "ruffle their heads in excesses of this kind." Eliot became a very old man; and it was his sorrow to live long enough to see devout deacons with their hair unclipped, and even reputable ministers of the gospel embellished with the wicked device of periwigs; and at last his opposition died away in this sigh of despair—"the lust is insuperable." [26]

Their scheme of legal punishments was a product of theology rather than of jurisprudence. They measured out penalties according to the moral and ecclesiastical odiousness of each crime, not according to its evil effects upon society. Toward the criminal the judges stood not alone as civil magistrates, punishing him in order to prevent others from becoming like him, but as ministers of divine wrath giving the wretch in this world a foretaste of the pains of hell. Thus blasphemy was to be punished with death; likewise the cursing of parents by any one above sixteen years of age. Sabbath-breaking, neglect of public worship, and idleness were grave offences. "Common fowlers, tobacco-takers, and all other persons who could give no good account of how they spent their time," were to be put into jail.[27] In their penal methods there was great versatility, and a logical fitness almost picturesque. We read that one man was ordered to carry turfs to the fort for being drunk; that another, for being guilty of "a light carriage," was admonished to take heed; that another was severely whipped and kept in hold for suspicion of slander, idleness, and stubbornness; that John Wedgewood was to be set in the stocks for being in the company of drunkards; that Robert Shorthose, for

---

[25] In Quincy, "Hist. Harv. Univ." I. 426.
[26] 1 Mass. Hist. Soc. Coll. VIII. 27.
[27] Hutchinson, "Hist. Mass. Bay," I. 443.

swearing by the blood of God, was to have his tongue put into a cleft stick and to stand so for the space of half an hour; that a servant, for making a fraudulent bargain with a child, had to stand for two hours with his hands tied up to a bar, and a basket of stones hanged about his neck; that a certain woman, for reproaching the magistrates, was sentenced to be whipped, and that "she stood without tying and bare her punishment with a masculine spirit, glorying in her suffering;" [28] that this same heroic dame, eight years afterward, "had a cleft stick put on her tongue half an hour, for reproaching the elders;" [29] that a man named Fairfield, for an atrocious act of shame, was sentenced to pay a fine of forty pounds, to be severely whipped at Boston, to be severely whipped again at Salem, then to return to Boston and have one nostril slit and seared, next to go back to Salem and have the other nostril slit and seared, then to be kept on Boston Neck so long as he lived, to wear a halter visibly about his throat during the remainder of his life, to be whipped if he should appear abroad without it, and to die if he repeated the original offence.

One other personal trait remains to be spoken of: these people inevitably were persecutors. They lived at a time when not many human beings in all the world had taken in the idea that an error in religious opinion may not be a crime; they believed with all their might that the religious opinions which they held were the true ones, and that having come out to the ends of the earth to found there for the glory of God a pure religious commonwealth, it would be impious as well as treasonable for them to tolerate among them the presence of any disbeliever. Among people of religious earnestness on both sides of the Atlantic, the word toleration was then a profligate and a scandalous word. "Toleration," said a leading member of the Westminster Assembly, "is so prodigious an impiety that this religious parliament cannot but abhor the meaning of it." [30] What more natural than that Thomas Dudley of Massachusetts, if he should write verses at all, should write these verses:

>"Let men of God in courts and churches watch
>O'er such as do a toleration hatch." [31]

[28] J. Winthrop, "Hist. N. E." I. 340.　[29] Ibid.
[30] Narr. Club Pub. III. Pref. xiii.　[31] "Magnalia," I. 134.

A saying was then current in New England, that "Antichrist was coming in at the backdoor by a general liberty of conscience." [32] "It is Satan's policy," said Thomas Shepard, "to plead for an indefinite and boundless toleration." [33] "Every toleration of false religions or opinions," said Nathaniel Ward, "hath as many errors and sins in it as all the false religions and opinions it tolerates." [34] Finally, John Norton, with the devout frankness of a Spanish inquisitor, declared that for the putting down of error, "the holy tactics of the civil sword should be employed." [35] All this was their sincere belief; and they were men who had the habit of standing by their sincere beliefs with a dreadful fidelity. One example will be enough. In 1644, the Baptist Church at Newport, Rhode Island, appointed three of its prominent members, John Clarke, John Crandall, and Obadiah Holmes, to pay a visit of Christian sympathy to an aged member of their church, named William Witter, who lived near Lynn, Massachusetts, and who had sent to them a request for such a visit. The delegates reached Lynn on Saturday; and on Sunday, for the comfort of their aged brother, they began to hold a religious service at his house, which stood about two miles from the town. They were in the midst of this service, when, as John Clarke writes, "two constables entered, who by their clamorous tongues made an interruption in my discourse, and more uncivilly disturbed us than the pursuivants of the old English bishops were wont to do." The three visitors were then rudely carried off by the constables, who exhibited a written warrant for the arrest; the next day they were taken to Boston and thrown into jail. Upon their trial before the Court of Assistants, Clarke pleaded the cause of himself and his associates; whereupon the governor, John Endicott, "stepped up and told us we had denied infant baptism, and, being somewhat transported, told me I had deserved death, and said he would not have such trash brought into their jurisdiction." The prisoners were sentenced to pay heavy fines, and in default of payment to be whipped. Clarke's fine was paid for him without his knowledge; Crandall was released after a time

---

[32] J. Chaplin, "Life of Henry Dunster," 186.   [33] Ibid. 185.
[34] "Simple Cobbler of Agawam," 8.
[35] J. Chaplin, "Life of Henry Dunster," 184. See also Longfellow's delineation of Norton, in "Tragedy of John Endicott," 13, 79.

upon condition; and Holmes, after lying in jail until the autumn, was taken out on occasion of the weekly religious lecture and publicly whipped in so barbarous a manner that "for a considerable time he could take no rest, except by supporting himself on his knees and elbows." [36]

Such, both on the bright and on the dark side, were the people who founded New England in the seventeenth century, and who helped, more than all other persons, to found American literature. Doubtless we shall be ready to say with Nathaniel Hawthorne: "Let us thank God for having given us such ancestors; and let each successive generation thank him not less fervently for being one step further from them in the march of ages." [37]

V

The outward arrangements which they had constructed for themselves—the visible framework of their lives in home and shop and field and court and school and church—were the authentic expression of their characters, and fitted them as the garment does the man who wears it: closely related communities; local self-government; only members of the church allowed any voice in the state; every man a soldier; every man a scholar; constant friction of mind with mind; not labor but idleness deemed a disgrace; and all this upon a hard soil and under a fierce sky. They were men who carried keen brains and despotic consciences throbbing in bodies toughened by toil; and what they worked out in the development of human nature and of human society, neither America nor the world can yet dispense with. At once a grim happiness began to sprout up out of the sturdy freedom and thrift which they made for themselves here. "We are all freeholders," was the proud message sent back to England by one of these early settlers; "the rent-day doth not trouble us; and all those good blessings we have, . . . in their seasons, for taking." [38] Many

[36] Narr. Club Pub. VI. 210–211, note, where full references are given to the original authorities for the above account. For the ablest modern extenuation of the conduct of these persecutors, see "As to Roger Williams," 119–122, by Henry Martyn Dexter.
[37] "The Snow Image, and Other Twice-Told Tales," 85.
[38] Young, "Chron. Pil." 250.

elements of civic felicity were soon there; and with time whatever elements were discordant with these, were sure to be sloughed off. One of the descendants of these first New-Englanders, a great statesman of the eighteenth century, being told by a Virginian that he wished that his own commonwealth were like New England, offered him "a receipt for making a New England in Virginia:" it consisted of four ingredients, "town-meetings, training-days, town-schools, and ministers." [39]

Did the people of New England in their earliest age begin to produce a literature? Who can doubt it? With their incessant activity of brain, with so much both of common and of uncommon culture among them, with intellectual interests so lofty and strong, with so many outward occasions to stir their deepest passions into the same great currents, it would be hard to explain it had they indeed produced no literature. Moreover, contrary to what is commonly asserted of them, they were not without a literary class. In as large a proportion to the whole population as was then the case in the mother-country, there were in New England many men trained to the use of books, accustomed to express themselves fluently by voice and pen, and not so immersed in the physical tasks of life as to be deprived of the leisure for whatever writing they were prompted to undertake. It was a literary class made up of men of affairs, country-gentlemen, teachers, above all of clergymen; men of letters who did not depend upon letters for their bread, and who thus did their work under conditions of intellectual independence. Nor is it true that all the environments of their lives were unfriendly to literary action; indeed for a certain class of minds those environments were extremely wholesome and stimulating. There were about them many of the tokens and forces of a picturesque, romantic, and impressive life: the infinite solitudes of the wilderness, its mystery, its peace; the near presence of nature, vast, potent, unassailed; the strange problems presented to them by savage character and savage life; their own escape from great cities, from crowds, from mean competitions; the luxury of having room enough; the delight of being free; the urgent interest of all the Protestant world in their undertaking; the hopes of humanity already looking thither; the coming to them of

[39] Works of John Adams, III. 400.

scholars, saints, statesmen, philosophers. Many of these factors in the early colonial times are such as cannot be reached by statistics, and are apt to be lost by those who merely grope on the surface of history. If our antiquarians have generally missed this view, it may reassure us to know that our greatest literary artists have not failed to see it. "New England," as Hawthorne believed, "was then in a state incomparably more picturesque than at present, or than it has been within the memory of man." [40] That, indeed, was the beginning of "the old colonial day" which Longfellow has pictured to us,

> "When men lived in a grander way,
> With ampler hospitality."

For the study of literature, they turned with eagerness to the ancient classics; read them freely; quoted them with apt facility. Though their new home was but a province, their minds were not provincial: they had so stalwart and chaste a faith in the ideas which brought them to America as to think that wherever those ideas were put into practice, there was the metropolis. In the public expression of thought they limited themselves by restraints which, though then prevalent in all parts of the civilized world, now seem shameful and intolerable: the printing-press in New England during the seventeenth century was in chains. The first instrument of the craft and mystery of printing was set up at Cambridge in 1639, under the auspices of Harvard College; and for the subsequent twenty-three years the president of that College was in effect responsible for the good behavior of the terrible machine. His control of it did not prove sufficiently vigilant. The fears of the clergy were excited by the lenity that had permitted the escape into the world of certain books which tended "to open the door of heresy;" [41] therefore, in 1662 two official licensers were appointed, without whose consent nothing was to be printed. Even this did not make the world seem safe; and two years afterward the law was made more stringent. Other licensers were appointed; excepting the one at Cambridge no printing-press was to be allowed in the colony; and if from the printing-press that was allowed, anything should be printed without the

[40] "The Snow Image," etc. 161.
[41] Isaiah Thomas, "Hist. Printing in Am." I. 58.

permission of the licensers, the peccant engine was to be forfeited to the government and the printer himself was to be forbidden the exercise of his profession "within this jurisdiction for the time to come." But even the new licensers were not severe enough. In 1667, having learned that these officers had given their consent to the publication of "The Imitation of Christ," a book written "by a popish minister, wherein is contained some things that are less safe to be infused amongst the people of this place," the authorities directed that the book should be returned to the licensers for "a more full revisal," and that in the meantime the printing-press should stand still. In the leading colony of New England legal restraints upon printing were not entirely removed until about twenty-one years before the Declaration of Independence.[42]

The chief literary disadvantages of New England were, that her writers lived far from the great repositories of books, and far from the central currents of the world's best thinking; that the lines of their own literary activity were few; and that, though they nourished their minds upon the Hebrew Scriptures and upon the classics of the Roman and Greek literatures, they stood aloof, with a sort of horror, from the richest and most exhilarating types of classic writing in their own tongue. In many ways their literary development was stunted and stiffened by the narrowness of Puritanism. Nevertheless, what they lacked in symmetry of culture and in range of literary movement, was something which the very integrity of their natures was sure to compel them, either in themselves or in their posterity, to acquire. For the people of New England it must be said that in stock, spiritual and physical, they were well started; and that of such a race, under such opportunities, almost anything great and bright may be predicted. Within their souls at that time the æsthetic sense was crushed down and almost trampled out by the fell tyranny of their creed. But the æsthetic sense was still within them; and in pure and wholesome natures such as theirs, its emergence was only a matter of normal growth. They who have their eyes fixed in adoration upon the beauty of holiness, are not far from the sight of all beauty. It is not permitted to us to doubt that in music, in painting, architecture, sculpture, poetry, prose, the highest art will be reached,

[42] Thomas, "Hist. Printing in Am." I. 16, 58, 59.

New England Traits

in some epoch of its growth, by the robust and versatile race sprung from those practical idealists of the seventeenth century—those impassioned seekers after the invisible truth and beauty and goodness. Even in their times, as we shall presently see, some sparkles and prophecies of the destined splendor could not help breaking forth.

Chapter VI

New England: Historical Writers

I. Early development of the historic consciousness in New England.
II. William Bradford—His career in England, Holland, and America—His History of Plymouth—Singular fate of the manuscript—His fitness for historical writing—Outline of the work—Condition and feelings of the Pilgrims when first ashore at Plymouth—Portrait of a clerical mountebank—The skins needed by the founders of colonies—Unfamiliar personal aspects of the Pilgrims—Their predominant nobility—Summary of this historian's traits.
III. Nathaniel Morton—His life—His "Memorial," and how he made it—Lack of originality in it and in him.
IV. The sailing of the Winthrop fleet—John Winthrop himself—His "Model of Christian Charity"—His "History of New England"—An historical diary—Its minute fidelity and graphic power—Examples—His famous speech.
V. Edward Johnson—His "Wonder-Working Providence"—How he came to write it—Reflects the greatness and pettiness of the New England Puritans—Examples—Its literary peculiarities.
VI. The literature of the Pequot War—John Mason its hero and historian—His book—His story of the Mystic fight.
VII. The high worth of Daniel Gookin—An American sage, patriot, and philanthropist—The trials and triumphs of his life—His two historical works relating to the Indians.

I

WE now enter upon the study of the earliest contributions made to American literature by New England. We begin with its historical writings—historical writings relating to New England, and produced

New England: Historical Writers

in New England, in its very first century, nay, in its very first generation. Of course history, as signifying the act by which the present reviews the past and utters a passionless, wise, and final verdict upon it, New England had not and could not have, either in its first generation or in its first century. But this it had, an historical consciousness; a belief, born with itself, in the large human significance of its great task of founding a new order of things in America; an assurance that what it was then doing the future would desire to know about, and therefore that for the benefit of the future the present should keep a record of itself. The history that the earliest men of New England wrote was what we may call contemporaneous history; it was historical diarizing; it was the registration of events as they went by, or as they yet lived in the memories of the living. Here, indeed, are extraordinary facts,—the early development of the historical consciousness in New England, the large number of historical writers that it produced in its primal age, the amount and the quality of the work that these writers did. We find in our first literary period no less than six writers who deserve mention as historians; and it is through a study of what they wrote that we can best make our way into the very heart of the intellectual life of the period, and qualify ourselves to judge of all its literary memorials.

II

William Bradford, of the Mayflower and Plymouth Rock, deserves the pre-eminence of being called the father of American history. We pay to him also that homage which we render to those authors who even by their writings give to us the impression that, admirable as they may be in authorship, behind their authorship is something still more admirable—their own manliness. He was born in Austerfield, Yorkshire, in 1588; * at the age of seventeen he became a zealous member of the little company of separatists who, under the ministry of the saintly John Robinson, fled from England into Holland; at the age of thirty-two † he appeared as a prominent man among that portion of John Robinson's flock who landed in New England in 1620; and from 1621 until his death in 1657 he was annually chosen

[* Changed to "1590."]   [† Changed to "thirty."]

governor of the colony, excepting on five occasions when "by importunity he got off." After he had been in America ten years and had seen proof of the permanent success of the heroic movement in which he was a leader, his mind seems to have been possessed by the historic significance of that movement; and thenceforward for twenty years he gave his leisure to the composition of a work in which the story of the settlement of New England should be told in a calm, just, and authentic manner. The result was his "History of Plymouth Plantation,"—a book which has had an extraordinary fate. It was left by its author in manuscript. After his death, it came into the hands of his nephew, Nathaniel Morton, by whom it was profusely used in the composition of his famous "New England's Memorial," published in 1669. Afterward, the manuscript belonged to Thomas Prince, who drew from it what he desired when writing his "Chronological History of New England." By Prince the old book was left at his death in his library in the tower of old South Church, Boston, where it was used by Thomas Hutchinson when engaged on his "History of Massachusetts Bay." During the occupation of Boston by the British troops in 1775 and 1776, Prince's library was plundered, and many precious historical documents were destroyed. Bradford's manuscript was known to have been in that library not long before; and as afterward it did not appear among the remains of the library, it was given up for lost, and was mourned over by American scholars for nearly a hundred years. In 1855, however, the long-lost treasure was discovered in England, in the Fulham library, the ancient and rich collection belonging to the Bishop of London. It was thereupon at once copied, and published in this country;[1] and by American historical students it was welcomed back into life with a sort of jubilant all-hail.

There is no other document upon New England history that can take precedence of this either in time or in authority. Governor Bradford wrote of events that had passed under his own eye, and that had been shaped by his own hand; and he had every qualification of a trustworthy narrator. His mind was placid, grave, well-poised; he was a student of many books and of many languages;[2] and being

[1] In 4 Mass. Hist. Soc. Coll. III.
[2] Besides his own language he knew Dutch, French, Latin, and Greek; and in

New England: Historical Writers

thus developed both by letters and by experience, he was able to tell well the truth of history as it had unfolded itself during his own strenuous and benignant career. His history is an orderly, lucid, and most instructive work; it contains many tokens of its author's appreciation of the nature and requirements of historical writing; and though so recently published in a perfect form, it must henceforward take its true place at the head of American historical literature, and win for its author the patristic dignity that we have ascribed to him.

The philosophical thoroughness of his plan is indicated at the very beginning of his book. In relating the history of Plymouth plantation he undertakes to go back to "the very root and rise of the same," and to show its "occasion and inducements;" and he avows his purpose to write "in a plain style, with singular regard unto the simple truth in all things." This plan of course conducts him into an account of the origin of religious dissent in England, and of the lamentable blunders of English churchmen and statesmen in their attempts to beat back that dissent into submission and to throttle its free voice. There is a charm in the simple English and in the quiet pathos of his words as he depicts the sufferings of these persecuted ones, particularly of the little congregation at Scrooby, with which the author himself was identified: "But after these things they could not longer continue in any peaceable condition, but were hunted and persecuted on every side, so as their former afflictions were but as flea-bitings in comparison of these which now came upon them. For some were taken and clapped up in prison; others had their houses beset and watched night and day, and hardly escaped their hands; and the most were fain to fly and leave their houses and habitations and the means of their livelihood. Yet these and many other sharper things which afterward befel them, were no other than they looked for, and therefore were the better prepared to bear them by the assistance of God's grace and spirit. Yet seeing themselves thus molested, and that there was no hope of their continuance there, by a joint consent they re-

---

his old age he was a diligent student of Hebrew. "Though I am grown aged, yet I have had a longing to see with mine own eyes something of that most ancient language and holy tongue, in which the law and oracles of God were writ, and in which God and angels spake to the holy patriarchs of old time." Bradford's "Dialogue," ed. by Charles Deane, Pref. viii.

solved to go into the Low-Countries, where they heard was freedom of religion for all men." [3] He then proceeds to tell "of their departure into Holland and their troubles thereabout, with some of the many difficulties they found and met withal;" [4] "of their manner of living and entertainment there;" [5] of "the reasons and causes of their removal" [6] across "the vast and furious ocean." "The place they had thoughts on was some of those vast and unpeopled countries of America, which are fruitful and fit for habitation, being devoid of all civil inhabitants, where there are only salvage and brutish men which range up and down, little otherwise than the wild beasts of the same." [7] There is something very impressive in the quiet, sage words in which he pictures the conflicts of opinion among the Pilgrims over this question of their removal to America, their clear, straight view of the perils and pains which it would involve, and finally the considerations that moved them, in spite of all the tremendous difficulties they foresaw, to make their immortal attempt. No modern description of these modest and unconquerable heroes can equal the impression made upon us by the reserve and the moral sublimity of the historian's words: "It was answered that all great and honorable actions are accompanied with great difficulties, and must be both enterprised and overcome with answerable courages. It was granted the dangers were great, but not desperate; the difficulties were many, but not invincible. For though there were many of them likely, yet they were not certain; it might be sundry of the things feared might never befall; others by provident care and the use of good means might in a great measure be prevented; and all of them, through the help of God, by fortitude and patience, might either be borne or overcome. True it was that such attempts were not to be made and undertaken without good ground and reason; not rashly or lightly as many have done for curiosity or hope of gain, and so forth. But their condition was not ordinary; their ends were good and honorable; their calling lawful and urgent; and therefore they might expect the blessing of God in their proceeding. Yea, though they should lose their lives in this action, yet might they have comfort

---

[3] "Hist. Plym. Plantation," 10. [4] Ibid. 11.
[5] Ibid. 16. [6] Ibid. 22. [7] Ibid. 24–25.

New England: Historical Writers

in the same, and their endeavors would be honorable." [8] A minute account is then given of their negotiations in England and in Holland for permission to settle in America; of their difficulties about money, ships, food, destination; and finally of their departure from Holland, their delays, toils, and risks, in getting free of the English coast, their long voyage over the sea, their groping and dubious approach to Plymouth harbor, and their final debarkation there. The language in which the historian describes their condition and their emotion on reaching shore is a noble specimen of simple, picturesque, and pathetic eloquence, and deserves an honorable place in the record of contemporaneous English style: "Being thus arrived in a good harbor and brought safe to land, they fell upon their knees and blessed the God of heaven, who had brought them over the vast and furious ocean, and delivered them from all the perils and miseries thereof, again to set their feet on the firm and stable earth, their proper element. And no marvel if they were thus joyful, seeing wise Seneca was so affected with sailing a few miles on the coast of his own Italy, as he affirmed, that he had rather remain twenty years on his way by land, than pass by sea to any place in a short time; so tedious and dreadful was the same unto him. But here I cannot but stay and make a pause, and stand half amazed at this poor people's present condition; and so I think will the reader too when he well considers the same. Being thus passed the vast ocean and a sea of troubles before, in their preparation, . . . they had now no friends to welcome them, nor inns to entertain or refresh their weather-beaten bodies, no houses or much less towns to repair to, to seek for succor. It is recorded in Scripture as a mercy to the apostle and his shipwrecked company, that the barbarians shewed them no small kindness in refreshing them; but these savage barbarians when they met with them . . . were readier to fill their sides full of arrows than otherwise. And for the season, it was winter; and they that know the winters of that country know them to be sharp and violent, and subject to cruel and fierce storms, dangerous to travel to known places, much more to search an unknown coast. Besides, what could they see but a hideous and desolate wilderness, full of wild beasts

[8] "Hist. Plym. Plantation," 26.

and wild men? And what multitudes there might be of them, they knew not. Neither could they, as it were, go up to the top of Pisgah, to view from this wilderness a more goodly country to feed their hopes; for which way soever they turned their eyes (save upward to the heavens) they could have little solace or content in respect of any outward objects. For summer being done, all things stand upon them with a weather-beaten face; and the whole country, full of woods and thickets, represented a wild and savage hue. If they looked behind them, there was the mighty ocean which they had passed, and was now as a main bar and gulf to separate them from all the civil parts of the world. . . . What could now sustain them but the spirit of God and his grace? May not, and ought not, the children of these fathers rightly say: 'Our fathers were Englishmen which came over this great ocean and were ready to perish in this wilderness; but they cried unto the Lord and he heard their voice and looked on their adversity. . . . When they wandered in the desert wilderness out of the way, and found no city to dwell in, both hungry and thirsty, their soul was overwhelmed in them. Let them confess before the Lord his loving-kindness, and his wonderful works before the sons of men.' " [9]

As the history proceeds year by year, few things are omitted that a noble curiosity could desire to look into, the bright and the sombre side of that primal life,—its inadequate shelter, its sickness, its weariness, its long pressure upon the verge of famine and assassination, its roughness, its grim toils, its ignoble wranglings and meannesses, its incongruous outbreaks of crime, its steady persistent ascent into prosperity through sagacious enterprise, hard work, and indomitable faith, its piety, its military exploits, its philanthropy, its acute diplomacy, its far-eyed statesmanship. As the book is composed in the form of annual records of experience, it has the privilege of stopping where it will without violating its own unity. The historian's hand kept moving upon this task for twenty years; and when at last old age and public cares rested too heavy upon it, the work, brought down to 1646, was finished so far as it went. Break off when it would, that work could not be a fragment.

The prevailing trait of its pages is of course grave; but at times this

[9] "Hist. Plym. Plantation," 78-80.

New England: Historical Writers

sedateness is relieved by a quaint and pithy emphasis of phrase that amounts almost to humor. But a writer like Bradford is more likely to condescend to a solemn sort of sarcasm than to humor; as, for instance, in his dealing with John Lyford, the mischievous clerical impostor who in 1624 found his way to Plymouth, and vexed the souls of the Pilgrims by the antics of his sly, sensual, and malignant life. Some lines in Bradford's sketch of this fawning swindler remind one of the more elaborate work of a mighty painter of human character in our own time, having particularly an amusing resemblance to that great artist's portrait of Uriah Heep. The historian ushers Lyford upon the stage under the ironical title of an "eminent person," and adds that when he "first came ashore, he saluted them with that reverence and humility as is seldom to be seen, and indeed made them ashamed, he so bowed and cringed unto them, and would have kissed their hands if they would have suffered him; yea, he wept and shed many tears, blessing God that had brought him to see their faces; and admiring the things they had done in their wants, and so forth, as if he had been made all of love, and the humblest person in the world." [10] In the early and doubtful days of the Plymouth colony, the true men were troubled by the querulous and paltry complaints which by some of the weaker brethren were sent back or carried back to England, and which had the effect of discouraging the flow of emigration thither. Many of these complaints seemed to a man like Bradford to be too despicable for serious notice, as this, "that the people are much annoyed with mosquitoes." His contemptuous answer was: "They are too delicate, and unfit to begin new plantations and colonies, that cannot endure the biting of a mosquito. We would wish such to keep at home till at least they be mosquito-proof." [11]

This old document brings into view some aspects of character now not commonly presented as belonging to those august personages whom we reverently name the Pilgrim Fathers. Through the thick haze of oratorical compliment that has so long enveloped their persons, we perhaps fail to see the literal and prosaic truth concerning them. They were not all of the saintly and heroic type, bearing every burden with speechless and devout endurance. Even while

[10] "Hist. Plym. Plantation," 171.   [11] Ibid. 163.

their feet had but just touched the sacred granite of Plymouth Rock, "discontents and murmurings" arose among some, and "mutinous speeches and carriages" among others.[12] Even some of the best of them, perhaps, would have seemed to us rather pragmatical and disputatious persons, with all the edges and corners of their characters left sharp, with all their opinions very definitely formed, and with their habits of frank utterance quite thoroughly matured. Certainly, in these pages, they do not seem to have been a company of gentle, dreamy, and euphemistical saints, with a particular aptitude for martyrdom, and an inordinate development of affability. The world, it appears, is indebted for much of its progress to uncomfortable and even grumpy people; and the Pilgrim Fathers had so implacable a desire to have things quite right according to their own austere standard, that even on the brink of any momentous enterprise, they would stop and argue the case, if a suspicion occurred to them that things were not quite right. This exacting and tenacious propensity of theirs was not a little criticised by some who had business connections with them. Thomas Weston of London, in his disgust at the first return of the Mayflower from Plymouth without any lading, told them by letter that "a quarter of the time" they "spent in discoursing, arguing, and consulting" would have enabled them to make a better showing of the commercial success of their expedition. The impetuous and noble-hearted Robert Cushman, with his practical eye, and his keen zest for unhindered action, complained of the interminable disputations of the Pilgrims when hovering upon the English coast preparatory to their famous ocean voyage: "We that should be partners of humility and peace shall be examples of jangling and insulting;" "there is fallen already amongst us a flat schism; and we are readier to go to dispute, than to set forward a voyage." [13]

Nevertheless, upon almost every page of this history there is some quiet trace of the lofty motives which conducted them to their great enterprise, and of the simple heroism of their thoughts in pursuing it. They had undertaken the voyage, "for the glory of God, and advancement of the Christian faith," and for the honor of their "king

[12] "Hist. Plym. Plantation," 90–91.   [13] Ibid. 57.

and country." [14] In computing the prodigious labors and sufferings of it, they deliberately judged themselves to be suitable to encounter them; for "it is not with us as with other men, whom small things can discourage, or small discontentments cause to wish themselves at home again." [15] "We are well weaned from the delicate milk of our mother-country, and inured to the difficulties of a strange and hard land, which yet in a great part we have by patience overcome." [16] With all their hard grip of the things of this world, their carefulness in bargains, their mechanic industry, their pecuniary thrift, they had a just estimate of the limited value of earthly possessions, and a sincere habit of unworldly-mindedness. Being baffled in one of their projects for getting to America, after having much trusted to this plan, they were greatly disappointed; and Bradford calls it "a right emblem, it may be, of the uncertain things of this world; that when men have toiled themselves for them, they vanish into smoke." [17] Upon their final departure from Leyden, he says: "So they left that goodly and pleasant city which had been their resting place near twelve years; but they knew they were pilgrims, and looked not much on those things, but lift up their eyes to the heavens, their dearest country, and quieted their spirits." [18]

Thus are made plain to us the commanding qualities of the mind and style of our first American historian,—justice, breadth, vigor, dignity, directness, and an untroubled command of strong and manly speech. Evidently he wrote without artistic consciousness or ambition. The daily food of his spirit was noble. He uttered himself, without effort, like a free man, a sage, and a Christian.

III

Nathaniel Morton, whose name we place next to that of William Bradford merely on account of the close personal connection between the two men, was born in England in 1613.* With his father's family he came to Plymouth in 1623. In 1624, his father died, and

[14] "Hist. Plym. Plantation," 89–90. [15] Ibid. 33. [16] Ibid. 32.
[17] Ibid. 41. [18] Ibid. 59.

[* This date is encircled and the notation occurs, "H. M. Dexter says this date rests on conjecture only."]

thenceforward Nathaniel was the object of paternal kindness from his illustrious uncle, Governor Bradford. In 1645, being thirty-two years old, he was elected secretary of Plymouth Colony, and continued to hold that office until his death forty years afterward.

The occupation of his life, his presence in the colony almost from the beginning, and his familiar acquaintance with its leading men, all directed his thoughts toward the composition of its history. The result was the publication at Cambridge, Massachusetts, in 1669, of "New England's Memorial," which the author himself describes as "a brief relation of the most memorable and remarkable passages of the providence of God manifested to the planters of New England in America, with special reference to the first colony thereof called New Plymouth." [19] He takes pains to mention that his principal authorities are the manuscript history of his uncle, and "certain diurnals of the honored Mr. Edward Winslow." The use which he made of these authorities was to transcribe large portions of them with almost literal exactness to his own pages.[20] Bradford's manuscript ends with 1646; Winslow's could not have continued later than 1649; and from about this time, Morton's history, deprived of the copious currents of their assistance, dwindles into a mere rill of obituary notices relating principally to godly ministers thereafter from time to time defunct.

Morton's modesty in alluding to his own literary merits would perhaps disarm us of severity in criticising him, even if we were not already intimidated by the quaint and tremendous dehortation with which he has undertaken to shield his book: "Let not the harshness of my style prejudice thy taste or appetite to the dish I present thee with. Accept it as freely as I give it. Carp not at what thou dost not approve, but use it as a remembrance of the Lord's goodness, to engage to true thankfulness and obedience; so it may be a help

[19] Title-page.

[20] The reader who cares to verify this statement may make comparison of the following passages, first in Davis's edition of Morton's "Memorial," and second in Bradford's History:

Pages 19–20 of Morton with pages 23–24 of Bradford.
" 23–24 " " " " 59–60 " "
" 30–32 " " " " 67–70 " "
" 35–36 " " " " 78–79 " "

to thee in thy journey through the wilderness of this world, to that eternal rest which is only to be found in the heavenly Canaan." [21]

We need not expect to find in an author who is a mere historical copyist, any individual force or originality. Morton was shaped plastically by the hand of his sect and of his locality; and wherever he utters anything that is not the echo of Bradford or of Winslow, it is likely to be the echo of the common opinion or passion of the community in which he passed his painstaking life. He squares off, for example, against poor Samuel Gorton—the favorite target of orthodox New England invectives in those days—and safely pommels with blows a man who was already down, and whom everybody else was pommelling.[22] A far greater man than Samuel Gorton, Roger Williams, was handled by the historian in the same manner, and apparently for the same reason.[23] The historian was in no respect superior to his age; and the venom and the pettiness of his age mix themselves with the ink that flows from his pen.

For nearly two hundred years his book has enjoyed the reputation of an original and a classic document in our early annals. Thomas Prince, the historian, indicates its great celebrity in his time by the remark that in his own childhood next to religious history he was instructed in the history of New England, and that the first book put into his hands upon the latter subject was Morton's "Memorial." [24] Since the recent publication of Bradford's history, however, that of Morton has declined rapidly toward the fate of being utterly unread. Henceforward they who wish to seek our earliest history at its head waters will of course pass by Nathaniel Morton, and draw from the same limpid and sweet well-spring that he drew from.

---

[21] Morton's "Memorial," 16.

[22] Ibid. 202–206. He describes Gorton as "a proud and pestilent seducer, and deeply leavened with blasphemous and familistical opinions."

[23] A letter of Roger Williams's has lately come to light, written in the very year in which Morton's "Memorial" was published, and referring with characteristic magnanimity and playfulness to Morton's habit of praising the saints who fitted the regnant fashion of New England piety, and of damning those who fitted it not. The letter is addressed to his dear friend, the younger Winthrop: "Sir, since I saw you, I have read Morton's 'Memorial,' and rejoice at the encomiums of your father and other precious worthies, though I be a reprobate, *contemptâ vilior algâ*." Narr. Club Pub. VI. 333.

[24] Prince, "Chron. Hist. N. E." Pref.

IV

In the early spring of the year 1630, a fleet of four vessels sailed out into the sea from a beautiful harbor in the Isle of Wight, their prows pointed westward. On board that fleet were the greatest company of wealthy and cultivated persons that have ever emigrated in any one voyage from England to America. They were prosperous English Puritans. They had in England houses and lands and social consideration. With all the faults of England, in church and state, they loved her still. Their departure from England was not the effort of poverty in an old country seeking to better itself in a new one, nor of smirched reputations fleeing away to find in distance the solace of being unknown, nor of uneasy spirits changing their abode on account of the mere frenzy for changing something. Their expatriation was their own act; and it was prompted both by the noblest self-denial and by the shrewdest statesmanship.

Foremost among them in intellectual power and in weight of character was John Winthrop, already chosen governor of the Massachusetts company, and qualified by every personal trait to be the conductor and the statesman of the new Puritan colony of Massachusetts Bay. He was then just forty-two years old. Born at Groton, in Suffolk, of a family honored in that neighborhood for its high character and its wealth, he had been trained to the law, as his father and his grandfather had been before him. He was a man of good books and of good manners; catholic in opinion and sympathy; a deeply conscientious man; not willing that his life should be a thing of extemporized policies and make-shifts, but building it up clear from the foundation on solid principle.

The little fleet that carried to New England John Winthrop and his fortunes, was more than two months upon the voyage; and he made such use of this sea-born leisure, that we have occasion to commemorate it yet. Brooding upon the new life they were about to begin in the new land, he saw that only in one way could it be saved from becoming base, discordant, and disappointing: that way was by their carrying into it, for every day and for every act, the Christlike spirit of disinterestedness. The thought grew in his mind and asserted itself in the form of a little treatise which he entitled "A

Model of Christian Charity." [25] It is an elaborate exposition of the Christian doctrine of unselfishness, and bears especially upon the condition awaiting the colonists in the new, perilous, and struggling life toward which they were going. It shows that if each man be for himself, their great enterprise would come to nothing. Only by mutual love and help, and a grand, patient self-denial, could they all meet the tasks that lay before them. "We must be knit together in this work as one man. We must entertain each other in brotherly affection. We must be willing to abridge ourselves of our superfluities for the supply of other's necessities. We must uphold a familiar commerce together in all meekness, gentleness, patience, and liberality. We must delight in each other; make other's conditions our own; rejoice together, mourn together, labor and suffer together, always having before our eyes our commission and community in the work as members of the same body." [26]

As John Winthrop, while upon the voyage, wrote this discourse to prepare the spirits of himself and his associates for the toils and frets and depressions of their pioneer life, so also immediately upon going on board ship he began another piece of writing, which he continued to work at not only during the rest of the voyage but during the rest of his life, and which is a treasure beyond price among our early historic memorials. It was on Easter Monday, March the twenty-ninth, 1630, his ships still riding in the harbor of Cowes, that he wrote the first record in that journal of his which grew to be "The History of New England." His plan was to jot down significant experiences in the daily life of his company, not only while at sea but after their arrival in America,—thus writing their history as fast as they should make it. Accordingly, the long voyage is registered in an almost daily chronicle, giving faithful mention of the changes of the winds, the various behavior of the ocean, the routine and the caprices of ship-life, the temperate diversion afforded by daily prayers and frequent sermons, the interchange of social courtesies between the passengers belonging to the different vessels, and such other items as were wont to fill up the sluggish days of sea-travel in the seventeenth century. At last, on the eighth of June, "we had sight of land to the north-west about ten leagues. . . . We had now fair sunshine

[25] Printed in 3 Mass. Hist. Soc. Coll. VII. 31-48.   [26] Ibid. 46-47.

weather, and so pleasant a sweet air as did much refresh us, and there came a smell off the shore like the smell of a garden." [27]

For one in Winthop's station the end of his voyage was the end of his leisure; and his journal thenceforward shows that he had too much to do every day to write much about it. Here are frequent breaks and blanks in the record, rallyings of remembrance, many a great day having to content itself with small mention, tokens enough that the resolute diarist was forced to wrestle continually with the temptation of yielding all to the overpowering encroachments of haste and fatigue. Yet, in spite of all, he kept on sturdily, making such headway as he could, fixing a date even when he could not expand a scene, and securing to us, notwithstanding all interruption and reticence, a clear, true story of the way in which the fathers and mothers of the commonwealth of Massachusetts labored and suffered in the days of that stern beginning. For almost twenty years the story went forward, from 1630 until a few weeks before the writer's death in 1649. It is quite evident that Winthrop wrote what he did with the full purpose of having it published as a history; but he wrote it amid the hurry and weariness of his unloitering life, with no anxiety about style, with no other purpose than to tell the truth in plain and honest fashion. The native qualities of the man were lofty, self-respecting, grave; by culture and habit he expressed himself spontaneously in dignified and calm words; and at times, when the thought lifted him, he rose to a stately unconscious eloquence. He was no artist, only a thinker and a doer. Of course he never aimed at effect. His moral qualities are plainly stamped upon his manner of expression—moderation, disinterestedness, reverence, pity, dignity, love of truth and of justice. The prevailing tone is judicial: he tells the truth squarely, even against himself. The greatest incidents in the life of the colony are reported; also the least. The pathos, and heroism, and pettiness of their life, all are here. "My son, Henry Winthrop, was drowned at Salem." [28] "A cow died at Plymouth, and a goat at Boston, with eating Indian corn." [29] "Monday we kept a court." [30] "The rivers were frozen up, and they of Charlestown

[27] John Winthrop, "Hist. N. E." I. 27.   [28] Ibid. I. 34.
[29] Ibid. 44.   [30] Ibid. 35.

New England: Historical Writers

could not come to the sermon at Boston till the afternoon at high water." [31] "Billington executed at Plymouth for murdering one." [32] "The governor and deputy and Mr. Nowell . . . went to Watertown to confer with Mr. Phillips, the pastor, and Mr. Brown, the elder of the congregation there, about an opinion which they had published that the churches of Rome were true churches. The matter was debated before many of both congregations, and by the approbation of all the assembly except three, was concluded an error." [33] "The night before, alarm was given in divers of the plantations. It arose through the shooting off some pieces at Watertown by occasion of a calf which Sir Richard Saltonstall had lost." [34] "At the same court one Henry Linne was whipped and banished for writing letters into England full of slander against our government and orders of our churches." [35] "The governor went on foot to Agawam, and because the people there wanted a minister, spent the Sabbath with them, and exercised by way of prophecy, and returned home the tenth." [36]

That last bit of narration is delightful for the clear glimpse it gives us of the spirit of early New England society, and of the plain devout ways of "the governor" himself. Again and again this good governor comes into the story, always in thoroughly modest reference. Once, he tells us, he got benighted in the woods, and had to pass the whole night there; and out of this arose an amusing little incident, which, with the peril it involved of having his moral reputation misconstrued, he faithfully relates, all unconscious of the somewhat comic aspect in which he would thus present himself for a moment to the contemplation of posterity: "The governor being at his farmhouse at Mistick, walked out after supper, and took a piece in his hand, supposing he might see a wolf; . . . and being about half a mile off, it grew suddenly dark, so as, in coming home, he mistook his path, and went till he came to a little house of Sagamore John, which stood empty. There he stayed; and having a piece of match in his pocket (for he always carried about him match and a compass, and in summer-time snake-weed) he made a good fire near the house,

---

[31] John Winthrop, "Hist. N. E." 47.
[32] Ibid. 43.
[33] Ibid. 70.
[34] Ibid. 59.
[35] Ibid. 73.
[36] Ibid. 154–155.

and lay down upon some old mats which he found there, and so spent the night, sometimes walking by the fire, sometimes singing psalms, and sometimes getting wood, but could not sleep. It was through God's mercy a warm night; but a little before day it began to rain, and having no cloak he made shift by a long pole to climb up into the house. In the morning there came thither an Indian squaw: but perceiving her before she had opened the door, he barred her out; yet she stayed there a great while, essaying to get in, and at last she went away, and he returned safe home, his servants having been much perplexed for him, and having walked about, and shot off pieces, and hallooed in the night; but he heard them not." [37]

There lived in those days near Medford a farmer named Dalkin; and to him and his wife there happened a grotesque experience to which they are indebted for being immortalized in Winthrop's usually solemn pages. They were coming home by night, and had to cross the river at the ford before the tide had fallen. "The husband adventured over, and finding it too deep persuaded his wife to stay awhile; but it raining very sore, she would needs adventure over, and was carried away with the stream past her depth. Her husband, not daring to go help her, cried out; and thereupon his dog, being at his house near by, came forth, and seeing something in the water swam to her; and she caught hold on the dog's tail, so he drew her to the shore and saved her life." [38]

There is in this history one vein of writing that is of deep interest to us now for its frank mention of certain strange psychological phenomena in the experience of our ancestors. Living as they did on a narrow strip of land, between the two infinities of the ocean and the wilderness, and under the consciousness that the mysteries of the unseen world were close about them, it is not strange that they fell into glooms and fantasies. They had overpowering manifestations of spiritual force; they heard awful voices in the air; strange sights glimmered before their eyes on the verge of the forest, or flitted along the sea. Of all this, here are characteristic examples: "About midnight three men coming in a boat to Boston, saw two lights arise out of the water near the north point of the town cove, in form like a man, and went at a small distance to the town, and so to the south

[37] John Winthrop, "Hist. N. E." I. 74–75.   [38] Ibid. II. 195.

point, and there vanished away. They saw them about a quarter of an hour, being between the town and the governor's garden. The like was seen by many, a week after, arising about Castle Island, and in one fifth of an hour came to John Gallop's Point. . . . A light like the moon arose about the north-east point in Boston, and met the former at Nottle's Island, and there they closed in one, and then parted, and closed and parted divers times, and so went over the hill in the island and vanished. Sometimes they shot out flames, and sometimes sparkles. This was about eight of the clock in the evening, and was seen by many. About the same time a voice was heard upon the water between Boston and Dorchester, calling out in a most dreadful manner, 'Boy! boy! come away! come away!' and it suddenly shifted from one place to another a great distance about twenty times. It was heard by divers godly persons." [39]

There is one portion of this History that has acquired great celebrity: it is the one embodying Winthrop's speech, in 1645, in the general court, on his being acquitted of the charge of having exceeded his authority as deputy-governor. The speech as a whole, especially when read in connection with the touching circumstances of its delivery, is one of great nobility, pathos, and grave eloquence; [40] and one passage of it, containing Winthrop's statement of the nature of liberty, is of pre-eminent merit, worthy of being placed by the side of the weightiest and most magnanimous sentences of John Locke or Algernon Sidney. A distinguished American publicist has declared that this is the best definition of liberty in the English language, and that in comparison with it what Blackstone says about liberty seems puerile. "The great questions," says Winthrop, "that have troubled the country, are about the authority of the magistrates and the liberty of the people. . . . Concerning liberty, I observe a great mistake in the country about that. There is a twofold liberty, natural, . . . and civil or federal. The first is common to man with beasts and other creatures. By this, man, as he stands in relation to man simply, hath liberty to do what he lists; it is a liberty to evil as well as to good. This liberty is incompatible and inconsistent with author-

[39] John Winthrop, "Hist. N. E." II. 184–185.
[40] For instances of European comment upon it, see "Life and Letters of John Winthrop," II. 342-343.

ity, and cannot endure the least restraint of the most just authority. The exercise and maintaining of this liberty makes men grow more evil, and in time to be worse than brute beasts: *omnes sumus licentiâ deteriores.*[41] This is that great enemy of truth and peace, that wild beast, which all the ordinances of God are bent against, to restrain and subdue it. The other kind of liberty I call civil or federal; it may also be termed moral, in reference to the covenant between God and man, in the moral law, and the politic covenants and constitutions amongst men themselves. This liberty is the proper end and object of authority, and cannot subsist without it; and it is a liberty to that only which is good, just, and honest. This liberty you are to stand for, with the hazard not only of your goods but of your lives, if need be. Whatsoever crosseth this, is not authority, but a distemper thereof. This liberty is maintained and exercised in a way of subjection to authority; it is of the same kind of liberty wherewith Christ hath made us free. . . . If you stand for your natural corrupt liberties, and will do what is good in your own eyes, you will not endure the least weight of authority, but will murmur, and oppose, and be always striving to shake off that yoke; but if you will be satisfied to enjoy such civil and lawful liberties, such as Christ allows you, then will you quietly and cheerfully submit unto that authority which is set over you, in all the administrations of it, for your good. Wherein, if we fail at any time, we hope we shall be willing by God's assistance to hearken to good advice from any of you, or in any other way of God; so shall your liberties be preserved in upholding the honor and power of authority amongst you." [42]

V

The explorer of our early literature meets at many a turn in his wanderings one title whose quaintness appeals to his imagination as well as to his curiosity: "The Wonder-Working Providence of Zion's Saviour in New England." The book to which this title belongs was written by a man who had made something of a name in his day for

[41] The governor thus recalled, with a slight variation in the order of the words, a line from Terence, Heautontimorumenos, III. 1, 74.
[42] John Winthrop, "Hist. N. E." II. 279–282.

quite other things than writing books, Captain Edward Johnson, immigrant in 1630 to New England from Herne Hill, in Kent; a man of property in both countries; principal founder of the town of Woburn, in Massachusetts, in 1640; and from that year until his death in 1672, entrusted by his fellow-townsmen with almost every responsible office they had to bestow—town-clerk, delegate to the general court, and so forth. He was a very devout and explicit Puritan; his square, stalwart common-sense made itself felt in public and private; he had a strong taste and aptitude for military affairs; and it is significant of his soundness of brain that, amid the general frenzy of the early witchcraft excitement, he was one of the few that kept their heads cool and opposed all judicial prosecution of those uncomely hags that were suspected of unlawful intimacy with the devil.

Had a man like this—a ship-carpenter and farmer, unlettered, unversed in affairs, a sort of rural alderman and militia-hero—lived anywhere else than in New England in the seventeenth century, we should by no means have suspected him of any inclinations toward authorship. But whatever inclinations of this kind he had he could not help; for there was so earnest and stimulating a quality in the grand tasks which these men of New England had undertaken in the world, that even ship-carpenters and country-politicians could not escape the occasional propensity to clutch the pen, and rough-hew a handful of sentences, especially when any good thing was to be accomplished by the job. It was no ambition of authorship that prompted Edward Johnson to write his book, but an important tangible result which could be achieved in no other way. He handled the pen as he did the sword and the broadaxe—to accomplish something with it; and the precise object just then before him was this. Through such unfriendly gossips as Sir Christopher Gardiner, Philip Ratcliff, and Thomas Morton, the people of England had been all along receiving ill tidings of the people of Massachusetts; and it was somebody's duty to put down these lies by the truth. The truth was well known to Edward Johnson. Why might it not be the duty of Edward Johnson to tell it? To him it seemed plain that the planting of God's church and state in New England was a thing that God himself had taken a very active part in, in fact was directly responsible for; that instead of being calumniated, it ought to be celebrated; and that the straightforward way of doing this would be merely to give a history of the wonder-working providence of God in the country spoken of.[43] This single object, held steadily before him as he wrote, gave an epic unity to his work, and makes it strong and interesting yet, notwithstanding the literary clumsiness of the author.

The significance and the glory of God's intervention in all that mighty business of erecting a great religious commonwealth in America could not be felt without a knowledge of the dismal state of England at the time God began to rescue his chosen ones from it. Accordingly, the book opens with a homely but graphic picture of "the sad condition of England when this people removed." It was in this dark time that "Christ the glorious king of his churches" came to their deliverance; and in 1628, he stirred up his heralds to make this proclamation: "All you, the people of Christ that are here oppressed, imprisoned, and scurrilously derided, gather yourselves together, your wives and little ones, and answer to your several names, as you shall be shipped for his service in the western world, and more especially for planting the united colonies of New England, where you are to attend the service of the King of Kings." [44]

Here we have the clue to the whole book. The departure from England, the long peril on "a dreadful and terrible ocean," and the erection of a pure church in "the far-remote and vast wilderness," are but the successive stages in a stupendous religious campaign, inaugurated by Christ for a hallowed purpose, and sustained by him with marvellous exhibitions of divine power. Their emigration was, in the author's view, not a secular act but a sacred one; they who went to New England went upon a spiritual crusade; they were not adventurers, wandering traders and agriculturists seeking earthly gain, but soldiers of Christ, doing battle under his banner, fighting in a holy war, and looking for their reward beyond the clouds. The

---

[43] His book, "Wonder-Working Providence of Zion's Saviour in New England," was first published anonymously in London in 1654; reprinted in 2 Mass. Hist. Soc. Col. II. III. IV. VII. VIII.; again reprinted, with elaborate introduction and notes by Wm. Frederick Poole, Andover, 1867.

[44] "Wonder-Working Providence," 2.

whole book is pervaded by this thought; and a thousand incidental phrases express it. The colonists are "brethren and fellow-soldiers;" [45] the addition at one time of forty-six freemen is the addition of so many "soldiers listed;" [46] in looking about upon their antagonists they "face to the right," they "face to the front," they "face to the left;" [47] and the great service of "this poor people" in populating the "howling desert," is simply "marching manfully on—the Lord assisting—through the greatest difficulties and forest labors that ever any with such weak means have done." [48]

Believing thus with a stanch and literal faith that they were volunteers in the immediate service of their "great Lord Paramount," they had the invincible cheer and courage of knowing that he "stood not as an idle spectator beholding his people's ruth and their enemies' rage, but as an actor in all actions, to bring to naught the desires of the wicked, . . . having also the ordering of every weapon in its first produce, guiding every shaft that flies, leading each bullet to his place of settling, and weapon to the wound it makes." [49]   Under such a leader, upon such a crusade, the humblest soldier was ennobled, and the pettiest undertaking made grand: "for the Lord Christ intends to achieve greater matters by this little handful than the world is aware of;" and "although it may seem a mean thing to be a New England soldier," yet some of them were to "have the battering and beating down, scaling, winning, and wasting the overtopping towers of the hierarchy." [50]   And as the august leadership and the sublime service under which they marched gave rank and stateliness to them and to their small doings, so it lifted them out of timidity and petulance, and armed them with a virtue that could defy both temptation and pain: "As Death, the King of Terror, with all his dreadful attendance inhumane and barbarous, tortures doubled and trebled by all the infernal furies, have appeared but light and momentary to the soldiers of Christ Jesus, so also the pleasure, profits, and honors of this world, set forth in their most glorious splendor and magnitude by the alluring Lady of Delight, proffering pleasant embraces, cannot

---

[45] "Wonder-Working Providence," 17.   [46] Ibid. 56.
[47] Ibid. 113.   [48] Ibid. 84–85.
[49] Ibid. 116.   [50] Ibid. 10–11.

History of American Literature

entice with her siren songs such soldiers of Christ, whose aims are elevated by him many millions above that brave warrior Ulysses." [51]

But from premises like these followed some stern and terrible conclusions; for if they were actual soldiers of Christ, and in a state of war, any toleration of disbelievers was an enormous military crime—it was giving aid and comfort to the enemy. Hence came, by a logic that had in it no flaw, the whole dire philosophy and ethics of persecution: "You are not set up for tolerating times, nor shall any of you be content with this that you are set at liberty; but take up your arms and march manfully on till all opposers of Christ's kingly power be abolished. And as for you who are called to sound forth his silver trumpets, blow loud and shrill to this chiefest treble tune—for the armies of the great Jehovah are at hand." [52]

It is in this spirit of rapt and austere Puritan confidence, that Edward Johnson wrote his history of New England from the establishment of Salem in 1628, to the time of John Endicott's governorship in 1651. His words are those of a spectator of most of the events which he describes. He omits many things which we should now like to read of, but which did not so immediately illustrate the religious significance of New England life. He tells particularly the story of the successive formation of towns and churches, as the people pushed inland, and up and down the coast. He chronicles the annual elections of governor and deputy-governor; the arrival of godly ministers from England; the troubles incident to all primitive settlements in a rough country and in a harsh climate; Indian wars; religious controversies; and, in general, the pangs and risks and deliverances of God's chosen troops in their appointed campaign in the wilderness.

The value of this book, of course, is not that which attaches to what we commonly call history. Here are lacking impartiality, coolness, comprehensiveness, critical judgment, and the delight of a masterly and sweet expression. It is crude enough in thought and style, avowedly partisan, and pitched upon a key of wild religious rhapsody. Yet with all its limitations, it is the sincere testimony of an eye-witness and an honest man; it preserves the very spirit and aroma of New England thought and experience in the seventeenth century; it sup-

---

[51] "Wonder-Working Providence," 25.   [52] Ibid. 7. See also 90, 91, 101.

plies us with a multitude of tints and tones which, without this book, we should not have; its very faults of diction, its grotesque and fanatic zeal, its narrowness, its harshness, its frank and bloodthirsty Hebraisms, its touching and sublime simplicity of trust, its choice of what is noble and everlasting in existence, its disdain of lies and toys and fleshly phantoms, all make it a most authentic and a priceless memorial of American character and life in the heroic epoch of our earliest men.

An admirable quality in the book is its concentrated sketches of the leading men of the time. Thus, John Endicott was "a fit instrument to begin this wilderness work, of courage bold, undaunted, yet sociable, and of a cheerful spirit, loving and austere, applying himself to either as occasion served." [53] His references to the great personages in secular life, Winthrop, Sir Harry Vane, Hopkins, Bradstreet, and others, are indeed laudatory, but they are cold in comparison with the intensity of his reverent language concerning the principal ministers of the young nation. The vocabulary of Puritan admiration is strained to give utterance to his laic affection and loyalty towards "the grave, godly, and judicious Hooker," "the reverend and much desired Mr. John Cotton," "the rhetorical Mr. Stone," "the reverend and holy man of God, Mr. Nathaniel Rogers," and "the holy, heavenly, sweet-affecting, and soul-ravishing minister, Mr. Thomas Shepard." The natural rebound of this rapturous enthusiasm for the ministers was an equally rapturous contempt for their opponents—the unsanctioned preachers, the heretics, babblers, and illiterate agitators who infested those pioneer communities; and in his opinion all that was odious in such talking vagrants was brought together in the person of the troublesome prophetess of New England, Anne Hutchinson. He seldom condescends to mention her by name; but he points at her with scornful allusions that are unmistakable. She is the "woman that preaches better gospel than any of your black-coats that have been at the Ninneversity;" [54] she is the "master-piece of women's wit, . . . backed with the sorcery of a second who had much converse with the devil;" [55] she is "the grand-

[53] "Wonder-Working Providence," 19. [54] Ibid. 96.
[55] Ibid. 100.

mistress of them all who ordinarily prated every Sabbath day." [56]

It would be true to say that there is hardly a trait of Puritanism, either noble or narrow or grim, that does not represent itself in some line of this book. Here, for example, we have in the author's description of what the ruling elders should be, the lofty confidence of Puritanism in the unseen and supernal Righteousness: they should be "not greedily given to hoard up for themselves, but by their own example leading others to liberality and hospitality, having the earth in low esteem, and faith in exercise when cattle and corn fail." [57] For the narrowness of Puritanism, the examples here at hand are of an embarrassing multitude; but this may serve. The belief in a present, watchful, and benign Providence, is the source of the sweetest comfort and the most perfect fortitude that can live in human nature; but when this belief intensifies itself into a microscopic and picayune Providence, to be interpreted in detail by man as an expression of the divine favor or wrath in the case of every falling tower, or launched thunderbolt, or capsized sail-boat, or lost cow, it becomes a creed ministering to abject superstition and vindictiveness. Thus, Edward Johnson mentions, as an instance of "the sad hand of the Lord" against a person, the case of a certain barber of Boston who was summoned one day to Roxbury to draw a tooth, and who, being overwhelmed upon the journey by a snow-storm, was found several days after frozen to death: "in which sad accident this was taken into consideration by divers people, that this barber was more than ordinary laborious to draw men to those sinful errors that were formerly so frequent, . . . he having a fit opportunity, by reason of his trade, so soon as any were set down in his chair, he would commonly be cutting off their hair and the truth together." [58] And for the grimness of Puritanism, the following passage will be likely to satisfy the most exacting. After describing the famous war of extermination against the Pequots, the author thus concludes: "The Lord in mercy toward his poor churches, having thus destroyed these bloody barbarous Indians, he returns his people in safety to their vessels, where they take account of their prisoners. The squaws and some young youths they brought home with them, and finding the

[56] "Wonder-Working Providence," 132.   [57] Ibid. 5.   [58] Ibid. 138.

New England: Historical Writers

men to be deeply guilty of the crimes they undertook the war for, they brought away only their heads." [59]

In a book like this we are not apt to expect much gayety; but one may find in it, here and there, some hint of an effort on the author's part to relax his visage into a smile. Thus, in one place he deigns to speak rather facetiously of so serious a thing as the Atlantic Ocean, which he calls in familiar style "the ditch between England and their now place of abode;" and he even proceeds to the playful remark that this ditch, forsooth, "they could not leap over with a lope-staff," [60]— doubtless the nearest approach to a jest that the author of "Wonder-Working Providence" was ever frivolous enough to indulge in.

But though he intended it not, the book is nevertheless somewhat mirth-inspiring. Its very seriousness has a comic aspect, most of all when it rises into the awful shape of verse; for, this retired ship-carpenter of Woburn hewed out poetry in a manner worthy of his original trade. His first official entry in the town records of Woburn took a metrical form; and in his history, no important person is introduced upon the scene without some brief poetic tribute. He has indeed a half abashed air, a virgin coyness, so to speak, as he brings forward these tiny trinkets in rhyme, as if he were himself remotely conscious of some impropriety in the manufacture of such things by a respectable man like himself; and yet, on the other hand, he seems to have a sturdy faith that since these things are poetry, there must be a sort of immortalizing virtue in them. "And now," says he, as he is about to hold up before us his poetic apostrophe to Governor John Endicott, "let no man be offended at the author's rude verse, penned of purpose to keep in memory the names of such worthies as Christ made strong for himself, in this unwonted work of his." [61] One couplet of this little poem will be quite enough:

> "Strong valiant John, wilt thou march on and take up station first,
> Christ called hath thee, his soldier be, and fail not of thy trust." [62]

The following lines are a portion of his "metre" composed "for the future remembrance" of the celebrated Hugh Peters:

[59] "Wonder-Working Providence," 117.*
[60] Ibid. 20.
[61] Ibid. 19.
[62] Ibid. 19.

"With courage, bold Peters, a soldier stout,
　In wilderness, for Christ, begins to war;
　Much work he finds 'mongst people, yet holds out;
　With fluent tongue he stops fantastic jar." [63]

But even from the literary aspect there are some qualities of this book that we may not use for our mirth, yea for our laughter, when we are waspish. It has not infrequently, even amid its most ungainly sentences, a charm of picturesque simplicity, an unconscious and unadorned beauty of honest speech. Speaking of the work they hoped to do in the fields when a certain long winter should have passed away, he says that they discoursed "between one while and another, of the great progress they would make after the summer's sun had changed the earth's white furred gown into a green mantle." [64] One of their Providential deliverances on the sea as they were nearing the American coast is thus pictured to us: "The night newly breaking off her darkness, and the daylight being clouded with a gross vapor, as if night's curtains remained half-shut, the seamen and passengers standing on the decks suddenly fixed their eyes on a great boat, as they deemed; and anon after, they spied another, and after that another; but musing on the matter, they perceived themselves to be in great danger of many great rocks. With much terror and affrightment they turned the ship about, expecting every moment to be dashed in pieces against the rocks. But He whose providence brought them in, piloted them out again, without any danger, to their great rejoicing." [65] In speaking of Christ's tenderness and care toward his persecuted church, the author has a sentence that anyone might take to be a bit of the prose of John Milton: "With his own blessed hands wiping away the tears that trickle down her cheeks, drying her dankish eyes, and hushing her sorrowful sobs in his sweet bosom." [66] In the following sentence, wherein he cheers up the good people of New England by reminding them of more helpers already on the way to them from England, one may hear a sort of plaintive and lingering melody: "There are for your further aid herein many more of these sincere soldiers floating upon the great ocean toward you." [67]

[63] "Wonder-Working Providence," 79.　　[64] Ibid. 20.
[65] Ibid. 35.　　[66] Ibid. 117.　　[67] Ibid. 118.

New England: Historical Writers

VI

In our first literary period there remain two other historical writers who have this in common, that their writings relate to the Indians of New England, and to the dreadful conflicts that raged there in the seventeenth century between those Indians and the white people who had undertaken to settle near them.

The ability of the English to establish themselves in New England in spite of the objections of the original inhabitants, was tested in a serious manner twice, and only twice. The first occasion was in 1637 and gave rise to the Pequot war; the second was in 1675 and brought on King Philip's war. Of course, at other times, before and afterward, there were innumerable petty collisions of the rival races, casual jets of murder, fitful paroxysms of wrath and vengeance on both sides; but these two were the only occasions on which the red men in that portion of the continent, alarmed and maddened by the danger ever swelling and darkening over them from the increasing multitude of their English invaders, deliberately combined in large numbers, formed comprehensive plans, and moved toward the extermination of the English colonists with a method in their ferocity, with a wide-reaching concert of action, with a skill and a ruthless vigor, that for a time threw some doubt over the possibility of preserving the English settlements there.

These events are now so far away from us that we do not realize their appalling character; but during the first century and a half of American history, the Indian peril was the one frightful fact perpetually hovering, by day and by night, near every white community. These two wars were the two great acts in early New England history. They marked the heroic epochs of colonial existence. The men who, in these two wars, led the colonists to victory and to safety were thenceforward the popular heroes, the persons of might and renown. It is not strange that each of these tremendous conflicts should have a literature of its own—a crop of writings commemorative of events that had brought to every cottage in New England so much both of agony and of exultation.

Of the first of these wars—that with the Pequots—Captain John Mason was the historian as well as the hero. On many accounts he is an interesting personage for us to look at in that early time. Though less famous now than Captain Miles Standish, he was in that age fully his equal in reputation, even as he fully equalled him in military service. Like Miles Standish, too, he had been trained to warfare in the Netherlands, where his commander was that Sir Thomas Fairfax who afterward became so distinguished as the leader of the parliamentary forces in the English civil wars; and who, while so engaged, remembered his ancient military pupil then in New England, and sent to him an invitation to come back to England and take a hand in the fight then going forward. But John Mason had important work to do in the new world; and he staid there, and did it. And he did his work so well that his very name became a terror to the Indian tribes, and was a wall of safety around the scattered farmhouses and the feeble villages of his pioneer countrymen. Moreover he lived to a good old age, honored to the last for the courage and the generous wisdom of his life.

It was at the request of the general court of Connecticut that he wrote "The History of the Pequot War," [68] a work of only thirty-three pages, giving a plain but vigorous narrative of a very plain and very vigorous campaign. Naturally enough, the historian writes not from documents, but from his own recollection of the events in which he bore so large a part. His style is that of a fighter rather than of a writer; there is an honest bluntness about it, an unaffected rough simplicity, a manly forth-rightness of diction, all the charm of authenticity and strength. It is fortunate that he dashed off his little book without the expectation of printing it: "I never had thought that this should have come to the press . . . ; if I had, I should have endeavored to have put a little more varnish upon it." [69] We like his bluff narrative all the more because the varnish was left off; and we like him all the more as we get acquainted with the modest and frank spirit in which he wrote it. "I shall only draw the curtain," he says, "and open my little casement, that so others of larger

[68] First printed by Increase Mather in 1677 in his "Relation of the Troubles" with the Indians, and by him erroneously attributed to John Allyn. In 1736 it was republished by Thomas Prince. Prince's edition is reprinted in 2 Mass. Hist Coll. VIII. 120-153, and the latter is the edition referred to in the present work.

[69] "The Hist. of the Pequot War," 128.

hearts and abilities may let in a bigger light; that so, at least, some small glimmering may be left to posterity, what difficulties and obstructions their forefathers met with in their first settling these desert parts of America." [70]

The history begins with an account of the first treacherous assaults of the Pequot Indians upon the English "about the year 1632," and of their further acts of perfidy and violence until, in the year 1637, they had drawn other Indian tribes into a conspiracy for the annihilation of the white settlements in Connecticut. The condition of the latter "did look very sad, for those Pequots were a great people, being strongly fortified, cruel, warlike, munitioned, and so forth; and the English but an handful in comparison." [71] In May, 1637, the English, knowing that the hour was come, gathered two little armies, one under Captain John Underhill, the other under Captain John Mason, and pushed swiftly into the country of the Pequots, and by night drew near to the fort at Mystic in which the most of the Pequot warriors were gathered. There the white men lay down, "much wearied with hard travel, keeping great silence; . . . the rocks were our pillows; yet rest was pleasant. . . . We appointed our guards and placed our sentinels at some distance, who heard the enemy singing at the fort, who continued that strain until midnight, with great insulting and rejoicing." [72] By daybreak, the Indians having sunk into a deep sleep, the whites awoke, crept up to the fort, forced their way into it, and got the savages within their grip. Sword and musket did their work too slowly. "The Captain told them that we should never kill them after that manner; . . . we must burn them; and immediately stepping into the wigwam . . . brought out a firebrand, and putting it into the mats with which they were covered, set the wigwams on fire. . . . When it was thoroughly kindled the Indians ran as men most dreadfully amazed. And indeed such a dreadful terror did the Almighty let fall upon their spirits, that they would fly from us and run into the very flames. . . . And when the fort was thoroughly fired, command was given that all should fall off and surround the fort. . . . The fire . . . did swiftly overrun the fort, to the extreme amazement of the enemy: . . . some of them

[70] "The Hist. of the Pequot War," 128.   [71] Ibid. 132.
[72] Ibid. 137-138.

climbing to the top of the palisado; others of them running into the very flames; many of them, gathering to windward, lay pelting at us with their arrows, and we repaid them with our small shot. Others of the stoutest issued forth, as we did guess, to the number of forty—who perished by the sword. . . . Thus were the stout-hearted spoiled, having slept their last sleep; and none of their men could find their hands. Thus did the Lord judge among the heathen, filling the place with dead bodies. . . . In little more than one hour's space was their impregnable fort, with themselves, utterly destroyed, to the number of six or seven hundred. . . . There were only seven taken captive, and about seven escaped." [73]

Such was the famous 'Mystic-fight,' a thorough piece of work, fought over again and again in talk around many a New England fire-side for a hundred years afterward, and never forgotten by the red men who were left alive to remember anything. With that fight the war was really over, even as all was over with the terrible tribe of the Pequots; and the book, after relating some minor incidents, more or less bloody, rises at the close into a Davidic chant of exultation at the victory of Jehovah over them that do evil, and at the glorious deliverance wrought by him for his people.[74]

VII

The reputation of Daniel Gookin has fallen among us far below his deserts. As we study his writings, we see shining through them the signals of a very noble manhood,—modesty, tenderness, strength, devoutness, a heart full of sympathy for every kind of distress, a hand able and quick to reach out and obey the promptings of his heart. Then, too, we are impressed by his uncommon intellectual value.

---

[73] "The Hist. of the Pequot War," 139–141.

[74] Other contemporaneous accounts of the Pequot war are: (a) "News from America," by Capt. John Underhill, London, 1638, reprinted in 3 Mass. Hist. Soc. Coll. VI. 1–28; (b) "Relation of the Pequot Wars," by Lion Gardener, first printed in 3 Mass. Hist. Soc. Coll. III. 131–160; (c) "A True Relation of the late Battle fought in New England between the English and the Pequot Savages," by the Rev. Philip Vincent, London, 1638,* reprinted in 3 Mass. Hist. Soc. Coll. VI. 29–43. All these have historical value, none that is literary.

[* Changed to "1637."]

New England: Historical Writers

We find that he had width and grip in his ideas; his mind was trained to orderly movement; his style rose clear and free above the turbid and pedantic rhetoric of his age and neighborhood; his reading was shown, not in the flapping tags of quotation, but in a diffused intelligence, fullness, and poise of thought; as an historian, he had the primary virtues—truth, fairness, lucidity.

Thus, as we begin to get acquainted with the man through his writings and to like him more and more, we turn with quite a new zest to the study of his personal history. His life, we find, was a noble one from end to end: not in all respects prosperous, but rugged and sometimes sorrowful; having in fact the veiled prosperities of hinderance, disappointment, struggle; but cheerful always with the firmness and brightness of high trust, manly pluck, and Christian resignation. Moreover, he belonged to that large type of manhood that England produced so many specimens of in the sixteenth and seventeenth centuries, Elizabethan men, who settled the antique quarrel between the life of thought and the life of action, by leading both lives. Over against this prosaic, old name of Daniel Gookin, it is right for us to set the two descriptive words that throw some gleam of poetry upon it—the words, author, soldier.

The date of his birth can be only approximately stated: it was about 1612. He probably came to America with his father in 1621. It is a notable thing about him that though he had grown up to manhood in the Cavalier colony of Virginia, in theology and in politics he was a very Puritan. But in the year 1643, Virginia had a renewed attack of the disease that was then epidemic throughout Christendom —the disease of religious intolerance; and under the paroxysms of this disease Virginia proceeded to expel from her borders certain persons who did not conform to the Episcopal church as there established. This seems to have been the cause of Gookin's removal to Massachusetts, where he was made a freeman of the colony in May, 1644; taking up his residence subsequently at Cambridge, which continued to be his home during the remainder of his long life. The aptitude of the man for public service was soon recognized; for he was thenceforward in constant employment in matters of war and peace, of piety and politics; he was made captain of militia, member of the house of deputies, speaker of the house of deputies, one of the general magistrates of the colony, a licenser of the printing press, and at last commander-in-chief of the colonial military forces. In 1655, and again in 1657, Gookin went to England, and spent two or three years there, enjoying the acquaintance and confidence of the Protector; for it was through Daniel Gookin that Cromwell sent to the men of Massachusetts his celebrated proposition, that they should abandon the rugged land in which they had settled and transfer themselves to the balm and bloom of Jamaica. Of all Daniel Gookin's public employments, the one that was most congenial to his humane spirit was that of superintendent of the Indians within the jurisdiction of Massachusetts. This position he held during the last thirty years of his life, performing its duties with a heartiness and fidelity that were more than official. During all those years he and the apostle Eliot went hand in hand in Christ-like labor and provident care for the Indians; and when in 1675 and 1676 the red men of New England under the lead of King Philip made their last great concerted effort to exterminate the white men who had taken possession of their hunting-fields, Gookin and Eliot were among the very few persons who did not give way to insane terror and exasperation. Almost alone, these two men stood up against the popular delirium, and they pleaded even then on behalf of the execrated copper-face the pleas of reason, and Christian pity, and common justice. For this crime Gookin especially was for a time punished with the popular hatred. He was hooted at in public places. He said from the bench where he sat as a magistrate that it was dangerous for him to walk along the streets. He was denounced as a traitor to his own kind. But it was not in Daniel Gookin, doing the right, to bend before any sort of storm; and at last the storm passed by; and he abode still. Later in his life, the same resolute obstinacy, under altered circumstances, brought to him a popularity as prodigious as had been his previous unpopularity; for, when that dogged political conflict with Randolph and Andros came on, and the people of New England were in danger of being robbed both of property and of freedom by those rapacious menials of James the Second, once more the undaunted courage and the rock-like firmness of Daniel Gookin were a power in the land. He fought Randolph and Andros upon every item of their demands. He opposed every concession to them. He opposed

New England: Historical Writers

the sending of agents to England. He opposed any submission to the acts of trade. He stood for a strict construction of the colonial charter. He nourished his patriotic jealousy for every specific American right, political or commercial. He was the originator and the prophet of that immortal dogma of our national greatness—no taxation without representation. Of course, in this bitter and perilous battle with the enemies of his own people, his own people at least * were with him; and he who ten years before had been so obnoxious to them that his name was "a by-word among men and boys," [75] and that jeers and threats pursued him along the streets, in his last years was permitted to taste the flavor of a public approbation that filled all the air about him and thronged after his footsteps wherever he went. Finally, in honor of this man, three things remain to be said. First, his piety was Puritanic without being vitriolic. Second, he had been in the public service a large part of his life; but he died so poor that his surviving friend, the apostle Eliot, wrote to the bountiful and wise Robert Boyle in England, asking him in charity to send over to the poor man's widow the sum of ten pounds. Third, he was a white man; yet the rumor of his death carried sorrow into every red man's wigwam in Massachusetts.

The writings left to us by this grand old American patriarch and sage are two treatises, both historical, and both relating to the Indians of New England. He had indeed worked out an admirable plan for a general history of New England,—the most comprehensive and philosophical plan, perhaps, that was projected by any one before the present century. He was about sixty-two years old when he gave to the public a description of this plan; and in doing so he used these interesting sentences of self-reference: "You may here see my design, which I earnestly desired might have been drawn by a more able pen; and I have often earnestly moved able persons to undertake it; but not knowing of any, and being unwilling that a matter of so great concernment for the honor of God and the good of men, should be buried in oblivion, I have adventured in my old age, and in a plain style, to draw some rude delineaments of God's beautiful work in this land. I have, through grace, travelled half way in this work,

[* Changed to "last."]
[75] "A Letter to London," quoted in Archæol. Am. II. 449, note.

as is said before; but in truth I find myself clogged with so many avocations, as my public employ among the English and Indians, and my own personal and family exercises, which by reason of my low estate in the world are the more obstructive and perplexing, so that I cannot proceed in this work so vigorously as I desire. Yet I shall endeavor, by God's assistance, if he please to spare me life and ability, to make what speedy progress I can. If this tract concerning the Indians find acceptance, I shall be the more encouraged to finish and send forth the other; which although it should prove very imperfect, by reason of the weakness and unworthiness of the author, yet I shall endeavor that it be drawn according to truth; and then, if it be of no other use, it may serve to inform my children, or possibly contribute some little help to a more able pen, to set forth the same thing, more exactly and exquisitely garnished, in after times." [76]

These sentences occur in the postscript of his first work, "Historical Collections of the Indians in New England," which he made ready for publication in 1674, and dedicated to Charles the Second. Though carefully finished for the press, the work slumbered in manuscript one hundred and eighteen years, and first awoke to the privilege of print in 1792, in the earliest volume of the Massachusetts Historical Society. It describes the several Indian nations of New England, their customs, their religious beliefs, their forms of government; it particularly tells of the Indians who had accepted Christianity; and it gives affectionate sketches of such noble white men as had devoted themselves to the task of helping the Indians to find the way to a better life. The author gathered his materials with care, and arranged them with clearness; and his book abounds in calm, pleasant, and judicial statements concerning those crabbed and forlorn creatures, earth-men, anthropoid animals, whose fate it seemed to be to wither and disappear before the breath of the pale-faces.

The second work written by Daniel Gookin was finished in 1677, and was dedicated to Robert Boyle. It was probably sent over to England for publication; and in England it remained in manuscript, and was lost, until the present century, when it was brought to the light once more, sent back to this country, and in the year 1836

[76] 1 Mass. Hist. Soc. Coll. I. 226.

New England: Historical Writers

printed for the first time.[77] This also relates to the Indians of New England; and its composition was prompted by certain incidents connected with King Philip's war, at that time but recently ended. That terrible war had kindled among the white inhabitants of New England a delirium of wrath against the Indians which cast away all pity, all justice; which embraced in an awful doom of destruction the Christian Indian and the pagan, the friend and the enemy. Against this brutal and indiscriminate fury, Daniel Gookin had all along protested; and he wrote this book for the purpose of showing that the Indians who had avowed themselves Christians, had taken no part in the conspiracy that their pagan kindred had formed for the extermination of the English. It was entitled "An Historical Account of the Doings and Sufferings of the Christian Indians in New England." It is written with tranquillity of tone, without bitterness even toward his own bitter assailants; and its calm and massive accumulation of facts rises to an irresistible and even pathetic vindication of the Christian Indians from the monstrous charges that had been cast against them. It shows that months before the war actually burst upon the white settlements, these true-hearted Indian disciples gave repeated warning of the coming danger; that when at last the war came on, they offered their services as soldiers, servants, scouts, and spies; that down to the very close of the war, they rendered invaluable aid to the English in many ways; and yet, that from the beginning to the end, they and their harmless families were treated by their white patrons with unmeasured contempt and distrust; that they were insulted everywhere, were denied the ordinary comforts of life, and that some of them were murdered atrociously in cold blood, even by white women; but that in spite of all these cruelties, they remained faithful to the English, and bore their hardships with a meekness and a fortitude which implied that these swarthy religious disciples of the white men had already got far beyond their teachers in the scholarship of the Christian graces. "I had need apologize," says the author, "for this long story concerning the Indians. But the true reason of being so particular is that I might, in the words of truth and soberness, clear the innocency of those Indians, unto

[77] By Am. Antiqu. Soc. in Archæol. Am. II. 423-534.

all pious and impartial men that shall peruse this script; and so far as in me lies, to vindicate the hand of God and religion that these Christians profess and practise; and to declare I cannot join with the multitude that would cast them all into the same lump with the profane and brutish heathen, who are as great enemies to our Christian Indians as they are to the English." [78]

In spite of old age, poverty, and public cares, Daniel Gookin completed his large scheme of a "History of New England;" but the manuscript, which at his death was left to a son, is supposed to have been burned some years afterward in the house of that son, in Sherburne, Massachusetts. This was probably the only existing copy of the work. The loss of it is a calamity to early American history.

[78] Archæol. Am. II. 461–462.

Chapter VII

New England: Descriptions of Nature and People in America

I. Sensitiveness of the first Americans to the peculiar phenomena of the new world.
II. "Journal" of Bradford and Winslow—First contact of the Pilgrims with America—Gropings—American thunder—Indian visits—An Indian king at home—Winslow's letter—His "Good News from New England"—History as cultivated by the Indians—Men who are not called to be colonists.
III. Francis Higginson, churchman, dissenter, immigrant—His "True Relation"—His "New England's Plantation"—Pictures of sea and land—The bright side of things in America.
IV. William Wood—His "New England's Prospect"—His uncommon literary ability—Analysis of his book—His defence of the honesty of travellers—His powers of description—Merit of his verses—Mirthfulness—Wolves, humming-birds, fishes—Eloquent and playful sketches of Indians.
V. John Josselyn—His kindred—No lover of the New England Puritans—His habits in America—A seventeenth century naturalist in our woods—His "New England's Rarities Discovered"—His "Two Voyages to New England"—The White Hills—His true value as a reporter of natural history—Generous gifts to the credulous reader—His friendly attitude toward the unknown.

I

A DELIGHTFUL group of writings belonging to our earliest age is made up of those which preserve for us, in the very words of the men themselves, the curiosity, the awe, the bewilderment, the fresh delight, with which the American Fathers came face to face for the first time with the various forms of nature and of life in the new world. We have already seen examples of this class of writings produced by the early men of Virginia; and among the founders of New England there was no lack of the same sensitiveness to the vast, picturesque, and novel aspects of nature which they encountered upon the sea and the land, in their first journeys hither. The evidence of this fact is scattered thick through all their writings, in letters, sermons, histories, poems; while there remain several books, written by them immediately after their arrival here, describing in the first glow of elated feeling the vision that unfolded itself before them, of the new realms of existence, the "vast and empty chaos,"[1] upon which they were entering.

II

The first of these books consists of a journal[2] kept by two renowned passengers upon the Mayflower, William Bradford and Edward Winslow, from the ninth of November, 1620, the day on which they caught their first glimpse of American land, until the return to England of the good ship Fortune, more than thirteen months afterward. Of course, in a book of this kind, made up of extemporized jottings, we ought not to look for careful literary workmanship; and yet, the deliberation and the conscientiousness of the Pilgrim character are stamped upon every line of it. It has the charm of utter sincerity, the effortless grace that we might expect in the language of noble-minded men casting their eyes for the first time, and with unhackneyed enthusiasm, upon the face of a new universe.

"After many difficulties in boisterous storms, at length, by God's providence . . . we espied land. . . . And the appearance of it much comforted us, especially seeing so goodly a land, and wooded to the brink of the sea."[3] Coming round "the spiral bending" of

[1] Robert Cushman, in Young, "Chron. Pil." 245.
[2] Long known under the ugly name of "Mourt's Relation," so called probably through a typographical error in the first edition. Reprinted in Young, "Chron. Pil." 109–229.
[3] Young, "Chron. Pil." 117.

New England: Descriptions of Nature

the outermost point of Cape Cod, they found themselves suddenly in "a good harbor and pleasant bay," "wherein a thousand sail of ships may safely ride."[4] Upon land "there was the greatest store of fowl that ever we saw. And every day we saw whales playing hard by us, of which in that place, if we had instruments and means to take them, we might have made a very rich return; which to our great grief we wanted."[5] Some of the pioneers going on shore for the purpose of discovering a place of habitation, they wondered at the density of the forests, and at the scarcity of the inhabitants. "We marched through boughs and bushes, and under hills and valleys, which tore our very armor in pieces, and yet could meet with none" of the inhabitants "nor their houses, nor find any fresh water." At last, "about ten o'clock we came into a deep valley, full of brush, wood-gaile, and long grass, through which we found little paths or tracks; and there we saw deer, and found springs of fresh water, of which we were heartily glad, and sat us down and drunk our first New England water, with as much delight as ever we drunk drink in all our lives."[6] "We went ranging up and down till the sun began to draw low, and then we hasted out of the woods, that we might come to our shallop, which . . . we espied a great way off, and called them to come unto us. . . . They were exceeding glad to see us. . . . So being both weary and faint, for we had eaten nothing all that day, we fell to make our rendezvous and get firewood. . . . By that time we had done, and our shallop come to us, it was within night; and we fed upon such victuals as we had, and betook us to our rest, after we had set our watch. About midnight we heard a great and hideous cry; and our sentinels called 'Arm! Arm!' So we bestirred ourselves, and shot off a couple of muskets, and the noise ceased. We concluded that it was a company of wolves or foxes; for one told us he had heard such a noise in Newfoundland. About five o'clock in the morning we began to be stirring. . . . After prayer we prepared ourselves for breakfast and for a journey; and it being now the twilight in the morning, it was thought meet to carry the things down to the shallop. . . . As it fell out, the water not being high enough, they laid the things down upon the shore and came up to breakfast. Anon, all upon a sudden, we heard a great and a strange cry, which

[4] Young, "Chron. Pil." 118.   [5] Ibid. 119.   [6] Ibid. 128–129.

we knew to be the same voices, though they varied their notes. One of our company, being abroad, came running in, and cried, 'They are men! Indians! Indians!' and withal their arrows came flying amongst us. Our men ran out with all speed to recover their arms. . . . In the meantime, Captain Miles Standish, having a snaphance ready, made a shot, and after him another. After they two had shot, other two of us were ready; but he wished us not to shoot till we could take aim, for we knew not what need we should have. . . . Our care was no less for the shallop. . . . We called unto them to know how it was with them; and they answered 'Well! Well!' every one, and 'be of good courage!' . . . The cry of our enemies was dreadful. . . . Their note was after this manner, *'Woach, woach, ha ha hach woach.'* . . . There was a lusty man, and no whit less valiant, who was thought to be their captain, stood behind a tree within half a musket-shot of us, and there let his arrows fly at us. He was seen to shoot three arrows, which were all avoided; for he at whom the first arrow was aimed, saw it, and stooped down, and it flew over him. The rest were avoided also. He stood three shots of a musket. At length, one took, as he said, full aim at him; after which he gave an extraordinary cry, and away they went all. We followed them about a quarter of a mile. . . . Then we shouted all together two several times, and shot off a couple of muskets and so returned. This we did that they might see we were not afraid of them, nor discouraged. Thus it pleased God to vanquish our enemies and give us deliverance." [7]

On Saturday, the third of March, "the birds sang in the woods most pleasantly. At one of the clock it thundered, which was the first we heard in that country. It was strong and great claps, but short; but after an hour it rained very sadly till midnight." [8]

On Friday, the sixteenth of March, "we determined to conclude of the military orders, which we had begun to consider of before. . . . And whilst we were busied hereabout, we were interrupted again; for there presented himself a savage, which caused an alarm. He very boldly came all alone, and along the houses, straight to the rendezvous; where we intercepted him, not suffering him to go in. . . . He saluted us in English and bade us 'welcome.' . . . He was a man free

[7] Young, "Chron. Pil." 154–158.   [8] Ibid. 181–182.

New England: Descriptions of Nature

in speech, so far as he could express his mind, and of a seemly carriage. We questioned him of many things; he was the first savage we could meet withal. He said he was not of these parts, but of Morattiggon, and one of the sagamores or lords thereof. . . . He discoursed of the whole country, and of every province, and of their sagamores, and their number of men, and strength. The wind beginning to rise a little, we cast a horseman's coat about him; for he was stark naked, only a leather about his waist, with a fringe about a span long or little more. He had a bow and two arrows. . . . He was a tall, straight man, the hair of his head black, long behind, only short before, none on his face at all. He asked some beer, but we gave him strong water, and biscuit, and butter, and cheese, and pudding, and a piece of mallard; all which he liked well. . . . All the afternoon we spent in communication with him. We would gladly have been rid of him at night, but he was not willing to go this night. . . . We lodged him that night at Stephen Hopkins's house, and watched him." [9]

On the twenty-second of March, the Pilgrims received a visit from the great sagamore, Massasoit. "After salutations, our governor kissing his hand, the king kissed him; and so they sat down. The governor called for some strong water, and drunk to him; and he drunk a great draught, that made him sweat all the while after. . . . All the while he sat by the governor, he trembled for fear. In his person he is a very lusty man, in his best years, an able body, grave of countenance, and spare of speech; in his attire little or nothing differing from the rest of his followers, only in a great chain of white bone beads about his neck. . . . The king had in his bosom, hanging in a string, a great long knife. He marvelled much at our trumpet, and some of his men would sound it as well as they could. Samoset and Squanto, they staid all night with us; and the king and all his men lay all night in the woods, not above half an English mile from us, and all their wives and women with them. That night we kept good watch; but there was no appearance of danger.[10]

"For the temper of the air here," writes Edward Winslow, in a letter appended to the journal from which we have been quoting, "it agreeth well with that in England; and if there be any difference at

[9] Young, "Chron. Pil." 182-185.   [10] Ibid. 193-195.

all, this is somewhat hotter in summer. Some think it to be colder in winter; but I cannot out of experience so say. The air is very clear, and not foggy, as hath been reported. I never in my life remember a more seasonable year than we have here enjoyed; and if we have once but kine, horses, and sheep, I make no question but men might live as contented here as in any part of the world. . . . The country wanteth only industrious men to employ; for it would grieve your hearts if, as I, you had seen so many miles together by goodly rivers uninhabited; and withal, to consider those parts of the world wherein you live to be even greatly burthened with abundance of people." [11]

Thus, with words of happy import, do these earliest Americans close up the story of their first year in their new home; and three years afterward, in 1624, Edward Winslow had a second report to make, which was published in London under the title of "Good News from New England." [12]

He takes up the narrative at the very point where the previous report had dropped it, and carries it forward in luminous and spirited style down to September, 1623. It is a story of the griefs and perils and escapes of the young settlement, of their various encounters, in amity and in enmity, with mean red men and meaner white ones; of the interior administration of the little commonwealth, and of its steady advancement through all obstructions into solid security; above all else, it is a description of the country, with reference to its desirableness as the seat of a new English community. Winslow was a brave man, most expert in dealing with the Indians, and was several times sent upon embassies to them; and his book abounds in vivid and amusing descriptions of these savages, and of the manner of their lives. In one place, for example, he gives this account of their mode of preserving the memory of historical events: "Instead of records and chronicles, they take this course. Where any remarkable act is done, in memory of it, either in the place or by some pathway near adjoining, they make a round hole in the ground, about a foot deep, and as much over; which when others passing by behold, they inquire the cause and occasion of the same, which being once known, they are careful to acquaint all men, as occasion serveth, therewith; and lest such holes should be filled or grown up by any

[11] Young, "Chron. Pil." 233–234.   [12] Printed in ibid. 270–375.

New England: Descriptions of Nature

accident, as men pass by, they will oft renew the same; by which means many things of great antiquity are fresh in memory. So that as a man travelleth, if he can understand his guide, his journey will be the less tedious, by reason of the many historical discourses [which] will be related unto him." [13] Perhaps nothing in all the book is more graphic or entertaining than his description of a journey which in the company of "one Master John Hamden, a gentleman of London, who then wintered with us," he made for the medical relief of Massasoit.[14]

The conclusion of the work is a racy and vigorous admonition addressed to Englishmen who might meditate emigration to America, and warning them against the danger of entering upon that grim business without sufficient consideration of its inevitable tasks and pains: "I write not these things to dissuade any that shall seriously, upon due examination, set themselves to further the glory of God and the honor of our country, in so worthy an enterprise, but rather to discourage such as with too great lightness undertake such courses; who peradventure strain themselves and their friends for their passage thither, and are no sooner there, than seeing their foolish imagination made void, are at their wit's end, and would give ten times so much for their return, if they could procure it; and out of such discontented passions and humors, spare not to lay that imputation upon the country, and others, which themselves deserve. As, for example, I have heard some complain of others for their large reports of New England, and yet, because they must drink water and want many delicates they here enjoyed, could presently return with their mouths full of clamors. And can any be so simple as to conceive that the fountains should stream forth wine or beer, or the woods and rivers be like butchers' shops or fishmongers' stalls, where they might have things taken to their hands? If thou canst not live without such things, and hast no means to procure the one, and will not take pains for the other, nor hast ability to employ others for thee, rest where thou art; for, as a proud heart, a dainty tooth, a beggar's purse, and an idle hand, be here [15] intolerable, so that person

---

[13] Young, "Chron. Pil." 367.   [14] Ibid. 313–323.
[15] In England, where the concluding paragraphs of the book appear to have been written.

that hath these qualities there, is much more abominable. If, therefore, God hath given thee a heart to undertake such courses, upon such grounds as bear thee out in all difficulties, namely, his glory as a principal, and all other outward good things but as accessories, . . . then thou wilt with true comfort and thankfulness receive the least of his mercies; whereas on the contrary, men deprive themselves of much happiness, being senseless of greater blessings, and through prejudice smother up the love and bounty of God; whose name be ever glorified in us, and by us, now and evermore. Amen." [16]

III

Among the Argonauts of the first decade of New England colonization there was perhaps no braver or more exquisite spirit than Francis Higginson, a graduate of St. John's College, Cambridge, who, entering the ministry of the Church of England, soon became noted for his eloquence, and who, turning away from very brilliant prospects of promotion, became a resolute non-conformist, and finally accepted the office of religious teacher to the little pioneer community of Salem, in Massachusetts. It was in April, 1629, that this saintly and gifted man, with his wife and eight little children, sailed away from England, on the Talbot, "a good and strong ship," carrying "above a hundred planters, six goats, five great pieces of ordnance, with meal, oatmeal, pease, and all manner of munition and provision for the plantation for a twelvemonth." [17]

Of this journey over the Atlantic, then a thing of great novelty and risk, Francis Higginson kept a journal, which he promptly sent back to England, and which was circulated in manuscript under the title of "A True Relation of the last Voyage to New England, declaring all circumstances, with the manner of the passage we had by sea, and what manner of country and inhabitants we found when we came to land, and what is the present state and condition of the English people that are there already; faithfully recorded, according to the very truth, for the satisfaction of very many of my loving friends, who have earnestly requested to be truly certified in these things." Arriving at Salem on the twenty-ninth of June, the author

[16] Young, "Chron. Pil." 373–374.
[17] F. Higginson's "Journal," in Young, "Chron. Mass. Bay," 213–238.

New England: Descriptions of Nature

passed the next three months in getting established in his new home, and in making himself acquainted with the youthful-seeming world he had come to live in. The results of his observations were compressed into a little book, entitled "New England's Plantation," giving a "description of the commodities and discommodities of that country." This work was instantly printed in London; and so eager was the thirst of the English people for information concerning their recent settlements in New England, that three editions of the book were called for within a single year. In a little more than thirteen months from his arrival in America, however, Francis Higginson died, in the prime of his life, and on the threshold of a great career.

Upon the title-page of his first book there is the hint of an apology to any "curious critic" who may look into it "for exactness of phrases;" and yet, unlabored as is the composition of both his books, we find in them a delicate felicity of expression, and a quiet, imaginative picturesqueness. Thus, for Wednesday, May thirteenth, he writes: "The wind still holding easterly, we came as far as the Land's End, in the utmost part of Cornwall, and so left our dear native soil of England behind us; and sailing about ten leagues further, we passed the isles of Scilly, and launched the same day a great way into the main ocean. And now my wife and other passengers began to feel the tossing waves of the western sea." [18]

Again, under the date of May twenty-seventh, he gives this forcible description of a storm: "About noon there arose a south wind which increased more and more, so that it seemed to us that are landmen, a sore and terrible storm; for the wind blew mightily, the rain fell vehemently, the sea roared, and the waves tossed us horribly; besides, it was fearful dark, and the mariner's mate was afraid, and noise on the other side, with their running here and there, loud crying one to another to pull at this and that rope. The waves poured themselves over the ship, that the two boats were filled with water. . . . But this lasted not many hours, after which it became a calmish day." [19] What pathos and simple beauty are in these words, which were written for Wednesday, the twenty-fourth of June: "This day we had all a clear and comfortable sight of America." [20]

[18] Young, "Chron. Mass. Bay," 221.   [19] Ibid. 225.   [20] Ibid. 231.

Two days afterward the author wrote the following sentences, so vivid and real in their descriptiveness, that they enable us to enjoy the very luxury of drawing near to America and of beholding it with the eyes of the Fathers themselves: "Friday a foggy morning, but after clear, and wind calm. We saw many schools of mackerel, infinite multitudes on every side of our ship. The sea was abundantly stored with rockweed and yellow flowers, like gillyflowers. By noon we were within three leagues of Cape Ann; and as we sailed along the coasts, we saw every hill and dale and every island full of gay woods and high trees. The nearer we came to the shore, the more flowers in abundance, sometimes scattered abroad, sometimes joined in sheets nine or ten yards long, which we supposed to be brought from the low meadows by the tide. Now, what with fine woods and green trees by land, and these yellow flowers painting the sea, made us all desirous to see our new paradise of New England, whence we saw such forerunning signals of fertility afar off." [21] On Monday, the twenty-ninth of June, "as we passed along, it was wonderful to behold so many islands, replenished with thick wood and high trees, and many fair, green, pastures. . . . We rested that night with glad and thankful hearts that God had put an end to our long and tedious journey through the greatest sea in the world. . . . Our passage was both pleasurable and profitable. For we received instruction and delight in beholding the wonders of the Lord in the deep waters, and sometimes seeing the sea round us appearing with a terrible countenance, and, as it were, full of high hills and deep valleys; and sometimes it appeared as a most plain and even meadow. And, ever and anon, we saw divers kinds of fishes sporting in the great waters, great grampuses and huge whales, going by companies, and puffing up water-streams. Those that love their own chimney-corner, and dare not go beyond their own town's end, shall never have the honor to see these wonderful works of Almighty God." [22]

In describing New England with reference to its fitness as the seat of an English commonwealth, the author arranges his facts, rather quaintly, under the topics of "the four elements—earth, water, air, and fire." All his pages are full of sunshine, and the fragrance of flowers, and the gladness of nature in New England during the balmy

[21] Young, "Chron. Mass. Bay," 232–233.   [22] Ibid. 234–237.

New England: Descriptions of Nature

season in which he came to it. Indeed, he was accused by some who came afterward, of having given too attractive a picture of the country; but for this he was hardly to blame. When he wrote, he had seen only the season of roses: no wonder that his descriptions were rosy. After a voyage of six weeks upon the ocean, any land seems good, much more a delicious, flowery summer-land; and Francis Higginson wrote in the first flush of excitement at being on shore, in a bounteous realm, in an exhilarating new life. It seems to him a paradise regained. All things are delightful. He even exults in the domestic felicity of having "already a quart of milk for a penny," [23] and in having candles of "the wood of the pine tree cloven in two little slices something thin, which . . . burn as clear as a torch." [24] Concerning the climate of the country, he declared that "a sup of New England's air is better than a whole draught of Old England's ale." [25] He was not long in making a study of the Indians, whom in one passage he describes with great zest, even weaving into his account a stroke of gentle raillery at a certain English fashion then prevalent, and very distasteful to the Puritans. The Indians "are a tall and strong-limbed people. Their colors are tawny. . . . Their hair is generally black, and cut before, like our gentlewomen, and one lock longer than the rest, much like to our gentlemen, which fashion, I think, came from hence into England." [26] But best of all, "we have here plenty of preaching, and diligent catechising, with strict and careful exercise. . . . And thus we doubt not but God will be with us; and if God be with us, who can be against us?" [27]

IV

A very sprightly and masterful specimen of descriptive literature, embodying the results of precise observation directed toward the

---

[23] Young, "Chron. Mass. Bay," 245.   [24] Ibid. 254.
[25] Ibid. 252.   [26] Ibid. 256–257.
[27] Ibid. 259. Some of the pleasantest portions of these writings of Francis Higginson have lately been made more accessible by their publication in Thomas Wentworth Higginson's "Book of American Explorers," 341–355. An early brochure, which has acquired considerable note in our time, is "Good News from New England," London, 1648, reprinted in 4 Mass. Hist. Soc. Coll. I. 195–218; a work of no little vigor, also of considerable antiquarian value, but in literary form inexpressibly crude. No clue to the authorship of it has yet been discovered.

topography, climate, and productions of the country, is "New England's Prospect," [28] published in London in 1634, and written by William Wood, whose residence in America is supposed to have begun five years before that date. It will not be easy for us to give a more felicitous account of the book than it gives of itself, when, upon its old title-page, it assures us that it is indeed "a true, lively, and experimental description" of the region that it treats of. The author had attained the fine art of packing his pages full of the most exact delineation of facts, without pressing the life and juice out of them; and, besides the extraordinary raciness and vivacity of his manner, he has an elegance of touch by no means common in the prose of his contemporaries. His style, indeed, is that of a man of genuine literary culture, and has the tone and flavor of the best Elizabethan prose-writers; almost none of the crabbedness of the sermon-makers and pamphleteers of his own day. There are dainty strokes of beauty in his sentences; a forceful imaginative vigor; gayety, and good-hearted sarcasm; all going to make up a book of genial descriptions of nature such as Izaak Walton must have delighted in, if perchance his placid eye ever fell upon it. The book is broken into two parts, the first being a description of the country, the second an account of its Indian inhabitants. Under the first division, we have in twelve chapters a sketch of the geographical features of New England; of the seasons; of the climate, "with the suitableness of it to English bodies for health and sickness;" of the soil; "of the herbs, fruits, woods, waters, and minerals;" "of the beasts that live on the land," or in the water, or both; finally, of the colonies already established there, and of the best preparations to be made by those who intended to remove into the new world. The second division of the work contains twenty chapters, all relating to the Indian tribes of New England; their places of abode; their apparel, ornaments, paintings; their food; their personal characteristics, such as friendship, fortitude, intellectual condition; their politics; their worship; their wars, diversions, domestic customs, and means of livelihood.

Thus the book has a wide range of topics and a multitude of details; but it moves easily through them all, with an alert and thorough

[28] Reprinted by the Prince Society, Boston, 1865.

New England: Descriptions of Nature

treatment, not once blundering out of the straight path or lapsing into dulness. In the preface, the author has a spirited passage avowing that in all his statements he had been careful of the truth, and wittily defending the reputation of travellers against the calumnies of those home-keeping souls who denounce as false whatever is beyond the petty sweep of their own horizons. "I would be loath to broach any thing which may puzzle thy belief, and so justly draw upon myself that unjust aspersion commonly laid on travellers; of whom many say, 'They may lie by authority, because none can control them;' which proverb had surely his original from the sleepy belief of many a home-bred dormouse, who comprehends not either the rarity or possibility of those things he sees not; to whom the most classic relations seem riddles and paradoxes; of whom it may be said, as once of Diogenes, that because he circled himself in the circumstance * of a tub, he therefore contemned the port and palace of Alexander, which he knew not. So there is many a tub-brained cynic, who because anything stranger than ordinary is too large for the strait hoops of his apprehension, he peremptorily concludes that it is a lie. But I decline this sort of thick-witted readers, and dedicate the mite of my endeavors to my more credulous, ingenious, and less censorious countrymen, for whose sake I undertook this work. . . . Thus, thou mayest, in two or three hours' travel over a few leaves, see and know that which cost him that writ it, years, and travel over sea and land, before he knew it."

It is a discovery soon made by us, as we turn over the pages of this writer, that in a book in which description needs to be the principal thing, his style is most happily descriptive. He seems to have the very gift of picture-making, describing objects so well that, as the Arabs say, the ear is converted into the eye. For example, having to tell us of Massachusetts Bay, he lets us look at it for ourselves. It "is both safe, spacious, and deep, free from such cockling seas as run upon the coast of Ireland, and in the channels of England. . . . The mariners . . . may behold the two capes embracing their welcome ships in their arms, which thrust themselves out into the sea in form of a half-moon, the surrounding shore being high, and showing many

[* Changed to "circumference."]

white cliffs in a most pleasant prospect. . . . This harbor is made by a great company of islands, whose high cliffs shoulder out the boisterous seas." [29]

Another literary trait of the author, which he shares with many of the writers of his period, is that of sprinkling verses along the landscape of his prose; and his verses have this singularity, that they are often of considerable poetic merit. In giving a description of the forest trees of New England, he compresses a multitude of particulars into these terse lines, in which the literary aptness and even imaginative force of his epithets are as striking as is their scientific precision:

> "Trees both in hills and plains in plenty be;
> The long-lived Oak, and mournful Cypress-tree;
> Sky-towering Pines, and Chestnuts coated rough,
> The lasting Cedar, with the Walnut tough;
> The rosin-dropping Fir, for masts in use;
> The boatmen seek for oars, light, neat-grown Spruce;
> The brittle Ash, the ever-trembling Asps,
> The broad-spread Elm, whose concave harbors wasps;
> The water-spongy Alder, good for naught;
> Small Eldern, by the Indian fletchers sought;
> The knotty Maple, pallid Birch, Hawthorns;
> The horn-bound tree, that to be cloven scorns,
> Which from the tender vine oft takes his spouse,
> Who twines embracing arms about his boughs.
> Within this Indian orchard fruits be some:
> The ruddy Cherry, and the jetty Plum,
> Snake-murthering Hazel, with sweet Saxifrage,
> Whose spurs, in beer, allays hot fever's rage.
> The dyer's Sumach, with more trees there be,
> That are both good to use, and rare to see." [30]

In his chapters on animals are many paragraphs illustrating an amusing quaintness and quiet mirthfulness of tone, as well as the author's power of condensed and graphic description in verse: "Having related unto you the pleasant situation of the country, the healthfulness of the climate, the nature of the soil, with his vegetatives and other commodities, it will not be amiss to inform you of such irra-

[29] "New England's Prospect," 2–3.   [30] Ibid. 18.

New England: Descriptions of Nature

tional creatures as are daily bred and continually nourished in this country, which do much conduce to the well being of the inhabitants, affording not only meat for the belly, but clothing for the back. The beasts be as followeth:

> The kingly Lion, and the strong-armed Bear,
> The large-limbed Mooses, with the tripping Deer;
> Quill-darting Porcupines and Raccoons be
> Castled in the hollow of an aged tree;
> The skipping Squirrel, Rabbit, purblind Hare,
> Immurëd in the selfsame castle are;
> Lest red-eyed Ferrets, wily Foxes should
> Them undermine, if rampired but with mould;
> The grim-faced Ounce, and ravenous, howling Wolf
> Whose meagre paunch sucks like a swallowing gulf;
> Black-glistering Otters, and rich-coated Beaver,
> The civet-scented Musquash smelling ever.

Concerning * lions I will not say that I ever saw any myself; but some affirm that they have seen a lion at Cape Ann, which is not above six leagues from Boston; some likewise being lost in woods have heard such terrible roarings as have made them much aghast; which must either be devils or lions; there being no other creatures which use to roar saving bears, which have not such a terrible kind of roaring. Besides, Plymouth men have traded for lions' skins in former times." [31] "The Porcupine is a small thing not much unlike a Hedgehog; something bigger, who stands upon his guard, and proclaims a 'Noli me tangere' to man and beast that shall approach too near him, darting his quills into their legs and hides." [32] "The beasts of offence be Skunks, Ferrets, Foxes, whose impudence sometimes drives them to the good-wives' hen roost to fill their paunch." [33] "The Oldwives be a fowl that never leave tattling day or night; something bigger than a duck." [34]

Altogether the most remarkable literary quality of this writer is shown in his delineation of objects in natural history: he has in these an extraordinary union of comprehensiveness, minute accuracy, brev-

[31] "New England's Prospect," 21.   [32] Ibid. 24.
[33] Ibid. 25.   [34] Ibid. 34.

[* Quotation marks were inserted before "Concerning" in the 1897 edition.]

151

ity, and pictorial vividness. Thus, in his account of wolves and hummingbirds are passages that indicate in the author an uncommon power of close and definite observation, together with an easy command of the words that are at once nicely, concisely, and poetically descriptive. Wolves "be made much like a mongrel, being big-boned, lank-paunched, deep-breasted, having a thick neck and head, prick ears, and long snout, with dangerous teeth, long staring hair, and a great bush-tail. It is thought of many that our English mastiffs might be too hard for them; but it is no such matter, for they care no more for an ordinary mastiff, than an ordinary mastiff cares for a cur; many good dogs have been spoiled with them. Once a fair greyhound hearing them at their howlings, run out to chide them, who was torn to * pieces before he could be rescued. One of them makes no more bones to run away with a pig than a dog to run away with a marrow bone. . . . Late at night and early in the morning they set up their howlings, and call their companies together at night to hunt, at morning to sleep; in a word they be the greatest inconveniency the country hath, both for matter of damage to private men in particular, and the whole country in general." [35] "The Humbird is one of the wonders of the country, being no bigger than a hornet, yet hath all the dimensions of a bird, as bill and wings, with quills, spider-like legs, small claws. For color she is as glorious as the rainbow; as she flies she makes a little humming noise like a humblebee: wherefore she is called the Humbird." [36]

"Having done with these," he says, "let me lead you from the land to the sea, to view what commodities may come from thence;" [37] and in the course of this description, he mentions with his usual excellence of apt epithets:

> "The king of waters, the sea-shouldering Whale;
> The snuffing Grampus, with the oily Seal;
> The storm-presaging Porpus; Herring-Hog;
> Line-shearing Shark, the Catfish, and Sea-Dog;

. . .

[35] "New England's Prospect," 26–27.   [36] Ibid. 31.
[37] Ibid. 35.

[* Changed to "in."]

New England: Descriptions of Nature

> The stately Bass, old Neptune's fleeting post
> That tides it out and in from sea to coast." [38]

It was not the author's plan to deal at any length with the history and social development of the colonies established in New England; yet he does not altogether pass them over, nor does he forget the needs of those in the mother-land who might be considering the project of coming to America. He speaks sarcastically of the ignorant questions often asked in England concerning the new land, as, "whether the sun shines there or no;" [39] and of the "groundless calumniations" of those who had come to the country with fantastic and impossible notions of what was to be found there, and had of course abandoned it in disgust: "I have myself heard some say that they heard it was a rich land, a brave country; but when they came there they could see nothing but a few canvas booths and old houses, supposing at the first to have found walled towns, fortifications * and cornfields, as if towns could have built themselves, or cornfields have grown of themselves without the husbandry of man. These men, missing of their expectations, returned home and railed against the country." [40] The second part of the book is devoted to the Indians, and is written, as the author says, "in a more light and facetious style, . . . because their carriage and behavior hath afforded more matter of mirth and laughter, than gravity and wisdom; and therefore I have inserted many passages of mirth concerning them, to spice the rest of my more serious discourse and to make it more pleasant." [41] But the author's merry eye, never failing to catch a glimpse of whatever is amusing, is likewise alert for whatever is instructive; and the really fine and wise sketch which he has given of the various savage tribes of New England, is not likely to be scorned by us, even though he may have committed the crime of paving the highway of knowledge with entertainment. His study of the Indians seems to have embraced not only their habits in this world, but their notions about the world to

---

[38] "New England's Prospect," 36. [39] Ibid. 61.
[40] Ibid. 52. [41] Ibid. "To the Reader."

[* In his correction copy of the first edition, Tyler seems to have queried the absence of a comma after this word, but the punctuation was not changed in later editions.]

come; and in his chapter on "their deaths, burials, and mourning," we find these nimble and affluent sentences, which, besides giving us considerable amusing information, reproduce for us the very manner of the best Elizabethan prose: "Although the Indians be of lusty and healthful bodies, not experimentally knowing the catalogue of those health-wasting diseases which are incident to other countries, . . . but spin out the thread of their days to a fair length, numbering three score, four score, some a hundred years, before the world's universal summoner cite them to the craving grave; but the date of their life expired, and death's arrestment seizing upon them, all hope of recovery being past, then to behold and hear their throbbing sobs and deep-fetched sighs, their grief-wrung hands, and tear-bedewed cheeks, their doleful cries, would draw tears from adamantine eyes, that be but spectators of their mournful obsequies. The glut of their grief being passed, they commit the corpse of their deceased friends to the ground, over whose grave is for a long time spent many a briny tear, deep groan * and Irish-like howlings. . . . These are the mourners without hope; yet do they hold the immortality of the never-dying soul, that it shall pass to the South-West Elysium, concerning which their Indian faith jumps much with the Turkish Alcoran, holding it to be a kind of paradise, wherein they shall everlastingly abide, solacing themselves in odoriferous gardens, fruitful cornfields, green meadows, bathing their tawny hides in the cool streams of pleasant rivers, and shelter themselves from heat and cold in the sumptuous palaces framed by the skill of Nature's curious contrivement; concluding that neither care nor pain shall molest them, but that Nature's bounty will administer all things with a voluntary contribution from the overflowing storehouse of their Elysian hospital." [42]

So vigilant an observer as was this author, would not be likely to let slip any trait that might illustrate the grotesque and droll effects wrought by the contact of English culture with the mental childhood of the Indians. Nothing in this kind has ever ministered more to the white man's mirth than the impression made upon the savages by our improvements in the arts, which of course seemed to them to

[42] "New England's Prospect," 104–105.

[* Tyler inserted a comma here in his correction copy, but no change was made.]

New England: Descriptions of Nature

be things enormous, superhuman, and dreadful: "These Indians being strangers to arts and sciences, and being unacquainted with the inventions that are common to a civilized people, are ravished with admiration at the first view of any such sight. They took the first ship they saw for a walking island, the mast to be a tree, the sail white clouds, and the discharging of ordnance for lightning and thunder, which did much trouble them; but this thunder being over, and this moving island steadied with an anchor, they manned out their canoes to go and pick strawberries there; but being saluted by the way with a broadside, they cried out 'what much hoggery,' 'so big walk,' and 'so big speak,' and 'by and by kill,' which caused them to turn back, not daring to approach till they were sent for. They do much extol and wonder at the English for their strange inventions, especially for a windmill, which in their esteem was little less than the world's wonder, for the strangeness of his whisking motion and the sharp teeth biting the corn (as they term it) into such small pieces. They were loath at the first to come near to his long arms, or to abide in so tottering a tabernacle, though now they dare go anywhere so far as they have an English guide." [43]

His chapter on the Aberginians, a tribe of savages renowned for their stalwart and superb physical proportions, furnishes us with another instance of his remarkable gift of concentrated, exact, and vivid description. They are "between five or six foot high, straight-bodied, strongly composed, smooth-skinned, merry-countenanced, of complexion something more swarthy than Spaniards, black-haired, high-foreheaded, black-eyed, out-nosed, broad-shouldered, brawny-armed, long- and slender-handed, out-breasted, small-waisted, lank-bellied, well-thighed, flat-kneed, handsome-grown legs, and small feet. In a word, take them when the blood brisks in their veins, when the flesh is on their backs, and marrow in their bones, when they frolic in their antique deportments and Indian postures, and they are more amiable to behold (though only in Adam's livery) than many a compounded fantastic in the newest fashion." [44] "But a sagamore with a humbird in his ear for a pendant, a black hawk on his occiput for his plume, mowhackees for his gold chain, good store of wampompeage begirting his loins, his bow in his hand, his quiver

[43] "New England's Prospect," 87.   [44] Ibid. 70.

at his back, with six naked Indian spatterlashes at his heels for his guard, thinks himself little inferior to the great Cham; he will not stick to say, he is all one with King Charles. He thinks he can blow down castles with his breath, and conquer kingdoms with his conceit." [45]

V

A writer of more pronounced scientific intentions, though of far less literary skill, was John Josselyn, who, belonging to an ancient and aristocratic family in England, had the distinction of being able to subscribe his name with the proud affix, "Gentleman." His father, Sir Thomas Josselyn, of Kent, was an associate of Sir Ferdinando Gorges in schemes of American colonization; his brother was that Henry Josselyn, who, from about the year 1634 onward for forty years, was a leading land-holder and magistrate in the province of Maine, and who, in life-long contests with white men and Indians, displayed an unslumbering activity of courage and of hate,—a characteristic exactly touched by Whittier in a single vivid line of Mogg Megone—

"Grey Jocelyn's eye is never sleeping."

John Josselyn, the author, was twice an inhabitant of this country. He came first in 1638, remaining only fifteen months; he came again in 1663, and remained eight years: in both cases passing the most of his time on his brother's plantation at Scarborough. In connection with his first arrival in Boston, he mentions a fact that gives us a pleasant glimpse of the intellectual exchanges already begun between the men of books in America and the men of books in England: he states that he first paid his respects to "Mr. Winthrop, the governor," and that he next called upon the great pulpit-orator, John Cotton, to whom he "delivered from Mr. Francis Quarles, the poet, the translation of the 16th, 25th, 51st, 88th, 113th, and 137th Psalms, into English metre, for his approbation." [46] Though his family in England

---

[45] "New England's Prospect," 74.
[46] "Two Voyages to N. E.," 225–226, reprinted in 3 Mass. Hist. Soc. Coll. III. 211–354.

New England: Descriptions of Nature

appear to have been attached to the Puritan party, he himself certainly had little sympathy with the Puritans of New England, concerning whom he in one place frees his mind, with a refreshing copiousness of frank words. Their leading men, he tells us, "are damnable rich, . . . inexplicably covetous and proud: they receive your gifts but as an homage or tribute due to their transcendency. . . . The chiefest objects of discipline, true religion, and morality, they want; some are of a linsey-woolsey disposition, . . . all like Ethiopians, white in the teeth only; full of ludification, and injurious dealing, and cruelty." [47]

There is no evidence that he engaged in any kind of business in America. He was probably a bachelor; and finding a comfortable home on his brother's estate, he had leisure to indulge his love of reading and particularly his fondness for researches in natural history. He made it his ambition, as he informs us, "to discover the natural, physical, and chirurgical rarities of this new-found world." [48] He appears to have wandered at his will in the forests and on the mountains of Maine, to have dropped his hook in many waters, and to have explored the islands along the coast, everywhere soliciting nature to deliver up to him her mysteries. Some of these mysteries, indeed, did not consent to be delivered up passively to the prying stranger, even for the advancement of science among mankind; as was made apparent, for example, in his somewhat too zealous investigation of that uneasy Americanism, a hornet's nest: "In the afternoon I walked into the woods . . . , and happening into a fine broad walk, . . . I wandered till I chanced to spy a fruit, as I thought, like a pine-apple plated with scales. It was as big as the crown of a woman's hat. I made bold to step unto it, with an intent to have gathered it. No sooner had I touched it, but hundreds of wasps were about me. At last I cleared myself from them, . . . but by the time I was come into the house, . . . they hardly knew me but by my garments." [49] This grim practical joke of the wasps at the expense of the learned naturalist, which must have long supplied food for bucolic mirth among the woodmen of New England, is

---

[47] "Two Voyages to N. E." 331. [48] "New England's Rarities," 35.*
[49] "Two Voyages to N. E." 231–232.

[* Tyler apparently used the edition published by William Veazie, Boston, 1865.]

deftly used by Longfellow in his "Tragedy of John Endicott," when he makes the troubled inn-keeper of Boston, Samuel Cole, exclaim:

"I feel like Master Josselyn when he found
The hornet's nest, and thought it some strange fruit,
Until the seeds came out, and then he dropped it." [50]

It is as a naturalist, and as the writer of two books embodying the results of his observations in that capacity, that John Josselyn has a place in our literary annals. He appears indeed to have been a man of some general learning. He quotes Pliny, Lucan, Isidore, and Paracelsus; all his Biblical citations are from the Vulgate; he brings in a proverb in the Italian; and among the writers of his own country, he has references to Drayton, Ben Jonson, Sir John Davies, Sylvester, George Sandys, Captain John Smith, and to Charles the First; to the last of whom, as the supposed author of "Eikon Basilike," he alludes in the sympathetic cant of the Restoration, as "the royal martyr." John Josselyn's first book, entitled "New England's Rarities Discovered in Birds, Beasts, Fishes, Serpents, and Plants of that Country," was published in London in 1672; his second book, considerably larger than the first, and entitled "An Account of Two Voyages to New England," was published in the same place in 1674.

Although his main purpose in these books was to give an account of American productions in natural history, he did not altogether leave out descriptions of the country in general. Thus he speaks of "a ridge of mountains . . . known by the name of the White Mountains, upon which lieth snow all the year, and is a landmark twenty miles off at sea." [51] One of the highest of these mountains is "called the Sugar Loaf, . . . a rude heap of massy stones piled one upon another. . . . From this rocky hill you may see the whole country round about: it is far above the lower clouds, and from hence we beheld a vapor, like a great pillar, drawn up by the sunbeams out of a great lake or pond into the air, where it was formed into a cloud. The country beyond these hills northward is daunting terrible, being full of rocky hills . . . and clothed with infinite thick woods." [52]

In dealing with objects in natural history, the most valuable part of his work is in botany. Of course that science was then in a crude

[50] "New England Tragedies," 35.   [51] "New England's Rarities," 35–36.
[52] Ibid. 36.

New England: Descriptions of Nature

condition, and it may be that even in that condition Josselyn had not perfectly mastered it. According to the decision of Professor Edward Tuckerman, Josselyn is "little more than a herbalist; but it is enough that he gets beyond that entirely unscientific character. He certainly botanized, and made botanical use of Gerard and his other authorities. The credit belongs to him of indicating several genera as new which were so, and peculiar to the American Flora. . . . There are important parts of his account of our plants, in which we know with certainty what he intended to tell us; and farther, that this was worth the telling." [53]

Beyond the realm of botany, his contributions to natural history are less esteemed. Indeed, even within that realm, he was capable of making the announcement that, in America, barley "commonly degenerates into oats," [54] and that "summer-wheat many times changeth into rye;" [55] while in the domain of the other sciences, he indulges in many assertions that exhibit the uncritical habits of even scientific observers in the seventeenth century. He informs us, with all gravity, that in their assemblies the Indians commonly carry on their discussions "in perfect hexameter verse," doing this "extempore." [56] He assures us that there is in New England a species of frog, "which chirp in the spring like sparrows, and croak like toads in autumn;" some of which "when they sit upon their breech are a foot high;" while "up in the country" they are "as big as a child of a year old." [57] He tells of swallows which, loving to dwell in chimneys, construct their nests so as to hang down "by a clew-like string a yard long." These swallows, he adds, "commonly have four or five young ones, and when they go away, which is much about the time that swallows use to depart, they never fail to throw down one of their young birds into the room by way of gratitude. I have more than once observed that, against the ruin of the family, these birds will suddenly forsake the house and come no more." [58] He gives a brilliant description of the Pilhannaw, "a monstrous great bird . . . four times as big as a goshawk, white-mailed, having two or three purple feathers in her head as long as geese's feathers; . . . her head is as big as a child's of a year old; a very princely bird. When she

[53] "New England's Rarities," 15–16. [54] Ibid. 143.
[55] "Two Voyages to N. E." 336. [56] "New England's Rarities," 38.
[57] Ibid. 76–77. [58] Ibid. 40.

History of American Literature

soars abroad, all sort of feathered creatures hide themselves; yet she never preys upon any of them, but upon fawns and jackals. She aeries in the woods upon the high hills of Ossapy." [59] These sentences upon the Pilhannaw are indeed delightful, the last one in particular being very sweet, with a certain far-off, appealing melody; and the artistic merit of the whole picture is perhaps enhanced by the consideration, that it seems to have been on his part an exploit of pure imagination, supplemented by some guess-work and hear-say, —this princely bird of Josselyn's being probably nothing but "a confused conception made up from several accounts of large birds" seen in different parts of America.[60]

It may not surprise us to ascertain that this author, whose scientific methods had in them so little severity, should have stopped occasionally to reproach his "skeptic readers" for "muttering out of their scuttle-mouths" expressions of derisive unbelief in his statements. As a student of nature, his own capacity for receiving at the hands of other narrators prodigious gift-horses which he was too polite to look very sharply in the mouth, implied in him at least this compensating merit—a tolerant and catholic mood. And is it not possible, after all, that in our search for knowledge, swiftness to reject may be as great an impediment to progress as swiftness to accept? If extreme credulity swallows down a good deal of error, may it not be that extreme incredulity spurns away a good deal of truth? At any rate, our gentle author seems to have had some such notion; for in his lifetime he walked quite freely about this earth, keeping his eyes and ears open for the discovery of such matters as he had not known before, and believing, as he tells us, "that there are many stranger things in the world than are to be seen between London and Stanes." [61]

---

[59] "New England's Rarities," 40–41.   [60] Professor E. Tuckerman, ibid. note.

[61] "Two Voyages to N. E." 229. Josselyn also published in London, in 1674, "Chronological Observations of America, from the year of the World to the year of Christ, 1673." It is reprinted in 3 Mass. Hist. Soc. Coll. III. 355–396; and is meagre and unimportant.*

[* A marginal note says, "Justin Winsor thinks that this note is misleading; & that the book here mentioned was a part of the 'Two Voyages.'" In blue pencil is "Added for new ed. 1896." What was added was: "Mr. Justin Winsor informs me that, in his opinion, the latter work originally appeared not by itself but as a part of the 'Two Voyages to N. E.'"]

Chapter VIII

New England: Theological and Religious Writers

I. The supremacy of the clergy in early New England—Their worthiness—Their public manifestations—How they studied and preached—The quality and vastness of the work they did.

II. Thomas Hooker one of the three greatest—His career in England—Comes to Massachusetts—Founds Hartford—A prolific writer—His commanding traits as a man and an orator—His published writings—Literary characteristics—His frankness in damnatory preaching—Total depravity—Formalism—Need of Christ—The versatility and pathos of his appeals.

III. New England's debt to Archbishop Laud—Thomas Shepard's animated interview with him, and its consequences—Shepard's settlement in America—Personal peculiarities—Illustrations of his theology and method of discourse.

IV. John Cotton—His brave sermon in St. Mary's Church, Cambridge—Becomes rector of St. Botolph's, Boston—His great fame in England—His ascendency in New England—Correspondence with Cromwell—His death announced by a comet—As a student and writer.

V. A group of minor prophets—Peter Bulkley founder of Concord—The man—His "Gospel Covenant"—John Norton—Succeeds John Cotton—His style as a writer—William Hooke—His life—His "New England's Tears for Old England's Fears"—Charles Chauncey's career in England and America—Becomes president of Harvard—Great usefulness as an educator—His scholarship, industry, old age—His "Plain Doctrine of Justification"—His unpublished writings made useful.

History of American Literature

I

AMONG the earliest official records of Massachusetts, there is a memorandum of articles needed there and to be procured from England. The list includes beans, pease, vine-planters, potatoes, hop-roots, pewter-bottles, brass-ladles, spoons, and ministers. It is but just to add that in the original document the article here mentioned last, stands first; even as in the seventeenth century, in New England, that article would certainly have stood first in any conceivable list of necessaries, for this world or the world to come. An old historian, in describing the establishment of the colony of Plymouth, gives the true sequence in the two stages of the process when he says, they "planted a church of Christ there and set up civil government."[1] In the year 1640, a company of excellent people resolved to found a new town in Massachusetts, the town of Woburn; but before getting the town incorporated, they took pains to build a meeting-house and a parsonage, to choose a minister, and to fix the arrangements for his support.[2] New England was a country, as a noted writer of the early time expresses it, "whose interests were most remarkably and generally enwrapped in its ecclesiastical circumstances;"[3] it followed that for any town within its borders the presence or absence of a "laborious and illuminating ministry" meant the presence or absence of external prosperity. Indeed, the same writer stated the case with delightful commercial frankness when he remarked: "The gospel has evidently been the making of our towns."[4] During the first sixty years, New England was a theocracy, and the ministers were in reality the chief officers of state. It was not a departure from their sphere for them to deal with politics; for everything pertaining to the state was included in the sphere of the church. On occasion of an exciting popular election, in 1637, Mr. John Wilson, one of the pastors of Boston, climbed upon the bough of a tree, and from that high pulpit, with great authority, harangued the crowd upon their political duties. The greatest political functionaries, recognizing the ministers as in some sense their superior officers, "asked their advice upon the most important occasions,"[5] and sometimes even appealed to them

---

[1] Edw. Johnson, "Wonder-Working Providence," 18.
[2] Ibid. W. F. Poole's Introd. xci.   [3] "Magnalia," I. 296.
[4] Ibid. I. 89.   [5] John Eliot, in 1 Mass. Hist. Soc. Coll. X. 1.

162

New England: Theological Writers

for the settlement of personal differences that had arisen among themselves. In 1632, the deputy-governor, Thomas Dudley, having a grievance against the governor, John Winthrop, made complaint to two ministers, John Wilson and Thomas Welde; whereupon a council of five ministers was convened to call before them the governor and the lieutenant governor, and to hear what they had to say for themselves; having heard it, the ministers "went apart for one hour," and then returned with their decision, to which the governor meekly submitted.[6] To speak ill of ministers was a species of sedition. In 1636, a citizen of Boston was required to pay a fine of forty pounds and to make a public apology, for saying that all the ministers but three preached a covenant of works.[7]

The objects of so much public deference were not unaware of their authority: they seldom abused it; they never forgot it. If ever men, for real worth and greatness, deserved such preëminence, they did; they had wisdom, great learning, great force of will, devout consecration, philanthropy, purity of life. For once in the history of the world, the sovereign places were filled by the sovereign men. They bore themselves with the air of leadership: they had the port of philosophers, noblemen, and kings. The writings of our earliest times are full of reference to the majesty of their looks, the awe inspired by their presence, the grandeur and power of their words.

Men like these, with such an ascendency as this over the public, could not come before the public too often, or stay there too long; and on two days in every seven, they presented themselves in solemn state to the people, and challenged undivided attention. Their pulpits were erected far aloft, and as remote as possible from the congregation, typifying the awful distance and the elevation of the sacred office which there exercised its mightiest function. Below, among the pews, the people were arranged, not in families, but according to rank and age and sex; the old men in one place, the old dames in another; young men and maidens prudently seated far apart; the boys having the luxury of the pulpit stairs and the gallery. Failure to attend church was not a thing to be tolerated, except in cases of utter necessity. People who stayed away were hunted up by the tithingmen: for one needless absence they were to be fined; for such absence

[6] J. Winthrop, "Hist. N. E." I. 98.   [7] T. Hutchinson, "Hist. Mass. Bay," I. 60.

persisted in four weeks, they were to be set in the stocks or lodged in a wooden cage. Within the meeting-house, the entire congregation, but especially the boys, were vigilantly guarded by the town constables, each one being armed with a rod, at one end of which was a hare's foot, and at the other end a hare's tail. This weapon they wielded with justice tempered by gallantry: if a woman fell asleep, it was enough to tingle her face gently with the bushy end of the rod; but if the sleeper were a boy, he was vigorously thumped awake by the hard end of it.[8]

In the presence of God and of his appointed ministers, it was not for man to be impatient; and the modern frailty that clamors for short prayers and short sermons had not invaded their sanctuaries or even their thoughts. When they came to church, they settled themselves down to a regular religious siege, which was expected to last from three to five hours. Upon the pulpit stood an hour-glass; and as the sacred service of prayer and psalm and sermon moved ruthlessly forward, it was the duty of the sexton to go up hour by hour and turn the glass over. The prayers were of course extemporaneous; and in that solemn act, the gift of long continuance was successfully cultivated: the preacher, rising into raptures of devotion and storming heaven with volleys of petitionary syllogism, could hardly be required to take much note of the hour-glass. "Mr. Torrey stood up and prayed near two hours," writes a Harvard student in the seventeenth century; "but the time obliged him to close, to our regret; and we could have gladly heard him an hour longer."[9] Their sermons were of similar longitude, and were obviously exhaustive—except of the desire of the people to hear more. John Winthrop mentions a discourse preached at Cambridge by Thomas Hooker when he was ill: the minister at first proceeded in his discourse for fifteen minutes, then stopped and rested half an hour, then resumed and preached for two hours.[10] Well might Nathaniel Ward, in his whimsical satire, make this propensity of himself and his brethren the theme of a confession which was at least half in earnest:

[8] T. W. Higginson, "Young Folks' Hist. U. S." 76–77.
[9] J. L. Sibley, "Harv. Grad." 566.
[10] J. Winthrop, "Hist. N. E." I. 366. This was the length of Hooker's sermon at a time when he was ill; the historian does not state how long he would have preached had his health been as good as usual.

New England: Theological Writers

"We have a strong weakness in New England that when we are speaking we know not how to conclude. We make many ends before we make an end. . . . We cannot help it, though we can; which is the arch infirmity in all morality. We are so near the west pole that our longitudes are as long as any wise man would wish, and somewhat longer. I scarce know any adage more grateful than 'Grata brevitas.' " [11]

In his theme, in his audience, in the appointments of each sacred occasion, the preacher had everything to stimulate him to put into his sermons his utmost intellectual force. The entire community were present, constituting a congregation hardly to be equalled now for its high average of critical intelligence: trained to acute and rugged thinking by their habit of grappling day by day with the most difficult problems in theology; fond of subtle metaphysical distinctions; fond of system, minuteness, and completeness of treatment; not bringing to church any moods of listlessness or flippancy; not expecting to find there mental diversion, or mental repose; but going there with their minds aroused for strenuous and robust work, and demanding from the preacher solid thought, not gushes of sentiment, not torrents of eloquent sound. Then, too, there was time enough for the preacher to move upon his subject carefully, and to turn himself about in it, and to develop the resources of it amply, to his mind's content, hour by hour, in perfect assurance that his congregation would not desert him either by going out or by going to sleep. Moreover, if a single discourse, even on the vast scale of a Puritan pulpit-performance, were not enough to enable him to give full statement to his topic, he was at liberty, according to a favorite usage in those days, to resume and continue the topic week by week, and month by month, in orderly sequence; thus, after the manner of a professor of theology, traversing with minute care and triumphant completeness the several great realms of his science. If the methods of the preacher resembled those of a theological professor, it may be added that his congregation likewise had the appearance of an assemblage of theological stu-

---

[11] "Simple Cobbler of Agawam," 91. Many early religious customs in New England are recorded in Thomas Lechford, "Plain Dealing, or News from New England," London, 1642: a book well described by its author as "these confused papers," 160.

dents; since it was customary for nearly every one to bring his notebook to church, and to write in it diligently as much of the sermon as he could take down. They had no newspapers, no theatres, no miscellaneous lectures, no entertainments of secular music or of secular oratory, none of the genial distractions of our modern life: the place of all these was filled by the sermon. The sermon was without a competitor in the eye or mind of the community. It was the central and commanding incident in their lives; the one stately spectacle for all men and all women year after year; the grandest matter of anticipation or of memory; the theme for hot disputes on which all New England would take sides, and which would seem sometimes to shake the world to its centre. Thus were the preachers held to a high standard of intellectual work. Hardly anything was lacking that could incite a strong man to do his best continually, to the end of his days; and into the function of preaching, the supreme function at that time in popular homage and influence, the strongest men were drawn. Their pastorships were usually for life; and no man could long satisfy such listeners, or fail soon to talk himself empty in their presence, who did not toil mightily in reading and in thinking, pouring ideas into his mind even faster than he poured them out of it.

Without doubt, the sermons produced in New England during the colonial times, and especially during the seventeenth century, are the most authentic and characteristic revelations of the mind of New England for all that wonderful epoch. They are commonly spoken of mirthfully by an age that lacks the faith of that period, its earnestness, its grip, its mental robustness; a grinning and a flabby age, an age hating effort, and requiring to be amused. The theological and religious writings of early New England may not now be readable; but they are certainly not despicable. They represent an enormous amount of subtile, sustained, and sturdy brain-power. They are, of course, grave, dry, abstruse, dreadful; to our debilitated attentions they are hard to follow; in style they are often uncouth and ponderous; they are technical in the extreme; they are devoted to a theology that yet lingers in the memory of mankind only through certain shells of words long since emptied of their original meaning. Nevertheless, these writings are monuments of vast learning, and of a stupendous intellectual energy both in the men who produced them and in the men who listened to them. Of course they can never be recalled to any vital human interest. They have long since done their work in moving the minds of men. Few of them can be cited as literature. In the mass, they can only be labelled by the antiquarians and laid away upon shelves to be looked at occasionally as curiosities of verbal expression, and as relics of an intellectual condition gone forever. They were conceived by noble minds; they are themselves noble. They are superior to our jests. We may deride them, if we will; but they are not derided.

II

Of all the great preachers who came to New England in our first age, there were three who, according to the universal opinion of their contemporaries, towered above all others,—Thomas Hooker, Thomas Shepard, John Cotton. These three could be compared with one another; but with them could be compared no one else. They stood apart, above rivalry, above envy. In personal traits they differed; they were alike in bold and energetic thinking, in massiveness of erudition, in a certain overpowering personal persuasiveness, in the gift of fascinating and resistless pulpit oratory.

Thomas Hooker, though not the eldest, died the first, namely in 1647, aged sixty-one. He had then been in America fourteen years. Before coming to America he had achieved in England a brilliant, influential, troubled career. He was a graduate of Emmanuel College, Cambridge; taking holy orders, he was for some years a preacher in London; in 1626, being forty years old, he became religious lecturer and assistant minister in Chelmsford; and there, if not before, he planted himself conspicuously upon grounds of non-conformity to several doctrines and usages of the established church. In no long time, of course, Bishop Laud was upon his track, storming with ecclesiastical fury. Hooker was cast out of the pulpit. At once he set up a grammar-school near Chelmsford, whence, however, once more the echoes of his eloquent and brave talk even in private, reached the ears of the bishop. Hooker had to flee for his life. Of course he fled to Holland; and there for two or three years he preached to English congregations at Delft and at Rotterdam. Already many of his friends had gone across the Atlantic to the great Puritan colony of Massachusetts Bay; and in 1633 he himself went thither, in the same ship with his illustrious compeer, John Cotton. For three years after his arrival in New England, he preached to the church in Cambridge; and in 1636 he led his entire flock, about a hundred families, westward through the wilderness to the lovely valley of the Connecticut, where they built the town of Hartford,—a town which then seemed to the people of Boston to be so close to the western verge of the world that, as they used to say, the last great conflict with antichrist would certainly take place there. Of this colony, Hooker was priest and king; and here, during the last eleven years of his life, he did perhaps his best work, studying hard, preaching hard, shaping for all time the character of the community which he founded, and pouring forth in swift succession through the press of London, those glowing and powerful religious treatises of his which at once became classics in Puritan literature. Soon after his death, a noble young minister, John Higginson, revering his genius, went through the toil of copying two hundred of Hooker's sermons, and sent them to England for publication. There, under various titles, about one half of them were printed. In 1830, one hundred and eighty-three years after Hooker's death, the old parsonage at Hartford was torn down, and in it were found large quantities of manuscripts, supposed to have been his. What they were, we know not. They may have contained letters, diaries, and other invaluable personal and historical memoranda; but there happened to be no one then in the city which Hooker founded, to give shelter to these venerable treasures, and to save them from the doom of being thrown into the Connecticut River.

In the living presence of Hooker there appears to have been some singular personal force, an air both of saintliness and kingliness, that lofty and invincible moral genius which the Hebrew prophets had, and with which they captivated or smote down human resistance. Even during his life-time and shortly afterward, there gathered about him the halo of spiritual mystery, a sort of supernatural prestige, anecdotes of weird achievement that in a darker age would have blossomed into frank and vivid legends of miraculous power. In his youth there was noticed in him "a grandeur of mind" that marked him out for something uncommon. As he came on into manhood, his person and bearing partook of peculiar majesty; the imperial dignity of his office made him imperial. "He was a person," they said, "who when he was doing his Master's work, would put a king into his pocket." People, seeing how fiery was his temper, marvelled at his perfect command of it: he governed it as a man governs a mastiff with a chain; "he could let out his dog," they said, "and pull in his dog as he pleased." [12] As he ruled himself, so he ruled other men, easily; they felt his right to command them. In his school near Chelmsford, a word or a look from him was all the discipline that was needed. His real throne was the pulpit. There he swayed men with a power that was more than regal. His face had authority and utterance in it; his voice was rich, of great compass and flexibility; every motion of him spoke. The impressiveness of his preaching began in his vivacity; he flashed life into any subject, no matter how dead before. He so grappled the minds of his hearers that they could not get away from him. While he preached at Chelmsford, an ungodly person once said to his companions: "Come, let us go hear what that bawling Hooker will say to us." The mocker went; but he was no longer a mocker. Hooker had that to say to him which subdued him: he became a penitent and devout man, and followed his conqueror to America.[13] Once Hooker was to preach in the great church at Leicester. A leading burgess of the town, hating the preacher and thinking to suppress him, hired fiddlers to stand near the church door and fiddle while Hooker should preach; but somehow Hooker's preaching was mightier and more musical than the fiddlers' fiddling. The burgess, astonished at such power, then went near to the door to hear for himself what sort of talking that was which kept people from noticing his fiddlers; soon even he was clutched by the magnetism of the orator, sucked in through the door in spite of himself, smitten down by stroke after stroke of eloquent truth, and converted. Hooker's personality had in it something which made it easy for his disciples to think, that the Almighty would require even the forces of nature to pay considerable deference to so wonderful a man. On his flight toward the sea-side, as he was escaping to Holland, an attendant, knowing that an officer was in full

[12] "Magnalia," I. 345.   [13] Ibid. I. 337.

chase not far behind, said anxiously: "Sir, what if the wind should not be fair when you come to the vessel?" "Brother, let us leave that with Him who keeps the wind in the hollow of his hand." And they noticed that, though the wind was against them before Hooker reached the vessel, as soon as he got aboard "it immediately came about fair and fresh," and swept the ship out to sea just in time to leave his pursuer panting and baffled upon the shore.[14] Hooker, like many another strong man, seems to have had a Cæsarean faith in himself and his fortunes. On the voyage to Holland the vessel struck by night upon the sands. A panic ran through the ship. Hooker, though unknown to them, by sheer force of personal greatness, restored them to quiet: he just told them not to be frightened; that they should surely be preserved.[15] They had to believe the man who could say that. Multitudes of his contemporaries supposed him to have the gift of prophecy. He himself assumed to have it. Long before the civil war in England he said openly in a sermon: "It has been told me from God, that God will destroy England, and lay it waste, and that the people shall be put unto the sword, and the temples burnt, and many houses laid in ashes."[16] When this man prayed, they noticed that there was some very strange power in it. "His prayer," says Cotton Mather, "was usually like Jacob's ladder, wherein the nearer he came to an end, the nearer he drew towards heaven."[17] Such praying as his, they were sure, God would take particular notice of. Once during a war between the weak Mohegans, who were our friends, and the strong Narragansetts, who were our enemies, this holy man prayed strenuously against the Narragansetts. "And the effect of it was," says the historian, "that the Narragansetts received a wonderful overthrow from the Mohegans."[18]

Every Monday was set apart by him as a day for private consultation upon cases of conscience. It was simply an involuntary Protestant confessional, born of the great need people had to tell their secrets to this particular man; and all sorts of perturbed beings came, and laid their spiritual maladies before him, and were comforted.

It is not to be supposed that, at the close of a life into which so

---

[14] "Magnalia," I. 338.   [15] Ibid.   [16] Ibid. 341.
[17] Ibid. 344.   [18] Ibid. 344.

New England: Theological Writers

many marvellous things had entered, death would come unheralded by supernatural tokens. On the last Sunday of his life, when he preached and administered the Lord's Supper, "some of his most observant hearers" perceived "an astonishing sort of a cloud" in the room, and among themselves "a most unaccountable heaviness and sleepiness . . . not unlike the drowsiness of the disciples when our Lord was going to die." In a few days the mystery was explained. After a short illness, "at last he closed his own eyes with his own hands, and gently stroking his own forehead, with a smile in his countenance, he gave a little groan, and so expired his soul into the arms of his fellow-servants, the holy angels." [19]

From all the communities of New England a wail of grief went up at the tidings of his death: this was the first one of their mighty leaders that had fallen in the wilderness. One writer mourned him in a Latin elegy, two lines of which have this sense in English:

> "The thought will come when o'er him thus we moan,
> That in his grave New England finds her own." [20]

One of his clerical brethren, Peter Bulkley, contenting himself with English verse, thus celebrated Hooker's traits as a preacher:

> "To mind he gave light of intelligence,
> And searched the corners of the conscience.
> To sinners stout, which no law could bring under,
> To them, he was a son of dreadful thunder,
> When all strong oaks of Bashan used to quake,
> And fear did Libanus his cedars shake.
> The stoutest hearts he fillëd full of fears;
> He clave the rocks, they melted into tears;
> Yet to sad souls, with sense of sin cast down,
> He was a son of consolation." [21]

His great contemporary, John Cotton, saluted him with tender congratulation:

[19] "Magnalia," I. 350.
[20] "Morte tua infandum cogor renovare dolorem Quippe tua videat terra Nov-Angla suam." This Latin poem, which was by Elijah Corlet, of Cambridge, is given by Mather, "Magnalia," I. 351.
[21] Morton, "New England's Memorial," 240.

"Now, blessed Hooker, thou art set on high,
Above the thankless world and cloudy sky;
Do thou of all thy labor reap the crown,
Whilst we here reap the seed which thou hast sown." [22]

Finally, the process of Protestant canonization was completed some time afterward, when one writer gave expression to the general belief, by calling him "Saint Hooker."

The published writings of Thomas Hooker number twenty-three titles.[23] Many of them are large treatises; all of them are on matters of theology, church-polity, or religious life. A noted English preacher of that age said, that to praise the writings of Hooker would be "to lay paint upon burnished marble, or add light unto the sun." [24] This of course is the rapture of contemporaneous enthusiasm; and yet even for us there remains in Hooker's words a genuine vitality, the charm of clearness, earnestness, reality, strength. Remembering what the man was, who once stood behind these words, we cannot much wonder at the effects produced by them. He has many of the traits common to the Puritan writers of his time: minute and multitudinous divisions and subdivisions; the anatomy of his discourse exposed on the outside of it; a formal announcement of doctrine, proofs, sequences, applications; showers of quotation from Scripture. He has also some exceptional literary advantages: a copious and racy vocabulary; an aptitude for strong verbal combinations; dramatic spirit; the gift of translating arguments into pictures; cumulative energy, oratorical verve. This orator is dead: his words after all are not dead.

What he wrote is literature meant for the ear, not the eye; having the rhythm and cadence of a good speech. It is constructed for swift practical effect on the minds, passions, resolutions of men. Its lines of thought are straight, rugged, bold; its movement is like the unhesitating tramp of an advancing army; it quite omits the graces of reserve, the dallying and tenderness of literary implication. We are apt to startle at the blunt integrity of his speech. His theology has

---

[22] Morton, "New England's Memorial," 238–239.

[23] A list of them is given in E. W. Hooker's "Life of T. Hooker," 172–175; also in Sprague, "Annals of Am. Pulpit," I. 36.

[24] Allen, "Biog. Dict." Art. T. Hooker.

New England: Theological Writers

a fierce and menacing side to it, the mention of which he takes no pains to conceal from ears polite. He uses frankly all the stern and haggard words of his sect. He awards punishment to sinners in good, round, English curses, that are plain and fructifying. He assures them of damnation right heartily. His pages gleam and blaze with the flashes of threatened hell-fire. His ink has even yet a smell of theological sulphur in it.

It was one part of his duty, as he thought, to "fasten the nail of terror deep into their hearts;" [25] and in rhetoric well-seasoned for the use of "proud sinners" he greatly excels: "Do you think to out-brave the Almighty? . . . Dost thou think to go to heaven thus bolt-upright? The Lord cannot endure thee here, and will he suffer thee to dwell with himself forever in heaven? What, thou to heaven upon these terms? Nay, . . . how did the Lord deal with Lucifer and all those glorious spirits? He sent them all down to hell for their pride." [26] "The Lord comes out in battle array against a proud person, and singles him out from all the rest, and . . . saith, 'Let that drunkard and that swearer alone a while, but let me destroy that proud heart forever. You shall submit in spite of your teeth, when the great God of heaven and earth shall come to execute vengeance." [27] "There must be subjection or else confusion. Will you out-brave the Almighty to his face, and will you dare damnation? . . . As proud as you, have been crushed and humbled. Where are all those Nimrods, and Pharaohs, and all those mighty monarchs of the world? The Lord hath thrown them flat upon their backs, and they are in hell this day." [28]

He gives sinners to understand, also, that the hell-torments which await them are none of those metaphorical and altogether tolerable hell-torments that are now usually signified by that term: "Judge the torments of hell by some little beginning of it, and the dregs of the Lord's vengeance by some little sips of it; and judge how unable thou art to bear the whole, by thy inability to bear a little of it. . . . When God lays the flashes of hell-fire upon thy soul, thou canst not endure it. . . . When the Lord hath let in a little horror of heart into the soul of a poor sinful creature, how he is transported with an insup-

[25] "Effectual Calling," 43. [26] "The Soul's Humiliation," 92.
[27] Ibid. 94. [28] Ibid. 223.

portable burden . . . roaring and yelling as if he were in hell already. . . . If the drops be so heavy, what will the whole sea of God's vengeance be?" [29]

The doctrine of the total depravity of man lay in his mind under a light of absolute certainty; and in commending this doctrine to his congregations, he did not dim it by any glozing or euphemistic words: "Thou art dead in trespasses and sins. What is that? A man is wholly possessed with a body of corruption, and the spawn of all abomination hath overspread the whole man. . . . All noisome lusts abound in the soul, and take possession of it, and rule in it, and are fed there. . . . No carrion in a ditch smells more loathsomely in the nostrils of man, than a natural man's works do in the nostrils of the Almighty." [30] "Alas, the devil hath power over you. As it is with a dead sheep, all the carrion crows in the country come to prey upon it, and all base vermin breed and creep there; so it is with every poor, natural, carnal creature under heaven—a company of devils, like so many carrion crows, prey upon the heart . . . and all base lusts crawl, and feed, and are maintained in such a wretched heart." [31]

His speech is vigorous in denunciation of religious formalism. He tells them that the outward duties are important, but that these without Christ cannot save any one. Forms are but the bucket; Christ is the well: "If you say your bucket shall help you, you may starve for thirst if you let it not down into the well for water; so, though you brag of your praying, and hearing, and fasting, and of your alms, and building of hospitals, and your good deeds, if none of these bring you to Christ, you shall die for thirst." [32] "I do not dishonor these ordinances, but I curse all carnal confidence in them. . . . Hell is full of hearers, and dissemblers, and carnal wretches that never had hearts to seek unto Christ in these duties, and to see the value of a Saviour in them." [33]

As outward forms of piety cannot save the sinner, neither can ministers of the gospel, potent as they are, save him: "Dost thou think that a few faint prayers, and lazy wishes, and a little horror of heart, can pluck a dead man from the grave of his sins, and a damned soul

---

[29] E. W. Hooker's "Life of T. Hooker," 206–7.
[30] "The Soul's Humiliation," 33–34.   [31] Ibid. 37.
[32] Ibid. 11.   [33] Ibid. 18.

New England: Theological Writers

from the pit of hell, and change the nature of a devil to be a saint? No, it is not possible. . . . We are as able to make worlds, and to pull hell in pieces, as to pull a poor soul from the paw of the devil." [34] "Should you pray till you can speak no more; and should you sigh to the breaking of your loins; should every word be a sigh, and every sigh a tear, and every tear a drop of blood, you would never be able to recover that grace which you lost in Adam." [35]

As he passes thus from realm to realm in the vast empire of Christian persuasion, he reaches at times those which appeal to nobler passions than terror or shame; and when he will, he can make a most gallant spiritual charge, and carry for his Master the batteries of self-respect, magnanimity, honor: "Christ must needs take this unkindly that you should give the devil the flower of your age, and give to Christ but the decrepit and infirm parts of your lives; that the devil should suck out the marrow of your youth, and only give God the dry bones, a palsy head, a dim eye, a weak body." [36]

He depicts dramatically, and with a soothing tenderness, the struggle of the soul to find its way to Christ and to be saved: "When a poor travelling man comes to the ferry, he cries to the other side, 'Have over! have over!' His meaning is he would go to the other side by a boat. . . . So Christ is in heaven; but we are here on earth . . . on the other side of the river. The ordinances of God are but as so many boats to carry us and to land us at heaven where our hopes are, and our hearts should be. . . . 'Have over! have over!' saith the soul. The soul desires to be landed at the stairs of mercy, and saith, 'Oh, bring me to speak with my Saviour.' " [37]

He tells them that if they have found Christ and have received his gifts, then are they rich with treasures outshining all the world's riches: "Though a man should beg his bread from door to door, if he can beg Christ and have it, and beg grace and have it, he is the richest man upon earth." [38]

He points out the true method of success in the Christian life, warning them, for example, against idleness, and against impatience: "Whilst the stream keeps running, it keeps clear; but let it stand still, it breeds frogs and toads and all manner of filth. So while you keep

[34] "The Soul's Humiliation," 37.   [35] "Effectual Calling," 15.
[36] Ibid. 70.   [37] "The Soul's Humiliation," 75.   [38] "Effectual Calling," 76.

going, you keep clear; but do but once flag in your diligence, and stand still, and oh! what a puddle of filth and sin thy heart will be." [39] "We must wait God's leisure, and stay his time for the bestowing of his favors. Beggars must not be choosers." [40]

He seeks to draw them to the higher spiritual life by the imagery of love and utmost tenderness: "Let us be led by all means into a nearer union with the Lord Christ. As a wife deals with the letters of her husband that is in a far country, she finds many sweet inklings of his love, and she will read these letters often and daily, . . . because she would be with her husband a little, and have a little parley with him in his pen, though not in his presence; so these ordinances are but the Lord's love-letters, and we are the ambassadors of Christ, and . . . we bring marvellous good news that Christ can save all poor broken-hearted sinners in the world." [41]

He assures them that in the grace of utter resignation they touch the very essence of felicity and victory: "Be content to want what God will deny, and to wait God's good pleasure, and to be at his disposing. . . . Whatsoever can or shall befall you by the devil and his instruments, and if every spire of grass were a devil, be humbled, and then be above all the devils in hell, and all temptations, and oppositions." [42] "God hath but two thrones; and the humble heart is one." [43] "An humble soul, a poor soul, a very beggar at the gate of mercy, the Lord will not only know him, . . . but he will give him such a gracious look as shall make his heart dance in his breast. Thou poor humbled soul, the Lord will give thee a glimpse of his favor, when thou art tried in thy trouble; and when thou lookest up to heaven, the Lord will look down upon thee." [44] "Men, brethren, and fathers, if there be any soul here that is content in truth and sincerity to be humbled, and to be at God's disposing, . . . do not you make too much haste to go to heaven; the Lord Jesus Christ will come down from heaven and dwell in your hearts." [45] "In thy distempers be humbled and yet comforted: Christ hath overcome the power of them. They may plague thee: they shall not prevail against thee. . . . The power of Christ's prayer will outlive thy life, and the life of

---

[39] "Effectual Calling," 13.
[40] "Christ's Last Prayer," 98.
[41] "The Soul's Humiliation," 73–74.
[42] Ibid. 144–145.
[43] Ibid. 213.
[44] Ibid. 214–215.
[45] Ibid. 220.

New England: Theological Writers

thy sins, and set heaven's gates open before thee." [46] "It is with the soul in this case as it is with a mariner; though his hand be upon the oar, yet he ever looks homeward to the haven where he would be." [47]

III

New England has perhaps never quite appreciated its great obligations to Archbishop Laud. It was his over-mastering hate of nonconformity, it was the vigilance and vigor and consecrated cruelty with which he scoured his own diocese and afterward all England, and hunted down and hunted out the ministers who were committing the unpardonable sin of dissent, that conferred upon the principal colonies of New England their ablest and noblest men. Indeed, without Laud, those principal colonies would perhaps never have had an existence. His dreadful name is linked to our early story by sickening memories of terror and brutal insult and grief, of darkened fire-sides, of foul prisons opened to receive saints instead of felons, of delicate women and little children set adrift in the world without shelter or protector; of good men—scholars, apostles—fleeing for their lives, under masks, under false names, skulking in the guise of criminals, from the land they were born in.

The short and easy way with dissenters that Laud adopted, is happily shown in his treatment of Thomas Shepard. In the year 1630, this gifted and consecrated man, then twenty-five years old, a graduate of Emmanuel College, Cambridge, and admitted to holy orders by the bishop of Peterborough, was preaching in the little town of Earles-Colne, in Essex. The odor of his Puritanical piety had reached the nostrils of Laud, then bishop of London. On the sixteenth of December, of the year just named, at about eight o'clock in the morning, the poor parson, in obedience to a citation, presented himself before the face of the bishop in his palace in the great city. Of the vivacious conversation that then ensued, the parson himself has left us a narrative.[48] "As soon as I came, . . . falling into a fit

---

[46] "Christ's Last Prayer," 203.   [47] "The Soul's Humiliation," 69.
[48] "*First printed from Shepard's manuscript, by Thomas Prince, "Chron. Hist. N. E." I. 338; and reprinted in Young, "Chron. Mass. Bay," 518–520.

[* The superfluous quotation marks appeared also in the 1881 and 1897 editions.]

of rage he asked me what degree I had taken in the university. I answered him, I was a Master of Arts. He asked, of what college? I answered, of Emmanuel. He asked, how long I had lived in his diocese. I answered, three years and upwards. He asked, who maintained me all this while, charging me to deal plainly with him; adding withal that he had been more cheated and equivocated with by some of my malignant faction than ever was man by Jesuit. At the speaking of which words he looked as though blood would have gushed out of his face, and did shake as if he had been haunted with an ague fit, to my apprehension, by reason of his extreme malice and secret venom. I desired him to excuse me. He fell then to threaten me, and withal to bitter railing, . . . saying, 'You prating coxcomb, do you think all the learning is in your brain?' He pronounced his sentence thus: 'I charge you that you neither preach, read, marry, bury, or exercise any ministerial function, in any part of my diocese; for if you do, and I hear of it, I'll be upon your back, and follow you wherever you go, in any part of the kingdom, and so everlastingly disenable you.' . . . I prayed him to suffer me to catechise in the Sabbath days in the afternoon. He replied, 'Spare your breath. I'll have no such fellows prate in my diocese. Get you gone; and now make your complaints to whom you will.' So away I went." Very naturally the young parson was at first somewhat dazed by the Laudean hurricane that had swept over him; and two days afterward, he met half a dozen of his clerical brethren who "consulted together," as he tells us, "whether it was best to let such a swine to root up God's plants in Essex, and not to give him some check." [49]

Unfortunately, in the present case, the mighty hunters were all on the side of the swine; and the check which the parsons had hoped to give to him was abundantly bestowed upon themselves. They were routed and scattered, this way and that. For four years Thomas Shepard was a wanderer in England, eager to preach the gospel and having a wonderful aptitude that way, but unable to find anywhere in England a spot that was not interdicted to him by Laud's unslumbering hostility. Accordingly, in 1635, resolving to put the ocean between himself and his enemy, he came to New England; and early

[49] Shepard's autobiography, in Young, "Chron. Mass. Bay," 521.

New England: Theological Writers

in the following year, he took charge of the church in Cambridge, and there remained until his death in 1649.

Even during his life-time his fame as a pulpit-orator and a writer rose high in both Englands; and it rose still higher after his death. In person he had some disadvantages. He lacked the bodily vigor, the massive proportions, the stateliness, of his two compeers, Thomas Hooker and John Cotton. His contemporaries describe him to us as a poor, weak, pale-complexioned man, whose physical powers were feeble but spent to the full. He was a cloistered student and an invalid, recoiling from the crisp breath of a New England winter; during which season, as he tells us, there was a near relation between him and the fireside.[50] But his fragile body was possessed by a spirit of uncommon beauty, devoutness, and power. He had a subtile and commanding intellect; he was a profound thinker; his style was in the main clear, terse, abounding in energy, with frequent flashes of eloquence; and the charm of his diction was enhanced by the manner of his speech, which was almost matchless for its sweet and lofty grace, its pathos, its thrilling intensity, its ringing fulness and force. His successor in office spoke of "the lively voice of this soul-melting preacher."[51] John Higginson described him as one who was both "a Timothy in his family" and a "Chrysostom in the pulpit."[52] His writings, which have been honored by a modern edition,[53] have had among theologians of his school a permanent reputation. He has been much read by his own profession. He may be described as the preacher's preacher. His brethren have paid to him the flattering tribute of lavishly borrowing both his ideas and his words. From a single one of Thomas Shepard's books, Jonathan Edwards, it is said, drew nearly a hundred citations for his celebrated "Treatise concerning Religious Affections."

The theology of Thomas Shepard, of course, derived its characteristic features not from him, but from his age and his sect: it was harsh, dark, inexorable; most sincere in its exaggerations of the sinfulness of man and the wrathfulness of God; placing on the throne of the universe a stark divine justice, upon which scarcely fell one

[50] "Clear Sunshine of the Gospel," 8. [51] Works of T. Shepard, II. 10.
[52] Ibid. I. clxxxii. [53] Three volumes, Boston, 1853.

glimmer of divine pity; copious in maledictions; having a marvellous alacrity in making its consignments of souls to the devil.

The doctrine, for example, that "in Adam's fall we sinned all," is expounded by this preacher with a courage and a candor that never flinched before considerations either of humanity or of commonsense: "We are all in Adam, as a whole country in a parliament man; the whole country doth what he doth." [54] To some, the felicity of this comparison may be damaged by the fact that, while the country chooses its parliament man to stand for it, "we made no particular choice of Adam to stand for us;" [55] but the reply is, that the choice was made not by us but on our behalf, ages before we were born, by a Being infinitely better and wiser than we are. This first step being made secure, every subsequent step is logical and easy. Each man, having thus fallen into sin thousands of ages before he was born, finds, on arriving to take possession of the existence thus blighted for him in advance, that his fall is an exceedingly complete one—dragging down with itself every faculty and atom of his nature. Nowhere else, perhaps, is the dogma of total depravity presented to us in braver, or more sprightly limning: "Every natural man and woman is born full of all sin, as full as a toad is of poison, as full as ever his skin can hold; mind, will, eyes, mouth, every limb of his body, and every piece of his soul, is full of sin; their hearts are bundles of sin." [56] "Thy mind is a nest of all the foul opinions, heresies, that ever were vented by any man; thy heart is a foul sink of all atheism, sodomy, blasphemy, murder, whoredom, adultery, witchcraft, buggery; so that if thou hast any good thing in thee, it is but as a drop of rose-water in a bowl of poison. . . . It is true thou feelest not all these things stirring in thee at one time . . . ; but they are in thee, like a nest of snakes in an old hedge." [57]

Certainly this is a dire condition of affairs; and it is entailed upon every man at his birth, in consequence of the personal misconduct of an individual, named Adam, who lived some sixty centuries ago; who was the moral representative of every man, but who was chosen as representative by no man. And what is to be done about it? Is there any escape? If the man be one of the elect, yes; if he be

[54] Works of T. Shepard, I. 24. [55] Ibid. I. 24.
[56] Ibid. 28. [57] Ibid.

New England: Theological Writers

not one of the elect, no. In the latter case, "God shall set himself like a consuming infinite fire against thee, and tread thee under his feet, who hast by sin trod him and his glory under foot all thy life. . . . I tell thee all the wisdom of God shall then be set against thee to devise torments for thee. . . . The torment which wisdom shall devise, the almighty power of God shall inflict upon thee; so as there was never such power seen in making the world, as in holding a poor creature under this wrath, that holds up the soul in being with one hand, and beats it with the other; ever burning like fire against a creature, and yet that creature never burnt up. Think not this cruelty: it is justice. What cares God for a vile wretch, whom nothing can make good while it lives? If we have been long in hewing a block, and we can make no meet vessel of it, put it to no good use for ourselves, we cast it into the fire. God heweth thee by sermons, sickness, losses and crosses, sudden death, mercies and miseries, yet nothing makes thee better. What should God do with thee, but cast thee hence? O consider of this wrath before you feel it. . . . Thou canst not endure the torments of a little kitchen-fire, on the tip of thy finger, not one half hour together. How wilt thou bear the fury of this infinite, endless, consuming fire, in body and soul, throughout all eternity?"[58] "Death cometh hissing . . . like a fiery dragon with the sting of vengeance in the mouth of it. . . . Then shall God surrender up thy forsaken soul into the hands of devils, who, being thy jailers, must keep thee, till the great day of account; so that as thy friends are scrambling for thy goods, and worms for thy body, so devils shall scramble for thy soul. . . . Thy forlorn soul shall lie moaning for the time past, now it is too late to recall again; groaning under the intolerable torments of the wrath of God present, and amazed at the eternity of misery and sorrow that is to come; waiting for that fearful hour, when the last trump shall blow, and body and soul meet to bear that wrath,—that fire that shall never go out."[59]

IV

Not far from the year 1612, the ancient church of Saint Mary, in Cambridge, was filled one day by a great concourse of persons,—

[58] Works of T. Shepard, I. 42–43.   [59] Ibid. 35–39.

under-graduates, fellows, professors,—who had been attracted thither by the brilliant reputation of a member of their own university, a fellow of Emmanuel College, John Cotton by name, then only about twenty-seven years old. This person had been in the university ever since he was a lad of thirteen; he had continually distinguished himself as a scholar; he had risen to be catechist, head-lecturer, and dean in the college to which he belonged. He was proficient in the logic and philosophy then taught in the schools; was a critical master of Greek; could converse fluently either in Latin or in Hebrew. Beyond all other things, he had genius for oratory, particularly the oratory of the pulpit. It was his extraordinary fame in that direction which had drawn together the great crowd to hear him on the occasion to which reference has been made. Several times before, he had preached in the presence of the whole university, always carrying off their applause; for he had never failed to give them the sort of sermons that were then in fashion,—learned, ornate, pompous, bristling with epigrams, stuffed with conceits, all set off dramatically by posture, gesture, and voice. Meantime, however, his religious character had been deepening into Puritanism. He had come to view his own preaching as frivolous, Sadducean, pagan. In preparing once more to preach to this congregation of worldly and witty folk, he had resolved to give them a sermon intended to exhibit Jesus Christ, rather than John Cotton. This he did. His hearers were astonished, disgusted. Not a murmur of applause greeted the several stages of his discourse as formerly. They pulled their shovel-caps down over their faces, folded their arms, and sat it out sullenly,—amazed that the promising John Cotton had turned lunatic or Puritan.

Evidently there was stuff in this man; and he it was who, twenty years later, came over to New England, and acquired there a marvellous ascendency, personal and professional,—an ascendency more sovereign, probably, than any other American clergyman has ever reached. The interval of twenty years that fell between that brave university-sermon, and his great career in New England, was by no means a blank. In fact it was a period for him very rich and intense in incident. He left the university to take charge of the great church of St. Botolph's, at Boston, in Lincolnshire, and there he remained till his removal to Boston, in New England. Year by year, while he

New England: Theological Writers

lived in the elder Boston, he grew in knowledge about the Bible, and in the science of God and man as seen through the dun goggles of John Calvin; his singular faculty as a preacher greatened every way, in force and splendor; his fame filled all the kingdom; and though he was far from being a good churchman, the powerful prelate, Lord Keeper Williams, told King James that Cotton was a good man and a good preacher, and got from the king a promise that Cotton should not be disturbed; finally, under the reign of Charles, the preacher drew upon himself the fatal eye of Bishop Laud. It was in 1633 that Laud became primate of England; which meant, among other things, that nowhere within the rim of that imperial island was there to be peace or safety any longer for John Cotton. Some of his friends in high station tried to use persuasive words with the archbishop on his behalf; but the archbishop brushed aside their words with an insupportable scorn. The earl of Dorset sent a message to Cotton, that if he had only been guilty of drunkenness, or adultery, or any such minor ministerial offence, his pardon could have been had; but since his crime was Puritanism, he must flee for his life.[60] So, for his life he fled, first hiding himself here and there about London, dodging his pursuers; and finally slipping out of England, after innumerable perils, like a hunted felon; landing in Boston in September, 1633.

His arrival filled the colony with exceeding joy. It was a thing they had been praying for. Even the name of Boston had been given to their chief town as a compliment and an enticement to him.

> "The lantern of St. Botolph's ceased to burn,
> When from the portals of that church he came
> To be a burning and a shining light,
> Here in the wilderness." [61]

At once, the most conspicuous pulpit was given to him; and from that hour till his death nineteen years afterward, he wielded with strong and brilliant mastership the fierce theocracy of New England. Laymen and clergymen alike recognized his supremacy, and rejoiced in it. He was the unmitred pope of a pope-hating commonwealth. "I hold myself not worthy," said an eminent minister of Massa-

[60] "Magnalia," I. 263.   [61] Longfellow, "New England Tragedies," 15.

chusetts, "to wipe his slippers." [62] Roger Williams wrote, evidently with a subdued smile, that some people in Massachusetts used to say that "they could hardly believe that God would suffer Mr. Cotton to err." [63] The contemporary historian, William Hubbard, states that whatever John Cotton "delivered in the pulpit was soon put into an order of court . . . or set up as a practice in the church." [64] Another clergyman of that day, trying to utter his homage for John Cotton, found the resources of prose inadequate:

> "A man of might at heavenly eloquence,
> To fix the ear and charm the conscience;
> As if Apollos were revived in him,
> Or he had learnëd of a seraphim.
>
> . . .
>
> Rocks rent before him, blind received their sight,
> Souls levelled to the dunghill stood upright." [65]

When in 1651, he, the mightiest man in New England, wrote to Cromwell, the mightiest man in old England, the latter promptly "took this liberty from business, to salute" John Cotton, as his "dear friend," to confess to him his own sense of unworthiness, and to inform him of the progress of events then big with the fulfilment of prophecies, adding, "We need your prayers in this as much as ever;" and closing with this cordial subscription, "Your affectionate friend to serve you." [66]

It was, of course, rather strange that the Almighty should permit such a man to die; but when at last death did come to him, the services of his interment, we are told, made "the most grievous and solemn funeral that was ever known perhaps upon the American strand." [67] Nay, it was commonly believed at the time, that even the heavens as

---

[62] Nathaniel Ward, quoted by J. W. Dean, "Memoir" of Ward, 83.
[63] Narr. Club Pub. IV. 42.   [64] Hubbard, "Gen. Hist. N. E." 182.
[65] The whole is given in Morton, "New England's Memorial," 254.
[66] Carlyle, "Oliver Cromwell's Letters and Speeches" (N. Y. 1859), II. 8–10; where Carlyle speaks of John Cotton as "a painful preacher, oracular of high gospels to New England; who in his day was well seen to be connected with the Supreme Powers of this universe; . . . was thought especially on his death-bed to have manifested gifts even of prophecy—a thing not inconceivable to the human mind that well considers prophecy and John Cotton."
[67] "Magnalia," I. 273.

New England: Theological Writers

well as the earth took note of the dreadful event, and that Providence set aflame in the sky an indubitable signal of it. "About the time of his sickness," says the historian, Nathaniel Morton, "there appeared in the heavens over New England a comet, giving a dim light; and so waxed dimmer and dimmer, until it became quite extinct and went out; which time of its being extinct was soon after the time of the period of his life: it being a very signal testimony that God had then removed a bright star, a burning and a shining light out of the heaven of his church here, unto celestial glory above." [68]

Although John Cotton was a prolific author, his place in our early literary history bears no proportion to his place in our early religious and political history. As a student, he was of the heroic pattern of the seventeenth century. A sand-glass which would run four hours stood near him when he studied, and being turned over three times, measured his day's work. This he called "a scholar's day." Esteeming John Calvin to be greater than all the fathers and all the schoolmen, he was accustomed to read in him last of all every evening: "I love to sweeten my mouth with a piece of Calvin before I go to sleep." [69] His grandson, Cotton Mather, who upon such a theme never lapsed into an understatement, tells us that John Cotton "was indeed a most universal scholar, and a living system of the liberal arts, and a walking library." [70]

Upon better testimony we know that he certainly had large reading, a retentive memory, great intellectual poise, agility, and self-command, all his accomplishments and accumulations at ready call; while the character and range of his work as a writer, during the nineteen years of his American life, may be seen by a glance over the mere titles of his principal publications: "The Bloody Tenet washed and made white in the Blood of the Lamb;" "A Brief Exposition upon Ecclesiastes;" "A Brief Exposition upon Canticles;" "The Covenant of Grace;" "An Exposition upon the Thirteenth Chapter of the Revelation;" "The Grounds and Ends of the Baptism of the Children of the Faithful;" "Of the Holiness of Church Members;" "The Keys of the Kingdom of Heaven;" "A Modest and Clear Answer to Mr. Ball's Discourse of Set Forms of Prayer;" "The New Covenant;" "A Prac-

[68] Morton, "New England's Memorial," 251–252.
[69] McClure, "Life" of Cotton, 271.   [70] "Magnalia," I. 273.

tical Commentary upon the First Epistle of John;" "Spiritual Milk for Babes;" "A Treatise of the Covenant of Grace as it is dispensed to the Elect Seed;" "The Way of the Congregational Churches Cleared;" "The Way of Life;" "A Treatise concerning Predestination." [71]

Let us open, now, any of these old books of John Cotton. At once, the immensity of his contemporaneous influence becomes a riddle to us. In the writings of his great associates, Hooker, Shepard, Peter Bulkley, William Hooke, and Charles Chauncey, at least some threads of immortal light, some lingering movements of a once glorious energy, some half-blurred foot-prints of a departed genius, may still be traced by us, after these two centuries; marks of literary superiority; quotable passages. The same can hardly be said of the writings of John Cotton. These are indeed clear and cogent in reasoning; the language is well enough; but that is all. There are almost no remarkable merits in thought or style. One wanders through these vast tracts and jungles of Puritanic discourse—exposition, exhortation, logic-chopping, theological hair-splitting—and is unrewarded by a single passage of eminent force or beauty, uncheered even by the felicity of a new epithet in the objurgation of sinners, or a new tint in the landscape-painting of hell.

Evidently the vast intellectual and moral force of John Cotton was a thing that could not be handed over to the printing-press or transmitted to posterity: it had to communicate itself in the living presence of the man himself. The traditions of that living presence are certainly notable. He was of medium size; his hair, brown in early years, with advancing time grew white as snow; and "in his countenance there was an inexpressible sort of majesty, which commanded reverence from all that approached him." Thus the inn-keeper at Derby, having once John Cotton for a guest, very naturally wished him gone from the house; since he "was not able to swear while that man was under his roof." [72] His voice was not powerful, but clear, mellow, sympathetic. One contemporary says that "Mr. Cotton had such an insinuating and melting way in his preaching that he would usually carry his very adversary captive after the triumphant chariot

[71] The Prince Library Catalogue, prepared by Justin Winsor, 17–18.
[72] "Magnalia," I. 280.

of his rhetoric." [73]   But the chariot of his rhetoric ceased to be triumphant when the master himself ceased to drive it.

V

Such were the three foremost personages among the theological and religious writers of New England, in our first literary period. In the throng of their professional associates—scholars, thinkers, devotees—were not a few others who did famous work in the one form of writing that then suited best the intellectual appetite of the people, and that still preserves best the very form and pressure of that unique time.

One of these men was Peter Bulkley, born in 1583, sometime fellow of St. John's College, Cambridge, a man of considerable estate and social position. For twenty-one years he was rector of Woodhill, Bedfordshire; but at last the hand of the terrible archbishop being laid heavily upon him, he came to Cambridge, Massachusetts, in 1635. The next year "he carried a good number of planters with him up further into the woods," [74] where they established the town of Concord, and where he abode as pastor until his death in 1659. He was a sufferer from bodily pains; his will was exacting, his temper quick, his tongue sharp; yet in heart and hand he was benignant and bountiful; noted even among Puritans for the superlative stiffness of his Puritanism, his austere looks, his prim dress, his incredible brevity of hair. He was a great scholar too; having, as Cotton Mather saith, "a competently good stroke at Latin poetry," [75] even down to old age blossoming oft into fragrant Latin epigrams. A large place in Puritan literature was held by him in his life-time and long afterward, on account of his book, "The Gospel Covenant, or the Covenant of Grace Opened," made up of a series of systematic sermons preached at Concord, first published in London in 1646; one of those massive, exhaustive, ponderous treatises into which the Puritan theologians put their enormous Biblical learning, their acumen, their industry, the fervor, pathos, and consecration of their lives. It deals with a topic which at that time stirred the minds of all men in New England,

---

[73] W. Hubbard, "Gen. Hist. N. E." 175.   [74] "Magnalia," I. 400.
[75] Ibid. I. 403.

which made and unmade reputations, which shook the whole commonwealth. The style, though angular, sharp-edged, carved into formal divisions, and stiff with the embroidery of Scriptural texts, is upon the whole direct and strong. The book has a peculiar interest for us still, on account of its occasional episodes of reference to the mighty things then taking place in England. Near the close of it, is this impressive appeal to the people of New England: "And for ourselves here, the people of New England, we should in a special manner labor to shine forth in holiness above other people. We have that plenty . . . of ordinances and means of grace, as few people enjoy the like. We are as a city set upon an hill, in the open view of all the earth; the eyes of the world are upon us because we profess ourselves to be a people in covenant with God. . . . Let us study so to walk that this may be our excellency and dignity among the nations of the world. . . . There is no people but will strive to excel in something. What can we excel in, if not in holiness? If we look to number, we are the fewest; if to strength, we are the weakest; if to wealth and riches, we are the poorest of all the people of God through the whole world. We cannot excel, nor so much as equal, other people in these things; and if we come short in grace and holiness too, we are the most despicable people under heaven. . . . Be we an holy people, so shall we be honorable before God, and precious in the eyes of his saints." [76]

The whole work carries momentum with it. It gives the impression of an athletic, patient, and orderly intellect. Every advance along the page is made with the tread of logical victory. No unsubdued enemies are left in the rear. It is a monumental book. It stands for the intellectual robustness of New England in the first age. It is an honor to that community of pioneers, drudging in the woods of Concord, that these profound and elaborate discourses could have been produced, and endured, among them.

Another man deserving at least a glance from posterity is John Norton. He came to New England in 1635, being then twenty-nine years of age, a Cambridge scholar, sometime domestic chaplain to Sir William Masham. Soon after his arrival in America he was settled at Ipswich; in 1653 he went to Boston as John Cotton's successor; ten

[76] "The Gospel Covenant," 431-432.

New England: Theological Writers

years later he went with Simon Bradstreet to England on an embassy of conciliation to Charles the Second; soon returning he died in 1663. He was remarkable for his early and brilliant attainments as a scholar, the thoroughness of his knowledge of Puritan theology, the multitude of his writings, and his frank advocacy of persecution for all who dared to live in New England without holding orthodox opinions. Longfellow, in his "Tragedy of John Endicott," permits Norton to describe himself as

> "A terror to the impenitent, and Death
> On the pale horse of the Apocalypse
> To all the accursëd race of heretics." [77]

Whosoever peeps into John Norton's writings will note their excessively technical character, the frequency and the hardness of their divisions, their dry and jagged diction. The most readable of his books is "The Life and Death of that deservedly famous man of God, Mr. John Cotton," published in London in 1658. Though promising to be a biography, it has the didactic and hortatory tone of a sermon; the thread of the narrative is strung thick with beads of moralizing; its statements are embellished with citations, from a wide range of history and literature; it abounds in the antitheses that were then in demand.

A thoroughly wholesome personage was William Hooke, a cousin of Oliver Cromwell and brother-in-law of Cromwell's general, Edward Whalley. He was born in 1601; was educated at Trinity College, Oxford; was for many years vicar of Axmouth, Devonshire; was emigrant to America for conscience' sake about the year 1636; was minister of Taunton, Massachusetts, from 1637 to 1644 or 1645; then, for about twelve years was teacher of the church in New Haven; having great inducements to return to England he went thither in 1656, and became chaplain to the Protector, master of the Savoy, and man of influence generally; in 1677, he died and was laid to rest in Bunhill Fields. His life in America made him a true American; and he never ceased to be one, even after his restoration to England, keeping always

---

[77] It by no means diminishes the accuracy of this self-description, that Norton himself had been dead two years at the date assigned to the Tragedy in which he figures as a very lively persecutor.

his interest warm in American affairs, and his "old brotherly affection" [78] for the young communities there, of which he had been for twenty years a strong and honored member. Not many of his writings ever got into print. Those of them that were printed are sermons, and are of singular interest to us now for their literary merit, and for a certain flavor of American thought and emotion that still lurks in them. Altogether the best is his sermon preached at Taunton, on the twenty-third of July, 1640, "on a day of public humiliation . . . in behalf of our native country in time of feared dangers." As observers of public affairs in England at that time, the people of America had, in their very distance in space, something of the advantage that is given to posterity by distance in time. They were a contemporaneous posterity; they had the knowledge possessed by those who were upon the spot, and the perspective enjoyed by those who were afar off. In that great year, 1640, the men and women of New England saw, perhaps more clearly than did their brethren in the old home, the meaning and the drift of events in England, then rushing forward into tears and blood. This sermon of William Hooke's is a striking instance of their foresight. Its title, "New England's Tears for Old England's Fears," worthily indicates the touching and passionate love for the mother-land which the whole sermon breathes. "Old England, dear England still, . . . left indeed by us in our persons, but never yet forsaken in our affections." [79] "There is no land that claims our name but England; . . . there is no nation that calls us countrymen but the English. Brethren, did we not there draw in our first breath? Did not the sun first shine there upon our heads? Did not that land first bear us, even that pleasant island, . . . that garden of the Lord, that paradise?" [80] But before the eyes of the preacher, as he spoke, seemed to be unrolled an appalling vision of the scenes that were to be enacted in the old land they had left,—the chaos, havoc, and misery of its oncoming civil war. One picture drawn by him of the horrors of a battlefield, has a realism and an intensity of coloring not easily to be matched in any prose. "Oh, the shrill, ear-piercing clangs of the trumpets, noise of drums, the animating voice of horse-captains and commanders, learned and learning to

[78] Letter from Hooke, 1671, in W. B. Sprague, "Annals of Am. Pulpit," I. 105.
[79] The sermon, 23.   [80] Ibid. 16.

destroy! . . . Here ride some dead men swagging in their deep saddles; there fall others alive upon their dead horses; death sends a message to those from the mouth of the muskets; these it talks with face to face, and stabs them in the fifth rib. In yonder file there is a man who hath his arm struck off from his shoulder; another by him hath lost his leg; here stands a soldier with half a face; there fights another upon his stumps, and at once both kills and is killed; not far off lies a company wallowing in their sweat and gore; such a man whilst he chargeth his musket is discharged of his life, and falls upon his dead fellow. Every battle of the warrior is with confused noise and garments rolled in blood. Death reigns in the field, and is sure to have the day, which side soever falls. In the meanwhile—O formidable!—the infernal fiends follow the camp to catch after the souls of rude nefarious soldiers . . . who fight themselves fearlessly into the mouth of hell, for revenge, for booty, or a little revenue. . . . A day of battle is a day of harvest for the devil." [81]

At least one more of these great New England preachers must be named here, Charles Chauncey, whose early and conspicuous influence upon American letters was such as to suggest to Cotton Mather the freak of calling him our Cadmus: [82] a great man in many ways, in originality, learning, brain-force, physical endurance, zest for work, enthusiasm, eloquence; a man of impetuous and stormy nature, apt to assert himself strongly and to expect immediate assent, lacking somewhat in tact, capable of lapses from heroism and of penitential agonies in consequence thereof. He was a boy of thirteen at Westminster School at the very time of Guy Fawkes's failure to blow up the adjacent parliament-house, and thereby lost his one opportunity of going to heaven or elsewhere in extremely aristocratic company. At Trinity College, Cambridge, Chauncey took his degrees; he became professor of Greek at his Alma Mater; and in 1627 he became vicar of Ware, where, with his views, he had not long to wait before getting into trouble. He sadly objected to the "Book of Sports;" for in that book the clergy were forbidden to preach on Sunday afternoons, and their parishioners were encouraged to employ that happy time in dancing, archery, vaulting, may-games, and other recreations. Chauncey tried to evade the prohibition by filling the Sunday after-

[81] The sermon, 20–21.   [82] "Magnalia," I. 464.

noons with a catechetical exercise for old and young; but this arrangement the bishop stamped on, telling him "that catechising was as bad as preaching." [83] In 1635, he got into a new difficulty. He was cited before the High Commission Court for the crime of objecting to a rail around the communion table, and to the act of kneeling in the communion service. For this he was thrown into prison, sentenced to pay heavy costs, and suspended from the ministry till he should recant. At last in open court he did recant, making confession "that kneeling at the receiving of the holy communion is a lawful and commendable gesture, and that a rail set up in the chancel of any church . . . is a decent and convenient ornament." [84] Of this inglorious act Chauncey was soon ashamed; and to the end of his days he lacerated himself for it, even saying in his will that he kept ever before him his "many sinful compliances with . . . vile human inventions, and will-worship, and hell-bred superstitions, and patcheries stitched into the service of the Lord which the English mass-book . . . and the Ordination of Priests . . . are fully fraught withal." [85]

Of course such a man could not then stay in England, except in jail; and he escaped to America, reaching Plymouth in 1638. There he stayed as minister three years. In 1641, he was invited to Scituate, and continued there thirteen years, preaching, teaching, practising medicine, studying many books, and encountering many griefs. Especially did he suffer from the rebuffs of opponents and of extreme poverty. So wretched was the support allowed him that he had to write to a friend, "deest quidem panis." At last, in 1654, Laud being quiet in his grave, and all things in England having a pleasant look for men like Chauncey, he resolved to go back thither; but on his way to the ship in Boston harbor, he was overtaken by an offer of the presidency of Harvard College in place of the noble-minded Henry Dunster, who had been driven from the office on account of his frank avowal of the Baptist heresy.[86] Chauncey, who also had some taint

---

[83] "Chauncey Memorials," 12.
[84] The whole document given in W. B. Sprague, "Annals of Am. Pulpit," I. 111.
[85] "Magnalia," I. 467.
[86] Wm. Hubbard, who graduated in President Dunster's first class, says that Dunster might have continued in the presidency "if he had been endowed with that wisdom . . . to have kept his singular opinion to himself, when there was little occasion for venting thereof;" ("Gen. Hist. N. E." 556) a significant remark,

New England: Theological Writers

of the same heresy, promised not to avow it, and was inducted into the great office. It proved to be the right place for him; and he filled it with illustrious success, not without sorrows, until his death in 1672 at the age of eighty. He was a great educating force in those years and long afterward. Neither labor nor age could quell his energy. He rose at four o'clock winter and summer; he outdid all his students in devotion to books; "wittily he moderated their disputations and other exercises;"[87] at College prayers he caused a chapter of the Hebrew Bible to be read in the morning, and of the Greek Testament in the evening, and upon these he always gave an extemporaneous comment in Latin; to all the students he was father, inspirer, guide; and he greatly helped to fill the land with scholars, gentlemen, and Christians. His old age was of the glorious, gritty kind. His friends begged him not to work so hard; but he gave the proud answer, "Oportet imperatorem stantem mori." One day, in winter, the fellows of the College were leading him toward the chapel where he was to preach; and hoping to dissuade him from the labor, they said, "Sir, you will certainly die in the pulpit." But this, so far from intimidating the grand old man, gave him a new delight; and pressing on more eagerly through the snow-drifts, he exclaimed, "How glad I should be if what you say might prove true!"[88]

His published writings are not many, and all are sermons excepting one—a controversial pamphlet, "Antisynodalia Scripta Americana," 1662. His most important work is a volume of twenty-six sermons, published in London, in 1659, and entitled, "The Plain Doctrine of the Justification of a Sinner in the Sight of God." On the title-page we are told that the doctrine is "explained . . . in a plain . . . and familiar way for the capacity and understanding of the weak and ignorant;" yet the leading title of the book is in Hebrew, the dedication is in Latin, and the discussion well sprinkled with quotations from Hebrew, Latin, and Greek, and with such technical terms as synecdoche, equipollent, and the like. In spite of this, the ideas are indeed as clear as crystal, and are generally stated in English that is

---

throwing some historical day-light upon clerical casuistry in New England in the early days, and suggesting visions of an outward orthodoxy accepted with various mental reservations, about which they prudently held their tongues.

[87] "Magnalia," I. 468. [88] Ibid. 470.

vigorous and keen. Though the formality of stiff topical divisions cramps the movement of his style, and denies him room for swing and flight, the author's mind breaks out often with genuine brightness and power. There are strokes of condensed force, flashes of imagination and passionate light, felicities of epithet and comparison, vivifying words, memorable sayings: "God . . . stabs the wicked as an enemy with his sword, but lances the godly as a surgeon does his patient with the lancet."[89] "As the moon is nearest to the sun when the least light doth outwardly appear; so is God nearest to the godly when they have the least outward light of comfort."[90] "Let all . . . careless wretches know that if justification be a state of blessedness, then their state is a state of cursedness."[91] "We are singing and chanting to the sound of the viol, while God sounds an alarum by the trumpet of war. We are dancing in jollity, while God is marching in battalia. We are drinking in the wine and strong drink, while God is letting out our blood."[92] "If death arrests you, how will you scramble for bail? How will you wish you had pleased God? . . . Oh, leave not that to the last gasp that should be done first. Thou mayest be great and rich and honorable, and yet not fit to live nor to die; but he that is justified is fit for both."[93] "It was unknown torment that our Saviour underwent. He encountered both the Father's wrath . . . and entered the lists with Satan and all the powers of darkness. . . . All the devils in hell were up in arms, and issued out of their gates; principalities and powers are all let loose against the Redeemer of the world."[94] "Then let us pursue our sins with all possible detestations. . . . Let us stab them to the heart, till they bleed their last, that drew the blood of Christ."[95]

The works of President Chauncey that were published, formed but a small portion of those that he wrote. His manuscripts descended to his eldest son, thence to his grandson, who dying left them in possession of his widow. This lady subsequently married again; and her new husband, a godly man, to wit, a deacon and pie-maker of Northampton, straightway proceeded to utilize the learned labors of the deceased president of Harvard, by putting those manuscripts at

---

[89] "The Plain Doctrine," etc. 64.   [90] Ibid. 96.   [91] Ibid. 42.
[92] Ibid. 43.   [93] Ibid. 46.   [94] Ibid. 55.   [95] Ibid. 84.

the bottom of his pies in the oven; and thus the eloquent and valuable writings of Charles Chauncey were gradually used up, their numerous Hebrew and Greek quotations, and their peppery Calvinism, doubtless adding an unwonted relish and indigestibility to the pies under which they were laid.

Chapter IX

New England:

Miscellaneous Prose Writers

I. Nathaniel Ward and his collisions with Laud—His position in early American literature—His large experience before coming to America—A reminiscence of Prince Rupert.

II. Career of Nathaniel Ward in New England—His "Simple Cobbler of Agawam"—Summary of the book—The author's mental traits—His attitude toward his age—Vindicates New England from the calumny that it tolerates variety of opinions—His satire upon fashionable dames in the colony and upon long-haired men—His discussion of the troubles in England—Literary traits of the book.

III. Roger Williams as revealed in his own writings—His exceptional attractiveness as an early New-Englander—What he stood for in his time in New England—A troublesome personage to his contemporaries and why—His special sympathy with Indians and with all other unfortunate folk.

IV. First visit of Roger Williams to England—His first book—His interest in the great struggle in England—His reply to John Cotton's justification of his banishment from Massachusetts—His book against a national church—His "Bloody Tenet of Persecution"—John Cotton's reply—Williams's powerful rejoinder—Other writings—His letters—Personal traits shown in them—His famous letter against lawlessness and tyranny.

I

IN the year 1631, William Laud, Bishop of London, faithfully harrying his diocese in search of ministers who might be so insolent as to deviate from his own high standard of doctrine and ceremony, be-

New England: Miscellaneous Prose

came aware of the presence, in one of his parishes, of an extremely uncomfortable parson named Nathaniel Ward, rector of Stondon Massey, Essex. Accordingly, on the twelfth of December of that year, this parson was brought before the bishop for inspection. Though he escaped that time, the bishop kept his inexorable eye upon him, and frequently thereafter cited him into his presence; and at last, in 1633, "left him under the sentence of excommunication." [1] This man, thus turned loose upon the world by the ungentle help of his bishop, naturally found his way very soon to New England, where arriving in 1634 he remained twelve years, and where by his incisive and stiff opinions, the weight of his unusual legal learning, his skill and pungency as a writer, and the flavor of his piquant individuality, he considerably influenced contemporary events, stamped some of his own features upon the jurisprudence of Massachusetts, and connected himself with our early literature by the composition of a book the most eccentric and amusing that was produced in America during the colonial period.

Perhaps no other Englishman who came to America in those days, brought with him more of the ripeness that is born, not only of time and study, but of distinguished early associations, extensive travel in foreign lands, and varied professional experience at home. He was graduated at Emmanuel College, Cambridge, in 1603, and is named by Fuller among the learned writers of that college who were not fellows. He at first entered the profession of the law, which he practised several years; he then spent several years upon the continent; and upon his return to England took holy orders, and was settled in the parish from which, after about ten years, he was ejected by Laud. His personal and professional standing may be partly inferred from his acquaintance with Sir Francis Bacon, with Archbishop Usher, and with the famous theologian of Heidelberg, David Paræus. It was during his residence upon the continent, that he was brought into relations of some sort with the family of the Princess Elizabeth, daughter of James the First, and wife of Frederick, elector Palatine; and in this way he came to have that immediate contact with infantile royalty which many years later suggested a characteristic passage in the book that we are soon to inspect. He took into

[1] Laud, quoted in J. W. Dean, "Memoir" of Ward, 39.

his arms the young child of Frederick and Elizabeth; and when, long afterward, that young child had expanded into the impetuous, swearing cavalier hero of the English civil war, the terrible Prince Rupert, the good old Puritan preacher, Nathaniel Ward, then far away beyond the sea in America, wrote of him these serious words: "I have had him in my arms; . . . I wish I had him there now. If I mistake not, he promised then to be a good prince; but I doubt he hath forgot it. If I thought he would not be angry with me, I would pray hard to his Maker to make him a right Roundhead, a wise-hearted Palatine, a thankful man to the English; to forgive all his sins, and at length to save his soul, notwithstanding all his God-damn-me's." [2]

II

Soon after his arrival in Massachusetts Nathaniel Ward became minister to a raw settlement of Puritans at Agawam.[3] His health here soon gave way; and in two or three years he surrendered his pastorate. But a man of so strong and various a culture as he, could not be left idle in New England. He was placed on a commission to form a code of laws for the colony, and in that capacity did some good service. Early in 1645, he commenced writing the remarkable book, "The Simple Cobbler of Agawam," which will keep for him a perpetual place in early American literature. This book appears to have been finished in the latter part of 1646, and was at once transmitted to London for publication, where it came from the press in January, 1647. It had the good fortune to fit the times and the passions of men; it was caught up into instant notice, and ran through four editions within the first year.

"The Simple Cobbler of Agawam" may be described as a prose satire upon what seemed to the author to be the frightful license of new opinions in his time, both in New England and at home; upon the frivolity of women and the long hair of men; and finally upon the raging storm of English politics, in the strife then going forward between sects, parties, parliament, and king. It is a tremendous

---

[2] "Simple Cobbler of Agawam," 66–67.

[3] The beautiful Indian name of that district, afterward foolishly exchanged for Ipswich.

New England: Miscellaneous Prose

partisan pamphlet, intensely vital even yet, full of fire, wit, whim, eloquence, sarcasm, invective, patriotism, bigotry. One would have to search long among the rubbish of books thrown forth to the public during those hot and teeming days, to find one more authentically representing the stir, the earnestness, the intolerance, the hope, and the wrath of the times than does this book. Thinly disguising his name under the synonym of Theodore de la Guard, the author speaks of himself as a humble English cobbler in America, quite unable to stick to his last, or to restrain his thoughts from brooding anxiously over the errors, follies, sins, griefs, and perils of his countrymen on both sides of the sea. The title-page is too racy and characteristic a part of the book to be omitted: "The Simple Cobbler of Agawam in America: willing to help 'mend his native country, lamentably tattered both in the upper-leather and sole, with all the honest stitches he can take; and as willing never to be paid for his work by old English wonted pay. It is his trade to patch all the year long gratis. Therefore I pray gentlemen keep your purses. By Theodore de la Guard. 'In rebus arduis ac tenui spe, fortissima quaeque consilia tutissima sunt.' Cic. In English:

> When boots and shoes are torn up to the lefts,
> Cobblers must thrust their awls up to the hefts;
> This is no time to fear Apelles' gramm:
> 'Ne sutor quidem ultra crepidam.'

London: Printed by J. D. and R. I. for Stephen Bowtell, at the sign of the Bible in Pope's Head Alley, 1647."

The assumed character of a humble cobbler digressing from his vocation of mending shoes to that of mending commonwealths, is one which the author succeeds in maintaining only upon the title-page and in certain formal divisions of his work: as where he puts on "a most humble heel-piece to the most honorable head-piece, the parliament of England;"[4] or where he drives in "half a dozen plain, honest, country hobnails, such as the martyrs were wont to wear."[5] In the body and tissue of the work, however, he makes no effort to write like a cobbler; on the contrary, in nearly every paragraph, the irrepressible individuality of Nathaniel Ward, Puritan gentleman, scholar,

[4] "The Simple Cobbler," etc. 82.   [5] Ibid. 85.

lawyer, clergyman, and bigot, urges itself to the surface in language which has the authenticity of a mental photograph.

The key-note of the entire work is struck in the opening sentence: "Either I am in an apoplexy, or that man is in a lethargy, who doth not now sensibly feel God shaking the heavens over his head and the earth under his feet. . . . The truths of God are the pillars of the world, whereon states and churches may stand quiet if they will; if they will not, he can easily shake them off into delusions and distractions enough." The remainder of the book is but an evolution and a reverberation of these two statements.

It must be admitted, on the evidence of this book, that Nathaniel Ward was a grumbler—a sincere, witty, and valiant grumbler. Everything and everybody seemed to him to be going wrong. The times were out of joint. "Sathan is now in his passions; . . . he loves to fish in roiled waters." [6] And the difficulty between Nathaniel Ward and the age he lived in, arose from the not uncommon fact that he shrank from the consequences of his own ideas. He was one of those unhappy persons with the brain of a radical and the temperament of a conservative. His own dissent from the teachings of the church on matters of doctrine and ceremony was incipient radicalism; but he failed to remember that having once set up reason against authority on some topics, it was illogical for him to deny to reason its dispute with authority upon all topics. He had himself been ejected for not conforming to the standard of Bishop Laud; and while crying out against that as an injustice, he was still prepared to eject all who did not conform to his own standard. Looking out over English Christendom, he saw nothing but a chaos of jangling opinions, upstart novelties, lawless manners, illimitable changes in codes, institutions, and creeds. All this filled him with alarm. It seemed to him that the Almighty was raining discord and confusion upon the earth in punishment for its departure from the truth—the truth as held by Nathaniel Ward. What was to be done? His book answers the question with a three-fold remedy. First, the exact truth must be announced, and no toleration shown to the wretches who might dispute it. Second, the sports, fashions, vanities, frivolities of men and women must be extinguished in a universal enforcement of Puritan

[6] "The Simple Cobbler," etc. 1.

New England: Miscellaneous Prose

primness and asceticism. Finally, there must be a speedy cessation of warfare in England, through a general agreement to purity and justice in church and state.

We shall find the discussion of the first subject, upon the whole, the most enjoyable. Hardly anything could be conceived more racy, frank, or droll, than the childlike ingenuousness with which the author deals out ferocious declamations against freedom of opinion, or gibbets the doctrine of religious toleration as the most damnable treason and blasphemy. Here, indeed, is the undisguised and undiluted logic of persecution for the crime of free thought. The fathers of the inquisition might have reveled over the first twenty-five pages of this Protestant book, that actually blaze with the eloquent savagery and rapture of religious intolerance. He desires at the outset to repel the infamous calumny that had somehow got abroad in old England, and that represented New England as a place where diversity of opinions was tolerated: "We have been reputed a colluvies of wild opinionists swarmed into a remote wilderness, to find elbow-room for our fanatic doctrines and practices. I trust our diligence past, and constant sedulity against such persons and courses, will plead better things for us. I dare take upon me to be the herald of New England so far as to proclaim to the world, in the name of our colony, that all Familists, Antinomians, Anabaptists, and other enthusiasts, shall have free liberty—to keep away from us; and such as will come—to be gone as fast as they can, the sooner the better." But though so foul a shame as religious toleration does not attach to New England, he confesses that there is an English colony, planted in a certain "West Indian Island," where are provided "free stable-room and litter for all kind of consciences, be they never so dirty or jadish," and where things have reached so vile a pass that it is "actionable, yea, treasonable, to disturb any man in his religion, or to discommend it, whatever it be." This, he tells us, is "profaneness;" it is laying "religious foundations on the ruin of true religion; which strictly binds every conscience to contend earnestly for the truth, to preserve unity of spirit, faith, and ordinances, to be all like-minded, of one accord; every man to take his brother into his Christian care, to stand fast with one spirit, with one mind, striving together for the faith of the Gospel, and by no means to permit heresies or erroneous opinions.

... Irregular dispensations dealt forth by the facilities of men, are the frontiers of error, the redoubts of schism, the perilous irritaments of carnal and spiritual enmity. My heart hath naturally detested four things: the standing of the Apocrypha in the Bible, foreigners dwelling in my country to crowd our native subjects into the corners of the earth, alchemized coins, tolerations of divers religions or of one religion in segregant shapes. . . . Poly-piety is the greatest impiety in the world. . . . To authorize an untruth by a toleration of state, is to build a sconce against the walls of heaven, to batter God out of his chair. To tell a practical lie is a great sin, but yet transient; but to set up a theorical untruth is to warrant every lie that lies from its root to the top of every branch it hath, which are not a few! . . . He that is willing to tolerate any religion or discrepant way of religion, besides his own, unless it be in matters merely indifferent, either doubts of his own, or is not sincere in it. He that is willing to tolerate any unsound opinion, that his own may also be tolerated, though never so sound, will for a need hang God's Bible at the Devil's girdle. . . . That state that will give liberty of conscience in matters of religion, must give liberty of conscience and conversation in their moral laws, or else the fiddle will be out of tune, and some of the strings crack. . . . There is talk of an universal toleration. I would talk as loud as I could against it, did I know," he adds with solemn irony, "what more apt and reasonable sacrifice England could offer to God for his late performing all his heavenly truths, than an universal toleration of all hellish errors; or how they shall make an universal reformation, but by making Christ's academy the Devil's university, where any man may commence heretique 'per saltum,' where he that is 'filius diabolicus' or 'simpliciter pessimus' may have his grace to go to hell 'cum publico privilegio,' and carry as many after him as he can. . . . It is said though a man have light enough himself to see the truth, yet if he hath not enough to enlighten others, he is bound to tolerate them. I will engage myself that all the devils in Britannia shall sell themselves to their shirts, to purchase a lease of this position for three of their lives, under the seal of the parliament. It is said that men ought to have liberty of their conscience, and that it is persecution to debar them of it. . . . Let all the wits under the heavens lay their heads together and find an assertion worse than this

New England: Miscellaneous Prose

(one excepted) I will petition to be chosen the universal idiot of the world." [7] Then, glancing across the sea toward England, and reflecting upon the happy tidings which had reached him of the Presbyterian ascendency there, he congratulates his brethren upon the goodly prospect of realizing in that country also this iron-clamped paradise of uniformity in opinions—opinions beaten into one shape by the sledge-hammer of the law: "I am rather glad to hear the Devil is breaking up house in England, and removing somewhither else. Give him leave to sell all his rags and odd-ends by the outcry; and let his petty chapmen make their market while they may: upon my poor credit it will not last long. . . . Fear nothing, gentlemen; . . . ye have turned the Devil out of doors; fling all his old parrel after him out at the windows, lest he makes an errand for it again." Having thus launched out into the pleasant task of giving advice, he continues to lavish it upon his readers under no less than ten heads. For example, he warns young men against the deadly risk of even listening to errorists: "Their breath is contagious, their leprey spreading. . . . He usually hears best in their meetings, that stops his ears closest; he opens his mouth to best purpose, that keeps it shut; and he doeth best of all, that declines their company as wisely as he may. . . . Here I hold myself bound to set up a beacon to give warning of a new-sprung sect of phrantastics, which would persuade themselves and others that they have discovered the Nor-West passage to Heaven. These wits of the game cry up and down in corners such bold ignotions of a new gospel, new Christ, new faith, and new gay-nothings, as trouble unsettled heads, querulous hearts, and not a little grieve the Spirit of God. I desire all good men may be saved from their lunatic creed by infidelity; and rather believe these torrid overtures will prove in time nothing but horrid raptures down to the lowest hell, from which he that would be delivered, let him avoid these blasphemers, a late fry of croaking frogs, not to be endured in a religious state; no, if it were possible, not an hour. . . . Since I knew what to fear, my timorous heart hath dreaded three things: a blazing star appearing in the air; a state-comet, I mean a favorite, rising in a kingdom; a new opinion spreading in religion." [8]

As the author comes within sight of the end of his diatribe against

[7] "The Simple Cobbler," etc. 3–12.   [8] Ibid. 13–21.

toleration, he bethinks him of his purpose "to speak a word to the women anon;" and being conscious of a good deal of pent-up invective within himself upon that subject, he thinks it merciful to stop and notify the women of what they are to expect: "in the meantime I entreat them to prepare patience." Notwithstanding this note of warning, the reader is quite unlikely to be prepared for the untempered fury, at once merciless and mannerless, with which this clerical barbarian proceeds to buffet the fashionable dames of the period. He explains why he treats of them in a separate division of the book: it is because they are "deficients or redundants, not to be brought under any rule;" and, besides, he "was loath to pester better matter with such stuff." Having decided, notwithstanding their insignificance, to give them a small corner in his book, he then makes bold "for this once to borrow a little of their loose-tongued liberty, and misspend a word or two upon their long-waisted but short-skirted patience." "I honor the woman that can honor herself with her attire; a good text always deserves a fair margent;" but as for a woman who lives but to ape the newest court-fashions, "I look at her as the very gizzard of a trifle, the product of a quarter of a cipher, the epitome of nothing; fitter to be kicked, if she were of a kickable substance, than either honored or humored. To speak moderately, I truly confess, it is beyond the ken of my understanding to conceive how those women should have any true grace or valuable virtue, that have so little wit as to disfigure themselves with such exotic garbs, as not only dismantles their native, lovely lustre, but transclouts them into gaunt bar-geese, ill-shapen shotten shell-fish, Egyptian hieroglyphics, or at the best into French flirts of the pastry, which a proper English woman should scorn with her heels. It is no marvel they wear drails on the hinder part of their heads; having nothing, it seems, in the forepart but a few squirrels' brains to help them frisk from one ill-favored fashion to another. . . . We have about five or six of them in our colony: if I see any of them accidentally, I cannot cleanse my fancy of them for a month after. . . . If any man think I have spoken rather merrily than seriously, he is much mistaken: I have written what I write with all the indignation I can, and no more than I ought."[9]

[9] "The Simple Cobbler," etc. 25–30.

New England: Miscellaneous Prose

It is not easy for one of these fierce prophets of Puritanism to pass from invectives against "short-skirted" women, without pouring a few drops of contemptuous ink upon long-haired men: "A short promise is a far safer guard than a long lock; it is an ill distinction which God is loath to look at, and his angels cannot know his saints by. Though it be not the mark of the beast, yet it may be the mark of a beast prepared to slaughter. I am sure men use not to wear such manes; I am also sure soldiers use to wear other marklets . . . in time of battle." [10]

From this point in the book the author passes to the discussion of the troubles in England: "Having done with the upper part of my work, I would now with all humble willingness set on the best piece of sole-leather I have, did I not fear I should break my awl, which though it may be a right old English blade, yet it is but little and weak." [11] He desires "to speak such a word over the sea" as may persuade "to a comely, brotherly, seasonable, and reasonable cessation of arms on both sides," and may put a stop to "these wearisome wars." In the original quarrel between the parliament and the king, he justifies the parliament; and he does not flinch at the avowal of the right of a people to take up arms against their king. To the objection that prayers and tears "are the people's weapons," he replies: "So are swords and pistols, when God and parliaments bid them arm. Prayers and tears are good weapons for them that have nothing but knees and eyes; but most men are made with teeth and nails; only they must neither scratch for liberties nor bite prerogatives, till they have wept and prayed as God would have them." [12] Yet Nathaniel Ward shrank from extreme democratic conclusions; and while he was willing to fight against the king in the wrong, he preferred to fight for him in the right. He sincerely yearned for the restoration of the king, first to correct opinions, and then to his throne. It seemed to him possible for a wise and courageous statesmanship "to cut an exquisite thread between kings' prerogatives and subjects' liberties of all sorts; so as Cæsar might have his due, and people their share, without such sharp disputes." [13] In pursuing this thought, he reaches at last the determination to make a manly ap-

---

[10] "The Simple Cobbler," etc. 32.　　[11] Ibid. 32–33.
[12] Ibid. 48–49.　　[13] Ibid. 53.

peal directly to the king himself, telling him with full voice some loyal truths that his courtiers had not courage to mention to him even in a whisper. His prayer to the king, conceived in no truculent spirit, but in that of sincere affection, is in some passages very noble: it has, throughout, a stern eloquence, and the grandeur of overpowering emotion; the author bravely telling the king, "I am resolved to display my unfurled soul in your very face, and to storm you with volleys of love and loyalty." [14]

Upon the whole, "The Simple Cobbler of Agawam" is a droll and pungent bit of early American prose, with many literary offences upon its head: an excessive fondness for antitheses; an untempered enjoyment of quirks and turns and petty freaks of phraseology; the pursuit of puns and metaphors beyond all decorum; the blurring of its sentences with great daubs and patches of Latin quotation; the willing employment of outlandish and uncouth words belonging to no language at all, sometimes huddled together into combinations that defy syntax and set all readers aghast. For example, he will be a bold man who can affirm at sight in what language this sentence is written, or what it means: "If the whole conclave of hell can so compromise exadverse and diametrical contradictions as to compolitize such a multimonstrous maufrey of heteroclites and quicquidlibets quietly, I trust I may say with all humble reverence, they can do more than the senate of heaven." [15] Any one who fairly reads the book, however, may see that the literary sins of its author are sins that he shared with most of the prose writers of his period, on both sides of the ocean; and that in his case they are partly redeemed by the utter sincerity of his work, its invincible ardor and power. In some particulars he was as a writer even superior to the most of his contemporaries; for there are usually in his periods a compactness, a directness, and a brevity not commonly to be seen in the prose style of the seventeenth century, in which vast, involved, amorphous sentences were wont to heave their huge bulks along the page—the verbal mastodons and megatheria of a primitive rhetorical epoch. Besides, Nathaniel Ward had courage of opinion, an unabashed enthusiasm for ideas—his own ideas, frankness, disdain of lisping, finical, and ambiguous utterance, a hearty and high-spirited mirth born

[14] "The Simple Cobbler," etc. 56. [15] Ibid. 22–23.

New England: Miscellaneous Prose

of a good conscience and a good digestion, a force of imagination that occasionally uttered itself in a rough but virile and genuine eloquence. Thus, in reproaching his contemporaries for turning away from old truths as if they were "superannuate and sapless, if not altogether antiquate," he exclaims with glorious indignation: "No man ever saw a gray hair on the head or beard of any truth, wrinkle or morphew on its face." [16] His faith in the omnipotence of truth rushes out in dashing phrases of defiance: "Ye will find it a far easier field to wage war against all the armies that ever were or will be on earth, and all the angels of heaven, than to take up arms against any truth of God." [17] Addressing the statesmen of England, "the architectors now at work," he makes an appeal, the earnest manliness of which is finely edged by its humor: "Most expert gentlemen, be entreated at length to set our head right on our shoulders, that we may once look upwards and go forwards, like proper Englishmen." [18]

After all, the one great trait in this book which must be to us the most welcome, is its superiority to the hesitant, imitative, and creeping manner that is the sure sign of a provincial literature. The first accents of literary speech in the American forests, seem not to have been provincial, but free, fearless, natural. Our earliest writers, at any rate, wrote the English language spontaneously, forcefully, like honest men. We shall have to search in some later period of our intellectual history to find, if at all, a race of literary snobs and imitators—writers who in their thin and timid ideas, their nerveless diction, and their slavish simulation of the supposed literary accent of the mother-country, make confession of the inborn weakness and beggarliness of literary provincials.

But proud, and nobly self-sufficient, as were the makers of American literature in our first age, they still loved England as their home; and they always spoke of it as such, with a sweet sincerity of passion that has in it both pathos and eloquence. Nathaniel Ward could

---

[16] "The Simple Cobbler," etc. 23.

[17] Ibid. 75. In writing this true and grand sentence, the author apparently did not observe how perfectly it annihilated his own doctrine against tolerance. Of course, if truth is thus irresistible, it hardly needs the protection of human force, and may be safely left to take care of itself in a free fight with error in all ages and over all the world.

[18] Ibid. 36.

not help calling England "that most comfortable and renowned island," [19] and "the stateliest island the world hath;" [20] and everywhere he makes it manifest that in leaving England he had not left behind him the tenderest and most patriotic solicitude for England, and for the triumph of the struggling patriots within it: "Go on, therefore, renowned gentlemen; fall on resolvedly, till your hands cleave to your swords, your swords to your enemies' hearts, your hearts to victory, your victories to triumph, your triumphs to the everlasting praise of Him that hath given you spirits to offer yourselves willingly, and to jeopard your lives in high perils, for his name and service' sake. And we, your brethren, though we necessarily abide beyond Jordan, and remain on the American sea-coasts, will send up armies of prayers to the throne of Grace that the God of power and goodness would encourage your hearts, cover your heads, strengthen your arms, pardon your sins, save your souls, and bless your families, in the day of battle. We will also pray that the same Lord of Hosts would discover the counsels, defeat the enterprises, deride the hopes, disdain the insolencies, and wound the hairy scalps of your obstinate enemies, and yet pardon all that are unwillingly misled." [21]

III

Roger Williams, never in anything addicted to concealments, has put himself without reserve into his writings. There he still remains. There if anywhere we may get well acquainted with him. Searching for him along the two thousand printed pages upon which he has stamped his own portrait, we seem to see a very human and fallible man, with a large head, a warm heart, a healthy body, an eloquent and imprudent tongue; not a symmetrical person, poised, cool, accurate, circumspect; a man very anxious to be genuine and to get at the truth, but impatient of slow methods, trusting gallantly to his own intuitions, easily deluded by his own hopes; an imaginative, sympathetic, affluent, impulsive man; an optimist; his master-passion benevolence; his mind clarifying itself slowly; never quite settled on all subjects in the universe; at almost every moment on the watch for

[19] "The Simple Cobbler," etc. 25.   [20] Ibid. 57.
[21] Ibid. 77.

New England: Miscellaneous Prose

some new idea about that time expected to heave in sight; never able by the ordinary means of intellectual stagnation to win for himself in his life-time the bastard glory of doctrinal consistency; professing many things by turn and nothing long, until at last, even in mid-life, he reached the moral altitude of being able to call himself only a Seeker—in which not ignoble creed he continued for the remainder of his days on earth.

It must be confessed that there is even yet in the fame of Roger Williams a singular vitality. While living in this world, it was his fate to be much talked about, as well as to disturb much the serenity of many excellent people; and the rumor of him still agitates and divides men. There are, in fact, some signs that his fame is now about to take out a new lease, and to build for itself a larger habitation. At any rate, the world, having at last nearly caught up with him, seems ready to vote—though with a peculiarly respectable minority in opposition—that Roger Williams was after all a great man, one of the true heroes, seers, world-movers, of these latter ages.

Perhaps one explanation of the pleasure which we take in now looking upon him, as he looms up among his contemporaries in New England, may be that the eye of the observer, rather fatigued by the monotony of so vast a throng of sages and saints, all quite immaculate, all equally prim and stiff in their Puritan starch and uniform, all equally automatic and freezing, finds a relief in the easy swing of this man's gait, the limberness of his personal movement, his escape from the paste-board proprieties, his spontaneity, his impetuosity, his indiscretions, his frank acknowledgments that he really had a few things yet to learn. Somehow, too, though he sorely vexed the souls of the judicious in his time, and evoked from them words of dreadful reprehension, the best of them loved him; for indeed this headstrong, measureless man, with his flashes of Welsh fire, was in the grain of him a noble fellow; "a man," as Edward Winslow [22] said, "lovely in his carriage." Evidently he was of a hearty and sociable turn, and had the gift of friendship. Some of the choicest spirits of that age were knit to him in a brotherly way, particularly the two Winthrops, John Milton, and Sir Henry Vane. Writing, in the winter of 1660, to the younger Winthrop, Roger Williams says: "Your loving lines in this

[22] "Hypocrisy Unmasked," 65.

cold, dead season were as a cup of your Connecticut cider, which we are glad to hear abounds with you, or of that western metheglin which you and I have drunk at Bristol together." [23] Here, indeed, was an early New-Englander that one could still endure to have an hour with, particularly at Bristol; in truth, a clubable person; a man whose dignity would not have petrified us, nor his saintliness have given us a chill.

From his early manhood even down to his late old age, Roger Williams stands in New England a mighty and benignant form, always pleading for some magnanimous idea, some tender charity, the rectification of some wrong, the exercise of some sort of forbearance toward men's bodies or souls. It was one of his vexatious peculiarities, that he could do nothing by halves—even in logic. Having established his major and his minor premises, he utterly lacked the accommodating judgment which would have enabled him to stop there and go no further whenever it seemed that the concluding member of his syllogism was likely to annoy the brethren. To this frailty in his organization is due the fact that he often seemed to his contemporaries an impracticable person, presumptuous, turbulent, even seditious. This it was that tainted somewhat the pleasantness of his relations with the colony of Massachusetts during his residence in it. For example, he had taken orders in the established church of England, but had subsequently come to the conclusion that an established church was necessarily a corrupt organization. He acted logically. He went out of it. He would hold no fellowship with it, even remotely or by implication. He became an uncompromising Separatist. Furthermore, on arriving in New England, the same uncomfortable propensity was put into action, by the spectacle of the white men helping themselves freely to the lands of the red men, and doing so on pretence of certain titles derived from a white king on the other side of the Atlantic. He was unable to see that even so great a monarch as the king of England could give away what did not belong to him. To Roger Williams it appeared that these lands actually belonged to the red men who lived on them; hence, that the white men's titles to them ought to come from the red men, and to be the result of a genuine and fair bargain with the red men. Thus, he

[23] Narr. Club Pub. VI. 306.

New England: Miscellaneous Prose

became an assailant of the validity, in that particular, of the New England charters. It happened, moreover, that his views in both these directions constituted offences, just then, for the colony of Massachusetts, extremely inopportune and inconvenient. But these were not his only offences. Roger Williams also held that it was a shocking thing—one of the abominations of the age—for men who did not even pretend to have religion in their hearts, to be muttering publicly the words of religion with their mouths; and that such persons ought not to be called on to perform any acts of worship, even the taking of an oath. Finally, he held another doctrine—at that time and in that place sadly eccentric and disgusting—that the power of the civil magistrate "extends only to the bodies and goods and outward state of men," and not at all to their inward state, their consciences, their opinions. For these four crimes, particularly mentioned by Governor Haynes in pronouncing sentence upon him, Massachusetts deemed it unsafe to permit such a nefarious being as Roger Williams to abide anywhere within her borders.

With respect to the sympathy of Roger Williams with the Indians, it concerns us, at present, to note that it did not exhaust itself in the invention of a legal opinion on their behalf: throughout his whole life, early and late, he put himself to much downright toil and self-denial for their benefit, both in body and in soul. He and John Eliot had come to New England in the same year, 1631; but at least a dozen years before John Eliot had entered upon his apostolic labors among the Indians,[24] Roger Williams had lodged "with them in their filthy, smoky holes . . . to gain their tongue," [25] and had preached to them in it. "My soul's desire," he said, "was to do the natives good." [26] Later, he knew from his own experience, that it was possible for the English to live at peace with the Indians; when, however, that peace was broken, though he wished the English to acquit themselves manfully and successfully, he evermore stood between them and their vanquished foes, with words of compassion. In 1637, amid the exasperation caused by the Pequot war, the voice of Roger Williams was heard imploring the victors to spare. "I much rejoice," he writes to the governor of Massachusetts, "that . . . some of the

[24] J. Hammond Trumbull, Pref. to R. W.'s "Key," etc. 3–6.
[25] Quoted in J. D. Knowles, "Mem. of R. W." 109.   [26] Ibid. 108.

chiefs at Connecticut, . . . are almost adverse from killing women and children. Mercy outshines all the works and attributes of Him who is the Father of Mercies." [27] In another letter he expresses the hope that all Christians who receive as slaves the surviving Pequots, may so treat them "as to make mercy eminent." [28] In still another letter he invokes mercy upon the miserable Pequots, "since the Most High delights in mercy, and great revenge hath been already taken." [29] This, to the end of his life, was his one cry in the midst of all storms of popular wrath and revenge.[30]

And the benignity of Roger Williams was large enough to go out toward other people than the Indians. His letters, public and private, are a proof that the sight of any creature in trouble, was enough to stir his heart and his hand for quick relief. His best clients appear to have been those who had no other advocate, and who could pay no fees: poor people; sick ones; wanderers; [31] "the dead, the widows, and the fatherless;" [32] and, especially, all who had been turned adrift for the crime of having an independent thought. Nay, his generosity threw its arms not only around those who were then actually unfortunate, but even around those who might ever become so; and for them, too, he tried to make tender provision. In 1662, the people of Providence resolved to divide among themselves the lands that still remained common. When Roger Williams heard of this, he wrote a warm-hearted and moving appeal to them, as his "loving friends and neighbors," beseeching them that as he first gave to them all the lands, so they would permit some to remain unappropriated, as a possession in reserve for such homeless persons as, driven from any country for conscience' sake, might thereafter flee to them for refuge: "I earnestly pray the town to lay to heart, as ever they look for a blessing from God on the town, on your families, your corn and cattle, and your children after you, . . . that after you have got over the black brook of some soul-bondage yourselves, you tear not down the bridge after you, by leaving no small pittance for distressed souls that may come after you." [33]

[27] Narr. Club Pub. VI. 36.
[28] Ibid. 80.
[29] Ibid. 87–88. See also 34, 35, 44, 47, 54.
[30] See his noble letter, ibid. 269–276.
[31] Ibid. 212, 213.
[32] Ibid. 208. See also entire letter, 206–209.
[33] Ibid. 318.

New England: Miscellaneous Prose

IV

In the early part of the year 1643, the four colonies, Massachusetts Bay, Plymouth, Connecticut, and New Haven, formed themselves into a snug confederacy called The United Colonies of New England, from which very naturally Rhode Island was excluded,—an incident that reminded the latter in a lively way of its perfect isolation among the peoples of this earth. As it had no recognized connection with its sister-colonies, so it had none with the mother-country. At once, it resolved to procure for itself such civic respectability as could be conveyed by a charter from England; and it summoned its foremost citizen, Roger Williams, to go thither and get it. This command he promptly obeyed, taking ship that very summer, not from Boston —in whose streets he was forbidden to set his foot—but from the friendly Dutch port of New Amsterdam. It was upon this long and leisurely sea-voyage, that he composed his first book, "A Key into the Language of America: or, An help to the language of the natives in that part of America called New England," which was given to the press soon after his arrival in London.[34] This work is primarily a phrase-book of the language of certain Indian tribes; but it is much more than that. Indeed, it is a most suggestive and racy description of those Indians themselves. Each chapter groups together the words pertaining to some one topic; with each group of words are connected comments, brief, pithy, instructive; at the end of each chapter is a series of verses upon its prevailing topic; and through all, whether in verse or prose, runs a gentle and liberal tone, that note of magnanimity, compassion, personal freedom and freshness, to be heard all along the life of this man. For instance, at the end of the chapter which gathers the words of salutation, is this stanza:

> "If nature's sons, both wild and tame,
> Humane and courteous be,
> How ill becomes it sons of God
> To want humanity!" [35]

---

[34] Reprinted in Narr. Club Pub. I. 1–222, and there edited by J. Hammond Trumbull.
[35] Ibid. 39.

In the chapter giving the words of entertainment is this comment: "It is a strange truth that a man shall generally find more free entertainment and refreshing amongst these barbarians, than amongst thousands that call themselves Christians;" [36] and he hints gratefully at the hospitality he had found among American savages even when he had experienced some lack of it among his own countrymen:

> "God's providence is rich to his,
> Let none distrustful be;
> In wilderness, in great distress,
> These ravens have fed me." [37]

Even in a book like this, he continually returns to themes of pity, forbearance, and faith, as if these were the chorus to his own psalm of life; and he sees among the wild beasts of the American forests, some traits that should shame Christians out of their ferocity and meanness: "The wilderness is a clear resemblance of the world, where greedy and furious men persecute and devour the harmless and innocent, as the wild beasts pursue and devour the hinds and roes." [38] "The wolf is an emblem of a fierce, blood-sucking persecutor; the swine of a covetous, rooting worldling. Both make a prey of the Lord Jesus in his poor servants." [39]

Upon reaching England, he of course found the country upheaved and aflame in civil war, John Hampden having not long before fallen in the fight. In such a controversy, the sympathy of Roger Williams could only be with the party that stood for some widening of human horizons; and though he never lost sight of the particular business that brought him to England, it was impossible for him even there to see so interesting a quarrel in progress and not take a hand in it. His participation in the strife was in two ways, the one physical, the other intellectual; both significant of the humane and efficient nature of him. First, as the winter came on, the poor of London began to suffer for want of fuel, and even to rise in mutiny,—the supply of coals from Newcastle having been cut off. This suggested to Roger Williams something to do. His American experience had taught him that there were several ways by which men could keep warm

---

[36] "Key," etc. 46. [37] Ibid. 46.
[38] Ibid. 130. [39] Ibid. 191.

New England: Miscellaneous Prose

in an emergency; and he at once put himself into the service of parliament for the supply of firewood to the shivering folk of the great city. But the intellectual aspects of the contest in England probably interested him even more than did its physical ones. It grieved him to think of men's bodies shivering with cold: it grived him far worse to think of their souls shivering with fear; and doubtless the one result that he hoped for out of all the havoc of those times, was that men would learn to abhor what he called the "body-killing, soul-killing, and state-killing doctrine" [40] of persecuting one another for their differences in opinion. At last, this had become his master-thought. Even upon the ocean, and while compiling a mere Indian vocabulary, he had been unable, as we have seen, to keep this great thought from thrusting itself forward among his word-lists; and it happened that, so long as he stayed in England, there came to him occasions for its more explicit utterance. He had not been a great while upon shore when, oddly enough, there appeared in print, in London, a letter which the celebrated John Cotton had written to him six years before, adroitly justifying the banishment of Roger Williams from Massachusetts. This letter it was fitting that Roger Williams should take notice of; and his notice of it swiftly came in the form of a little book, called "Mr. Cotton's Letter Lately Printed, Examined and Answered;" [41] a manly and self-restrained piece of work, giving frankly his own side of the story, emitting an occasional jet of indignation at the harshness of the treatment that had been visited upon him, and standing by every one of the ideas for which he had been driven, in midwinter, from his home and friends, into the wilderness: "I . . . hope that as I then maintained the rocky strength of them, . . . so through the Lord's assistance I shall be ready for the same grounds, not only to be bound and banished, but to die also in New England." [42] At the very time when, in both Englands, many of the greatest di-

---

[40] Narr. Club Pub. I. 328.

[41] First printed, London, 1644, and reprinted in Narr. Club Pub. I. 313–396. Cotton's "Letter" is also printed in the same volume.

[42] Narr. Club Pub. I. 324–325, where he cites the four charges against him as summed up by Governor Haynes. In defence of Massachusetts for its treatment of Roger Williams, all that can be fairly urged by the utmost learning and the utmost ingenuity has been urged by Henry Martyn Dexter, in his powerful monograph, "As To Roger Williams."

vines, both among the Congregationalists and the Presbyterians, were outspoken for the suppression of heresy by force, denouncing the word toleration as a word of infamy, Roger Williams declared it to be "a monstrous paradox, that God's children should persecute God's children, and that they that hope to live eternally together with Christ Jesus in the heavens, should not suffer each other to live in this common air together." [43] "Persecutors of men's bodies," he exclaimed, "seldom or never do these men's souls good." [44]

He had not long finished his answer to John Cotton when he saw need to speak forth again. Standing in the thick of the strifes that then engaged all Englishmen, viewing them with his American eyes and from his American experience, he was able to discern, better than most Englishmen could do, the inevitable drift of things, and to give resounding forenotice of some dangers ahead. The illustrious Westminster Assembly of Divines had been in session since July, 1643. Already the Presbyterians in it had come to hard blows with the Congregationalists in it, with respect to the form of church government to be erected in England upon the ruins of the Episcopacy. On that subject Roger Williams had a very distinct opinion. While some were for having the new national church of this pattern, and others were for having it of that, Roger Williams boldly stepped two or three centuries ahead of his age, and affirmed that there should be no national church at all. Putting his arguments into the deferential form of mere questions, he published, in 1644, what he called "Queries of Highest Consideration." [45] The introduction to this little book is a direct address to both houses of parliament, and speaks to them with the noble Miltonic accent: "Most renowned patriots, you sit at helm in as great a storm as e'er poor England's commonwealth was lost in; yet be you pleased to remember that, excepting the affairs . . . of religion, . . . all your consultations, conclusions, executions, are not of the quantity of the value of one poor drop of water. . . . It shall never be your honor, to this or future ages, to be confined to the patterns of either French, Dutch, Scotch, or New-English churches. . . . If he whose name is Wonderful, Counsellor, be consulted, . . . we are confident you shall exceed the acts and

[43] Narr. Club Pub. I. 319.   [44] Ibid. 327–328.
[45] Reprinted in ibid. II. 241–275.

patterns of all neighbor nations." Then, in the book itself, turning to the ecclesiastical champions who confronted one another in the Westminster Assembly, he puts to them twelve great questions. These questions pierce to the core of all ecclesiastical disputes then and since then. They contain the germs of all truths that go to the erection upon this earth of a majestic human commonwealth, in which all souls shall be utterly free. Observe the foresight and the glorious audacity of this seventeenth century American: "We query where you now find one footstep, print, or pattern, in this doctrine of the Son of God, for a . . . national church. . . . Again we ask, whether in the constitution of a national church it can possibly be framed without a racking and tormenting of the souls as well as of the bodies of persons. . . . It seems not possible to fit it to every conscience: sooner shall one suit of apparel fit everybody, one law-precedent every case, or one size or last every foot. . . . Whether it be not the cause of a world of hypocrites, the soothing up of people in a formal state-worship to the ruin of their souls, the ground of persecution to Christ Jesus in his members, and sooner or later the kindling of the devouring flames of civil wars. . . . Since you profess to want more light, and that a greater light is yet to be expected, . . . we query how you can profess and swear to persecute all others as schismatics, heretics, and so forth, that believe they see a further light, and dare not join with either of your churches. . . . Whether . . . it be not a true mark . . . of a false church to persecute; it being the nature only of a wolf to hunt the lambs and sheep, but impossible for a lamb or sheep, or a thousand flocks of sheep to persecute one wolf. . . . Whether there can possibly be expected the least look of peace in these fatal distractions and tempests raised, but by taking counsel of the greatest and wisest politician that ever was, the Lord Jesus Christ." [46]

All this, of course, was stark and dreadful heresy; but it was heresy for which Roger Williams had already suffered loss and pain, and was prepared to suffer more. Whatever were the faults of this man, indifference to the sacred prerogatives of personality was not among them. He could not bear the weight of any fetters upon his own soul; and the spectacle of them upon any other soul, filled him with

[46] Narr. Club Pub. II. 264–274.

pity and great wrath. Very likely in his early manhood he had been, both in speech and deed, hot, precipitate, destructive. But, for him, time, meditation, sorrow, solitude, the presence of nature, a larger acquaintance with mankind, had been doing their work, chastening and mellowing him; and though nothing could quench the fire of his spirit, or tame him into a safe, calculating, and conventional person, —pulling judiciously in any regulation-traces,—he had certainly grown in patience, and in the justice which patience gives. Above all, however, his nature had become absolutely clear in its adjustment of certain grand ideas, of which the chief was soul-liberty. On behalf of that idea, having now an opportunity to free his mind, he resolved to do so, keeping nothing back; and accordingly, almost upon the heels of the little book that has just been mentioned, he sent out another—not a little one; a book of strong, limpid, and passionate argument, glorious for its intuitions of the world's coming wisdom, and in its very title flinging out defiantly a challenge to all comers. He called it "The Bloody Tenet of Persecution for Cause of Conscience." [47]

This book, which had two editions within its first year, and quickly attained the honor of martyrdom in the flames of a Presbyterian auto-da-fé, was written, the author tells us, while he was busy with his task of procuring fuel for the poor of London, "in change of rooms and corners, yea sometimes . . . in variety of strange houses, sometimes in the fields, in the midst of travel; where he hath been forced to gather and scatter his loose thoughts and papers." It is a treatise in the form of a dialogue, the interlocutors being two angelic and sorrowful fugitives, Truth and Peace, who, after long separations and friendless wanderings over the earth, have at last met in some dusky corner of it, where they confer together mournfully over those errors and passions which blind men, and fill the world with tumult and misery. The conversation between these heavenly personages goes forward at great length, and covers the entire field of the doctrine of intellectual freedom. In the very year in which this book was published, in London, John Milton likewise gave to the public, in the same place, his majestic plea for soul-liberty, "Areopagitica;" but even Milton's vision of this sublime truth had not then acquired the

[47] First published, London, 1644. Reprinted in Narr. Club Pub. III. 1-425.

New England: Miscellaneous Prose

breadth and clearness with which it was revealed to Roger Williams. Milton asks only that "many be tolerated rather than all be compelled," and immediately suggests this fatal limitation: "I mean not tolerated Popery and open superstition, which as it extirpates all religions and civil supremacies, so itself should be extirpate." [48] How much nobler and more spacious is the declaration of Roger Williams! "It is the will and command of God, that . . . a permission of the most Paganish, Jewish, Turkish, or Antichristian consciences and worships, be granted to all men, in all nations and countries; and they are only to be fought against with that sword which is only, in soul-matters, able to conquer, to wit, the sword of God's Spirit, the word of God." [49]

It may be that this great work had not even passed from the hands of the printer, when the author of it, having fully accomplished the business that brought him to England, had set out upon his return to Rhode Island, where he arrived in the autumn of 1644. His book, having likewise set out upon its travels, reached in due time the library of John Cotton, and stirred him up to make a reply, which was published in London in 1647, and which bore a title reverberating that given by Roger Williams to his book: "The Bloody Tenet washed and made white in the Blood of the Lamb." Cotton's book quickly found Roger Williams, at his home in Rhode Island, and of course aroused him to write a rejoinder. This he sent to England for publication; but it did not get into print until his own second visit there, in 1652. Its title is a reiteration of that given to his former work, and is likewise a characteristic retort upon the modification of it made by his antagonist: "The Bloody Tenet yet more Bloody, by Mr. Cotton's Endeavor to wash it white in the Blood of the Lamb." [50]

As usual, this book has several prefaces. The first one, addressed "to the most honorable, the parliament of the commonwealth of England," is written with great power. It is a magnificent and soul-stirring appeal, a noble chant of spiritual liberty, an overture in sonorous word-music to the mighty strain that rolls stormily through the book, an invocation to the rulers of England to practise the magnanimity of a complete enfranchisement of human souls within all

---

[48] "Areopagitica," Arber's ed. 76.   [49] Narr. Club Pub. III.
[50] Reprinted in ibid. IV. 1–547.

the realms swayed by their authority: "O ye, the prime of English men and English worthies, whose senses have so oft perceived the everlasting arms of the invincible and eternal King, when your ship's hold hath been full with water, yea with blood, . . . when she hath beaten upon some rocky hearts and passages as if she would have staved and split into a thousand pieces. Yet this so near . . . foundered, sinking nation, hath the God of heaven, by your most valiant and careful hands, brought safe to peace, her harbor. Why, now, should any duty possible be impossible? Yea, why not impossibilities possible? Why should your English seas contend with a neighbor Dutchman, for the motion of a piece of silk, . . . and not ten thousand fold much more your English spirits with theirs, for the crown of that state-piety and wisdom which may make your faces more to shine, . . . with a glory far transcending all your fairest neighbors' copies. The States of Holland, having smarted deeply and paid so dearly for the purchase of their freedoms, reach to . . . the world a taste of such of their dainties. And yet (with due reverence to so wise a state and with due thankfulness for mercy and relief to many poor oppressed consciences) I say, their piety nor policy could ever yet reach so far, nor could they in all their school of war . . . learn that one poor lesson of setting absolutely the consciences of all men free. . . . But why should not such a parliament as England never had . . . outshoot and teach their neighbors, by framing a safe communication of freedom of conscience in worship, even to . . . the Papists and Arminians themselves? . . . The Pope, the Turk, the King of Spain, the Emperor, and the rest of persecutors, build among the eagles and the stars; yet, while they practise violence to the souls of men and make their swords of steel corrivals with the two-edged spiritual sword of the Son of God, the basis of their highest pillars, the foundation of their glorious palaces are but dross and rottenness. And however, in our poor arithmetic, their kingdoms' number seem great, yet in the only wise account of the Eternal, their ages are but minutes, and their short periods are near accomplished. . . . But light from the Father of Lights hath shined on your eyes, mercy from the Father of Mercies hath softened your breasts, to be tender of the tenderest part of man, his conscience." [51]

[51] Narr. Club Pub. IV. 9–13.

New England: Miscellaneous Prose

This book is the most powerful of the writings of Roger Williams. Its range of topics is dictated by the line of discussion adopted by John Cotton. There are three principal matters argued in it,—the nature of persecution, the limits of the power of the civil sword, and the tolerance already granted by parliament. Like its author's previous book, this work has an abundance of literary faults. It conforms to the manner of the controversial prose of the seventeenth century: its sentences are often involved, lumbering, diffuse; it is entirely lacking in reticence; it defies proportion; it moves onward and onward in unpruned and boundless loquacity; eternity seems not long enough for the entire perusal of it. Nevertheless, here also are some of the best qualities that can be in a book: ripeness of judgment, uttermost sincerity, all-consuming earnestness, the inspiration of being in the right and of knowing it, the rebound of a strong, generous, and brilliant nature against the thrusts of an able antagonist. Here, in a most benign service, are ample erudition, logic, imagination, noble emotion, humor, pathos, sarcasm, invective, torrents of eager and irresistible speech. The closing passage of this book is, at once, the summary and the climax of all the argument and passion that have enlightened and kindled its pages: a stately, an appalling arraignment, before the tribunal of divine, angelic, and human reason, of the doctrine of persecution. Having now, against that doctrine, argued the case in full, and from every point of view; having proved it to be heavy and accursed with the weight of every impolicy and of every crime, the author seems to gather up all his powers of thought, feeling, and utterance for one final onset; and he proceeds to hurl upon the tenet, which he execrates, these fierce, crashing sentences: "And for myself, I must proclaim before the most holy God, angels, and men, that . . . yet this is a foul, a black, and a bloody tenet; a tenet of high blasphemy against the God of peace, the God of order, who hath of one blood made all mankind to dwell upon the face of the earth; . . . a tenet warring against the Prince of Peace, Christ Jesus; . . . a tenet fighting against the sweet end of his coming, which was not to destroy men's lives for their religions, but to save them; . . . a tenet lamentably guilty of his most precious blood, shed in the blood of so many hundred thousand of his poor servants by the civil powers of the world, pretending to suppress blasphemies, heresies, idolatries, superstition, and so forth; a tenet fighting against the spirit of love, holiness, and meekness, by kindling fiery spirits of false zeal and fury; . . . a tenet against which the blessed souls under the altar cry aloud for vengeance, this tenet having cut their throats, torn out their hearts, and poured forth their blood, in all ages, as the only heretics and blasphemers in the world; a tenet, which no uncleanness, no adultery, incest, sodomy, or bestiality can equal,—this ravishing and forcing . . . the very souls and consciences of all the nations and inhabitants of the world; . . . a tenet loathsome and ugly . . . with the palpable filths of gross dissimulation and hypocrisy; . . . a tenet that fights against the common principles of all civility, and the very civil being and combinations of men . . . by commixing . . . a spiritual and civil state together; . . . a tenet that kindles the devouring flames of combustions and wars in most nations of the world; . . . a tenet all besprinkled with the bloody murders, stabs, poisonings, pistollings, powder-plots, and so forth, against many famous kings, princes, and states; . . . a tenet all red and bloody with those most barbarous and tigerlike massacres of so many thousand and ten thousands, formerly in France and other parts, and so lately and so horribly in Ireland; . . . a tenet that stunts the growth and flourishing of the most likely and hopefulest commonweals and countries; . . . a tenet that corrupts and spoils the very civil honesty and natural conscience of a nation; since conscience to God, violated, proves, without repentance, ever after a very jade, a drug, loose and unconscionable in all converse with men; lastly, a tenet in England most unseasonable, as pouring oil upon those flames which the high wisdom of the parliament, by easing the yokes on men's consciences, had begun to quench. In the sad consideration of all which, . . . let heaven and earth judge of the washing and color of this tenet. . . . For me, . . . I must profess, while heaven and earth lasts, that no one tenet that either London, England, or the world, doth harbor, is so heretical, blasphemous, seditious, and dangerous, to the corporal, to the spiritual, to the present, to the eternal good of men, as the bloody tenet (however washed and whited) . . . of persecution for cause of conscience." [52]

With Roger Williams, the mood for composition seems to have

[52] Narr. Club Pub. IV. 493–501.

New England: Miscellaneous Prose

come in gusts. His writings are numerous; but they were produced spasmodically and in clusters, amid long spaces of silence. He is known to have written two or three works which were never printed at all, and which are now lost. In 1652, during his second visit to England, he published, in addition to his rejoinder to John Cotton, two small treatises, "The Hireling Ministry None of Christ's," and "Experiments of Spiritual Life and Health." From that time, no book of his was given to the press until the year 1676, when he published at Boston a quarto volume of nearly three hundred and fifty pages, embodying his own report of a series of stormy public debates, which he had held in Rhode Island, not long before, with certain robust advocates of Quakerism. This book bears a punning title, "George Fox digged out of his Burrows." [53] By his contemporaries, it was read with intense interest; and it is interesting still, at least for its many local and personal allusions, and as an authentic and unpleasant memorial of the anger, the barbarous discourtesy, the vituperation, with which in those ages even kindly men engaged in intellectual controversy.[54] Most readers nowadays, who may find themselves by chance near this huge book, will gaze down into it for a moment as into some vast tank into which have poured the drippings of a furious religious combat in the olden time,—theological nick-names, blunt-headed words of pious abuse, devout scurrilities, the rancid vocabulary of Puritan billingsgate, that diction of hearty and expressive dislike which Roger Williams himself pleasantly described as "sharp Scripture language." [55]

Besides those of his writings that were intended for books, there are many in the form of letters, some addressed to the public, most of them to his personal friends. In these letters,[56] which cover his whole life from youth to old age, we seem to get very near to the man himself. They are upon all sorts of subjects, often hurriedly written, always cheerful, seldom mirthful; they are full of urbanity, tenderness, generosity; they show an habitual upwardness of mental move-

---

[53] Reprinted in Narr. Club Pub. V. 1–503.
[54] Think of the controversial writings of such true-souled gentlemen as Sir Thomas More and John Milton.
[55] For examples of his energetic candor see Narr. Club Pub. V. 84, 193, 203, 226, 227, 233, 243, 366, 417, 491.
[56] Many of them are given in Narr. Club Pub. VI. 1–420.

ment; they grow rich in all gentle, gracious, and magnanimous qualities as the years increase upon him. Especially do they please us by the tokens they furnish of the noble friendships that he was capable of. His letters to the younger Winthrop are peculiarly affable and tender; nowhere else in his writings do we meet so many passages of benediction and aspiration, sweet, brief phrases of comfort. In one letter he begins with this greeting: "Best respects and love presented to yourself and dearest." [57] In another he says: "Above the sun is our rest, in the Alpha and Omega of all blessedness, unto whose arms of everlasting mercy I commend you." [58] In another he says: "This instant before sunrise as I went to my field," I met "an Indian running back for a glass, bound for your parts;" I use him to carry "this hasty salutation to your kind self and dear companion." [59] In another letter to the same friend, is preserved an amusing reminiscence both of his familiar and thoughtful friendliness, and of a certain imperious domestic necessity that civilization has at last succeeded in making us unconscious of: "Sir, hearing want of pins, I crave Mrs. Winthrop's acceptance of two small papers, that, if she want not herself, she may pleasure a neighbor." [60]

The letters of Roger Williams also show that, to the very end of his days, he kept his mind open and alert to nearly all that was passing among men, at home and abroad, especially in wars, politics, and divinity. Even more vividly than in his books, we see in them likewise the habits of his mind in the grasp and expression of thought. His was not a dry, hard, or acute mind, but sensitive, imaginative, comprehensive, with great fertility of ideas, moved by energies rushing into it from the heart. Evidently he had no objections to laughter, but the humor of his letters is of the lurking and delicate kind; as when he says that Prince Rupert was one "whose name in these parts sounds as a north-east snow-storm," [61] or when he describes his friend Gregory Dexter as "an intelligent man . . . and conscionable (though a Baptist)." [62] All his writings, and especially his letters, abound in quotable sentences, masses of thought heaved to the surface by its own natural action: "Better an honorable death than a

[57] Narr. Club Pub. VI. 200.
[58] Ibid. 174.
[59] Ibid. 319.
[60] Ibid. 200.
[61] Ibid. 197–198.
[62] Ibid. 332.

New England: Miscellaneous Prose

slave's life." [63] "I fear not so much iron and steel as the cutting of our throats with golden knives." [64] "Oh, how sweet is a dry morsel and a handful, with quietness from earth and heaven." [65] "The counsels of the Most High are deep concerning us poor grasshoppers hopping and skipping from branch to twig in this vale of tears." [66] In the moral perspectives of life he has some notable sayings. He speaks of "the vain and empty puff of all terrene promotions;" [67] and of "that life which is eternal when this poor minute's dream is over." [68] "Alas, sir, in calm midnight thoughts, what are these leaves and flowers, and smoke and shadows, and dreams of earthly nothings, about which we poor fools and children, as David saith, disquiet ourselves in vain." [69] "In my poor span of time, I have been oft in the jaws of death, sickening at sea, shipwrecked on shore, in danger of arrows, swords, and bullets; and yet, methinks, the most high and most holy God hath reserved me for some service to his most glorious and eternal majesty." [70]

Finally, he conceived truth in its concrete forms; his propositions were often uttered in images; he could settle a long debate by the authority of a luminous comparison. A noble example of this habit of his mind, is that celebrated letter to the people of Providence, written by him, in 1655, as President of Rhode Island, with the purpose of correcting a perversion, just then attempted, of his own strong championship of soul-liberty: "There goes many a ship to sea, with many hundred souls in one ship, whose weal and woe is common, and is a true picture of a commonwealth or a human combination or society. It hath fallen out sometimes that both Papists and Protestants, Jews and Turks, may be embarked in one ship; upon which supposal I affirm, that all the liberty of conscience that ever I pleaded for, turns upon these two hinges—that none of the Papists, Protestants, Jews, or Turks, be forced to come to the ship's prayers or worship, nor compelled from their own particular prayers or worship, if they practise any. I further add, that I never denied that, notwithstanding this liberty, the commander of this ship ought to command the ship's course, yea, and also command that justice, peace, and so-

---

[63] Narr. Club Pub. VI. 15.
[64] Ibid. 15.
[65] Ibid. 165.
[66] Ibid. 158–159.
[67] Ibid. 101.
[68] Ibid. 242.
[69] Ibid. 343.
[70] Ibid. 242.

briety, be kept and practised, both among the seamen and all the passengers. If any of the seamen refuse to perform their services, or passengers to pay their freight; if any refuse to help, in person or purse, toward the common charges or defence; if any refuse to obey the common laws and orders of the ship, concerning their common peace or preservation; if any shall mutiny and rise up against their commanders and officers; if any should preach or write that there ought to be no commanders or officers, because all are equal in Christ, therefore no masters nor officers, no laws nor orders, nor corrections, nor punishments;—I say, I never denied, but in such cases, whatever is pretended, the commander or commanders may judge, resist, compel, and punish such transgressors, according to their deserts and merits. This, if seriously and honestly minded, may, if it so please the Father of Lights, let in some light to such as willingly shut not their eyes. I remain, studious of your common peace and liberty, Roger Williams." [71]

The supreme intellectual merit of this composition is in those very qualities that never obtrude themselves upon notice—ease, lucidity, completeness. Here we have the final result of ages of intellectual effort, presented without effort; a long process of abstract reasoning made transparent and irresistible in a picture. With a wisdom that is both just and peaceable, it fixes, for all time, the barriers against tyranny on the one side, against lawlessness on the other. It has the moral and literary harmonies of a classic. As such, it deserves to be forever memorable in our American prose.*

[71] Narr. Club Pub. VI. 278–279.

[* A penciled note states: "In 1896, inserted foot-note concerning the recovered tract in R I Hist Tracts No 14, 1881." The note added in 1897 was as follows:

"Two years after the first publication of this book, a long-lost tract by Roger Williams, entitled 'Christenings Make Not Christians,' London, 1645, was discovered by Henry Martyn Dexter in the library of the British Museum, where, having been bound together with eight or ten other pamphlets, it had somehow escaped being catalogued. In 1881, this noble-hearted monograph, along with certain letters of Williams believed to have been previously unpublished, was printed as No. 14 of the 'Rhode Island Historical Tracts.' An important contribution to the study of the position of Roger Williams in the development of American civilization, has been made by Oscar S. Straus, in his 'Roger Williams the Pioneer of Religious Liberty,' New York, 1894."]

Chapter X

New England: The Verse-Writers

I. The attitude of Puritanism toward Art—Especially toward Poetry—The unextinguished poetry in Puritanism.
II. The Puritans of New England universally addicted to versification—The mirth of their elegies and epitaphs—The poetical expertness of Pastor John Wilson.
III. The pleasant legend of William Morrell—His poem in Latin and English on New England.
IV. The prodigy of "The Bay Psalm Book"—Its Reverend fabricators—Their conscientious mode of proceeding—A book fearfully and wonderfully made.
V. Anne Bradstreet the earliest professional poet of New England—First appearance of her book—Her career—Her prose writings—Her training for poetry—Her guides and masters the later euphuists in English verse—List of her poetical works—Analysis of "The Four Elements"—"The Four Monarchies"—The fundamental error in her poetry—Her "Contemplations"—The first poet of the Merrimac—Her devout poems—Her allusions to contemporary politics—Her championship of women—Final estimate.

I

A HAPPY surprise awaits those who come to the study of the early literature of New England with the expectation of finding it altogether arid in sentiment, or void of the spirit and aroma of poetry. The New-Englander of the seventeenth century was indeed a typical Puritan; and it will hardly be said that any typical Puritan of that century was a poetical personage. In proportion to his devotion to the ideas that won for him the derisive honor of his name, was he at war with nearly every form of the beautiful. He himself believed that there was an inappeasable feud between religion and art; and hence, the duty of suppressing art was bound up in his soul with the master-purpose of promoting religion. He cultivated the grim and the ugly. He was afraid of the approaches of Satan through the avenues of what is graceful and joyous. The principal business of men and women in this world seemed to him to be not to make it as delightful as possible, but to get through it as safely as possible. By a whimsical and horrid freak of unconscious Manichæism, he thought that whatever is good here is appropriated to God, and whatever is pleasant, to the devil. It is not strange if he were inclined to measure the holiness of a man's life by its disagreeableness. In the logic and fury of his tremendous faith, he turned away utterly from music, from sculpture and painting, from architecture, from the adornments of costume, from the pleasures and embellishments of society; because these things seemed only "the devil's flippery and seduction" to his "ascetic soul, aglow with the gloomy or rapturous mysteries of his theology." [1] Hence, very naturally, he turned away likewise from certain great and splendid types of literature,—from the drama, from the playful and sensuous verse of Chaucer and his innumerable sons, from the secular prose writings of his contemporaries, and from all forms of modern lyric verse except the Calvinistic hymn.

Nevertheless, the Puritan did not succeed in eradicating poetry from his nature. Of course, poetry was planted there too deep even for his theological grub-hooks to root it out. Though denied expression in one way, the poetry that was in him forced itself into utterance in another. If his theology drove poetry out of many forms in which it had been used to reside, poetry itself practised a noble revenge by taking up its abode in his theology. His supreme thought was given to theology; and there he nourished his imagination with the mightiest and sublimest conceptions that a human being can entertain—conceptions of God and man, of angels and devils, of Providence and duty and destiny, of heaven, earth, hell. Though he stamped his foot in horror and scorn upon many exquisite and delicious types of literary art; stripped society of all its embellishments, life of all its

[1] E. C. Stedman, "Victorian Poets," 12.

New England: The Verse-Writers

amenities, sacred architecture of all its grandeur, the public service of divine worship of the hallowed pomp, the pathos and beauty of its most reverend and stately forms; though his prayers were often a snuffle, his hymns a dolorous whine, his extemporized liturgy a bleak ritual of ungainly postures and of harsh monotonous howls; yet the idea that filled and thrilled his soul was one in every way sublime, immense, imaginative, poetic—the idea of the awful omnipotent Jehovah, his inexorable justice, his holiness, the inconceivable brightness of his majesty, the vastness of his unchanging designs along the entire range of his relations with the hierarchies of heaven, the principalities and powers of the pit, and the elect and the reprobate of the sons of Adam. How resplendent and superb was the poetry that lay at the heart of Puritanism, was seen by the sightless eyes of John Milton, whose great epic is indeed the epic of Puritanism.[2]

II

Turning to Puritanism as it existed in New England, we may perhaps imagine it as solemnly declining the visits of the Muses of poetry, sending out to them the blunt but honest message—'Otherwise engaged.' Nothing could be further from the truth. Of course, Thalia, and Melpomene, and Terpsichore could not under any pretence have been admitted; but Polyhymnia—why should not she have been allowed to come in? especially if she were willing to forsake her deplorable sisters, give up her pagan habits, and submit to Christian baptism. Indeed, the Muse of New England, whosoever that respectable damsel may have been, was a muse by no means exclusive; such as she was, she cordially visited every one who would receive her, —and every one would receive her. It is an extraordinary fact about these grave and substantial men of New England, especially during our earliest literary age, that they all had a lurking propensity to write what they sincerely believed to be poetry,—and this, in most cases, in unconscious defiance of the edicts of nature and of a predetermining Providence. Lady Mary Montagu said that in England, in her time, verse-making had become as common as taking snuff:

[2] Taine, "Hist. Eng. Lit." I. 420, calls it "the Protestant epic of damnation and grace."

in New England, in the age before that, it had become much more common than taking snuff—since there were some who did not take snuff. It is impressive to note, as we inspect our first period, that neither advanced age, nor high office, nor mental unfitness, nor previous condition of respectability, was sufficient to protect any one from the poetic vice. We read of venerable men, like Peter Bulkley, continuing to lapse into it when far beyond the grand climacteric. Governor Thomas Dudley was hardly a man to be suspected of such a thing; yet even against him the evidence must be pronounced conclusive: some verses in his own handwriting were found upon his person after his death. Even the sage and serious governor of Plymouth wrote ostensible poems. The renowned pulpit-orator, John Cotton, did the same; although, in some instances, he prudently concealed the fact by inscribing his English verses in Greek characters upon the blank leaves of his almanac. Here and there, even a town-clerk, placing on record the deeply prosaic proceedings of the selectmen, would adorn them in the sacred costume of poetry. Perhaps, indeed, all this was their solitary condescension to human frailty. The earthly element, the passion, the carnal taint, the vanity, the weariness, or whatever else it be that, in other men, works itself off in a pleasure-journey, in a flirtation, in going to the play, or in a convivial bout, did in these venerable men exhaust itself in the sly dissipation of writing verses. Remembering their unfriendly attitude toward art in general, this universal mania of theirs for some forms of the poetic art—this unrestrained proclivity toward the "lust of versification"—must seem to us an odd psychological freak. Or, shall we rather say that it was not a freak at all, but a normal effort of nature, which, being unduly repressed in one direction, is accustomed to burst over all barriers in another; and that these grim and godly personages in the old times fell into the intemperance of rhyming, just as in later days, excellent ministers of the gospel and gray-haired deacons, recoiling from the sin and scandal of a game at billiards, have been known to manifest an inordinate joy in the orthodox frivolity of croquet? As respects the poetry which was perpetrated by our ancestors, it must be mentioned that a benignant Providence has its own methods of protecting the human family from intolerable misfortune; and that the most of this poetry has perished.

New England: The Verse-Writers

Enough, however, has survived to furnish us with materials for everlasting gratitude, by enabling us in a measure to realize the nature and extent of the calamity which the divine intervention has spared us.

It will be natural for us to suppose that, at any rate, poetry in New England in the seventeenth century could not have been a *Gaya Sciencia,* as poetry was called in Provence in the thirteenth century.[3] Even this, however, is not quite correct; for no inconsiderable part of early New England poetry has a positively facetious intention,—that part, namely, which consists of elegies and epitaphs. Our ancestors seem to have reserved their witticisms principally for tombstones and funerals. When a man died, his surviving friends were wont to conspire together to write verses upon him—and these verses often sparkled with the most elaborate and painful jests. Thus, in 1647, upon the death of the renowned Thomas Hooker of Hartford, his colleague in the pastorate, Samuel Stone, wrote to an eminent minister in Massachusetts certain words of grave and cautious suggestion: "You may think whether it may not be comely for you and myself and some other elders, to make a few verses for Mr. Hooker, and transcribe them in the beginning of his book. I do but propound it."[4] The appeal was effectual; and when, a few years later, it came Samuel Stone's turn to depart this life, those who outlived him rendered to his memory a similar service, his name furnishing an unusually pleasant opportunity for those ingenuities of allusion and those literary quirks and puns that were then thought to be among the graces of a threnody. Thus, the deceased brother was

> "A stone more than the Ebenezer famed;
> Stone, splendent diamond, right orient named;
> A cordial stone, that often cheerëd hearts
> With pleasant wit, with gospel rich imparts;
> Whetstone, that edgified the obtusest mind;
> Loadstone, that drew the iron heart unkind;
> A ponderous stone, that would the bottom sound
> Of Scripture depths, and bring out arcans found;
> A stone for kingly David's use so fit,

[3] Geo. Ticknor, "Hist. Spanish Lit." I. 103.
[4] The entire letter in W. B. Sprague, "Annals of Am. Pulpit," I. 35.

> As would not fail Goliath's front to hit;
> A stone, an antidote, that brake the course
> Of gangrene error by convincing force;
> A stone acute, fit to divide and square;
> A squarëd stone became Christ's building rare." [5]

The death of Samuel Danforth, of Roxbury, occurred just after that excellent person had preached through the Gospel of St. Luke in course, and also just after a new and more spacious meeting-house had been erected by his congregation,—interesting personal items which found their appropriate mention in his epitaph:

> "Our minds with gospel his rich lectures fed;
> Luke and his life at once are finishëd,
> Our new-built church now suffers too by this,
> Larger its windows, but its lights are less." [6]

Connecticut had for one of its early governors the generous Edward Hopkins, as a proof of whose devoutness it is recorded that his prayers were so fervent "that he frequently fell a bleeding at the nose, through the agony of spirit with which he labored in them." [7] After his death, an epitaph was written upon him, in which his glorious resurrection is predicted in this spirited legal metaphor:

> "But Heaven, not brooking that the earth should share
> In the least atom of a piece so rare,
> Intends to sue out, by a new revise,
> His *habeas corpus* at the grand assize." [8]

In the year 1668, there died in Cambridge "that super-eminent minister of the gospel, Mr. Jonathan Mitchell," and upon his "deplored death" the following epitaph was composed:

> "Here lies the darling of his time,
> Mitchell expirëd in his prime;
> Who four years short of forty-seven,

---

[5] Part of "A Threnodia upon our churches' second dark eclipse, happening July 20, 1663, by death's interposition between us and that great light and divine plant, Mr. Samuel Stone, late of Hartford, in New England," preserved in Morton, "New England's Memorial," 302–3. The poem is signed "E. B.," and is attributed to Edward Bulkley, son of Peter Bulkley of Concord.

[6] "Magnalia," II. 62.   [7] Ibid. I. 145.   [8] Ibid. 148.

New England: The Verse-Writers

>Was found full ripe and plucked for heaven;
>Was full of prudent zeal and love,
>Faith, patience, wisdom from above;
>New England's stay, next age's story,
>The churches' gem, the college glory.
>Angels may speak him—ah! not I,—
>Whose worth's above hyperbole.
>But for our loss, wer't in my power,
>I'd weep an everlasting shower." [9]

Of all the manufacturers of this kind of verse, probably no one, in that period, displayed an alacrity and perseverance equal to John Wilson, the first pastor of Boston, who, as Cotton Mather says, "had so nimble a faculty of putting his devout thoughts into verse, that he signalized himself by . . . sending poems to all persons, in all places, on all occasions, . . . wherein if the curious relished the piety, sometimes, rather than the poetry, the capacity of the most therein to be accommodated must be considered." [10] He was matchless in skill to detect allegories, to invent anagrams, to work out acrostics, and to twist puns and conceits into consolatory verses on mournful occasions; and these verses, steadfastly held to be poetry, were cherished as sacred by the recipients, even as were "the handkerchiefs carried from Paul to uphold the disconsolate." [11] It was most fitting therefore that these shining poetic services of the faithful pastor should be remembered by the poet, who, after John Wilson's death, sought to embalm his memory in some congenial verses, and who addressing New England exclaims:

>"this father will return no more
>To sit the moderator of thy sages.
>But tell his zeal for thee to after ages,
>His care to guide his flock and feed his lambs
>By words, works * prayers, psalms, alms, and anagrams." [12]

[9] In Morton, "New England's Memorial," 341, signed "J. S.," supposed to be either Joshua Scottow, or the Rev. John Sherman of Watertown.
[10] "Magnalia," I. 302.
[11] This comparison is by John Wilson's son, "Magnalia," I. 303.
[12] "Magnalia," I. 320.

[* The comma was still missing in 1897.]

III

Over the early literary annals of New England, there hovers one poetic reminiscence, very slight, perhaps, and dim, but altogether gracious, and worthy of being saved from fading into entire forgetfulness. It is of the presence among our ancestors, for a little while, of a noble-minded clergyman of the English Church, an accomplished scholar, a pleasant Christian gentleman, William Morrell, who came to live in New England in 1623, with the colony under Captain Robert Gorges, at Wessagusset, and who abode in that colony during its brief and unfortunate existence. Upon the failure of the enterprise that had brought him hither, William Morrell, who had in fact come armed with a commission to exercise a superintendency over the churches which should be established in New England, went to the little village of Plymouth; and dwelt there quietly for a whole year among the Pilgrims; he, the English churchman, holding genial fellowship with those peaceful separatists, and courteously forbearing even to mention to them his commission until he was upon the point of leaving them. He was a gentle, meditative, brotherly man; and while living among them, he spent his time chiefly in studying New England—the country, the climate, the white people and the Indians, and in writing an elaborate Latin poem upon the subject.[13] This poem, entitled "Nova Anglia," was published by him in London, in 1625, the Latin text being accompanied by a version, in English rhymed pentameters, done by himself. He wrote good Oxford Latin of the period, and in versification that is blameless. His English rendering of his own Latin, is less a translation than a wide and wandering paraphrase of it; having some felicities here and there, but in the main clumsy and tuneless. He was an Englishman having the accomplishment, not unusual among scholars in that time, of being more expert in the dead language of Rome than in the living language of his own country; for which, probably, he had to thank his English university, then contemptuous of everything English in language and in literature. He introduces his poem by an address to the reader, which at least has the grace of literary humility and of entire accuracy of judgment:

[13] Reprinted in 1 Mass. Hist. Soc. Coll. I. 125-139.

New England: The Verse-Writers

>"If thou, Apollo, hold'st thy sceptre forth
> To these harsh numbers, that's thy royal worth.
> Vain is all search in these to search that vein
> Whose stately style is great Apollo's strain.
> Minerva ne'er distilled into my muse
> Her sacred drops; my pumice * wants all juice.
> My muse is plain, concise; her fame's to tell
> In truth and method. Love or leave. Farewell."

At the opening of the poem, one finds this not unpleasant description of New England:

>"Fear not, poor muse, 'cause first to sing her fame,
> That's yet scarce known, unless by map or name;
> A grand-child to earth's paradise is born,
> Well-limb'd, well-nerv'd, fair, rich, sweet, yet forlorn.
> Thou blest director, so direct my verse
> That it may win her people, friends, commerce;
> Whilst her sweet air, rich soil, blest seas, my pen
> Shall blaze, and tell the natures of her men.
>
> . . .
>
> Westward a thousand leagues, a spacious land
> Is made, unknown to them that it command,
> Of fruitful mould, and no less fruitless main,
> Inrich with springs and prey, highland and plain;
> The light, well-tempered, humid air, whose breath
> Fills full all concaves betwixt heaven and earth,
> So that the region of the air is blest
> With what earth's mortals wish to be possessed."

He thus proceeds to give, at considerable length, a series of pictures —somewhat lacking in distinctness and color—of the climate and productions of the country, of its recent inhabitants, and more particularly of the Indians. The poem culminates in an impassioned appeal for Christian pity and help, on behalf of these dark-minded savages, whose nature

>"Retains not one poor sparkle of true light;"

and in view of their inevitable doom unless rescued by Christian intervention, he utters this sorrowful cry:

[* Changed to "pomace" in 1897.]

> "And now what soul dissolves not into tears,
> That hell must have ten thousand thousand heirs,
> Which have no true light of that truth divine,
> Or sacred wisdom of the eternal Trine!"

His closing lines, which express the author's modest but very noble purpose in writing the poem, leave with us an impression of the lovableness and benignity of his heart, and especially of his generous compassion for the rude and neglected land beyond the western ocean, where he had thus dwelt for a time a gentle and friendly spectator:

> Si mea barbaricae prosint conamina genti;
> Si valet Anglicanis incompta placere poesis,
> Et sibi perfaciles hac reddere gente potentes,
> Assiduosque pios sibi persuadere colonos;
> Si doceat primi vitam victumque parentis;
> Angli si fuerint Indis exempla beate
> Vivendi, capiant quibus ardua limina coeli;
> Omnia succedunt votis; modulamina spero
> Haec mea sublimis fuerint praesagia regni.

His English version of these lines is much closer to the original than is usual with him, and is by no means despicable as poetry:

> "If these poor lines may win this country love,
> Or kind compassion in the English move,
> Persuade our mighty and renownëd state
> This poor blind people to commiserate,
> Or painful men to this good land invite,
> Whose holy works these natives may inlight;
> If heaven grant these, to see here built, I trust,
> An English kingdom from this Indian dust."

IV

There has descended to us from our first literary period one very considerable specimen of English verse, "The Bay Psalm Book," which will be forever memorable among us as a sort of prodigy in that kind,—a poetic phenomenon, happily unique, we may hope, in all the literatures of English speech. This portentous metrical fabric

New England: The Verse-Writers

was the joint production of "the chief divines in the country," [14] each of whom took a separate portion of the original Hebrew for translation; the workmen most conspicuous in the sacred job being Thomas Welde, John Eliot, and Richard Mather. To the one last named was also assigned the duty of writing a preface for the work, in order to explain and commend to the churches the achievement which had been thus prepared for their edification. This preface is a characteristic bit of Puritan prose, very Hebraic in learning, very heroic in conscientiousness, sharp and minute in opinion, quaint in phrase. Of course, he had to deal with the question, then somewhat disturbing, whether the Psalms should be sung "in their own words or in such words as English poetry is wont to run into;" and of course, he establishes the propriety of the latter method. But in thus turning the Psalms of David into verses "which," as he rather hesitantly puts it, "are commonly called metrical," "it hath been one part of our religious care and faithful endeavor to keep close to the original text. . . . If, therefore, the verses are not always so smooth and elegant as some may desire or expect, let them consider that God's altar needs not our polishings, for we have respected rather a plain translation than to smooth our verses with the sweetness of any paraphrase; and so have attended conscience rather than elegance, fidelity rather than poetry." The work thus accurately described, was published at Cambridge, Massachusetts, in 1640,—the first book in English, probably, that ever issued from any printing-press in America.[15] It is entitled "The Whole Book of Psalms, faithfully translated into English Metre," and undoubtedly deserves the preëminence conceded to it by John Nichol,[16] of being "the worst of many bad." In turning over these venerable pages, one suffers by sympathy something of the obvious toil of the undaunted men who, in the very teeth of nature, did all this; and whose appalling sincerity must, in our eyes, cover a multitude of such sins, as sentences wrenched about end for end, clauses heaved up and abandoned in chaos, words disembowelled or split quite in two in the middle, and

---

[14] "Magnalia," I. 407.
[15] The first book, not the first printed production. "The Freeman's Oath" was the first; an almanac was the second; both in 1639. Next came "The Bay Psalm Book." Thomas, "Hist. Printing in Am." I. 46.
[16] In Encyc. Brit. 9th ed. I. 720.

dissonant combinations of sound that are the despair of such poor vocal organs as are granted to human beings. The verses, indeed, seem to have been hammered out on an anvil, by blows from a blacksmith's sledge. Everywhere in the book, is manifest the agony it cost the writers to find two words that would rhyme—more or less; and so often as this arduous feat is achieved, the poetic athlete appears to pause awhile from sheer exhaustion, panting heavily for breath. Let us now read, for our improvement, a part of the Fifty-Eighth Psalm:

> "The wicked are estranged from
>   the womb, they goe astray
> as soone as ever they are borne;
>   uttering lyes are they.
> Their poyson's like serpents poyson:
>   they like deafe Aspe, her eare
> that stops. Though Charmer wisely charme,
>   his voice she will not heare.
> Within their mouth doe thou their teeth
>   break out, o God most strong,
> doe thou Jehovah, the great teeth
>   break of the lions young."

It is pathetic to contemplate the tokens of intellectual anxiety scattered along these pages; the prolonged baffling, perspiration, and discouragement which these good men had to pass through, in order to overcome the metrical problems presented, for example, by the Fifty-First Psalm:

> "Create in mee cleane heart *at* last
>   God: a right spirit in me new make.
> Nor from thy presence quite me cast,
>   thy holy spright not from me take.
> Mee thy salvations joy restore,
>   and stay me with thy spirit free.
> I will transgressors teach thy lore,
>   and sinners shall be turned to thee." [17]

[17] The specimens here given of "The Bay Psalm Book," I take from the copy of the first edition once owned by Thomas Prince, and now in the Boston Public Library.

New England: The Verse-Writers

V

It will not be difficult for the reader to believe that the examples of early American verse that have now been laid before him, were the productions of persons whom it is a charity to call amateurs in the art of poetry. There was, however, belonging to this primal literary period, one poet who, in some worthy sense, found in poetry a vocation. The first professional poet of New England was a woman.

In the year 1650,—a full twelvemonth after the head of Charles the First had fallen upon the block in front of his palace at Whitehall, the very year in which Oliver Cromwell was giving to the Presbyterian Scots on the field of Dunbar a strong dose of English Congregationalism,—there was published, in London, a book of poems written by a gifted young woman of the New England wilderness, Anne Bradstreet by name. This book bore one of those fantastic and long-winded title-pages, at once a table of contents and a printer's puff, that the literary folk of the sixteenth and seventeenth centuries greatly delighted in. It reads thus: "The Tenth Muse lately sprung up in America; or, Several Poems, compiled with great variety of wit and learning, full of delight; wherein especially is contained a complete discourse and description of the four elements, constitutions, ages of man, seasons of the year; together with an exact epitome of the four monarchies, viz., the Assyrian, Persian, Grecian, Roman; also, a dialogue between Old England and New concerning the late troubles; with divers other pleasant and serious poems. By a gentlewoman in those parts. Printed at London, for Stephen Bowtell, at the sign of the Bible, in Pope's Head Alley, 1650." [18]

Perhaps that year, 1650, was not the friendliest year that could be imagined for any Tenth Muse to get the attention of the world, even though she had "lately sprung up in America," and even though the poems she sang were "compiled with great variety of wit and learning, full of delight." Not the Muses, one would say, but rather the Furies had the field just then; and the dulcet notes of any gentle word-music had little chance of being heard, amid the universal din of the crash-

[18] The entire works of Anne Bradstreet, in prose and verse, edited by John Harvard Ellis, were published in sumptuous form at Charlestown, Mass., in 1867; to which volume I refer in the present chapter.

ing footsteps of Mars striding angrily up and down the island, while, in the pauses of his wrathful spasms, the politicians were bent on filling the air with their clamorous and sullen jargon. But whether the time were fortunate, or otherwise, for the publication of Anne Bradstreet's poems, not greatly did it concern Anne Bradstreet herself, far away from London in her rustic mansion, amid the picturesque hills and rough woods of Andover, and within sound of the murmurs of the Merrimac.

She was born in England, in 1612. Her father, Thomas Dudley, an austere Puritan, a man of much study and stern will, had settled down, after some military experience, as steward of the estates of the Puritan nobleman, the Earl of Lincoln. It was while he was in that responsible service, that his brilliant young daughter passed some of her girlhood in the earl's castle of Sempringham; and we may not doubt that a mind so eager for knowledge as was hers, made high festival over the various treasures of books that were gathered there. In the year 1628, when she had reached the age of sixteen, she married the man in whose loving and grave companionship she passed the remainder of her life, Simon Bradstreet, nine years older than herself, of a good family in Suffolk, a graduate of Emmanuel College, Cambridge, educated to business by her own father, a man of Puritan faith and demeanor, God-fearing, and fearing no man. Two years later, the young people joined the great company of wealthy and cultivated Puritans who sailed away to New England, where, thenceforward, Simon Bradstreet steadily advanced in importance, and came to take a great part in matters of church and state, living out a long career there as colonial secretary, judge, legislator, governor, ambassador, and royal councillor, dying at last in great honor, at the great age of ninety-four, the white-haired and wise-tongued Nestor of the Puritan commonwealth.

This coming away from old England to New England was, for many of these wealthy emigrants, a sad sacrifice of taste and personal preference; and for none of them, probably, was it more so than for this girl-wife, Anne Bradstreet, who, with a scholar's thirst for knowledge, and a poet's sensitiveness to the elegant and the ugly, would have delighted in the antique richness and the mellow beauty of English life, as much as she recoiled from the savage surroundings, the scant privileges, the crude, realistic, and shaggy forms of society in America. "After a short time," she says in an autobiographic sketch, "I changed my condition and was married, and came into this country, where I found a new world and new manners, at which my heart rose. But after I was convinced it was the way of God, I submitted to it." [19] But though she thus submitted to her fate, the effort was one that had to be ever-renewed; and in her own writings, as in the writings of her contemporaries, one hears, between the lines, the plaintive cry of their consciousness of being, for a sacred duty and by God's unmistakable will, in a remote exile:

"Remember, Lord, thy folk, whom thou
To wilderness hast brought." [20]

It took several years for her husband and herself to find their way to their permanent home; but in 1644, after many settlements, they settled finally near Andover, where, upon a farm which is still pointed out as the Bradstreet farm, amid noble and inspiring natural scenery, and within the distance of only a mile and a quarter from the Merrimac, she passed the remainder of her life, dying in 1672, at the age of sixty.

So, whatever work this writer wrought, whether good or bad, she wrought in the midst of circumstances that did not altogether help her, but hindered her rather. She was the laborious wife of a New England farmer, the mother of eight children, and herself from childhood of a delicate constitution. The most of her poems were produced between 1630 and 1642, that is, before she was thirty years old; and during these years, she had neither leisure, nor elegant surroundings, nor freedom from anxious thoughts, nor even abounding health. Somehow, during her busy life-time, she contrived to put upon record compositions numerous enough to fill a royal octavo volume of four hundred pages,—compositions which entice and reward our reading of them, two hundred years after she lived.

Perhaps her prose writings, by no means many or long, are likely to be more attractive to the altered tastes of our time, than her poems can be. They consist of a brief sketch of her own life, called "Religious Experiences," and of a series of aphorisms bearing the title

---

[19] Works of Anne Bradstreet, 5.   [20] Ibid. 34.

of "Meditations Divine and Moral." It is in the latter work that we find the best examples of her strength of thought, and of her felicity in condensed and pungent expression: "A ship that bears much sail, and little or no ballast, is easily overset; and that man whose head hath great abilities and his heart little or no grace, is in danger of foundering." [21] "Authority without wisdom, is like a heavy axe without an edge, fitter to bruise than polish." [22] "Iron, till it be throughly heat, is uncapable to be wrought; so God sees good to cast some men into the furnace of affliction, and then beats them on his anvil into what frame he pleases." [23] "We read in Scripture of three sorts of arrows,—the arrow of an enemy, the arrow of pestilence, and the arrow of a slanderous tongue. The two first kill the body, the last the good name; the two former leave a man when he is once dead, but the last mangles him in his grave." [24] "Sore laborers have hard hands, and old sinners have brawny consciences." [25] "We often see stones hang with drops, not from any innate moisture, but from a thick air about them. So may we sometimes see marble-hearted sinners seem full of contrition; but it is not from any dew of grace within, but from some black clouds that impends them, which produces these sweating effects." [26] "Dim eyes are the concomitants of old age; and short-sightedness in those that are eyes of a republic, foretells a declining state." [27] "Ambitious men are like hops, that never rest climbing so long as they have anything to stay upon; but take away their props, and they are of all, the most dejected." [28]

It was, however, as a poet only, that Anne Bradstreet was known in literature to her contemporaries. Our expectations of finding high poetic merit in her work, are not increased by ascertaining the lines of culture through which she trained herself for her calling as poet. Literature, for her, was not a republic of letters, hospitable to all forms of human thought, but a strict Puritan commonwealth, founded on a scheme of narrow ascetic intolerance, and excluding from its citizenship some of the sublimest, daintiest, and most tremendous types of literary expression. Evidently, in her mind, Wil-

[21] Anne Bradstreet, 48.   [22] Ibid. 50.   [23] Ibid. 54.
[24] Ibid. 55.   [25] Ibid. 56.   [26] Ibid. 58–59.
[27] Ibid. 55.   [28] Ibid. 55.

New England: The Verse-Writers

liam Shakespeare, play-wright and actor, was an alien, and a godless person; and Ben Jonson, Massinger, Beaumont and Fletcher, Webster, Ford, Shirley, and all the rest of that superb group of masters, were sons of Belial. Furthermore, while her imagination thus lost the witchery and the stimulation of the great English dramatists, she was taught to seek for the very essence of poetry in the quirks, the puns, the contorted images, the painful ingenuities of George Wither * and Francis Quarles, and especially of "The Divine Weeks and Works" of the French poet Du Bartas, done into English by Joshua Sylvester. In short, she was a pupil of the fantastic school of English poetry—the poetry of the later euphuists; the special note of which is the worship of the quaint, the strained, the disproportionate, the grotesque, and the total sacrifice of the beautiful on the altar of the ingenious. Harmony, taste, dignity, even decency, were by this school eagerly cast away, if only an additional twist could be given to the turn of a metaphor, or still another antithesis could be wrenched from the agonies of a weary epithet. It is easy enough to find in the writings of Anne Bradstreet grotesque passages, preposterous stuff, jingling abominations; but we shall only mislead ourselves, if we look upon these as traits peculiarly characteristic of this writer, or of American verse-writing in the seventeenth century. They were, rather, the symptoms of a wider and far deeper literary disease —a disease which, originating in Italy in the sixteenth † century, swept westward and northward like the plague, desolating for a time the literatures of Spain, of France, and of England. The worst lines of Anne Bradstreet and of the other American verse-writers in the seventeenth century, can be readily matched for fantastic perversion, and for the total absence of beauty, by passages from the poems of John Donne, George Herbert, Crashaw, Cleveland, Wither,‡ Quarles, Thomas Coryat, John Taylor, and even of Herrick, Cowley, and Dryden.[29]

[* Changed to "George Herbert." A penciled question mark appears in the margin of the correction copy.]

[† Changed to "fifteenth."]

[‡ Changed to "Waller." A marginal note reads: "Prof Lounsbury thinks Wither is wrongly classed as of the 'metaphysical poets': & he is right."]

[29] The later English euphuists were called by Dr. Johnson "the metaphysical poets," a description that does not describe them. Perhaps Milton's phrase is

Glancing over the entire field of Anne Bradstreet's poems, we find them to include, first, a number of minor pieces, such as elegies, epitaphs, and complimentary verses; second, two longer poems entitled "A Dialogue between Old England and New," and "Contemplations;" and third, a series of huge and heavy poems wherein the topics are grouped together in quaternions. The first of these quaternions is named "The Four Elements;" and some description of this poem will give us a sufficient idea of the method and spirit of all the poems that constitute the group. The personages of the poem are four, Fire, Air, Earth, and Water; and upon occasion they

> "did contest
> Which was the strongest, noblest, and the best,
> Who was of greatest use and mightiest force." [30]

Each of these potent beings is represented as having a very high opinion of her own merits, and as disposed to assert this opinion with all the loquacity and controversial vehemence of a theological wrangle in the seventeenth century:

> "All would be chief, and all scorned to be under;
> Whence issued winds and rains, lightning and thunder.
> The quaking earth did groan, the sky looked black;
> The Fire, the forcëd Air, in sunder crack;
> The sea did threat the heavens, the heavens the earth,
> All lookëd like a chaos or new birth:
> Fire broilëd Earth, and scorchëd Earth it choked:
> Both by their darings Water so provoked
> That roaring in it came, and with its source
> Soon made the combatants abate their force.
> The rumbling, hissing, puffing was so great,
> The world's confusion it did seem to threat." [31]

All this smoke and pother are over the small question of priority between the Four Elements, in the privilege of making the harangues

---

the best one—the "fantastics." What Donne and his poetic associates were to English literature, that were Marini to Italian literature, Gongora to Spanish, Du Bartas to French. For accounts of the "conceited" epoch in English Literature, see Henry Morley, "First Sketch of Eng. Lit." 526–532; Thomas Arnold, "Manual of Eng. Lit." 160–164; Taine, "Hist. Eng. Lit." I. 201–206.

[30] Works of Anne Bradstreet, 103.   [31] Ibid. 103.

New England: The Verse-Writers

in which each is to let forth her own preëminent merits, and to denounce, after the good old fashion of theological debaters, the vices and impotencies of all competitors. The difficulty is at last composed by an agreement that Fire should have the floor first, and be followed, in order, by Earth, Water, and Air. Whereupon Fire springs to her feet, and makes a hot and learned speech, recounting her valuable services in the mechanic arts, in warfare, in cookery, in chemistry, and in other mundane employments; then waxing self-complacent, and leaving these lowly utilities, she proceeds to claim the glory and the beauty of the warm and illuminating orbs that blaze in the sky:

> "my flame aspires
> To match on high with the celestial fires." [32]

She asserts for herself, in particular, the honor of the annual blessing which the sun works upon the Earth:

> "How doth his warmth refresh thy frozen back,
> And trim thee brave in green, after thy black.
> Both man and beast rejoice at his approach,
> And birds do sing to see his glittering coach." [33]

After much discourse about her astrological operations, she boasts of her volcanic eruptions, and of all the mighty cities that she has consumed, and points prophetically to her final and most triumphant exertion of power when all things upon earth shall surrender to her flames:

> "And in a word, the world I shall consume,
> And all therein, at that great day of doom." [34]

Having made this glowing speech, Fire takes her seat, and Earth mounts the rostrum, showing herself not inferior to Fire in valiant braggadocio, and in the will to retort upon Fire in many a characteristic taunt and quip. Then,

> "Scarce Earth had done, but the angry Water moved:
> Sister, quoth she, it had full well behoved

[32] Works of Anne Bradstreet, 105. [33] Ibid. 106.
[34] Ibid. 108.

245

> Among your boastings to have praisëd me,
> Cause of your fruitfulness as you shall see.
>
> . . .
>
> Not one of us, all knows, that's like to thee—
> Ever in craving from the other three.
> But thou art bound to me above the rest,
> Who am thy drink, thy blood, thy sap and best.
> If I withhold, what art thou? Dead, dry lump,
> Thou bearest nor grass nor plant nor tree nor stump.
> Thy extreme thirst is moistened by my love
> With springs below and showers from above;
> Or else thy sunburnt face and gaping chops
> Complain to the heavens if I withhold my drops." [35]

The speech of Water, though rather a dry one, is equal to the others, perhaps, in the flow of its fanfaronade. By the dire calamity of droughts she argues, in converse fashion, her own utility to man and beast; she mentions proudly all her "fountains, rivers, lakes, and ponds," her "sundry seas, black and white," her various curative waters, her mysterious tides, her dews, the value of her oceans and rivers to the traffic of the world; and, finally, she illustrates her greatness by the destruction and havoc worked upon the world through her great floods, those of Deucalion, Noah, and others. At last she ends:

> "Much might I say of wracks, but that I'll spare
> And now give place unto our sister, Air." [36]

Upon the whole, Madam Air is rather the most voluble and expert of all, in this contest of braggart speech-making. With a sort of meek self-complacency, as thanking God for her humility, she thus sets out upon her oration:

> "Content, quoth Air, to speak the last of you,
> Yet am not ignorant first was my due.
> I do suppose you'll yield without control,
> I am the breath of every living soul.
> Mortals, what one of you that loves not me
> Abundantly more than my sisters three?
>
> . . .

[35] Works of Anne Bradstreet, 114.   [36] Ibid. 118.

New England: The Verse-Writers

> I ask the man condemned, that's near his death,
> Now gladly should his gold purchase his breath.
>
> . . .
>
> No, Earth, thy witching trash were all but vain
> If my pure air thy sons did not sustain.
>
> . . .
>
> Nay, what are words which do reveal the mind?
> Speak who or what they will, they are but wind.
> Your drums, your trumpets, and your organs' sound,
> What is't but forcëd air which doth rebound?
> And such are echoes and report of th' gun
> That tells afar the exploit which it hath done.
> Your songs and pleasant tunes, they are the same,
> And so's the notes which nightingales do frame.
> Ye forging smiths, if bellows once were gone,
> Your red-hot work more coldly would go on.
> Ye mariners, 'tis I that fill your sails
> And speed you to your port with wishëd gales.
> When burning heat doth cause you faint, I cool;
> And when I smile, your ocean's like a pool.
> I help to ripe the corn, I turn the mill,
> And with myself I every vacuum fill.
> The ruddy, sweet sanguine is like to Air,
> And youth and spring, sages to me compare." [37]

In continuing this rehearsal of her merits, she gives a list of her "fowls"—the feathery inhabitants of her empire; she speaks of her force when offended, as shown in fevers and in pestilences, and especially in tempests, exclaiming:

> "How many rich-fraught vessels have I split?
> Some upon sands, some upon rocks, have hit;
> Some have I forced to gain an unknown shore;
> Some overwhelmed with waves and seen no more." [38]

There is no little poetic vividness in her picture of the airy battles sometimes fought in her sky, and of the dreadful signals which these high phenomena hold out over the earth:

[37] Works of Anne Bradstreet, 119–120. [38] Ibid. 121.

"Then what prodigious sights I sometimes show:
As battles pitched in th' air, as countries know,
Their joining, fighting, forcing, and retreat,
That earth appears in heaven, O wonder great!
Sometimes red, flaming swords and blazing stars,
Portentous signs of famines, plagues, and wars,
Which make the mighty monarchs fear their fates,
By death or great mutation of their states." [39]

The last poem of this series, "The Four Monarchies," is by far the longest and most ambitious. It is simply a rhymed chronicle of ancient history from Nimrod to Tarquinius Superbus, following very closely Sir Walter Raleigh's "History of the World." Heavy as the poem seems to us, to the first generation of her readers, doubtless, it seemed the most precious issue of her genius. It commended itself to the sturdy and careful minds of her Puritan constituency, as useful poetry. They could read it without any twinges of self-reproach; it was not too pleasant; it was not trivial or antic or amusing; they were in no danger of losing their souls, by being borne away on the vain and airy enticements of frivolous words; then, best of all, it was not poetic fiction, but solid fact. Very likely, they gave to her their choicest praise, and called her, for this work, a painful poet; in which compliment every modern reader will most cordially join.

Of course, Anne Bradstreet had ample precedents in English literature for this form of poetry.[40] Of course, too, she was grossly misled; since poetry is nothing, if it is nothing more than rhymed historical teaching. The fatal taint in all her poetical life was that, badly instructed by her literary guides, she too generally drew her materials from books rather than from nature. How much better, had she bravely looked within her own heart, and out upon the real world, and given voice to herself rather than to mere erudition! What she could have done in this way, she has partly shown in "Contemplations," the very best of her poems. It was written late in her life, at her home in Andover, and is a genuine expression of poetic feeling

---

[39] Works of Anne Bradstreet, 122.

[40] For example, "The Mirror for Magistrates," Daniel's "History of the Civil Wars," and Drayton's "Barons' Wars," to say nothing of the early chronicles, many of which were in verse.

New England: The Verse-Writers

in the presence of nature; not a laborious transfusion into metre of leaden historical items.

She stands confronting the gorgeous array of the forests when robed in their October tints:

> "Sometime now past in the autumnal tide,
> When Phœbus wanted but one hour to bed,
> The trees all richly clad, yet void of pride,
> Were gilded o'er by his rich golden head." [41]

Her eye advances from one glorious object to another, "the stately oak," "the glistering sun," and from each she evokes some noble suggestion:

> "Silent, alone, where none or saw or heard,
> In pathless paths I led my wandering feet;
> My humble eyes to lofty skies I reared
> To sing some song my mazëd muse thought meet." [42]

At last, she reaches the banks of the beautiful river whose massive, potent, and calm presence must often have been to her a soothing and strengthening refuge:

> "Under the cooling shadow of a stately elm,
> Close sat I by a goodly river's side,
> Where gliding streams the rocks did overwhelm;
> A lonely place, with pleasures dignified.
> I once that loved the shady woods so well,
> Now thought the rivers did the trees excel,
> And if the sun would ever shine, there would I dwell.
>
> While on the stealing stream I fixed mine eye,
> Which to the longed for ocean held its course,
> I marked nor crooks, nor rubs, that there did lie,
> Could hinder aught, but still augment its force:
> O happy flood, quoth I, that holds thy race
> Till thou arrive at thy belovëd place.
> Nor is it rocks or shoals that can obstruct thy pace.
>
> Nor is't enough that thou alone may'st slide,
> But hundred brooks in thy clear waves do meet;

[41] Works of Anne Bradstreet, 370.   [42] Ibid. 372.

So hand in hand along with thee they glide
  To Thetis' house, where all embrace and greet.
Thou emblem true of what I count the best,
O could I lead my rivulets to rest,
So may we pass to that vast mansion, ever blest.

. . .

While musing thus, with contemplation fed,
  And thousand fancies buzzing in my brain,
The sweet-tongued Philomel perched o'er my head,
  And chanted forth a most melodious strain,
Which rapt me so with wonder and delight,
I judged my hearing better than my sight,
And wished me wings with her awhile to take my flight." [43]

This strain of music from the "merry bird" draws, likewise, from the poet a rapturous eulogy upon the free, sweet life of the songster, that

"Feels no sad thoughts, nor cruciating cares."

With this, she contrasts the worried and baffled existence of man, who nevertheless clings to that which is so unsatisfying:

"And yet this sinful creature, frail and vain,
  This lump of wretchedness, of sin and sorrow,
This weather-beaten vessel wracked with pain,
  Joys not in hope of an eternal morrow." [44]

Through this rather conventional path of reflection she proceeds till, in the final stanza of the poem, she rises to an altitude of noble and even stately song:

"O Time, the fatal wrack of mortal things,
That draws oblivion's curtains over kings:
Their sumptuous monuments, men know them not;
Their names without a record are forgot;
Their parts, their ports, their pomps, all laid in th' dust:
Nor wit, nor gold, nor buildings, scape time's rust.
But he whose name is graved in the white stone
Shall last and shine, when all of these are gone." [45]

[43] Works of Anne Bradstreet, 377.   [44] Ibid. 380.
[45] Ibid. 381.

New England: The Verse-Writers

This poem of "Contemplations" is not the only one in which Anne Bradstreet, liberated from her book-learning, has shown the power that was in her of giving strong and poetic expression to her own feeling. There is a little poem written within a few months of her death, entitled "Longing for Heaven," which has in it some lines of genuine pathos, simplicity, and verbal grace:

> "As weary pilgrim now at rest
> Hugs with delight his silent nest;
> His wasted limbs now lie full soft,
> That miry steps have trodden oft;
> Blesses himself to think upon
> His dangers past, and travails done;
>
> . . .
>
> A pilgrim I, on earth perplexed,
> With sins, with cares and sorrows vexed,
> By age and pains brought to decay,
> And my clay house mouldering away,
> Oh, how I long to be at rest
> And soar on high among the blest." [46]

Very naturally, she was a writer of hymns; and of these we must frankly say that they are bad enough. Nevertheless, when compared with the cacophonous and jagged productions of her hymnological contemporaries in New England, they seem marvels of music, and of fluent skill.

It is interesting to trace in her poems the tokens of the opinions she held concerning the politics of those times, by which must be meant the affairs of church as well as of state, in England as well as in America. In her poem of "Old England and New," she has given a vigorous statement of the questions then at issue in the mother-land. Though she sided with parliament, she was by no means inclined to democratic opinions. On the ecclesiastical side of politics, however, she held without reserve the most sweeping anti-Romanist, and anti-Ritualist conclusions:

> "These are the days the church's foes to crush,
> To root out Popelings, head, tail, branch, and rush.

[46] Works of Anne Bradstreet, 42–43.

History of American Literature

> Let's bring Baal's vestments forth to make a fire,
> Their mitres, surplices, and all their tire,
> Copes, rochets, crosiers, and such empty trash,
> And let their names consume, but let the flash
> Light Christendom and all the world, to see
> We hate Rome's Whore with all her trumpery." [47]

The invective of these ringing lines, verging well toward satire, is not a solitary example of her capacity in that direction. Indeed, a sort of grim mirth now and then relaxes the severity of her verse, and expresses itself in a half-playful sarcasm. Thus,

> "one would more glad
> With a tame fool converse, than with a mad." [48]

The traditional disparagement by men, of the intelligence of her sex, of course she felt,—the sting of it, the wrong of it; and she resented it, sometimes in the form of a sarcastic reference, sometimes in that of an ironical admission that hers was indeed "a less noble gender," and sometimes in that of a superb and defiant denial. For instance, as a woman, she seemed to take vast pleasure in the magnificent career of Queen Elizabeth:

> "She hath wiped off the aspersion of her sex,
> That women wisdom lack to play the Rex." [49]

Appealing to the universal and enthusiastic pride of Englishmen in the imperial greatness of their recent woman-monarch, the poet, in a flash, retaliates upon masculine detraction, with this keen and glorious thrust:

> "Now say, have women worth, or have they none?
> Or had they some, but with our Queen is't gone?
> Nay, masculines, you have thus taxed us long;
> But she, though dead, will vindicate our wrong.
> Let such as say our sex is void of reason,
> Know 'tis a slander now, but once was treason." [50]

Upon the whole, it is impossible to deny that Anne Bradstreet was sadly misguided by the poetic standards of her religious sect and of

[47] Works of Anne Bradstreet, 340–341.   [48] Ibid. 145.
[49] Ibid. 359.   [50] Ibid. 361.

New England: The Verse-Writers

her literary period, and that the vast bulk of her writings consists not of poetry, but of metrical theology and chronology and politics and physics. Yet, amid all this lamentable rubbish, there is often to be found such an ingot of genuine poetry, as proves her to have had, indeed, the poetic endowment. Of her own claims as a writer of verse, she kept for herself a very modest estimate; and in the Prologue to her volume, she speaks of her writings in diffident lines, whose merit alone would prompt us to grant to her a higher poetic rank than she herself asks for:

"And oh, ye high flown quills that soar the skies,
And ever with your prey still catch your praise;
If e'er you deign these lowly lines your eyes,
Give thyme and parsley wreaths: I ask no bays.
This mean and unrefinëd ore of mine
Will make your glistering gold but more to shine." [51]

[51] Ibid. 102. In the last line but one I have substituted "ore" for "ure," which, in spite of the explanation of the latest editor of her works, I think to be a misprint in the first edition. This may be a suitable place in which to mention the interesting fact that among the lineal descendants of this noble personage—this "Gentlewoman of New England" as she was designated on the title-page of the first edition of her poems, this "peerless gentlewoman" as John Norton calls her—are included the Channings, the Buckminsters, Eliza B. Lee, Richard H. Dana the poet, Richard H. Dana the prose-writer, Wendell Phillips, and Oliver Wendell Holmes.

SECOND COLONIAL PERIOD: 1676–1765

AMERICAN LITERATURE

SECOND COLONIAL PERIOD: 1676–1765

Writers of Narration and Description
- Thomas Budd
- William Byrd
- Daniel Coxe
- Jonathan Dickenson, of Pa.
- Daniel Denton
- Lewis Evans
- Richard Frame
- Hugh Jones
- Sarah Kemble Knight
- John Lawson
- Mary Rowlandson
- Patrick Tailfer
- Gabriel Thomas
- John Williams

Historical and Biographical Writers
- Robert Beverley
- Benjamin Church
- Cadwallader Colden
- John Callender
- Thomas Clap
- William Douglass
- William Hubbard
- Increase Mather
- Cotton Mather
- Samuel Mather
- Samuel Niles
- Samuel Penhallow
- Thomas Prince
- William Smith, of N. Y.
- Samuel Smith
- William Stith
- Ebenezer Turell

Theological and Religious Writers
- James Blair
- Mather Byles
- John Barnard
- Charles Chauncey
- Benjamin Colman
- Thomas Clap
- Jonathan Dickinson, of N. J.
- Samuel Davies
- Jonathan Edwards
- Alexander Garden
- John Higginson
- William Hubbard
- Samuel Johnson
- Increase Mather
- Cotton Mather
- Samuel Mather
- Jonathan Mayhew
- Urian Oakes
- Thomas Prince
- William Smith, of Pa.
- Samuel Sewall
- Solomon Stoddard
- William Stoughton
- Samuel Willard

AMERICAN LITERATURE

SECOND COLONIAL PERIOD: 1676–1765—*Continued*

Writers upon Science
- John Banister
- John Bartram
- John Clayton
- Cadwallader Colden
- Thomas Clap
- William Douglass
- Jonathan Edwards
- Jared Eliot
- Benjamin Franklin
- Alexander Garden, M.D.
- Samuel Johnson
- James Logan
- John Mitchell
- John Winthrop, of Harvard Coll.

Miscellaneous Prose Writers
- Nathaniel Ames
- Robert Calef
- Jeremiah Dummer
- Benjamin Franklin
- Daniel Leeds
- William Livingston
- Lewis Morris
- William Smith, of Pa.
- Samuel Sewall
- Joshua Scottow
- John Webbe
- John Wise

Writers of Verse
- John Adams
- Joseph Breintnal
- Henry Brooke
- Mather Byles
- Benjamin Colman
- Ebenezer Cook
- Peter Folger
- Thomas Godfrey
- Joseph Green
- Francis Knapp
- William Livingston
- John Maylem
- Nicholas Noyes
- John Norton
- Urian Oakes
- Peter Oliver
- John Osborn
- Authors of Pietas et Gratulatio
- Aquila Rose
- John Rogers
- John Seccomb
- Joseph Shippen
- Jane Turell
- Benjamin Tompson
- Jacob Taylor
- George Webb
- Michael Wigglesworth
- Samuel Wigglesworth
- Roger Wolcott

Chapter XI

New England. The Verse-Writers

I. The two literary periods in our colonial age—Their points of distinction—The times and the men—Our intended line of march through the second period.

II. John Norton—His poem on the death of Anne Bradstreet—John Rogers—His poetic praise of Anne Bradstreet.

III. Urian Oakes—His high literary gifts—His elegy on the death of Thomas Shepard.

IV. Peter Folger, the ballad-writer—Benjamin Tompson, the satirist.

V. Michael Wigglesworth, the sturdy rhymer of New England Calvinism—His great popularity—Puts into verse the glooms and the comforts of the prevailing faith—The realistic poet of hell-fire—"God's Controversy with New England"—"Meat out of the Eater"—"The Day of Doom"—Synopsis of the latter poem—Its wide diffusion and influence—His son, Samuel Wigglesworth, a true poet—"A Funeral Song" by the latter.

VI. Nicholas Noyes, the last and greatest of our Fantastics—His fine personal career—The monstrosities of his muse—Prefatory poem on the "Magnalia"—Lines on John Higginson—Elegy on Joseph Green—Verses on the painful malady of a Reverend friend.

VII. Strong influence in America of the contemporary English poets, especially Pope, Blackmore, Watts, Thomson, Young—Echoes of them in Francis Knapp, Benjamin Colman, Jane Turell, Mather Byles—The career and poetry of Roger Wolcott—His Connecticut epic—His "Poetical Meditations."

VIII. Humorous poetry—John Seccomb and his burlesque verses—The facetiousness of Joseph Green—His impromptus—His "Entertainment for a Winter Evening."

IX. War-verses—Popular ballads—"Lovewell's Fight"—Tilden's "Miscellaneous Poems"—John Maylem, Philo-Bellum—His "Conquest of Louisburg"—His "Gallic Perfidy."

X. A group of serious singers—John Adams—His accomplishments and poetry—"Poems by Several Hands"—Peter Oliver, the literary politician—His poem in honor of Josiah Willard.

XI. "Pietas et Gratulatio"—Its occasion—Its authors—A burst of American loyalty to the English monarchs—Its Greek and Latin verses—Its English verses—Apotheosis of George the Second—Salutation to George the Third.

I

I HAVE taken the year sixteen hundred and seventy-six as the year of partition between the two periods into which our colonial age seems to fall. By a coincidence that is almost dramatic, that year proved to be one of spacious import for both the great English communities then planted in America, and then holding within themselves the types and the hopes of all possible English civilization in the new world. Alike for Virginia and for New England, it was a year in which most doleful mischief, long gathering force from the crimes and the blunders of men, came to its culmination, exploded, and passed away;—a year of fright, of fury, of outcry and blood and battle-agony, and at last of the sort of silence that is called peace. In that year, Virginia saw the crisis and close of the patriotic insurrection of its own people under the hero, Nathaniel Bacon; in that year, New England saw the crisis and close of the conspiracy of its exasperated Indians under the hero, Philip. For those two central English communities in America, and for all other English communities that should afterward be grouped around them or issue from them, the year sixteen hundred and seventy-six established two very considerable facts, namely, that English colonists in America could be so provoked as to make physical resistance to the authority of England; and, second, that English colonists in America could, in the last resort, put down any combination of Indians that might be formed against them. In other words, it was then made evident that English colonists would certainly be safe in the new world, and also that they would not always be colonists. That year completed the proofs that

New England: The Verse-Writers

a certain uncounted throng of articulating bipeds, known as Americans—together with the words that they should articulate—were to be endured on this planet, for some ages to come.

Let us turn away, now, from the significance of those events which, at the end of a long and troubled sequence, came to an issue in sixteen hundred and seventy-six, and glance for a moment at the men and women who, in that year, constituted the larger part of the population of the English colonies. Here, at length, we confront a new race of beings under the sun: people who loved England, but had never seen England; who always called England home, but had never been at home; who spoke and wrote the English language, but had learned to do so three or four thousand miles from the island in which that language had been hitherto cooped up. Before sixteen hundred and seventy-six, the new civilization in America was principally in the hands of Americans born in England; after sixteen hundred and seventy-six, it was principally in the hands of Americans born in America, and the subjects of such training as was to be had here. Our first colonial period, therefore, transmits to us a body of writings produced by immigrant Americans; preserving for us the ideas, the moods, the efforts, the very phrases, of the men who founded the American nation; representing to us, also, the earliest literary results flowing from the reactions of life in the new world upon an intellectual culture formed in the old world. Our second colonial period does more; it transmits to us a body of writings, produced in the main by the American children of those immigrants, and representing the earliest literary results flowing from the reactions of life in the new world upon an intellectual culture that was itself formed in the new world.

Our first colonial period, just seventy years long, we have now studied with full and earnest care; we have held up before our eyes the tattered and time-stained memorials of its literary activity; we have listened attentively to its multitudinous voices, hushed by death two centuries ago. Each reader has now before him the materials out of which to construct for himself the praise, or the contempt, which he is willing to bestow upon that period. For my part, I have no apology to make for it: I think it needs none. It was a period principally engaged in other tasks than the tasks of the pen; it laid, quietly and well, the foundation of a new social structure that was to cover a hemisphere, was to give shelter and comfort to myriads of the human race, was to endure to centuries far beyond the gropings of our guesswork. Had it done that deed alone, and left no written word at all, not any man since then could have wondered; still less could any man have flung at it the reproach of intellectual lethargy or neglect. But if, besides what it did in the founding of a new commonwealth, we consider what it also did in the founding of a new literature—the muchness * of that special work, the downright merit of it—we shall find it hard to withhold from that period the homage of our admiration.

From the year sixteen hundred and seventy-six, when our first colonial period ends, there stretches onward a space of just eighty-nine years, at the end of which the American colonies underwent a swift and portentous change,—losing, all at once, their colonial content, and passing suddenly into the earlier and the intellectual stage of their struggle for independence. This space of eighty-nine years forms, of course, our second colonial period; and it is this which we are now to study.

For the most of this period, and for most purposes of investigation, our history is but a bundle of anecdotes telling of detached groups of communities,—each group working out its own life in its own way, and uttering in some fashion of frank speech its own uppermost thought. Here, at the farthest north, we rest our eyes upon the New England group of communities; thence, passing along the coast, we encounter the group of the middle colonies, New York, New Jersey, Pennsylvania; finally, the southern group, Maryland, Virginia, the two Carolinas, and Georgia. Between the several members of each group there were, perhaps, special intimacies, domestic, commercial, military, religious; but between the several groups there were almost no intimacies at all.

Moving across this tract of time, we shall make research for whatever writings were produced within it by these clustered populations of Americans. It will be convenient for us to begin with New England, and to proceed in geographical order southward.

Of nearly all the writers that we are now to deal with, it may be

[* Changed to "largeness."]

New England: The Verse-Writers

said that they did their most significant work within the limits which we have assigned to our second colonial period; and yet some of them, the eldest, began their work before that period began; and others, the youngest, perhaps continued their work after that period ended. In order to give a satisfactory account of them, we shall occasionally find ourselves flitting back, and committing trespass upon the territory which we profess to have abandoned, or even, it may be, advancing into that territory to which in this volume we shall not try to lay claim.

The topic that last engaged our notice, in the literary period just closed, was the verse-writers of New England; and this topic is the one with which we shall begin our study of the period now to be opened,—thus taking up the thread of the story at the very point where we laid it down. We became somewhat acquainted with the poet, Anne Bradstreet, the only person of an avowed and special vocation in poetry that New England had in its earliest age. The first two poets that we meet on the threshold of our new studies, were men who had grown up in New England under the influence of Anne Bradstreet's fame; who were, in some sense, her literary children; and who have left verses in praise of her, that constitute their own best title to praise.

II

Of these two poets, one was John Norton, nephew of the famous Boston minister of the same name; born in 1651; graduated at Harvard in 1671; pastor of the first church at Hingham from 1678 till his death in 1716; during all that time publishing only an election sermon, in 1708, and still earlier, in 1678, a poem occasioned by the death of Anne Bradstreet. It is this poem, "A Funeral Elogy upon that pattern and patron of virtue," that will preserve for him a high and permanent memory among the few real singers of our colonial time. We know not what else he did in verse; but, certainly, the force and beauty that are in this little poem could not have been caught at one grasp of the hand. His poetical strokes were by no means sure; the literary taint of the time had smitten him; and even in this sorrowful and stately chant, he once or twice slipped into grotesqueness of conceit, and funereal frivolity. Yet, here is something more than mechanic poetry, something other than inspiration of the thumbnail. To this young American scholar and poet, just then at the opening of his active career, his mind brimming with the imagery of the antique classics, the death of Anne Bradstreet—their one glorious example of poetic power in New England—seemed to come as a sort of elemental loss, a bereavement and a darkening of the earth, at which the sky itself and all its splendid tenants would put on mourning. Therefore, with the fine exaggerating speech of his passion, he cries out:

> "Ask not why the great glory of the sky,
> That gilds the stars with heavenly alchemy,
>
> . . .
>
> Ask not the reason of his ecstasy,
> Paleness of late, in midnoon majesty;
> Why that the pale-faced Empress of the night
> Disrobed her brother of his glorious light.
> Did not the language of the stars foretell
> A mournful scene, when they with tears did swell?
> Did not the glorious people of the sky
> Seem sensible of future misery?
>
> . . .
>
> Behold how tears flow from the learnëd hill;
> How the bereavëd Nine do daily fill
> The bosom of the fleeting air with groans
> And woful accents, which witness their moans."

As he dwells upon it, her death seems so cruel a theft from the world of what the world could ill spare, that his grief passes into wrath:

> "Some do for anguish weep; for anger, I,
> That Ignorance should live, and Art should die.
> Black, fatal, dismal, inauspicious day!
>
> . . .
>
> Be it the first of miseries to all,
> Or last of life defamed for funeral.
> When this day yearly comes, let every one
> Cast in their urn the black and dismal stone.

New England: The Verse-Writers

>   Succeeding years, as they their circuit go,
>   Leap o'er this day, as a sad time of woe."

Then, as this indignant gust has uttered itself, he turns in direct and reverent salutation to the dead poet, for whom he mourns:

>   "Grave Matron, whoso seeks to blazon thee,
>   Needs not make use of wit's false heraldry;
>   Whoso should give thee all thy worth, would swell
>   So high, as 'twould turn the world infidel.
>
>   .   .   .
>
>   To write is easy; but to write on thee,
>   Truth would be thought to forfeit modesty.
>
>   .   .   .
>
>   Virtue ne'er dies: time will a poet raise,
>   Born under better stars, shall sing thy praise.
>   Praise her who list, yet he shall be a debtor;
>   For Art ne'er feigned, nor Nature framed, a better.
>   Her virtues were so great, that they do raise
>   A work to trouble fame, astonish praise.
>
>   .   .   .
>
>   Beneath her feet, pale Envy bites her chain,
>   And Poison-Malice whets her sting in vain.
>   Let every laurel, every myrtle bough,
>   Be stript for leaves to adorn and load her brow:
>   Victorious wreaths, which, 'cause they never fade,
>   Wise elder times for kings and poets made.
>   Let not her happy memory e'er lack
>   Its worth in Fame's eternal almanac,
>   Which none shall read, but straight their loss deplore,
>   And blame their fates they were not born before." [1]

Somewhat older than John Norton, but associated with him in poetic genius and in devotion to Anne Bradstreet, was John Rogers; a strong and famous man in his day; one of the early presidents of Harvard College; in his own person an example of that versatility of gifts which American life has always had in it some peculiar force to develop,—preacher, physician, linguist, scientist, educator, poet. In

---

[1] The entire poem is in "The Works of Anne Bradstreet," J. H. Ellis's ed. 409–413.

1649, at the age of eighteen, he was graduated at Harvard College; from 1656 to 1683, he lived at Ipswich, physician both to the bodies and to the souls of men; in August, 1683, he was inaugurated as president of Harvard College; and on the second of July, 1684, during an eclipse of the sun, he died. The tradition of him brings to us a man of uncommon grace of mind and sweetness of temper, of all gentlemanly and scholarly accomplishments; in fact, "a treasury of benevolence, a storehouse of theologic learning, a library of the choicest literature, a living system of medicine, an embodiment of integrity, a repository of faith, a pattern of Christian sympathy, a garner of all virtues." [2] Of course, his portrait hangs upon the walls of the "Magnalia," [3]—a portrait to which is attached the inevitable Matheresque ear-mark, as follows. One day, while president of the college, it happened that his prayer in chapel was only about half as long as usual,—a phenomenon agreeable, doubtless, to the students, but quite inexplicable to them. Indeed, at the moment, no human being knew why that presidential prayer had come to an end so soon; but, as Cotton Mather judiciously remarks, "Heaven knew the reason." The college was on fire; and had it not been for the inspired brevity of the president's devotions that day, it "had been irrevocably laid in ashes." One almost shudders now to contemplate the fascinating motive to collegiate incendiarism, which this memorable providence must have suggested thenceforward, for many generations, to the undergraduate mind,—a possible explanation, indeed, of the numerous conflagrations which, since that time, have desolated the Harvard Yard.

Nearly all memorials of John Rogers's work as a writer have perished. One little poem of his, however, remains, a poem addressed to Anne Bradstreet, and, probably, first published in 1678; a monument of the keen enthusiasm which the writings of that admirable woman awakened among the bright young scholars of New England, during the latter part of her own life and for some years afterward; a monument, also, of its author's literary culture, and of his really high faculty of poetic utterance. The framework of this poem is a

[2] As may be imagined, this quotation is originally from his tomb-stone; in spite of which, there is reason to believe that it is, in the main, true.
[3] Volume II. 16–17.

modified form of the Chaucerian stanza, the variation being very sweet and effective; the order of the rhymes is slightly changed, and the seventh line rolls on into a sonorous Alexandrine. Though, in one place, the poem lapses into a conceit that is gross, and, in fact, damnable, upon the whole it is very noble; it is of high and sustained imaginative expression; it shows, likewise, that this Puritan scholar of our little college in the New England wilderness, had not only conversed to good purpose with the classics of pagan antiquity, but had even dared to overleap the barriers interposed by his own sect between themselves and the more dreadful Christian classics of the Elizabethan singers:

> "Madam, twice through the Muses' grove I walked,
>   Under your blissful bowers, I shrouding there.
> It seemed with nymphs of Helicon I talked;
>   For there those sweet-lipped sisters sporting were;
> Apollo with his sacred lute sate by;
> On high they made their heavenly sonnets fly;
> Posies around they strewed, of sweetest poesy.
>
> Twice have I drunk the nectar of your lines,
>   Which high sublimed my mean-born fantasy.
> Flushed with these streams of your Maronian wines,
>   Above myself rapt to an ecstasy,
> Methought I was upon Mount Hybla's top,
> There where I might those fragrant flowers lop,
> Whence did sweet odors flow, and honey-spangles drop.
>
> . . .
>
> Nor barking satyr's breath, nor dreary clouds,
>   Exhaled from Styx, their dismal drops distil
> Within these fairy, flowery fields; nor shrouds
>   The screeching night-raven, with his shady quill;
> But lyric strings here Orpheus nimbly hits,
> Orion on his saddled dolphin sits,
> Chanting as every humor, age, and season fits.
>
> Here silver swans with nightingales set spells,
>   Which sweetly charm the traveller, and raise
> Earth's earthèd monarchs from their hidden cells,
>   And to appearance summon lapsèd days.

There heavenly air becalms the swelling frays,
And fury fell of elements, allays,
By paying every one due tribute of his praise.

This seemed the site of all those verdant vales,
   And purlëd springs, whereat the nymphs do play;
With lofty hills where poets read their tales
   To heavenly vaults, which heavenly sounds repay
By echo's sweet rebound; here ladies kiss,
Circling, nor songs nor dance's circle miss;
But whilst those sirens sung, I sunk in sea of bliss.

      .   .   .

Your only hand, those posies did compose;
   Your head, the source whence all those springs did flow;
Your voice, whence change's sweetest notes arose;
   Your feet, that kept the dance alone, I trow.
Then vail your bonnets, poetasters all;
Strike lower amain, and at these humbly fall,
And deem yourselves advanced to be her pedestal.

Should all with lowly congés laurels bring;
   Waste Flora's magazine, to find a wreath,
Or Peneus' banks, 'twere too mean offering:
   Your muse a fairer garland doth bequeath
To guard your fairer front: here 'tis your name
Shall stand immarbled; this, your little frame,
Shall great Colossus be, to your eternal fame." [4]

III

   The same class of college-boys that produced, in John Rogers, a poet and a Harvard president, produced, likewise, in Urian Oakes, another poet and another Harvard president. The latter, born in 1631, was reared in the woods of Concord—an air, then and since then, quickening to fine and rugged thought. Though of diminutive body, he gave evidence from childhood of a large and gracious intellect; in college he won high reputation for scholarship; when

   [4] This noble poem is reprinted in N. E. Hist. and Geneal. Reg. V. 138; and in Works of Anne Bradstreet, J. H. Ellis's ed. 93–96. I have quoted from the latter.

New England: The Verse-Writers

but nineteen years old, he published a set of astronomical calculations, prefixed by this motto of modest reference to himself and his brochure:

"Parvum parva decent, sed inest sua gratia parvis."

Upon his graduation, he devoted himself to theology, and began to preach. Soon, however, yielding to the attractions of England under the Protectorate, he went thither, and accepted the living of Titchfield, Hampshire, where he remained until the year of expulsion, 1662. Nevertheless, he continued to find in England both protection and clerical employment; but in 1671, upon urgent solicitation, he returned to this country, and became pastor of the church at Cambridge. In 1675, he added to his duties as pastor of that church, those of president of Harvard College. In 1681, in the full splendor of his powers and of his usefulness, he died.

A study of the writings of this man, will be likely to convince any one that there is less than the usual mortuary extravagance in the sentence of Increase Mather, that Urian Oakes "was one of the greatest lights that ever shone in this part of the world, or that is ever like to arise in this horizon." [5] He seems to have been what another contemporary [6] called him, a man of great "art and grace," as well as "a delightful, loving, profitable, fast, and faithful friend." He was distinguished in his day for the unsurpassed elegance and fluency of his Latin; and with respect to his English, it is, perhaps, the richest prose style,—it furnishes the most brilliant examples of originality, breadth, and force of thought, set aglow by flame of passion, by flame of imagination, to be met with in our sermon-literature from the settlement of the country down to the Revolution.[7]

But the splendid literary capacity of this early American—this product of our pioneer and autochthonous culture—is seen in this: as his sermons are among the noblest specimens of prose to be met with, in that class of writings, during the colonial time, so the one example that is left to us of his verse, reaches the highest point touched by American poetry, during the same era. The poem thus referred to, is an elegy upon the death of a man to whom the poet

[5] Mather's Preface to Oakes's Fast Day Sermon, published 1682.
[6] John Sherman, in Preface to Oakes's Second Artillery-Sermon, published 1682.
[7] As a sermon-writer, Urian Oakes is particularly noticed in Chapter XV.

seems to have been bound by the tenderest friendship, Thomas Shepard, minister of the church in Charlestown, a man of great gifts and of great influence, who died in December, 1677, at the age of forty-two. It was within a few days after the death of this friend, that Oakes published his elegy,—a poem in fifty-two six-lined stanzas; not without some mechanical defects; blurred also by some patches of the prevailing theological jargon; yet, upon the whole, affluent, stately, pathetic; beautiful and strong with the beauty and strength of true imaginative vision:

> "Reader! I am no poet; but I grieve.
> Behold here what that passiön can do,
> That forced a verse, without Apollo's leave,
> And whether the learnëd Sisters would or no.
>   My griefs can hardly speak; my sobbing muse
>   In broken terms our sad bereavement rues.
>
>   . . .
>
> Oh! that I were a poet now in grain!
> How would I invocate the Muses all
> To deign their presence, lend their flowing vein,
> And help to grace dear Shepard's funeral!
>   How would I paint our griefs! and succors borrow
>   From art and fancy, to limn out our sorrow.
>
> Now could I wish—if wishing would obtain—
> The sprightliest efforts of poetic rage,
> To vent my griefs, make others feel my pain,
> For this loss of the glory of our age.
>   Here is a subject for the loftiest verse
>   That ever waited on the bravest hearse.
>
> And could my pen ingeniously distil
> The purest spirits of a sparkling wit,
> In rare conceits, the quintessence of skill
> In elegiac strains—none like to it—
>   I should think all too little to condole
>   The fatal loss to us of such a soul.
>
> Could I take highest flights of fancy; soar
> Aloft; if wit's monopoly were mine;

New England: The Verse-Writers

All would be too low, too light, too poor,
To pay due tribute to this great divine.
   Ah! wit avails not, when the heart's like to break;
   Great griefs are tongue-tied, when the lesser speak.

Away, loose-reined careers of poetry;
The celebrated Sisters may be gone;
We need no mourning women's elegy,
No forced, affected, artificial tone;
   Great and good Shepard's dead! Ah! this alone
   Will set our eyes abroach, dissolve a stone.

Poetic raptures are of no esteem;
Daring hyperboles have here no place;
Luxuriant wits on such a copious theme
Would shame themselves, and blush to show their face.
   Here's worth enough to overmatch the skill
   Of the most stately Poet Laureate's quill.

. . .

As when some formidable comets blaze,
As when portentous prodigies appear,
Poor mortals with amazement stand and gaze,
With hearts affrighted and with trembling fear;
   So are we all amazëd at this blow,
   Sadly portending some approaching woe.

. . .

Art, nature, grace, in him were all combined,
To show the world a matchless paragon;
In whom, of radiant virtues no less shined
Than a whole constellation; but he's gone!
   He's gone, alas! Down in the dust must lie
   As much of this rare person as could die.

If to have solid judgment, pregnant parts,
A piercing wit, and comprehensive brain;
If to have gone the round of all the arts,
Immunity from death could gain;
   Shepard would have been death-proof, and secure
   From that all-conquering hand, I'm very sure.

If holy life, and deeds of charity,
If grace illustrious, and virtue tried,
If modest carriage, rare humility,
Could have bribed Death, good Shepard had not died.
 Oh! but inexorable Death attacks
 The best men, and promiscuous havoc makes.

. . .

Farewell, dear Shepard! Thou art gone before,
Made free of heaven, where thou shalt sing loud hymns
Of high, triumphant praises evermore,
In the sweet choir of saints and seraphims.

. . .

My dearest, inmost, bosom-friend is gone!
Gone is my sweet companion, soul's delight!
Now in an huddling crowd I'm all alone,
And almost could bid all the world—Good-night."

IV

Thus, we gather some notion of the sort of literary accomplishments that were imparted to the earliest men reared in the American forests; the first growths of the highest culture to be had here in the days of the pioneers. Let us listen, now, to a man who stood for the lower forms of culture in New England in those days, its virile intelligence, its free-mindedness, the breadth of its manhood.

In the spring of 1676, while New England was absorbed in the fright and wrath of its great conflict with the Indians, there came out from the heart of the sea-mists hanging over the island of Nantucket, a clear strong voice, speaking against the one enormous sin of New England, for which, as the speaker thought, Providence was once more smiting the land with peril and pain. Peter Folger, an able and godly man, surveyor, school-master, and lay-assistant to Thomas Mayhew in missionary work among the Indians upon that island, felt it in him, in that hour of stress, to bear some rhymed testimony to a great principle, which then had much need of being uttered both in prose and rhyme—the principle of religious toleration. It seemed to him to be plain enough, that King Philip and his lusty scalp-fumblers were but so many cords braided into that knotted

New England: The Verse-Writers

lash with which the Almighty was then scourging dreadfully, even unto the bone, the Christians of New England, for their behavior toward Christian brethren who differed from them in opinion, to wit, Baptists, Quakers, and other lovers and users of free speech. Peter Folger's testimony upon this occasion streamed forth in one long jet of manly, ungrammatical, valiant doggerel,—a ballad, just fit to be sung by "some blind crowder, with no rougher voice than rude style,"—called "A Looking-Glass for the Times; or, The former spirit of New England revived in this generation." [8] He asks what the sin is, for which God is angry against them.   This is his answer:

> "Sure, 'tis not chiefly for those sins
>   That magistrates do name,
> And make good laws for to suppress
>   And execute the same.
> But 'tis for that same crying sin
>   That rulers will not own,
> And that whereby much cruelty
>   To brethren hath been shown.
> The sin of persecution
>   Such laws establishëd;
> By which laws they have gone so far
>   As blood hath touchëd blood."

This ballad, though without one sparkle of poetry, is great in frankness and force; and as the author of it had seen fit to arraign and censure the mightiest personages in the land—magistrates and ministers—he nobly declined all shirking of responsibility in the affair, but just wove his name and his place of abode into the tissue of his verse, thereby notifying all who might have any issues to try with him, precisely who he was and where he was to be found, in case of need:

> "I am for peace, and not for war,
>   And that's the reason why,

[8] Printed in 1676; reprinted in 1763; printed again in full in Duyckinck, "Cycl. Am. Lit." Simons's ed. 58–61.*

[* This note was changed in 1897 to read as follows:
"No printed copy earlier than that of 1763 is now known to exist. I use the copy given in Duyckinck, I. 58–61."]

> I write more plain than some men do,
>   That use to daub and lie.
> But I shall cease, and set my name
>   To what I here insert;
> Because, to be a libeller,
>   I hate it with my heart.
> From Sherbon town, where now I dwell,
>   My name I do put here;
> Without offence, your real friend,
>   It is Peter Folger."

This strong-brained and free-hearted old surveyor of Nantucket was blessed with sons and daughters nine; and the youngest of his daughters became the mother of Benjamin Franklin. The grandson, when he undertook to write his autobiography, did not ignore the honorable memory of his ancestor; by a few quiet strokes of description he has secured him against being ever forgotten.

At the very time when Peter Folger, in his sea-girdled solitude, was preaching from the terrible text of the Indian conflict his blunt sermon for toleration, there lived, probably at Charlestown, a schoolmaster named Benjamin Tompson, born at Braintree in 1640, graduated at Harvard in 1662, who was pondering the same text, and who wrought from it a sermon in smoother verse, called "New England's Crisis." [9] This poet's best vein is satiric,—his favorite organ

---

[9] My most diligent search for this book through public and private libraries, and even by advertisements in the public journals, has failed to bring it to my view. All that is at present known of it, appears to be derived from Samuel Kettell ("Specimens of Am. Poetry," I. Introd. xxxvii.–xlii. and III. 379), who says that he "discovered" it, and then gives an analysis of its contents and two long passages from it. I can hear of no one since then who has seen the book. What became of Kettell's copy? *

[* This note has been crossed out in blue pencil with the notation: "This note omitted: a new one substituted 1896." Two loose slips appear in Tyler's copy of the book at this point: one has a typed and corrected version of the note which, with somewhat changed wording, was printed in 1897; the other bears two references to "Dr. Green's contributions," which were incorporated in the note as published in 1897. The final form of the note was as follows:

"The only copy of the poem under this title, so far as is known to me, belongs to the Boston Athenæum, and is probably the copy used before my time by Kettell and Duyckinck. When making my studies on Tompson, I did not know of its existence there, and for my citations from it was obliged to depend on the

being the rhymed pentameter couplet, with a flow, a vigor, and an edge obviously caught from the contemporaneous verse of John Dryden. He has the partisanship, the exaggeration, the choleric injustice, that are common in satire; and like other satirists, failing to note the moral perspectives of history, he utters over again the stale and easy lie, wherein the past is held up as wiser and holier than the present. Though New England has had a life but little more than fifty years long, the poet sees within it the tokens of a hurrying degeneracy, in customs, in morals, in valor, in piety. He turns back, with reverent and eyeless homage, to the good old times of the Founders, when the people dwelt

>"Under thatch'd huts, without the cry of rent,
>And the best sauce to every dish—content;"

when

>"Deep-skirted doublets, Puritanic capes,
>Which now would render men like upright apes,
>Was comelier wear, our wiser fathers thought,
>Than the cast fashions from all Europe brought;"

when, at table,

>"an honest grace would hold
>Till an hot pudding grew at heart a cold;
>And men had better stomachs at religion,
>Than I to capon, turkey-cock, or pigeon;
>When honest sisters met to pray, not prate,
>About their own, and not their neighbors' state;"

when Indian impertinence was not tolerated for an instant, and

>"No sooner pagan malice peepëd forth,
>But valor snibbed it. Then were men of worth,
>Who by their prayers slew thousands; angel-like,
>Their weapons are unseen, with which they strike."

---

extracts given by Kettell. Through the diligence and acumen of Dr. Samuel A. Green, 'New England's Crisis' has been identified as a different edition of the poem called 'New England's Tears for her Present Miseries,'—a unique copy of the latter being among the treasures of the library of Mr. John Nicholas Brown. Other verses by Tompson have also been brought to light by Dr. Green, as may be noted in 2 Mass. Hist. Soc. Proc., V. 2–3; VIII. 387–389; X. 263–284; 369–371."]

Alas, those flawless times—that never were—those

> "golden times, too fortunate to hold,
> Were quickly sinned away for love of gold;"

and in retribution, God is sending upon New England the wrath and anguish of the Indian wars:

> "Not ink, but blood and tears now serve the turn,
> To draw the figure of New England's urn."

Other and slighter poetic work of Benjamin Tompson's is to be met with, safely lodged in the pages of some of his contemporaries.[*] Among the complimentary verses prefixed to the "Magnalia," [10] are two little poems by him, one in Latin, one in English; and in the text of that work, he has a rhymed eulogy "upon the Very Reverend Samuel Whiting." [11] Moreover, in William Hubbard's "Indian Wars," is a prefatory poem, signed "B. T.," that is undoubtedly Tompson's, and that has some sprightly and characteristic lines,—as these, addressed to the historian:

> "I took your muse for old Columbus' ghost,
> Who scraped acquaintance with this Western Coast." [12]

V

In contemporaneous renown, far above all other verse-writers of the colonial time, was Michael Wigglesworth, the explicit and unshrinking rhymer of the Five Points of Calvinism; a poet who so perfectly uttered in verse the religious faith and emotion of Puritan New England that, for more than a hundred years, his writings had universal diffusion there, and a popular influence only inferior to that of the Bible and the Shorter Catechism.

No one holding a different theology from that held by Michael Wigglesworth, can do justice to him as a poet, without exercising

[10] Vol. I. 20.   [11] Ibid. 510-511.
[12] W. Hubbard, "Indian Wars," I. 24, S. G. Drake's ed.

[* A marginal note says: "Robt. C. Winthrop has two Odes by Thomson (sic), on the death of the two Ct. Governor Winthrops. One Ode is in MS; the other in print."]

New England: The Verse-Writers

the utmost intellectual catholicity; otherwise, disgust and detestation for much of this poet's message, will drown all sense of the picturesqueness, the imaginative vigor, the tremendous realism, of many of the conceptions under which his message was delivered. It is necessary, likewise, if we would not fail in true insight as we study him, to distinguish between the essence of poetry and its form. There was in him the genius of a true poet; his imagination had an epic strength,—it was courageous, piercing, creative; his pages are strewn with many unwrought ingots of poetry. Yet, he had given up to a narrow and a ferocious creed what was meant for mankind; in his intense pursuit of what he believed to be the good and the true, he forgot the very existence of the beautiful; finally, not having served his poetic apprenticeship under any of the sane and mighty masters of English song, he was himself forever incapable of giving utterance to his genius—except in a dialect that was unworthy of it.

His verse is quite lacking in art; its ordinary form being a crude, swinging ballad-measure, with a sort of cheap melody, a shrill, reverberating clatter, that would instantly catch and please the popular ear, at that time deaf to daintier and more subtle effects in poetry. He was, himself, in nearly all respects, the embodiment of what was great, earnest, and sad, in colonial New England; even in his limitations, he was true to it, and was the better qualified to be its poetic voice. In spite, however, of all offences, of all defects, there are in his poetry an irresistible sincerity, a reality, a vividness, reminding one of similar qualities in the prose of John Bunyan; and had these forces in our poet gained for themselves a nobler literary expression, they would have gained for him a high and permanent fame.

Coming to this country in 1638, a child of seven years, he grew up in his father's household at New Haven; in 1651, he was graduated at Harvard College, and served for a time as tutor there; in 1656, he was made pastor of the church at Malden, Massachusetts; and there he remained, as pastor and physician, until his death in 1705. In body he was slight and delicate—"a feeble, little shadow of a man;" [18] all his life he had sorrow and pain; yet there was in him an intensity

[18] Cotton Mather, in Funeral Sermon, 26.

of spirit that triumphed over all physical ills, and a tenderness of sympathy that made him, after the somewhat dreary manner of those days, "a man of the beatitudes," [14] and a comforter to all who, like himself, knew the touch of grief.

As a poet, Michael Wigglesworth stands for New England Puritanism confronting with steady gaze the sublime and hideous dogmas of its creed, and trying to use those dogmas for the admonition and the consolation of mankind by putting them into song. A sensitive, firm, wide-ranging, unresting spirit, he looks out mournfully over the throngs of men that fill the world,—all of them totally depraved, all of them caught, from farthest eternity, in the adamantine meshes of God's decrees; the most of them, also, being doomed in advance, by those decrees, to an endless existence of ineffable torment,—and upon this situation of affairs, the excellent Michael Wigglesworth proposes to make poetry. Such as it is, it is absolutely sincere, grim, pathetic, horrible. He chants, with utter frankness, the chant of Christian fatalism, the moan of earthly vanity and sorrow, the physical bliss of the saved, the physical tortures of the damned.

In the multitude of his verses, Michael Wigglesworth surpasses all other poets of the colonial time, excepting Anne Bradstreet. Besides numerous minor poems, he is the author of three poetical works of considerable length.

One of these, "God's Controversy with New England," was "written in the time of the great drought," 1662,—a calamity of which the author takes advantage for the purpose, as he tells the reader, of

> "pointing at those faults of thine
> Which are notorious." [15]

The argument of the poem is this: "New England planted, prospered, declining, threatened, punished." The poet holds the opinion, common enough in his day, that before the arrival of the English in America, this continent had been the choice and peculiar residence of the Devil and his angels:

---

[14] The Rev. A. P. Peabody's description of him, cited in J. W. Dean, "Sketch of the Life of Michael Wigglesworth," 10.

[15] This poem was first printed in Mass. Hist. Soc. Proc. for 1871–1873, 83–93; from which I make my quotations.

New England: The Verse-Writers

> "A waste and howling wilderness,
>   Where none inhabited,
> But hellish fiends, and brutish men,
>   That devils worshippëd.
>
> This region was in darkness placed,
>   Far off from heaven's light,
> Amidst the shadows of grim death
>   And of eternal night."

At last, in this doleful realm, arrive the Lord's forces from England:

> "The dark and dismal western woods,
>   The Devil's den whilere,
> Beheld such glorious gospel-shine,
>   As none beheld more clear."

The poet then pictures the entrance of the English into America, in language similar to that used in Scripture to describe the entrance of the Jews into Canaan; he chronicles the zeal of the first generation, next its decay; after which, as he informs us,

> "The air became tempestuous;
>   The wilderness gan quake;
> And from above, with awful voice,
>   The Almighty, thundering, spake."

What the Almighty then spake, is faithfully reported by the poet,—a quaintly eloquent and very Puritanic address to the people of New England, closing with a dire menace of immediate retribution:

> "Thus ceased his dreadful, threatening voice,
>   The high and lofty One.
> The heavens stood still, appalled thereat;
>   The earth beneath did groan.
>
> Soon after I beheld and saw
>   A mortal dart come flying;
> I looked again, and quickly saw
>   Some fainting, others dying;"

and the poet goes on to give, with the exactness of a medical man in full practice, a catalogue of the various diseases then most prevalent in his neighborhood; he also draws a picture of the barrenness of the fields in consequence of the long drought; and he concludes with a pathetic appeal to the "many praying saints" still left in New England.

Another large poem of Wigglesworth's is "Meat out of the Eater; or, Meditations concerning the necessity, end, and usefulness of afflictions unto God's children, all tending to prepare them for and comfort them under the Cross." Here we have simply the Christian doctrine of comfort in sorrow, translated into metrical jingles. With nearly all sensitiveness to literary form torpid in New England, and with devout feeling warm and alert, it is not strange that this clumsy but sympathetic poem should have found there a multitude of admirers. It was first published, probably, in 1669; ten years afterward, it had passed through at least four editions; and during the entire colonial age, it was a much-read manual of solace in affliction. And, indeed, it is such poetry as might still serve that purpose, at least by plucking from the memory, for a moment, a rooted sorrow, and substituting a literary anguish in place of it.

But the master-piece of Michael Wigglesworth's genius, and his most delectable gift to an admiring public, was that blazing and sulphurous poem, "The Day of Doom; or, A poetical description of the great and last Judgment." In summoning to himself the inspiration necessary for the composition of the work, the poet flouts at all pagan help, and utters "a prayer unto Christ the Judge of the world":

> "Thee, thee alone, I'll invocate;
> For I do much abominate
> To call the Muses to mine aid.
>
> . . .
>
> Oh! what a deal of blasphemy,
> And heathenish impiety,
> In Christian poets may be found,
> Where heathen gods with praise are crowned!
> They make Jehovah to stand by,
> Till Juno, Venus, Mercury,
> With frowning Mars, and thund'ring Jove,
> Rule earth below, and heaven above.

> But I have learned to pray to none,
> Save unto God in Christ alone;
> Nor will I laud, no, not in jest,
> That which I know God doth detest.
> I reckon it a damning evil,
> To give God's praises to the Devil.
> Thou, Christ, art he to whom I pray;
> Thy glory fain I would display.
> Oh! guide me by thy sacred Sprite,
> So to indite, and so to write,
> That I thine holy name may praise,
> And teach the sons of men thy ways."

The opening stanzas of the poem give a rather brisk picture of the heedlessness and sensual ease of the world, just before the Judgment:

> "Still was the night, serene and bright,
>   When all men sleeping lay;
> Calm was the season, and carnal reason
>   Thought so 'twould last for aye."

Upon this scene of carnal security, suddenly bursts the world's doom:

> "For at midnight breaks forth a light,
>   Which turns the night to day,
> And speedily an hideous cry
>   Doth all the world dismay."

At this dreadful noise, all sleeping sinners are abruptly wakened:

> "They rush from beds with giddy heads,
>   And to their windows run,
> Viewing this light, which shines more bright
>   Than doth the noonday sun."

At once, in appalling state, appears Christ, the Judge:

> "Before his face the heavens give place,
>   And skies are rent asunder,
> With mighty voice and hideous noise,
>   More terrible than thunder.
>   . . .

No heart so bold but now grows cold
    And almost dead with fear;
No eye so dry but now can cry,
    And pour out many a tear.
Earth's potentates and powerful states,
    Captains and men of might,
Are quite abashed, their courage dashed,
    At this most dreadful sight.

. . .

All kindreds wail, all hearts do fail;
    Horror the world doth fill
With weeping eyes and loud outcries,—
    Yet knows not how to kill.

Some hide themselves in caves and delves,
    In places under ground;
Some rashly leap into the deep
    To scape by being drowned;
Some to the rocks—O senseless blocks!—
    And woody mountains run,
That there they might this fearful sight
    And dreaded Presence shun.

. . .

The mountains smoke, the hills are shook,
    The earth is rent and torn,
As if she should be clear dissolved,
    Or from her centre borne.
The sea doth roar, forsakes the shore,
    And shrinks away for fear;
The wild beasts flee into the sea,
    So soon as he draws near."

After this, the trump is sounded; at which, the dead rise from their graves, the living are "changed," and all are brought before the vast tribunal:

"His wingëd hosts fly through all coasts,
    Together gathering
Both good and bad, both quick and dead,
    And all to judgment bring.

New England: The Verse-Writers

> Out of their holes, those creeping moles
>   That hid themselves for fear,
> By force they take, and quickly make
>   Before the judge appear."

Immediately, the sheep are parted from the goats; the former are briefly described; then the latter, as follows:

> "At Christ's left hand, the goats do stand:
>   All whining hypocrites,
> Who for self-ends did seem Christ's friends,
>   But fostered guileful sprites;
>
> . . .
>
> Apostates base, and run-aways,
>   Such as have Christ forsaken,
> Of whom the Devil, with seven more evil,
>   Hath fresh possession taken;
>
> . . .
>
> Blasphemers lewd, and swearers shrewd,
>   Scoffers at purity,
> That hated God, contemned his rod,
>   And loved security;
> Sabbath-polluters, saints-persecutors,
>   Presumptuous men, and proud,
> Who never loved those that reproved;
>   All stand among this crowd.
>
> . . .
>
> False-witness bearers, and self-forswearers,
>   Murderers, and men of blood,
> Witches, enchanters, and ale-house haunters,
>   Beyond account there stood.
>
> . . .
>
> There stand all nations and generations
>   Of Adam's progeny,
> Whom Christ redeemed not, whom he esteemed not,
>   Through infidelity.
>
> . . .
>
> These numerous bands, wringing their hands,
>   And weeping all stand there,
> Fillëd with anguish, whose hearts do languish,

>   Through self-tormenting fear.
> Fast by them stand, at Christ's left hand,
>   The lion fierce and fell,
> The dragon bold, that serpent old,
>   That hurried souls to hell.*
> There also stand, under command,
>   Legions of sprites unclean,
> And hellish fiends, that are no friends
>   To God, nor unto men.
>
> With dismal chains, and strongest reins,
>   Like prisoners of hell,
> They're held in place before Christ's face,
>   Till he their doom shall tell.
> These void of tears, but filled with fears,
>   And dreadful expectation
> Of endless pains and scalding flames,
>   Stand waiting for damnation."

Then proceeds the business of the court. The saints are first attended to: they draw near, and receive their benign award, and are at once comfortably placed on thrones to join with Christ in judging the wicked. Then, of course, the wicked have their turn; and in reply to the indictment against them all, different classes of them put in their defences, and "the judge uncaseth them." Thus, in order, are considered "hypocrites," "civil honest men," "those that pretend want of opportunity to repent," those who "plead examples of their betters," "heathen men," and others, until, at last, "reprobate infants" are reached:

> "Then to the bar, all they drew near
>   Who died in infancy,
> And never had, or good or bad,
>   Effected personally,
> But from the womb unto the tomb
>   Were straightway carriëd,
> Or, at the least, ere they transgressed,—
>   Who thus began to plead."

[* In the early editions the page ended here. Apparently the stanza break should have come four lines above, after "fear."]

New England: The Verse-Writers

These poor little babes, breaking from the muteness of their terror over all these horrid proceedings, argue, with a truly precocious logical acumen, against the injustice of their being cast into hell forever and ever, on account of a sin committed by Adam,—particularly as Adam himself was even then seated in quiet bliss in one of the most agreeable and conspicuous of those thrones among the saints. With these infantile pleadings, however, the poet is in no respect embarrassed; and in his poem he has "their arguments taken off" with great promptness and severity—a severity mitigated, indeed, by one indulgent concession. The judge says to these infants, in conclusion:

> "You sinners are; and such a share
>   As sinners, may expect;
> Such you shall have, for I do save
>   None but mine own elect.
> Yet to compare your sin with their
>   Who lived a longer time,
> I do confess yours is much less,
>   Though every sin's a crime.
>
> A crime it is; therefore in bliss
>   You may not hope to dwell;
> But unto you I shall allow
>   The easiest room in hell."

Thus the last word of argument is spoken; Christ begins

> "To fire the earth's foundation;"

and to this enormous conflagration are the shrieking victims of God's omnipotent fury then formally doomed:

> "Ye sinful wights and cursëd sprites,
>   That work iniquity,
> Depart together, from me forever,
>   To endless misery;
> Your portion take in yonder lake
>   Where fire and brimstone flameth;
> Suffer the smart which your desert
>   As its due wages claimeth.
>
>   . . .

Then might you hear them rend and tear
    The air with their outcries;
The hideous noise of their sad voice
    Ascendeth to the skies.
They wring their hands, their caitiff-hands,
    And gnash their teeth for terror;
They cry, they roar, for anguish sore,
    And gnaw their tongues for horror.

But get away without delay;
    Christ pities not your cry;
Depart to hell, there may you yell
    And roar eternally.

    . . .

As chaff that's dry, as dust doth fly
    Before the northern wind,
Right so are they chasëd away
    And can no refuge find.
They hasten to the pit of woe
    Guarded by angels stout,
Who to fulfil Christ's holy will
    Attend this wicked rout;

Whom having brought, as they are taught,
    Unto the brink of hell;
(That dismal place, far from Christ's face,
    Where Death and Darkness dwell,
Where God's fierce ire kindleth the fire
    And vengeance feeds the flame,
With piles of wood and brimstone flood,
    So none can quench the same;)

With iron bands they bind their hands
    And cursëd feet together;
And cast them all, both great and small,
    Into that lake forever;
Where day and night, without respite,
    They wail and cry and howl,
For torturing pain which they sustain,
    In body and in soul.

New England: The Verse-Writers

> For day and night, in their despite,
>   Their torment's smoke ascendeth;
> Their pain and grief have no relief,
>   Their anguish never endeth.
> There must they lie and never die,
>   Though dying every day;
> There must they, dying, ever lie,
>   And not consume away.
>
> Die fain they would, if die they could,
>   But death will not be had;
> God's direful wrath their bodies hath
>   Forever immortal made.
> They live to lie in misery
>   And bear eternal woe;
> And live they must whilst God is just,
>   That he may plague them so."

The last strains of the poem are singularly appropriate; they celebrate the felicity of the saints, "who rejoice to see judgment executed upon the wicked world."

This great poem, which, with entire unconsciousness, attributes to the Divine Being a character the most execrable and loathsome to be met with, perhaps, in any literature, Christian or pagan, had for a hundred years a popularity far exceeding that of any other work, in prose or verse, produced in America before the Revolution. The eighteen hundred copies of the first edition were sold within a single year; which implies the purchase of a copy of "The Day of Doom" by at least every thirty-fifth person then in New England,—an example of the commercial success of a book never afterward equalled in this country. Since that time, the book has been repeatedly published; at least once in England, and at least eight times in America—the last time being in 1867.[16]

Happily, this frightful and blasphemous delineation of the government exercised over us by the Good God, has at last, in civilized society, lost its cruel power over the human mind, and may now be read merely as a curious literary phenomenon,—as a dreadful example, indeed, of the distressing illusions once inflicted upon them-

[16] This is the ed. from which I have drawn the foregoing extracts.

selves, in the name of religion, by the best of men. But no narrative of our intellectual history during the colonial days, can justly fail to record the enormous influence of this terrible poem during all those times. Not only was it largely circulated in the form of a book, but it was hawked about the country, in broadsides, as a popular ballad; it "was the solace," as Lowell playfully says, "of every fireside, the flicker of the pine-knots by which it was conned perhaps adding a livelier relish to its premonitions of eternal combustion;" [17] its pages were assigned in course to little children, to be learned by heart, along with the catechism; as late as the present century, there were in New England many aged persons who were able to repeat the whole poem; for more than a hundred years after its first publication, it was, beyond question, the one supreme poem of Puritan New England; and Cotton Mather predicted that it would continue to be read in New England until the day of doom itself should arrive.

Among the sons of Michael Wigglesworth, was one, Samuel, who in early life gave brilliant proof of having high poetic genius. In 1707, when he was eighteen years of age, he was graduated at Harvard; then, for two years, he remained near the college, pursuing further studies; then, after an experience of fluctuation between the claims of medicine, pedagogy, and divinity, he gave himself to the latter profession, and in its pursuit passed the remainder of his long life, dying in 1768. It was in 1709, while he was but a youth of twenty and near the end of his post-graduate studies at college, that he wrote a few verses which, alone, are sufficient to show him to have had a true and fine endowment for poetry. These verses are entitled "A Funeral Song." They were written in commemoration of a gifted young man, Nathaniel Clarke, who, after taking the Master's degree at Harvard, had paid a visit to England, but, on the voyage homeward, had died, and been buried in the sea. Here, indeed, in this song of friendship and of sorrow, we trace once more the touch of a real poet. Even to his eyes, glad with the gladness of his youth,

---

[17] "Harvard Book," II. 158. The humor of Lowell's remark should not give us the impression that "The Day of Doom" was often perused with any humorous feeling, by the first three or four generations of readers,—to whom, indeed, all its fearful words seemed only the literal truth. Joseph T. Buckingham mentions that even after the Revolution he read it, as a lad, with great excitement and fright. His "Personal Memoirs," I. 19.

New England: The Verse-Writers

the once radiant world, now that his friend has gone from it, wears a sorrowful and impoverished look; he grieves, too, because into the mysteries and silences of death his friend has been hurried, at a time when no pressure of the hand, no whisper of affection, could tell him of the love and the grief of those who were left behind. Therefore, the poet, unable to endure the anguish of this thought, would pursue his friend, even into the far heavens whither he is gone; would make outcry and inquest for him through the remotest spaces of the universe; and convey to him, wheresoever he may be, the passionate message that had been unspoken here:

>"Vain poet's license! now, if thou canst soar
>Above mount Sinai's top, 'bove things revealed,
>Put on the winged morn, and speed amain
>Where increate eternity's revealed;
>
>Fancy thyself shot through the ethereal world,
>Translated from thy clay, amidst the seats
>Of highest angels, mighty seraphim,
>Of thrones, dominions, princes, potentates;
>
>Find there a saint in milk-white robes arrayed,
>Clothed with the sun, adorned with grace and love,
>Who not long since bade this vile world adieu,
>To fill the number of the choir above.
>
>Tell him who now is glorified above,
>How rivulets of tears have drowned our eyes;
>Our hopes are all thrown overboard with him,
>Our tumid thoughts becalmed in a surprise.
>
>Put on thy graces, court the vestal soul
>To a relapse of things; with all thy might
>Sing an encomium of terrestrial joys,
>Try if thou canst recall her winged flight.
>
>At least ascend and view the orbs above,
>See where he pierced heaven's powdered canopy;
>Perhaps his soul left her idea there,
>Or stopped to hear the spheric harmony.

> Behold the starry train—those rolling lamps
> That burn fierce anthems to the eternal light;
> Number those morning sons, and find him there;
> Look, look, and see him, with extreme delight,
>
> . . .
>
> Warbling divinest airs, and shouting forth
> Loud hallelujahs to the Immortal King,—
> The God whose breath first formed the heavenly hosts,
> And quickening gave to every living thing.
>
> Descend, my soul, to the Elysian bowers,
> The imaginary shades, where up and down
> The blessed ghosts do rove and pass the hours,
> In grateful pastimes till the eternal dawn.
>
> Trace every verdant grove, each flowery bank,
> Whose wanton edges curl the silver streams;
> Search every silent grot, each peaceful vale,
> Each circling walk in those enameled greens.
>
> Ask all the rural powers and infant swains
> That range in those luxurious paths of bliss,
> Ask if or no a comely, gentle youth
> Has flown of late into their paradise."

But, suddenly, in the midst of this brave scheme of communication with the dead, there falls upon the poet the thought of its impossibility. Death outwits us! Death despoils us and there is no remedy! Death, "an angry foe," "a lawless, tearless enemy,"

> "Murders us with an unrelenting hand,
> And reaps impartial both the green and dry.
>
> He shrinks not at the manly grace:
> See, here he rudely takes their breath:
> See, see, the valiant soul gives place
> Unto all-conquering Time and Death."

Then, the fierceness of this invective having spent itself, the poem ends with one short strain of altered melody, exquisite in beauty and pathos:

New England: The Verse-Writers

"Add one kind drop unto his watery tomb:
Weep, ye relenting eyes and ears;
See, Death himself could not refrain—
But buried him in tears." [18]

The genius that produced this dainty music, and that might have achieved a high career in poetry, soon became wrapped in the occupations of a country-pastor, and was content to utter itself, during the subsequent fifty-nine years of its earth-life, in the commonplaces of theologic talk.

VI

We are now well entered upon the eighteenth century, and are next to stand before a most notable poetic personage, Nicholas Noyes of Salem. His distinction in our literature will be that he was the last and the greatest of our poetical punsters and image-manglers, reproducing in America, even during the earlier years of the eighteenth century, the most grotesque traits of a form of poetry that had died out in England, near the middle of the century before.

Whatever we may have to conclude respecting the poetry of Nicholas Noyes, we shall agree that his personal qualities were fine and strong. He was born in Massachusetts in 1647; was graduated at Harvard in 1667, at the tail of his class in social rank, at the head of it in scholarship; he was minister of Haddam from 1670 until 1683; in the latter year, he was made colleague of the venerable John Higginson at Salem; and at Salem he passed the remainder of his life, which came to its close in 1717. This celebrated town was described by a physician, thirty years after Nicholas Noyes lived in it, as one in which "hypochondriac, hysteric, and other maniac disorders prevail," indeed, "seem to be endemical." [19] There, in an especial manner, appeared the frenzy of witchcraft, and the still wilder frenzy of persecuting it; and in this latter madness the brain of poor Nicholas Noyes was sadly entangled for a time. It does one good to mention that, when at last his lunacy passed off and he saw the folly and the

---

[18] The entire poem is in N. E. Hist. and Geneal. Reg. IV. 89–90, and is dated Charlestown, Aug. 15, 1709.
[19] W. Douglass, "Summary," I. 448.

cruelty of his conduct, he spoke out like a man and confessed it—naught extenuating, and went about among the people, humbly making all possible reparation to the persons whom he had wronged. This was, perhaps, the only cloud that ever darkened his long, benignant, studious life,—a life that seemed to lie outspread in a lovelier and still brighter light, when its solitary shadow was withdrawn. To his contemporaries, he appeared to be a reader of all literatures, to bring into his most common talk great entertainment and utility, and to be faithful and even illustrious in his sacred office; a true friend and helper of his kind.

Doubtless he had little expectation of being remembered in our literary history; for in his coyness, though he wrote much, he shrank from the publicity of print. In prose, only two productions of his have been found,—a pleasant biographical sketch contributed by him to the "Magnalia," [20] and an election sermon for the year 1698.[21] It is his verse that is phenomenal in our literary annals; for, even in his old age, he continued to write the sort of poetry that, in his youth, had been the fashion, both in England and in America,—the degenerate euphuism of Donne, of Wither,* of Quarles, of George Herbert. To this appalling type of poetry, Nicholas Noyes faithfully adhered, even to the end of his days, unseduced by the rhythmical heresies, the classic innovations, of John Dryden and Alexander Pope.

When Cotton Mather launched his "Magnalia," Nicholas Noyes was one of the admiring friends who stood about and huzzaed, as the huge and dreadful hulk glided down the well-greased stocks into the sea. He produced, in fact, "a prefatory poem on that excellent book," particularly addressed "to the candid reader." The first half of the poem is an argument for the enormous value

[20] Vol. I. 483–488.
[21] Entitled "New England's Duty and Interest to be an Habitation of Justice and a Mountain of Holiness."

[* Changed to "Crashaw." Apparently there was some confusion over the spelling of this name. Tyler wrote "Crashawe" here and then crossed out the final "e." In the text and notes "Crashawe" seems to have been used for William and "Crashaw" for Richard, but the index used the shorter form for both men.]

New England: The Verse-Writers

"of such a scribe as Cotton Mather,
Whose piety, whose pains, and peerless pen,
Revives New England's nigh-lost origin;"

and the argument is based upon the indisputable fact that the American aborigines, whatever else they may have had, had no such scribe as Cotton Mather, and that, in consequence, their history had perished. Concerning all these miserable and Matherless nations we ask, and we ask in vain,

"Who was their father, Japhet, Shem, or Cham;
And how they straddled to the antipodes
To look another world beyond the seas;
And when, and why, and where they last broke ground,
What risks they ran, where they first anchoring found?
. . .
What charters had they; what immunities;
What altars, temples, cities, colonies,
Did they erect; who were their public spirits?"

But since, in Cotton Mather, the white inhabitants of America had at last found a worthy historian, such oblivion can never fall upon them:

"Heads of our tribes, whose corps are under ground,
Their names and fames in chronicles renowned,
Begemmed on golden ouches he hath set,
Past envy's teeth and time's corroding fret." [22]

Perhaps there were then in New England other persons that could equal Nicholas Noyes in the writing of "prefatory poems;" but, throughout all the colonial times, he had no rival there as an epitaph-maker, and as a fabricator of punning elegies. In this realm of service, he seems to have possessed a skill that not art alone, that only genius with art, could have given him, at perfectly emptying his verses of the last atom of beauty, and at so packing them with quirks, quibbles, conceits, and the most unexpected contortions of unlovely imagery, as to impart to them a sort of horrible fascination—a mirth-

[22] "Magnalia," I. 19.

fulness in the presence of which the reader writhes in pain and disgust.

When, in 1708, his aged associate, the noble John Higginson, died, Nicholas Noyes lovingly described him as one who

> "For rich array cared not a fig,
> And wore Elisha's periwig;
> At ninety-three had comely face
> Adorned with majesty and grace;
> Before he went among the dead,
> He children's children's children had."

In 1715, there died in Salem a much younger man than Higginson, the Reverend Joseph Green; and as his name presented a boundless opening for an elegiac punster, his brother Noyes poured out over his memory nine pages of most whimsical and distracting verses:

> "In God's house we of late did see
> A Green and growing olive tree.
> 'Twas planted by a living spring
> That always made it flourishing,
> Filled it with sap and oily juice
> That leaves and fruit and light produce;
> An holy tree, whose very wood
> For temple-use was choice and good."

Thus the poet goes forward, pitilessly ringing changes on the verdant name of the dead gentleman; speaking of "Green olive leaves," of "pastures Green;" saying that

> "Summer and Winter, Green was he,
> Most like the noble olive tree;"

and at last taking leave of him with this relenting couplet:

> "His Master's work he did so ply,
> He did but just get time to die." [23]

The supreme poetic opportunity in the career of Nicholas Noyes occurred, however, some years earlier, when a Reverend friend of his, James Brayley of Roxbury, became afflicted with the Stone. To

[23] This elegy is in the library of the Mass. Hist. Soc.

this unhappy man the poet, accordingly, sent some verses, both consolatory and congratulatory, which certainly ought to establish the fame of Nicholas Noyes as the most gifted and brilliant master ever produced in America, of the most execrable form of poetry to which the English language was ever degraded. In this poem, the author flatteringly expresses astonishment, not only at the fortitude of his friend, but at his versatility, both in doing and in suffering:

> "What! in one breath both live and die,
> Groan, laugh, sigh, smile, cry, versify?
> Is this the Stone? Are these the pains
> Of that disease that plagues the reins?
> That slyly steals into the bladder,
> Then bites and stings like to the adder?
> Is this the scourge of studious men,
> That leaves unwhipt scarce five of ten?"

He then advances into the merits of his theme, using the name of his friend's disease as a pivot on which to revolve the antic and frantic creations of his fancy:

> "For if thou shouldst be Stoned to death,
> And this way pelted out of breath,
> Thou wilt like Stephen fall asleep,
> And free from pain forever keep."

The poet then proceeds to spiritual exhortation:

> "That Stone which builders did refuse,
> For thy foundation choose and use.
> Yea, think what Christ for thee hath done,
> Who took an harder, heavier, Stone
> Out of thine heart;"

and he asks him to remember this comforting truth, that, great as may be the sufferings inflicted on him by the Stone in this world, they are vastly less than the sufferings of the damned in the next, some of whom

> "roll the Sisyphean Stone."

With this joyous reflection, he also invites him to anticipate the bliss of heaven, where

"shall hid manna be thy fare,
In which no grit nor gravel are;
Yea, Christ will give thee a White Stone
With a New Name engraved thereon." [24]

VII

For a considerable time before Nicholas Noyes had ceased from his detestable labors, the new school of poetry in England, represented first by Dryden and then by Pope, had found sympathetic pupils in America. With the advancing years of the first half of the eighteenth century, the authority of this school became complete among us. The unloveliness of the earlier manner of poetry disappeared; and, in place of it, we find the smooth and mechanic melody, the shallow elegance, the monotonous grace, that, to a large extent, served as substitutes for real thought and passion. During the earlier portion of the century, an English scholar, Francis Knapp, a graduate of St. John's college, Oxford, lived the life of a literary recluse, at Watertown, Massachusetts; and glorying in a personal acquaintance with Alexander Pope, he attempted to reproduce, on "the bleak Atlantic shore," and amid "solitudes obscene," the poetic notes of his master.[25] The two eloquent preachers, Benjamin Colman and Mather Byles, both caught the new tune in English verse; and for nearly fifty years, with a fatal facility, to the vast admiration of their parishioners, they both continued to evolve twaddling variations upon it. The gifted daughter of Benjamin Colman, Jane Turell, was instructed by her father to regard Sir Richard Blackmore as a poet "far above all her praises," and, next "after the Reverend

---

[24] This monstrous production was printed in "The Boston News-Letter," August 4-11, 1707, from which I copy these extracts.*

[25] Poem by Francis Knapp, among the "Recommendatory Poems," prefixed to Pope's works. See, also, "Biographical Sketches," by Samuel L. Knapp, 140-143; and Duyckinck's "Cycl. of Am. Lit." 77-78, Simons's ed.

[* Penciled changes were made in this note and marked in blue pencil: "Inserted correction in revised ed." The final form of the note, which varies somewhat from the form in Tyler's correction copy, follows:

"This monstrous production was printed in broadside, and in that form was bound with the file of 'The Boston News Letter' now in possession of the New York Historical Society. It thus follows No. 173, for Aug. 4-11, 1706."]

New England: The Verse-Writers

Doctor Watts," as "the laureate of the Church of Christ;" [26] and to this knightly and medicinal bard she addressed verses—not unworthy of his own pen.[27]

In Roger Wolcott, we have still another early example of the American knack of doing a great many things, and of doing them tolerably well,—a knack that does not become intolerable, except when it thrusts itself, as it has a dangerous fondness for doing, into the sphere of poetry. Born in Windsor, Connecticut, in 1679, in a wild frontier settlement, he had never school or school-master for a day; at the age of twelve, he was bound as an apprentice to a trade; at the age of twenty-one, he set up for himself in business in his native town; he was diligent, thrifty, studious; he turned his attention to public affairs, military and political, and became great in both; in a campaign for the conquest of Canada, in 1711, he was commissary of the Connecticut troops; at the capture of Louisburg in 1745, he was major-general; he also rose through many stages of civil promotion, becoming member of the colonial assembly and of the colonial council, county-judge, deputy-governor, chief-justice of the superior court; at last, in 1751, he became governor, and continued so for four years; he died in 1767, a wise, strong, apt, devout, and wholesome man. He began life in ignorance and poverty; he ended it, at nearly ninety years of age, crowned with earthly prosperity, full of honor and knowledge, a Nestor, a patriot, a sage.

His one human frailty lurked in an invincible illusion that he was a poet; and, surely, the man who could storm and carry so many heights of difficulty—might he not hope to carry by storm the heights of Parnassus also? Other poets had found inspiration in patriotic memories; he also. Accordingly, in commemoration of the early valor and statesmanship of his own Connecticut, he wrote a long poem, with a title almost as prosaic, if possible, as the poem to which it belongs: "A Brief Account of the Agency of the Honorable John Winthrop, Esquire, in the Court of King Charles the Second, A.D., 1662, when he obtained a Charter for the Colony of Connecticut."

This great historical poem, the author forbore to publish in his

[26] "Memoirs of Mrs. Jane Turell," by E. Turell, 29–30.
[27] Ibid. 28–29.

lifetime;[28] but upon one occasion, even during his lifetime, he did venture into print with specimens of his verse, to wit, "Poetical Meditations, being the Improvement of some vacant Hours," published at New London in 1725.* Probably the best passage in the book is this, entitled "The Heart is Deep":

> "He that can trace a ship making her way
> Amidst the threatening surges of the sea;
> Or track a towering eagle in the air;
> Or on a rock find the impressions there
> Made by a serpent's footsteps; who surveys
> The subtle intrigues that a young man lays
> In his sly courtship of a harmless maid,
> Whereby his wanton amours are conveyed
> Into her breast; 'tis he alone that can
> Find out the cursëd policies of man." [29]

The ordinary stroke and height of its art may be seen in these lines, on Man:

> "For having once rebelled against his duty,
> Opacous sin soon blasted all his beauty;" [30]

or in these lines, on Pride:

> "Pride goes before destruction,
>   And haughtiness before a fall;
> Whoever pores his merits on,
>   Shall be endangered there withal." [31]

[28] The honor of first publishing it fell to the Mass. Hist. Soc. See their Collections, first series, IV. 262-298.†
[29] "Poetical Meditations," 12.   [30] Ibid. 5.
[31] Ibid. 7.

[* "Corrected in new Ed. 1896" to read: "This great historical poem, the author forbore not to publish even in his lifetime, but courageously gave it to the world, along with other specimens of his verse, in a volume called 'Poetical Meditations, being the Improvement of some vacant Hours,' published at New London in 1725."]

[† In Tyler's correction copy a crossed-out notation opposite this note reads: "No. Robt. C. Winthrop writes that it had been already printed. He has a copy." In 1897 the original note was changed to: "It was reprinted by the Massachusetts Historical Society in their Collections, first series, IV. 262-298."]

New England: The Verse-Writers

Upon the whole, the "Poetical Meditations" of Roger Wolcott are sad rubbish. He himself described them as "the improvement of some vacant hours." One finds it hard to imagine by what possibility such things could have been an improvement upon any sort of vacancy likely to occur in this good man's hours. For ourselves, we could have been content, had his hours remained vacant; and putting our own interpretation on his words, we thoroughly agree with the author himself when, in one place, he drops the judicious observation,

> "These very Meditations are
> Quite insupportable to bear." [32]

VIII

Among writers of poetry intended to be humorous, we encounter, in this period, at least two that may require a moment's notice. One of these is John Seccomb, the author of "Father Abbey's Will," and of "The Letter to the Widow Abbey,"—a writer, who, by some untoward accident, has had an extraordinary notoriety in our early literary history. He was graduated at Harvard College in 1728, at the age of twenty; was pastor of a church in the town of Harvard from 1733 to 1757; then, vexed by a calumny born, it is said,[33] of the jealous imagination of his wife, he withdrew from that parish and from the colony likewise, and betook himself as far as possible from the rumor of the scandal that had besmirched him, settling in Chester, Nova Scotia; where he served as minister, apparently in clean repute, during the remainder of his long life, dying in 1793. Had there been in him any germ of literary force, the extreme popularity, both in England and in America, achieved by his two effusions of metrical balderdash, would have prompted him to rise to something better, even in the vein of humorous verse. He lived more than sixty years after the perpetration of the ballads referred to; but he appears never again to have issued into print, excepting twice, each time for the publication of a sermon, the first at an ordination,

---

[32] "Poetical Meditations," 16.
[33] J. L. Sibley, in his ed. of "Father Abbey's Will," 8–9.

the second at a funeral, neither discourse being of any notable merit. It was in 1730, while he was still at Cambridge awaiting his second degree, that a queer old personage named Matthew Abdy, for many years sweeper, bed-maker, and bottle-washer to the college, came to his death; and John Seccomb conceived the harmless idea of celebrating the event by writing a pretended will, wherein the old fellow is made to bequeath to his widow all his real and personal estate, the several paltry items of which are reeled off in some fourteen stanzas of doggerel, the flatness and vulgarity of which may be sufficiently ascertained by a single one of them:

"A greasy hat,
My old ram cat,
A yard and half of linen,
A woolen fleece,
A pot of grease,
In order for your spinning."

This miserable stuff, well enough for an obscure escapade of rustic satire or of under-graduate wit, happened to catch the attention of the governor of Massachusetts, who, deeming it something wonderful, sent it to England. Strangely enough, it was at once published there, both in "The Gentleman's Magazine" and in "The London Magazine;" and it seems to have been widely read in the mother-country, as a just specimen of the poetic attainments and of the general literary taste of the Americans. It is hardly to be wondered at, that, instructed by such tokens, the English people should have formed very chastened expectations of the poetic destinies of their American children; or, that, nearly a hundred years afterward, one famous English poet should have written to another one, with reference to an American then in England, "I suppose an American enquires for live poets as you or I should do in America for a skunk or an opossum." [34] The uncommon notice paid in England to Seccomb's lines, naturally increased their celebrity in America: they were circulated here in newspapers and in broadsides; several imita-

[34] Robert Southey to Walter Scott, in Life of Southey by his Son, Harper's ed 364.

New England: The Verse-Writers

tions of them were produced; and New England mothers, we are told, were wont to recite them for the diversion of their children,—a service, indeed, in which they may have been not ineffective, since they rise, perhaps, to the intellectual altitude of the nursery. The author's true place as a melodist seems to be among the tuneful posterity of Mother Goose.

A humorist of far more palpable merit was Joseph Green, who was born in Boston in 1706; was graduated at Harvard when twenty years old; became a successful merchant in his native city; took some interest in colonial politics; upon the rupture with England became a loyalist, went into exile, and passed the last years of his life in England, dying there in 1780. In his time, he had great reputation for wit, particularly in the form of satirical verse. His favorite view of things was the facetious one; he was convivial and hilarious; he loved to mitigate by his waggeries the sombre tints of life at the Puritan metropolis; and neither religion nor death, it was believed, could awe him into gravity, as is partly intimated in this epitaph, which one of his friends wrote for his tomb-stone, long before he had need of one:

"Siste, Viator! Here lies one,
Whose life was whim, whose soul was pun;
And if you go too near his hearse,
He'll joke you, both in prose and verse."

It may be that, upon inspection of such examples of his wit as have floated down to us, we shall find that they scarcely justify the ecstasies of laughter with which, when first delivered, they seem to have been greeted; but, besides the fact that the pungency of personal satire always evaporates with time and distance, we need to reflect that Joseph Green's fellow citizens were not exactly persons abandoned to mirthful ways, and that they are, upon the whole, to be pardoned if they did welcome, at its full value, any honest effort for their diversion. Of his merit, no small part lay in his facility; and long after he was gone, the people of Boston kept alive there the memory of his exploits of extemporized witticism in verse. Thus, one day, while passing along the street, he observed that the Fourth Latin School of Boston was being taken down, in order to make room for the enlargement of an adjoining church; upon which incident, Green instantly composed this epigram:

> " 'A fig for your learning! I tell you the town,
> To make the church larger, must pull the school down.'
> 'Unluckily spoken,' replied Master Birch;
> 'Then learning, I fear, stops the growth of the church.' " [35]

On another occasion, a club of good fellows in Boston, of whom Green was prince, went to call upon one of their own number, named John Checkley, who was just then recovering from a long and dangerous illness. This gentleman, it appears, was noted for the ugliness of his countenance, at that time rendered still more forbidding by the ravages of disease. During the visit, it was agreed that as a mark of their satisfaction over Checkley's recovery, his portrait should be painted by Smibert; and Green was appointed to write a few appropriate verses to be inscribed beneath the portrait. Without waiting for the artist to do his work, the wit immediately drew forth his notebook, and, inspired by the countenance of poor Checkley, at once performed his part of the task, to the general satisfaction:

> "John, had thy sickness snatched thee from our sight
> And sent thee to the realms of endless night,
> Posterity would then have never known
> Thine eye, thy beard, thy cowl and shaven crown;
> But now, redeemed by Smibert's faithful hand,
> Of immortality secure you stand.
> When nature into ruin shall be hurled,
> And the last conflagration burn the world,
> This piece shall then survive the general evil,—
> For flames, we know, cannot consume the Devil." [36]

His satirical wit sometimes took a more deliberate and a larger flight, as is shown in several rather notable pieces of his that have been preserved. One of these is a parody on a hymn—a beautiful

---

[35] Given in S. Kettell, "Specimens of Am. Poetry," I. 139.
[36] Samuel L. Knapp "Biographical Sketches of Eminent Lawyers, Statesmen, and Men of Letters," 135.

New England: The Verse-Writers

and impressive hymn—written at sea by Mather Byles;[37] another is "A Mournful Lamentation for the sad and deplorable death of Mr. Old Tenor;"[38] another is "The Grand Arcanum Detected; or, A wonderful phenomenon explained, which has baffled the scrutiny of many ages; by Me, Phil. Arcanos, Gent. Student in Astrology;"[39] and still another is "An Entertainment for a Winter Evening," being a satire upon an ostentatious Masonic celebration in Boston on Saint John's day. In the latter, the poet notices, particularly, the march of the brotherhood from the tavern to the church, the chaplain's discourse there, and then the march of the brotherhood back again from the church to the tavern:

> "Come, goddess, and our ears regale
> With a diverting Christmas tale.
> O come, and in thy verse declare
> Who were the men, and what they were,
> And what their names, and what their fame,
> And what the cause for which they came,
> To house of God from house of ale,
> And how the parson told his tale;
> How they returned, in manner odd,
> To house of ale, from house of God."[40]
>
> . . .
>
> Masons at church! Strange auditory!
> And yet we have as strange in story.
> For saints, as history attests,
> Have preached to fishes, birds, and beasts.
>
> . . .
>
> So good Saint Francis, man of grace,
> Himself preached to the braying race;
> And further, as the story passes,
> Addressed them thus—'My brother asses.' "[41]

---

[37] Both the hymn and its parody are in "The Belknap Papers," 5 Mass. Hist. Soc. Coll. II. 70–72.

[38] Originally printed in 1750, on a half-sheet of foolscap paper; reprinted in "Am. Journal of Numismatics," April, 1871, 80–81.

[39] S. Kettell, "Specimens of Am. Poetry," III. 382.

[40] Second edition, 5–6.   [41] Ibid. 7–8.

History of American Literature

His version of the discourse is somewhat ludicrous; and in depicting the march back to the tavern, he gives burlesque portraits of conspicuous and well-known personages in the procession. One of these personages, a worthy citizen by the name of Pue, distinguished for habits that gave a brilliant color to his nose, is thus described:

> "Who's he comes next? 'Tis Pue by name,
> Pue by his nose well known to fame;
> This, when the generous juice recruits,
> Around a brighter radiance shoots.
> So, on some promontory's height,
> For Neptune's sons the signal light
> Shines fair, and fed by unctuous stream
> Sends off to sea a livelier beam." [42]

IX

During the entire colonial age, Americans lived under some menace of harm, either from the Indians, or from the French, or from both. Hence, they lived in a state of constant war, or of constant readiness for war. As might be expected, the vehement martial spirit engendered by such conditions, found voice and stimulation in numerous war-songs that made up at least in ferocity for what they lacked in poetical merit; while the most memorable incidents in all these military campaigns were enacted over again in rough popular ballads, such as "The Gallant Church," "Smith's Affair at Sidelong Hill," "The Godless French Soldier," and especially "Lovewell's Fight." [43]

In the year 1756, there appeared a little book, without mention of the place of publication or of the author's Christian name, bearing this title: "Tilden's Miscellaneous Poems on Divers Occasions, chiefly

---

[42] "An Entertainment for a Winter Evening," 2nd ed. 13.

[43] These titles are in R. W. Griswold, "Curiosities of Am. Lit." 26. "Lovewell's Fight" is printed in that book; also, in Samuel Penhallow, "Indian Wars," 129–136. A song-writer deserving some slight mention is John Osborn, born 1713, graduated at Harvard 1735; and died 1753. His most notable production is "A Whaling Song," said to have been long in use among our sailors. It is reprinted in S. Kettell, "Specimens Am. Poetry," I. 120–122. It is fortunate that his verses were acceptable on the sea—they had small chance of being so on land. He was probably a poet among sailors, and a sailor among poets.

New England: The Verse-Writers

to animate and rouse the soldiers." In his preface, the author describes himself as a man above seventy years of age. He excuses himself "for digging up rusty talents out of the earth, so long lain hid," by saying that, when young, he "was bashful and could not stand the gust of a laugh," but, that having for sixty years seen many an old scribbler come off with impunity, he was at last emboldened to venture upon authorship himself. How much the soldiers must have been animated and roused by "Tilden's Miscellaneous Poems," may be inferred from the following specimen of them:

> "Kind sirs, if that you will accept
> This petty pamphlet as a gift,
> With all the powers I have left,
>   I will consult your honor;
> But if you throw her quite away,
> As I confess you justly may,
> I've nothing further for to say,
>   But spit and tread upon her." [44]

Another poet, whom we are now to speak of, should be ushered into this history with the blast of a bugle and the roar of artillery; for, by his own account, he was, above all other things, a battle-bard, revelling in rhymes and bloodshed and the blaze of war. He published two very military and sonorific poems, upon the title-pages of which he proclaimed himself as "John Maylem, Philo-Bellum." The first of these poems is "The Conquest of Louisburg," [45] and is a narrative, in rhymed pentameters, of the exhilarating effort of New England heroism, indicated by the title. The whole poem is tumultuous, gory, and gigantesque, as these lines may show:

> "But lo! while ready for the charge they stood,
> Death, blunderbuss, artillery, and blood!
> Blue smoke and purple flame around appear,
> And the hot bullets hail from front to rear.
> Tremendous Fate by turns incessant flies,
> While the black sulphur clouds the azure skies,
> And ghastly savages, with fearful yell,
> Invoke their kindred of profoundest hell."

[44] "Tilden's Miscellaneous Poems," 18.   [45] Boston, 1758.

This gusty warrior, who could hardly have moved upon his enemy with any weapons more awe-inspiring or destructive than his own verses, published another poem, named "Gallic Perfidy." [46] In this work, he tells the story of the capture of himself and his military companions, at the hands of Indians and Frenchmen under Montcalm; of his own great sufferings during his captivity; finally, of his redemption and return. He begins by informing us that he is the same poetic individual,

"who, of late, in epic strains essayed,
And sung the hero on Acadia's plains;"

also, that he now intends to sing again, and about something else:

"But yet in rougher strain; for softer rhyme
Seems not adapt to this my solemn theme." [47]

Having thus given a timely hint of the peculiarly awful nature of the subject to be sung about, he pauses in order to invoke an inspiration that shall be appropriate. Certainly, no common one will answer the present purpose:

"Not to invoke
A vulgar muse,—ye powers of Fury, lend
Some mighty frenzy to enrage my breast
With solemn song, beyond all nature's strain!
For such the scene of which I mean to sing." [48]

His prayer appears to have been instantaneously answered; for, in the very next line, he is able to chronicle this state of things:

"Enough! I rave!—the Furies rack my brain!
I feel their influence now inspire my song!
My laboring muse swells with the raving god!
I feel him here! My head turns round!—'twill burst!
So have I seen a bomb, with livid train,
Emitted from a mortar, big with death,
And fraught, full fraught, with hell's combustibles,
Lay dreadful on the ground; then with a force
Stupendous, shiver in a thousand atoms!
But, on, my muse!" [49]

[46] Boston, 1758.   [47] "Gallic Perfidy," 2.   [48] Ibid. 3.
[49] Ibid. 3. For this remarkable poet our literature is indebted to Harvard Col-

New England: The Verse-Writers

X

In the year 1740, there died at Cambridge, at the age of thirty-six, a man named John Adams, who as scholar, preacher, and poet, had won high reputation for himself. He was the son of a Nova-Scotian; was of the Harvard class of 1721; had served as minister in Newport and in Philadelphia; seemed to his friends to be quite a prodigy of genius and learning, being a master of nine languages, and familiar with the best writings in ancient and modern literatures; during his lifetime had gained special glory by his verses, particularly a satirical poem on the love of money. His death came as a premature and cruel ending of a career that promised very considerable things. Five years afterward, the principal fragments of his poetic estate were gathered up and printed in a book, entitled "Poems on Several Occasions." It contains translations from the Bible and from Horace, and such not unprecedented things as verses on "Melancholy," "Contentment," "Joy," "Society," "The Perfection of Beauty," and "The King of Zion;"—poems not absolutely indispensable to the world's continued existence or peace of mind. Doubtless, the Reverend John Adams was an accomplished, pious, and pleasant gentleman in his time; but in poetry he sounded no note that was not conventional and imitative.

In the year 1744, there came from the press in Boston a little book of somewhat ambitious aspect, "A Collection of Poems by Several Hands." Being the product of a literary combination, it was doubtless looked upon at the time as a work representative of the poetic taste and skill then attained in the land; and it has since been described as a landmark of literary progress up to that date. If it had such significance, the indications are rather depressing; they report little more than weak reverberations of the imagery and the syllables of Alexander Pope. The book seems, in fact, to have been the offspring of an amiable conspiracy on the part of some literary friends of Mather Byles, to accomplish—and with his own entire approbation—the poetical apotheosis of that gentleman, and to induce the

---

lege, where he was graduated in 1715. The ordinary accounts of him say that he died in 1742. As, however, the capture of Louisburg did not take place until 1745, and as he wrote a poem on that affair, it seems somewhat improbable that he was then dead. Indeed, I have come across no satisfactory evidence to show that he is dead yet.

public to believe that one of the most gifted of its pulpit orators was likewise a very great poet. The first poem, attributed to the Reverend John Adams, is a metrical gush of adulation directed toward Byles. The latter is the

> "charming poet whose distinguished lays
> Excite our wonder, and surmount our praise;" [50]

and he is explicitly told to his face that there are points of striking resemblance between himself and John Milton:

> "You imitate his airy rapid flights,
> And mount with ardor to his godlike heights." [51]

Another poem, extending the personal comparison, asserts that Byles,

> "Harvard's honor, and New England's hope,
> Bids fair to rise and sing and rival Pope." [52]

Another poem, after reciting the reproaches that had been cast upon New England for poetic barrenness, finds in the lofty genius of Byles the prospect of New England's speedy vindication:

> "At length our [Byles] aloft transfers his name,
> And binds it on the radiant wings of fame." [53]

Another poem, written by a lady, declares that a certain

> "pleased goddess triumphs to pronounce
> The name of [Byles], Pope, Homer, all at once." [54]

Among the treasures of this volume, not directly referring to Mather Byles, we find a dulcet and platitudinous pastoral introducing our well-remembered friends, "Belinda," and "Strephon;" also "circling arms," "surrendering charms," several "swains," a fair as-

[50] "A Collection of Poems," etc. 3.   [51] Ibid. 3.   [52] Ibid. 13.
[53] Ibid. 13. In examining these poems, I have used the volume that belonged first to Mather Byles himself, then to his daughter, "Th. Byles, given her by her father, Feb. 14, 1763," then to George Ticknor, then to Charles Deane, and finally by the generosity of the latter to the Mass. Hist. Soc. In some passages where Byles is referred to, five asterisks are given instead of the letters of his name; but in the volume used by me, his name is written over these asterisks, apparently by himself.
[54] Ibid. 44.

sortment of "pangs," besides one "yielding fair," who is "abandoned to despair," together with numerous other things of a similar nature. Here, also, are a couple of puerile ballads on military events, some unusually silly nursery-rhymes, and even—so low does the book descend—"A Commencement Ode." Upon the other hand, there are a very few pieces that are not contemptible, the best one being entitled "The Comet." It is attributed to Mather Byles himself, and is in his usual style when serious and eloquent.

Peter Oliver, whose name in our civil history rests under the shadow of unpatriotic subservience to the English crown in the great struggle of the Americans for their rights, had an earlier fame among us of a gentler and pleasanter kind; a fame procured by his uncommon talents as a writer. He was born in 1713, was graduated at Harvard in 1730, and settling upon his estate at Middleborough, devoted his life for many years to agriculture, literature, and politics. The most satisfactory token that remains to us of his gifts, is a poem, published at Boston in 1757, in honor of an accomplished and noble-minded colonial statesman, Josiah Willard, who had died at an advanced age the year before. The poem, though clad in the orthodox metrical garb of the day,—especially having some vestments borrowed from the wardrobes of Thomson and of Young,—has likewise a strength of its own, an individual spirit not quite smothered under its conventionalisms.

XI

King George the Second died in October, 1760; and the English people, who, since the downfall of the Stuarts, had seen upon their throne an almost unbroken succession of foreign monarchs, now welcomed with universal joy the accession of a king of England who was also a native of England. This joy, abundant throughout the three kingdoms both in noise and in heartiness, was, in the American colonies of England, certainly not less hearty or noisy; and among many other forms of expression, it uttered itself here in one most elaborate and most sumptuous literary form. The oldest college in America, observing that the English universities had laid before his Majesty "their poetical oblations," conceived the idea of conveying to the king its own loyal emotion in the same reputable manner. Accordingly, there was a strong muster to the undertaking, of all the available culture and genius of Harvard College, among both its faculty and its graduates, with the worthy intent of producing a series of poems in Latin, Greek, and English, that should bewail the exit of one king and belaud the advent of another, and at the same time represent to Europe the progress thus far made, in the new world, in the most elegant studies.

Unfortunately, the inspiration that gives birth to great poetry does not often come from its vasty deep in response to the call of any sort of ceremonial subpœna. Without doubt, this planet of ours bears upon it at present the beautiful burden of innumerous volumes of official poetry,—tomes throbbing with most metrical and sonorous joy and sorrow, carefully compounded in deference to high command; but seldom is such a thing as "Lycidas" to be met with among these fabrications. Let us, therefore, with our expectations well chastened, draw near to this noble and famous quarto, in which Harvard College, on a fitting occasion, enshrined its very filial and very colonial grief and gladness; in which, likewise, it deposited the evidence of the mechanical expertness then attained in America in the manufacture of books and of poetry: "Pietas et Gratulatio Collegii Cantabrigiensis Apud Nov-Anglos. Bostoni-Massachusettensium. Typis J. Green & J. Russell.—MDCCLXI."

The work is introduced by a graceful letter in prose, addressed to the new king, and signed by the president and fellows of Harvard. It makes modest reference to the remoteness and obscurity of the college, and expresses great loyalty to the English crown, and great hope respecting the generosity and justice of the monarch who had just begun to wear it: "Your Majesty is raised by heaven to provide in the new world a retreat for the wretched inhabitants of the old,—an asylum to which they may retire from the reach of war, and set themselves down in peace, sure to reap the fruits of industry, secure in the enjoyment of their civil and religious liberties, and exempt from the miseries which distress most other countries." The letter does not altogether omit to remind his Majesty of the propriety of some "royal favor and patronage" for the college; it utters likewise the belief that America is now to become "a more interesting object to Great Britain" than ever before—a belief that was entirely justi-

New England: The Verse-Writers

fied by events; and it concludes with a promise on the part of the college so to educate its pupils "that they may be in their future stations grateful as well as useful subjects to the best of kings"—a promise not entirely justified by events.

The book contains one hundred and six pages of typography, which is exquisite; and thirty-one pieces of poetry, the exquisiteness of which is less obvious. Of these poems, three are in Greek, sixteen in Latin, twelve in English; all the writers save one—Sir Francis Bernard—being scholars of American birth and training.[55] Glancing, first, at the poems produced in the ancient languages, we find that the Greek odes show a fondness for Homeric words and forms; that they are Homeric even in their deviations from the syntax of Attic Greek; and that they contain some metrical irregularities, corresponding to those met with in Sappho, and the other lyric poets belonging to the archaic period of the language. Of the Latin odes, the classical purity is in the main unexceptionable; though there are a few faulty constructions, besides a tendency to use certain words and phrases in meanings unusual in classical Latin, together with a habit of placing some words out of their regular positions in the sentence.[56] As regards their versification, it may be said that the hexameters and pentameters have no positive blemishes, unless unmusical lines be counted as such; but that in the Alcaic and Sapphic stanzas there are a few notable faults in metre, in rhythm, and even in quantity.[57]

Naturally, our principal interest is in the English poems of the book; and we note, first of all, the entire conformity of the writers to the poetic manner then prevalent in England—a dialect fluent, automatic, insincere. Making allowance for this fault—a venial one—we find the work, even as poetry, in some respects creditable; a fact all the more surprising, since the incidents that called this poetry into existence,—the death of an individual like George the Second,

---

[55] Respecting the authorship of particular pieces, there are several traditions; but as these traditions are conflicting, I have not here mentioned any of them. The chief value of the book is in its aggregate character as representing the most advanced stage of classical and literary culture reached in America in the colonial time.

[56] For example, que is in these odes out of its regular position as many as ten or twelve times.

[57] As ĕlegantioris.

and the accession of another individual like George the Third,—are incidents supremely unpoetic. Undoubtedly, the mourning in these poems is official. Here is the full, round chant of formal laudation and ceremonious sorrow; tears that flow only from impossible eyes, and groans that no one utters except from a sense of duty, and then only in verse. Compared with the poetry produced in England with reference to the same events, very likely this, born in America, was especially honest,—having, in fact, the genuineness of feeling that comes of provincial ignorance, and the enchantment about monarchs that is one of the many advantages of being at a distance from them.

In celebrating the glory of the dead king, his American eulogists point to the material prosperity of England under his reign:

"Commerce, o'er the broad-backed sea
Extending far on floating isles,
Imported India's wealth, and rich
Peruvian spoils." [58]

But the death of George the Second seems to these ingenuous poets to be an event so vast and so disastrous as to call for some very sympathetic recognition on the part of Nature:

"thy noontide ray,
Phœbus, suspend; ye clouds, obscure the day;
Her face let Cynthia veil;
Thick darkness spread her wing,
And the night-raven sing;
While Britons their sad fate bewail." [59]

In her sorrow at the death of George the Second, Britannia herself is observed on "her sea-girt shore," "with head reclined":

"White * Melancholy on her brow
Sat brooding, with her raven wing
Shading those features which till then
With majesty unrivalled shone." [60]

[58] "Pietas et Gratulatio," 14.   [59] Ibid. 17.   [60] Ibid. 43.

[* Changed to "While." A marginal note says: "Justin Winsor gives me this correction from a slip of errata in Harv. Lib. copy."]

New England: The Verse-Writers

And, indeed, all these pathetic demonstrations were most appropriate both for Nature and for Britannia, if the dead king had been endowed even with a tithe of the personal and kingly virtues here attributed to him. It seems to be conceded by these New England bards that there were indeed a few great heroes and great kings before George the Second; and yet the greatest of them, Cæsar and Alexander, are mentioned, only to give emphasis to the fact that they are quite unworthy of being brought into comparison with the one English king and hero lately deceased:

> "No more let ancient times their heroes boast,
> Since all their fame in George's praise is lost;
> Not Greece—her Alexanders; Cæsars—Rome.
> For worth and virtue, view our monarch's tomb.
> Restless ambition dwelt in Cæsar's mind;
> He murdered nations and enslaved mankind,
> He found a generous people great and free,
> And gave them tyrants for their liberty.
> The glorious Alexander, half divine,
> Whose godlike deeds in ancient records shine,
> Dropt his divinity at every feast,
> And lost the god and hero in the beast.
> Shall, then, our monarch be with these compared?
> Or George's glory with a Cæsar shared?
> No—we indignant spurn the unworthy claim;
> George shines unrivalled in the lists of fame." [61]

In fact, to these rapturous American poets even Death seems rather insolent in having presumed to aim his dart at such a king as George the Second:

> "Insulting victor! boast this trophy won!
> That your broad shade hath darkened Britain's sun;
> But, know! such kings as George but take their way
> Through your thick darkness to immortal day.
> Indulgent Heaven with splendor rayed him down
> To swell the lustre of the British crown;
> But virtues, such as his, are not confined
> To small domains; they encircle all mankind.

---

[61] "Pietas et Gratulatio," 21–22.

Bourbons to humble, Brunswicks were ordained:
Those mankind's rights destroyed, but these regained." [62]

But for all the grief consequent upon the death of the king, there is at least some consolation: if one George be snatched away, Heaven is merciful to this extent, that another George remains:

"In the forehead of the East
See the gilded morning star—
Of glad day the harbinger.
Sighing, now, and tears are ceased:
Still George survives; his virtues shine
In him who sprung alike from Brunswick's royal line." [63]

Another of these colonial rhapsodists, not dreaming of the rough blows with which the near future was to shatter all these illusions of transatlantic fealty to the Georges, exclaims:

"But say, my muse, say, who is he
The scarcely vacant throne who fills?
'Tis he! the heaven-inspirëd youth!
The falling purple robe who caught,
And all the virtues of the grandsire claims;" [64]

while still another poet speaks of the joy with which the whole British empire sees

"ascend the throne
A blooming monarch who is all her own." [65]

No one who duly considers this magnificent effusion of provincial gush and king-worship, from the most accomplished gentlemen in America in 1761,—this premeditated and ostentatious torrent of adulatory drivel with reference to such dull fellows as the Brunswicks,—will ever imagine that our war for independence came upon us a moment too soon; indeed, it appears to have been as necessary for our intellects, as it was for our liberties.

---

[62] "Pietas et Gratulatio," 11–12. It is amusing to remember how, a very few years afterward, the opinion * expressed in the last couplet was, in American opinion, exactly reversed.   [63] Ibid. 18.   [64] Ibid. 50.   [65] Ibid. 24.

[* Changed to "thought" in 1897. Tyler wrote and crossed out "idea," "sentiment," and "judgment" before deciding upon "thought."]

Chapter XII

New England: The Dynasty of the Mathers

I. The founder of the dynasty, Richard Mather—His flight from England and career in America—His traits—His writings—An ecclesiastical politician—His love of study.

II. Increase Mather—His American birth and breeding—His residence in Ireland and England—Returns to New England—His great influence there—Pulpit-orator, statesman, courtier, college president—His learning—His laboriousness in study—His manner in the pulpit—The literary qualities of his writings—Specimens—Number and range of his published works—His "Illustrious Providences"—Origin of the book—Its value.

III. Cotton Mather—His preëminence—The adulation received by him —His endowments—His precocity—The development of his career— His religious character and discipline—His intellectual accomplishments—His habits as a reader—The brilliancy of his talk—Contemporaneous admiration—The watchword of his life—The multitude of his books—Characteristic titles—The fame of his "Magnalia"—His anxieties respecting its publication—Its scope—His advantages and disadvantages for historical writing—Estimate of the historical character of the "Magnalia"—The best of his subsequent writings—"Bonifacius"—. "Psalterium Americanum"—"Manuductio ad Ministerium"—Its counsels to a young prophet—Study of Hebrew, of history, of natural philosophy—Assault on Aristotle—The place of Cotton Mather in American literature—The last of the Fantastics in prose—Traits of his style —Pedantry—His style not agreeable to his later contemporaries—His theory of style—Defence of his own style against his critics.

IV. Samuel Mather—His days and deeds—A stanch patriot—The end of the dynasty.

I

IN the year 1634, the Archbishop of York, being of an honest mind to snip the pestiferous weeds of dissent that were then sprouting up in his province, sent forth his visitors into Lancashire, for the prosecution of the good work. Straightway, these pleasant gentlemen, holding court at Wigan, summoned before them one Richard Mather, who humbly confessed that he had been minister of the church at Toxteth for fifteen years, and yet had never in all that time worn a surplice; whereupon, one of these reverend visitors "swore, 'It had been better for him that he had begotten seven bastards.'"[1] Not having any such extenuating achievements to plead in his behalf, the poor parson, much against his will, "betook himself to a private life;" and in April, of the following year, he made his way stealthily, and in disguise, to Bristol, and thence got ship for Boston, where he arrived on the seventeenth of August, 1635. The long voyage was for him both tedious and perilous; but it brought to him, likewise, its compensations,—one being a spectacle that forever relieved his mind of some previous carnal embarrassment in connection with the difficult story of Jonah: "In the afternoon we saw mighty whales spewing up water in the air, like the smoke of a chimney, and making the sea about them white and hoary, as it is said in Job; of such incredible bigness that I will never wonder that the body of Jonah could be in the belly of a whale."[2]

At the time of his arrival in Boston, Richard Mather was thirty-nine years of age; a man of extensive and precise learning in the classics, in the Scriptures, and in divinity; already a famous preacher. "His voice," we are told, "was loud and big; and uttered with a deliberate vehemency, it procured unto his ministry an awful and very taking majesty."[3] It was of him that the illustrious Thomas Hooker had said, "My brother Mather is a mighty man."[4] No wonder that, upon the arrival in New England of this same mighty man, together with his loud and big voice, there was among the churches some brotherly strife for the possession of him. Dorchester, as it chanced, was the fortunate church; for, in 1636, he ac-

---

[1] "Magnalia," I. 448. [2] Young, "Chron. Mass. Bay," 465.
[3] "Magnalia," I. 452. [4] Ibid.

New England: Dynasty of the Mathers

cepted its call, and in its service he abode, until April the twenty-second, 1669, when "he quietly breathed forth his last; after he had been about seventy-three years a citizen of the world, and fifty years a minister in the church of God." [5]

This man, "the progenitor of all the Mathers in New England," [6] and the first of a line of great preachers and great men of letters that continued to hold sway there through the entire colonial era, had in himself the chief traits that distinguished his family through so long a period;—great physical endurance, a voracious appetite for the reading of books, an alarming propensity to the writing of books, a love of political leadership in church and state, the faculty of personal conspicuousness, finally, the homiletic gift.

His numerous writings were, of course, according to the demand of his time and neighborhood;—sermons, a catechism, a treatise on justification, public letters upon church government, several controversial documents, the preface to the Old Bay Psalm Book, and many of the marvels of metrical expression to be viewed in the body of that work.[7]

In recognition of his prominence and power in ecclesiastical politics, one of his contemporaries wrote this epitaph for him: "Vixerat in synodis, moritur moderator in illis." [8] Yet, as was the case with each of his famous descendants, his true life seemed to be among his books; and he did his share to create the tradition of heroic studiousness attaching to the clergy of colonial New England. On "the morning before he died, he importuned the friends that watched with him, to help him into the room where he thought his usual works and books expected him. To satisfy his importunity, they began to lead him thither; but finding himself unable to get out of his lodging-room, he said, 'I see I am not able. I have not been in my study several days; and is it not a lamentable thing that I should lose so much time?'" [9]

This dying speech of the first of the Mathers was, in its spirit, the living speech of all the rest of them, for more than a hundred years. Above all other things, they were a bookish clan. To them, that

---

[5] "Magnalia," I. 456.   [6] Young, "Chron. Mass. Bay," 480, note.
[7] A list of his writings in W. B. Sprague, "Annals of Am. Pulpit," I. 78–79.
[8] John Eliot, "Biograph. Dict." 306.   [9] "Magnalia," I. 453.

moment seemed lost, in which, if not publicly preaching or privately plotting, they were not either reading a book, or writing one.

II

Of the six sons of Richard Mather, four became famous preachers, two of them in Ireland and in England, other two in New England; the greatest of them all being the youngest, born at Dorchester, June twenty-first, 1639, and at his birth adorned with the name of Increase, in grateful recognition of "the increase of every sort, wherewith God favored the country about the time of his nativity." [10]

Even in childhood he began to display the strong and eager traits that gave distinction and power to his whole life, and that bore him impetuously through the warfare of eighty-four mortal years. At twelve, he entered Harvard College, taking his Bachelor's degree at seventeen. His Latin oration, at Commencement, was so vigorous an assault upon the philosophy of Aristotle, that President Chauncey would have stopped him, had not the Cambridge pastor, Jonathan Mitchell—a man of great authority—cried out in intercession, "Pergat, quaeso, nam doctissime disputat." In 1657, on his nineteenth birthday, he preached in his father's pulpit his first sermon,—a sermon so able in matter and in manner, that it greatly added to the general belief that here was a youth from whom more was to be heard by and by. Twelve days afterward, he sailed for Dublin, where his eldest brother, Samuel, was a noted preacher, and where, entering himself as a student of Trinity College, he took, with high reputation, his Master's degree in the following year,—declining a fellowship. During the subsequent three years, he exercised his talents as a preacher, with great effect, in various parts of England and in Guernsey; and in 1661, not deeming the outlook an agreeable one, just then, for dissenters in the mother-country, he abandoned his purpose of making a career there, and returned to his native land.

At once, invitations poured in upon him from "as many places as there are signs for the sun in the Zodiac." Declining to be settled anywhere in haste, he divided his services between his father's church at Dorchester and the North Church of Boston; and at last,

[10] C. Mather, "Parentator," 1–5.

New England: Dynasty of the Mathers

in May, 1664, he consented to be made minister of the latter church, which, thenceforward, to the end of his own life, and to the end of the life of his more famous son, continued to be the tower and the stronghold of the Mathers in America.

Thus, before his twenty-sixth birthday, Increase Mather had found the place of his work for life,—a prominent pulpit in the chief town of the New England theocracy. There, wielding the most tremendous weapon of influence known in such a community, he continued to fulminate, to the delight of his adherents, to the great terror of his foes, for almost sixty years; and by force of his learning, his logic, his sense, his eloquence, his tireless energy, his adroitness in intrigue, his sagacity and audacity in partisan command, he became, during the first thirty years of that time, the most powerful man in all that part of the world. In the desperate conflict in which Massachusetts contended with James the Second for its own existence, Increase Mather was a potent counsellor of the people; and for several years, as the representative of his colony at the court of James, and of William and Mary, the Boston pastor proved himself an able and successful diplomate. For sixteen years, also, he filled the high office of president of Harvard College, without ceasing to be pastor of North Church. From about 1694 and until his death in 1723, his political prestige, even his ecclesiastical prestige, greatly declined; yet to the last, he was a sovereign man throughout New England, illustrious for great talents and great services, both at home and abroad.

Here, then, was a person, born in America, bred in America,—a clean specimen of what America could do for itself in the way of keeping up the brave stock of its first imported citizens; a man every way capable of filling any place in public leadership made vacant by the greatest of the Fathers; probably not a whit behind the best of them in scholarship, in eloquence, in breadth of view, in knowledge of affairs, in every sort of efficiency.

As to learning, it has been said [11] that he even exceeded all other New-Englanders of the colonial time, except his own son, Cotton. On the day when he was graduated at our little rustic university, he had the accomplishments usual among the best scholars of the best

[11] By Enoch Pond, "Life of I. Mather," 142.

universities of the old world; he could converse fluently in Latin, and could read and write Hebrew and Greek; and his numberless publications in after life bear marks of a range of learned reading that widened as he went on in years, and drew into its hospitable gulf some portions of nearly all literatures, especially the most obscure and uncouth.

His habits as a student were those of the mighty theologians and pulpit-orators among whom he grew up. He had the appalling capacity of working in his study sixteen hours a day. One now contemplates with a mixture of admiration and horror—alleviated by incredulity—the picture that has been left us by filial hands, of one of this man's ordinary working-days: "In the morning, repairing to his study (where his custom was to sit up very late, even until midnight and perhaps after it) he deliberately read a chapter, and made a prayer, and then plied what of reading and writing he had before him. At nine o'clock, he came down and read a chapter, and made a prayer with his family. He then returned unto the work of the study. Coming down to dinner, he quickly went up again, and begun the afternoon with another prayer. There he went on with the work of the study till the evening. Then with another prayer he again went unto his Father; after which he did more at the work of the study. At nine o'clock, he came down to his family sacrifices. Then he went up again to the work of the study, which anon he concluded with another prayer; and so he betook himself unto his repose." [12]

His power as a pulpit-orator was very great, and it was bought at a great price. On Monday morning he began his sermons for the next Sunday, and continued to work upon them diligently until Friday night; on Saturday he committed them to memory. Of course, on Sunday, armed thus at every point, he could march into his pulpit with confident tread. Using no manuscript, he spoke without hesitation, "with a grave and wise deliberation," often with impassioned vehemence. He had, like his father, a commanding voice; and he used it with great effect, at times, indeed, "with such a tonitruous cogency that the hearers would be struck with an awe, like what would be produced on the fall of thunderbolts." [13] It was

[12] C. Mather, "Parentator," 181.   [13] Ibid. 216.

New England: Dynasty of the Mathers

a common saying of his contemporaries, that Increase Mather was "a complete preacher."

From a literary point of view, his writings certainly have considerable merit. His style is far better than that of his son,—simpler, more terse, more sinewy and direct, less bedraggled in the dust of pedantry; it has remarkable energy; in many places it is so modern in tone that it would not seem strange in any pulpit now, except for the numerous quotations from Scripture, as well as for an occasional use of some Latin or Greek or Hebrew phrase. Thus, depicting the victory of Christ over the Devil, the preacher exclaims: "He has led captivity captive. He has disarmed the Devil and all his angels, and, as it were, tied them to his triumphal chariot, and exposed them openly in the sight of heaven and earth." [14] The worth of a human soul—that enticing and ineffable theme of pulpit-rhetoric in every age—he proclaims in this pithy and vivid manner: "One soul is of more worth than all the world. . . . Every man has . . . a body that must die, and shall die, and a soul that shall never die. To save such a soul is a mightier thing than to save all the bodies in the world." [15] In the battle of life, here upon the earth, we are not engaged, he tells us, in an obscure field, or unwatched by throngs of spectators: "Let us always remember what eyes are upon us. There are glorious eyes, which, though we see not them, are observing us in all our motions. The eyes of holy angels are upon us. . . . And the eyes of Jesus Christ, the Son of God, behold us. . . . And the eyes of God behold us. . . . It is reported of a faithful minister of Christ, that there was written on the walls of his study, 'Deus videt, angeli adstant, conscientia testabitur,'—God seeth thee, angels are by thee, thy own conscience will be a witness how thou dost behave thyself." [16] Sometimes, he casts his thought into an illustration so luminous and so shrewd that it makes further argument unnecessary; as when he says of the government of Massachusetts under Sir Edmund Andros: "The Foxes were now made the administrators of justice to the Poultry."

The publications of Increase Mather defy mention, except in the form of a catalogue. From the year 1669, when he had reached the

[14] "Several Sermons," 13. [15] Ibid. 13–14.
[16] Sermon on death of Rev. John Baily, 6–7.

age of thirty, until the year 1723, when he died, hardly a twelvemonth was permitted to pass in which he did not solicit the public attention through the press. An authentic list of his works would include at least ninety-two titles.[17] The most of these works are sermons; but as sermons, they sweep the entire circuit of themes, sacred and secular, on which men employed their thoughts in those days,—divinity, ethics, casuistry, church government, law, English and American politics, history, prophecy, demonology, angelology, crime, poverty, ignorance, dancing, the Indian question, earthquakes, comets, winds, conflagrations, drunkenness, and the small-pox.

Of all the great host of Increase Mather's publications, perhaps only one can be said to have still any power of walking alive on the earth,—the book commonly known by a name not given to it by the author, "Remarkable Providences." The origin of this book is worth mention. As early as 1658, a number of Puritan ministers in England and in Ireland combined to put on record, and finally to publish, authentic accounts of extraordinary interpositions of Providence in recent human affairs. After some progress had been made in the work, it was dropped. Subsequently, the manuscript was sent to New England, probably by Milton's friend, Samuel Hartlib. For many years it lay in obscurity in Boston, until, by good fortune, it fell into the energetic hands of Increase Mather. The plan was exactly suited to a mind like his; and after communicating it to his clerical brethren, and receiving their cordial encouragement to go on with it, he sent forth proposals through New England, calling upon ministers and other reputable persons to forward to him written narratives of Providential events that had occurred under their own observation. In 1684, the book was published, under the title of "An Essay for the Recording of Illustrious Providences." [18] Thus the work is simply a compilation of anecdotes sent to the editor, or culled by him from his own observation and from books, the whole being plentifully decorated with comments and speculations of his own. The materials are classified under these topics: "remarkable sea-deliverances;" "some other remarkable preservations;" "remark-

[17] One list is given in W. B. Sprague, "Annals of Am. Pulpit," I. 156–157; another and better list in J. L. Sibley, "Harv. Grad." I. 438–463.
[18] Reprinted, London, 1856.

ables about thunder and lightning;" "things preternatural which have happened in New England;" "demons and possessed persons;" "apparitions;" "deaf and dumb persons;" remarkable tempests, earthquakes, and floods in New England; remarkable judgments upon Quakers, drunkards, and enemies of the church; finally, "some remarkables at Norwich in New England." It cannot be denied that the conception of the book is thoroughly scientific; for it is to prove by induction the actual presence of supernatural forces in the world. Its chief defect, of course, is its lack of all cross-examination of the witnesses, and of all critical inspection of their testimony, together with a palpable eagerness on the author's part to welcome, from any quarter of the earth or sea or sky, any messenger whatever, who may be seen hurrying toward Boston with his mouth full of marvels. The narratives, often vividly told, are tragic, or amusing, or disgusting, now and then merely stupid; in several particulars they anticipate the phenomena of modern spiritualism; while the philosophical disquisitions of the author are at once a laughable and an instructive memorial of the mental habits of very orthodox and very enlightened people in Protestant Christendom, in the seventeenth century.

III

In the intellectual distinction of the Mather family, there seemed to be, for at least three generations, a certain cumulative felicity. The general acknowledgment of this fact is recorded in an old epitaph, composed for the founder of the illustrious tribe:

> "Under this stone lies Richard Mather,
> Who had a son greater than his father,
> And eke a grandson greater than either."

This overtopping grandson was, of course, none other than Cotton Mather, the literary behemoth of New England in our colonial era; the man whose fame as a writer surpasses, in later times and especially in foreign countries, that of any other pre-Revolutionary American, excepting Jonathan Edwards and Benjamin Franklin.

The twelfth of February, 1663, was the happy day on which he was bestowed upon the world,—the eldest of a family of ten children, his mother being the only daughter of the celebrated pulpit-orator, John Cotton. In himself, therefore, the forces and graces of two ancestral lines renowned for force and for grace, seemed to meet and culminate.

From his earliest childhood, and through all his days, he was gazed at and belauded by his immediate associates, as a being of almost supernatural genius, and of quite indescribable godliness. That his nature early became saturated with self-consciousness, and that he grew to be a vast literary and religious coxcomb, is a thing not likely to astonish any one who duly considers, first, the strong original aptitude of the man in that direction, and, secondly, the manner of his mortal life from the cradle to the grave,—the idol of a distinguished family, the prodigy both of school and of college, the oracle of a rich parish, the pet and demi-god of an endless series of sewing-societies.

It may be said of Cotton Mather, that he was born with an enormous memory, an enormous appetite for every species of knowledge, an enormous zeal and power for work, an enormous passion for praise. At his birth, also, he came into a household of books and of students. The first breath he drew was air charged with erudition. His toys and his playmates were books. The dialect of his childhood was the ponderous phraseology of philosophers and divines. To be a scholar was a part of the family inheritance. At eleven years of age, he was a freshman in Harvard College; having, however, before that time, read Homer and Isocrates, and many unusual Latin authors, and having, likewise, entered upon the congenial employment of exhorting his juvenile friends to lives of godliness, and even of writing "poems of devotion" for their private use. At fifteen, on taking his first degree, he had the pleasure of hearing the president of the college address to him, by name, in the presence of the great throng at commencement, a glowing compliment,—admirably constructed to ripen in this precocious and decidedly priggish young gentleman his already well-developed sense of his own importance. At eighteen, on taking his second degree, he delivered a learned and persuasive thesis, on "the divine origin of the Hebrew points."

One year before the event last mentioned, he began to preach.

New England: Dynasty of the Mathers

Being oppressed by a grievous habit of stammering, he was on the point of abandoning the ministry for the medical profession, when "that good old school-master, Mr. Corlet," told him that he could cure himself of his trouble, if he would but remember always to speak "with a dilated deliberation." He adopted the suggestion, and was cured.[19] At the age of twenty-two, he was made an associate of his father in the pastorship of North Church, Boston. There, in the pauseless prosecution of almost incredible labors, literary, philanthropic, oratorical, and social, he continued to the end of his days on earth. He departed this life in 1728, having been permitted to contemplate, for many years and with immense delight, the progress of his own fame, as it reverberated through Christendom.

Upon the whole, the picture of Cotton Mather, given to us in his own writings, and in the writings of those who knew him and loved him, is one of surpassing painfulness. We see a person whose intellectual endowments were quite remarkable, but inflated and perverted by egotism; himself imposed upon by his own moral affectations; completely surrendered to spiritual artifice; stretched, every instant of his life, on the rack of ostentatious exertion, intellectual and religious, and all this partly for vanity's sake, partly for conscience' sake—in deference to a dreadful system of ascetic and pharisaic formalism, in which his nature was hopelessly enmeshed.

In his fourteenth year, he began the habit of frequent fasts and vigils, to which he attached a superstitious importance, and which he kept up with increasing intensity to the end of his life. He desired "to resemble a rabbi mentioned in the Talmud, whose face was black by reason of his fastings;" [20] and it was computed that, in the course of his life, the number of his special fast-days amounted to four hundred and fifty.[21] Once, in his old age, he abstained from all food three days together, and spent the time, as he expressed it, "in knocking at the door of heaven."

Moreover, he prescribed to himself a scheme of minute rules for the association of devout thoughts with every occurrence of the day or the night: "When he heard a clock strike, he could not help think-

---

[19] S. Mather, "Life of C. Mather," 26.
[20] W. B. O. Peabody, "Life of C. Mather," 176.
[21] S. Mather, "Life of C. Mather," 110.

ing and wishing that he might so number his days as to apply his heart to wisdom." "When he knocked at a door, the faith of our Saviour's promise was awakened in him—'Knock and it shall be opened unto you.'" "When he mended his fire, it was with a meditation how his heart and life might be rectified, and how, through the emendations of divine grace, his love and zeal might flame more agreeably." "When he put out his candle, it must be done with an address to the Father of Lights, that his light might not be put out in obscure darkness." "In drinking a dish of tea—of which he was a great admirer—he would take occasion for these thoughts, . . . that should have many sweet acknowledgments of the glorious Jesus in them. And whatever delight any of his senses took, it was soon sanctified and rendered more delightful, by his making such an improvement of it." "When the Doctor waked in the night, he would impose it as a law upon himself, ever, before he fell asleep again, to bring some glory of his Saviour into his meditations, and have some agreeable desire of his soul upon it." "When he washed his hands, he must think of the clean hands, as well as pure heart, which belong to the citizens of Zion." "And when he did so mean an action as paring his nails, he thought how he might lay aside all superfluity of naughtiness." "He had many years a morning cough; it every morning 'raised' proper dispositions of piety in him." "Upon the sight of a tall man, he said, 'Lord, give that man high attainments in Christianity; let him fear God above many:' a negro, 'Lord, wash that poor soul; make him white by the washing of thy Spirit:' a man going by without observing him, 'Lord, I pray thee help that man to take a due notice of Christ.'" [22] In his early days, Cotton Mather was a great sufferer from toothache; and, of course, "in these pains," instead of inferring that some of his teeth were decayed and needed to be pulled out, "he would set himself, as well as he could, to try his ways. He considered whether or no he had not sinned with his teeth. How? By sinful and excessive eating; and by evil speeches, for there are 'literae dentales' used in them." [23] One would like to suppose that, at least in the matter of love and marriage, Cotton Mather gave himself some slight release from these fanatic pedantries. Not so; for we read that "he thought it advisable in his twenty-

[22] S. Mather, "Life of C. Mather," 101 et seq.   [23] Ibid. 61.

New England: Dynasty of the Mathers

fourth year to marry. He first looked up to Heaven for direction, and heard the counsel of his friends. The person he first pitched upon, was"[24]—the one who had the honor of marching for a few years at the head of his procession of three wives.

If, now, we may be permitted to stand, for some moments, in the presence of this great man, and to make a study of his literary significance in our annals, it is very likely that we shall be impressed, first of all, even as his contemporaries were, by his vast industry, the variety of his acquisitions, and his almost illimitable prolificacy.

At the age of sixteen, he had drawn up for himself systems of all the sciences. Besides the ancient languages, Hebrew, Latin, Greek, which he used with facility, he knew French, Spanish, and even one of the Indian tongues, and prided himself on having composed and published works in most of them. It was his ambition to be acquainted with all branches of knowledge, with all spheres of thought; to get sight of all books. His library was the largest private collection on the American continent. They who called upon him in his study, were instructed by this legend written in capitals above the door: "Be Short." He had no time to waste. He was always at work. They who beheld him marvelled at his power of dispatching most books at a glance, and yet of possessing all that was in them. "He would ride post through an author."[25] "He pencilled as he went along, and at the end reduced the substance to his commonplaces, to be reviewed at leisure; and all this with wonderful celerity."[26] The results of all his omnivorous readings were at perfect command; his talk overflowed with learning and wit: "he seemed to have an inexhaustible source of divine flame and vigor. . . . How instructive, learned, pious, and engaging was he in his private converse; superior company for the greatest of men. . . . How agreeably tempered with a various mixture of wit and cheerfulness."[27] The readers of his books may, indeed, infer from them something of his splendid powers of intellect; but they cannot "imagine that extraordinary lustre of pious and useful literature, where-

---

[24] S. Mather, "Life of C. Mather," 12.
[25] Ibid. 68.
[26] T. Prince, Pref. to "Life of C. Mather," by S. Mather.
[27] T. Prince, Sermon on Death of C. Mather, 20-21.

with we were every day entertained, surprised, and satisfied, who dwelt in the directer rays, in the more immediate vision." [28] The people in daily association with him were, indeed, constantly amazed at "the capacity of his mind, the readiness of his wit, the vastness of his reading, the strength of his memory, . . . the tenor of a most entertaining and profitable conversation." [29]

On his death-bed, he gave to his son, Samuel, this final charge: "Remember only that one word—'Fructuosus.' " [30] It seemed the hereditary motto of the Mathers. He himself could have uttered no word more descriptive of the passion and achievement of his own life. There is a chronological list [31] of the publications made in America during the colonial time; and it is swollen and overlaid by the name of Cotton Mather, and by the polyglot and arduous titles of his books. We are told that in a single year, besides doing all his work as minister of a great metropolitan parish, and besides keeping sixty fasts and twenty vigils, he published fourteen books. The whole number of his separate writings published during his lifetime, exceeds three hundred and eighty-three. No wonder that his contemporaries took note of such fecundity. One of them exclaimed:

"Is the blest Mather necromancer turned?" [32]

Another one declared:

"Play is his toil, and work his recreation." [33]

Very likely, however, the astonishment we may feel at the multitude of his productions, will be considerably tempered if we force ourselves to the exertion of looking into them; for not many of these productions are large works, or represent labor beyond his direct preparations for the pulpit. As our eyes run along the columns crowded with the names of his books, we seem to get nearer to the intellectual character of the writer of them, and of the age he lived in, to find under what remote and freakish designations even very

[28] T. Prince, Pref. to "Life of C. Mather," by S. Mather.
[29] Joshua Gee, Sermon on Death of C. Mather, 18.
[30] S. Mather, "Life of C. Mather," 156.
[31] By S. F. Haven, Jr. Archæol. Am. VI. 309–666.
[32] B. Tompson, in "Magnalia," I. 20.   [33] Ibid. 19.

commonplace subjects are announced: "Adversus Libertinos; or, Evangelical Obedience Described;" "Boanerges, A Short Essay to strengthen the Impressions Produced by Earthquakes;" "Christianus per Ignem; or, a Disciple Warming of Himself and Owning of his Lord;" "Coheleth, A Soul upon Recollection coming into Incontestable Sentiments of Religion;" "Hatzar-Maveth, Comfortable Words, the Comforts of One Walking through the Valley of the Shadow of Death;" "Nails Fastened; or, Proposals of Piety Complied Withal;" "Ornaments for the Daughters of Zion, A Discourse which Directs the Female Sex how to Express the Fear of God, and Obtain Temporal and Eternal Blessedness;" "Orphanotrophium; or, Orphans Well-provided for in the Divine Providence;" "Fasciculus Viventium, Essay on a Soul Bound up in the Bundle of Life;" "Ecclesiæ Monilla, The Peculiar Treasure of the Almighty King Opened."

The most famous book produced by him,—the most famous book, likewise, produced by any American during the colonial time,—is one to which, in these pages, we have often gone for curious spoils: "Magnalia Christi Americana; or, The Ecclesiastical History of New England, from its first planting, in the year 1620, unto the year of our Lord 1698." [34]

From the diary [35] of Cotton Mather, it appears that he conceived the design of this work in 1693, he being then thirty years of age; that in 1695, he published a prospectus of it; that in August, 1697, he set apart a day for secret thanksgiving to God for divine help in finishing it; and that thenceforward until 1702, when the book came from the press in London, he had innumerable prayers, tears, prostrations, and elevations, respecting its safe transmission to England and its slow and dubious struggle into print. On the twenty-seventh of November, 1697, "I did, at the close of the day, prostrate on my study-floor, joyfully receive . . . assurances from Heaven, . . . that there are good news coming to me from England . . . about the future publication of my 'Church History.'" The twelfth of January,

---

[34] First published in one folio volume, London, 1702; republished in America, in two vols. Hartford, 1820; second Am. ed. 1853. The ed. last mentioned is the one referred to throughout the present work.

[35] Still in manuscript, and inaccessible to me. For my present extracts from it, I am indebted to an interesting paper by Charles Deane, in Mass. Hist. Soc. Proc. for 1862–1863, 404–414.

1698, "I set apart . . . for the exercise of a secret fast before the Lord," for "the direction of Heaven about my 'Church History,' the time and way of my sending it into Europe, and the methods of its publication." On the fourth of March, 1698, "in the close of the day, as I lay prostrate on my study-floor, in the dust, before the Lord, . . . it was told me from heaven that" my Church History "shall be carried safe to England, and there employed for the service of my glorious Lord." On the sixth of June, 1701, "the Lord supports and comforts my faith about my 'Church History.'" On the thirteenth of June, 1701, "I received letters from London. . . . My 'Church History' is a bulky thing. . . . The impression will cost about six hundred pounds. The booksellers in London are cold about it." On the twelfth of February, 1702, though the publication of the book has been "thus long delayed and obstructed and clogged," "an heavenly afflatus causes me sometimes to fall into tears of joy, assured that the Lord has heard my supplications about this matter." On the fourth of April, 1702, "I was in much distress . . . concerning my 'Church History.' . . . Wherefore, I set apart a vigil this night. . . . Accordingly, in the dead of the night, I first sang some agreeable psalms; and then, casting myself prostrate into the dust, on my study-floor, before the Lord, I confessed unto him the sins for which he might justly reject me and all my services." On the eleventh of April, in a vigil, "my mind is irradiated with celestial and angelical influences, assuring of me that my 'Church History' shall not be lost, but shall come abroad." On the twenty-ninth of October, 1702, "I first saw my 'Church History,' since the publication of it. A gentleman arrived here from Newcastle in England, that had bought it there." Wherefore, the following day "I set apart . . . for solemn thanksgiving unto God for his watchful and gracious providence over that work, and for the harvest of so many prayers and cares and tears and resignations as I had employed upon it."

The "Magnalia" is, indeed, what the author called it, "a bulky thing,"—the two volumes of the latest edition having upwards of thirteen hundred pages. Its scope may be sufficiently seen by a glance at the subjects of the seven books into which it is divided. The first book is a history of the settlement of New England; the second contains "the lives of the governors and the names of the magistrates that have been shields unto the churches of New England;" the third recounts "the lives of sixty famous divines, by whose ministry the churches of New England have been planted and continued;" the fourth is devoted to the history of Harvard College, and of "some eminent persons therein educated;" the fifth describes "the faith and order of the churches;" the sixth speaks of "many illustrious discoveries and demonstrations of the Divine Providence in remarkable mercies and judgments;" and the seventh, entitled "A Book of the Wars of the Lord," narrates "the afflictive disturbances which the churches of New England have suffered from their various adversaries"—the Devil, Separatists, Familists, Antinomians, Quakers, clerical impostors, and Indians.

Here is an imposing array of historical topics; and for the treatment of them, no other man ever had, or ever can have, such advantages as had Cotton Mather:—multitudes of original papers of all sorts within easy reach, that have since perished; personal acquaintance with all the great New England leaders or with those who had personally known them; finally, access to innumerable and most valuable oral traditions, which afterward would have died for lack of record. On the other hand, it must be said that for the performance of careful and disinterested historical work, few men that have undertaken it, ever had greater disadvantages; since there were in him traits that constituted an intellectual and moral inability to be either accurate or fair. He had an insuperable fondness for tumultuous, swelling, and flabby declamation, and for edifying remarks, in place of a statement of the exact facts in the case; infinite credulity; infinite carelessness; finally, a disposition to stain the chaste pages of history with the tints of his family friendships and his family feuds.

Upon the whole, as an historian, he was unequal to his high opportunity. The "Magnalia" has great merits; it has, also, fatal defects. In its mighty chaos of fables and blunders and misrepresentations, are of course lodged many single facts of the utmost value, personal reminiscences, social gossip, snatches of conversation, touches of description, traits of character and life, that can be found nowhere else, and that help us to paint for ourselves some living picture of the great men and the great days of early New England; yet herein, also, history and fiction are so jumbled and shuffled together, that it is never possible to tell, without other help than the author's, just where the fiction ends and the history begins. On no disputed question of fact is the unaided testimony of Cotton Mather of much weight; and it is probably true, as a very acute though very unfriendly modern critic of his has declared, that he has "published more errors of carelessness than any other writer on the history of New England." [36]

Though the fame of the "Magnalia" overshadows that of all the other writings produced by its author, it was the book of a young man —if, indeed, we are permitted to suppose that Cotton Mather ever was a young man. Of the books he wrote after that, and especially in his later years, several are more readable, and perhaps also more valuable, than the work on which his literary renown principally rests.

One of these is "Bonifacius, An Essay upon the Good that is to be Devised and Designed, with Proposals of unexceptionable Methods to do Good in the World:"—a book quite remarkable for the clear ingenuity and the fascinating power with which it reduces charity to an exact science, and plans the systematic transaction of good deeds on business principles; a book to which Benjamin Franklin,[37] in his old age, paid the highest tribute—saying, that it had largely directed his conduct through life, and had done much to make him a useful citizen of the world; a book which holds the germs and hints of nearly all those vast organizations of benevolence that have been the glory of the years since it was written.

Upon the great and agitating theme of psalmody in his time, Cotton Mather obviously needed to be heard; and in 1718, he expressed himself on the subject, with his usual explicitness, in "Psalterium Americanum," which is simply "The Book of Psalms" translated from the Hebrew into English blank-verse. In his introduction to the work, he laments that in all the many versions of the Psalms before his own, "those rich things which the Holy Spirit of God speaks in the original Hebrew," are confounded with the rubbish of human inventions, and all this "merely for the sake of preserving the clink

[36] James Savage, in J. Winthrop, "Hist. N. E." II. 28, note.
[37] Works, X. 83.

New England: Dynasty of the Mathers

of the rhyme, which after all is of small consequence unto a generous poem, and of none at all unto the melody of singing,—but of how little, then, in singing unto the Lord." [38]

Probably the most vigorous and entertaining book that he ever wrote, is one that is also the most characteristic expression of his later mental development, "Manuductio ad Ministerium,"—a manual of "directions for a candidate of the ministry," published at Boston in 1726, only two years before the author's death. It describes, first, what the religious character of the candidate should be; secondly, what course he should take for his intellectual improvement; and, thirdly, what should be his "conduct after his appearance in the world,"—all intended to make him "a skilful and useful minister of the gospel." The book is written heartily, with real enthusiasm for the subject, and with greater directness and simplicity of style than the author has shown in any other work. Of course, being written by Cotton Mather, it is ostentatious of his vast reading and of his heroic grasp of all studies; it is, also, in some measure, an index to the state of literature, of science, of criticism, of general culture, in New England at that time; and, in many places, it is positively sprightly and amusing.

As would be expected, he draws out a generous scheme of study for his clerical protégé; summons him to make all knowledge tributary to his splendid vocation; bids him scorn the shallow and ignorant notions of professional attainment then spreading in New England. He urges him, for instance, to become a master of Hebrew; although that language "is fallen under so much disrepute as to make a learned man almost afraid of owning that he has anything of it, lest it should bring him under the suspicion of being an odd, starved, lank sort of a thing, who had lived only on Hebrew roots all his days." [39]

He urges upon the young minister the need of mastering the lessons of history, and yet to be on his guard against the falsehoods of history—a theme on which Cotton Mather had an uncommon right to speak: "The instances wherein false history has been imposed upon the world are what cannot be numbered. Historians have generally taken after their father, Herodotus; . . . though they have

[38] Introd. vii.   [39] "Manuductio," etc. 30.

not all of them always been such mercenary villains . . . as that scandalous fellow, who . . . hired himself out as an history-writer for the highest bidder. . . . Yea, there are historians of whom one can scarcely tell, which to admire most, the nature of their lies, or their manner of telling them—I mean, the impudence with which they tell them. . . . Be sure, the late historians that pretend unto an History of England, . . . write with such flagrant partialities, and are such evident leasing-makers, . . . that one may as well believe the 'True History' of a Lucian, as yield any credit unto them. . . . Indeed, the historians never keep closer to the way of lying, than in the relation they give of those twenty years which passed after the beginning of our Civil Wars. . . . Among these, the romance that goes under the title of 'The History of the Grand Rebellion,' and is fathered on the Earl of Clarendon, I would have you more particularly treat with the disregard that is proper for it." [40]

In directing his pupil to the study of natural philosophy, he passes into a satirical denunciation of Aristotle: "When I said natural philosophy, you may be sure I did not mean the Peripatetic. . . . It is, indeed, amazing to see the fate of the writings which go under the name of Aristotle. First, falling into the hands of those who could not read them, and yet for the sake of the famous author were willing to keep them, they were for a long while hid under ground, where many of them deserved a lodging. And from this place of darkness, the torn and worn manuscripts were anon fetched out, and imperfectly and unfaithfully enough transcribed, and conveyed from Athens to Rome. . . . The Saracens by and by got them. . . . When learning revived under Charlemagne, all Europe turned Aristotelian; yea, in some universities, they swore allegiance to him; and, O monstrous! if I am not misinformed, they do, in some universities at this day, foolishly and profanely on their knees continue to do so. With the vile person that made himself the head of the Church at Rome, this muddy-headed pagan divided the empire over the Christian world; but extended his empire further than he, or even Tamerlane. The very Jews themselves became his vassals. . . . And though Europe has, with fierce and long struggles about it, begun to shake off the shackles, he does to this day . . . continue

[40] "Manuductio," etc. 60–63.

New England: Dynasty of the Mathers

to tyrannize over human understanding in a great part of the oriental world. No mortal else ever had such a prerogative to govern mankind as this philosopher, who, after the prodigious cartloads of stuff that has been written to explain him, . . . he yet remains in many . . . things sufficiently unintelligible, and forever in almost all things unprofitable. Avicen, after he had read his Metaphysics forty times over, and had them all by heart, was forced after all to lay them aside in despair of ever understanding them." [41]

In this fatherly talk of an elderly prophet with one of his professional sons, he does not always succeed in keeping upon the level of ordinary discourse, but occasionally ascends to the grand style that is most natural to him; as when he imparts to the youth this consoling assurance: "I will not now suppose a quinquarticular controversy, but rather propose a ternaticular period of all controversies." [42]

The true place of Cotton Mather in our literary history is indicated when we say, that he was in prose writing, exactly what Nicholas Noyes was in poetry,—the last, the most vigorous, and, therefore, the most disagreeable representative of the Fantastic school in literature; and that, like Nicholas Noyes, he prolonged in New England the methods of that school even after his most cultivated contemporaries there had outgrown them, and had come to dislike them. The expulsion of the beautiful from thought, from sentiment, from language; a lawless and a merciless fury for the odd, the disorderly, the grotesque, the violent; strained analogies, unexpected images, pedantries, indelicacies, freaks of allusion, monstrosities of phrase;— these are the traits of Cotton Mather's writing, even as they are the traits common to that perverse and detestable literary mood that held sway in different countries of Christendom during the sixteenth and seventeenth centuries. Its birthplace was Italy; New England was its grave; Cotton Mather was its last great apostle.

His writings, in fact, are an immense reservoir of examples in Fantastic prose. Their most salient characteristic is pedantry,—a pedantry that is gigantic, stark, untempered, rejoicing in itself, unconscious of shame, filling all space in his books like an atmosphere. The mind of Cotton Mather was so possessed by the books he had read, that his most common thought had to force its way into utter-

[41] "Manuductio," etc. 47–49.   [42] Ibid. 119.

ance through dense hedges and jungles of quotation. Not only every sentence, but nearly every clause, pivots itself on some learned allusion; and by inveterate habit he had come to consider all subjects, not directly, but in their reflections and echoes in books. It is quite evident, too, that, just as the poet often shapes his idea to his rhymes * and is helped to an idea by his rhyme, so Mather's mind acquired the knack of steering his thought so as to take in his quotation, from which in turn, perhaps, he reaped another thought.

That his manner of writing outlived the liking of his contemporaries, especially his later contemporaries, is plain. The best of them,—Jeremiah Dummer, Benjamin Colman, John Barnard, Mather Byles, Charles Chauncey, Jonathan Mayhew, rejected his style, and formed themselves, instead, upon the temperate and tasteful prose that had already come into use in England; while, even by his most devoted admirers, the vices of his literary expression were acknowledged. Thomas Prince, for example, gently said of him: "In his style he was something singular, and not so agreeable to the gust of the age." [43] Even his own son, Samuel Mather, regretted his fault of "straining for far-fetched and dear-bought hints." [44]

But Cotton Mather had not formed his style by accident, nor was he without a philosophy to justify it. In early life he described his compositions as ornamented "by the multiplied references to other and former concerns, closely couched, for the observation of the attentive, in almost every paragraph;" and declared that this was "the best way of writing." [45] And in his old age, nettled by the many sarcastic criticisms that were made upon his style by presumptuous persons even in his own city, he resumed the subject; and in a simple and trenchant passage, of real worth not only for itself but for its bearing upon the literary spirit of the period, he proudly defended his own literary manner, and even retorted criticism upon the literary manner of his assailants: "There has been a deal of ado about a style. . . . There is a way of writing, wherein the author endeavors that the reader may have something to the purpose in every paragraph. There is not only a vigor sensible in every sentence, but the

[43] Sermon on Death of Cotton Mather, 24.
[44] S. Mather, "Life of C. Mather," 69.   [45] "Magnalia," I. 31.

[* The "s" on this word is marked for deletion, but the change was not made.]

New England: Dynasty of the Mathers

paragraph is embellished with profitable references, even to something beyond what is directly spoken. Formal and painful quotations are not studied; yet all that could be learned from them is insinuated. The writer pretends not unto reading, yet he could not have writ as he does if he had not read very much in his time; and his composures are not only a cloth of gold, but also stuck with as many jewels as the gown of a Russian ambassador. This way of writing has been decried by many, and is at this day more than ever so, for the same reason that in the old story the grapes were decried, 'That they were not ripe.' A lazy, ignorant, conceited set of authors would persuade the whole tribe to lay aside that way of writing, for the same reason that one would have persuaded his brethren to part with the encumbrance of their bushy tails. But, however fashion and humor may prevail, they must not think that the club at their coffee-house is all the world. But there will always be those who will in this case be governed by indisputable reason, and who will think that the real excellency of a book will never lie in saying of little; that the less one has for his money in a book, 'tis really the more valuable for it; and that the less one is instructed in a book, and the more of superfluous margin and superficial harangue, and the less of substantial matter one has in it, the more 'tis to be accounted of. And if a more massy way of writing be never so much disgusted at this day, a better gust will come on. . . . The blades that set up for critics, appear to me, for the most part, as contemptible as they are a supercilious generation. . . . Nor can you easily find any one thing wherein they agree for their style, except perhaps a perpetual care to give us jejune and empty pages. . . . There is much talk of a florid style obtaining among the pens that are most in vogue; but how often would it puzzle one, even with the best glasses, to find the flowers. . . . After all, every man will have his own style, which will distinguish him as much as his gait." [46]

IV

Samuel Mather, the son of Cotton Mather, was born in 1706; was graduated at Harvard College in 1723; and in 1732, became one of

[46] "Manuductio," etc. 44-46.

the pastors of the church in the service of which his father and his grandfather had spent their lives. In 1741, in consequence of disaffection in that church, he led off a portion of it, and formed a new church, of which he continued to be the pastor until his death, in 1785. In him, evidently, the ancestral fire had become almost extinct. He had abundant learning; was extremely industrious; published many things—discourses, a biography of his father, theological and historical treatises, even a poem; but there was not in them, as there was not in him, the victorious energy of an original mind, or even the winning felicity of an imitative one. In the strifes of the Revolution his course was both patriotic and bitter: he differed from some of his kindred, by taking the side of the colonies against the king; he disinherited his only son for loyalty to the Crown; he described his loyalist brother-in-law, Governor Thomas Hutchinson, as a "misguided and avaricious" man, and as "doomed to perpetual infamy;" and the whole "body of Tories and Refugees," he denounced, in the language of William Pitt, as "the most infamous scoundrels on the face of the earth." [47] He was a sturdy and a worthy man. He left no successor to continue the once-splendid dynasty of his tribe. He was the last, and the least, of the Mathers.

[47] S. G. Drake's Introd. to I. Mather's "Hist. of King Philip's War," xviii.–xxii.

Chapter XIII

New England:

Topics of Popular Discussion

I. Early literary prominence of the clergy—Growth of the laity in intellectual influence—The range of the people's thought and talk during the second colonial period.

II. The mournful reminiscences of Joshua Scottow—The witchcraft spasm—Robert Calef and "More Wonders of the Invisible World."

III. The diary in literature—Sarah Kemble Knight—Her "Journal"—Pictures of travel and of rustic manners early in the eighteenth century.

IV. Samuel Sewall—His brave life—The man—His attitude toward witchcraft and slavery.—His "Selling of Joseph"—Among the prophets—"A Description of the New Heaven"—The New Jerusalem to be in America—A gallant champion of the immortality of the souls of women.

V. John Wise—His inadequate fame—His genius as a writer—His career as preacher, muscular Christian, and opponent of despotism—The first great American expounder of democracy in church and state—His victorious assault upon a scheme for clerical aggrandizement—"The Churches' Quarrel Espoused"—The logic, wit, and eloquence of the book—His "Vindication of the Government of New England Churches"—Analysis of the book—Traits of his mind and style.

VI. Jeremiah Dummer—His early fame—Short career as a preacher—Goes to London and becomes courtier, barrister, and colonial agent—A faithful American always—His "Letter to a Noble Lord"—His "Defence of the New England Charters"—The elegance and strength of his style.

VII. The almanac in modern literature—Its early prominence in America—Its function—Wit and wisdom in almanacs not originated by

Franklin—Nathaniel Ames, the greatest of our colonial almanac-makers—His "Astronomical Diary and Almanac," an annual miscellany of information and amusement—Its great popularity and utility—Its predictions—Its shrewd and earnest appeals to the common mind—Its suggestions concerning health—Its original verses—Predicts the Day of Judgment—A noble prophecy of universal peace—Vision of the coming greatness of America—A friendly address to posterity.

I

IN the history of literature in New England during the colonial time, one fact stands out above all others,—the intellectual leadership of the clergy, and that, too, among a laity neither ignorant nor weak. This leadership was in every sense honorable, both for the leaders and the led. It was not due alone to the high authority of the clerical office in New England; it was due still more to the personal greatness of the men who filled that office, and who themselves made the office great. They were intellectual leaders because they deserved to be; for, living among a well-educated and high-spirited people, they knew more, were wiser, were abler. than all other persons in the community. Of such a leadership, it was an honor even to be among the followers. And in our record of the literary achievements of New England in the colonial time, the clergy fill by far the largest space, because, in all departments of writing, they did by far the largest amount of work.

After the first half century of New England life, another fact comes into notice,—the advance of the laity in literary activity. By that time, many strong and good men, who had been educated there in all the learning of the age, either not entering the clerical profession or not remaining in it, began to organize and to develop the other learned professions—the legal, medical, and tuitionary—and, appealing to the public through various forms of literature, to divide more and more with the clergy the leadership of men's minds. Moreover, in the last decade of the seventeenth century, an attempt was made to establish a newspaper in New England. The attempt failed. In the first decade of the eighteenth century, another attempt was made, and did not fail; and long before the end of our colonial epoch, a new profession had come into existence, having a

New England: Popular Discussion

power to act on the minds of men more mightily than any other,— the profession of journalism.

Thus, as public discussion grew in the number of those who were participators in it, so also did it increase in the variety of its methods, and in the range of its themes. Henceforward we may trace the intellectual life of New England, not merely in sermons, in formal theological treatises, in grave narratives of civil and military experience, in sombre and painful religious poetry, but likewise in compact literary essays, in pamphlets sprightly or brutal or stupid, in satires, in almanacs, in popular songs, in editorial articles. Public discussion became secularized. At last, even this world began to receive some attention, and to be written about. Witchcraft, statecraft, the small-pox, the behavior of the royal governors, the words and deeds of preachers, quarrels of churches, quarrels of towns and of colonies, agriculture, the currency, repudiation, manufactures, the training of soldiers, the founding of colleges, Whitefield, religious mania, dress, drunkenness, wars with the Indians, wars with the French, earthquakes, comets, the new wonders of science, the impiety of averting lightning by the "electrical points," the truth of Christianity, the damnation of infants, the right to think, the conquest of Canada, the consolidation of the English colonies in America, the grand future of the American continent, the virtues of the English kings, the love and loyalty of America for England,—these were some of the subjects that, year by year, along our second colonial period, possessed the thoughts of men and women in New England, and found some sort of utterance in literature.

II

In 1691, a thrifty old merchant of Boston, Joshua Scottow,[1] who had grown up with the colony almost from the beginning, published a little book of senile lamentations over the degeneracy of the age. It was called "Old Men's Tears for their own Declensions."[2] Encouraged by this stroke at authorship, he gave to the press, three

[1] Born probably 1615, died 1698. Sketch of him in 2 Mass. Hist. Soc. Coll. IV. 100-104.

[2] A second edition was published in 1749, but without the best part of it, the "Address to the Reader."

years afterward, "A Narrative of the Planting of the Massachusetts Colony,"[3] beginning with 1628, and particularly accenting the fact of "the Lord's signal presence the first thirty years." Both books have some historical and psychological value, but as literature are worthless. His method of expression is spasmodic, ecstatic, full of apocalyptic symbols, cant, forced allusions, and the croakings of decrepitude. In the dedication of his second book to Simon Bradstreet, he had the good sense to anticipate that his writings might be pronounced "the delirious dotage of his puerile and superannuated brains."

The paroxysms of terror and of frenzy into which, during the last decade of the seventeenth century, multitudes of people in New England were thrown by the witchcraft excitement, gave birth to numerous publications, chiefly hortatory, minatory, and inflammatory; and to one publication that was at least rational, "More Wonders of the Invisible World," published in London in 1700, and written by a merchant of Boston, Robert Calef, then forty-eight years of age.[4] Though the book is quite destitute of literary expertness; is without symmetry in substance or felicity in form; is, indeed, a hodge-pudding of facts, hints, queries, and conjectures; it is not destitute of expertness of other kinds,—particularly that kind of expertness which, in a time of general enravishment, may enable one cool head to be an antidote to a multitude of hot ones. It is a reservoir of weird psychological phenomena, first frankly described in the credulous speech of the brotherhood and sisterhood of victims, then chilled and taken to pieces by a process of Sadducean counter-evidence and cross-examination. It is, also, a monument of the moral courage and the intellectual poise of its author; of his firm, placid tenacity in demanding some real evidence as the price of his belief; of his obstinate incredulity to the end; all this in contrast with the intolerant eagerness of his contemporaries to rush headlong into folly; their hectic mental spasms; and their appetency—at once voracious and ferocious—for marvels, born in malice or in madness, and ending in infamy and in death. For the chief clerical leaders in the witchcraft excitement, especially the two Mathers, this book,

[3] Reprinted in 4 Mass. Hist. Soc. Coll. IV. 279–330.
[4] N. E. Hist. and Gen. Reg. XXX. 461.

both by its scepticism and by its personal irreverence, was most exasperating. The younger of these two divines wreaked his rage upon the book by calling it "a firebrand thrown by a madman;"[5] and the elder of them, at that time president of Harvard College, tried to extinguish the book by having it publicly burned in the college-yard. But its peculiar power could not be stifled in a hangman's smudge; and one may truly say of it, that it went far to unmadden a whole population of devout and learned lunatics.

III

There is one form of writing—the diary—that costs little to produce; that is usually valued at little by its producers; but that often gathers incalculable worth with time, outlives many laborious and ambitious literary monuments, and becomes a storehouse of treasures for historians, poets, and painters. It cannot be said that our ancestors failed to write diaries. Unluckily, however, the diaries that they wrote in great abundance, were generally records of events which took place only inside of them; psychological diaries, more or less mystical and unhealthy; chronicles of tender, scrupulous, introverted natures, misled into gratuitous self-torture; narratives of their own spiritual moods fluctuating hour by hour, of the visitations of Satan, of dulness or of ecstasy in prayer, of doubts or hopes respecting their share in the divine decrees; itineraries of daily religious progress, aggravated by overwork, indigestion, and a gospel of gloom.

There has come down to us, however, from our second literary period, one specimen of the diary, which, though crude enough in texture, is refreshingly carnal, external, and healthy. It is "The Journal" kept by Mistress Sarah Kemble Knight, a dame of Boston—buxom, blithe, and debonair—who in October, 1704, being then thirty-eight years of age, a wife and a mother, travelled on horseback from Boston through Rhode Island and southern Connecticut to New Haven, a journey of five days; thence, in December, to New York, a journey of two days; returning home by the same route, and reaching Boston in March, 1705. In the pauses of her journey each day, she carefully jotted down her adventures and her own com-

[5] C. Mather, "Some Few Remarks upon a Scandalous Book," 5.

ments upon them, doing this with no little sprightliness and graphic power. The roads were rough, often uncertain; the crossings of the rivers were perilous; the inns were abominable; the manners of the people churlish, their speech a jargon of disgusting slang. Her "Journal," published for the first time in 1825,[6] is an amusing little book, and has special value as a realistic picture of rural manners in New York and New England in the first decade of the eighteenth century. She had no companions upon her expedition, except as she hired them or fell in with them by the way; and she bore the annoyances of the journey with a sort of mocking and recalcitrant resignation, which was only saved from going to pieces altogether by help of an eye quick to see the ludicrous aspects of disagreeable things—particularly as soon as they were past. Her note-book, indeed, was a sovereign safety-valve to her, forming a harmless conduit through which she could pour her hourly vexations, in playful little puffs of prose and verse. Thus, having to cross a certain river, and not daring to do so by fording it on horseback, she went over it in a wretched canoe—a far less safe ferry-boat than her horse would have been. "The canoe was very small and shallow, so that when we were in," it "seemed ready to take in water, which greatly terrified me, and caused me to be very circumspect, sitting with my hands fast on each side, my eyes steady, not daring so much as to lodge my tongue a hair's breadth more on one side of my mouth than t'other, nor so much as think on Lot's wife; for a wry thought would have overset our wherry."[7] On another day, as she relates, the road was furnished even worse than usual "with accommodations for travellers, so that we were forced to ride twenty-two miles by the post's account, but nearer thirty by mine, before we could bait so much as our horses, which I exceedingly complained of. But the post encouraged me by saying we should be well accommodated anon at Mr. Devil's, a few miles further; but I questioned whether we ought to go to the Devil to be helped out of affliction. However, like the rest of deluded souls that post to the infernal den, we made all possible speed to this Devil's habitation; where, alighting in full assurance of

[6] Edited by Theodore Dwight. Reprinted, with new preface and additional information about her, Albany, 1865.
[7] "Journal," 15–16.

New England: Popular Discussion

good accommodation, we were going in; but meeting his two daughters, (as I supposed, twins—they so nearly resembled each other, both in features and habit, and looked as old as the Devil himself, and quite as ugly,) we desired entertainment, but could hardly get a word out of them, till with our importunity . . . they called the old sophister; who was as sparing of his words as his daughters had been. . . . He differed only in this from the old fellow in t'other country —he let us depart. However, I thought it proper to warn poor travellers to endeavor to avoid falling into circumstances like ours, which at our next stage I sat down and did, as followeth:

> May all that dread the cruel Fiend of Night
> Keep on, and not at this curst mansion light.
> 'Tis hell; 'tis hell; and Devils here do dwell;
> Here dwells the Devil—surely this is hell.
> Nothing but wants—a drop to cool your tongue
> Can't be procured these cruel fiends among.
> Plenty of horrid grins, and looks severe,
> Hunger and thirst; but pity's banished here.
> The right hand keep, if hell on earth you fear!" [8]

IV

A strong, gentle, and great man was Samuel Sewall, great by almost every measure of greatness,—moral courage, honor, benevolence, learning, eloquence, intellectual force and breadth and brightness. Both his father and his grandfather were among the pioneers of New England colonization; although his father, who founded the town of Newbury, Massachusetts, seems to have passed and repassed between England and America without bringing hither his wife and children, until 1661, when the boy, Samuel, was nine years old. This boy, destined to great usefulness and distinction in the new world, thus came to it in time to have that personal shaping for his life here, only to be got from early and direct contact with it. He had the usual education of a New England gentleman in those days. He was graduated at Harvard College. He tried his hand for a time at preaching,—a vocation for which he was well qualified, but from

[8] "Journal," 25-26.

which he was diverted into a prosperous and benign secular career. He became a member of the board of assistants, then of the council, judge of the supreme court, and finally its chief-justice, holding the latter office until 1728, two years after which date he died. He was a man built, every way, after a large pattern. By his great wealth, his great offices, his learning, his strong sense, his wit, his warm human sympathy, his fearlessness, his magnanimity, he was a visible potentate among men in those days.

> "Stately and slow, with thoughtful air,
> His black cap hiding his whitened hair,
> Walks the Judge of the great Assize,
> Samuel Sewall, the good and wise.
> His face with lines of firmness wrought,
> He wears the look of a man unbought,
> Who swears to his hurt and changes not;
> Yet touched and softened nevertheless
> With the grace of Christian gentleness;
> The face that a child would climb to kiss;
> True and tender and brave and just,
> That man might honor and woman trust." [9]

He had the courage to rebuke the faults of other people; he had the still greater courage to confess his own. Having, in 1692, fallen into the witchcraft snare, and having from the bench joined in the sentence of condemnation upon the witches, five years later—when more light had broken into his mind—he made in church a public confession of his error and of his sorrow. The Indians of Massachusetts had then no wiser or more generous friend than he; and he was, perhaps,* the first of Americans to see and renounce and denounce the crime of negro slavery as then practised in New England. In 1700, he spoke out plainly on this subject, publishing a tract named "The Selling of Joseph;" [10] an acute, compact, powerful statement of the case against American slavery, leaving, indeed, almost

[9] J. G. Whittier, "Prophecy of Samuel Sewall." Works, II. 141.
[10] First printed in a folio of three pages, at Boston, 1700. Reprinted in Mass. Hist. Soc. Proc. for 1863–1864, 161–165. I quote from the reprint.

[* Tyler replaced "perhaps" with "one of" and then apparently changed his mind and crossed out the correction.]

New England: Popular Discussion

nothing new to be said a century and a half afterward, when the sad thing came up for final adjustment. In this pamphlet one sees traces both of his theological and his * legal studies; it is a lawyer's brief, fortified by Scriptural texts, and illuminated by lofty ethical intuitions. Within those three pages he has left some strong and great words—immortal and immutable aphorisms of equity: "Liberty is in real value next unto life; none ought to part with it themselves or deprive others of it, but upon most mature consideration." [11] "All men, as they are the sons of Adam, are co-heirs, and have equal right unto liberty, and all other outward comforts of life." [12] "Originally and naturally there is no such thing as slavery." [13] "There is no proportion between twenty pieces of silver and liberty." [14]

All his lifetime he made the Biblical prophecies his favorite study,—a study out of which all manner of marvels, not always edifying, may be educed upon occasion; and the special marvel drawn from them by this sagacious Puritan judge was their palpable predictions of America as the final "rendezvous for Gog and Magog," and as the true seat of the New Jerusalem. In his "Phaenomena Quaedam Apocalyptica; . . . or . . . a Description of the New Heaven as it makes to those who stand upon the New Earth," a book first published in 1697,[15] he unfolds this theory, going over the applicable prophecies clause by clause. Toward the end of his book, he replies to the objections that might be urged against his doctrine,—one of them being that in America the human race inevitably deteriorates, becomes barren, dies off early. The accusation he repels with an affluence of facts illustrating the productiveness and longevity of the human family here; and having done so, he rises into this rhythmical and triumphant passage, which in its quaint melody of learned phrase, and in a gentle humor that lurks and loses itself in the stiff folds of his own solemnity, has a suggestion of the quality of Sir Thomas Browne: "As long as Plum Island shall faithfully keep the commanded post, notwithstanding all the hectoring words and hard blows of the proud and boisterous ocean; as long as any salmon or sturgeon shall swim in the streams of Merrimac, or any perch or

[11] "The Selling of Joseph," 161.   [12] Ibid. 161.
[13] Ibid. 162.   [14] Ibid. 162.   [15] Reprinted, Boston, 1727.

[* "Of" was inserted between "and" and "his" in 1897.]

pickerel in Crane Pond; as long as the sea-fowl shall know the time of their coming, and not neglect seasonably to visit the places of their acquaintance; as long as any cattle shall be fed with the grass growing in the meadows, which do humbly bow down themselves before Turkey-Hill; as long as any sheep shall walk upon Old-Town Hills, and shall from thence pleasantly look down upon the River Parker, and the fruitful marshes lying beneath; as long as any free and harmless doves shall find a white oak or other tree within the township, to perch, or feed, or build a careless nest upon, and shall voluntarily present themselves to perform the office of gleaners after barley-harvest; as long as Nature shall not grow old and dote, but shall constantly remember to give the rows of Indian corn their education by pairs; so long shall Christians be born there, and being first made meet, shall from thence be translated to be made partakers of the inheritance of the saints in light." [16]

It gives still another charm to the memory of this practical and hard-headed mystic of New England, this wide-souled and speculative

"Puritan,
Who the halting step of his age outran,"

to discover, that, in a matter of very serious concern, he had the chivalry to come forward as the champion of woman. He tells us that once, while "waiting upon a dear child in her last sickness," he took up a book to read. It was a book called "The British Apollo." Presently, his eye fell upon a startling question, worded thus: "Is there now, or will there be at the resurrection, any females in heaven; since there seems to be no need of them there?" Very likely he then closed the book; and there, by the death-bed of his daughter, over whose resurrection this question threw its cold shadow, his mind set to work upon the problem thus presented; and afterward he fully resolved it, in an essay bearing this delectable title: "Talitha Cumi; or, An Invitation to Women to look after their Inheritance in the

---

[16] "Phaenomena," etc. 63. The reader will recall the use of this passage made by Whittier in his delightful poem, "The Prophecy of Samuel Sewall." The old Puritan's prose in this case is more poetic than the poet's metrical paraphrase of it. Whittier speaks of Newbury as Sewall's "native town;" but Sewall was born at Horton, England. He also describes Sewall as an "old man," "propped on his staff of age" when he made this prophecy; but Sewall was then forty-five years old.

New England: Popular Discussion

Heavenly Mansions." He begins by quoting the question that he had met with; then he proceeds to say: "This malapert question had not patience to stay for an answer, as appears by the conclusion of it —'since there seems to be no need of them there.' 'Tis most certain there will be no needless, impertinent persons or things in heaven. Heaven is a roomy, a most magnificent palace, furnished with the most rich and splendid entertainments; and the noblest guests are invited to partake of them. But why should there seem to be no need of women in heaven? . . . To speak the truth, God has no need of any creature. His name is exalted far above all blessing and praise. But by the same argument there will be no angels nor men in heaven, because there is no need of them there." He then discusses, with judge-like care and fulness, all the arguments, on both sides, that may be drawn from reason, Scripture, and the ancient and modern theologians, reaching at last this assertion: "There are three women that shall rise again,—Eve, the mother of all living; Sarah, the mother of the faithful; and Mary, the mother of our Lord. And if these three rise again, without doubt all will." In the course of the discussion he meets the objection that, upon a certain branch of his subject, "the ancients are divided in their opinions." His answer to this objection comes edged by a flash of wit: "If we should wait till all the ancients are agreed in their opinions, neither men nor women would ever get to heaven." [17]

V

When Chaucer visited the house of the goddess Fame, he observed that the outer gate

> "so well y-corven was,
> That never suche another nas;
> And yit it was be aventure
> Ywrought, as often as be cure." [18]

[17] Selections from Sewall MSS. Mass. Hist. Soc. Proc. for 1873, 380–384. Other published writings of Sewall's are "Answer to Queries respecting America," 1690; "Proposals Touching Accomplishment of Prophecies," 1713. Voluminous manuscripts of his, including his diary for about forty years, are now in possession of the Mass. Hist. Soc., and are rich materials for the illustration of those times.
[18] Works of Chaucer, Aldine ed. V. 248.

It is an illustration of the caprice which everywhere prevails in the domain of this goddess, that the one American who, upon the whole, was the most powerful and brilliant prose-writer produced in this country during the colonial time, and who in his day enjoyed a sovereign reputation in New England, should have passed since then into utter obscurity; while several of his contemporaries, particularly Increase and Cotton Mather, who were far inferior to him in genius, have names that are still resounding in our memories. This writer was John Wise, born at Roxbury, probably in 1652; graduated at Harvard College in 1673; and, from 1680 until his death in 1725, minister of the Second Church of Ipswich. He had almost every quality that gives distinction among men. He was of towering height, of great muscular power, stately and graceful in shape and movement; in his advancing years, of an aspect most venerable. His parishioners long remembered with pride how a certain famous and blustering hero from Andover, the mighty wrestler of all that region, once came down to Ipswich for the purpose of challenging their stalwart parson to a friendly trial of strength at wrestling; and how the parson, after much solicitation, at last reluctantly consented, but had scarcely wrapped his arms in iron hug around his antagonist, when the latter lay outstretched upon the earth, with his curiosity respecting the Reverend Mr. Wise completely satisfied.

The soul of this man was of the same large and indomitable make. He had a robust joy in nature and in human nature; the creed of a democrat, without fear and without truculence: to him the griefs of the oppressed and the aggressions of the oppressor were alike insupportable. In 1687, when Sir Edmund Andros sent down to Ipswich his lawless order for a province-tax, the young parson braved the tyrant's anger, by advising his people not to comply with that order; for which he was arrested, tried, deposed from the ministry, fined, and thrown into prison. In 1689, when Sir Edmund was overthrown, John Wise was back again in his parish; and, both there and in Boston, he was at the front among the bravest, who then sought to prevent the recurrence of such despotism, by making examples of the petty English despot and of his still pettier American accomplices. In 1690, when the new governor of Massachusetts, Sir William Phips, led an expedition against Canada, John Wise, by

New England: Popular Discussion

request of the colonial legislature, accompanied him as chaplain, distinguishing himself in the campaign by feats of heroism, endurance, and military skill, as well as by fidelity in preaching and praying.

Thus far in his life, he had been noted chiefly for traits of physical and moral greatness, a devout, benignant, valiant, and blameless manhood; but within a few years afterward, there came upon the country an event that made him famous for the exertion of intellectual powers, both in thought and speech, the most rugged, versatile, and splendid.

In the year 1705, on the fifth of November—ominous day!—there was issued at Boston a very shrewd document, without any signature attached,* but purporting to have been framed by an association of ministers in and near that city. It was addressed to the churches and ministers of New England. It bore the unassuming title of "Question and Proposals." Masked under deferential and harmless phrases, it was really a project for taking away the power of the laity in all the churches of New England, for annulling the independence of each church, and for substituting in place of both the will of the clergy. The document was understood to have been the work of the two Mathers, backed by a coterie of clerical admirers, and representing an inclination widely cherished, even if concealed. The document had a meek look, innocuous, even holy; it sought only the glory of God and the good of man; it was not loud, peremptory, dogmatic; it only asked and suggested. But John Wise, from his rural study in Ipswich, saw its true character,—a plot for an ecclesiastical revolution, and a revolution backward; and having given ample time for the scheme to work its way into general discussion, at last he lifted up his hand, and, at one blow, crushed it. His blow was a book, "The Churches' Quarrel Espoused," published at Boston in 1710,—a book that by its learning, logic, sarcasm, humor, invective, its consuming earnestness, its vision of great truths, its flashes of triumphant eloquence, simply annihilated the scheme which it assailed.

His introduction is planned with exceeding art to conciliate the reader, to rouse the suspicion of the public against the men who had

[* "Without any signature attached" is underscored in the correction copy, and a cross appears in the margin. No change occurred in later printings.]

proposed the revolutionary scheme, and to confirm the popular conviction that the order of church-government already established, had upon the whole worked satisfactorily: "The scheme seems to be the spectre . . . of Presbyterianism; . . . yet if I don't mistake, in intention there is something considerable of Prelacy in it. . . . There is also something in it which smells very strong of the infallible chair. . . . For the clergy to monopolize both the legislative and executive part of canon law, is but a few steps from the chair of universal pestilence; and by the ladder here set up, clergymen may, if they please, clamber thus high. . . . Who can limit their power, or shorten their arm in their executions? Their Bulls can now, upon any affront, bellow and thunder out a thousand terrible curses; and the poor affrighted and envassaled laity . . . must forfeit their salvation, if they don't tamely submit." [19]

He then takes up, one by one, the several proposals; and exposes the danger and folly of each, with great power of logic, humor, and sarcasm. Thus, in commenting upon the proposed mode of receiving candidates into the ministry, he argues that it will surely lead to the evils of clerical corruption seen elsewhere: "How oft is it repeated that poor, sordid, debauched wretches are put into holy orders, whenas they were fitter to be put into the stocks, or sent to Bridewell for madmen, than to be sent with their testimonials to work in Christ's vineyard! How long have the Indies, the seas, the provinces, and many other parts of the empire, groaned under this damnable way of cheating God of his glory and the world of salvation!" [20]

It was, however, objected that under the present system, candidates often got into the ministry too young. He replies: "What then? . . . If Christ be preached, all is well. . . . Despise not the day of small things. All men must have a beginning, and every bird which is pretty well fledged must begin to fly. And ours are not of the nest where Icarus was hatched, whose feathers were only glued on; but these belong to the angelic host, and their wings grow out from their essence; therefore, you may allow them with the lark now and then to dart heavenward, though the shell or down be scarce off from their heads." [21]

[19] "The Churches' Quarrel Espoused," 38–39. [20] Ibid. 65.
[21] Ibid. 66.

New England: Popular Discussion

It was urged, likewise, that the scheme has quite a harmless look; and in reply, he shows that, in spite of that, it involves the possibility of great expansion into mischief: "Though it be but a calf now, yet in time it may grow—being of a thrifty nature—to become a sturdy ox that will know no 'whoa,' and, it may be, past the churches' skill then to subdue it. For if I am not much mistaken, . . . that great and terrible Beast with seven heads and ten horns . . . was nothing else, a few ages ago, but just such another calf as this is. It was, indeed, finely shaped and of neat limbs, . . . insomuch that the great potentates of the earth were much ravished with its aspect and features; some offered to suckle it on the choicest cows amongst all the herds of royal cattle, . . . hoping to stock their own countries with the breed; and when it was grown to a considerable magnitude, to render it more shapely and fair, they put iron tips on to its horns, and beset its stupendous bulk with very rich ornaments. . . . But alas, poor men! they have paid dear for their prodigality and fondness; for this very Creature, that was but a calf when they first begun to feed it, is now grown to be such a mad, furious, and wild Bull, that there is scarce a Christian monarch on earth . . . —the best horseman or huntsman of them all—that dare take this Beast by the horns, when he begins to bounce and bellow. Indeed the Emperor, within these few years, has recovered so much courage that he took him by the tail, to drive him out of his royal granges, being quite angry and weary with his cropping and browsing on the flowers of his imperial crown. But, otherwise, the Beast generally goes at large, and does what he will in all princes' dominions, and keeps them in awe. Therefore, to conclude, . . . 'Obsta principiis!' It is wisdom to nip such growths in the bud, and keep down by early slaughter such a breed of cattle." [22]

The document that he is exposing, is dated "November the fifth." He does not let this incident slip; and having, with wonderful effectiveness, developed his argument that the scheme contained in that document is a treasonable conspiracy, he proceeds to give the authors of it a terrible thrust. Beginning with some "astrological remarks" upon the document, he says: "I find its nativity full of favorable aspects to English churches. The fifth day of November has been

[22] "The Churches' Quarrel Espoused," 81–82.

History of American Literature

as a guardian angel to the most sacred interest of the empire; it has rescued the whole glory of church and state from the most fatal arrest of hell and Rome. . . . Had I been of the cabal . . . which formed these proposals, so soon as I had seen . . . the date, . . . I should have cried out, 'Miserere nostri Deus,'—the good Lord have mercy upon us. This is the 'gun-powder-treason day;' and we are every man ruined, being running Fawkes's fate! Why, gentlemen, have you forgot it? It is the day of the gun-powder-treason, and a fatal day to traitors. . . . I have such an awe upon my mind of this very day, that I have made a settled resolution, that of all the days of the whole year, I will never conspire treason against my natural prince, nor mischief to the churches, on the fifth day of November. And so, farewell, gentlemen; for I dare not join with you in this conspiracy." [23] But again, in the discussion, he returns to this date, and he addresses to it a fervid and brilliant apostrophe: "Blessed! thrice blessed day! uphold and maintain thy matchless fame in the calendar of time; and let no darkness or shadow of death stain thee; let thy horizon comprehend whole constellations of favorable and auspicious stars, reflecting a benign influence on the English monarchy; and upon every return, in thy anniversary circuits, keep an indulgent eye open and wakeful upon all the beauties, from the throne to the footstool, of that mighty empire! And when it is thy misfortune to conceive a Monster, which may threaten any part of the nation's glory, let it come crippled from the womb, or else travail in birth again, with some noble hero or invincible Hercules, who may conquer and confound it." [24]

This noble passage is near the victorious close of the book; and having thus abundantly implied the infamous character of the conspiracy, he magnanimously tells the conspirators themselves that, for the present, and on their good behavior, they are safe; for he will not reveal their names: "Where the place was, or the persons who were present in this rendezvous, shall never be told by me, unless it be extorted by the rack. And though I have endeavored with freedom of argument to subvert the error, I will never stain their personal glory by repeating or calling over the muster-roll. Therefore, as Noah's sons cast a garment upon their father's nakedness, so . . . their

[23] "The Churches' Quarrel Espoused," 82. [24] Ibid. 114.

names for me shall repose under a mantle of honorable pity and forgetfulness." [25]

Upon the whole, this book has extraordinary literary merit. It is, of its kind, a work of art; it has a beginning, a middle, and an end, —each part in fit proportion, and all connected organically. The author is expert in exciting and in sustaining attention; does not presume upon the patience of his readers; relieves the heaviness and dryness of the argument by gayety and sarcasm; and has occasional bursts of grand enthusiasm, of majestic and soul-stirring eloquence. In tone it is superior to its time; keen and urgent in its reasoning, showing no pity for opposing principles, it is full of forbearance and even of urbanity for opposing persons. It is a piece of triumphant logic, brightened by wit, and ennobled by imagination; a master-specimen of the art of public controversy.

"The Churches' Quarrel Espoused" is an exposition of the theory of democracy, in the Christian church, but the argument is developed according to the exigencies of a special occasion. In 1717, seven years after the publication of that book, John Wise published a systematic treatise upon the same subject, expounding in a formal and didactic way the principles of ecclesiastical polity then adopted in New England. He entitled this work, "A Vindication of the Government of New England Churches."

His theory of the best government for the church derives its character from his fundamental ideas of what is the best government for the state; and the treatment of the latter subject leads him into a broad discussion of the rights of man, the nature of civil obligation, and the various forms of civil polity.

He first deals with man in his natural state, "as a free-born subject under the crown of Heaven, and owing homage to none but God himself. . . . He is the favorite animal on earth, in that this part of God's image, namely, reason, is congenerate with his nature, wherein by a law immutable, enstamped upon his frame, God has provided a rule for men in all their actions, obliging each one to the performance of that which is right, . . . the which is nothing but the dictate of right reason founded in the soul of man. . . . The second great immunity of man is an original liberty enstamped upon

[25] "The Churches' Quarrel Espoused," 115.

his rational nature. . . . I shall waive the consideration of man's moral turpitude, but shall view him" as "the most august animal in the world. . . . Whatever has happened since his creation, he remains at the upper-end of nature." Man's natural liberty consists in three things: first, man has "a faculty of doing or omitting things according to the direction of his judgment;" second, "every man must be conceived to be perfectly in his own power and disposal, and not to be controlled by the authority of any other;" third, there is "an equality amongst men, which is . . . to be cherished and preserved to the highest degree, as will consist with all just distinctions amongst men of honor, and shall be agreeable with the public good. For man has a high valuation of himself, and the passion seems to lay its first foundation, not in pride, but really in the high and admirable frame and constitution of human nature. . . . Since, then, human nature agrees equally with all persons, and since no one can live a sociable life with another that does not own and respect him as a man, it follows as a command of the law of nature, that every man esteem and treat another as one who is naturally his equal, or who is a man as well as he. . . . The noblest mortal in his entrance on the stage of life is not distinguished by any pomp . . . from the lowest of mankind; and our life hastens to the same general mark. Death observes no ceremony, but knocks as loud at the barriers of the court as at the door of the cottage. . . . Nature having set all men upon a level and made them equals, no servitude or subjection can be conceived without inequality, and this cannot be made without usurpation in others, or voluntary compliance in those who resign their freedom and give away their degree of natural being." [26]

In treating of man in a civil state, he shows that "the true and leading cause of forming governments and yielding up natural liberty, and throwing man's equality into a common pile . . . was . . . to guard themselves against the injuries men were liable to interchangeably; for none so good to man as man, and yet none a greater enemy. So that the first . . . original of civil power is the people. . . . The formal reason of government is the will of a community, yielded up and surrendered to some other subject, either of one particular person or more." [27] He, then, speaks of "the three forms of

[26] "A Vindication," etc. 32–43. [27] Ibid. 43–44.

a regular state,"—democracy, aristocracy, and monarchy; and of the first he says: "This form of government appears in the greatest part of the world to have been the most ancient. . . . Reason seems to show it to be most probable that when men . . . had thoughts of joining in a civil body, they would without question be inclined to administer their common affairs by their common judgment, and so must necessarily . . . establish a democracy." [28]

Having thus spoken of each of these civil forms, he next deals with their analogous forms in church organization. He begins with the ecclesiastical monarchy, and of course finds this embodied in the Papacy: "It is certain his Holiness, either by reasonable pleas or powerful cheats, has assumed an absolute and universal sovereignty; this fills his cathedral chair, and is adorned with a triple crown." His claim is that "the Almighty has made him both key-keeper of heaven and hell, with the adjacent territories of purgatory, and vested in him an absolute sovereignty over the Christian world. . . . He therefore decks himself with the spoils of the divine attributes, styling himself, Our Lord God, 'Optimum, maximum, et supremum numen in terris;' a God on earth, a visible Deity, and that his power is absolute, and his wisdom infallible. And many of the great potentates of the earth have paid their fealty as though it was really so. . . . He has placed his holy foot on the monarch's profane neck, as crushing a vermin crawling out of the stable of his sovereignty; and others very frequently kiss his toes with very profound devotion. . . . But the sad inquiry is, whether this sort of government has not plainly subverted the design of the gospel, and the end for which Christ's government was ordained, namely, the moral, spiritual, and eternal happiness of men. But I have no occasion to pursue this remark with tedious demonstrations. It is very plain; it is written with blood in capital letters, to be read at midnight by the flames of Smithfield and other such like consecrated fires,—that the government of this ecclesiastical monarch has, instead of sanctifying, absolutely debauched the world, and subverted all good Christianity in it. . . . Without the least show of any vain presumption, we may infer that God and wise Nature were never propitious to the birth of this Monster." [29]

[28] "Vindication," etc. 47.   [29] Ibid. 54–56.

As regards the aristocratic form of church government, which he finds embodied in the Episcopacy, he thinks that Christianity "has been peeled, robbed, and spoiled" by it—"so doleful a contemplation is it to think the world should be destroyed by those men who by God were ordained to save it." [30]

He then comes to the ecclesiastical democracy, and of course advocates it, doing so with calm, rational, and powerful arguments: "This is a form of government which the light of nature does highly value, and often directs to, as most agreeable to the just and natural prerogatives of human beings." [31]

Throughout this entire work, the author shows abundant learning; but always he is the master of his learning, and not its victim. He lays out his propositions clearly and powerfully; marshals his arguments with tact and effect; is nowhere freakish, or extravagant; never fails in good temper, or in good sense.

Upon the whole, no other American author of the colonial time is the equal of John Wise in the union of great breadth and power of thought with great splendor of style; and he stands almost alone among our early writers for the blending of a racy and dainty humor with impassioned earnestness.

His force and brilliance in statement cannot be fully represented in sentences torn from their connection; yet on almost every page one meets terse and quotable sayings, here and there long passages grand for their nobility of feeling, their truth, and the music of their words. "Order," says he, "is both the beauty and safety of the universe. Take away the decorum whereby the whole hangs together, the great frame of nature is unpinned, and drops piece from piece; and out of a beautiful structure we have a chaos." [32] "If men are trusted with duty," he exclaims, "they must trust that, and not events. If men are placed at helm to steer in all weather that blows, they must not be afraid of the waves or a wet coat." [33]

Here is his stately and passionate chant of homage to religion: "Religion, in its infallible original, the wisdom and authority of God; in its Infinite Object, the ineffable Persons and Perfections of the Divine Essence; in its means, the gospel of salvation; in its in-

[30] "Vindication," etc. 59–60.   [31] Ibid. 60.
[32] "The Churches' Quarrel Espoused," 40.   [33] Ibid. 53.

New England: Popular Discussion

spired wakeful and capacious ministry; in its subject, the inestimable immortal soul of man; in its transcendent effects, in time the charming peace and joys of conscience, in eternity the joyful retreat and shouts of glory;—is the most incomparable gift of Palladium which ever came from heaven. Amongst all the favors of the Father of Lights, there is none parallel with this; when disclosed in its beauty, it ravisheth all the intellects of the universe; and challenge may be made that the prerogatives and glory belonging to all the crowned heads in the world, do bow and wait upon its processions through the earth, to guard it from its innumerable and inveterate enemies. . . . It is certain that the church of Christ is the pillar of truth, or sacred recluse and peculiar asylum of Religion; and this sacred guest, Religion, which came in the world's infancy from heaven to gratify the solitudes of miserable man, when God had left him, hath long kept house with us in this land, to sweeten our wilderness-state; and the renowned churches here are her sacred palaces. Then, certainly, it is not fair for her lovers, under pretence of maintaining her welcome in greater state, to desolate her pleasing habitations, though they stand somewhat low like the myrtle grove." [34]

Perhaps even greater than the distinction he deserves for his brilliant writing, is the distinction due him for the prophetic clearness, the courage, and the inapproachable ability with which, in that unfriendly time, he, almost alone among Americans, avowed his belief in civil governments founded on the idea of human equality. He was the first great American democrat. In the earlier years of the eighteenth century, he announced the political ideas that, fifty years later, took immortal form under the pen of Thomas Jefferson. Indeed, in 1772, when the doctrine of human right had come to be a very urgent and very practical one among men, the two books of John Wise were called for in Boston by the Revolutionary leaders; they were reprinted in response to this call; and they proved an armory of burnished weapons in all that stern fight. "The end of all good government is to cultivate humanity and promote the happiness of all, and the good of every man in all his rights, his life, liberty, estate, honor, and so forth, without injury or abuse to any." [35] No wonder that the writer of that sentence was called up from his

[34] "The Churches' Quarrel Espoused," 75–76.   [35] "Vindication," etc. 42.

grave, by the men who were getting ready for the Declaration of Independence!

VI

Not long before the Revolutionary War, a distinguished clergyman of Boston, Charles Chauncey, then an aged man, said, in a letter to President Stiles, that of all the eminent men he had known in New England, Jeremiah Dummer was "for extent and strength of genius" one of the three greatest. By all contemporary allusions it is evident that this man was regarded in his day as having extraordinary ability. Certainly no other American of that period began life with more brilliant promise; perhaps none ended it under sadder disappointment. He was born in Boston about 1679, of a family prominent and honorable in the country from its earliest settlement. He was graduated at Harvard College in 1699, where his student-life was long perpetuated in splendid tradition. Being at that time of a singularly devout spirit, he chose theology for his profession, and entered upon the study of it with his usual ardor and thoroughness. He soon went abroad for larger opportunities of instruction, taking his doctor's degree at the University of Utrecht; [36] and upon his return to New England, probably in 1704, he brought with him testimonials to his industry and blameless life while in Europe. To his friends and to himself he now probably seemed fully ripe for the illustrious service among the churches of New England to which he had been destined. He began to preach in the pulpits of Boston; but somehow, in spite of all his genius and all his vast academic preparation, his preaching did not make any impression. It was without fault, and without effect. Thus, on the twenty-ninth of October, 1704, he preached "A Discourse on the Holiness of the Sabbath Day." It was immaculate for orthodoxy, fitting even the most ascetic Puritan variety of that article; it had an abundance of Biblical, theological, and classical learning in it; it was smooth and liquid in style; indeed, it had nearly every quality of a speech, except

[36] In the Prince Library are copies of four of his university theses, in Latin, printed in Holland in 1702 and 1703, and showing his minute and large acquisitions in philological and theological learning.

New England: Popular Discussion

fitness for being spoken. It was simply a labored literary essay, quite too bookish, ornate, and fine to have any practical effect either on saints or sinners. The sermon, however, was at once published,[37] under the high sanction of the venerable Increase Mather, who, in the preface, spoke of Dummer's unequalled success as a student at home and abroad, and of his personal excellence in creed and deed, but concluded with the alarming intimation that unless the churches of New England should make haste to possess themselves of this clerical prodigy, he would be very likely to withdraw into some other quarter of the universe.

The menace was unheeded. Dummer preached here and there for a time, but found no acceptable pulpit to which he was acceptable; and at last he gave up the quest. Five years later, 1709, he once more emerged into view. This time it was in London, in a new character, on a new theme. He had dropped his theological profession, and his theology, and, very likely, his religion; he had gone to England to be a politician, and to make for himself there a great career in secular life. He had arrived not long before the formation of the Tory ministry under Harley and St. John; and to the anguish of his friends in America, he soon allied himself with the latter powerful and profligate statesman; adopted his politics, and even his morals; served him in various secret negotiations; and had from him promises of high promotion. But, in 1714, the Queen died; Bolingbroke fled in disgrace to France; and poor Dummer, damned by such an alliance, found all his hopes of a political career in England blasted.[38] It was impossible for him to confess his failure by a return to his native land; and in England he remained during the rest of his days, becoming a member of the Middle Temple, and indulging in certain respectable laxities of conduct more suggestive of his later friends than of his earlier ones; at last, in 1739, he died, without ever grasping any of that glory in the world for which he had so laboriously qualified himself, almost unknown in the country which he had adopted, and long before forgotten in the country in which he was born.

Yet on behalf of Jeremiah Dummer it remains to be said, that what-

[37] Republished, Boston, 1763.
[38] T. Hutchinson, "Hist. Mass. Bay," II. 170, note.

ever else, of true and good, he may have given up when he turned his back upon his own country, he never gave up his love for that country, or his passion to promote her welfare by his best labors. From 1710 to 1721, he served Massachusetts as its agent in London; and when that office was taken from him, he continued to serve her still, without appointment and without pay, whenever he found occasion. However much of an Englishman he may have become, he never ceased to be an American. Whatever he wrote for the public, is upon American topics; and his letters to his friends in this country showed at times a pensive and affectionate regret for the land and the life that he could never return to.

His memory as a writer will rest upon two publications, both being proofs not only of his fine literary accomplishments, but of his vigilant and laborious zeal for his country. The first was printed, in London, in 1709,[39] and is entitled, "A Letter to a Noble Lord concerning the late Expedition to Canada," wherein he makes three points: first, that the conquest of Canada was of great importance to England; second, that the late expedition was wisely planned; third, that its failure cannot be charged upon New England. It is an able and convincing essay, written in urbane and graceful style, everywhere bright and readable. It contains some striking illustrations of the adroitness with which the French missionaries in Canada aided the political designs of France; for instance, teaching their Indian converts that "the Virgin Mary was a French lady, and that her Son, the Saviour of the world, was crucified by the English." The book also denotes how early and passionate among the English colonies in America was the dread of the American power of France; thus, even in 1709, he says that those colonies can never be easy or happy "whilst the French are masters of Canada." [40]

But the second of Dummer's political publications is much the abler: "A Defence of the New England Charters." It was published in London in 1728,[41] at a time when there was danger of a bill passing the House of Commons, annulling the charters granted to the New

---

[39] Reprinted, Boston, 1712.

[40] 'A Letter to a Noble Lord,' etc. 4.

[41] Republished in London by J. Almon, in 1766, on account of its pertinence to colonial topics then under discussion.

New England: Popular Discussion

England colonies. It opens with a fine sketch of the origin and growth of those colonies, and of the circumstances under which the charters were given to them; and then proceeds to establish these four propositions: first, that the charter-governments have a good right to their charters; second, that they have not forfeited them; third, that if they had, it would not be the interest of the crown to accept the forfeitures; and, fourth, that it is inconsistent with justice to disfranchise the charter-colonies by act of parliament. It is an admirable specimen of argumentative literature; strict in logic, strong in fact, clear, flowing, graceful, occasionally rising into noble enthusiasm, but always temperate, courteous, and cosmopolitan.

VII

No one who would penetrate to the core of early American literature, and would read in it the secret history of the people in whose minds it took root and from whose minds it grew, may by any means turn away, in lofty literary scorn, from the almanac,—most despised, most prolific, most indispensable of books, which every man uses, and no man praises; the very quack, clown, pack-horse, and pariah of modern literature, yet the one universal book of modern literature; the supreme and only literary necessity even in households where the Bible and the newspaper are still undesired or unattainable luxuries.

The earliest record of this species of literature in America carries us back to the very beginning of printed literature in America; for, next after a sheet containing "The Freeman's Oath," the first production that came from the printing-press in this country was "An Almanac calculated for New England, by Mr. Pierce," and printed by Stephen Daye, at Cambridge, in 1639.[42] Thenceforward for a long time, scarcely a year passed over that solitary printing-press at Cambridge, without receiving a similar salute from it. In 1676, Boston itself grew wise enough to produce an almanac of its own. Ten years afterward, Philadelphia began to send forth almanacs—a trade in which, in the following century, it was to acquire special glory. In 1697, New York entered the same enticing field of enterprise. The

[42] I. Thomas, "Hist. of Printing in Am." I. 46.

first almanac produced in Rhode Island, was in 1728; the first almanac produced in Virginia, was in 1731.[43] In 1733, Benjamin Franklin began to publish what he called "Poor Richard's Almanac," to which his own personal reputation has given a celebrity surpassing that of all other almanacs published anywhere in the world. Thus, year by year, with the multiplication of people and of printing-presses in this country, was there a multiplication of almanacs, some of them being of remarkable intellectual and even literary merit. From the first, they contained many of the traits that had become conventional in printed almanacs in Europe, ever since their first publication there in the fifteenth century; particularly astrological prophecies, or, as they were called, "prognostications," relating both to mankind and to the weather, and representing the traditional belief in the influence of the heavenly bodies upon mundane affairs. Gradually, to these were added other things,—scraps of wisdom, crumbs of history, snatches of verse, proverbs, jests, all scattered through the little book according to the convenience of the printer and the supposed benefit of the reader. Throughout our colonial time, when larger books were costly and few, the almanac had everywhere a hearty welcome and frequent perusal; the successive numbers of it were carefully preserved year after year; their margins and blank pages were often covered over with annotations, domestic and otherwise. Thus, John Cotton, it will be remembered, used the blank spaces in his almanacs as depositories for his stealthy attempts at verse. So, also, the historian, Thomas Prince, recorded in his almanacs the state of his accounts with his hair-dresser and wig-maker. A writer of some note,[44] born in Connecticut during the American Revolution, has left a vivid description of his own excitement, as a child, in reading again and again the literary treasures of the household, consisting, in large part, of a file of almanacs for fifty years.

One of the numerous myths still prevailing in the world with reference to Benjamin Franklin, describes him as the first founder of an

---

[43] For several of the above dates I depend upon Ainsworth R. Spofford, in "Am. Almanac" for 1878, 23–25.

[44] Joseph T. Buckingham, "Personal Memoirs," etc. I. 20.

New England: Popular Discussion

almanac blending those qualities of shrewd instruction and keen mother-wit, that are to be seen in his famous series; a French encyclopædist, for example, declaring that Franklin "put forth the first popular almanac which spoke the language of reason." [45] In truth, much of the wisdom and wit introduced by Franklin into his almanac was borrowed from Bacon, Rabelais, Rochefoucauld, Steele, Swift, De Foe, and others: [46] but even the idea of introducing into an almanac wit and wisdom whether original or borrowed, had been thought of and put into practice before Franklin's "Poor Richard" was born. In 1728, five years before that event, Franklin's brother, James, sent forth the first number of "The Rhode Island Almanac;" and in its pages, year by year, one may find no little of that sagacity, humor, and knack of phrase, that did so much for the fortunes of his own runaway apprentice. But even three years before James Franklin's almanac appeared, Nathaniel Ames,[47] a physician and innkeeper of Dedham, Massachusetts, a man of original, vigorous, and pungent genius, began the publication of his "Astronomical Diary and Almanac;" which he continued to publish till his death in 1764; which, under his management, acquired an enormous popularity throughout New England; and which, from the first, contained in high perfection every type of excellence afterward illustrated in the almanac of Benjamin Franklin. Indeed, Ames's almanac was in most respects better than Franklin's, and was, probably, the most pleasing representative we have of a form of literature that furnished so much entertainment to our ancestors, and that preserves for us so many characteristic tints of their life and thought.

Nathaniel Ames made his almanac a sort of annual cyclopædia of information and amusement,—a vehicle for the conveyance to the public of all sorts of knowledge and nonsense, in prose and verse, from literature, history and his own mind, all presented with brevity, variety, and infallible tact. He had the instinct of a journalist; and, under a guise that was half-frolicsome, the sincerity and benignant

---

[45] "Am. Almanac," for 1878, 25.

[46] A delightful account of "Poor Richard's Almanac" is in James Parton's "Life and Times of Benjamin Franklin," I. 227–240.

[47] He was the father of the celebrated orator and statesman, Fisher Ames.

passion of a public educator. He carried into the furthest wildernesses of New England some of the best English literature; pronouncing there, perhaps for the first time, the names of Addison, Thomson, Pope, Dryden, Butler, Milton; and repeating there choice fragments of what they had written. Thus, eight years before Benjamin Franklin had started his almanac, Nathaniel Ames was publishing one that had all of its best qualities,—fact and frolic, the wisdom of the preacher without his solemnity, terse sayings, shrewdness, wit, homely wisdom, all sparkling in piquant phrase.

As the public expected the almanac-maker to be a prophet, Nathaniel Ames gratified the public; and he freely predicted future events, but always with a merry twinkle in his eye, and always ready to laugh the loudest at his own failure to predict them aright. He mixes, in delightful juxtaposition, absurd prognostications, curt jests, and aphorisms of profound wisdom, the whole forming a miscellany even now extremely readable, and sure, at that time, to raise shouts of laughter around thousands of fireplaces where food for laughter was much needed. Thus,

January 1. "About the beginning of the year expect plenty of rain or snow."
"Warm and clears off cold again."
May 22. "Some materials about this time are hatched for the clergy to debate on."
October 21. "He that lives by fraud is in danger of dying a knave."
November 9. "These aspects show violent winds and in winter storms of driving snow; mischiefs by Indians, if no peace; and among us, feuds, quarrels, bloody-noses, broken pates—if not necks."
November 24. "If there was less debating and more acting, 'twould be better times."
December 7–10. "Ladies, take heed,
　　　　　Lay down your fans,
　　　　　And handle well
　　　　　Your warming-pans."
December 15–18. "This cold, uncomfortable weather
　　　　　Makes Jack and Gill lie close together."
December 20–22. "The lawyers' tongues—they never freeze,
　　　　　If warmed with honest clients' fees." [48]

[48] Almanac for 1749.

New England: Popular Discussion

Having been laughed at for his false predictions, he uses the almanac for 1729 to join in the laugh, and to turn the occasion of it into a witty and instructive home-thrust at every reader:

> "Man was at first a perfect, upright creature,
> The lively image of his great Creator.
> When Adam fell, all men in him transgressed;
> And since that time they err that are the best.
> The printer errs; I err,—much like the rest.
> Welcome's that man for to complain of me,
> Whose self and works are quite from errors free."

Sometimes, in a more serious tone, he gives his real opinion about this traditional department of the almanac, and helps to lift his readers above the demand for it: "He who has foreordained whatsoever comes to pass, knows, and he only knows with absolute certainty, what will come to pass. The Book of Fate is hid from all created beings. . . . Indeed, the Devil does not know so much of future events, as many expect an almanac-maker should foretell; although it must be owned that they are willing to allow him the help of the Devil for his information." [49]

But everywhere it is plain enough that the author wears his mask of jester, only to hide a most earnest and friendly face; and having by his mirth gained admission to every New England cabin, he sits down with the family around the great crackling fire, and helps them to a wisdom that will enable them to keep on laughing. Thus, in the almanac for 1754, he has a preliminary address to the reader, uttered in the tone of a Cobbett or a Greeley,—a born tribune of the people: "I have filled the two last pages with an essay on regimen. I don't pretend to direct the learned; the rich and voluptuous will scorn my direction, and sneer or rail at any that would reclaim them; but since this sheet enters the solitary dwellings of the poor and illiterate, where the studied ingenuity of the learned writer never comes, if these brief hints do good, it will rejoice the heart of your humble servant, Nathaniel Ames."

February 24–27. "If you fall into misfortunes, creep through those bushes which have the least briers."

[49] Almanac for 1763.

March 21–23. "Expectation waits to know whether the mountain bears a mouse or no."

October 25–28. "There are three faithful friends—an old wife, an old dog, and ready cash."

November 6–8. "Were things done twice, many would be wise." [50]

July 16–27. "Every man carries a fool in his sleeve; with some he appears bold, with some he only pops out now and then, but the wise keep him hid."

September 12–16. "To some men their country is their shame; and some are the shame of their country." [51]

He sprinkles his pages with wholesome suggestions about health-getting and health-keeping. For September, 1762, he says: "This month is a proper season to recruit the unhealthy, by taking Dr. Horse and riding long journeys—though moderately." The gospel that he preaches is the gospel of health, virtue, economy, industry, content; he shows that always grumbling is either a vice or a disease, and that whichever it be, the first duty of every man is to rid himself of it:

> "As for myself, whom poverty prevents
> From being angry at so great expense,
>
> . . .
>
> I choose to labor, rather than to fret;
> What's rage in some, in me goes off in sweat.
> If times are ill, and things seem never worse,
> Men, manners, to reclaim,—I, take my horse:
> One mile reforms 'em; or, if aught remain
> Unpurged—'tis but to ride as far again.
> Thus on myself in toils I spend my rage:
> I pay the fine, and that absolves the age.
> Sometimes, still more to interrupt my ease,
> I take my pen, and write such things as these;
> Which, though all other merit be denied,
> Show my devotion still to be employed.
>
> . . .
>
> And since midst indolence, spleen will prevail,
> Since who do nothing else, are sure to rail,

[50] Almanac for 1758.   [51] Almanac for 1763.

New England: Popular Discussion

> Men should be suffered thus to play the fool
> To keep from hurt, as children go to school." [52]

The almanac for 1736 ends with a brief prose essay, which is an amusing miscellany of physical learning and humor, all intended to interest the reader and to advertise the merits of a certain invaluable medicine—worm-seed for children; concluding with this paragraph worthy of the shrewdness of Poor Richard himself: "Some nurses are so superstitious that they dare not give their children worm-seed without pounding and sifting it, affirming that every seed that escapes being bruised in the mortar will become a live worm in the bowels of the child. But, by the by, it is an excellent medicine for the purpose, and they need not be afraid to use it; for, if they will prove that it can breed worms in children, I can as easily prove that it can breed children in women; and so those unhappy persons who have had the ill-luck to have children without fathers, need not lie under the imputation of scandal, if they can produce sufficient evidence that they have taken worm-seed."

His pages are sprinkled with verses from the English poets and from his own pen,—the latter often of great vigor and sprightliness. For 1736, he spreads over the almanac a poem of twelve stanzas, one stanza being prefixed to each month. The subject of the poem is the Day of Judgment, and is so vivid and powerful in its descriptions, and is so blended with ominous references to the stars and to the warring elements, that it must have carried awe into many impressible minds, as if the omniscient almanac-maker intended actually to announce the coming of the awful day that very year. This is the stanza for January:

> "The muses tremble with a faltering wing,
>   While nature's great catastrophe they sing;
>   For Helicon itself, their sacred throne,
>   Must to the womb of chaos back return.
>   The cheerful region of the earth and air
>   Is filled with horror, darkness, and despair."

So, with fascinating gloom opens the year; and thus it proceeds, with variations of poetic horror, month by month. In March, we

[52] Almanac for 1757.

have this mystic and dreadful description of the moon and stars:

> "No more she rules as regent of the night,
>   But fills her orb with blood instead of light;
>   And dissolution reigns both near and far,
>   Through heaven's wide circuit round. Each shining star
>   His intricate nocturnal mazes stops,
>   And from his place assigned in heaven down drops."

In the following month things grow rapidly worse. The stars, it will be remembered, have fallen:

> "Their light extinct, nature in darkness ends,
>   Except what light hell's horrid bosom sends
>   Around the sky; her baneful torches come
>   To light dissolving nature to her tomb.
>   The earth with trembling agonies doth roll,
>   As though she mixed her centre with the pole."

In May,

> "The seas do roar; and every peaceful lake
>   And wandering rivers horrid murmurings make;
>   The rocks explode, and trembling mountains nod,
>   And valleys rise at the approaching God;
>   From heaven's high court angelic throngs descend;
>   Myriads this great solemnity attend."

It must have given some relief to sensitive readers to cast the eye further down the page, and to read in the author's prose his cheerful prophecies concerning the course of the weather for that very month; for he assures them of "a fine pleasant air, with gentle gales," and of "fair, pleasant, growing weather." And although there is an ominous threat of combustibility during the last week—"This week will afford heat and thunder"—yet the prospect is redeemed by the subsequent promise of "now and then a sprinkling of rain,"—which, of course, must defer the general conflagration. The stanza for July concludes with this couplet:

> "A rending sound from the expanded skies
>   Commands the dead, the sleepy dead, to rise;"

which harmonizes admirably with the weather probabilities for the same time; "The month ends with thunder and hot weather."

The almanac for 1749, the year succeeding the close of King George's War, has a fine literary tone, and its poetic motto, on the title-page, is a noble prophecy of peace in the world:

> "No heroes' ghosts, with garments rolled in blood,
> Majestic stalk; the golden age renewed,
> No hollow drums in Flanders beat; the breath
> Of brazen trumpets rings no peals of death.
> The milder stars their peaceful beams afford,
> And sounding hammer beats the wounding sword
> To ploughshares now; Mars must to Ceres yield,
> And exiled Peace returns and takes the field."

The essay at the end of the almanac for 1758, is of unusual merit for thought and vivacity of expression. It is a fine specimen of what we now call a leading editorial article—terse, epigrammatic, vigorous, formed to catch and to hold the attention; and it is a very creditable example of literary style. It was written in the midst of the struggle between France and England for the empire of America. It is upon "America—its Past, Present, and Future State." With reference to the Past, he says: "Time has cast a shade upon this scene. Since the creation, innumerable accidents have happened here, the bare mention of which would create wonder and surprise; but they are all lost in oblivion. The ignorant natives, for want of letters, have forgot their stock, and know not from whence they came, or how, or when they arrived here, or what has happened since." Then glancing at the events that have happened in America since the arrival of the Europeans, he describes the magnificent territory of the North-West then in dispute: "Time was when we might have been possessed of it; at this time two mighty kings contend for this inestimable prize. Their respective claims are to be measured by the length of their swords. The poet says, 'the Gods and Opportunity ride post;' that you must take her by the forelock, being bald behind. Have we not too fondly depended upon our numbers? Sir Francis Bacon says, 'The wolf careth not how many the sheep be.' But numbers, well-spirited, with the blessing of heaven, will do wonders when by military skill and discipline the commanders can actuate, as by one soul, the most numerous bodies of armed people. Our numbers will not avail till the colonies are united. . . . If we do not join heart and hand in the common cause against our exulting foes, but fall to disputing amongst ourselves, it may really happen as the governor of Pennsylvania told his assembly, 'We shall have no privilege to dispute about, nor country to dispute in.' "

His treatment of the Future State of America shows a remarkable grasp of facts relating to the physical resources of the continent, and an unusual power of reason in constructing the possibilities of civil and material development, especially in the West: "Here we find a vast stock of proper materials for the art and ingenuity of man to work on,—treasures of immense worth, concealed from the poor, ignorant, aboriginal natives. . . . As the celestial light of the gospel was directed here by the finger of God, it will doubtless finally drive the long, long night of heathenish darkness from America. . . . So arts and sciences will change the face of nature in their tour from hence over the Appalachian Mountains to the Western Ocean; and as they march through the vast desert, the residence of wild beasts will be broken up, and their obscene howl cease forever. Instead of which, the stones and trees will dance together at the music of Orpheus, the rocks will disclose their hidden gems, and the inestimable treasures of gold and silver be broken up. Huge mountains of iron ore are already discovered; and vast stores are reserved for future generations. This metal, more useful than gold and silver, will employ millions of hands, not only to form the martial sword and peaceful share alternately, but an infinity of utensils improved in the exercise of art and handicraft amongst men. . . . Shall not then these vast quarries that teem with mechanic stone,—those for structure be piled into great cities, and those for sculpture into statues, to perpetuate the honor of renowned heroes—even those who shall now save their country?" He then closes with this appeal to posterity: "O ye unborn inhabitants of America! should this page escape its destined conflagration at the year's end, and these alphabetical letters remain legible when your eyes behold the sun after he has rolled the seasons round for two or three centuries more, you will know that in Anno Domini, 1758, we dreamed of your times."

Chapter XIV

New England: History and Biography

I. Further development of the historic spirit in New England—Biography and biographers—Ebenezer Turell—His biographies of Jane Turell and of Benjamin Colman.
II. William Hubbard—Picture of him by John Dunton—His literary culture and aptitude—Qualities of his style—His "General History of New England"—His "Indian Wars"—Celebrity of the latter—Its faults and merits—Represents the wrath of the people against the Indians—Portrait of a noble savage.
III. Other literary memorials of the long conflict with the Indians—Mary Rowlandson and her thrilling "Narrative" of Indian captivity—"The Redeemed Captive," by John Williams of Deerfield—Benjamin Church—His history of King Philip's War and of other struggles with the Indians—Interest of his narratives—Samuel Penhallow—His history of Indian wars—Pictures of heroism and cruelty—His reminiscences of classical study—Samuel Niles—His "History of the Indian and French Wars."
IV. Thomas Prince—His eminent career—His special taste and training for history—Has the cardinal virtues of an historian—His "Chronological History of New England"—Thoroughness of his methods—Salient features of the book—Its worthiness.
V. John Callender—His careful sketch of the first century of Rhode Island's history.
VI. William Douglass—The life and the singularities of the man—A literary Ishmaelite—His ability and self-confidence—His sarcastic account of the medical profession in America—His "Summary"—A passionate, heterogeneous, able book—Its style and scope—Its drolleries

History of American Literature

—His dislike of the Indians, of the French, of Whitefield, of Bishop Berkeley, and of paper-money—General estimate of his book.

I

THE one form of secular literature for which, during the entire colonial age, the writers of New England had the most authentic vocation, is history.

All persons of devout, brooding, and introverted natures are apt to keep records of themselves,—to have the historic feeling; for to such persons life seems so costly and venerable a thing, that they would hold the memory of it from lapsing into that grave of the past, whither life itself every moment is hurrying. The men and women who founded the sturdy little commonwealths of New England, had such natures; they reverenced themselves, they reverenced their lives, they reverenced the stupendous task to which they were giving their lives. By a law as deep as their own souls, they were, inevitably, from the first, a race of diarists, chroniclers, biographers, autobiographers, historians. And their children and their children's children were like unto them. The historic feeling did not perish, or even abate, with the passing of the generations. It throve rather, and grew lustier, nourishing itself on a finer and broader acceptance of life, and on the sweet memory of its own heroic age.

Our second literary period produced four considerable historians, —William Hubbard, Cotton Mather, Thomas Prince, Thomas Hutchinson: the first two excelling, in popularity, all other historians of the colonial time; the last two excelling all others in specific training for the profession of history, and in the conscious accumulation of materials for historic work.[1]

Of that species of history that is devoted to the lives of individuals rather than of communities, there were many specimens produced in the colonial epoch; such, for example, as biographies of John Cotton, Richard Mather, Increase Mather, Cotton Mather, and of the great army of divines, heroes, and sages that abide eternally in the

---

[1] Of these four historians, it will be most convenient to deal with the last, Thomas Hutchinson, in another volume, to be devoted to the literature of the American Revolution.

New England: History and Biography

"Magnalia." But it is a singular fact that, in literary quality, the biographies written in colonial New England are far inferior to its histories.

The best example of its biographical work is "The Life and Character of the Reverend Benjamin Colman," by his son-in-law, Ebenezer Turell, published in Boston, in 1749. Even this distinction, however, does not imply exalted merit. In its construction, the book imitates a bad model,—Samuel Mather's "Life of Cotton Mather," —wherein the narrative is arranged, not in the natural order of time, but in the artificial one of topics. The style of Turell's book is superior to Samuel Mather's, being pure and pleasant; and his admiration for his subject, while it is hearty and reverent, never betrays him into hyperboles of laudation.[2]

II

William Hubbard was born in England in 1621; came to New England in his childhood; and was one of that remarkable group of nine young men whom Harvard College sent forth, in 1642, as the first specimens of high culture achieved in the woods of America. By training, by strong aptitude, and by prevailing engagements, he was almost a professional man of letters. The most of his life he passed as minister of the First Church at Ipswich, Massachusetts, where his learning and eloquence won for him a commanding reputation. But his distinction points to the literary rather than to the theological side of personal greatness. Indeed, the breadth of his thought, his geniality, and his tolerance seems well-nigh to have cracked the shell of clerical propriety in which he was encased. Thomas Hutchinson[3] speaks of him as having "a good degree of catholicism," which, as that historian suggests, "was not accounted the most valuable part of his character in the age in which he lived."

---

[2] Turell also published, in 1735, "Memoirs of the Life and Death of the Pious and Ingenious Mrs. Jane Turell." The book is largely made up of her writings, especially her poetry. She was the literary phenomenon of an admiring circle of friends; but she died before she had outgrown the feebleness of poetic imitation. Indeed, she left no proofs of poetic genius, more notable than are to be found in the desk of almost any spirited school-girl with a tendency toward emotional effervescence in verse.

[3] "Hist. Mass. Bay," II. 136, note.

He resided in his parish of Ipswich to the great age of eighty-three; and from contemporary allusions we may picture him to ourselves as a stately, affable, and accomplished gentleman, the ideal country-pastor in a highly intellectual community,—passing the most of his time in his library, and filling the long quiet spaces of his life with various culture. The eccentric London bookseller, John Dunton, who made a voyage of business to New England in 1686, has left a lively picture of Hubbard, by whom the bookseller was hospitably received on his visit to Ipswich: "The benefit of nature and the fatigue of study have equally contributed to his eminence; neither are we less obliged to both than himself, for he fully communicates of his learning to all who have the happiness to share in his converse. In a word, he is learned without ostentation and vanity, and gives all his productions . . . a delicate turn and grace." [4] Like nearly all his clerical associates in those days, he published occasional sermons; and these, having the unusual quality of verbal elegance, did much to form his reputation as a writer of genuine literary skill.[5] But his most important work was done as an historian; and as such he represents a clear advance, at least in the literary quality of his labor. He had an ear for style, something of poetic feeling, a conscious purpose of art. His hand loved to form sentences that had precision in them, a liquid flow, the lingering echo of pleasant sounds, imaginative meanings.

In his capacity of historian, Hubbard wrote two works, considerable in size, very unequal in merit. The less valuable one is "A General History of New England from the Discovery to 1680," left by him in manuscript, and not put into print until the present century.[6]

---

[4] J. Dunton, "Life and Errors," I. 134.

[5] I think, however, that the praise of Hubbard as a writer has been overdone. Thus, John Eliot, in his "Biographical Dictionary," speaks of Hubbard as "superior to all his contemporaries as a prose writer;" and James Savage, in N. A. Review, II. 221–230, speaks of Hubbard's election-sermon as surpassed in style by "no work of the two next generations." That sermon is able and impressive; its diction is smooth and dignified; yet it is far inferior, in all respects, to the sermons of Urian Oakes, John Barnard, Benjamin Colman, Jonathan Mayhew, or Mather Byles. His own fellow-townsman, John Wise, was vastly his superior as a prose writer.

[6] First published by Mass. Hist. Soc. 1815; reprinted by the same Society in 1848, under the editorial care of Thaddeus Mason Harris.

New England: History and Biography

Of this work, many pages are transferred solidly from Morton's "New England's Memorial;" and for the period between 1630 and 1650, the larger part of Hubbard is but a literal repetition of Winthrop. The book seems to have been done as a mere literary job.

A more agreeable task awaits us when we come to the study of Hubbard's "Narrative of the Troubles with the Indians in New England,"[7] from the earliest white settlement to the year 1677. If, in the seventeenth century, was produced in America any prose work which, for its almost universal diffusion among the people, deserves the name of an American classic, it is this work. The author evidently wrought upon it with genuine zest. It is not without serious faults. As a whole the narrative would now seem tedious, being clogged by petty items, often wandering into digressions, lacking a continuous and culminating power. Moreover, the work has a still greater blemish; it is inaccurate. An antiquarian of our time calls the author "the careless Hubbard;"[8] and one of his own contemporaries says, with some exaggeration, of the work now before us, "the mistakes are judged to be many more than the truths in it."[9] In spite of all this, however, as a narrative embodying the spirit of early New England heroism, it has qualities that still give to it something of the interest which it had for its original readers. In many passages the style is strong, picturesque, dramatic, enlivened by an occasional touch of sarcasm or humor; detached incidents are often told with thrilling effect. It is not impossible for us even now to understand why, during several generations, the book had an absorbing fascination for its readers in New England, to whom these Indian stories brought home again the traditions of dreadful experience and daring achievement on the part of their own kindred.

In one thing, certainly, the book is authentic; it represents the im-

---

[7] First published, both in Boston and in London, in 1677. The London edition is the more accurate, and probably had the personal supervision of the author, who, there is reason to think, went to London with a copy of his work. The best reprint of the work is one edited by S. G. Drake, 2 vols. Roxbury, 1865. My quotations, however, are from the Stockbridge reprint, 1803; but I have collated them with the corresponding passages in Drake's ed.

[8] Alexander Young, "Chron. Pilg." 334, note.

[9] John Cotton of Plymouth, in lette. to Increase Mather, 4 Mass. Hist. Soc. Coll. VIII. 232.

measurable rage against the Indians, that had at last taken possession of the white inhabitants of New England,—their final purpose to count out those bipeds from the list of human beings, and to wipe them out from the face of the earth. Here Hubbard is the frank voice of his contemporaries. He utters words about the red men, that are rasping and fell; such as one hears still, upon the same topic, on the American frontiers. In his pages, the Indians are "treacherous villains," [10] "the dross of mankind," [11] "the dregs and lees of the earth," [12] "faithless and ungrateful monsters," [13] "children of the Devil, full of all subtlety and malice," [14] and Philip himself is "this treacherous and perfidious caitiff." [15] "Subtlety, malice, and revenge seem to be as inseparable from them as if it were a part of their essence. Whatever hopes may be of their conversion to Christianity in after time, there is but little appearance of any truth in their hearts at present, where so much of the contrary is ordinarily breathed out of their mouths." [16] Of the fate of certain Indians taken in battle, he has this quiet and classic description: "The men . . . were turned presently into Charon's ferry-boat, under the command of skipper Gallop, who dispatched them, a little without the harbor." [17]

Along these old pages, which almost quiver with fury against the Indians, and are strewn with words that seem to weary the vocabulary of execration and contempt, we now and then come to a portrait of some Indian who is neither brute nor caitiff, but for pride and fortitude towers into a hero, and renders credible Dryden's conception of "the noble savage." One day, during King Philip's War, some white men and a few Indian allies, resting in front of their camp in the woods, caught sight, at a distance, of a stalwart Indian, of princely air, running swiftly as if from pursuit. They "guessed by the swiftness of his motion, that he fled as if an enemy." They instantly joined in the chase; and one of them, an Indian named Catapazet, "put him so hard to it, that he cast off, first his blanket, then his silver-laced coat and belt of peag, which made Catapazet conclude it was the right bird. . . . So as they forced him to take

[10] "Indian Wars," 18. [11] Ibid. 18. [12] Ibid. 18.
[13] Ibid. 118. [14] Ibid. 120. [15] Ibid. 69.
[16] Ibid. 359–360. [17] Ibid. 42.

New England: History and Biography

the water, through which as he overhastingly plunged, his foot slipping upon a stone, it made him fall into the water so deep as it wetted his gun; upon which accident, he confessed soon after, that his heart and his bowels turned within him, so as he became like a rotten stick, void of strength; insomuch as one Monopoide, a Pequod, swiftest of foot, laid hold of him within thirty rod of the riverside, without his making any resistance; though he was a very proper man, of goodly stature and great courage of mind, as well as strength of body. One of the first English that came up with him was Robert Stanton, a young man that scarce had reached the twenty-second year of his age; yet adventuring to ask him a question or two, to whom this manly sachem, looking with a little neglect upon his youthful face, replied in broken English, 'You much child, no understand matters of war; let your brother or your chief come, him I will answer;' and was as good as his word, acting herein as if, by a Pythagorean metempsychosis, some old Roman ghost had possessed the body of this western pagan. . . . He continuing in the same his obstinate resolution, was carried soon after to Stonington, where he was shot to death by some of his own quality. . . . This was the confusion of a damned wretch, that had often opened his mouth to blaspheme the name of the living God, and those that made profession thereof. . . . And when he was told his sentence was to die, he said he liked it well; that he should die before his heart was soft, or had spoken anything unworthy of himself." [18]

III

Of the sorrowful conflict in New England between Englishmen and Indians, reaching its reddest crisis in 1676, there is no more graphic or more exquisite literary memorial than a little book written by a woman—who had in her own person a frightful experience of it—Mary Rowlandson, wife of the pastor of the church at Lancaster, then an outpost of civilization. In the bitterness of winter, February the tenth, 1676, while her husband was absent in Boston, the town in which she lived was suddenly assaulted and destroyed by Indians; and she, with her children, was carried away into captivity,

[18] "Indian Wars," 167–169.

experiencing horrible treatment. After eleven weeks and five days, with money raised for the purpose by the women of Boston, she was ransomed; and while all the anguish of her fright and suffering was still fresh in her memory, she wrote a narrative of her captivity, which was first printed in New England in 1682, was reissued in London the same year, and has been repeatedly published since then.[19] It is a series of life-like pictures of the wild and sorrowful scenes that she had encountered; is most effective in its artless touches of pathos; and is such an exhibition of Indian barbarity as must have driven still deeper into the minds of the New-Englanders their hate of the red men, and their quiet purpose of giving them over to doom. The diction of this little book is admirable,—the pure, idiomatic, and sinewy English of a cultivated American matron.

Another powerful picture of Indian cruelty, but referring to a time nearly thirty years later, is "The Redeemed Captive," by John Williams,[20] who, in 1686, at the age of twenty-two, had entered upon his life-long pastorate at Deerfield, Massachusetts. This village was then on the furthest edge of the white settlements, and was protected from Indian assaults only by a rude picketed fort. Sentinels kept guard every night; even in the daytime, no one left his doorsteps without a musket; and neighborly communication between the houses was kept up principally by underground passages from cellar to cellar. In the winter of 1704, the inhabitants had received warning of unusual danger approaching them; and at their request twenty soldiers had been sent to them as a special guard. On the night of February twenty-eighth, the watch patrolled the streets until just before dawn, when, unfortunately, they yielded to the desire for sleep; upon which, three hundred Frenchmen and Indians from Canada, who had been skulking in the neighborhood, waiting for such an opportunity, got into the hapless town. What followed, in that hideous winter-darkness, when savage and fiendish lusts were at once let loose upon victims who were absolutely powerless, is told, with genuine pathos, by the pastor, himself and family being among

---

[19] The first ed. is entitled "The Sovereignty and Goodness of God: A Narrative of the Captivity and Restoration of Mrs. Mary Rowlandson." The 6th ed. appeared in 1828.

[20] Born at Roxbury, 1664; graduated at Harvard, 1683.

New England: History and Biography

the chief sufferers.[21] In the same touching manner, he narrates the whole story of his captivity: his long, faint march through the snows to Canada; the cruelties and the courtesies he experienced there; his efforts to recover his children from the Indians; the adroit and persistent attempts of the Jesuits to induce him to apostatize from his faith; and finally, after a bondage of more than two years, his redemption and return home, with all his children, excepting one, a daughter, who remained the rest of her life among her captors.[22] In the year following his restoration, he published his famous narrative, which has since then been six times reprinted, and has contributed its tinge of horror and hate to the white man's memory of the Indian.

In the lineage of New England military prowess, a true descendant of Miles Standish and of John Mason was Colonel Benjamin Church; born at Plymouth, Massachusetts, in 1639; founder of Little Compton, where he died in 1718; a matchless guerilla-leader; the most famous Indian-fighter of his day; especially renowned as the conqueror of King Philip, and as the invincible champion of the white men in five other wars against the Indians. In his old age, he put into the hands of his son, Thomas, the memoranda he had kept of his campaigns, and he caused to be written and published, in 1716, "Entertaining Passages Relating to Philip's War . . . as also of Expeditions more lately made against the Common Enemy and Indian Rebels in the Eastern Parts of New England;"[23] a book that stirred the very heart of New England, holding "children from play and old men from the chimney-corner," having indeed a spell almost beyond the reach of literary art. It is a soldier's bluff narrative of his own dangerous and enticing adventures; it is full of individual incidents—risks, grapplings, bloodshed, leaps in the dark, all man-

---

[21] "Redeemed Captive," 10–17.

[22] This daughter was Eunice, then ten years old. She could not afterward be induced to leave the Indians, having herself become an Indian in habit and language, and having been smitten by the almost incurable fascination of savage life. She married an Indian; and their supposed grandson or great-grandson was Eleazer Williams, once notorious in this country for his claim to be the lost Dauphin, son of Louis XVI. and Marie Antoinette.

[23] Reprinted, with elaborate and careful editing by Henry Martyn Dexter, Boston, first part, 1865; second part, 1867.

ner of stern things. The reader seems to be a listener, and to be sitting by the side of this scarred and ancient paladin of the New England bush-whackers, and to hear his very talk, as he narrates, frankly, vividly, and always with a strong man's modesty, the deeds that once saved every New England man's door-post from being bespattered with the blood of his own wife and children.

Another fine old chronicler of the Indian troubles was Samuel Penhallow, born in England in 1665, and educated at the celebrated dissenting academy of Charles Morton in Newington Green, where he may have had Daniel De Foe for a school-mate. In 1686, with his teacher, he came to New England, intending to complete his studies for the Christian ministry; instead of which, however, he married a young woman of great wealth at Portsmouth, New Hampshire; and thenceforward resided there, devoting himself to the care of his property, and to the public service. He built a stately mansion; lived in the grand manner of our colonial gentry; practised a boundless hospitality; acquired great influence in the province; was for many years its treasurer; and died, as its chief-justice, in 1726. New Hampshire, being then a frontier colony, had in its outlying settlements no rest, day or night, from the peril of an Indian massacre; and in the very year in which Penhallow died, he published, in Boston, "The History of the Wars of New England with the Eastern Indians," [24] covering the period from 1703 to 1726,—a realistic and vivid story of all that time of anguish, of the various assaults of the Indians upon the habitations of white men, especially of several stiff and dreadful fights in which the two races grappled together in the woods. He himself says of his book that he might have named it, after Orosius, "De Miseriâ Hominum," since it is "no other than a narrative of tragical incursions perpetrated by bloody pagans, who are monsters of such cruelty that the words of Virgil may not unaptly be applied to them:

> Tristius haud illis monstrum, nec saevior ulla
> Pestis et ira deûm." [25]

[24] Reprinted in Boston, 1826; also in N. H. Hist. Soc. Coll. I.; also in Philadelphia, 1859. My references are to the reprint last named.
[25] "The History," etc. 13.

New England: History and Biography

He indicates the cruelty of the savages rather by harrowing facts than by epithets; yet the flow of the history is sometimes broken by a sentence in which one almost hears a sob of grief and rage. No veil is cast by him over ghastly and blood-clotted things; our sensibilities are never spared; we come face to face, constantly, with the hard and the horrible. In one place, we read the proclamation of the government offering from ten to fifty pounds for every Indian scalp that shall be brought in; in another, we see a procession of white captives driven onward through the woods, fainting by the way, some of them knocked on the head, "teeming women in cold blood . . . ript open, others fastened to stakes and burnt alive." [26] We have a glimpse, too, of a scene like this: A group of Indians one day skulking near the negligent garrison of Haverhill, and taking it by surprise; the sentinel is slain; the only white person at all adequate being a brave woman, who "perceiving the misery that was attending her, and having boiling soap on the fire," throws it over the assailants, scalding one of them to death. But she is carried off by the savages; after a few days of weariness and cruelty she is delivered of a child; "but the babe soon perished . . . by the cruelty of the Indians, who, as it cried, threw hot embers in its mouth." [27] On another page, we are made acquainted with a most gritty hero, one Lieutenant Robbins, who, being mortally wounded in Lovewell's famous fight, is about to be left on the field by his retreating companions; but "being sensible of his dying state, desired one of the company to charge his gun and leave it with him, being persuaded that the Indians by the morning would come and scalp him, but was desirous of killing one more before he died." [28]

It lends a sort of charm to this unshrinking narrative of human wretchedness, that the author often dashes his story with reminiscences of his early classical studies, giving to it a gentle flavor of pedantry, and especially suggesting a piquant contrast between lettered and elegant peace and the savagery of the facts which he records. He quotes Virgil, Horace, Plutarch. Now and then he finds a parallelism between these fatal incidents done in the American wilderness, and others done to immortal remembrance in Greek or Roman story:

[26] "The History," etc. 47. [27] Ibid. 23. [28] Ibid. 113.

as, that two aged men, "Mr. Phipenny and Mr. Kent," were attacked by Indians, "and soon fell by their fury; for, being advanced in years, they were so infirm that I might say of them, as Juvenal did of Priam, they had scarce blood enough left to tinge the knife of the sacrifice." [29] This conjuction * of Priam and Mr. Phipenny is unexpected, at the least.

We must make room for one more of these historians of New England's agony of effort against its foes,—Samuel Niles, who was a Harvard graduate, an eminent minister, and the author of a few books on theology and church-polity. His special drift was toward history. In 1747, he published a narrative, in crude verse, of the reduction of Louisburg; and he left in manuscript a voluminous "History of the Indian and French Wars." [30] The life of the author stretched from before the time of King Philip's War until after the time of the conquest of Canada; and from his own memory he was able to compose large portions of this work. He used freely, besides, the labors of others. The book is written with some vigor and verbal skill; but the narrative is straggling and long-drawn, and the interest of the reader soon perishes in a wilderness of petty details.

IV

Thomas Prince was born at Sandwich, Massachusetts, in 1687; was graduated at Harvard in 1707; and from 1718 to 1758,—the last forty years of his life,—was pastor of the South Church, Boston; during all those years filling a high and great space in the thoughts of his contemporaries. He had prepared himself for the public service by diligent study at home, and by eight years of observation abroad; he was a man of most tolerant and brotherly spirit; his days were filled by gentle and gracious and laborious deeds; he was a great scholar; he magnified his office and edified the brethren by publishing a large number of judicious and nutritious sermons; he also revised and improved the New England Psalm Book, "by an endeavor

[29] "The History," etc. 20.
[30] Printed in 3 Mass. Hist. Soc. Coll. VI. 154–279, and in 4 Mass. Hist. Soc. Coll. V. 309–589.

[* Corrected to "conjunction."]

New England: History and Biography

after a yet nearer approach to the inspired original, as well as to the rules of poetry;" [31] he took a special interest in physical science, and formed quite definite opinions about earthquakes, comets, "the electrical substance," and so forth. For all these things, he was deeply honored in his own time, and would have been deeply forgotten in ours, had he not added to them very unique performances as an historian. No American writer before Thomas Prince, qualified himself for the service of history by so much conscious and specific preparation; and though others did more work in that service, none did better work than he.

The foundation of his character as an historian was laid in reverence, not only for truth, but for precision, and in willingness to win it at any cost of labor and of time. He likewise felt the peculiar authority of originals in historical testimony, and the potential value, for historical illustration, of all written or printed materials whatsoever; and while he was yet a college-boy, driven by the sacred avarice of an antiquarian and a bibliographer, he began to gather that great library of early American documents, which kept growing upon his hands in magnitude and in wealth as long as his life lasted, and which, notwithstanding the ravages of time, of British troops, of book-borrowers, and of book-thieves, still remains for him a barrier against oblivion, and for every student of early American thought and action, a copious treasure-house of help.[32]

Even in childhood, Thomas Prince had felt the attractions of American history; even then he had noted some blemishes in the attempts thus far made to write it; and later, during his residence in Europe, he had become conscious of the ambition to give his life to its pursuit: "In my foreign travels I found the want of a regular history of this country everywhere complained of, and was often moved to undertake it; though I could not think myself equal to a work so noble as the subject merits. . . . And yet I had a secret thought that, upon returning to my native country, in case I should fall into a state of leisure, . . . I would attempt a brief account of

---

[31] Part of title-page, first ed. Boston, 1758.

[32] The Prince Library is now in the careful and generous custody of the Boston Public Library. An admirable catalogue of it has been published under the superintendence of Justin Winsor, Boston, 1870.

facts at least, in the form of annals." [33]   But the pastorship of a great church in Boston was not a state of leisure; and it was not until eighteen years had passed, after his return to New England, that he was able in any measure to gratify his cherished passion. In 1736, he gave to the public the first volume of his "Chronological History of New England, in the Form of Annals,"—the most genuine and the most meritorious piece of historical work published in America up to that date.

His plan was to write a history somewhat in the manner of Archbishop Usher's Annals; the principal features being exactness, brevity, and a statement of events in the order of time: an austere scheme, both for writer and for reader, "comprising only facts in a chronological epitome, to enlighten the understanding," and repelling all "artificial ornaments and descriptions to raise the imagination and affections." [34]

He was a devotee to historical accuracy, a knight-errant of precise and unadorned fact, an historical sceptic before the philosophy of historical scepticism was born: "I would not take the least iota upon trust, if possible; I examined the original authors I could meet with." [35] "Some may think me rather too critical; others that I relate some circumstances too minute. . . . As for the first, I think a writer of facts cannot be too critical. It is exactness I aim at, and would not have the least mistake if possible pass to the world." [36] "In short, I cite my vouchers to every passage; and I have done my utmost, first to find out the truth, and then to relate it in the clearest order. I have labored after accuracy; and yet I dare not say that I am without mistake; nor do I desire the reader to conceal any he may possibly find. But on the contrary I offer this work to the public view, that it may be perused with the most critical eye, that every error may be discovered, and the correction published." [37]

Such was his attitude toward historical accuracy. Now let us see what was his attitude toward historical fairness. In another noble passage of self-revelation, he says: "As to impartiality, I know it is usual for the writers of history to assert it, some in their prefaces,

[33] "Chron. Hist. N. E." Pref. ii.   [34] Ibid. Dedication.
[35] Ibid. Pref. iv.   [36] Ibid. ix.   [37] Ibid. xi.

others in the front of their works; some in the strongest terms, who have been notoriously guilty of the contrary; and I am apt to think that many are partial who are insensible of it. For myself, I own I am on the side of pure Christianity; as also of civil and religious liberty, and this for the low as well as high, for the laity as well as the clergy; I am for leaving every one to the freedom of worshipping according to the light of his conscience; and for extending charity to every one who receives the gospel as the rule of his faith and life; I am on the side of meekness, patience, gentleness, and innocence. And I hope my inclination to these great principles will not bias me to a misrecital of facts, but rather to state them as I really find them for the public benefit." [38]

In carrying out his plan of writing the history of his own country, it seemed to him right to present it in its relations to the precedent history of all the world; for he held that the story of New England was not some isolated and forlorn chapter in the appendix of the book of time, but an integral part of that book, bound up in a volume with the rest in logical and chronological sequence: "It may be grateful to many readers to see the age of the world when this part of the earth came to be known to the other; and the line of time, with the succession of the principal persons, events, and transactions, which had been running on from the creation to the settlement of this country by a colony from England." [39] Accordingly, with great pains and great accuracy, and upon a close study of all the leading systems of chronology, as well as of all the original authors in Hebrew, Greek, and Roman history, he proceeds to give the succession of the world's great events, from Adam, "year one, first month, sixth day," down to the accession of James the First of England, year sixteen hundred and three, third month, twenty-fourth day. At last, having completed this immense introduction, which has its utility, but involved a sad miscalculation of the time at his disposal, and likewise proved to be a porch of inordinate size for his unfinished edifice, he reaches the chronology of New England, of which the first part extends from the accession of James the First to the settlement of Plymouth, December the thirty-first, 1620; and the second part,

[38] "Chron. Hist. N. E." Pref. x.   [39] Ibid. Introd. 1.

from that date to events in New England history as late as August the fifth, 1633.[40]

Throughout the work he is faithful to his promise of giving only nude facts, spurning all embellishments. His entries are made in the hard and compact form of a register, absolutely unimaginative and unemotional; yet as he reaches certain great epochs of history, he seems unable to keep back at least a sentence throbbing with suppressed feeling, or darting with the thrust of a sarcasm. Sometimes, indeed, this parenthetical sentence broadens into a paragraph, and breathes the music of a temperate and fine eloquence. Thus, when about to usher in the discovery of America, he gives himself pause, and says: "We are now to turn our eyes to the west, and see a new world appearing in the Atlantic Ocean, to the great surprise and entertainment of the other. Christopher Columbus or Colonus, a Genoese, is the first discoverer. . . . He becomes possessed with a strong persuasion that in order to balance the terraqueous globe and proportion the seas and lands to each other, there must needs be formed a mighty continent on the other side, which boldness, art, and resolution would soon discover. . . . Ferdinand and Isabella, . . . after five years' urging, are at last prevailed upon to furnish him with three ships and ninety men for this great enterprise; which, through the growing opposition of his fearful mariners, he at length accomplishes, to his own immortal fame and the infinite advantage of innumerable others." [41]

As he draws near to the time of the settlement of New England, he again stops, and takes a long view, and draws a long breath: "Having passed through the seven great periods of time from the creation to the beginning of the British empire, with the discovery of that Indian shore which is soon to be the theatre of our Chronology, a new face of things appears both to the western parts of Europe and the eastern of America. . . . Divers attempts are made to settle this

---

[40] His first volume abruptly closed at Sept. 7, 1630, on warning from the printer that, if he went further, it would become "too unsizable;" and the remainder of his fragment, comprising three numbers, was afterward published in pamphlets. These are reprinted in 2 Mass. Hist. Soc. Coll. VII. 189–295; also in S. G. Drake's ed. of "Chron. Hist. N. E." 1852.

[41] "Chron. Hist. N. E." Introd. 78.

rough and northern country; first by the French, . . . and then by the English, and both from mere secular views. But such a train of crosses accompany these designs of both nations, that they seem to give it over as not worth the planting; till a pious people of England, not there allowed to worship their Maker according to his institutions only, . . . are spirited to attempt the settlement." [42] "So there were just one hundred and one who sailed from Plymouth in England; . . . and this is the solitary number who for an undefiled conscience and the love of a pure Christianity, first left their native and pleasant land, and encountered all the toils and hazards of the tumultuous ocean, in search of some uncultivated region in North Virginia, where they might quietly enjoy their religious liberties, and transmit them to posterity, in hopes none would follow to disturb or vex them." [43]

Passages like these, occurring in the midst of long and arid patches of chronological registration, have a sweet and stirring tone; yet the predominant effect of the book is depressing. The publication of it was a disappointment and a failure. A long list of subscribers had shown their interest in the inception of his great work: few had any interest to show in its continuance. Of course the author was discouraged. Nearly twenty years passed by before he had the heart to go on with his task; and then age, illness, public occupations, were too heavy upon him. Nevertheless, even as a fragment the "Chronological History of New England" is the most scholarly piece of literary work wrought in America during the colonial time; and in the particular sphere of historical writing, it represents not only a great advance upon all that had been achieved among us before its time, but the true method, and the prophecy, of all that was to be achieved among us afterward.

V

In 1739, three years after the publication of the great historical treatise of Thomas Prince, appeared an historical brochure, which deserves remembrance for the worthy quality of its work, and as a

[42] "Chron. Hist. N. E." Part I. 1–3.   [43] Ibid. 86.

token of the spread among us of genuine methods of historical inquiry. This is "An Historical Discourse" by John Callender,[44] minister of the First Baptist Church of Newport, Rhode Island. It is a careful and well-written sketch of the history of Rhode Island for the first century of its existence; and is especially notable for its fine antiquarian spirit, for its catholicity of tone, and for the poise and amenity with which the author refers to those painful facts in the early history of Massachusetts that had, in fact, produced the early history of Rhode Island. His prevalent magnanimity of statement gives greater edge and power to his occasional references to the intolerance which had once embittered human life in the elder commonwealth: "In reality the true grounds of liberty of conscience were not then known or embraced by any sect or party of Christians. . . . So that it was not singular or peculiar in those people at the Massachusetts to think themselves bound in conscience to use the sword of the civil magistrate to open the understandings of heretics. . . . These were not the only people who thought they were doing God good service, when smiting their brethren and fellow-servants. All other Christian sects acted generally as if they thought this was the very best service they could do to God, and the most effectual way to promote the gospel of peace, and prove themselves the true and genuine disciples of Jesus Christ—of Jesus Christ, who hath declared his kingdom was not of this world, who had commanded his disciples to call no man master on earth, who had forbidden them to exercise lordship over each other's consciences." [45]

VI

A work which has made for itself a prominent place in the literature of this period, and which, through the notice taken of it by Adam Smith, has been lifted into some European celebrity, is the "Summary, Historical and Political, of . . . the British Settlements in North America." [46] Its author was William Douglass, a Scotsman,

---

[44] Born 1707; graduated at Harvard 1723; minister at Newport from 1731 till his death in 1748; his "Historical Discourse" was written in 1738; printed in 1739; reprinted in R. I. Hist. Soc. Coll. IV. 45–176.

[45] The Discourse, in R. I. Hist. Soc. Coll. IV. 70–71.

[46] Published in 2 vols. Boston, 1748–1753.

New England: History and Biography

who, after an ample training in medicine at Leyden and at Paris, came to Boston in 1718, he being then about twenty-seven years of age. In Boston he established himself as a physician; and there he died in 1752. He was a man of large but heterogeneous knowledge, and blessed with a sovereign confidence in himself and his own opinions; and being also dogmatic, intolerant, of quick temper and boundless energy, fiery as a friend, still more fiery as an enemy, fond of strife, glib in speech, with a passion for rushing into print, his life was one prolonged and blissful warfare with all persons whom he could pick a quarrel with,—chiefly, his own professional brethren, likewise the clergy, the magistrates, and the successive governors of the colony.

He had great sagacity and shrewdness, and a pitiless way of dissecting fashionable enthusiasms and prejudices; a keen, racy, original diction; infinite courage in utterance. In a land still dominated by Calvinistic orthodoxy, he avowed himself a rationalist, saying that "the wise and thinking part of mankind" had at last learned "to regulate themselves by natural religion only." [47] He praised David Brainerd as "a true and zealous missionary," but said that allowances must be made for "his weak, enthusiastic turn of mind." [48] He condescended to call the apostle Eliot a good man, but added that it was a sheer waste of labor for him to translate the Bible into the language of a petty tribe of Indians who could not read and were soon to be extinct.[49] In the midst of the devout raptures of the people over Whitefield's preaching, Douglass coolly computed the marketable value of the time spent by them in listening to this "vagrant enthusiast," and announced that every exhortation of Whitefield in Boston, by diverting laborers from the work by which they supported their families, was a damage to that town to the extent of about a thousand pounds sterling. No sphere of life was safe from his intrusions; no topic escaped the puncture of his criticisms; he was always ready to proclaim his opinions; and even when those opinions failed to be justified by events, he had a Falstaffian assurance in standing by them still, and a Falstaffian wit in covering up the awkwardness of his discomfiture. For example, on account of his hostility to the men at that time in power, he publicly ridi-

[47] "Summary," I. 438.   [48] Ibid. II. 117.   [49] Ibid. I. 172.

culed the New England expedition for the capture of Cape Breton, declaring that the scheme was a folly, and would be a failure; and when, in due time, the news came that Cape Breton had been captured, he was not in the least disconcerted, merely remarking that he was entirely right in his conjectures, but that "fortune would always wait upon blunderers and quacks." [50]

The larger part of mankind seemed to be alike in this, that they were the objects of his contempt; none more so than the practitioners of medicine in New England in his time: "In our plantations, a practitioner, bold, rash, impudent, a liar, basely born and educated, has much the advantage of an honest, cautious, modest gentleman. In general the physical practice in our colonies is so perniciously bad, that excepting in surgery, and some very acute cases, it is better to let nature under a proper regimen take her course, . . . than to trust to the honesty and sagacity of the practitioner. Our American practitioners are so rash and officious, the saying in . . . Ecclesiasticus . . . may with much propriety be applied to them: 'He that sinneth before his Maker, let him fall into the hand of the physician.' Frequently there is more danger from the physician than from the distemper. . . . But sometimes, notwithstanding of malpractice, nature gets the better of the doctor, and the patient recovers. Our practitioners deal much in quackery and quackish medicines, as requiring no labor of thought or composition, and highly recommended in the London quack-bills—in which all the reading of many of our practitioners consists. . . . In the most trifling cases they use a routine of practice. When I first arrived in New England, I asked . . . a noted, facetious practitioner, what was their general method of practice. He told me their practice was very uniform: bleeding, vomiting, blistering, purging, anodyne, and so forth; if the illness continued, there was 'repetendi;' and finally 'murderandi;' nature was never to be consulted or allowed to have any concern in the affair. What Sydenham well observes, is the case with our practitioners: 'Æger nimiâ medici diligentiâ ad plures migrat.' " [51]

As an illustration of the amusing audacity of quacks in the English colonies, he also cites a medical advertisement, in which, among other nostrums, the doctor announces "an elegant medicine to pre-

[50] J. Thacher, "Am. Med. Biography," I. 256. [51] "Summary," II. 351–352.

vent the yellow fever and dry gripes in the West Indies;" and this, Douglass thinks, is only to be equalled by a similar advertisement published in Jamaica, immediately after an earthquake had done great destruction there. The physician offered to the public "pills to prevent persons or their effects suffering by earthquakes." [52]

During all the long warfare of his career in New England, William Douglass kept his pen constantly wet with ink, producing newspaper articles, pamphlets, medical books; and it was but natural that a man of his versatile and irrepressible activity should try his hand upon what he called history. The book which we have already mentioned, and for which Douglass is now principally remembered, is the evidence of this. He sincerely believed it to be history; and with an amusing unconsciousness of his own traits, he ascribes to himself nearly all the qualities of a great historian, scarcely one of which he was in possession of: "I have no personal disregard or malice, and do write of the present times as if these things had been transacted a hundred years since." [53] On the contrary, he was nothing if not partisan and malignant; and his reports of contemporaneous events are saturated with the fury of contemporaneous passions. In truth, he is not an historian at all; he lacks the calmness of history, its disinterestedness, its caution and reserve, its thoroughness, its accuracy, its nobility of expression. His style is hurried, slipshod, irregular; his materials jumbled together in the hotchpotch manner; he flits from topic to topic as the gust strikes him; with all his asserted intellectual humility, he delights to exhibit his polyglot proficiency, and covers his pages with specks of quotation from foreign languages, especially Latin and French. He is essentially a journalist and pamphleteer. He is hot, personal, caustic, capricious; and his history is only a congeries of pungent and racy editorial paragraphs.

On the first page of the first volume of his "Summary," he announces his plan for making the book interesting: "Descriptions and bare relations, although accurate and instructive, to many readers are insipid and tedious; therefore a little seasoning is used. Where a 'mica salis' occurs, may it not be disagreeable: it is not designed with any malicious, invidious view. For the same reason, a small digression, but not impertinent to the subject, is now and then made

[52] "Summary," II. 352, note.   [53] Ibid. I. 356.

use of; as also some short illustrations." As the history proceeds, he abundantly fulfils his promise of putting "a little seasoning" into the insipid dish of plain narrative—the seasoning of egotistic and sarcastic personalities. Moreover, he constantly acts as the chorus to his own play; he stops its movement, in order to explain something, to justify his method, to express the hope that he is not getting tedious, or to regret that he is violating his intended brevity, and that he is "prolix," and that his summary "swells too much." His favorite literay method is digression; and he employs it so frequently that when he does chance to revert to historical narration, the latter seems a sort of lapse from the main purpose of the book. But, as usual with him, finding this method convenient to himself, he stanchly defends it as the only proper one: "This Pindaric or loose way of writing ought not to be confined to lyric poetry; it seems to be more agreeable by its variety and turns, than a rigid, dry, connected account of things." [54]

Perhaps his most readable passages are the foot-notes, which are very numerous, and are reservoirs for his private opinions—if he can be said to have had any—his whims, hobbies, and hostilities. He is also very droll in such passages of the text as contain his reasons for not devoting himself to a minute and wearisome study of original authorities upon American history. Thus, on approaching the history of New England, and on surveying the vast extent and complexity of the subject, he relieves himself by the following comical preliminary groan of indignant criticism: "This is a laborious affair, being obliged to consult manuscript records. The many printed accounts are: 1. Too credulous and superstitious. 2. Too trifling. Must the insipid history of every brute . . . or man-animal be transmitted to posterity? 3. The accounts of every white man and Indian mutually killed or otherwise dead, would swell and lower history so much as to render the perusal of such histories (excepting with old women and children) impracticable. 4. The succession of pious pastors, elders, and deacons in the several townships, parishes, or congregations I leave to ecclesiastic chronologers; canonization or sainting seems not consistent with our Protestant principles. 5. The

[54] "Summary," I. 310.

New England: History and Biography

printed accounts in all respects are, beyond all excuse, intolerably erroneous."[55]

Whether right or wrong in his opinions, he is never wanting in explicitness in stating them. He has a multitude of petted animosities,—the Indians, the French, the Reverend George Whitefield, the Bishop of Cloyne and that prelate's nostrum of tar-water, paper-money, and so forth; and whenever, in the zigzag progress of his discourse, he catches a glimpse of any of these detested objects, he discharges at them the slugs and hot-shot of his vituperation.

As for the Indians, "excepting speech, which is natural to mankind, they seem to have been only a gregarious sort of man-brutes; that is, they lived in tribes or herds and nations, without letters, or arts further than to acquire the necessaries of life;" and until the white men came to America and brought it into connection with the civilized world, "America and the moon were much upon the same footing with respect to Europe, Asia, and Africa."[56]

As for the French, they "are the common nuisance and disturbers of Europe, and will in a short time become the same in America, if not mutilated at home, and in America fenced off from us by ditches and walls, that is, by great rivers and impracticable mountains. . . . Their promises and faith are by them used only as a sort of scaffolding, which, when the structure is finished, or project effected, they drop. In all public treaties they are 'gens de mauvaise foi.' "[57]

As for the Reverend George Whitefield, he is "an insignificant person, of no general learning, void of common prudence. His journals are a rhapsody of Scripture-texts and of his own cant expressions. . . . The strength of his arguments lay in his lungs. . . . He and his disciples seemed to be great promoters of impulses, ecstasies, and wantonness between the sexes. Hypocritical professions, vociferations, and itineracies, are devotional quackery."[58]

As for the Bishop of Cloyne, he "was an enthusiast in many affairs of life, not confined to religion and the education of youth. He invaded another of the learned professions, Medicine. . . . He published a book called 'Siris, . . . or Tar-Water.' . . . He ought to

[55] "Summary," I. 361-362.
[56] Ibid. 116.
[57] Ibid. I. 2-3.
[58] Ibid. II. 141-142.

have checked this officious genius (unless in his own profession-way he had acquired this nostrum by inspiration) from intruding into the affairs of a distinct profession." [59]

As for paper-money, it is the "fallacious and designed cheat of a plantation government," [60] an "iniquitous or base money currency," [61] an "accursed affair." [62] "I desire readers . . . may excuse prolixity; when this vile chimera or monster comes in my way, I cannot contain myself." [63]

Upon the whole, William Douglass may be said to have succeeded in his attempt at being amusing, if not at being instructive. His book contains an enormous mass of miscellaneous but untrustworthy information relating to America and the rest of the world; and our present interest in it is chiefly due to its representation of the author himself; who, certainly, was a very definite, positive, original, and self-centred person, never the echo or the shadow of one.

[59] "Summary," I. 149–151.   [60] Ibid. I. 310.   [61] Ibid. I. 334.
[62] Ibid. II. 13.   [63] Ibid. I. 499.

Chapter XV

New England:
The Pulpit in Literature

I. Continued ascendency of the clergy—Their full maintenance of the grand traits of their predecessors,—manliness, scholarship, thoughtfulness, eloquence—Their improvement upon their predecessors in breadth, and in social and literary urbanity.

II. John Higginson—Sketch of him by John Dunton—The power of his character and of his long life—His election-sermon—His "Attestation" to the "Magnalia."

III. William Stoughton, preacher and statesman—His "Narrative of the Proceedings of Andros"—His discourse on "New England's True Interest not to Lie"—Its literary ability—Its courage.

IV. Urian Oakes—His greatness in prose as well as in verse—Contemporaneous estimates of him—His first artillery-sermon—Its great eloquence—Its delineation of the Christian soldier—His election-sermon—His second artillery-sermon.

V. Samuel Willard—His "Complete Body of Divinity"—His career—His theological lectures—Their great influence—Their publication in 1726 in the first American folio—Strong qualities of the book.

VI. Solomon Stoddard—His activity as a writer—His special reputation for soundness of judgment—His "Answer to Some Cases of Conscience respecting the Country"—The sinfulness of long hair and of periwigs—Condemnation of other frivolities.

VII. Benjamin Colman—His great contemporaneous influence in church and state—His fine culture—His residence in England—His particular friendships there—His return to Boston—His long and prosperous public career—His discourses—Their literary polish—His charitable spirit.

History of American Literature

VIII. John Barnard of Marblehead—His versatile culture—His eminence—His intellectual traits—His volumes of sermons—His gentlemanly treatment of sinners.

IX. Jonathan Edwards—Outline of his life—His qualities, spiritual and intellectual—His precocity in metaphysics, and in physics—His juvenile writings—His more mature studies in science—His spiritual self-discipline—His resolutions—The sorrows of his life—Habits as a student and thinker—His power as a preacher—Analysis of his method in discourse—"Sinners in the Hands of an Angry God"—His literary characteristics.

X. Mather Byles—A scene in Hollis Street Church early in the Revolution—His brilliant career before the Revolution—His versatility—The misfortune of his later reputation as a jester—A great pulpit-orator—His literary qualities—His exposition of the preacher's character—His favorite themes—Passages from his sermons.

XI. Jonathan Mayhew—The lines of his influence—Estimate of him by John Adams—Charles Chauncey—His traits—His hatred of inaccurate and emotional utterance—His contempt for Whitefield—His discourse on "Enthusiasm"—His "Seasonable Thoughts"—His portrait of the enthusiast.

I

IN our progress over the various fields of literature in New England during the colonial time, we encounter not one form of writing in which we are permitted to lose sight of the clergy of New England,—their tireless and versatile activity, their learning, their force of brain, their force of character. But we are now to resume our study of their writings in the field that was peculiarly their own,—that of theological and religious exposition.

As we have already seen, the immigrant clergy of New England—the founders of this noble and brilliant order—were, in nearly all qualities of personal worth and greatness, among the greatest and the worthiest of their time, in the mother-country,—mighty scholars, orators, sages, saints. And by far the most wonderful thing about these men is, that they were able to convey across the Atlantic, into a naked wilderness, all the essential elements of that ancient civilization out of which they came; and at once, to raise up and educate, in the new world, a line of mighty successors in their sacred office,

New England: The Pulpit

without the least break in the sequence, without the slightest diminution in scholarship, in eloquence, in intellectual energy, in moral power.

It cannot be doubted, indeed, that the great divines of the immigrant period—those heroic pastors who led forth their flocks into the American forests and founded here a new empire—had in that very fact an enormous historical advantage over their successors in the ministry,—an inapproachable prestige and renown. Nevertheless, a study of all the writings produced by the New England clergy, from the years of the settlement to the years of the Revolution, cannot fail to convince us that the men who came after the Founders were as great as they: nay, that while in any particulars the sons and the sons' sons equalled the Fathers, in some particulars they outdid them; they fully maintained all the strong and lofty traits of the first generation—manliness, scholarship, thoughtfulness, eloquence, purity—and even added to these traits, those of intellectual breadth, of secular culture, of social and literary urbanity.

II

In the year 1686, John Dunton of London paid a visit to Salem, and there saw the senior minister of that place, the aged John Higginson. "All men look on him," wrote Dunton,[1] "as a common father; and on old age for his sake as a reverend thing. He is eminent for learning, humility, charity, and all those shining graces that adorn a minister. His very presence and face puts vice out of countenance. He is now in his eightieth year, yet preaches every Sunday; and his conversation is a glimpse of heaven." This benign old man was then just ten years younger than Dunton stated; but after that, he lived just twenty-two years, the last of the New England pioneers, the father of all the faithful, manifesting to the end the sweetness and strength of character that covered with unwonted majesty his patriarchal years.

In 1629, a year before Boston was founded, he had come to Salem, a boy of thirteen, with his father, Francis Higginson; he had received his education in the new world; after many years of service

[1] "Life and Errors of J. Dunton," I. 127–128.

as school-master and preacher in Connecticut, he had returned to Salem, in 1659; and there he remained the rest of his days, in charge of the church that his father had founded. He had great authority in all the land—the authority of goodness, of wisdom, and of ability. His earliest publication is the election-sermon of 1663, entitled "The Cause of God and his People in New England;" a sturdy effort to check what seemed to him the torrent of worldliness and wealth-seeking there, by recalling to the people the purpose for which they and their fathers had founded New England: "If any man amongst us make religion as twelve and the world as thirteen, let such an one know he hath neither the spirit of a true New England man nor yet of a sincere Christian." [2] It is a sermon that has the impressiveness imparted by a clear, earnest, consecrated mind; but is without special literary superiority. His other publications, seven in number, are all upon religious topics, either expository or historical; the most notable being his "Attestation" to the "Magnalia," dated 1697, and printed as one of the prefaces of that book. Many sentences of this production are very noble; having especially some of the antique qualities of thought and style that were then dying out of English prose,—massiveness of meaning, confidence in the invisible goodness and truth, unconsciousness of cynicism, a seer-like earnestness of tone, the quaint diction of dead sages and saints, a gravity and reverberating fulness of phrase, the expectation of intellectual fortitude in those who read.

III

During the last thirty years of the seventeenth century, William Stoughton was a conspicuous statesman of New England,—his great wealth, talent, learning, dignity, and public spirit, winning for him a large measure of the public confidence. He held, at various times, all the great offices in the commonwealth; and it was his misfortune to be chief-justice in the fatal time of the witchcraft delusion. Unfortunately, his own cool judgment was utterly overborne in that epidemic of fury and of folly; and he became a protagonist among

[2] The Sermon, 11.

New England: The Pulpit

the persecutors. The pitiless and gratuitous savagery of his acts as a magistrate, toward those innocent and helpless creatures who fell under a public accusation half malignant and half lunatic, have smirched his noble name with uncleansable dishonor.

He had in him the power to make for himself a great place in American letters; but he spent his principal force in outward affairs. Graduated at Harvard in 1650, at the age of nineteen, and afterward fellow of New College, Oxford, he began his public career as a minister; and having in that profession acquired much reputation, he passed out of it into politics. Two specimens of his ability as a writer have come down to us, representing the two fields of sacred and secular activity to which in succession he devoted his life. The later and inferior specimen is "A Narrative of the Proceedings of Andros," published in 1691,[3]—a clumsy and dull performance. The earlier and better specimen is, indeed, one of the landmarks of literature in New England for that time,—the election-sermon preached by him in Boston, in 1668. It bears the striking title, "New England's True Interest, not to Lie." A powerful document it must have been, in its day; eloquent after the fashion of those times; conservative in thought, able in statement; courageously confronting New England with its high obligations to God and to itself, and accusing it of a drift toward shameful degeneracy in morals, piety, and manners; and it contains one sentence that has become classic among us. The doctrine of the discourse, he first expounds in the minute and technical style of the seventeenth century sermon-builders; and as usual, the chief interest is reserved for the application. Here, he charges the people of New England with an extraordinary responsibility,—a responsibility derived from their own extraordinary character. They were picked men, he tells them; selected by God himself out of the common herd of mortals: "God sifted a whole nation that he might send choice grain over into this wilderness." [4] Hence, "it is a solemn conviction and charge against us to have it spoken, as it must be spoken in the name of the Lord this day, O New England,

---

[3] Included also among the reprints known as the "Andros Tracts," 3 vols. Boston, 1868–1874.
[4] The Sermon, 19.

thy God did expect better things from thee and thy children; not worldliness and an insatiable desire after perishing things; not whoredoms and fornications; not revilings and drunkenness; not oaths and false swearings; not exactions and oppressions; not slanderings and backbitings; not rudeness and incivility—a degeneracy from the good manners of the Christian world; not formality and profaneness, to loathe manna, to despise holy things, to grow sermon-proof and ordinance-proof; not contentions and disorders; not an itching after new things and ways; not a rigid Pharisaical spirit; not a contempt of superiors; not unthankfulness and disrespect to instruments of choice service; not a growing weary of government, and a drawing loose in the yoke of God; not these things, but better things, O New England, hath thy God expected from thee." [5]

IV

In our study of the verse-writers of New England, we have already met with Urian Oakes, whose "Elegy upon the Death of Thomas Shepard" we found to be among the few examples of genuine poetry produced in America in the colonial time. But his principal activity was as a sermon-writer; and in that capacity he had no superior among us during the seventeenth or the eighteenth century. For once, Cotton Mather's fancifulness struck the happy note in naming him "the Lactantius of New England;" [6] and when, in another place, this same provincial pedant declared that Urian Oakes "was an Orpheus that would have drawn the very stones to discipline," [7] he only smothered under an antic hyperbole the long-cherished tradition concerning those marvellous fascinations of living speech, which were wielded by the Cambridge pastor, and which did not perish even when uttering themselves in the cold oratory of print. I find in him an alert and forcible intelligence, civility, cosmopolitan range; an expression, affluent, nervous, flexible; a condensed energy of phrase; the epithets that are born of original and poetic insight; the gift of culminating and bright statement, crystallizing into epigram.

It was in 1672, the first year after the return of Urian Oakes from

[5] The Sermon, 20.   [6] "Magnalia," II. 124.   [7] Ibid. 116.

his long residence in the mother-country, that he was selected to give the annual sermon [8] before the artillery company of Boston,—an association composed of the first gentlemen in the colony, and intended to cherish here the chivalric traits of military discipline and honor. In speaking to such an audience, the orator naturally took as his theme the parallelisms existing between the true soldier and the true Christian. Here his rhetoric has a martial movement; his sentences ring like bugle-notes. There is high exhilaration—the dauntless ecstasy of heroism and triumph—in the words with which he sets forth the attributes of the warrior of Christ: "He is a man of war from his birth. Neither is he a poor naked creature; . . . but he comes into the new world in his suit of armor, armed 'cap-a-pie,' with a complete armor of proof, being vested with the graces of the spirit of Christ. He hath his excellent and invincible General, . . . and hath taken his 'sacramentum militare,' his oath of fidelity and obedience to the great Lord General. He hath also . . . his company that he is listed into. . . . He hath his banner to fight under. . . . He hath his arms and weapons, offensive and defensive, to fight withal. He hath his soldierly qualifications and military accomplishments,—courage, skill, patience, hope of victory, faithfulness to . . . his General, orderliness, disposition to endure hardship, or whatever else may be mentioned, . . . a soldier well appointed . . . to dispute it out with any adversary." [9]

Then, too, as every good man is a soldier, so, by a sad antithesis, is every bad man a soldier likewise; "but he fights against God, strengthens himself and stretches out his hand against the Almighty. . . . He puts on the whole armor of the Devil, that he may be able to stand against all the shocks of conscience, or encounters of the word and spirit of God, and fight it out to the last with the Infinite Majesty, to the everlasting ruin of his immortal soul." [10] In the long, bitter battle which is waging here, they who are Christ's men find that their enemy, "the world, can put on two faces, and change its countenance as occasion serves. If feigned, flattering smiles will not do, then

---

[8] This was printed at Cambridge 1674, and bore a title characteristic of the age rather than of the man: "The Unconquerable, All-conquering, and more than Conquering Soldier."

[9] The Sermon, 5.   [10] Ibid. 5.

killing frowns shall, if it be possible." [11] But, indeed, this will not be possible; for Christians "may be opposed, combated, and contended withal, but never routed, run down, totally defeated, or overthrown." [12] "Death may kill them but cannot conquer them." [13] And the supreme moment for all Christian soldiers is, of course, that endless one, which comes after the fierce campaigns of earth are over, and when they pass under triumphal arches to the repose of victory in heaven. They "have fought their fight, and finished the course of their warfare, and are . . . out of push of pike or gunshot, far enough removed out of the reach of their adversaries. They are marched out of the field, and discharged from any further service, and enjoying their reward." [14]

It is not strange that the new pastor of Cambridge, having made so thrilling and masterly an oration at the great military anniversary of the colony, should have been summoned to be the orator at its next great political anniversary. Accordingly, in 1673, we find him giving the election-sermon, taking as his subject the moral perils that then hung over New England. He entitled his discourse, "New England Pleaded With;" [15] a brave and manly exposition of the evil tendencies then developed there,—formality, spiritual listlessness, immorality, irreverence, worldliness, greed of wealth, sensualism, love of display in dress, vanity, ostentation. As a literary effort, this discourse is not so brilliant as the artillery-sermon; has not so many majestic and resounding passages; but it is very searching, pungent, and strong, and must have produced a vast impression as its invectives first leaped, in passionate and pathetic tones, from the lips of the prophet, and glanced down among a people most sensitive to such accusations. There are in it also some sentences of broad scope, worthy to become national aphorisms. This is one: "It is the property of Englishmen, much more of religious Englishmen, and should be most of all of religious New-Englishmen, to be tenacious and tender of their liberties." [16]

Four years afterward, this matchless preacher stood forth again as the orator of the artillery-company, giving them a sermon on "The

[11] The Sermon, 9. [12] Ibid. 2. [13] Ibid. 16.
[14] Ibid. 4. [15] Printed, Cambridge, 1673.
[16] The Sermon, 50.

New England: The Pulpit

Sovereign Efficacy of Divine Providence." [17] Addressing the foremost military organization in the country, and reviewing the havoc and agony of the war just closed with the Indians under Philip, he confesses his humiliation, that with all their own military training and their various other superiorities, they could have been so terrified and so injured by such enemies; but he warns his fellow-countrymen of obligations even more sacred than those of a soldier, and of a hostility even more terrible than that of the red men: "New England hath enemies enough on earth and in hell; woe to us if we make God in heaven our enemy also." [18]

V

In the year 1726, the men of books in New England noted with considerable exultation, as a sign of national progress, the issue from an American printing-press, of a huge folio volume,—the largest that had ever been printed in this country. It bore this well-deserved title, "A Complete Body of Divinity." Within its nine hundred and fourteen pages,—each page having two columns in small and compact type,—it held "two hundred and fifty expository lectures on the Assembly's Shorter Catechism," all written out and delivered in order by one busy man, during a period of nineteen years. That man was Samuel Willard, himself, like his book, a body of divinity; a man of inexpressible authority, in those days, throughout all the land. He was born in 1640, in the woods of Concord; in 1659 he was graduated at Harvard; he was settled in the ministry, first at Groton, and then at the South Church, Boston; he opposed the witchcraft persecutions; he succeeded Increase Mather in the presidency of Harvard College, adding that service to his work as pastor; all his lifetime, he was most fruitful in religious writings, printed and unprinted; and he died in 1707. At his funeral, Ebenezer Pemberton, his colleague, stood up and spoke of him, as one "who had been for so long a time the light, joy, and glory of the place," and whose death was "an awful rebuke of heaven upon this whole land."

Nineteen years before his death, he began to give at his own

[17] Printed in 1682, after the author's death, with a preface by John Sherman.
[18] The Sermon, 40.

church, on Tuesday afternoons, once a month, an elaborate lecture on theology. His was a mind formed for theological method. He did not desire to impose upon himself or upon any one a slavish submission to a theological system; he only wished to get for himself and others the clearness and vigor and practical utility that come from putting one's most careful ideas into orderly combination. He was a theological drill-sergeant. He was also a truly great divine. In the lectures upon systematic theology, which he thus began in 1688, and continued unflinchingly till he died, his object was to move step by step around "the whole circle of religion." The fame of his lucid talks on those great themes, soon flew abroad, and drew to him a large, permanent audience of the learned and the unlearned; and after his death, theological students and others kept clamoring for the publication of those talks. In 1726, all such persons were gratified.

"A Complete Body of Divinity" is a vast book, in all senses; by no one to be trifled with. Let us salute it with uncovered heads. The attempted perusal of all these nine hundred and fourteen double-columned pages, was, for many a theological scholar of the last century, a liberal education—and a training in every heroic and heavenly virtue. Along the pages of the venerable copy that I have used —the copy which Jeremiah Dummer, of the Middle Temple, London, sent over in 1727 as a gift to Yale College—I find fading memorials of the toil, and aspiration, and triumph, with which numerous worthy young divines of the last age grappled with the task of reading the book through; but on the blank leaf at the end, are only two inscriptions of final victory: "Lyman perlegit, 1742," and "Timothy Pitkin perlegit, A.D., 1765." Doubtless, both these heroes have long since had their reward, and have entered into rest, which they sorely needed; and the others perished by the way.

The thought and expression of this literary mammoth are lucid, firm, close. The author moves over the great spaces of his subject with a calm and commanding tread, as of one well assured both of himself and of the ground he walked on. His object seemed to be, not merely to enlighten the mind, but to elevate the character and the life; and whenever, in the discussion of a topic, he has finished the merely logical process, he advances at once to the practical bearings of it, and urges upon his hearers the deductions of a moral logic, always doing this earnestly, persuasively, and in a kingly way. The whole effect is nutritious to brain and to moral sense; and the book might still serve to make men good Christians as well as good theologians—if only there were still left upon the earth the men capable of reading it.

VI

Solomon Stoddard was born in Boston, in 1643, his father being an eminent merchant and politician of that city, and his mother a sister of Sir George Downing. He was graduated at Harvard College in 1662, and was settled in the ministry at Northampton from 1669 until his death in 1730: a man of reverend look, strong judgment, industry, learning, uncommon logical faculty; "for some years the most aged minister in the province, . . . a Peter here among the disciples and ministers of our Lord Jesus, very much our primate and a prince among us." [19] He seems not to have published anything until he was past fifty years of age; but from that time onward, his publications were numerous, in the form of sermons, controversial pamphlets, and treatises relating to theology and to personal conduct. His mental vision was a singularly clear one; and persons enveloped in various sorts of theological and ethical fog, were much inclined to depend on his superior eyesight. Thus, in 1722, he published a little book called "An Answer to Some Cases of Conscience respecting the Country;" wherein he solves ten great questions appertaining to New England casuistry. Some of these questions are: "What right doth belong to the Sabbath?" "At what time of the evening doth the Sabbath begin?" "Did we any wrong to the Indians, in buying their land at a small price?" "Is it lawful for men to set their dwelling-houses at such a distance from the place of public worship that they and their families cannot attend it?" Above all, "Is it lawful to wear long hair?" Upon this latter agitating theme, the excellent Mr. Stoddard has no uncertainty. The thing "seems utterly unlawful. . . . It is a great burden and cumber; it is effem-

---

[19] Benjamin Colman, Sermon on Death of Stoddard, quoted in W. B. Sprague, "Annals of Am. Pulpit," I. 174.

inacy and a vast expense, . . . a moral evil. . . . It was a part of the calamity that came upon Nebuchadnezzar that his hairs were grown like eagles' feathers, and his nails like birds' claws." [20] But the ingenuity of Satan is tireless; and being routed in the argument concerning long hair, he suggests to the depraved minds of men that, even if they must crop their heads close, they may still cover them up with periwigs: therefore, "Is it lawful to wear periwigs?" "I judge there is abundance of sin in this country in wearing periwigs. Particularly in these two things: First, when men do wear them needlessly, in compliance with fashion. Their own hair is sufficient for all those ends that God has given hair for. One man's hair is comelier than another's. . . . Some cut off their own because of the color —it is red or gray; some because it is straight; and some only because it is their own. Secondly, when those that may have just occasion to wear them, do wear them in such a ruffianly way as it would be utterly unlawful to wear their own hair in. Some of them are of an unreasonable length; and generally they are extravagant as to their bushiness. . . . The practice seems to me to have these four evils in it: 1. It is an uncontentedness with that provision that God has made for men. . . . When God has given to men such hair as is suitable to answer the ends of hair, it seems to be a despising of the goodness of God to cut it off, in compliance with a vain fashion. 2. It is wastefulness. . . . 3. It is pride. . . . 4. It is contrary to gravity. . . . This practice makes them look as if they were more disposed to court a maid than to bear upon their hearts the weighty concernments of God's kingdom." [21] "There be many other practices that are plainly contrary to the light of nature. Hooped petticoats have something of nakedness; mixed dances are incentives to lust; compotations in private houses is a drunken practice." [22]

VII

For nearly the entire first half of the eighteenth century, there was in Boston a minister of one of its churches, Benjamin Colman, who, by an exquisite union of strength and tenderness, the tact of the politician, the sincerity of the saint, the magical and captivating

[20] "An Answer,' etc. 4–5.   [21] Ibid. 6–7.   [22] Ibid. 15.

New England: The Pulpit

might of the orator, held an unsurpassed ascendency over his contemporaries. He was organized to be a conqueror of his kind, through their brains and their hearts. In person above the common height, delicate in shape, of fair complexion, with the dress and bearing of an accomplished gentleman, he had a "peculiar flame and dignity in his eye;" his presence instantly unlocked all minds as by something benign, graceful, and venerable. Some of his associates, who outlived him, and who wrote the introduction to his biography that appeared two years after his death, say that no written description can convey an idea of his personal charm and power, either in private or in public. They speak of his conversation as "admirably polished and courtly;" of his incomparable eloquence in the pulpit; of his earnestness and refinement; the inimitable power and sweetness of his elocution; the ardor of his imagination; the rapture of his impassioned and devout speech. As a clergyman, there were utilities in his life that reached far beyond those usually exerted by those in his profession; and in times of need, he was a pillar of state. Passing his days in an atmosphere charged with theological sullenness and acrimony, he was both orthodox and charitable; his personal breadth burst the hoops of his creed; he was human first, and clerical afterward.

His education was a wise and happy one—the education of books and of life. He was born in Boston, in 1673; was graduated at Harvard, in 1692; and after three years of theological study, with some real work as a preacher, he set out for Europe, intending to gain wisdom by looking upon the wisdom of the world. It was a time of war between England and France; and on the voyage, his ship was captured by a French privateer, after a hard battle, during which the pale young preacher fought bravely on deck among the bravest. Being made a prisoner, he was clothed in rags, thrown into the hold among the sailors, taken to France, and suffered there most barbarous treatment during a captivity of several weeks. At last, he was exchanged; he made his way to England, where he remained four years. He was heartily welcomed there by the most eminent of the dissenting clergymen; went much into society; preached with great acceptance at Cambridge, Bath, and elsewhere; and had many inducements to remain permanently in the mother-country. He was a particular favorite in the family of Sir Henry Ashurst, with whose daughter he appears to have conducted, for a time, a gentle and clerical flirtation. This young lady once desired him to write for her a poem; and in response to her commands, he produced some playful verses called "A Quarrel with Fortune," wherein, comparing her to a taper and himself to a fly, he intimates his own peril in fluttering so near a damsel of her exalted rank:

> "So have I seen a little, silly fly,
> Upon a blazing taper dart and die.
> The foolish insect, ravished with so bright
> And fair a glory, would devour the light.
> At first, he wheels about the threatening fire,
> With a career as fleet as his desire;
> This ceremony past, he joins the same,
> In hopes to be transformed, himself, to flame;
> The fiery, circumambient sparkles glow,
> And vainly warn him of his overthrow,
> But resolute he'll to destruction go.
> So, mean-born mortals, such as I, aspire,
> And injure, with unhallowëd desire,
> The glory we ought only to admire.
> We little think of the intense, fierce flame,
> That gold alone is proof against the same;
> And that such trash as we, like drossy lead,
> Consume before it, and it strikes us dead." [23]

Subsequently, in England, he became the victim of a far deeper and more serious passion. During his residence in Bath, he first met a beautiful and accomplished young woman, Elizabeth Singer of Frome, who, under the pseudonym of "Philomela," was just then beginning to attract notice by her poems, and who afterward, rejecting the suit of Matthew Prior, married one Thomas Rowe, and had a somewhat distinguished career as a writer, both of prose and of verse. Colman's acquaintance with this brilliant woman soon became very intimate and interesting; had he been willing to remain in England, it is said that he could have married her; and the memory of the passionate friendship thus formed with her, cast a tint of

[23] E. Turell, Life of B. Colman, 24–25.

romance over the remainder of his life, passed beyond the sea. Long after his return to America, he continued his correspondence with her; and even so late as 1708, her letters to him manifest ardent emotion: she called him her "guardian angel;" said that only "the language of heaven" could express "a friendship so noble" as theirs; and assured him that, after death, her friendship for him should "commence a more exalted ardor." [24]

Postponing, however, the consummation of this friendship to the leisure to be expected in paradise, Benjamin Colman returned, in 1699, to the more urgent vocation that awaited him in Boston, where he took charge of a new church founded on a somewhat liberal platform; serving it with preëminent success as long as he lived, nearly half a century; solacing himself, meantime, for the temporary loss of the society of his English Philomela, by three very excellent American wives.

During this long public career, his contributions to the literature of his country were most abundant, and mainly in the form of sermons. His style in these sermons is fluent, polished, modern in tone, Addisonian, with a rich and ample movement. He had formed his literary manner by the study of English literature, and in his sermons he often refers to the masters of English pulpit-eloquence,—to Bishop Pearson, to John Howe, to "the late excellent Archbishop Tillotson," whom he calls "that most reverend person, the greatest example of charity and moderation that the age produced." [25] His discourses abound in terse and felicitous terms. He speaks of "the dreggy, cheap pleasures of sin;" he says that the worldling acts as if he "esteemed himself only of the upper order of brutes, to graze with and perish like them." Describing the power of religion to adorn the body: "I once saw a poor old man in this country, who made no figure but for his piety, who seemed, already on his death-bed, to have changed his wrinkled face for Moses's shining one; and I am sure, were the vainest persons by, in all their tawdry ornaments of body as well as real beauty, they would have looked but uncomely and deformed compared with this venerable man." Describing the spiritual warfare of the Christian, he says: "Men must wrestle against

[24] E. Turell, Life of B. Colman, 49.
[25] "Discourses upon the Parable of the Ten Virgins," 57.

the importunities of flesh and blood, and against the power and policy of hell; against the cravings of a vitiated nature fomented by the world and the devil." [26]

There is a manly and sweet catholicity of tone in his writings,—a unique quality then: "It is indeed best to err on the charitable side; and no temper is more hateful than a censorious, jealous, judging one; suspecting everybody of evil but ourselves and a few we are fond of; confining the Church of Christ to a narrow compass, and salvation to those only of our own persuasion. . . . There are some practices and principles that look catholic, which, though I cannot reason myself into, yet I bear a secret reverence to in others, and dare not for the world speak a word against. Their souls look enlarged to me; and mine does so the more to myself, for not daring to judge them." [27]

VIII

A man of heroic mould both in body and in mind—one of the clerical Titans of our later colonial period—was John Barnard, who, in the year 1770, at the age of eighty-nine, died at Marblehead, after sixty-eight years of service as a preacher in New England, after fifty-six years of service as a preacher in that particular town. Tall, of graceful proportions, erect even under the burden of nearly ninety years, he had the imperial bearing of our elder New England clergy, the stateliness of a king, touched by the intellectuality of a scholar, and the tenderness of a saint. "His countenance was grand," wrote his associate, William Whitwell, "and his mien majestic; and there was a dignity in his whole deportment. . . . His presence restrained every imprudent sally of youth; and when the aged saw him, they arose and stood up." [28]

After taking his first degree at Harvard College in 1700, he devoted himself, at his father's house in Boston, to a wide range of studies in preparation for the Christian ministry; he began preaching, in 1701;

[26] "Discourses upon the Parable of the Ten Virgins," 90–91.
[27] Ibid. 56–57.
[28] Funeral Sermon by W. Whitwell, quoted in W. B. Sprague, "Annals of Am. Pulpit," I. 254.

New England: The Pulpit

he did some good service for his country as a military chaplain, in 1707; he paid a visit to England, in 1709, remaining there sixteen months; and at last, in 1714, ripened by multifarious contact with life and with books, he began his pastorate at Marblehead; where he advanced year by year to a commanding reputation throughout the country. His great trait was energy, physical and mental, impelling him to the mastery of all human knowledge. He had the usual scholarly attainments in the ancient languages; he was able to deal with the most subtle and rugged problems in Biblical criticism and in divinity; all his life, he pursued the study of the higher mathematics, for which he had peculiar aptitude; he was an expert in the theory and practice of music; he gave great attention to architecture; and living in a town where the building and sailing of ships were the principal employments of the people, he astonished them by his knowledge of their own mysteries, and was able to serve them by the execution of the most artistic and improved models for ships.

His intellectual activity, shown in so many other directions, was shown also in authorship. He published, in 1752, a metrical version of the Psalms; he wrote, in 1768, a sketch of the eminent ministers he had known in New England; and besides numerous isolated sermons, he issued, in 1727, a volume entitled "Sermons on Several Subjects," and in 1747, another volume entitled "The Imperfection of the Creature and the Excellency of the Divine Commandment."

The foremost impression now made upon one by these writings, is that of the robustness, the intellectual virility, of the man. He delights in hardy tasks of thought; he has the habit of confronting real difficulties of the mind. There is a mathematical thoroughness, a lawyer-like sense, in his handling of sacred subjects; he grips them with the clutch of conscious power. His great gift lies in his logic. He excels in the argumentative presentation and defence of Christian doctrine. Yet, having first dealt with his topic as a thing in debate, and having vindicated the reasonableness of his cause, he casts off severity of style and often becomes in expression ample, glowing, and affluent.

It marks the literary culture of the man, that in his writings one sees traces of his familiarity not only with Calvin and the great

Puritan divines, but with the more liberal writers of the Anglican church, such as Tillotson, Stillingfleet, and More;[29] and that he should even enforce his statements by the authority of Epictetus.[30] Though his style is by no means a rich or imaginative one, it is never beggarly or harsh; at times, it has a tone of delicate grace, the artful force of amenity in phrase; as, when he speaks of one who "hath made some progress in the mysterious art, the divine lesson, of self-denial;[31] or when he asks: "Is there anything more unbecoming a rational creature than to be a slave to sense, or than for a heaven-born soul to be the Devil's drudge?"[32] "A man may very much stifle and suppress the remonstrances of his own mind by the hurry and noise and diversions of the world; but can he always command silence in his own breast, and stop the just clamors of conscience against himself?"[33] He has a felicity of urbane statement, sometimes even a quiet sarcasm, which blend effectively with the vigor of stern denunciation; but always this preacher is a gentleman, even in his frankest professional arraignment of sinners.

IX

Jonathan Edwards, the most original and acute thinker yet produced in America, was born at East Windsor, Connecticut, in 1703; was graduated at Yale College in 1720; was a preacher in New York for about eight months prior to April, 1723; was a tutor in Yale College from the summer of 1724 until the summer of 1726; in 1727, became pastor of the church at Northampton, and so continued until 1750; from 1751 until 1758, was missionary to the Indians near Stockbridge; on the sixteenth of February, 1758, was installed as president of the College of New Jersey; and died a few weeks afterward, namely, on the twenty-second of March.

Both by his father and by his mother, he came of the gentlest and most intellectual stock in New England. In early childhood, he began to manifest those powerful, lofty, and beautiful endowments, of mind and of character, that afterward distinguished him,—spirit-

---

[29] "Sermons on Several Subjects," 11, 38, 40, 41, 42, 120. [30] Ibid. 91.
[31] Ibid. 90.   [32] "The Imperfection of the Creature," etc. 230.
[33] Ibid. 231.

uality, conscientiousness, meekness, simplicity, disinterestedness, and a marvellous capacity for the acquisition of knowledge and for the prosecution of independent thought. It is, perhaps, impossible to name any department of intellectual exertion, in which, with suitable outward facilities, he might not have achieved supreme distinction. Certainly, he did enough to show that had he given himself to mathematics, or to physical science, or to languages, or to literature—especially the literature of imagination and of wit—he would have become one of the world's masters. The traditions of his family, the circumstances of his life, the impulses derived from his education and from the models of personal greatness before his eyes, all led him to give himself to mental science and divinity; and in mental science and divinity, his achievements will be remembered to the end of time.

As a mere child, he read not only the ordinary writings in Latin, Greek, and Hebrew, but the most abstruse and subtile writings in English; and at the age of fourteen, being then a sophomore in Yale College, his eye, for the first time, fell upon Locke's "Essay on the Human Understanding,"—a book which made an era in the history of his mind, and which he read, even at that youthful period, with a delight greater, he tells us, "than the most greedy miser finds when gathering up handfuls of silver and gold from some newly discovered treasure." [34] Several years before that event, however, he had trained himself always to read with pen in hand; that is, to be productive as well as receptive in reading, and not only to think for himself as he went along, but to put his thinking into exact language. The result of such training as that upon such genius as his, was a precocity, both in original thought and in the expression of it, that is perhaps not surpassed, if it is equalled, in the case of any other intellectual prodigy.

Thus, when Jonathan Edwards was not more than twelve years old, he heard that some one in the neighborhood, probably an older boy, had advanced the opinion that the soul is material and remains with the body till the resurrection. Instead of debating the question in crude, antagonistic fashion, our young metaphysician wrote to his friend a playful letter, in which he ironically professes to be on

[34] Works of J. Edwards, I. 30.

the point of adopting the new opinion, and humbly submits for solution a few difficulties that still stood in his way, but that really constituted a most ingenious and effective exposure of the logical absurdities of the doctrine proposed: "I am informed that you have advanced a notion that the soul is material, and attends the body till the resurrection. As I am a professed lover of novelty, you must imagine I am very much entertained by this discovery; which, however old in some parts of the world, is new to us. But suffer my curiosity a little further. I would know the manner of the kingdom before I swear allegiance. First, I would know whether this material soul keeps with [the body] in the coffin; and if so, whether it might not be convenient to build a repository for it. In order to which, I would know what shape it is of, whether round, triangular, or four-square, or whether it is a number of long fine strings reaching from the head to the foot; and whether it does not live a very discontented life. I am afraid when the coffin gives way, the earth will fall in and crush it. But if it should choose to live above ground, and hover about the grave, how big it is; whether it covers all the body, or is assigned to the head, or breast, or how. If it covers all the body, what it does when another body is laid upon it; whether the first gives way, and, if so, where is the place of retreat. But suppose that souls are not so big but that ten or a dozen of them may be about one body, whether they will not quarrel for the highest place; and as I insist much upon my honor and property, I would know whether I must quit my dear head, if a superior soul comes in the way. But, above all, I am concerned to know what they do where a burying place has been filled twenty, thirty, or an hundred times. If they are a top of one another, the uppermost will be so far off that it can take no care of the body. I strongly suspect they must march off every time there comes a new set. I hope there is some other place provided for them but dust. The undergoing so much hardship and being deprived of the body at last, will make them ill-tempered. I leave it with your physical genius to determine whether some medicinal applications might not be proper in such cases; and subscribe your proselyte— when I can have solution of these matters." [35]

This discussion by two New England boys, of a profound and com-

[35] Works of J. Edwards, I. 20–21.

New England: The Pulpit

plex problem in psychology, is interesting as an illustration of the educational effects wrought on the people of New England, by their rugged theological drill. They had become a population of acute philosophers. Even their children, it seems, were ready to interrupt the delights of playing at tag or of capturing woodchucks, in order to exchange arguments over the question of the materiality of the human soul. We see, also, in the present example, some of the chief peculiarities of the mind of Jonathan Edwards,—his keenness in analysis, his faculty of seeing the logical absurdities involved in a false proposition, his power of setting forth these absurdities in a way at once fair and irresistible, his gift of raillery, his freedom from arrogance of tone, his use of the Socratic strategy of a deferential manner in debate.

While still an under-graduate, and therefore before his eighteenth year, he began to put into precise shape, in his note-book, the conclusions he had come to on leading topics in mental philosophy,—such as cause, existence, space, substance, matter, thought, motion, union of mind with body, consciousness, memory, personal identity, duration, and so forth. In one of these notes, on "The Place of Minds," he comes back to that sharp study of the nature and physical relations of the spirit that had employed his mind some years before: "Our common way of conceiving of what is spiritual, is very gross, and shadowy, and corporeal, with dimensions, and figure, and so forth. If we would get a right notion of what is spiritual, we must think of thought, or inclination, or delight. How large is that thing in the mind which they call thought? Is love square, or round? Is the surface of hatred rough, or smooth? Is joy an inch, or a foot, in diameter? These are spiritual things; and why should we then form such a ridiculous idea of spirits, as to think them so long, so thick, or so wide, or to think there is a necessity of their being square, or round, or some other certain figure?" [36]

In another of these juvenile notes, he thus discusses "Nothing": "That there should absolutely be Nothing at all, is utterly impossible. The mind, let it stretch its conceptions ever so far, can never so much as bring itself to conceive of a state of perfect Nothing. It puts the mind into mere convulsion and confusion, to think of such

[36] Works of J. Edwards, I. 678.

a state; and it contradicts the very nature of the soul, to think that such a state should be. It is the greatest of contradictions, and the aggregate of all contradictions, to say that Thing should not be. It is true, we cannot so distinctly show the contradiction in words; because we cannot talk about it, without speaking stark nonsense, and contradicting outselves at every word; and because Nothing is that whereby we distinctly show other particular contradictions. . . . If any man thinks that he can conceive well enough how there should be Nothing, I will engage that what he means by Nothing, is as much Something, as anything that he ever thought of in his life; and I believe that if he knew what Nothing was, it would be intuitively evident to him that it could not be. . . . Absolute Nothing is the aggregate of all the contradictions in the world: a state, wherein there is neither body, nor spirit, nor space, neither empty space nor full space, neither little nor great, narrow nor broad, neither infinite space nor finite space, not even a mathematical point, neither up nor down, neither north nor south. . . . When we go about to form an idea of perfect Nothing, we must shut out all these things; . . . nor must we suffer our thoughts to take sanctuary in a mathematical point. When we go to expel being out of our thoughts, we must be careful not to leave empty space in the room of it; and when we go to expel emptiness from our thoughts, we must not think to squeeze it out by anything close, hard, and solid; but we must think of the same that the sleeping rocks do dream of; and not till then, shall we get a complete idea of Nothing." [37]

It is in these wonderful memoranda, penned by this lad of sixteen or seventeen, that we find his first avowal of that philosophy of Idealism, with which the name of Berkeley has since been associated. At the end of an argument respecting "Being," Jonathan Edwards says: "What, then, is to become of the universe? Certainly, it exists nowhere but in the Divine mind. . . . Those beings which have knowledge and consciousness are the only proper, and real, and substantial beings; inasmuch as the being of other things is only by these. From hence we may see the gross mistake of those who think material things the most substantial beings, and spirits more like a shadow; whereas

[37] Works of J. Edwards, I. 706–707.

New England: The Pulpit

spirits only are properly substance." [38] In another note, he says: "The material universe exists only in the mind. . . . All material existence is only idea." [39]

The precocity of Jonathan Edwards in physical science, appears to have been not less wonderful than was his precocity in metaphysical science. His father had a correspondent, probably in England, who was much interested in natural history; and for this gentleman, Jonathan Edwards, when twelve years of age or perhaps younger, wrote an elaborate paper, giving with great exactness of statement, and with great force of reasoning, the results of his own observations upon spiders. "May it please your Honor," writes this modest and marvellous boy, "There are some things that I have happily seen of the wondrous way of the working of the spider. Although everything belonging to this insect is admirable, there are some phenomena relating to them more particularly wonderful. Everybody that is used to the country, knows their marching in the air from one tree to another, sometimes at the distance of five or six rods. Nor can one go out in a dewy morning, at the latter end of August and the beginning of September, but he shall see multitudes of webs, made visible by

---

[38] Works of J. Edwards, I. 708.

[39] Ibid. I. 676. Some of the sentences that I have quoted to illustrate Edwards's early avowal of Idealism, are also quoted by Professor A. C. Fraser (Works of Berkeley, IV. 182), to illustrate his statement that "Jonathan Edwards, the most subtle reasoner that America has produced," was "an able defender of Berkeley's great philosophical conception in its application to the material world." On another page (ibid. 190), Professor Fraser adds, that Berkeley's "direct influence is now, however, hardly to be found in the history of American thought, though his philosophy was professed by two of the greatest American thinkers, Samuel Johnson and Jonathan Edwards." It is certain that Johnson derived his Idealism from Berkeley, and in consequence of Berkeley's visit to America; and the impression likely to be made by Professor Fraser's words, is that the same was the case with Edwards. But this is by no means certain. The above sentences from Edwards, avowing Idealism, were written nine or ten years before Berkeley came to America. Moreover, Edwards was not the man to conceal his intellectual obligations; and the name of Berkeley nowhere occurs, so far as I can discover, in all the ten volumes of Edwards's printed writings. It seems more probable that the peculiar opinions which Edwards held in common with Berkeley, were reached by him through an independent process of reasoning and somewhat in the same way that they were reached by Berkeley, who, as Professor Fraser says (ibid. 35), "proceeded in his intellectual work on the basis of postulates which he partly borrowed from Locke, and partly assumed in antagonism to him."

the dew that hangs on them, reaching from one tree, branch, and shrub to another. . . . But these webs may be seen well enough in the daytime by an observing eye, by their reflection in the sunbeams. Especially, late in the afternoon may these webs that are between the eye and that part of the horizon that is under the sun, be seen very plainly, being advantageously posited to reflect the rays. And the spiders themselves may be very often seen travelling in the air, from one stage to another amongst the trees, in a very unaccountable manner. But I have often seen that which is much more astonishing. In very calm and serene days in the forementioned time of year, standing at some distance behind the end of an house or some other opaque body, so as just to hide the disk of the sun and keep off his dazzling rays, and looking along close by the side of it, I have seen a vast multitude of little shining webs, and glistening strings, brightly reflecting the sunbeams, and some of them of great length, and of such a height that one would think they were tacked to the vault of the heavens, and would be burnt like tow in the sun. . . . But that which is most astonishing is, that very often appears at the end of these webs, spiders sailing in the air with them. . . . And since I have seen these things, I have been very conversant with spiders, resolving if possible to find out the mysteries of these their astonishing works. And I have been so happy as very frequently to see their manner of working; that when a spider would go from one tree to another, or would fly in the air, he first lets himself down a little way from the twig he stands on by a web; . . . and then laying hold of it by his forefeet, and bearing himself by that, puts out a web . . . which is drawn out of his tail with infinite ease, in the gently moving air, to what length the spider pleases; and if the farther end happens to catch by a shrub or the branch of a tree, the spider immediately feels it, and fixes the hither end of it to the web by which he lets himself down, and goes over by that web which he put out of his tail." He then describes minutely how the spider moves from tree to tree; and how, in the fall of the year, they sustain themselves in the air and are carried upon the westerly winds to the sea, and are "buried in the ocean, and leave nothing behind them but their eggs for a new stock next year." [40]

[40] Works of J. Edwards, I. 23–28. The manuscripts from which these extraor-

New England: The Pulpit

The interest of Jonathan Edwards in physical science did not pass away with his childhood; and while a student at Yale College, and especially while a tutor there, he prosecuted his physical researches with great diligence. He even wrote a series of notes on natural science, intended as the basis of a book. In these notes, he dealt with the principal topics in physics and astronomy, many of his remarks being very acute, ingenious, and original. He suggested that "there is in the atmosphere some other ethereal matter considerably rarer than atmospheric air;" that water is a compressible fluid—a fact not publicly announced by scientific men until thirty years afterward; that water in freezing loses its specific gravity; and that "the existence of frigorific particles" is doubtful. In explaining the phenomena of thunder and lightning, without any knowledge of the electric fluid, and long before the invention of the Leyden jar, he rejected the notions then prevalent upon the subject, and came nearer to the theory afterward discovered by Franklin than any other human mind had then done. He made important suggestions relative to a theory of atoms; he demonstrated that the fixed stars are suns; he explained the formation of river-channels, the different refrangibility of the rays of light, the growth of trees, the process of evaporation, and the philosophy of the lever; and he made important observations on sound, on electricity, on the tendency of winds from the coast to bring rain, and on the cause of colors.[41]

The intense intellectual discipline to which, almost from infancy, this wonderful person subjected himself, was accompanied by a moral and spiritual discipline, begun as early in life, and in its rigor equally intense. In the "resolutions" that he wrote out for himself while a very young man, one now finds, amid many tokens of the gratuitous and puerile severity of his age and his sect, the traits of a personal character full of all nobility: "To live with all my might while I do live;" "When I feel pain, to think of the pains of martyrdom and of

---

dinary specimens of juvenile thought and expression are printed, were in the possession of Sereno E. Dwight, when editing the works of Edwards; and are described by him as in "handwriting of the earliest and most unformed cast;" the essay relative to the materiality of the soul being "without pointing or any division into sentences," and having "every appearance of having been written by a boy just after he had learned to write." Ibid. 20.

[41] Works of J. Edwards, I. 53–54; 702–761.

hell;" "Never to do anything out of revenge;" "In narrations, never to speak anything but the pure and simple verity;" "Never to give over nor in the least to slacken my fight with my corruptions, however unsuccessful I may be." [42] On the twenty-third of September, 1723, he wrote: "I observe that old men seldom have any advantage of new discoveries, because they are beside the way of thinking to which they have been so long used. Resolved, if ever I live to years, that I will be impartial to hear the reasons of all pretended discoveries, and receive them if rational, how long soever I have been used to another way of thinking." [43] About one month afterward, he wrote: "To follow the example of Mr. B., who, though he meets with great difficulties, yet undertakes them with a smiling countenance, as though he thought them but little; and speaks of them, as if they were very small." [44] On the sixth of June, 1724, while a tutor at Yale, he wrote: "I have now abundant reason to be convinced of the troublesomeness and vexation of the world, and that it never will be another kind of world," [45]—an observation confirmed, doubtless, by the experience of many another Yale tutor, since that date.

Such, in intellectual attainments and in spiritual quality, was Jonathan Edwards, when, at the age of twenty-four, he entered upon his work as minister of a parish on the frontiers of civilization. The remainder of his life was what he expected it to be,—an experience of labor and of sorrow; but always borne by him with meek and cheerful submission. He had ill health, domestic griefs, public misrepresentation, alienation of friends, persecution, even poverty. In 1751, he was so poor that his daughters had to earn money for household expenses by making fans, laces, and embroidery; and he himself, for lack of paper, had to do his writing, mostly on the margins of pamphlets, on the covers of letters, and on the remnants that his daughters could spare him from the silk-paper used by them in the manufacture of fans.

Nevertheless, through it all, he bated not a jot of heart or hope, but still bore up and steered right onward. His chief business was in his study; and there he usually worked thirteen hours a day. Even out of the study, his mind was not at rest; when, for exercise, he rode

[42] Works of J. Edwards, I. 68–72. [43] Ibid. 94.
[44] Ibid. 100. [45] Ibid. 103.

New England: The Pulpit

on horseback, or walked in the woods, he kept on at his tasks of thought; in order that he might not forget anything that he had wrought out in these excursions, he was accustomed to pin a bit of paper upon his coat, for every idea that was to be jotted down on his return; and it was noticed that, sometimes, he would come home with his coat covered over with these fluttering memorials of his intellectual activity.

The problems upon which his mind was constantly at work, were the great problems of theology,—especially those in immediate debate, at that time, in New England. Of course, he held the theology that was then and there orthodox,—that ganglion of heroic, acute, and appalling dogmas commonly named after John Calvin. To the defence of that theology, in all its rigors, in all its horrors, Jonathan Edwards brought his unsurpassed abilities as a dialectician.

We need not discredit the traditions that have come down to us, of the agonizing effects produced upon men and women, by such an advocate as he, giving statement to such doctrines as those. He was not an orator. In the pulpit, he generally held his little "manuscript volume in his left hand, the elbow resting on the cushion or the Bible, his right hand rarely raised but to turn the leaves, and his person almost motionless." [46] Yet such was the power of his sincerity, of his solemnity, and of his logic, that he wrought results not surpassed in their kind even by the oratory of Whitefield. His first sermon at Princeton, in the College Hall, was two hours long; but it so enchained the audience that they were astonished and disappointed that it closed so soon. One person, who heard him preach concerning the Day of Judgment, testified that "so vivid and solemn was the impression made on his own mind, that he fully supposed that, as soon as Mr. Edwards should close his discourse, the Judge would descend, and the final separation take place." [47] Once, at Enfield, Connecticut, he came into an assemblage that was unusually listless and indifferent; but before his sermon was ended, the people were bowed down in agony and terror. "There was such a breathing of distress and weeping, that the preacher was obliged to speak to the people, and desire silence that he might be heard." [48]

[46] S. E. Dwight, Works of J. Edwards, I. 605–606.
[47] Ibid. 604. [48] Ibid. 605.

The sermon through which he so moved the people of Enfield, had this terrifying title, "Sinners in the Hands of an Angry God;" and an analysis of his method in that discourse, will serve to show us enough of his method in all his discourses. It is upon the text, "Their feet shall slide in due time." After a concise and solemn exposition of the original use of the words, he deduces from them this proposition: "There is nothing that keeps wicked men, at any one moment, out of hell, but the mere pleasure of God." He then proceeds to justify the proposition by a series of ten considerations, each stated with great sharpness and force, and all accumulating upon this central thought an indescribable emphasis: 1. There is no want of power in God to cast wicked men into hell at any moment. 2. They deserve to be cast into hell. 3. They are already under a sentence of condemnation. 4. They are now the objects of that very same anger and wrath of God, that is expressed in the torments of hell. 5. The Devil stands ready to fall upon them and seize them as his own, at what moment God shall permit him. 6. There are in the souls of wicked men those hellish principles reigning, that would presently kindle and flame out into hell-fire, if it were not for God's restraints. 7. It is no security to wicked men, for one moment, that there are no visible means of death at hand. 8. Natural men's care to preserve their own lives, or the care of others to preserve them, does not secure them a moment. 9. All wicked men's pains and contrivance to escape hell, while they continue to reject Christ, do not secure them from hell one moment. 10. God has laid himself under no obligation, by any promise, to keep any natural man out of hell one moment.[49]

These several considerations follow, one after another, with dreadful swiftness and force, each hurled by calm, merciless logic, and by an overwhelming intensity of realism. He then reaches the application, where the urgency of reasoning, of menace, of consternation, becomes intolerable. No wonder that human nature gave way under it; that men and women sighed and sobbed, as the ghastly preacher, himself trembling at his own argument, went on and on with the horrible thing: "If God should let you go, you would immediately sink, and sinfully descend, and plunge into the bottomless

[49] Works of J. Edwards, VII. 163-168.

New England: The Pulpit

gulf. . . . Were it not for the sovereign pleasure of God, the earth would not bear you one moment; for you are a burden to it; the creation groans with you; the creature is made subject to the bondage of your corruption not willingly; the sun does not willingly shine upon you to give you light, to serve sin and Satan; the earth does not willingly yield her increase to satisfy your lusts; nor is it willingly a stage for your wickedness to be acted upon; the air does not willingly serve you for breath to maintain the flame of life in your vitals, while you spend your life in the service of God's enemies. . . . And the world would spew you out, were it not for the sovereign hand of him who hath subjected it in hope." [50]

His power over the people whom he addressed, consisted partly in his minuteness of imaginative detail,—bringing forward each element in the case one by one; so that drop after drop of the molten metal, of the scalding oil, fell steadily upon the same spot, till the victim cried out in shrieks and ululations of agony: "The bow of God's wrath is bent, and the arrow made ready on the string, and justice bends the arrow at your heart, and strains the bow, and it is nothing but the mere pleasure of God, and that of an angry God, without any promise or obligation at all, that keeps the arrow one moment from being drunk with your blood." [51] "The God that holds you over the pit of hell, much as one holds a spider or some loathsome insect over the fire, abhors you, and is dreadfully provoked; . . . he looks upon you as worthy of nothing else but to be cast into the fire. . . . You are ten thousand times more abominable in his eyes, than the most hateful, venomous serpent is in ours." [52] "You hang by a slender thread, with the flames of divine wrath flashing about it, and ready every moment to singe it and burn it asunder." [53] "If you cry to God to pity you, he will be so far from pitying you in your doleful case, or showing you the least regard or favor, that instead of that, he will only tread you under foot. And though he will know that you cannot bear the weight of omnipotence treading upon you, yet he will not regard that; but he will crush you under his feet without mercy; he will crush out your blood, and make it fly, and it shall be sprinkled on his garments, so as to stain

[50] Works of J. Edwards, VII. 169.
[51] Ibid. 170.
[52] Ibid. 170.
[53] Ibid. 171.

all his raiment. He will not only hate you, but he will have you in the utmost contempt; no place shall be thought fit for you, but under his feet to be trodden down as the mire of the streets."[54]

In the latter part of his life, Jonathan Edwards chanced to open and to read so frivolous a book as a novel—"Sir Charles Grandison." The delight that he found in that work, led him to analyze the sources of his pleasure, and especially to consider the power of mere style in the expression of thought; and to say to his son that he regretted his own neglect of it. As a theologian, as a metaphysician, as the author of "The Inquiry into the Freedom of the Will," as the mighty defender of Calvinism, as the inspirer and the logical drill-master of innumerable minds in his own country, and in Great Britain, he, of course, fills a large place in ecclesiastical and philosophical history. But even from the literary point of view, and in spite of his own low estimate of his literary merits, he deserves high rank. He had the fundamental virtues of a writer,—abundant thought, and the utmost precision, clearness, and simplicity in the utterance of it; his pages, likewise, hold many examples of bold, original, and poetic imagery; and though the nature of his subjects, and the temper of his sect, repressed the exercise of wit, he was possessed of wit in an extraordinary degree, and of the keenest edge. In early life, he was sadly afflicted by the burden of checking the movements of this terrible faculty; but later, it often served him in controversy, not as a substitute for argument, but as its servant; enabling him, especially in the climaxes of a discussion, to make palpable the absurdity of propositions that he had already shown to be untenable.[55]

X

In the year 1776, shortly after the evacuation of Boston by the British troops, a somewhat dramatic scene was presented one day, in one of the churches of that city, known as the Hollis Street Church. Its patriotic members, having returned from the outlying villages to which they had fled the year before, had determined to come to stern

[54] Works of J. Edwards, VII. 173.
[55] A notable instance of his wit in logical ridicule, is his exposure of the absurdity of Chubb's notion of "an act." Works of J. Edwards, II. 199–200.

New England: The Pulpit

issues with their pastor, the Reverend Mather Byles, a distinguished and powerful divine, but an incorrigible Tory, then just seventy years old. All along, from the opening of the controversy between the colonies and the king, he had taken sides with the king against the colonies. Although in the pulpit he never, in those days, referred to politics, out of the pulpit he referred to little else; and he made unsparing use of his acuteness and of his sarcastic wit, to baffle and scourge the political designs of his own people. During the occupation of the city by the king's soldiers, he had remained there, and had given them his aid and comfort; and he still affronted his congregation by praying, in their presence, for the prosperity of the monarch whose troops had desolated the town, had slaughtered their brethren, and were preparing to enslave the whole country. For forty-three years, Mather Byles had ministered to that one church, faithfully, ably, with great renown;[56] yet they could endure his political perversity no longer. Resting their public accusations against him, however, on his faults as a pastor, and not on his faults as a patriot, they drew up their charges in writing, and notified him of their wish for a public interview upon the subject. On the day appointed, the male members of the congregation, with grim resolution, yet with no little dread of the awful eye and the no less awful tongue of the great man who had been their spiritual lord so long, assembled early at the church. The pews had been removed by the troops from the floor of the house; and perhaps with a mute sense of greater safety in the approaching interview, the men took their seats in one of the lofty galleries, and there awaited in silence the arrival of the mighty person, whose wrath they were about to invoke upon themselves. "In due time," says the son [57] of one who witnessed the scene, "the door opened slowly, and Dr. Byles entered the house with an imposing solemnity of manner. He was dressed in his ample, flowing robes and bands, under a full bush-wig that had been recently powdered, surmounted by a large three-cornered hat. He walked from the door to the pulpit with a long and measured tread, ascended

---

[56] He was born in Boston in 1706, graduated at Harvard in 1725, ordained pastor of Hollis Street church in 1733.

[57] Samuel J. May, of Syracuse, in W. B. Sprague, "Annals of Am. Pulpit," I. 380–381.

the stairs, hung his hat upon the peg, and seated himself. After a few moments, he turned with a portentous air toward the gallery, where his accusers sat, and said,—'If ye have aught to communicate, say on.'" Upon this, one of the deacons, a very little man with a very little voice, stood up and began to read: "The church of Christ in Hollis Street"——"Louder!" roared the frowning orator, with awful, leonine voice. The puny deacon began again, and with still greater effort of articulate squeak: "The church of Christ in Hollis Street"——"Louder!" once more shouted the preacher, with terrible emphasis. The miserable little man, now trembling with fright as well as with great stress of vocal impotence, began once more, and was permitted to proceed through three or four of the specifications, when the insulted pastor arose, indignation darkening all his face and giving dreadful resonance to his voice, and thundered out,—" 'Tis false; 'tis false; 'tis false; and the church of Christ in Hollis Street knows that 'tis false." Upon this, he took down his hat, put it upon his head, and descending the pulpit, as an angry monarch would his throne, he stalked proudly out of the church, never to enter it again; leaving to the little deacon and his brethren, the contemptuous privilege of making the most of their specifications against him.

Thus, in great bitterness of popular aversion, ended the public career of a man, who, until his loyalty to his king made him disloyal to his country, had held a very high place in the admiration of his contemporaries. To them he had seemed a man of extraordinary brilliance, in many different characters,—wit, poet, man of letters, theologian, pulpit-orator; but it was as pulpit-orator only that he was really great, to the service of that single character subordinating whatever gifts he possessed for all the others.

The traditions of his wit have, since then, choked out nearly all memory of the central gravity and strength of his character; and he stands in our history merely as a Tory punster and a clerical buffoon. His jocoseness, after all, was not the principal part of him. He jested much; and yet he was much more than a jester; he was an earnest and devout Christian minister.[58]

[58] A collection of the jests of Mather Byles may be made from the following sources: William Tudor, "Life of James Otis," 156–160; "The Belknap Papers," in 5 Mass. Hist. Soc. Coll. II. 285, 471; III. 51, 234; W. B. Sprague, "Annals of Am. Pulpit," I. 377, 378, 382.

New England: The Pulpit

His great strength was in the pulpit. He was perhaps as great a master of the amenities and the potencies of pious persuasion as New England had in its colonial age, after the days of Hooker, Shepard, John Cotton, and Urian Oakes. His presence was stately and commanding; he was at once aristocrat and apostle; in dress and manner, one of the first gentlemen of his time. Very early in life, he had shown a propensity to purely literary work; he was in correspondence with some of the chiefs of literature in England; Pope sent to him a splendid copy of his translation of the Odyssey. His own literary facility was notable: he had poetic sensitiveness, an ear for the strokes and cadences of the Popean verse; no inconsiderable facility in the manufacture of that verse; all of which, without making him more than a minor poet, gave him uncommon skill in the modulation of his prose sentences for oratory. His sermons are invariably marked by neatness of phrase, and expertness in the manipulation of his materials; by fresh and striking views of things, by the avoidance of uncomfortable length, by courtesy of tone, by common sense. He had paid much attention to the æsthetics of his profession. His own idea of "a finished minister" included all the accomplishments, both of society and of books. The preacher, he said, should be a person of "graceful deportment, elegant address, and fluent utterance. He must study an easy style, expressive diction, and tuneful cadences. . . . Nothing can be more finished oratory than many of Paul's sermons. . . . Rattling periods, uncouth jargon, affected phrases, and finical jingles—let them be condemned; let them be hissed from the desk and blotted from the page." [59] The old Puritan traditions of the enormous studiousness of the preacher, were sanctioned by this preacher—at least in the impartation of advice to others: "The study of the minister is the field of battle. Here he plays the hero, tries the dangers of war, and repeats the toils of combat. . . . How often must he watch when others sleep; and his solitary candle burn when the midnight darkness covers the windows of the neighborhood." [60] He deemed it worth his while, also, to accentuate the rather obvious ethical requirements of the sacred calling: "What an inconsistent thing is a wicked minister! An unholy divine; a blind watchman; a wolfish shepherd; an ignorant angel;—

---
[59] Sermon at the ordination of his son, New London, 1758, 11–12.
[60] Ibid. 14.

what nonsense is this! An ungodly man of God—what a solecism! what a monster!" [61]

The distinctive gift of Mather Byles was homiletical; he originated no ideas, he constructed no new arrangement of ideas; his function lay in the strength, warmth, and vivacity with which he grasped for himself the great familiar propositions in faith and conduct, and then, for others, held them forth in a succession of splendid and powerful pictures that inevitably drew the eyes of men, and stirred their hearts into fellowship of fervor. He smote men with the sword of their own accepted ideas; into speech he put without reserve his imagination and his emotion; he loved those generic and universal topics—ancient but never old—which exercised his own uncommon faculty of sublime and tender description: the impotence of man, the insignificance of this world, the grandeur of the eternal state, the dissonance and emptiness that are in all things whatsoever save virtue and truth and God. Repeating that melancholy, tired text,—the very hyperbole and half-truth of mortal weariness and pain,—"Verily every man at his best estate is altogether vanity," the preacher, in one sermon,[62] interprets it in dramatic colloquy with an imaginary disputant, and charges each word of his text with an explicit burden of gloom. At another time, he draws this picture of the physical future of his hearers: "In a few years the most beauteous and learned and pious head will grin a hideous skull. Our broken coffins will show nothing but black bones, or black mould, and worms, and filth." [63] He pours scorn on the emptiness of all human pretension: "A creature drooping to dust, and falling into a filthy grave, to set up for strength and beauty, honor and applause! Was ever anything more absurd and ridiculous? So might an emmet crawl in state, and value itself upon its imaginary possessions, and conceited accomplishments. So might a shadow, lengthened by the setting sun, admire to find itself grown so tall, while in the same moment it was going to vanish, blended in the gathering twilight, and lost in night and darkness." [64]

The Bible is the storehouse for this preacher's themes, and for

[61] Sermon at the ordination of his son, New London, 1758, 8.
[62] Funeral Sermon on Wm. Dummer, 3-4.
[63] "The Present Vileness of the Body," 9.
[64] Funeral Sermon on Wm. Dummer, 20-21.

New England: The Pulpit

much of his imagery; and his gift of description, as it exercises itself on man's pettiness, so is it put forth for the display of God's greatness. Taking up one of the Scriptural titles of God, "the Lord of hosts," the orator proceeds to this amplification of it: "This is one of the magnificent and favorite titles which he wears; and it is about two hundred times applied to him in the inspired writings. The Lord of hosts, he is the King of glory: the Lord of hosts is his name. Take a view of his extended and potent armies, and see him in his glory at the head of all. The heavenly hosts are his. So are the angels in all their shining forms and unnumbered regiments. An immeasurable front, and an endless rear! No army of so exact discipline, such invincible courage and fatal execution. Our painted troops are a mere mock-show, to these resistless legions. Our chariots and horses make no figure at all before these chariots of fire and horses of fire. The chariots of God are twenty thousand thousands of angels; and he maketh his angels spirits and his ministers a flame of fire. A whole host of our mortal warriors shall wither in a night before one of them, and strew the pale camp with an hundred and four score and five thousand corpses. Beneath these, the stars keep their military watch, the out-guards of the celestial army. And what a glittering host of them range themselves over the blue plains of ether! . . . These in all their immense dominions are under his absolute command. . . . How mysterious and unknown are the laws of those unnumbered squadrons; and how irresistible their movements! Canst thou bind the sweet influences of Pleiades, or loose the bands of Orion? Canst thou bring forth Mazzaroth in his season, or canst thou guide Arcturus with his sons? But he, the great monarch of all, commands with infinite ease; and every rolling world submits with exact obedience. . . . Below these, and sailing along our atmosphere, the clouds make their majestic appearance, a flying camp, or a moving magazine of divine artillery. . . . There the northern tempests plant their impetuous batteries; there the fierce engines of the sky play in various forms of destruction. He is alike the Lord of the terrestrial hosts, while every species of creature and every individual are under his exact command. But who can call over the list of these extended cohorts? Is there any number of his armies? The earth is full of his legions; so also is the great and wide sea, with all the tribes and colonies there. . . . And where's the creature which he cannot commission, or that dares to mutiny against his sovereign edicts? . . . Behold what a Lord of hosts is here! Even the wind and the seas obey him! He rules

'amidst the war of elements,
The wrecks of matter, and the crush of worlds.'

Even the devils are subject to him. . . . He is the Lord of our hosts; and not an army gathers in this earth without his counsels and providence. . . . He unfurls his ensigns, and calls for the march of nations in universal tumult, and ranges half the globe on a side, confederated to a decisive battle." [65]

XI

On the border-line, between the colonial age and the age of the Revolution, we confront two great men, Jonathan Mayhew and Charles Chauncey, who belong to both ages, and who represent, not only the vast political influence of the New England clergy in the agitations of those times, but the broadest intellectual training, the most rational and the most catholic sentiment, then reached by any of their class. These two men we shall meet again, and study more fully, when we come to the literature of the Revolution; but our record of the high and splendid intellectual development of the clergy of New England, during the colonial time, would lack some essential factors, if we did not at least point to their names and to the significance of their lives, even in the period now under view.

Jonathan Mayhew, the younger of the two, who also died first, was for the last nineteen years of his short life, minister of a church in Boston. He was, in the pulpit, a sort of tribune of the people. He impressed himself upon his contemporaries as a thinker of much originality and boldness, as a preacher of extraordinary power, as a writer of great elegance, force, and wit. In the history of his time, he stands for two things: first, the impulse he gave to bold and manly political conduct among his fellow-countrymen; and second, the impulse he gave to the emancipation of their minds from the despotism

[65] Artillery-sermon for 1740, 9–14.

New England: The Pulpit

of the old theological dogmas. John Adams, who knew him well, predicted that the writings of Jonathan Mayhew would preserve his reputation "as long as New England shall be free, integrity esteemed, or wit, spirit, humor, reason, and knowledge admired." [66]

In a long life, which began almost with the beginning of the eighteenth century, and did not end until the stress and peril of the American Revolution were all passed, Charles Chauncey,[67] pastor of the first church of Boston, lived among men as their natural leader. He was a man of leonine heart, of strong, cool brain, of uncommon moral strength. He bore a great part in the intellectual strife of the Revolution; but before that strife was opened, he had moulded deeply the thought of his time, both by his living speech and by his publications. These were mostly sermons; but as sermons they had an extraordinary sweep of topics, from early piety and the lessons of affliction, to earthquakes in Spain, murder, religious compulsion, Presbyterian ordination, legislative knavery, the encouragement of industry, and the capture of Cape Breton.

The prevailing trait of the man was intellectual genuineness in all things, and utter scorn of its opposite in anything. He had a massive, logical, remorseless understanding, hardy in its processes, and unwilling to take either fact or opinion at second hand. On the great themes that were then in debate among men, he put himself to enormous research. One of these themes was the Episcopacy. He gave four years of hard reading to it, first in the Scriptures and in the Fathers, then in all modern books on both sides of the controversy. Other themes were the doctrines of human depravity, retribution, and the like. He settled himself down for seven years to the study of these doctrines in the New Testament, especially in the epistles of St. Paul, and finally in all other books within reach; and he thus worked his way "into an entirely new set of thoughts" [68] on those matters. He was an orthodox rationalist; and he stood in the line of that intellectual development among the clergy of New England, which at a later day culminated in Unitarianism.

---

[66] Works of J. Adams, IV. 29.
[67] Born in Boston 1705, graduated at Harvard 1721, pastor in Boston from 1727 to his death in 1787.
[68] "Chauncey Memorials," 70.

In the midst of the popular spasms and rhapsodies excited by the preaching of Whitefield and his imitators, the peculiar qualities of Charles Chauncey were strongly revealed. He had an ineffable contempt for all slipshod, giddy, gaseous minds; for ejaculatory and rhetorical folk; for that oratory which makes up for absence of ideas by vehemence of assertion. Whitefield himself, he regarded as a clerical mountebank, ignorant, shallow, presumptuous, injurious, "never so well pleased as with the hosannas of ministers and parishioners in these parts of the earth;" [69] "the grand promoter of all the confusion there has been in the land." [70] To Chauncey it seemed that the people were being led by Whitefield and his kind into all manner of disorder and folly; that inevitable reaction would come, by and by, in every shape of moral disaster; and that it was the duty of every sound brain to help to check the epidemic of lunacy. With his usual thoroughness he first undertook to gather the facts; he travelled hundreds of miles to observe for himself the proceedings of the itinerants and of the people who were affected by them; and being convinced that the fruits were delusion, anarchy, self-righteousness, and all uncharitableness, he published, in 1742, a tremendous sermon entitled "Enthusiasm," and in the following year, a still more powerful treatise, entitled, "Seasonable Thoughts on the State of Religion in New England."

A remarkable passage in the former of these works, is his description of the enthusiast; a full-length portrait for all ages and all lands. The original being just then very conspicuous in the streets of Boston, the fidelity of this portrait must have rendered it extremely effective at that time: "The enthusiast is one who has a conceit of himself as a person favored with the extraordinary presence of the Deity. He mistakes the workings of his own passions for divine communications; and fancies himself immediately inspired by the Spirit of God, when all the while he is under no other influence than that of an overheated imagination.

"The cause of this enthusiasm is a bad temperament of the blood and spirits. 'Tis properly a disease, a sort of madness. . . . None are so much in danger of it, as those in whom melancholy is the prevailing ingredient in their constitution. In these it often reigns, and

---

[69] "Chauncey Memorials," 65.   [70] Ibid. 68.

sometimes to so great a degree, that they are really beside themselves, acting as truly by the blind impetus of a wild fancy, as though they had neither reason nor understanding.

"And various are the ways in which their enthusiasm discovers itself. Sometimes, it may be seen in their countenance. A certain wildness is discernible in their general look and air. . . . Sometimes, it strangely loosens their tongues and gives them such an energy, as well as fluency and volubility in speaking, as they themselves, by their utmost efforts, cannot so much as imitate when they are not under the enthusiastic influence. Sometimes, it affects their bodies, throws them into convulsions and distortions, into quakings and tremblings. . . . Sometimes, it will unaccountably mix itself with their conduct, and give it such a tincture of that which is freakish and furious, as none can have an idea of, but those who have seen the behavior of a person in a frenzy. Sometimes, it appears in their imaginary peculiar intimacy with heaven. They are, in their own opinion, the special favorites of God; have more familiar converse with him than other good men; and receive immediate, extraordinary communications from him. . . . And what extravagances, in this temper of mind, are they not capable of, and under the specious pretext too of paying obedience to the authority of God? Many have fancied themselves acting by immediate warrant from heaven, while they have been committing the most undoubted wickedness. There is, indeed, scarce anything so wild, either in speculation or practice, but they have given in to it; they have, in many instances been blasphemers of God and open disturbers of the peace of the world. But in nothing does the enthusiasm of these persons discover itself more, than in the disregard they express to the dictates of reason. They are above the force of argument, beyond conviction from a calm and sober address to their understandings. As for them, they are distinguished persons; God himself speaks inwardly and immediately to their souls. . . . And in vain will you endeavor to convince such persons of any mistakes they are fallen into They are certainly in the right, and know themselves to be so. . . . They are not, therefore, capable of being argued with; you had as good reason with the wind. And as the natural consequence of their being thus sure of everything, they are not only infinitely stiff and tenacious, but impatient of contradiction, censorious, and uncharitable. . . . Those . . . who venture to debate with them about their errors and mistakes, their weaknesses and indiscretions, run the hazard of being stigmatized by them as poor, unconverted wretches, without the Spirit, under the government of carnal reason, enemies to God and religion, and in the broad way to hell. . . . The extraordinary fervor of their minds, accompanied with uncommon bodily motions, and an excessive confidence and assurance, gains them great reputation among the populace; who speak of them as men of God, in distinction from all others, and too commonly hearken to and revere their dictates, as though they really were, as they pretend, immediately communicated to them from the Divine Spirit." [71]

[71] The sermon, 3–6.

Chapter XVI

Literature in the Middle Colonies

1. NEW YORK AND NEW JERSEY

I. Traits of life in New York before it became English—After it became English—A many-tongued community—Metropolitan indications—Education neglected—Literary effort only in spasms.

II. Daniel Denton, a pioneer of American Literature there—His "Brief Description of New York"—His pictures of nature and of social felicity—Thomas Budd, of New Jersey, another pioneer writer—His "Good Order established in Pennsylvania and New Jersey"—William Leeds, a refugee from Philadelphia—His "News of a Trumpet sounding in the Wilderness."

III. Lewis Morris of Morrisania—His vivacious boyhood—Turns vagabond—Settlement into steady courses—A powerful politician—His literary inclinations—His letters from London—Provincial loyalty disenchanted by going to the metropolis.

IV. Cadwallader Colden—His long career—Manifold activity—Extraordinary range of his studies and of his writings—His "History of the Five Indian Nations"—Its characteristics—Its descriptions of the savage virtues.

V. Daniel Coxe of New Jersey—His "Description of the English Province of Carolana"—His statesmanly view of colonial affairs—Anticipates Franklin's plan of a union of the colonies.

VI. Jonathan Dickinson, pulpit-orator, physician, teacher, author—First president of the College of New Jersey—His personal traits—His eminence as a theological debater—His "Familiar Letters."

VII. William Livingston—His "Philosophic Solitude"—Manner and spirit of the poem—Antithesis between his ideal life and his real one—His strong character—Outward engagements—His activity as a pamphleteer and as a writer in the journals—His burlesque definition of his own creed—His "Review of the Military Operations in North America"—His "Verses to Eliza."

VIII. William Smith—The course of his life—His special interest in the history of his native province—His "History of New York"—Criticisms upon it—Samuel Smith and his "History of the Colony of Nova Cæsarea or New Jersey."

2. PENNSYLVANIA

I. The founders of Pennsylvania—The high motives of their work—Their social severity—Intellectual greatness of William Penn—Justice and liberality imparted by him to the constitution of his province—Education provided for—First impulses to literary production in Pennsylvania—The development of a literary spirit in Philadelphia.

II. Gabriel Thomas—A brisk Quaker—His "Account" of Pennsylvania and of West New Jersey—His enthusiasm for his province—Its freedom from lawyers and doctors—Its proffer of relief to the distressed in the old world—Richard Frame—His "Short Description of Pennsylvania"—John Holme—His "True Relation of the Flourishing State of Pennsylvania"—Jonathan Dickenson—His "God's Protecting Providence Man's Surest Help."

III. James Logan—Penn invites him to America and trusts to him his affairs there—His fidelity to the Penns and to the people—Difficulties of his position—His great intellectual attainments—His writings published and unpublished.

IV. William Smith—His influence upon intellectual culture in the middle colonies—Arrival at New York—His "General Idea of the College of Mirania"—Is invited to Philadelphia—His useful career as educator, preacher, and writer.

V. A succession of small writers—Jacob Taylor—Henry Brooke—Samuel Keimer—Aquila Rose—James Ralph—George Webb and his "Bachelors' Hall"—Joseph Breintnal—A poem from "Titan's Almanac" for 1730—Joseph Shippen—John Webbe—Lewis Evans.

VI. Samuel Davies—Born and educated in Pennsylvania—Acquires in Virginia great fame as a pulpit-orator—His mission to England—Becomes president of the College of New Jersey—His death—Great popularity of his published sermons down to the present time—His traits as a preacher—Passage from his sermon on "The General Resurrection."

Literature in the Middle Colonies

VII. Thomas Godfrey, the poet—Connection of his father's family with Franklin—His early life and death—Publication of his "Juvenile Poems" * His "Prince of Parthia," the first American drama—A study of it.

VIII. Benjamin Franklin, the first man of letters in America to achieve cosmopolitan fame—His writings during our present period—His great career during the subsequent period.

I. NEW YORK AND NEW JERSEY

I

NEAR the middle of the year 1664, the Dutch town of New Amsterdam was suddenly transformed into the English town of New York,—being then just forty-one years old, and having a population of fifteen hundred souls. The whole province, of course, shared the new name and the new mastership that had overtaken its chief town.

The Dutch, who founded both town and province, had thriven there from the beginning, according to the habit of their race,—a patient, devout, labor-loving, wealth-getting, stolid community. Though popular education was neglected, and intellectual life ran sluggish and dull, there were among them many men of strong brains and scholarly attainments: [1] Van der Donck, Megapolensis, and De Vries, who wrote history; Stuyvesant, Beeckman, and Van Rensselaer, whose letters show considerable learning; Van Dincklagen, and Van Schelluyne, who were wise in the law; Jacob Steendam, Henricus Selyns, and Nicasius De Sillè, who wrote poetry; [2] and besides these, several theologians and physicians who were well-read in their own sciences.

Though the prevailing race in New Amsterdam was Dutch, from an early day the town had been an attractive one to men of other races. Twenty-one years before it fell into the hands of the English, it had, within it and near it, a population speaking eighteen different

---

[1] J. R. Brodhead, "Hist. N. Y." I. 748.

[2] "Anthology of New Netherland; or, Translations from the early Dutch poets of New York, with memoirs of their lives," by Henry C. Murphy. New York, 1865.

[* The dash was omitted here in the early editions, perhaps because this was the end of the line.]

439

languages.[3]   After it fell into the hands of the English, its attractiveness to men of many languages certainly did not diminish; and it became, what its best historian calls it, "the most polygenous of all the British dependencies in North America." [4]   In the first twenty-four years of its existence under English sway, its population was nearly quadrupled; and by the end of the colonial time, it had increased almost twenty-fold.   A community of many tongues, of many customs, of many faiths,—there was, doubtless, in that fact a prophecy of metropolitan largeness and generosity, in store for it somewhere in the future.

Nevertheless, we shall greatly err if we imagine that, during the larger part of the colonial time, New York was much more than a prosperous and drowsy Dutch village, perplexed by polyglot interference and the menace of intellectual illumination; the scene of a petty life; ravaged by sectarian and provincial bigotries, and by vulgar competitions in society and in politics; very slowly moving toward the discovery that, in all the world, there is any other pursuit so noble as the pursuit of wealth.   The historian, William Smith, writing in 1757, mentions that, for a long time, his own father and James De Lancey "were the only academics" in the province; and that, as late as 1745, there were only thirteen more.[5]   "What a contrast," he exclaims, "in everything respecting the cultivation of science, between this and the colonies first settled by the English!" [6] "Our schools are of the lowest order—the instructors want instruction; and through a long and shameful neglect of all the arts and sciences, our common speech is extremely corrupt; and the evidences of bad taste, both as to thought and language, are visible in all our proceedings, public and private." [7]

The history of literature in such a community, at such a period, must be the record, not of any concentrated and continuous literary activity, but of the occasional efforts of cultivated men to express themselves, for practical purposes, in some literary form.

[3] J. R. Brodhead, "Hist. N. Y." I. 374.
[5] Wm. Smith, "Hist. N. Y." II. 113.
[7] Ibid. I. 328.
[4] Ibid. II. 387.
[6] Ibid. 379.

Literature in the Middle Colonies

II

Daniel Denton, the son of a minister in Connecticut, removed in 1644 into the province of New York, where he rose to distinction both as a land-owner and as a politician. In 1670, apparently with the view of attracting immigration to that province, he published, in London, "A Brief Description of New York,"[8]—a book of twenty-two pages, uncommonly graphic and animated. He kept closely to the facts that had come under his own eyes, prudently declining to say anything about those portions of the province that lay "to the northward yet undiscovered," or in "the bowels of the earth not yet opened." Even on the basis of literal and visible fact, however, he had enough, both useful and beautiful, to justify his enthusiasm for the land which he sought to make known to English emigrants. He gives an account of its fitness for all sorts of industrial success; not forgetting to describe its natural charms, as in May, when "you shall see the woods and fields so curiously bedecked with roses, and an innumerable multitude of delightful flowers, . . . that you may behold nature contending with art, and striving to equal if not excel many gardens in England;"[9] and "divers sorts of singing-birds, whose chirping notes salute the ears of travellers with an harmonious discord; and in every pond and brook, green, silken frogs, who, warbling forth their untuned tunes, strive to bear a part in this music."[10] Having given a sufficient account of the natural and social advantages of the province, he seeks to win inhabitants for it by appealing to the English love of personal independence and domestic thrift: "If there be any terrestrial happiness to be had by people of all ranks, especially of an inferior rank, it must certainly be here. Here any one may furnish himself with land, and live rent-free; yea, with such a quantity of land that he may weary himself with walking over his fields of corn and all sorts of grain. . . . Here those which Fortune hath frowned upon in England to deny them an inheritance amongst their brethren, or such as by their utmost labors can scarcely procure a living, . . . may procure here inheritances of lands and possessions, stock themselves with all sorts of cattle, enjoy the benefit of

---

[8] Reprinted, New York, 1845, ed. by Gabriel Furman.
[9] "A Brief Description," etc. 4.   [10] Ibid. 5–6.

them whilst they live, and leave them to the benefit of their children when they die. Here you need not trouble the shambles for meat, nor bakers and brewers for beer and bread, nor run to a linen-draper for a supply. . . . If there be any terrestrial Canaan, 'tis surely here, where the land floweth with milk and honey. The inhabitants are blessed with peace and plenty, blessed in their country, blessed in their fields, blessed in the fruit of their bodies, in the fruit of their grounds, in the increase of their cattle, horses, and sheep, blessed in their basket and in their store; in a word, blessed in whatsoever they take in hand, or go about, the earth yielding plentiful increase to all their painful labors." [11]

Precisely fifteen years after the publication of Daniel Denton's winsome sketch of the province of New York, Thomas Budd, of New Jersey, a worthy Quaker, and a man of much importance in his own neighborhood, published, likewise at London, a little book entitled "Good Order established in Pennsylvania and New Jersey in America." [12] The purpose of this book, like that of Daniel Denton, was to catch the eye of emigrants; and for that purpose it perhaps did not need, as certainly it did not have, much literary merit.

Another book belonging to this pioneer period of literature in New York and its neighborhood, is a very curious one: "News of a Trumpet sounding in the Wilderness; or, The Quakers' ancient testimony revived, examined, and compared with itself, and also with their new doctrine—whereby the ignorant may learn wisdom and the wise advance in their understandings;" published by William Bradford in 1697, and written by Daniel Leeds, once a Quaker and an early settler in Pennsylvania. This man, having quarrelled with his brethren there, abandoned them and finally their province, and established himself in New York, probably in 1693, where, for about thirty years, he continued in his famous almanacs that warfare against the Quakers which he had begun in his book.

III

Lewis Morris, born in 1671, on the paternal estate of Morrisania, lived a long and vigorous life as colonial politician in New York and

[11] "A Brief Description," etc. 19–21.
[12] Reprinted, New York, 1865, ed. by Edward Armstrong.

Literature in the Middle Colonies

New Jersey; was, for more than twenty years, chief-justice of the former province, and died, in 1746, as royal governor of the latter; a man of large inherited wealth, of high social consideration, of bold and somewhat unscrupulous talent; a natural intriguer. Though he settled into manhood sufficiently sedate, his youth was uncommonly vivacious, and sparkled long afterward in a trail of amusing traditions. Being left an orphan in his infancy, he came under the care of an uncle, who seems to have found the boy hard to tame into industry and propriety. At one time, he had for his tutor an enthusiastic Quaker, one Hugh Coppathwaite, who enjoyed much of the divine presence through various inward and outward communications. The boy conceived the happy thought of helping his preceptor to a new revelation, and himself to a holiday; and, accordingly, hiding in the branches of a tree under which the Quaker was used to walk, the lad called out to him in solemn tones, and commanded him to go away at once, and preach the gospel among the Mohawks. The good man accepted the mandate as the very voice of heaven, and was on the point of setting out to obey it, when, unluckily for the boy, the trick was discovered, and his studies were not interrupted.[13] Subsequently, breaking away from all restraints, he roamed into Virginia to see the world, thence to the West Indies, picking up a living as best he could; after some years, the vagabond came home, was pardoned by his uncle, married, and entered soon upon his distinguished public career. He was an able speaker; loved power over men, and the arts by which it is gained; and though his own contact with books must have been casual and irregular, he greatly enjoyed literature and the society of literary men.[14] There remains a letter of his to his London bookseller, for the year 1739, containing a list of books which he desired, and indicating that, even at the age of sixty-eight, his mind was reaching out toward new studies, as well as old ones: law books, political treatises, theological writings, histories, a Hebrew grammar, an Arabic grammar, and an edition of John Milton.[15]

He wrote nothing that he thought of as literature; but the brightness and vigor of his mind are shown in his correspondence, and in his state-papers. He appears to have been not incapable even of

[13] Wm. Smith, "Hist. N. Y." ed. 1814, 202.   [14] Ibid.
[15] "Papers of Lewis Morris," 47.

sportive rhymes on occasion. For instance, in 1709, in sending to the governor of New York, Lord Lovelace, a memorial for the board of trade, he added a private address on his own account, beginning with these lines:

> "As kings at their meals sit alone at a table,
> Not deigning to eat with the lords of the rabble,
> So the great Lewis Morris presents an address
> By himself, all alone, not one else of the mess." [16]

In 1735, he went to England, to make complaint to the parliament and ministry respecting the conduct of William Cosby, at that time governor of New York, under royal appointment; and his letters to friends at home are good examples of the sprightliness of his mind. The visit of this American politician to the metropolis, appears to have been the means of a rough disenchantment, robbing him of many beautiful provincial illusions respecting the tender and paternal care with which English statesmen were supposed to deal with Americans and their affairs: "You have very imperfect notions of the world on this side of the water—I mean that world with which I have to do. They are unconcerned at the sufferings of the people in America.... It may be you will be surprised to hear that the most nefarious crime a governor can commit is not, by some, counted so bad, as the crime of complaining of it; the last is an arraigning of the ministry that advised the sending of him." [17] "We talk in America of applications to parliaments. Alas! my friend, parliaments are parliaments everywhere; here, as well as with us, though more numerous. We admire the heavenly bodies which glitter at a distance; but should we be removed into Jupiter or Saturn, perhaps we should find it composed of as dark materials as our own earth.... We have a parliament and ministry, some of whom, I am apt to believe, know that there are plantations and governors—but not quite so well as we do. Like the frogs in the fable, the mad pranks of a plantation governor is sport to them, though death to us; and [they] seem less concerned in our contests than we are at those between crows and

[16] "Papers of Lewis Morris," 322.*   [17] Ibid. 24–25.

[* In 1897 a sentence was added to Note 16: "By 'N. J. Archives,' III. 381–382, pub. 1881, it appears that these lines were written at Morris, and not by him."]

king-birds. Governors are called the king's representatives; and when by repeated instances of avarice, cruelty, and injustice, they extort complaints from the injured, in terms truly expressive of the violence committed and injuries suffered, it must be termed a flying in the face of government; the king's representative must be treated with softness and decency; the thing complained of is nothing near so criminal in them, as the manner of complaint in the injured. And who is there that is equal to the task of procuring redress? Changing the man is far from an adequate remedy, if the thing remains the same; and we had as well keep an ill, artless governor we know, as to change him for one equally ill, with more art, that we do not know. One of my neighbors used to say that he always rested better in a bed abounding with fleas after they had filled their bellies, than to change it for a new one equally full of hungry ones; the fleas having no business there but to eat. The inference is easy." [18]

IV

Cadwallader Colden was the son of a Presbyterian minister in Scotland, but was himself accidentally born in Ireland. He was educated at the University of Edinburgh; after studying medicine there and in London, he emigrated to America in 1710, and settled at Philadelphia for the practice of his profession. In 1718, at the friendly solicitation of General Robert Hunter, the governor of New York, he removed to that province, where he received the office of surveyor-general; became proprietor of a large estate in lands; was made a member of the king's council, and in the latter part of his life, lieutenant-governor, with frequent exercise of the duties of governor; and died, in September, 1776, aged eighty-eight, a loyalist to his king, and bitterly hated by the people whom he had served so long, but whose later movements toward revolution he had felt it his duty to resist.

Thus, the life of Cadwallader Colden, though it had a patriarchal length, had not the patriarchal quietude; it was a life of manifold outward occupation, and latterly of political turmoil and rancor; and yet, so valiant and craving was his spirit, that he found time, dur-

[18] "Papers of Lewis Morris," 23–24.

ing all those busy lustrums of his, to be not only a cultivator of various learning, but one of the leaders of mankind in its cultivation. A monument of his industry and of his versatility, remains to us in the vast mass of his writings, published and unpublished, which deal, acutely and philosophically, with almost every great topic of human interest,—divinity, ethics, metaphysics, politics, mathematics, history, geology, botany, optics, zoölogy, medicine, agriculture, and even certain improvements in the mechanic arts, as stereotypy.[19]

The one production of his that most nearly approaches a purely literary effort, is "The History of the Five Indian Nations." Of this work, the first part, bringing the narrative down to 1688, was originally published in New York, in 1727;[20] and the second part, continuing the narrative to the peace of Ryswick, 1697, was published in London, in 1747.[21] The book is principally a sketch of five powerful allied Indian tribes then residing in the northern part of the province of New York,—their forms of government, their wars with hostile tribes, their conflicts and treaties with Frenchmen, Dutchmen, and Englishmen; upon the whole, a very slender, not altogether accurate, and not in the least interesting account of sundry parcels of savages, of their steady employment in scalping and in getting scalped, mitigated by occasional interludes of palaver with one another and with white men. Though the author writes with ease, and generally with verbal correctness, it is impossible for him to redeem his book from the curse of being a history of what deserves no history. A single episode, giving the exploits of the Algonquin chief, Piscaret, has some dramatic vividness, even though also the flavor of palpable myth;[22] while the best piece of writing in the book, is its dedication to William Burnet, the governor of New York,—particularly, the passage wherein the author celebrates the austere virtues of the savages whose history he records: "The Five Nations are a poor, barbarous people, under the darkest ignorance; and yet a bright and noble

---

[19] The rich Colden MSS. are in possession of the N. Y. Hist. Soc., and well deserve careful editing and publication.

[20] An exact reprint of this edition, with an introduction and notes by John Gilmary Shea, was made in N. Y. in 1866.

[21] A very corrupt edition, however, containing omissions and additions unauthorized by Colden.

[22] "The History of the Five Indian Nations," Shea's ed. 12–15.

genius shines through these black clouds. None of the greatest Roman heroes have discovered a greater love to their country, or a greater contempt of death, than these barbarians have done, when life and liberty came in competition. Indeed, I think our Indians have outdone the Romans in this particular; for some of the greatest Romans have murdered themselves, to avoid shame or torments; whereas our Indians have refused to die, meanly, with the least pain, when they thought their country's honor would be at stake by it, but gave their bodies willingly up to the most cruel torments of their enemies, to show that the Five Nations consisted of men whose courage and resolution could not be shaken." [23]

The hope that these vivacious sentences awaken in us, of some broad and fine human interest connected with the history of the author's nude patriots and stoics, is not fulfilled.

V

In the year 1722, there was published in London a book respecting America, which deserved the deep attention of English and American statesmen at that time, and which, on one account, is still worthy of remembrance by us. It bore this formidable title: "A Description of the English Province of Carolana, by the Spaniards called Florida, and by the French La Louisiane; as also the great and famous river, Meschacebe or Mississippi, the five vast navigable lakes of freshwater, and the parts adjacent; together with an account of the commodities, of the growth and production of the said province; and a preface containing some considerations on the consequences of the French making settlements there."

The author was Daniel Coxe, a man of wealth, and of high social and political influence in New Jersey, who had inherited from his father a claim to the vast territory described in his book. It is the preface of the book, however, that is now of special interest to us; for in that preface, the author discussed, at great length and with great ability, the condition and the perils of the English colonies in America, the legal right of the English to the interior of the continent, and especially, the strategy to be pursued by enlightened

[23] "The History of the Five Nations," Dedication, 3–4.

statesmanship in realizing that right in opposition to the competing claims of the Spanish and the French. The chief element in the strategy proposed by him, is described in one word—union. Thus, in 1722, Daniel Coxe publicly explained and advocated a plan of union among the American colonies,—the details of which closely resemble those brought forward by Franklin, thirty-two years afterward, at the famous congress of Albany: "That all the colonies . . . be united under a legal, regular, and firm establishment; over which . . . a lieutenant or supreme governor may be . . . appointed to preside on the spot, to whom the governors of each colony shall be subordinate;" that the council or assembly of each province elect anually two delegates "to a great council or general convention of the estates of the colonies;" that the latter "consult and advise for the good of the whole." "A coalition or union of this nature," adds Daniel Coxe, in his earnest argument for it, "tempered with and grounded on prudence, moderation, and justice, and a generous encouragement given to the labor, industry, and good management of all sorts and conditions of persons, . . . will, in all probability, lay a sure and lasting foundation of dominion, strength, and trade, sufficient not only to secure and promote the prosperity of the plantations, but to revive and greatly increase the late flourishing state and condition of Great Britain." [24]

VI

Jonathan Dickinson was born at Hatfield, Massachusetts, in 1688; and was graduated at Yale College, in 1706. In 1708, he went to Elizabethtown, New Jersey; and there, for the subsequent thirty-nine years, he lived a most energetic life, as minister, physician, educator, and author, displaying great ability in all these spheres, and acquiring a commanding influence through the whole land. He was a leader in ecclesiastical politics in the middle colonies; he was a fascinating and mighty pulpit-orator; he was the principal founder of the College of New Jersey, and its first president; in person he was

---

[24] "A Description," etc. ed. 1726, Pref. It may be mentioned that, in 1697, William Penn had suggested a similar plan of union among the colonies. Hildreth, "Hist. U. S." II. 444.

Literature in the Middle Colonies

of so saintly and impressive an aspect, "that the wicked seemed to tremble in his presence;" [25] his long life was so pure, consistent, and noble, that "the memory of it is still fragrant on the spot where he lived," and the descendants "of those who knew and loved him cherish an hereditary reverence for his name and his grave." [26]

He was a voluminous author, his chief distinction pointing toward skill in theological controversy. He had the talent of a logician; he was an intrepid debater; as a protagonist for Calvinism, he stood in reputation among American theologians of his time, next to Jonathan Edwards; and a great Scottish divine [27] testified that even "the British Isles had produced no such writers on divinity in the eighteenth century," as were these two men,—both born on the confines of the New England forests, and both bred at Yale College.

Perhaps the most interesting specimen of his literary and dialectical gifts, is his "Familiar Letters to a Gentleman, upon a Variety of seasonable and important Subjects in Religion;" [28] in which are these sentences, portraying the logical difficulties to be assumed by any one who shall reject the historical verity of the New Testament: "If this history be not true, then all the known laws of nature were changed; all the motives and incentives to human actions, that ever had obtained in the world, have been entirely inverted; the wickedest men in the world have taken the greatest pains and endured the greatest hardship and misery, to invent, practise, and propagate the most holy religion that ever was; and not only the apostles and first preachers of the gospel, but whole nations of men and all sorts of men, Christian, Jew, and pagan, were—nobody can imagine how or why —confederated to propagate a known cheat, against their own honor, interest, and safety; and multitudes of men, without any prospect of advantage, here or hereafter, were brought most constantly and tenaciously to profess what they knew to be false, to exchange all the comforts and pleasures of life for shame and contempt, for banishments, scourgings, imprisonments, and death; in a word, voluntarily to expose themselves to be hated both of God and man, and that without any known motive whatsoever." [29]

---

[25] David Austin, in W. B. Sprague, "Annals of Am. Pulpit," III. 17.
[26] Ibid. 17. [27] Dr. John Erskine, ibid. 17. [28] Boston, 1745.
[29] "Familiar Letters," etc. 58.

VII

In the year 1747, was published in New York a little book entitled "Philosophic Solitude; or, The Choice of a Rural Life,"—a poem of nearly seven hundred lines, announcing itself as the production of "a gentleman educated at Yale College." This gentleman proved to be William Livingston, then twenty-four years old, just beginning the practice of the law in New York, and destined to a long and illustrious career as a statesman in the era of the Revolution. During his whole life, he was absorbed in stormy and agitating public movements; yet he found time to retain an uncommon intimacy with the best literature, and to exercise in many ways his own remarkable aptitude for literary work. This poem is obviously the effort of a rhyming apprentice, still in bondage to the methods of his master, Alexander Pope; yet he catches the knack of his master with a cleverness proving the possibility of original work, on his own account, by and by. It illustrates, likewise, a trait of human nature, that this young lawyer and politician, having given himself to a practical career in the thick of the world's affairs, and one made tumultuous by his own aggressive spirit, should have begun it by depicting, in enthusiastic verse, his preference for a life of absolute retirement and serene meditation:

> "Let ardent heroes seek renown in arms,
> Pant after fame, and rush to war's alarms;
> To shining palaces, let fools resort,
> And dunces cringe to be esteemed at court:
> Mine be the pleasures of a rural life,
> From noise remote, and ignorant of strife;
> Far from the painted belle, the white-gloved beau,
> The lawless masquerade and midnight show;
> From ladies, lapdogs, courtiers, garters, stars,
> Fops, fiddlers, tyrants, emperors, and czars." [30]

He then pictures for us the situation of the home in the country, in which he would spend his tranquil life,—its furniture, its surroundings; he sings over again his love of solitude; he mentions the sort of friends whom he would have within call; he portrays the

[30] "Philosophic Solitude," 13.

Literature in the Middle Colonies

frame of devotion and calm contemplation which should abide with him. His hermitage should be far from

>"Prime-ministers, and sycophantic knaves,
>Illustrious villains, and illustrious slaves." [31]

There, he would

>"live retired, contented, and serene,
>Forgot, unknown, unenvied, and unseen." [32]

He would have books for his most intimate friends; he would have Virgil as prince of the classic bards; he would be surrounded by Milton, Pope, Dryden, and "the gentle Watts;" also, by Locke, Raleigh, Denham; among philosophers, he would give the place of honor to Newton. Moreover, he would alleviate his solitude by the presence of a wife. This being should be none of those "ideal goddesses" who

>"to church repair,
>Peep through the fan, and mutter o'er a prayer;
>. . .
>Or, deeply studied in coquettish rules,
>Aim wily glances at unthinking fools." [33]

She is to be not an ideal goddess, but a literal one, an absolutely faultless being, who having accepted his addresses becomes, he says,

>"Imparadised within my eager arms."

He then reaches the climax of his poem by depicting the crowning experience of his "philosophic solitude"—a solitude the peculiar rigors of which would not seem to have required a vast exertion of philosophy to endure:

>"With her I'd spend the pleasurable day,
>While fleeting minutes gayly danced away:
>. . .
>I'd reign the happy monarch of her charms;
>Oft in her panting bosom would I lay,
>And, in dissolving raptures, melt away;

[31] "Philosophic Solitude," 16. [32] Ibid. 17. [33] Ibid. 40–41.

Then lulled by nightingales to balmy rest,
My blooming fair should slumber at my breast." [34]

The voluptuous languors of this poem, report a quality in the author that did not control him; and henceforward, through nearly half a century, his real life was a battle for stern and great ideas. He was of Scottish ancestry; and if he had within him the romantic intensity of his race, he had likewise its intellectual ruggedness, its iron grasp of conviction, its unsubmissiveness, its onrushing and most fervid pleasure in strife, its nerve of invincible endurance,—a double strain sent down to him from the old Scottish ballad-makers and from the old Scottish covenanters. The practice of his profession did not consume his energy; he was felt, as a pamphleteer and as a journalist, in all the topics that came up for debate in the colony in those years, especially those connected with the denominational control of King's College, with military operations, and with the establishment of an American Episcopate. He was a resolute member of the Reformed Dutch Church. By his newspaper articles against the efforts of the Episcopalians to obtain the mastery of King's College, he had brought upon himself the charges of atheism, deism, and Presbyterianism; and with reference to these imputations, he retorted upon his opponents with his usual wit and vigor, in a travesty on the Thirty-nine Articles: "1. I believe the Scriptures of the Old and New Testament, without any foreign comments or human explanations but my own; for which I should, doubtless, be honored with martyrdom, did I not live in a government which restrains that fiery zeal which would reduce a man's body to ashes, for the illumination of his understanding. . . . 5. I believe that the word orthodox is a hard, equivocal, priestly term that has caused the effusion of more blood than all the Roman emperors put together. . . . 7. I believe that to defend the Christian religion is one thing, and to knock a man on the head for being of a different opinion is another thing. . . . 11. I believe that he who feareth God and worketh righteousness, will be accepted of Him, even though he refuse to worship any man or order of men into the bargain. . . . 13. I believe that riches, ornaments,

[34] "Philosophic Solitude," 45.

and ceremonies were assumed by churches for the same reason that garments were invented by our first parents. . . . 15. I believe that a man may be a good Christian, though he be of no sect in Christendom. . . . 17. I believe that our faith, like our stomachs, may be overcharged, especially if we are prohibited to chew what we are commanded to swallow. . . . 38. I believe that the virulence of some of the clergy against my speculations, proceeds not from their affection to Christianity, which is founded on too firm a basis to be shaken by the freest inquiry, and the divine authority of which I sincerely believe,—without receiving a farthing for saying so; but from an apprehension of bringing into contempt their ridiculous claims and unreasonable pretensions, which may justly tremble at the slightest scrutiny, and which I believe I shall more and more put into a panic, in defiance of both press and pulpit." [35]

His most serious effort as a prose writer, during this period of our literary history, was "A Review of the Military Operations in North America," from 1753 to 1756. This work is in the form of a letter addressed to a nobleman, and was first published, without the author's name, in London, in the year 1756. Its historical value is considerable,—principally, as embalming the fury of partisanship that raged, at that time, between the great families of the colony of New York, and that drew within its folds the reputations of Sir William Johnson on the one hand, and of Governor William Shirley on the other. As a literary work, the book rises far above the mob of political pamphlets. Though somewhat lacking in concentration, it is written with much elegance; and it is especially remarkable for its elaborate portraits of the great men of the day. The painter of these portraits makes no pretence of impartiality, but tints his canvas at will with the frankness of his love or of his hate.

It is not disagreeable to be reminded, once more, of the tender and gallant vein that streaked the nature of this robust political combatant; and to find that, even amid the rancors of his strenuous career, there were moods in which he could dash off verses so graceful and so sprightly as these:

[35] From No. 46 of "The Independent Reflector," as reprinted in T. Sedgwick, "Life of W. Livingston," 86–87.

"Soon as I saw Eliza's blooming charms,
  I longed to clasp the fair one in my arms.
Her every feature proved a pointed dart
  That pierced with pleasing pain my wounded heart;
And yet, this beauty—it transcends belief—
  This blooming beauty is an arrant thief.
Attend: her numerous thefts I will rehearse
  In honest narrative and faithful verse.

From the bright splendor of the noonday sky,
  She stole the sparkling lustre of her eye.
Her cheeks, though lovely red, still more to adorn,
  She filched the blushes of the orient morn.
To embalm her lips, she robbed the honey-dew;
  To increase their bloom, the rose-bud of its hue.

. . .

Her voice, enchanting to the dullest ears,
  She pillaged from the music of the spheres;
To make her neck still lovelier to the sight,
  She robbed the ermine of its spotless white;
From Virgil's Juno, Jove's fictitious mate,
  She stole the queen-like and majestic gait.
Of all her charms, she robbed the Cyprian queen,
  And, still insatiate, stripped the Graces of their mien.

But now, to perfect an harmonious whole,
  With those internal charms that can't be stole,
Kind Heaven, without her thieving, took delight
  To grant supernal grace, and inward light:
To charms angelic, it vouchsafed to impart
  Angelic virtues, and an angel heart.
Thus fair in form, embellished thus in mind,
  All beauteous outward, inward all refined,
What could induce Eliza still to steal,
  And make poor plundered me her theft to feel?
For, last, she stole (if with ill-purposed art
  I'll ne'er forgive the theft) she stole—my heart;
Yes, yes, I will, if she will but incline
  To give me half of hers, for all the whole of mine." [36]

[36] T. Sedgwick, "Life of W. Livingston," 117–118.

Literature in the Middle Colonies

VIII

William Smith was the son of an eminent lawyer of New York, where he was born in 1728. He was graduated at Yale College, in 1745. Devoting himself to the professions of law and of politics, he speedily rose to distinction in both. During the Revolutionary War, he was a loyalist; in 1783, he went to England, and three years later, was rewarded for his fidelity to the crown, by the appointment of chief-justice of Canada. In Canada, he died in 1793.

While still a very young man, he gave great attention to the legal and political records of his native province,—an experience that led him to write a "History of New York, from the First Discovery to the Year 1732." This work, which was first published in London, in 1757,[37] is a strong and clear piece of work, with the tone of a scholar and a gentleman, somewhat dashed by provincialism. Himself a New York politician, and the son of one, it was not easy for him, in dealing with the story of New York politics, wholly to suppress his partisan prejudices; and his narrative, as he admitted, "deserves not the name of a history."[38] It is an able and sturdy historical pamphlet, aggravated by vast public documents quoted in bulk. Although he believed that in his book the laws of truth had not been infringed, either "by positive assertions, oblique, insidious hints, wilful suppressions, or corrupt misrepresentations," and that in his writing of it he had chosen "rather to be honest and dull than agreeable and false,"[39] he was charged by a contemporary, Cadwallader Colden,[40] with having "wilfully misrepresented" some things; while in our own time, the ablest of the historians of New York, John Romeyn Brodhead,[41] has declared that, in several instances, William Smith gave utterance to "fabulous" statements.

In his book, it is interesting to note the tokens of American sensitiveness, even in that age, to the infinite and serene ignorance prevalent among the people of England concerning their own plantations in America: "The main body of the people conceive of these planta-

---

[37] It has been several times reprinted; but the only satisfactory edition is that published by the N. Y. Hist. Soc., in 2 vols., 1829. In this edition, the work is brought down by the author to 1762.
[38] Pref. to ed. of 1814, xiv. [39] Ibid. xiv.
[40] N. Y. Hist. Soc. Coll. for 1868, 181. [41] "Hist. N. Y." I. 44, note.

tions under the idea of wild, boundless, inhospitable, uncultivated deserts; and hence, the punishment of transportation hither, in the judgment of most, is thought not much less severe than an infamous death." [42] His portraits of the long line of royal governors who had in succession preyed upon the province, are drawn with the vivacity of genuine feeling; in the ardor of his filial pride and affection, he has painted a glowing picture of the learning and eloquence of his own father; [43] and his sketches of society in New York in his time, particularly of the steady preference there of the pursuits of wealth to those of mere knowledge, have a courageous authenticity, perhaps not altogether obsolete even yet.[44]

In the year 1765, was published "The History of the Colony of Nova Cæsarea, or New Jersey;" the author being Samuel Smith, an honest, solid Quaker, a native of the region that he wrote about, himself then forty-five years old. His book is a dry, ponderous performance, a compilation of dull documents and dull facts; the whole written, doubtless, with great patience, and only to be read by an abundant exercise of the same virtue.

2. PENNSYLVANIA

I

A sagacious English student of American history has said that "the most remarkable of the American colonies after the New England group, is Pennsylvania." [45] In spite of all outward differences, of all mutual dislikes, there was an inward kinship between the Quakers of Pennsylvania and the Puritans of New England. "I came for the Lord's sake," said William Penn, in 1682.[46] "Our business here in this new land," said one of the first Pennsylvanians, "is not so much to build houses, and establish factories, and promote trade and manufactures that may enrich ourselves, . . . as to erect temples of holiness and righteousness, which God may delight in; to lay such lasting foundations of temperance and virtue, as may support the

---

[42] "Hist. of N. Y." ed. of 1814, Pref. ix.   [43] Ibid. ed. of 1829, II. 48–50.
[44] Ibid. I. 328, 367; II. 3, 282, 384.
[45] Goldwin Smith, "On the Foundation of the American Colonies," 26.
[46] R. Proud, "Hist. Pa." I. 210.

Literature in the Middle Colonies

superstructures of our future happiness, both in this and the other world." [47]

The society that these men founded in Pennsylvania was, of course, serious, laborious, economic, monotonous, prim, especially pained by the pleasures of existence. Thomas Chalkley abhorred music as a thing "of evil consequence;" he denounced cards "as engines of Satan;" and of dancing he said, that "as many paces or steps as the man or woman takes in the dance, so many paces or steps they take toward hell." [48]

On the other hand, William Penn was a man of great intellectual foresight, and swayed by a passion to be both just and humane; and he began by inoculating his young commonwealth with the idea of civic generosity: "We have, with reverence to God and good conscience to men, to the best of our skill contrived and composed the frame of this government to the great end of all government,—to support power in reverence with the people, and to secure the people from the abuse of power." [49] "Whoever is right," said he, "the persecutor must be wrong." [50] From the beginning, a part of the fundamental law of Pennsylvania was the law of liberty for the souls of men. Through every turnpike in that province, ideas travelled toll-free.

But were there, in that province, any ideas inclined to travel? The founder of Quakerism, being himself able to get all necessary wisdom by the facility of an inward flash, quite naturally despised those who had to get it by the slow process of study; he despised books, also, and schools; and he declared that "God stood in no need of human learning." [51] William Penn, however, and many of his associates in the settlement of Pennsylvania, had never yielded to that barbaric mood of their religious teacher; and being themselves men of considerable learning,[52] they at once devised means for the spread of learning among others. "Before the pines had been cleared from

[47] Given in J. W. Leeds, "A Hist. U. S." 212-213.
[48] T. Chalkley, Works, 4.   [49] J. Grahame, "Hist. U. S." I. 506.
[50] W. Hepworth Dixon, "Wm. Penn," etc. 52.
[51] Ibid. 53.
[52] Job R. Tyson, "The Social and Intellectual State of the Colony of Pa. prior to the year 1743," 46.

457

the ground," they "began to build schools and set up a printing-press." [53] It was their noble ambition, "inter silvas quaerere verum." [54] The first school in Pennsylvania was founded during the first year of the existence of Pennsylvania; and in the sixth year of its existence, there was in Philadelphia an academy at which even those who had no money, might get knowledge without price.

The first impulse to the production of any sort of literature in Pennsylvania was given by a desire to publish through the world the advantages of that commonwealth. Very soon, the fierceness of religious controversy set other pens to work,—though with results too crude and too brutal to be called literature. Science, also, and the slavery-question, and the Indian-question prompted others to write. Near the end of the first quarter of the eighteenth century,—about the time that Benjamin Franklin commenced his career there,—Philadelphia, though still dominated by the Quakers, had become the seat of a large population who were not Quakers; it had something of the liberal tone of a metropolis,—where men of cultivation, of vivacity, of literary aptitude, had begun to realize the presence of one another, and of a common literary purpose. By the close of the colonial age, Philadelphia had grown to be the centre of a literary activity more vital and more versatile than was to be seen anywhere else upon the continent, except at Boston. In the ancient library of Philadelphia, there are "four hundred and twenty-five original books and pamphlets that were printed in that city before the Revolution." [55]

II

In 1681, in the first ship that sailed from England to the great American province of William Penn, was the pleasant Quaker, Gabriel Thomas, who, for the next seventeen years, lent a strong and willing hand to the task of building up there a generous drab commonwealth; and who returning to England in 1698, probably for a brief visit, carried with him and published in London, in that year,

---
[53] W. Hepworth Dixon, "Wm. Penn," etc. 207.
[54] T. I. Wharton, "The Prov. Lit. of Pa.," in Pa. Hist. Soc. Mem. I. 109.
[55] Ibid. 124.

Literature in the Middle Colonies

"An Historical and Geographical Account of the Province and Country of Pennsylvania and of West New Jersey." The book, which is written with Quaker-like frankness and simplicity, and with an undercurrent of playfulness not exactly Quaker-like, is full of information for the guidance of the poor in the old world to a good refuge in the new; and in the author's opinion, no better spot could be found anywhere along the vast American coast than that happily obtained by William Penn: "For though this country has made little noise in story or taken up but small room in maps, yet, . . . the mighty improvements . . . that have been made lately there, are well worth communicating to the public. . . . This noble spot of earth will thrive exceedingly." [56] "The air here is very delicate, pleasant, and wholesome; the heavens serene, rarely o'ercast, bearing mighty resemblance to the better part of France." [57] In delineating the natural characteristics of the country, he passes now and then into a semi-facetious intensity, into a droll largeness of statement, from which even the demureness of his sect did not save him, and which thus early show themselves as traits of American humor; saying, for example, that the bullfrog in Pennsylvania "makes a roaring noise hardly to be distinguished from that well known of the beast from whom it takes its name." [58] His pictures of the new social conditions formed there, have elements of uncommon attractiveness; as when he remarks: "Of lawyers and physicians I shall say nothing, because this country is very peaceable and healthy. Long may it so continue, and never have occasion for the tongue of the one nor the pen of the other, both equally destructive of men's estates and lives." [59]

Once again, also, we catch in this book the tender American note of sympathy with men and women in Europe who have a hard lot there; a cheery voice from this side of the Atlantic sounding out clear above the countless laughter of its billows, and telling all who need a new chance in life that at last they can have it: "Reader, what I have here written is not a fiction, flam, whim, or any sinister design, either to impose upon the ignorant or credulous, or to curry favor with the rich and mighty; but in mere pity and pure compas-

[56] Preface.
[58] Ibid. 16.
[57] "Account," etc. 7.
[59] Ibid. 32.

sion to the numbers of poor laboring men, women, and children in England—half-starved visible in their meagre looks—that are continually wandering up and down, looking for employment without finding any, who here need not lie idle a moment, nor want due encouragement or reward for their work, much less vagabond or drone it about. Here are no beggars to be seen, . . . nor, indeed, have any here the least occasion or temptation to take up that scandalous lazy life." [60]

A desire to bear public testimony to the delights and benefits of life in Pennsylvania, took possession of several others among its first inhabitants; and unfortunately, in some cases, this testimony sought utterance in verse. Thus, Richard Frame, probably a Quaker, published at Philadelphia, in 1692, "A Short Description of Pennsylvania; or, A relation what things are known, enjoyed, and like to be discovered in the said province." [61] So, also, John Holme, who came to Pennsylvania in 1686, and died there about the year 1701, wrote "A True Relation of the Flourishing State of Pennsylvania." [62] Both of these works are very slight as specimens of descriptive literature; and as examples of verse, they scarcely rise to the puerile—they approach the idiotic.

A piece of narration and description, happily in honest prose, and having the merit of being uncommonly interesting, is "God's Protecting Providence Man's surest Help and Defence in Times of greatest Difficulty and most eminent Danger," by Jonathan Dickenson, an English Quaker of property and education, who, after some sojourn in Jamaica, sailed thence, in 1696, for Pennsylvania, having with him his wife, an infant child, and several negro servants. On the voyage, they were cast away on the coast of Florida, and after suffering almost incredible hardships, not only "from the devouring waves of the sea" but "also from the cruel, devouring jaws of the inhumane cannibals of Florida," they made their way to Philadelphia. Of this frightful and most afflictive experience, Dickenson wrote an account, under the title already given,—telling his story in a modest, straight-

---

[60] "Account," etc. 44–45.
[61] Published in fac-simile from the copy, supposed to be unique, in possession of the Library Company of Philadelphia, 1867.
[62] Printed in Pa. Hist. Soc. Mem. for 1848, 161–180.

forward, manly way, like a hero and a Christian. He remained in Pennsylvania the rest of his life, became chief-justice of the province, and died there in 1722.[63]

III

In 1699, when William Penn was on the point of sailing for the second time to his province, he became deeply interested in a young Irishman of Scottish descent, named James Logan, who, though highly educated, and with strong aptitudes for literary and scientific pursuits, had recently embarked in trade at Bristol. Penn saw in this young man one whom he could safely lean upon, and whom he greatly needed; and after urgent solicitation, Logan gave up his own plans, and putting his fate into Penn's keeping, went with him to America. There he remained all the rest of his days; and there he died in 1751, at the age of seventy-seven.

That second visit of William Penn to Pennsylvania proved, also, to be his last; and when, in 1701, he went on board the ship that was to carry him away from the province forever, he wrote these words to the man whom he had commissioned to stand there in his place: "I have left thee in an uncommon trust, with a singular dependence on thy justice and care, which I expect thou wilt faithfully employ in advancing my honest interest. . . . For thy own services I shall allow thee what is just and reasonable. . . . Serve me faithfully as thou expects a blessing from God, or my favor, and I shall support thee to my utmost, as thy true friend."[64] Thenceforward, James Logan's letters to his patron and to his patron's family, are the letters of a man who deserved such trust; for he served them with flawless fidelity.

His office proved to be a most laborious and vexatious one. Year by year his troubles as Penn's agent thickened. In 1704, he wrote to his master: "I wish thou could be here thyself, for I cannot bear up under all these hardships; they break my rest, and I doubt will sink

[63] His book was first published, in Philadelphia, in 1699; it was reprinted in London, in 1700; an illustrated edition in Dutch was published at Leyden, in 1710. So strong and clinging is the human interest inspired by this pathetic book, that even so late as 1803 it was reprinted in English, probably for the sixth time.

[64] Pa. Hist. Soc. Mem. IX. 59–61.

me at last. . . . I have been so true to thee, that I am not just to myself; and had I now a family, it would appear that there has scarce been a greater knave in America to another's affairs, than I have been to my own." [65]

But though James Logan was through all his life thus faithful to the proprietors of Pennsylvania, he was never unfaithful to the people of Pennsylvania. He held in succession the leading offices in the province; from 1736 to 1738, as president of the council, he was really governor; and while, at times, he drew upon himself great unpopularity, he served the people better than they knew, in all their highest interests, in peace and even in war.

His long life and his great influence went especially for the public enlightenment; and in all possible ways he helped to build up good literature in Pennsylvania. His own intellectual accomplishments were extraordinary. Almost from childhood he had been familiar with the principal languages, ancient and modern; at the age of sixteen he began that enthusiastic study of the higher mathematics which he prosecuted all his life; and there seemed to be no topic in science or literature that did not have his attention. He carried on an extensive correspondence with the most illustrious scholars in Europe and America; and in these letters as well as in the mass of private papers that he left behind him, he discussed, with originality and precision, the leading subjects that then engaged the minds of learned men. "Sometimes Hebrew or Arabic characters and algebraic formulas roughen the pages of his letter-books. Sometimes his letters convey a lively Greek ode to a learned friend; and often they are written in the Latin tongue." [66]

The larger part of his writings still remain unprinted; but during his lifetime were published, besides several Latin treatises by him upon scientific subjects, his "Translation of Cato's Distichs into English Verse," and his more celebrated translation of "M. T. Cicero's Cato Major; or, Discourse on Old Age,"—works that not only denoted his own elegant literary taste, but also tended to develop such

[65] Pa. Hist. Soc. Mem. IX. 325.
[66] J. F. Fisher, in Sparks's ed. of Works of Franklin, VII. 24–27, note. For my account of the unpublished writings of Logan, I depend chiefly on J. F. Fisher, as above; and on J. F. Watson, "Annals of Phila." I. 523–526.

Literature in the Middle Colonies

taste in others. His correspondence with the Penn family, from 1700 to 1750, has been recently made public;[67] and though much of it is taken up with uninteresting details respecting business and politics, it is also a great storehouse of information respecting men and manners in Pennsylvania during that period. Everywhere this correspondence reveals the carefulness and the intellectual breadth of James Logan; and occasionally one finds in it a passage of general discussion, in which the clear brain and the noble heart of the writer utter themselves in language of real beauty and force.[68]

IV

In 1751, the very year in which James Logan died, there came to America another man of the same Scottish stock, and of the same Scottish vigor for various intellectual work, who, in the middle colonies, and especially in Pennsylvania, was to carry forward, during the second half of the eighteenth century, many of the wholesome scientific and literary influences with which the life of James Logan had been identified, during the first half of that century. This man was William Smith, born at Aberdeen about 1726, and graduated at its university in 1747. In New York, where he spent the first two years after his arrival in America, he found the leading men greatly occupied with the project of founding a college there; and in the discussion of this subject he skilfully participated by publishing "A General Idea of the College of Mirania," a sort of educational romance, written in graceful style, and unfolding with much vigor the author's notions of what a college in America should be.

A copy of the book soon fell under the eye of Benjamin Franklin, who was, at that time, also deeply engaged in plans for a college at Philadelphia; and was even then looking about for some one competent to take charge of it. Not long afterward, the ambitious young Scotchman was invited to Philadelphia for that purpose. He immediately went to England for holy orders; and returning to Philadelphia in 1754, he entered upon his duties at the head of the institution which, in the following year, took the name of a college. From that time onward until his death in 1803, William Smith, as educator,

[67] Pa. Hist. Soc. Mem. IX–X.   [68] For example, ibid. IX. 226–229.

politician, clergyman, and man of letters, was a tireless, facile, and powerful representative in Philadelphia of the higher intellectual interests of society. Under his care the little college grew apace; and by his own example as an eloquent writer, by his enthusiasm for good literature, and by his quick and genial recognition of literary merit in the young men who were growing up around him, he did a great work for the literary development of his adopted country.[69]

V

We find in Pennsylvania, during the first sixty years of the eighteenth century, a succession of persons swayed somewhat by literary inclinations, and addicted, in a small and rather amateur way, to literary utterance, in prose or rhyme.

One of these persons was Jacob Taylor, who served the public in the various capacities of school-master, surveyor, doctor, almanac-maker, and poet. His verses usually appeared in his almanacs; and it is said [70] that, "in harmony and spirit," some of them "nearly approached to the poetry of standard authors." One of his poems is entitled "Pennsylvania;" another, "The Story of Whackum," being a satire on country quacks. He died in 1736.

A man of considerable sprightliness and social grace was Henry Brooke, younger son of Sir Henry Brooke of Cheshire, for some time collector of customs in Pennsylvania, and during many years a leading politician in the province. In 1704, James Logan, in a letter to William Penn, described him as "a young man of the most polite education and best natural parts . . . thrown away on this corner of the world." [71] His gift as a writer of smooth and spirited verse may be seen in a little poem of his addressed to Robert Gracie, and entitled "A Discourse of Jests." [72]

Many of these small writers would have found long since the repose in utter oblivion to which they have so valid a claim, had it not

---

[69] His most important writings in our present period were published in a volume entitled "Discourses on Public Occasions in America," 2d ed. London, 1762.

[70] By J. F. Fisher, "Early Poets and Poetry of Pa." 67.

[71] Pa. Hist. Soc. Mem. IX. 311.

[72] A fragment of it is in R. W. Griswold's "Poets and Poetry of Am." 22.

Literature in the Middle Colonies

been for such incidental mention as is made of them by Franklin, in his "Autobiography." Thus, he records that, on his first arrival in Philadelphia as a runaway apprentice, he sought employment in the printing-office of one Samuel Keimer, a long-bearded, semi-literary, very mystical, and altogether preposterous adventurer, whom he found engaged in putting into type an elegy composed by the printer himself, on one Aquila Rose, also a printer and poet, who had but recently died. The latter was of English birth and education; and after his death, at the age of twenty-eight, "many of his best pieces" were loaned by his widow to her friends, and in consequence were lost; but in 1741, such of his verses as could then be obtained were collected by his son, Joseph Rose, and published in a pamphlet, under the title of "Poems on Several Occasions."

James Ralph, probably born in America and near the beginning of the eighteenth century, was another of that group of witlings and poetasters whose names are strung like glass beads upon the thread of Franklin's story of his own early career in Philadelphia. At the time of Franklin's first appearance upon the scene, Ralph was a young fellow of fine appearance, glib tongue, poetic aspirations, and superficial accomplishments. In 1724, he resolved to give the British metropolis the benefit of his talents. Being then encumbered with a wife and a young child, but not with a conscience, he quietly abandoned the former, and with Franklin for a companion, went to London as a literary adventurer, where, with sharp alternations of poverty and prosperity, he remained the rest of his life, a prolific and notorious literary hack; emitting with incontinent speed political pamphlets, newspaper articles, odes, epics, plays, satires, and histories; achieving the ludicrous immortality of a niche in Pope's pantheon of dunces; [73] and honored long after his death by the strong applause of Charles James Fox.[74] From the moment of his first arrival in London, however, Ralph succeeded so perfectly in casting off all topics that were connected with his native country and in taking on all those themes and modes that were peculiar to a London Bohemian, that his remarkable career as a writer seems to have no significance in relation to American literature. We cordially surren-

[73] "The Dunciad," Book III. 164–165.
[74] See Allibone's "Dict. of Authors," II. 1731.

der him, therefore, to the exclusive possession of our English kinsmen.

On Franklin's return from the expedition that he had made to London in the company of James Ralph, he found in Keimer's printing-office, "in the situation of a bought servant," one George Webb, "an Oxford scholar," and a native of Gloucester, England, who, having run away from college and fallen into distress in London, had obtained passage to Philadelphia on condition of doing four years' service after his arrival there. "He was lively, witty, good-natured, and a pleasant companion, but idle, thoughtless, and imprudent to the last degree."[75] He had a smattering of knowledge and some cleverness at verse-making; and having made his way into respectable society, he appears to have attracted considerable local attention by the merry little poems that he dashed off frequently enough. One of these is a poem of about a hundred lines, published by Franklin in 1736, and entitled "Bachelors' Hall." The name of the poem was that of a famous club-house built in the fields in Kensington by a set of Philadelphia bachelors, and long held in ill repute as the supposed seat of gluttonous and lascivious revels.[76] Webb's poem was an effort to placate public opinion, on behalf of the offending edifice:

> "Say, goddess, tell me,—for to thee is known
> What is, what was, and what shall e'er be done,
> Why stands this dome erected on the plain?
> For pleasure was it built, or else for gain?
> For midnight revels was it ever thought?
> Shall impious doctrines ever here be taught?
> Or else for nobler purposes designed,
> To cheer and cultivate the mind,
> With mutual love each glowing breast inspire,
> Or cherish friendship's now degenerate fire?
>
> . . .
>
> Tired with the business of the noisy town,
> The weary bachelors their cares disown;
> For this loved seat they all at once prepare,
> And long to breathe the sweets of country-air.
>
> . . .

[75] "Life of Franklin," etc., ed. by John Bigelow, I. 171–173.
[76] J. F. Watson, "Annals of Phila." I. 432–433.

Literature in the Middle Colonies

'Tis not a revel or lascivious night
That to this hall the bachelors invite;
Much less shall impious doctrines here be taught,
Blush, ye accusers, at the very thought!
For other, oh, for other ends designed,
To mend the heart and cultivate the mind.
Mysterious nature here unveiled shall be,
And knotty points of deep philosophy.

. . .

But yet sometimes the all-inspiring bowl
To laughter shall provoke and cheer the soul;
The jocund tale to humor shall invite,
And dedicate to wit a jovial night:
Not the false wit the cheated world admires,
The mirth of sailors, nor of country squires;
Nor the gay punster's, whose quick sense affords
Naught but a miserable play on words;
Nor the grave quidnunc's, whose enquiring head
With musty scraps of journals must be fed;
But condescending, genuine, apt, and fit;
Good nature is the parent of true wit.

. . .

Then, music, too, shall cheer this fair abode—
Music, the sweetest of the gifts of God;
Music, the language of propitious love;
Music, that things inanimate can move.

Ye winds be hushed, let no presumptuous breeze
Now dare to whistle through the rustling trees;
Thou, Delaware, awhile forget to roar,
Nor dash thy foaming surge against the shore;
Be thy green nymphs upon thy surface found,
And let thy stagnant waves confess the sound;
Let thy attentive fishes all be nigh,—
For fishes were always friends to harmony;
Witness the dolphin which Arion bore,
And landed safely on his native shore.

Let doting cynics snarl; let noisy zeal
Tax this design with act or thought of ill;
Let narrow souls their rigid morals boast,

Till in the shadowy name the virtue's lost;
Let envy strive their character to blast,
And fools despise the sweets they cannot taste,—
This certain truth let the inquirer know:
It did from good and generous motives flow." [77]

At least one more of Franklin's early literary companions must be named by us,—Joseph Breintnal, "a copyer of deeds for the scriveners, a good-natured, friendly, middle-aged man, a great lover of poetry, reading all he could meet with, and writing some that was tolerable, very ingenious in many little knickknackeries, and of sensible conversation." [78] When Franklin undertook to write for a weekly newspaper, a series of didactic and satirical essays called "The Busy Body," he was assisted in the work by the friendly pen of Breintnal, who, in fact, continued the series for several months after Franklin had ceased to take an interest in it.[79]

In "Titan's Almanac" for 1730 is an anonymous poem in praise of Pennsylvania, which may interest us still, not only as a token of the ordinary poetic manner of that time and place, but especially for its reference to the literary preëminence then attained, or confidently expected, on the part of Philadelphia:

"Stretched on the bank of Delaware's rapid stream,
Stands Philadelphia, not unknown to fame.
Here the tall vessels safe at anchor ride,
And Europe's wealth flows in with every tide.

. . .

'Tis here Apollo does erect his throne;
This his Parnassus, this his Helicon.
Here solid sense does every bosom warm;
Here noise and nonsense have forgot to charm.
Thy seers how cautious, and how gravely wise!
Thy hopeful youth in emulation rise;

---

[77] I cite these lines from a reprint of the poem in Thompson Westcott's "History of Philadelphia," published in serial form in the "Sunday Despatch" of that city.

[78] "Life of Franklin," etc. ed. by John Bigelow, I. 183.

[79] They appeared in "The Weekly Gazette," beginning with February 4, 1729. It is supposed that Breintnal wrote nearly all after the eighth essay; possibly, also, the sixth and seventh.

Literature in the Middle Colonies

Who, if the wishing muse inspired does sing,
Shall liberal arts to such perfection bring,
Europe shall mourn her ancient fame declined,
And Philadelphia be the Athens of mankind." [80]

A daintier poetic skill was reached by a later poet of Philadelphia, Joseph Shippen, who wrote so well that in his case we experience the unwonted regret that he did not write more. His most famous poem is a love-song, "The Glooms of Ligonier," published in 1759, and popular for many years afterward.[81] He also wrote some graceful verses on seeing a portrait, painted by Benjamin West, of a beautiful young lady. In this poem, having first extolled the exquisite charm of the portrait itself, he is upon the point of charging the artist with an exaggeration of the beauty of the original:

"Yet, sure, his flattering pencil's unsincere;
  His fancy takes the place of bashful truth;
And warm imagination pictures here
  The pride of beauty and the bloom of youth.

Thus had I said, and thus, deluded, thought,
  Had lovely Stella still remained unseen,
Whose grace and beauty, to perfection brought,
  Make every imitative art look mean." [82]

About the year 1741, John Webbe published in Philadelphia the first of an intended series of tracts, on the financial questions that agitated the American colonies during many war-making and wasteful years. He entitled his essay, "A Discourse concerning Paper-money." The style is compact and clear; but the literary merit of the production is unimportant by comparison with the argumentative feat that the author professes to have accomplished in it, namely, the demonstration of "a method, plain and easy, for introducing and continuing a plenty" of paper-money, "without lessening the present value of it."

In 1755, Lewis Evans, a surveyor in Pennsylvania, in order to help the public to understand the bearings of the strife, then waxing

[80] I cite these lines from the poem as reprinted in "The Hist. Magazine," IV. 344.
[81] R. W. Griswold. "Poets and Poetry of America," 24.   [82] Ibid. 24.

hot, between the English and the French for possession of the American continent, published "A General Map of the Middle British Colonies in America;" and, at the same time, an "Analysis" [83] of the map, in the form of a descriptive and argumentative essay, written with fulness of knowledge, and rising, toward the end, to a statesmanly view of the whole problem then coming to a solution by the two races.

VI

Probably the most brilliant pulpit-orator produced in the colonial time, south of New England, was Samuel Davies, born in Newcastle County, Delaware, in 1723. His classical education was obtained chiefly at the famous school founded by Samuel Blair, at Fogg's Manor, in Chester County; and there, also, he pursued the study of theology. He began to preach in 1746; and in the following year, he visited Virginia, where his earnestness, his imaginative rhetoric, and his impassioned elocution won for him a sudden and extensive popularity. In 1748, he accepted an invitation to settle in that colony; and during the subsequent five years, what before was popularity deepened into fame and a most benign influence, and filled the whole country. In 1753, in the company of Gilbert Tennent, he went to England to solicit aid for the College of New Jersey. He remained there about eleven months, having great success in his mission, and winning for himself high reputation as an orator. On his return, he resumed his labors in Virginia. In 1759, he succeeded Jonathan Edwards as president of the College of New Jersey; and upon him there fell the fate of speedy death, which, for a time, seemed to be the inevitable portion of those who should accept that office. He died in 1761.

During his life, many of his sermons were published, and were widely diffused. One of them, preached in Virginia, in 1755, shortly after the defeat of General Braddock, is remarkable for its prophetic allusion to the destiny of George Washington: "I may point out to the public that heroic youth, Colonel Washington, whom I cannot but hope Providence has hitherto preserved in so signal a manner, for

[83] A second ed. was published in the same year.

Literature in the Middle Colonies

some important service to his country." [84] Not long after his death, a collection of his sermons was published in three large volumes; and these have been repeatedly printed since that time.[85]

A glance at any page of these discourses reveals the fact that the author of them was, above all other things, an orator. He prepared his sermons with the utmost care; for he "always thought it to be a most awful thing to go into the pulpit and there speak nonsense in the name of God." What he prepared, however, was meant for the ear rather than for the eye. He had all the physical qualifications for oratory—voice, gesture, temperament; and in appearance he was so commanding that "he looked like the ambassador of some great king." As uttered by himself, these discourses must have been vivid and thrilling orations; but they suffer from the revelations of type. The thought is often loose; the imagery is sometimes confused; the sentences are frequently swollen into verbosity.

As we read, however, some of his eloquent sentences,—for example, these from his sermon on "The General Resurrection,"—we may easily imagine ourselves in the presence of the orator himself, and borne away beyond criticism, on the tide of his heroic faith and his passionate declamation: "They shall come forth. Now methinks I see, I hear, the earth heaving, charnel-houses rattling, tombs bursting, graves opening. Now the nations under ground begin to stir. There is a noise and a shaking among the dry bones. The dust is all alive, and in motion, and the globe breaks and trembles, as with an earthquake, while this vast army is working its way through and bursting into life. The ruins of human bodies are scattered far and wide, and have passed through many and surprising transformations. A limb in one country, and another in another; here the head and there the trunk, and the ocean rolling between. Multitudes have sunk in a watery grave, been swallowed up by the monsters of the deep, and transformed into a part of their flesh. Multitudes have been eaten by beasts and birds of prey, and incorporated with them; and some have been devoured by their fellow-men in the rage of a desperate hunger, or of unnatural cannibal appetite, and digested into a part of them. Multitudes have mouldered into dust, and this

---

[84] "Sermons" of S. Davies, ed. by W. B. Sprague, III. 101, note.
[85] One ed. is by Albert Barnes, N. Y. 1841; another by W. B. Sprague, Phila. 1864.

dust has been blown about by winds, and washed away with water, or it has petrified into stone, or been burnt into brick to form dwellings for their posterity; or it has grown up in grain, trees, plants, and other vegetables, which are the support of man and beast, and are transformed into their flesh and blood. But through all these various transformations and changes, not a particle that was essential to one human body has been lost, or incorporated with another human body, so as to become an essential part of it. . . . The omniscient God knows how to collect, distinguish, and compound all those scattered and mingled seeds of our mortal bodies. And now, at the sound of the trumpet, they shall all be collected, wherever they were scattered; all properly sorted and united, however they were confused; atom to its fellow-atom, bone to its fellow-bone. Now methinks you may see the air darkened with fragments of bodies flying from country to country to meet and join their proper parts. . . . Then, my brethren, your dust and mine shall be reanimated and organized. . . . And what a vast improvement will the frail nature of man then receive? Our bodies will then be substantially the same; but how different in qualities, in strength, in agility, in capacities for pleasure or pain, in beauty or deformity, in glory or terror, according to the moral character of the person to whom they belong! . . . The bodies of the saints will be formed glorious, incorruptible, without the seeds of sickness and death. . . . Then will the body be able to bear up under the exceeding great and eternal weight of glory; it will no longer be a clog or an incumbrance to the soul, but a proper instrument and assistant in all the exalted services and enjoyments of the heavenly state. The bodies of the wicked will also be improved, but their improvements will all be terrible and vindictive. Their capacities will be thoroughly enlarged, but then it will be that they may be made capable of greater misery; they will be strengthened, but it will be that they may bear the heavier load of torment. Their sensations will be more quick and strong, but it will be that they may feel the more exquisite pain. They will be raised immortal that they may not be consumed by everlasting fire, or escape punishment by dissolution or annihilation. In short, their augmented strength, their enlarged capacities, and their immortality, will be their eternal curse; and they would willingly exchange them for the fleeting duration of a fading flower, or the faint sensations of an infant. The only power they would rejoice in is that of self-annihilation." [86]

VII

Upon the fascinating pages of Franklin's "Autobiography," one meets several times the name of an ingenious and philosophical glazier of Philadelphia, named Thomas Godfrey. It was this glazier and his family, who, upon Franklin's return to Philadelphia after his first pilgrimage to London, shared with the economical young printer the space and the expense of his hired house "near the market;" it was the wife of this glazier, who, with much feminine diplomacy, tried to make a match between Franklin and one of her own relations, and was so offended at Franklin's intractableness in the affair, that she and her family removed from his house; again, it was the glazier himself who, in 1744, was enrolled as "a mathematician" among the nine original members of the American Philosophical Society.[87]

Among the children of this astute and worthy man, was a son, likewise named Thomas, who left such proofs of poetic genius, that his name will always have a prominent place in the story of our colonial literature. The expression of his genius, however, was inadequate; for he had the three misfortunes—stinted education, poverty, an early death. He was born at Philadelphia, in 1736. Being left an orphan at the age of thirteen, he was soon taken from school and apprenticed to a watch-maker—a trade that he did not like. His heart was in music, and especially in poetry; and to these he gave whatever time he could purloin from the business that was to him a servitude. In 1758, having reached his majority, he became a lieutenant in the Pennsylvania militia and served through the campaign that resulted that year in the capture by the English of Fort Duquesne. In 1759, he went to North Carolina, and remained there under engagement as a factor for three years. At the end of that time, being still un-

[86] "Sermons" of S. Davies, ed. by H. B. Sprague,* I. 498–502.
[87] "Life of Franklin," etc. ed. by John Bigelow, I. 181, 204, 276.

[* "H. B. Sprague" was corrected to "W. B. Sprague."]

473

settled, he made journeys to Philadelphia and to New Providence; then returned to North Carolina; and there, on the third of August, 1763, he suddenly died. Two years after his death, his writings, collected and edited by another young poet, Nathaniel Evans, were published at Philadelphia under this title: "Juvenile Poems on Various Subjects; with the Prince of Parthia, a Tragedy."

The poems called "juvenile," doubtless deserve that term. They have no original manner or matter; they are merely tentative and preparatory; those of them that failed to receive correction from his scholarly friends, reveal, in their imperfect metre, false accent, and false syntax, his own lack of scholarship. The topics are the usual ones in the case of poetic fledglings: "A Cure for Love;" "Ode on Friendship;" "A Dithyrambic on Wine." There are also some pastorals, and as many as seven or eight love-songs; and besides these, an ambitious and not discreditable poem in pentameter couplets, entitled "The Court of Fancy," obviously suggested by Chaucer and Pope.

These alone would not have gained for Thomas Godfrey any remembrance. There is in the volume, however, a tragedy—the first drama, probably, ever produced in this country—that has very considerable merit, and assures us of the presence in him of a constructive genius in poetry from which, very likely, great things would have come, had the stars befriended him.

This poem is in blank verse. It is an oriental story of love and lust, of despotism, ambition, and jealousy. A certain king of Parthia, Artabanus, has three sons. The eldest, Arsaces, is a military hero and an idol of the populace; he is also the object of consuming envy on the part of the second son, Vardanes, and of loyal affection on the part of the third son, Gotarzes. The first scene is in the temple of the sun, and represents the joy of this youngest son,* over a great victory recently gained by the Prince Arsaces in a battle with the Arabians. The second scene represents the envious brother, Vardanes, and his friend Lysias, as talking together of the rage they both felt at the success of Arsaces and at his enormous popularity.

[* A penciled correction in Tyler's copy makes this "brother," apparently because "sun" appears in the preceding line, but the change was not made in subsequent printings.]

Literature in the Middle Colonies

In the course of this conversation, it appears that Vardanes is in love with a beautiful Arabian captive, named Evanthe, who, however, is betrothed to Arsaces. The third scene introduces the queen, Thermusa, who reveals to an attendant her hatred of Arsaces and her desire for his destruction; likewise, her wrath at the beautiful captive, Evanthe, with whom the king himself has fallen in love. In the fourth scene, Evanthe herself appears, and talks with her maid, Cleone, of the popular enthusiasm for her beloved Arsaces, and of her own eagerness for his return:

> "How tedious are the hours which bring him
> To my fond, panting heart! For oh, to those
> Who live in expectation of the bliss,
> Time slowly creeps, and every tardy minute
> Seems mocking of their wishes. Say, Cleone,—
> For you beheld the triumph,—midst his pomp,
> Did he not seem to curse the empty show,
> The pageant greatness—enemy to love—
> Which held him from Evanthe? Haste to tell me,
> And feed my greedy ear with the fond tale."

In this conversation, while waiting for her lover, Evanthe tells the story of her early life and of her captivity. Her father, a high officer at court, and a great general,

> "was reputed,
> Brave, wise, and loyal; by his prince beloved.
> Oft has he led his conquering troops, and forced
> From frowning Victory her awful honors."

One day, while

> "bathing in Niphate's silver stream,
> Attended only by one favorite maid,
> As we were sporting on the wanton waves,
> Swift from the wood a troop of horsemen rushed;
> Rudely they seized and bore me trembling off.
> In vain Edessa with her shrieks assailed
> The heavens; for heaven was deaf to both our prayers."

Her captor, a cruel and lustful wretch, was afterward killed in battle by Arsaces, and thus Evanthe fell into his gallant keeping. In this scene, hearing that other Arabian captives had been brought in from the recent battle, she desires to get news of her father. The fifth scene presents the king in state, surrounded by his princes and officers, and in the act of reproaching a brave Arabian captive, named Bethas, who is before him in chains. To the king's hard words, Bethas answers:

> "True I am fallen, but glorious was my fall;
> The day was bravely fought; we did our best;
> But victory's of heaven. Look o'er yon field.
> See if thou findest one Arabian back
> Disfigured with dishonorable wounds!
> No, here, deep on their bosoms, are engraved
> The marks of honor! 'Twas through here their souls
> Flew to their blissful seats. Oh! why did I
> Survive the fatal day? To be this slave—
> To be the gaze and sport of vulgar crowds;
> Thus, like a shackled tiger, stalk my round,
> And grimly lower upon the shouting herd.
> Ye Gods!—

KING.

> Away with him to instant death.

ARSACES.

> Hear me, my lord. Oh, not on this bright day—
> Let not this day of joy blush with his blood;
> Nor count his steady loyalty a crime;
> But give him life. Arsaces humbly asks it,
> And may you e'er be served with honest hearts." [88]

The king grants the request of his eldest son, and Bethas is sent to prison. Thus closes the first Act. The second Act opens with a scene wherein the malignant brother, Vardanes, is contriving with Lysias a plot to destroy Arsaces. Their plan is to induce the king to believe that Arsaces is intending to slay him and to win the throne, and that the intercession of the prince on behalf of Bethas was for the purpose of securing the help of that great soldier. The talk of

[88] "Juvenile Poems," etc. 120–121.

the two conspirators is by night, and in the gloomy prison, of which
Lysias has charge; and it proceeds in the midst of a fearful storm:

> "VARDANES.
> Heavens! what a night is this!
>
> LYSIAS.
> 'Tis filled with terror;
> Some dread event beneath this horror lurks,
> Ordained by fate's irrevocable doom,—
> Perhaps Arsaces' fall; and angry heaven
> Speaks it in thunder to the trembling world.
>
> VARDANES.
> Terror indeed! It seems as sickening Nature
> Had given her order up to general ruin:
> The heavens appear as one continued flame;
> Earth with her terror shakes; dim night retires,
> And the red lightning gives a dreadful day,
> While in the thunder's voice each sound is lost.
> Fear sinks the panting heart in every bosom;
> E'en the pale dead, affrighted at the horror,
> As though unsafe, start from their marble jails,
> And howling through the streets are seeking shelter.
> . . .
>
> LYSIAS.
> I saw a flash stream through the angry clouds,
> And bend its course to where a stately pine
> Behind the garden stood; quickly it seized
> And wrapped it in a fiery fold; the trunk
> Was shivered into atoms, and the branches
> Off were lopped, and wildly scattered.
>
> VARDANES.
> Why rage the elements? They are not cursed
> Like me! Evanthe frowns not angry on them;
> The wind may play upon her beauteous bosom,
> Nor fear her chiding; light can bless her sense,

And in the floating mirror she beholds
Those beauties which can fetter all mankind.

. . .

LYSIAS.

My lord, forget her; tear her from your breast.
Who, like the Phœnix, gazes on the sun,
And strives to soar up to the glorious blaze,
Should never leave ambition's brightest object,
To turn, and view the beauties of a flower.

VARDANES.

O Lysias, chide no more, for I have done.
Yes, I'll forget the proud disdainful beauty;
Hence with vain love:—ambition, now, alone,
Shall guide my actions. Since mankind delights
To give me pain, I'll study mischief too,
And shake the earth, e'en like this raging tempest.

LYSIAS.

A night like this, so dreadful to behold,—
Since my remembrance' birth, I never saw.

VARDANES.

E'en such a night, dreadful as this, they say,
My teeming mother gave me to the world.
Whence by those sages who, in knowledge rich,
Can pry into futurity, and tell
What distant ages will produce of wonder,
My days were deemed to be a hurricane.

. . .

LYSIAS.

Then, haste to raise the tempest.
My soul disdains this one eternal round,
Where each succeeding day is like the former.
Trust me, my noble prince, here is a heart
Steady and firm to all your purposes;
And here's a hand that knows to execute
Whate'er designs thy daring breast can form,
Nor ever shake with fear."

Literature in the Middle Colonies

It is on this conspiracy, hatched by night and amid the storm, that the plot turns. From that point, the action moves on swiftly; the entanglements and cross-purposes and astute villanies are well presented; Bethas proves to be the father of Evanthe; the conspirators nearly succeed; they murder the king and are about to murder Arsaces and Bethas, and they have Evanthe in their power, when suddenly, the youngest brother arrives with a great army. A battle is fought in the streets of the city. Evanthe sends Cleone to a tower to see how the contest is going, and especially, to ascertain the fate of Arsaces. Cleone sees a hero slain, whom she mistakes for Arsaces, and rushes down with the dreadful news. Upon this, Evanthe takes poison; Arsaces, who has won the battle, rushes in, and the beautiful maiden dies in his arms. At once he kills himself; and the kingdom passes to the loyal and loving brother, Gotarzes.

The whole drama is powerful in diction and in action. Of course, there are blemishes in it,—faults of inexperience and of imperfect culture: but it has many noble poetic passages; the characters are firmly and consistently developed; there are scenes of pathos and tragic vividness; the plot advances with rapid movement and with culminating force. Thomas Godfrey was a true poet; and "The Prince of Parthia" is a noble beginning of dramatic literature in America.

VIII

On the tenth of May, 1762, David Hume writing from Edinburgh to Benjamin Franklin in London, used these words: "I am very sorry that you intend soon to leave our hemisphere. America has sent us many good things,—gold, silver, sugar, tobacco, indigo, and so forth; but you are the first philosopher, and indeed the first great man of letters, for whom we are beholden to her." [89] Even eight years before that time, an eminent French scholar, in sending to Franklin, at Philadelphia, the greetings of Buffon, Fonferrière, Marty, and the other great savans of Paris, had added this testimony,—"Your name is venerated in this country." [90]

Thus, before the close of its colonial epoch, America had produced

[89] Works of Franklin, VI. 244.   [90] Ibid. 194.

one man of science and of letters who had reached cosmopolitan fame. Yet, within the period here treated of, the renown of Franklin was that of a great scientific experimenter, rather than of a great writer. He had, indeed, very early in life acquired that mastery of style—that pure, pithy, racy, and delightful diction—which he never lost, and which makes him still one of the great exemplars of modern English prose. He had, likewise, before 1765, written many of his best productions;—essays on politics, commerce, education, science, religion, and the conduct of life; multitudes of wise and witty scraps of literature for his newspaper, his almanacs, and his friends; anecdotes, apologues, maxims; above all, many of those incomparable letters for his private correspondents, to the reading of which, since then, the whole world has been admitted, greatly to its advantage in wisdom and in happiness. Nevertheless, all his writings had been composed for some immediate purpose, and if printed at all, had been first printed separately, and as a general thing without the author's name. In 1751, however, a partial collection of his writings was published in London without his knowledge,—the book consisting of the papers on electricity sent by him to his friend, Peter Collinson. But these papers, valuable and even celebrated as they were as contributions to science, could give to the public no idea of the various and the marvellous powers of Franklin as a contributor to literature.

At the close of our colonial epoch, Benjamin Franklin, then fifty-nine years of age, was the most illustrious of Americans, and one of the most illustrious of men; and his renown rested on permanent and benign achievements of the intellect. He was, at that time, on the verge of old age; his splendid career as a scientific discoverer and as a citizen seemed rounding to its full; yet there then lay outstretched before him—though he knew it not—still another career of just twenty-five years; in which his political services to his country and to mankind were to bring him more glory than he had gained from all he had done before; and in which he was to write one book—the story of his own life—that is still the most famous production in American literature, that has an imperishable charm for all classes of mankind, that has passed into nearly all the literary languages of the globe, and

Literature in the Middle Colonies

that is "one of the half-dozen most widely popular books ever printed." [91] It will be most profitable for us to defer our minute study of the literary character of this great writer, until, in a subsequent volume of this work, we can view his literary career as a whole.

[91] John Bigelow, in "Life of Franklin," etc. I. 26.

Chapter XVII

Literature in Maryland, Virginia, and the South

1. MARYLAND

I. Ebenezer Cook, Gentleman—A rough satirist—His "Sot-Weed Factor"—Outline of the poem—Lively sketches of early Maryland life—Hospitality—Manners—Indians—A court-scene—Encounter with a Quaker and a lawyer—Swindled by both—His curse upon Maryland—His "Sot-Weed Redivivus."

2. VIRGINIA

I. James Blair, the true founder of literary culture in Virginia—His coming to Virginia—Forcible qualities of the man—His zeal for education—Founds the College of William and Mary—First president of it—The Commencement celebration in 1700—His writings—"The Present State of Virginia and the College"—His published discourses on the Sermon on the Mount—His literary qualities—Passages from his sermons.

II. Robert Beverley—Parentage—Education in England—His study of the history of Virginia—How he came to write it—The blunders of Oldmixon—Reception of Beverley's book—The author himself seen in it—A noble Virginian—A friend of the Indians—His love of nature—His style—Humor—Hatred of indolence—Virginia hospitality and comfort—Calumnies upon its climate.

III. Hugh Jones, clergyman, teacher, and school-book maker—His "Present State of Virginia"—Objects of the book—Its range—Its sarcasms upon the other colonies—Its criticisms upon Virginia—Suggestions for improvement.

...wis, C.S. - <u>Of Other Worlds</u>
823.912
L585.

...oorman, Charles
<u>Arthurian Triptych</u>
828
~~A~~ Ar 7 Z M

~~...alan, Jane~~
~~C.S. Lewis in Narnia~~

...illy, Robert J.
<u>Romantic Religion</u>
<u>in the Work of Owen</u>
<u>Barfield, C.S. Lewis,</u>
<u>Charles Williams,</u>
<u>and J.R.R. Tolkien</u>
820.912
R273.

Literature in the South

IV. William Byrd of Westover—His princely fortune and ways—His culture—Foreign travel—Public spirit—His writings—"History of the Dividing Line"—The humor and literary grace of the book—Amusing sketch of early history of Virginia—The Christian duty of marrying Indian women—Sarcasms upon North Carolina—Notices of plants, animals, and forest-life—The praise of ginseng—His "Progress to the Mines"—His "Journey to the Land of Eden."

V. William Stith—Various utilities of his life—His "History of Virginia"—Defects of the work—Its good qualities—Bitter description of James the First.

3. NORTH CAROLINA

I. John Lawson—His picture of Charleston in 1700—His journey to North Carolina—What he saw and heard by the way—Becomes surveyor-general of North Carolina—His descriptions of that province—Its coast—Sir Walter Raleigh's ship—A land of Arcadian delight—The playful alligator—A study of Indians—Amiability and beauty of their women—An ancient squaw—A conjuror—Indian self-possession—The author's fate—His "History of North Carolina."

4. SOUTH CAROLINA

I. Alexander Garden, rector of St. Philip's, Charleston—The force of his character—Greatness of his influence—His abhorrence of Whitefield—His sermons and letters against Whitefield—Their bitterness and their literary merit.

5. GEORGIA

I. Georgia's entrance into our literature—A conflict with Oglethorpe—The expert and witty book of Patrick Tailfer and others—"A True and Historical Narrative of the Colony of Georgia"—Outline of it—A masterly specimen of satire—Its mock dedication to Oglethorpe.

1. MARYLAND

I

A VEIN of genuine and powerful satire was struck in Maryland in the early part of the eighteenth century by a writer calling himself "Ebenezer Cook, Gentleman." Who he was, what he was, whence he came, whither he went,—are facts that now baffle us. His book is an obvious extravaganza; and the autobiographic narrative involved in the plot, is probably only a part of its robust and jocular mirth. It is entitled, "The Sot-Weed Factor; or, A Voyage to Maryland,—a satire, in which is described the laws, government, courts, and constitutions of the country, and also the buildings, feasts, frolics, entertainments, and drunken humors of the inhabitants in that part of America."

The author pretends to be an Englishman, under doom of emigrating to America:

> "Condemned by fate to wayward curse
> Of friends unkind and empty purse,—
> Plagues worse than filled Pandora's box,—
> I took my leave of Albion's rocks;
> With heavy heart concerned, that I
> Was forced my native soil to fly,
> And the old world must bid good-bye.
> . . .
> Freighted with fools, from Plymouth sound
> To Maryland our ship was bound." [1]

After a three months' voyage, they arrived in Maryland. Intending "to open store," he brought on shore his goods, and at once the "sot-weed factors," or tobacco agents, swarmed around him:

> "In shirts and drawers of Scotch cloth blue,
> With neither stockings, hat, nor shoe,
> These sot-weed planters crowd the shore,
> In hue as tawny as a Moor.
> Figures so strange, no god designed
> To be a part of human kind;
> But wanton nature, void of rest,
> Moulded the brittle clay in jest." [2]

He wonders who and what they are:

> "At last a fancy very odd
> Took me, this was the land of Nod;
> Planted at first when vagrant Cain
> His brother had unjustly slain;

[1] "The Sot-Weed Factor," 1.   [2] Ibid. 2.

Literature in the South

> Then conscious of the crime he'd done,
> From vengeance dire he hither run;
> . . .
> And ever since his time, the place
> Has harbored a detested race,
> Who when they could not live at home
> For refuge to these worlds did roam;
> In hopes by flight they might prevent
> The devil and his full intent,
> Obtain from triple-tree reprieve,
> And heaven and hell alike deceive." [3]

He thinks it best to give an account of his entertainment,

> "That strangers well may be aware on
> What homely diet they must fare on,
> To touch that shore where no good sense is found,
> But conversation's lost and manner's drowned." [4]

He crosses the river in a canoe; after some trouble, he finds in a cottage lodging and rough but cordial hospitality. This leads him to describe his host, the furniture, the customs of the house, and his own futile attempts at sleeping that night—pestered by mosquitoes and so forth. After breakfast, he is kindly sent on his journey, and goes to a place called Battletown. On his way he meets an Indian:

> "No mortal creature can express
> His wild fantastic air and dress.
> . . .
> His manly shoulders, such as please
> Widows and wives, were bathed in grease
> Of cub and bear." [5]

He proceeds on his journey, discussing with his companion the origin of Indians; and at last he reaches a place where court is in session, and a great crowd of strange people are assembled:

> "Our horses to a tree we tied,
> And forward passed among the rout
> To choose convenient quarters out;
> But being none were to be found,

[3] "The Sot-Weed Factor," 2.   [4] Ibid. 2–3.   [5] Ibid. 8.

History of American Literature

> We sat like others on the ground,
> Carousing punch in open air,
> Till crier did the court declare.
> The planting rabble being met,
> Their drunken worships being likewise set,
> Crier proclaims that noise should cease,
> And straight the lawyers broke the peace.
> Wrangling for plaintiff and defendant,
> I thought they ne'er would make an end on't,
> With nonsense, stuff, and false quotations,
> With brazen lies and allegations;
> And in the splitting of the cause,
> They used such motions with their paws,
> As showed their zeal was strongly bent
> In blows to end the argument." [6]

A mêlée ensues, in which judges, jury, clients and all take a hand; and thus the court breaks up for that session:

> "The court adjourned in usual manner,
> With battle, blood, and fractious clamor." [7]

The poet then describes the scenes of riot, debauchery, fighting, and robbery that filled the next night; tells how he lost his shoes, his stockings, his hat, and wig, how his friend was also stripped, and how after getting supplied anew, he and his friend rode away in disgust to the home of the latter:

> "There with good punch and apple-juice
> We spent our hours without abuse,
> Till midnight in her sable vest
> Persuaded gods and men to rest." [8]

After various other experiences, he thinks it time to sell his wares:

> "To this intent, with guide before,
> I tripped it to the Eastern Shore.
> While riding near a sandy bay,
> I met a Quaker, yea and nay;
> A pious, conscientious rogue,
> As e'er wore bonnet or a brogue;

---

[6] "The Sot-Weed Factor," 12.   [7] Ibid. 13.   [8] Ibid. 15.

Literature in the South

> Who neither swore nor kept his word,
> But cheated in the fear of God;
> And when his debts he would not pay,
> By Light Within he ran away." [9]

By this drab scoundrel the poet is basely swindled; and in his rage he goes to a lawyer, who was also a doctor,

> "an ambidexter quack
> Who learnedly had got the knack
> Of giving glisters, making pills,
> Of filling bonds, and forging wills,
> And with a stock of impudence,
> Supplied his want of wit and sense;
> With looks demure amazing people;
> No wiser than a daw in steeple."

To this versatile gentleman the poet offers a great fee:

> "And of my money was so lavish,
> That he'd have poisoned half the parish,
> And hanged his father on a tree,
> For such another tempting fee." [10]

In the litigation which followed, the author is cheated by his lawyer even worse than he had been by the Quaker; and at last, mad with rage, he hurries away from the country, leaving this curse upon it as his legacy:

> "May cannibals, transported over sea,
>   Prey on these shores as they have done on me;
> May never merchant's trading sails explore
>   This cruel, this inhospitable shore;
> But left abandoned by the world to starve,
> May they sustain the fate they well deserve.
> May they turn savage; or, as Indians wild,
> From trade, converse, and happiness exiled,
> Recreant to heaven, may they adore the sun,
> And into pagan superstitions run,
> For vengeance ripe;
> May wrath divine then lay these regions waste,
> Where no man's faithful, and no woman's chaste." [11]

[9] "The Sot-Weed Factor," 18.   [10] Ibid. 19.   [11] Ibid. 20-21.

This work was published in London, a quarto of twenty-one pages, in 1708.[12] Twenty-two years afterward, a writer, professing to be the same rough satirist, published at Annapolis another poem, entitled "Sot-Weed Redivivus; or, The Planter's Looking-Glass, in burlesque verse, calculated for the meridian of Maryland,"—a quarto of twenty-eight pages. The first poem has, indeed, an abundance of filth and scurrility, but it has wit besides; the second poem lacks only the wit.

2. VIRGINIA

I

Probably no other man in the colonial time did so much for the intellectual life of Virginia, as did the sturdy and faithful clergyman, James Blair, who came into the colony in 1685, and who died there in 1743, having been a missionary of the Church of England fifty-eight years, the commissary of the Bishop of London fifty-four years, the president of the College of William and Mary fifty years, and a member of the king's council fifty years.

Born in Scotland in 1656, and graduated at the University of Edinburgh in 1673, he was rector of Cranston until the year 1682, when he went into England in the hope of finding preferment there; but was induced by the Bishop of London to give up his life to the service of God and of man in Virginia.

On his arrival there, he was pained not only at the disorderly and ineffective condition of the church, but at the almost universal neglect of education. Henceforward, the story of his life is a story of pure and tireless labors for the rectification of both these evils. He was a man of great simplicity and force of character, very positive, very persistent, with an abundance of Scottish shrewdness as well as of Scottish enthusiasm, actuated by a lofty, apostolic determination to be useful to his fellow-creatures—whether, at the moment, they liked it or not. "He could not rest until school-teachers were in the land;"[13] and he did not rest until there was a college in the land, also.

---

[12] Reprinted in 1866 in "Shea's Early Southern Tracts," edited by Brantz Mayer, who says that the poem was reprinted at Annapolis in 1731, with an additional poem on Bacon's Rebellion.

[13] Edward D. Neill, "Notes on the Va. Colonial Clergy," 23.

For the latter, he toiled mightily, and with invincible hopefulness. First, he induced the Virginians themselves to put their names to subscriptions for a college, to the amount of twenty-five hundred pounds sterling. Next, having secured for the plan of a college the approbation of the colonial assembly, he crossed the ocean, and against all official resistance gained for it the approbation of the monarchs of England also,—in whose honor the little college was named William and Mary. Then, returning to Virginia in 1693, with a royal charter for the college and a royal endowment, the indefatigable man laid its foundations, and he served it with dauntless fidelity the next fifty years. In the year 1700, the Commencement was celebrated there with much éclat: "There was a great concourse of people. Several planters came thither in coaches, and others in sloops from New York, Pennsylvania, and Maryland,—it being a new thing in that part of America to hear graduates perform their exercises. The Indians themselves had the curiosity, some of them, to visit Williamsburg upon that occasion; and the whole country rejoiced as if they had some relish of learning." [14]

Thus, James Blair may be called the creator of the healthiest and the most extensive intellectual influence that was felt in the southern group of colonies before the Revolution. Moreover, his direct contributions to American literature were by no means despicable. He was, probably, the principal writer of a book upon the title-page of which the names of Henry Hartwell and Edward Chilton are joined with his own, and which was published in London in 1727: "The Present State of Virginia and the College." It is expertly written; is neat and vigorous in style; abounds in facts respecting the condition of civilization in the colony at that time; and is not lacking in the courage of plain speech: "As to all the natural advantages of a country," Virginia "is one of the best, but as to the improved ones, one of the worst, of all the English plantations in America. When one considers the wholesomeness of its air, the fertility of its soil, the commodiousness of its navigable rivers and creeks, the openness of its coast all the year long, the conveniency of its fresh-water runs and springs, the plenty of its fish, fowl, and wild beasts, the variety of its simples and dyeing-woods, the abundance of its timbers, minerals,

[14] C. Campbell, "Hist. Va." 361–362.

wild vines, and fruits, the temperature of its climate; . . . in short, if it be looked upon in all respects as it came out of the hand of God, it is certainly one of the best countries in the world. But, on the other hand, if we enquire for well-built towns, for convenient ports and markets, for plenty of ships and seamen, for well-improved trades and manufactures, for well-educated children, for an industrious and thriving people, or for an happy government in church and state, and in short for all the other advantages in human improvements, it is certainly, for all these things, one of the poorest, miserablest, and worst countries in all America, that is inhabited by Christians." [15]

But James Blair's chief claim to remembrance in our literary history is based upon a series of one hundred and seventeen discourses on "Our Saviour's Divine Sermon on the Mount," which were twice published in London during the author's lifetime, and which received public applause from the great English theologian, Daniel Waterland.[16] In these discourses the range of topics is as wide as that of the wonderful discourse upon which they are founded. The thought is fully wrought out; the divisions are sharp and formal; each discourse is short and to the point. The tone of the author's mind is moderate, judicial, charitable, catholic; he is not brilliant; his style is smooth, simple, honest, earnest; there is no display; he is trying to make people good. The drift of his argument is steadily toward practical results. "An error in morals," he says, "is more dangerous than a mere speculative error. . . . It is only the practical errors, the transgressions of morality, which our Saviour degrades into the lowest rank. . . . Speculative errors, which have no influence on the life and conversation, cannot be near so dangerous as those errors which lead men out of the way of their duty. As in a voyage at sea, the master and seamen and passengers may chance to see several objects, and very friendly and innocently may differ in their opinions about the names, and natures, and colors, and shapes, and properties of them; and yet none of all these opinions, the most true or the most erroneous, either furthers or hinders their voyage. But if they

[15] "The Present State," etc. 1–2.

[16] First published in London in 1722 in five vols.; republished there in 1740 in four vols., with a preface by Dr. Waterland. The work is extremely rare in this country. I have used the incomplete copy of the second ed. in the State Library at Albany.

should be in an error in using a bad compass, or in not knowing the tides and currents, the rocks and shelves; if they should run rashly on the shore in the night-time, by not keeping a right reckoning, thinking themselves far enough from land;—these are errors of fatal consequence, such as may endanger the ship and voyage. Just so it is in errors of opinion." [17]

While he insists upon the highest excellence in outward conduct, he shows that all moral significance attaches to the inward state of a man: "It is the great secret of Christian morals, which our Saviour drives at in all duties whatsoever, and is the principal thing which distinguishes the righteousness of a good Christian, from the righteousness of the Scribes and Pharisees." [18] "Particularly, has Christ interpreted the law in a more spiritual sense, killing vice in the seed, and strictly forbidding the feeding the very thoughts and imaginations with it. Then, let us employ a great part of our care in the good government of our heart and thoughts, that when wicked fancies or imaginations start up in our minds, or are thrown in by the Devil, we may take care not to harbor them, but to throw them quickly out, before they sprout out into bad resolutions and designs, or ripen into wicked actions and evil habits." [19]

II

Virginia had been in existence a hundred years before it produced an historian of its own. This was Robert Beverley, of an ancient family in England, himself born in Virginia. His father, likewise Robert Beverley, a man of considerable fortune at Beverley in Yorkshire, had removed to the colony in time to become a prominent politician in 1676, acting resolutely, amid the tumults of that year, on the side of Sir William Berkeley against Nathaniel Bacon. The younger Beverley was sent to England for his education; and early in life seems to have been employed by his father and an elder brother as assistant in charge of the colonial records. This circumstance turned his thoughts toward the study of his country's history.[20] Happening to be in London in 1703, his bookseller told him of a new

[17] Discourses, II. 48–49.
[18] Ibid. III. 67.
[19] Ibid. II. 24–25.
[20] Pref. to "Hist. Va." xvii.

work just then in press,—Oldmixon's "British Empire in America," —and gave him for inspection, the sheets relating to Virginia and Carolina. These sheets the young Virginian began to read, with his pen in hand for the purpose of jotting down any corrections that might be necessary; but he soon gave up that task in despair,—the new book being quite beyond the reach of correction. Prompted by this experience, and having with him his own memoranda of studies upon the subject, Beverley at once undertook to write a history of his native colony. This was first published in London, in 1705; was published in a French translation, both at Paris and at Amsterdam, in 1707; and was brought out in London in a second English edition, much enlarged and improved, in 1722.[21]

The traits of the man confront us on every page of this book. He had large wealth in lands, in houses, and in slaves, high social position, intense affection for Virginia, a sturdy pride in it; and he was as independent in mind as he was in circumstances. The robust virtues—simplicity, thrift, industry, enterprise, economy—had not died out of him in the soft air of Virginia. He lived upon his great estate with Spartan plainness; [22] and in his book he never misses the opportunity of rasping his countrymen for their luxury, their supineness, and the indolent use they were making of the overflowing bounties of nature. He gives first the history of the colony, then an account of the country itself, then a description of the Indians, finally a picture of the political and industrial condition of the colony in his own time. He writes not like a book-man or a theorist, but like a country-gentleman and a man of affairs. He speaks out plainly what he thinks; he has respect to limits, never loses himself in pedantries or long stories; he interprets all things, past and present, with shrewd, practical sense. In his style there is no flavor of classical study, or even of modern letters; yet it has the promptness, lucidity, and raciness of real talk among educated men of the world. It continues to be interesting. In some places, his history degenerates into a partisan pamphlet; for he inherited his father's hate of the Virginia governors,—Lord Culpepper and the Earl of Effingham,—having

[21] Reprinted in 1855 at Richmond, with introduction by Charles Campbell.
[22] Descriptions of his home in 1715 may be read in James Fontaine's "Memoirs of a Huguenot Family," 265.

Literature in the South

also a plenty of hate on his own account for Francis Nicholson. He is not heedless of accuracy; yet he has not a few errors. He knew the Indians well: in fact, in his first edition he identified himself with them by playfully calling himself an Indian; and the portion of his book devoted to them is written with love of the subject and full mastery of it. All his notices of natural objects also, are sharp and full. His eye was quick to see the characteristics of all sorts of dumb creatures, in the midst of whose haunts he passed his manly life; as may be illustrated in his graphic and amusing stories of the snake in the act of charming and swallowing a hare,[23] and of the fish-hawk pursued by a bald eagle.[24]

The whole work is fresh, original; not weighed down by documents; the living testimony of a proud and generous Virginian. Without apparent effort, he often hits upon strong and happy phrases, as when he speaks of "the almighty power of gold"—anticipating the more famous expression of Washington Irving. There is a tonic enjoyment in his under-flavor of humor and in his crisp sarcasms. He expresses a sort of contemptuous surprise at the "prodigious phantasms" with respect to Virginia, which he found cherished among the English; as, "that the servants in Virginia are made to draw in cart, and plough as horses and oxen do in England, and that the country turns all people black who go to live there." [25] As to his own country, he has a smile of quiet ridicule for its military development: "The militia are the only standing forces in Virginia. They are happy in the enjoyment of an everlasting peace, which their poverty and want of towns secure to them." [26] But if their military power was small, their hospitality certainly was not small; and he speaks of it with satisfaction: "The inhabitants are very courteous to travellers, who need no other recommendation but the being human creatures. A stranger has no more to do but to inquire upon the road where any gentleman or good housekeeper lives; and there he may depend upon being received with hospitality. This good nature is so general among their people, that the gentry when they go abroad order their principal servant to entertain all visitors with everything the plantation affords. And the poor planters who

[23] "Hist. Va." 245–246. [24] Ibid. 121.
[25] Ibid. Pref. xvii. [26] Ibid. 217.

have but one bed will often sit up, or lie upon a form or couch all night, to make room for a weary traveller to repose himself after his journey. If there happen to be a churl that, either out of covetousness or ill nature, won't comply with this generous custom, he has a mark of infamy set upon him, and is abhorred by all." [27] The author exults in the fact that "nobody is poor enough to beg or want food;" but checks himself with the confession, that "they have abundance of people that are lazy enough to deserve it. I remember the time when five pounds was left by a charitable testator to the poor of the parish he lived in; and it lay nine years before the executors could find one poor enough to accept of this legacy; but at last it was given to an old woman." [28] When he thinks of the charms of the climate of Virginia, he is indignant at the calumnies heaped upon it by those English merchants who had visited it, but who, with insular obstinacy, persisted there in all the habits that they were used to in a very different climate: "Many of the merchants and others that go thither from England, make no distinction between a cold and hot country; but wisely go sweltering about in their thick clothes all the summer, because forsooth they used to do so in their northern climate; and then unfairly complain of the heat of the country. They greedily surfeit with their delicious fruits, and are guilty of great intemperance therein, through the exceeding plenty thereof, and liberty given by the inhabitants; by which means they fall sick, and then unjustly complain of the unhealthiness of the country. In the next place, the sailors, for want of towns there, were put to the hardship of rolling most of the tobacco a mile or more to the water-side; this splinters their hands sometimes, and provokes them to curse the country. Such exercise and a bright sun made them hot, and then they imprudently fell to drinking cold water, or perhaps new cider, which in its season they found in every planter's house; or else they greedily devour the green fruit and unripe trash they met with, and so fell into fluxes, fevers, and the bellyache; and then, to spare their own indiscretion, they in their tarpaulin language cry, God d—n the country." [29]

[27] "Hist. Va." 258.   [28] Ibid. 223.   [29] Ibid. 241.

Literature in the South

III

In 1724, there came out in London a book of a hundred and fifty-one pages, entitled "The Present State of Virginia." Its author was a Virginia clergyman, Hugh Jones, born in England, but naturalized in the new world by a life of versatile and energetic usefulness there; rector of Jamestown, mathematical professor in William and Mary College, and chaplain to the colonial assembly. He was one of the earliest Americans to appease the demand for elementary text-books in our schools, serving well the advancing generations by his "English Grammar," his "Accidence to Mathematics," and his "Accidence to Christianity." His book on Virginia, which appears to have been published during some visit of the author to the mother-country, evidently had a philanthropic intention. He sets forth the condition of Virginia up to latest dates, in the hope of arousing and directing a more intelligent coöperation in England with the efforts of good men in the new world who were trying to build up there a prosperous and benign commonwealth. His book is that of an earnest, downright, and rather original man, intent on getting some good done in his part of the world, and having clear views as to the methods of doing it. He describes frankly the sort of material then extant in Virginia to make a nation of—Indians, negroes, Englishmen; its next door neighbors, also—the North Carolinians and the Marylanders; likewise, the schemes he had formed for promoting learning, religion, and trade in those regions. It is a book of solid facts and solid suggestions, written in a plain, positive style, just sufficiently tinctured with the gentlemanly egotism of a Virginian and of a Churchman.

His eulogiums upon his adopted colony are not incapable of a sarcastic edge when turned toward the other colonies in America: "If New England be called a receptacle of dissenters, and an Amsterdam of religion, Pennsylvania the nurse of Quakers, Maryland the retirement of Roman Catholics, North Carolina the refuge of runaways, and South Carolina the delight of buccaneers and pirates, Virginia may be justly esteemed the happy retreat of true Britons and true Churchmen." [30]

Yet he is nowhere blind to the blemishes of his own noble colony

[30] "The Present State of Va." 48.

and its people; he particularly sees its weakness in the great matters of popular education, individual discipline, public spirit, industry, and the like. The Virginians themselves, he tells us, "have good natural notions and will soon learn arts and sciences; but are generally diverted, by business or inclination, from profound study and prying into the depth of things. . . . Through their quick apprehension they have a sufficiency of knowledge and fluency of tongue, though their learning for the most part be but superficial. They are more inclinable to read men by business and conversation, than to dive into books." "As for education, several are sent to England for it." "The common planters, leading easy lives, don't much admire labor or any manly exercise except horse-racing, nor diversion except cock-fighting. . . . This easy way of living and the heat of the summer makes some very lazy, who are then said to be climate-struck." "They are such lovers of riding, that almost every ordinary person keeps a horse; and I have known some spend the morning in ranging several miles in the woods to find and catch their horses, only to ride two or three miles to church, to the court-house, or to a horse-race." [31]

He laments the poverty and consequent ineffectiveness of the College of William and Mary: "For it is now a college without a chapel, without a scholarship, and without a statute; there is a library without books, comparatively speaking; and a president without a fixed salary till of late." [32]

He makes valuable suggestions for the religious improvement of Virginia, and draws portraits of the sort of clergymen who are needed there: not "quarrelsome and litigious ministers who would differ with their parishioners about insignificant trifles," nor "mere scholars and stoics," nor "zealots too rigid in outward appearance," but pure, devout, sensible, and friendly men, fitted to deal successfully with a warm-hearted and high-spirited people who "are for moderate views neither high nor low," and who "never refuse to shout,

> "God * bless the church, and George its defender,
> Convert the fanatics, and balk the Pretender." [33]

[31] "The Present State of Va." 44, 45, 48, 49. [32] Ibid. 83.
[33] Ibid. 95–96.

[* Quotation marks before "God" were deleted in 1879.]

Literature in the South

IV

Perhaps the most accomplished and the wittiest Virginian of the colonial time was William Byrd of Westover, a man of princely fortune and of princely ways. He was born in the colony in 1674, and died there in 1744. His father, having the same name, had come to Virginia in early life; had founded a great estate there; during the latter part of the seventeenth century, had been conspicuous in public affairs; and finding this son to be endowed with every personal quality corresponding to the great position that awaited him in life, had given him the amplest training in the schools and in the society of Europe. He was educated in England, under the particular care of Sir Robert Southwell; "was called to the bar in the Middle Temple; studied for some time in the Low Countries; visited the court of France; and was chosen Fellow of the Royal Society." In England, he had "the acquaintance of many of the first persons of the age for knowledge, wit, virtue, birth, or high station, and, particularly, contracted a most intimate and bosom friendship with the learned and illustrious Charles Boyle, Earl of Orrery." [34]

On returning to his native land, he entered upon a long career of public and private usefulness. He was made receiver-general of the king's revenues; for thirty-seven years he was a member of the council, and at last its president; three times he was sent as the agent of Virginia to the court of England; he founded the two famous cities of Richmond and Petersburg; as the proprietor of tracts of land vast enough for a royal domain, he was active in the development of the agricultural and mineral resources of the colony; best of all, he was "the constant enemy of all exorbitant power, and hearty friend to the liberties of his country." [35] His course in private life was equally brilliant and attractive. On his estate at Westover he lived in a style of great magnificence. He was a student of science, a man of wit, of letters, of elegant tastes; and he had "the best and most copious collection of books" [36] in that part of America.

Of course, such a man, absorbed by manifold engagements, and living in a whirl of gayety and of hospitable pleasures, was not likely to

---

[34] "Byrd Manuscripts," I. xi. [35] Ibid.
[36] Wm. Stith, "Hist. Va." Pref. v.

devote himself to any deliberate literary work. Yet his mind was an active and fertile one; and stirred by outward incidents, he dashed off two or three bits of writing that have extraordinary merit,—representing the geniality of his nature, his wit, and the facility and grace of his style.

In the early part of the year 1729, in obedience to an appointment by the governor of Virginia, William Byrd joined an expedition for fixing the dividing line between that colony and North Carolina. The party consisted of two other commissioners for Virginia, the commissioners for North Carolina, a chaplain, several surveyors, and numerous attendants and laborers. The expedition occupied six weeks in the spring of that year; it was then abandoned on account of the hot weather; and being resumed in the autumn, it occupied ten weeks more. Beginning at a point on the sea-coast, the line was run westward six hundred miles, through the Great Dismal Swamp, through "marshes . . . and great waters," "over steep hills, craggy rocks, and thickets hardly penetrable." Of the two expeditions that accomplished this labor, William Byrd kept a journal, which, after lying in manuscript upwards of a century, was first published in 1841, under the title given to it by its author,—"The History of the Dividing Line." [37]

In the peculiar qualities that distinguish this little book, it is almost unique in our colonial age; and it is, without question, one of the most delightful of the literary legacies which that age has handed down to ours. Here we have the off-hand, daily jottings of a very clever Virginia gentleman of the early time, who has travelled much, read much, been long in the best company; and who, with a gayety that will not yield to any hardship or vexation, travels for several weeks through a wilderness, accompanied by a little army of very miscellaneous and very queer people, encountering Indians, semi-savage whites, wild beasts, insects, reptiles, every sort of fatigue and discomfort, the horrors and the grandeurs of nature in its wildest state.

As he is to record the story of a definite partitionment from Vir-

---

[37] This was then printed with other papers of Colonel Byrd under the general title of "The Westover Manuscripts." A more complete and a more accurate publication of his writings, edited by T. H. Wynne, was made in 1866, under the better title of "Byrd Manuscripts."

ginia of land that once belonged to it, he begins with a sparkling sketch of the history of Virginia up to that time; particularly showing how all English America was once Virginia, and how all other English colonies have been formed by being "carved out of Virginia." He sets off, with much humor, the traits of the first inhabitants of Virginia; saying that the original colony consisted of "about an hundred men, most of them reprobates of good families;" [38] and that at Jamestown, "like true Englishmen, they built a church that cost no more than fifty pounds, and a tavern that cost five hundred." [39] He points out the great mistake made by the first colonists in not intermarrying with the Indians: "Morals and all considered, I can't think the Indians were much greater heathens than the first adventurers, who, had they been good Christians, would have had the charity to take this only method of converting the natives to Christianity. For, after all that can be said, a sprightly lover is the most prevailing missionary that can be sent amongst these, or any other infidels. Besides, the poor Indians would have had less reason to complain that the English took away their land, if they had received it by way of portion with their daughters. . . . Nor would the shade of the skin have been any reproach at this day; for if a Moor may be washed white in three generations, surely an Indian might have been blanched in two." [40] "I may safely venture to say, the Indian women would have made altogether as honest wives for the first planters, as the damsels they used to purchase from aboard the ships. It is strange, therefore, that any good Christian should have refused a wholesome, straight bedfellow, when he might have had so fair a portion with her, as the merit of saving her soul." [41]

Very much of his journal, especially the earlier portion of it, is taken up with sarcastic comments upon North Carolina,—its backwardness in civilization, the idleness, ignorance, and poverty of its inhabitants; he heaps innumerable jokes upon them. Some of the people, he says, were sunken into absolute savagery. He tells of a poor wretch on the South Shore,—"a Marooner, that modestly called himself a hermit, though he forfeited that name by suffering a wanton female to cohabit with him. His habitation was a bower covered

[38] "Byrd Manuscripts," I. 4.   [39] Ibid. 5.   [40] Ibid. 5.
[41] Ibid. 77.

with bark after the Indian fashion. . . . Like the ravens, he neither ploughed nor sowed, but subsisted chiefly upon oysters, which his handmaid made a shift to gather from the adjacent rocks. Sometimes, too, for change of diet, he sent her to drive up the neighbors' cows, to moisten their mouths with a little milk. But as for raiment, he depended mostly upon his length of beard, and she upon her length of hair, part of which she brought decently forward, and the rest dangled behind quite down to her rump, like one of Herodotus's East Indian Pigmies. Thus did these wretches live in a dirty state of nature, and were mere Adamites, innocence only excepted." [42]

He has many sarcasms on the irreligion of North Carolina: " 'Tis natural for helpless man to adore his Maker in some form or other; and were there any exception to this rule, I should suspect it to be among the Hottentots of the Cape of Good Hope and of North Carolina." [43] The religious service held there by the chaplain of the Virginia party, "was quite a new thing to our brethren of North Carolina, who live in a climate where no clergyman can breathe, any more than spiders in Ireland." [44] "They account it among their greatest advantages that they are not priestridden, not remembering that the clergy is rarely guilty of bestriding such as have the misfortune to be poor." [45] "One thing may be said for the inhabitants of that province, that they are not troubled with any religious fumes, and have the least superstition of any people living. They do not know Sunday from any other day, any more than Robinson Crusoe did; which would give them a great advantage, were they given to be industrious. But they keep so many Sabbaths every week, that their disregard of the seventh day has no manner of cruelty in it, either to servants or cattle." [46] He suggests that, once in two or three years, the clergy of Virginia should "vouchsafe to take a turn among these gentiles. . . . 'Twould look a little apostolical; and they might hope to be requited for it hereafter,—if that be not thought too long to tarry for their reward." [47]

He has occasion to speak of Edenton, the capital of North Carolina, which he describes as consisting of "forty or fifty houses, most of them small and built without expense. A citizen here is counted extrava-

---

[42] "Byrd Manuscripts," I. 26–27. [43] Ibid. 43. [44] Ibid. 44.
[45] Ibid. 44. [46] Ibid. 44–45. [47] Ibid. 64.

gant if he has ambition enough to aspire to a brick-chimney. Justice herself is but indifferently lodged, the court-house having much the air of a common tobacco-house. I believe this is the only metropolis in the Christian or Mohammedan world, where there is neither church, chapel, mosque, synagogue, or any other place of public worship, of any sect or religion whatsoever." [48] In North Carolina, "they pay no tribute, either to God or to Cæsar." [49]

As to food, "provisions here are extremely cheap, and extremely good; so that people may live plentifully at a trifling expense. Nothing is dear but law, physic, and strong drink, which are all bad in their kind, and the last they get with so much difficulty, that they are never guilty of the sin of suffering it to sour upon their hands." [50] He does, however, criticise their excessive use of pork: "The truth of it is, the inhabitants of North Carolina devour so much swine's flesh, that it fills them full of gross humors. . . . They are commonly obliged to eat it fresh, and that begets the highest taint of scurvy." This disease often develops into a worse one,—"the yaws, called there very justly the country-distemper. . . . First it seizes the throat, next the palate, and lastly shows its spite to the poor nose, of which 'tis apt, in a small time, treacherously to undermine the foundation. This calamity is so common and familiar here, that it ceases to be a scandal; and in the disputes that happen about beauty, the Noses have in some companies much ado to carry it. Nay, 'tis said that once, after three good pork years, a motion had like to have been made in the house of burgesses, that a man with a nose should be incapable of holding any place of profit in the province; which extraordinary motion could never have been intended without some hopes of a majority." [51]

He amuses himself, likewise, over the indolence of the people. He speaks of "the Carolina felicity of having nothing to do." [52] Drones are common in North Carolina, but they are all men; the women "spin, weave, and knit, all with their own hands, while their husbands, depending on the bounty of the climate, are slothful in everything but getting of children, and in that only instance make themselves useful members of an infant-colony." [53] The men "make their

[48] "Byrd Manuscripts," I. 59.   [49] Ibid. 65.   [50] Ibid. 60.
[51] Ibid. 32–33.   [52] Ibid. 60.   [53] Ibid. 41.

wives rise out of their beds early in the morning, at the same time that they lie and snore, till the sun has run one-third of his course, and dispersed all the unwholesome damps. Then, after stretching and yawning for half an hour, they light their pipes, and under the protection of a cloud of smoke venture out into the open air; though, if it happens to be never so little cold, they quickly return shivering into the chimney corner. When the weather is mild, they stand leaning with both their arms upon the cornfield fence, and gravely consider whether they had best go and take a small heat at the hoe, but generally find reasons to put it off till another time. Thus, they loiter away their lives, like Solomon's sluggard, with their arms across, and at the winding up of the year scarcely have bread to eat." [54]

As the expedition moves westward, the author's attention is taken up by other things than the drolleries of North Carolina society; and he jots down admirable notices of rare plants and animals, racy sketches of Indian character, amusing stories of forest-adventure, a learned digression upon music, and vivacious pictures of the country through which they pass. He becomes a great enthusiast over the virtues of the plant, ginseng: "Though practice will soon make a man of tolerable vigor an able footman, yet, as a help to bear fatigue, I used to chew a root of ginseng as I walked along. This kept up my spirits, and made me trip away as nimbly in my half jack-boots as younger men could in their shoes. This plant is in high esteem in China, where it sells for its weight in silver. . . . Indeed, it is a vegetable of so many virtues, that Providence has planted it very thin in every country that has the happiness to produce it. Nor, indeed, is mankind worthy of so great a blessing, since health and long life are commonly abused to ill purposes. . . . Its virtues are, that it gives an uncommon warmth and vigor to the blood, and frisks the spirits beyond any other cordial. It cheers the heart even of a man that has a bad wife, and makes him look down with great composure on the crosses of the world. It promotes insensible perspiration, dissolves all phlegmatic and viscous humors that are apt to obstruct the narrow channels of the nerves. It helps the memory, and would quicken even Helvetian dulness. 'Tis friendly to the lungs, much

[54] "Byrd Manuscripts," I. 56–57.

more than scolding itself. It comforts the stomach, and strengthens the bowels, preventing all colics and fluxes. In one word, it will make a man live a great while, and very well while he does live. And what is more, it will make even old age amiable, by rendering it lively, cheerful, and good humored." [55]

Three years after these journeys across the debatable ground between Virginia and North Carolina, the author made another journey, of much less difficulty and of much less public importance, the leading incidents of which he has chronicled in some very piquant and charming memoranda, entitled "A Progress to the Mines." [56] In the autumn of the following year, 1733, with a party of four gentlemen, five woodmen, four negroes, and three Indians, he made a journey to a vast tract of land owned by him, near the River Dan in North Carolina. His diary of this expedition is called "A Journey to the Land of Eden," [57] the latter phrase being the somewhat ironical name of the region referred to. Both of these narratives are full of merriment; nearly every sentence has some jovial touch; and pervading all, is the perfect and ingrained gentlemanliness of the writer. One day, he arrived at a place where were two mills belonging to himself: "I had the grief to find them both stand as still for the want of water, as a dead woman's tongue, for want of breath." [58] At one house he was detained for a day or two on account of bad weather; and in his account of the way in which he and his friends amused themselves during their imprisonment, by reading the second part of "The Beggars' Opera," which he found in that remote Virginia mansion, we catch a glimpse of the early presence of the Queen Anne writers even in our American forests, as well as of William Byrd's familiar acquaintance with the current literary gossip of London.[59] Continuing that journey under a promise of better weather, he mentions his arrival at "the homely dwelling of the Reverend Mr. Marij," by "a path as narrow as that which leads to heaven, but much more dirty." [60] Further on, he tells how, one night, himself and another gentleman, after positively declaring against it, were induced by the ladies of the house to eat a hearty supper,—upon which he has this

[55] "Byrd Manuscripts," I. 161–162.
[56] Ibid. II. 41–82.
[57] Ibid. 1–39.
[58] Ibid. 41.
[59] Ibid. 47–48.
[60] Ibid. 48.

comment: "So very pliable a thing is frail man, when women have the bending of him." [61] He was a devout Churchman, and a faithful friend of the clergy of Virginia; and for the latter he shows his good-will by never missing an opportunity of playfully remarking upon their personal and professional characteristics. Thus, of a visit one Sunday to Brunswick church: "Mr. Betty, the parson of the parish, entertained us with a good, honest sermon; but whether he bought it, or borrowed it, would have been uncivil in us to inquire. Be that as it will, he is a decent man, with a double chin that fits gracefully over his band, and his parish, especially the female part of it, like him well. . . . When church was done, we refreshed our teacher with a glass of wine, and then receiving his blessing, took horse and directed our course to Major Embry's." [62]

V

William Stith, who was born in Virginia in 1689 and died in 1755, began late in his life to write the history of that colony; being particularly moved to the task by noticing "how empty and unsatisfactory" was everything at that time published upon the subject, excepting, as he said, "the excellent but confused materials" of Captain John Smith.[63] He had been a busy person in his day,—clergyman, master of the grammar school of William and Mary College, chaplain of the house of burgesses, president of the college, and man of public utility in general. Being related to several of the most eminent families in Virginia, and in constant association with its leading men, he was from his youth familiar with all its historical traditions; he had access to many rare manuscripts relating to its past; and, finally, he had won for himself "perfect leisure and retirement." All things seemed to favor his ambition to give to Virginia what it greatly needed—a history of itself. "Such a work," said he, "will be a noble and elegant entertainment for my vacant hours, which it is not in my power to employ more to my own satisfaction, or the use and benefit of my country." [64] Accordingly, in 1747, he published at Williamsburg, in a volume of three hundred and thirty-

---

[61] "Byrd Manuscripts," II. 67.   [62] Ibid. 34.
[63] "Hist. Va." Pref. iii.   [64] Ibid. iv.

Literature in the South

one pages, the first part of "The History of the First Discovery and Settlement of Virginia," carrying the narrative down only to the year 1624. Though he lived eight years longer, this first part of his history proved to be also its last part.[65] The book is not ill-written. It is, indeed, projected upon a scale too large for its subject; it fills up the canvas with small incidents; it seeks to give historical memory to the petty doings of politicians, pioneers, and savages, that carry in themselves the necessity of being forgotten. Nevertheless, while the interest of the story is often swamped in a deluge of details, and the whole book is a sin against artistic proportion and the limits of human life, the reader will be likely to pronounce unjust the verdict of Thomas Jefferson,[66] who says that Stith, though "very exact," had "no taste in style," and that his writing is "inelegant." The author founds his work chiefly upon the narratives of Captain John Smith, in whom he confides with a blissful faith that is now amusing: "I take him to have been a very honest man and a strenuous lover of truth."[67] The historian protests his own impartiality: "I declare myself to be of no party, but have labored solely with a view to find out and relate the truth."[68] Yet his account of the early governor, Samuel Argall, is so hostile that he has been accused of yielding unduly to partisan documents against that personage, and even of adding "bitter and groundless accusations of his own."[69] Against King James the First, who vexed the affairs of the colony by his ceaseless and senseless interference, the historian speaks with a frankness of contempt that leaves an unwonted animation upon his pages: "If more than a century is not enough to un-Solomonize that silly monarch, I must give up all my notions of things. . . . I take it to be the main part of the duty and office of an historian, to paint men and things in their true and lively colors; and to do that justice to the vices and follies of princes and great men after their death, which it is not safe or proper to do whilst they are alive. And herein, as I judge, chiefly consist the strength and excellency of Tacitus and Suetonius. Their style and manner are far inferior to Livy's, and

---

[65] The only other publication of his that I can hear of, is a sermon on "The Nature and Extent of Christ's Redemption," Williamsburg, 1753.
[66] "Complete Works," VIII. 415.   [67] "Hist. Va." Pref. iv.
[68] Ibid. vii.   [69] 4 Mass. Hist. Soc. Coll. IX. 5, note.

the writers of the Julian and Augustan ages; but they have more than painted and exposed alive to view the greatest train of monsters that ever disgraced a throne, or did dishonor to human nature. . . . King James the First fell, indeed, far short of the Cæsars' superlative wickedness and supremacy in vice. He was at best only very simple and injudicious, without any steady principle of justice and honor; which was rendered the more odious and ridiculous by his large and constant pretensions to wisdom and virtue. And he had, in truth, all the forms of wisdom,—forever erring very learnedly, with a wise saw or Latin sentence in his mouth; for he had been bred up under Buchanan, one of the brightest geniuses and most accomplished scholars of that age, who had given him Greek and Latin in great waste and profusion—but it was not in his power to give him good sense. That is the gift of God and nature alone, and is not to be taught; and Greek and Latin without it only cumber and overload a weak head, and often render the fool more abundantly foolish. I must, therefore, confess that I have ever had, from my first acquaintance with history, a most contemptible opinion of this monarch; which has perhaps been much heightened and increased by my long studying and conning over the materials of this history. For he appears in his dealings with the company to have acted with such mean arts and fraud, and such little tricking, as highly misbecome majesty. And I am much mistaken if his arbitrary proceedings and unjust designs will appear from any part of his history more fully than from these transactions with the company and colony. . . . I think and speak of him with the same freedom and indifferency that I would think and speak of any other man long since dead; and therefore I have no way restrained my style in freely exposing his weak and injurious proceedings." [70]

A good example of Stith's descriptive manner is his account of the dreadful massacre of the white people in Virginia by the Indians, in 1622—a passage of genuine dignity, pathos, and graphic power.[71]

[70] "Hist. Va." Pref. vi–vii.   [71] Ibid. 208–212.

Literature in the South

3. NORTH CAROLINA

I

"In the year 1700," writes a genial and enterprising young Englishman named John Lawson,[72] "when people flocked from all parts of the Christian world to see the solemnity of the grand jubilee at Rome, my intention at that time being to travel, I accidentally met with a gentleman who had been abroad and was very well acquainted with the ways of living in both Indies; of whom having made inquiry concerning them, he assured me that Carolina was the best country I could go to, and that there then lay a ship in the Thames in which I might have my passage. I laid hold on this opportunity, and was not long on board before we fell down the river and sailed to Cowes, where having taken in some passengers we proceeded on our voyage." Thus a very useful and notable man found his way to the new world, arriving at Charlestown,[*] South Carolina, early in September, 1700. Of this place and its people, just as they appeared to him in that closing year of the seventeenth century, he has left us a goodly picture: "The town has very regular and fair streets, in which are good buildings of brick and wood; and since my coming thence, has had great additions of beautiful, large brick buildings, besides a strong fort and regular fortifications made to defend the town. The inhabitants, by their wise management and industry, have much improved the country, which is in as thriving circumstances at this time as any colony on the continent of English America. . . . They have a considerable trade both to Europe and to the West Indies, whereby they become rich. . . . Their cohabiting in a town has drawn to them ingenious people of most sciences, whereby they have tutors amongst them, that educate their youth alamode. . . . All enjoy at this day an entire liberty of their worship; . . . it being the lord-proprietors' intent that the inhabitants of Carolina should be as free from oppression as any in the universe. . . . They have a well-disciplined militia. . . . Their officers, both infantry and cavalry, generally appear in scarlet mountings, and as rich as in most regiments belonging to

---

[72] "Hist. N. C." Introd. xi.

[* Changed to "Charleston" in 1879.]

the crown, which shows the richness and grandeur of this colony. They are a frontier, and prove such troublesome neighbors to the Spaniards, that they have once laid their town of St. Augustine in ashes, and drove away their cattle. . . . The merchants of Carolina are fair, frank traders. The gentlemen seated in the country are very courteous, live very noble in their houses, and give very genteel entertainment to all strangers and others that come to visit them." [73]

After staying in this delightful community nearly four months, the young immigrant determined, for some reason, to seek his fortunes in North Carolina; and on the third day after Christmas, 1700, he began his voyage thither along the coast, going in a large canoe, and having in his company five white men and four Indians. Upon this journey, he went by sea only as far as the Santee river; he then struck inland and wandered in zigzag fashion toward the north, paddling up rivers or wading across them, pushing through highlands and morasses, among savages, serpents, wild beasts, and white pioneers, and encountering in good humor all manner of hardships and perils. This long strain of travel in those woods, in those times, proved altogether a revelation to John Lawson, fresh and tender from the beatitudes of a civilized English home; and he had the good sense to keep a faithful record of it. He put down on paper what he saw and experienced day by day as he went along: mishaps, prosperities; descriptions of the country, rivers, plants, trees, animals; their own talk by the way; their occasional entertainment in the hovels of white settlers and of Indians; especially such traits of the latter as seemed to him novel, picturesque, or amusing. He is particularly minute and facetious in his account of the Indian women that they met; telling some broad stories of the intrigues of his own party with these tawny beauties,—wherein the supposed distinction in morals between Christian and pagan seems to become effaced, or, if possible, to be in favor of the pagan. At last, however, after "a thousand miles' travel among the Indians," he and his associates arrived safe in North Carolina; "where," he says, "being well received by the inhabitants and pleased with the goodness of the country, we all resolved to continue." [74]

A man of John Lawson's intelligence was of course a boon to that

[73] "Hist. N. C." Introd. xiii–xvii.   [74] Ibid. 105.

colony. He was especially useful by his ability to survey land. Accordingly, they soon made him their surveyor-general; and for the next twelve years he was kept busy in that function, going in every direction through the wilderness, and having his eyes open all the time for information about man and nature—much of which he carefully noted down in his journal. He had some skill in natural history, and compiled minute descriptions of birds, fishes, beasts, minerals, and the flora of the country. The country itself, however, its beauty and fertility, and the charms of its climate, bred in him an enthusiasm. Its coast, he tells us, in fine imagery, is "a chain of sandbanks, which defends it from the violence and insults of the Atlantic ocean; by which barrier a vast sound is hemmed in, which fronts the mouths of the navigable and pleasant rivers of this fertile country, and into which they disgorge themselves." [75] He gives a picture of the spot where the first hapless colonists sent by Sir Walter Raleigh had their fatal residence; and he adds to it this sweet and poetic story "that passes for an uncontested truth amongst the inhabitants of this place, . . . that the ship which brought the first colonists does often appear amongst them, under sail, in a gallant posture, which they call Sir Walter Raleigh's ship." [76]

As to North Carolina, it is "a delicious country, being placed in that girdle of the world which affords wine, oil, fruit, grain, and silk, with other rich commodities, besides a sweet air, moderate climate, and fertile soil. These are the blessings, under Heaven's protection, that spin out the thread of life to its utmost extent, and crown our days with the sweets of health and plenty, which, when joined with content, renders the possessors the happiest race of men upon earth. The inhabitants of Carolina, through the richness of the soil, live an easy and pleasant life; the land being of several sorts of compost; . . . one part bearing great timbers; others being savannahs or natural meads, where no trees grow for several miles, adorned by nature with a pleasant verdure and beautiful flowers, . . . yielding abundance of herbage for cattle, sheep, and horses. The country in general affords pleasant seats, the land, except in some few places, being dry and high banks, parcelled out into most convenient necks by the creeks; . . . whereby, with a small trouble of fencing, almost every

[75] "Hist. N. C." 107. [76] Ibid. 109.

man may enjoy to himself an entire plantation, or rather park. . . . I may say the universe does not afford such another." [77]

In his office of colonial surveyor he often had to live a rough and solitary life in the far-off woods; and his experience was fruitful in adventures, instructive and amusing for him and for us. Thus, in giving a description of the alligator, he narrates this incident, which occurred at an early period of his residence in North Carolina, and before he had become intimately acquainted with the playful ways of that interesting monster: "This animal in these parts sometimes exceeds seventeen feet long. It is impossible to kill them with a gun, unless you chance to hit them about the eyes, which is a much softer place than the rest of their impenetrable armor. They roar and make a hideous noise against bad weather, and before they come out of their dens in the spring. I was pretty much frightened with one of these once. . . . I had built a house about a mile from an Indian town on the fork of Neuse River, where I dwelt by myself, excepting a young Indian fellow, and a bull dog that I had along with me. I had not then been so long a sojourner in America as to be thoroughly acquainted with this creature. One of them had got his nest directly under my house, which stood on pretty high land and by a creek side, in whose banks his entering-place was, his den reaching the ground directly on which my house stood. I was sitting alone by the fireside, about nine o'clock at night, sometime in March, the Indian fellow being gone to the town to see his relations, so that there was nobody in the house but myself and my dog; when, all of a sudden, this ill-favored neighbor of mine set up such a roaring, that he made the house shake about my ears. . . . The dog stared as if he was frightened out of his senses; nor indeed could I imagine what it was. . . . Immediately again I had another lesson, and so a third. Being at that time amongst none but savages, I began to suspect they were working some piece of conjuration under my house, to get away my goods. . . . At last my man came in, to whom when I had told the story, he laughed at me and presently undeceived me." [78]

Of course he had great opportunities of studying the Indians, whom he always speaks of with a sort of gentle liking, especially their women. Among the latter, he says, "it seems impossible to find a

[77] "Hist. N. C." 135–136.   [78] Ibid. 209–210.

Literature in the South

scold; if they are provoked or affronted by their husbands or some other, they resent the indignity offered them in silent tears, or by refusing their meat. Would some of our European daughters of thunder set these Indians for a pattern, there might be more quiet families found amongst them." [79] "When young and at maturity, they are as fine-shaped creatures . . . as any in the universe. They are of a tawny complexion; their eyes very brisk and amorous; their smiles afford the finest composure a face can possess; their hands are of the finest make with small, long fingers, and as soft as their cheeks; and their whole bodies of a smooth nature. They are not so uncouth . . . as we suppose them, nor are they strangers or not proficients in the soft passion. . . . As for the report that they are never found unconstant, like the Europeans, it is wholly false; for were the old world and the new one put into a pair of scales, in point of constancy, it would be a hard matter to discern which was the heavier." [80] "The woman is not punished for adultery; but 'tis the man that makes the injured person satisfaction. . . . The Indians say that the woman is a weak creature and easily drawn away by the man's persuasion; for which reason, they lay no blame upon her, but the man (that ought to be master of his passion) for persuading her to it." [81]

At one time he saw this prodigy amongst the Indians,—"the strangest spectacle of antiquity I ever knew, it being an old Indian squaw, that, had I been to have guessed at her age by her aspect, old Parr's head (the Welsh Methusalem) was a face in swaddling clouts to hers. Her skin hung in reaves, like a bag of tripe. By a fair computation, one might have justly thought it would have contained three such carcasses as hers then was. . . . By what I could gather she was considerably above one hundred years old, notwithstanding she smoked tobacco and eat her victuals, . . . as heartily as one of eighteen." [82]

He tells in another place of an interview with the king of the Santee Indians, who came to him attended by his conjuror, or doctor,—the latter being a shrewd quack remarkably successful, like his brethren in Christendom, in living upon the credulity of his victims. This doctor himself had in former time been afflicted with a certain dangerous and disreputable disease; and in order to treat himself

[79] "Hist. N. C." 67.
[80] Ibid. 299.
[81] Ibid. 306.
[82] Ibid. 55.

for it in secret, he had withdrawn into the woods, having with him but a single companion, who was suffering from the same distemper. The conjuror succeeded in effecting a cure for both of them, but only at the expense of the noses of both; and, at last, "coming again amongst their old acquaintance so disfigured, the Indians admired to see them metamorphosed after that manner, inquired of them where they had been all that time, and what were become of their noses. They made answer that they had been conversing with the white man above—meaning God Almighty; . . . he being much pleased with their ways, . . . had promised to make their capacities equal with the white people in making guns, ammunition, and so forth; in retaliation of which, they had given him their noses. The verity of which they yet hold." [83]

The author greatly admired the dignity and self-contained power of the Indians: "Their eyes are commonly full and manly, and their gait sedate and majestic. They never walk backward and forward as we do, nor contemplate on the affairs of loss and gain, the things which daily perplex us. They are dexterous and steady, both as to their hands and feet, to admiration. They will walk over deep brooks and creeks on the smallest poles, and that without any fear or concern. Nay, an Indian will walk on the ridge of a barn or house, and look down the gable end, and spit upon the ground, as unconcerned as if he was walking on terra firma." [84]

The fate of this admirable observer was sufficiently mournful. Continuing his career as public surveyor of North Carolina as late as 1712, he went out in that year upon an expedition into the wilderness, in the company of a Swiss nobleman, Baron de Graffenried, who had plans for bringing a colony thither. They fell into the hands of hostile Indians, who burned Lawson at the stake, [85] and permitted the escape of the baron only upon his payment of a ransom. But John Lawson, though slain thus miserably, had made good use of his time in the Carolinas; and three years before his death, he had pub-

---

[83] "Hist. N. C." 37–40. [84] Ibid. 281.
[85] Col. Byrd, "Dividing Line," 174, gives a somewhat different version of the circumstances of Lawson's death. He says that the Indians were angry at Lawson for surveying their lands, and that "they waylaid him and cut his throat from ear to ear."

lished in London a quarto volume embodying the story of his adventures and observations in the new world, under the rather inapt title of "The History of North Carolina," [86]—an uncommonly strong and sprightly book.

4. SOUTH CAROLINA

I

There were in South Carolina in the eighteenth century three distinguished men of the name of Alexander Garden; one a physician and naturalist; another, his son, an officer in the Revolutionary War, and the author of a book of anecdotes respecting that contest; the third, perhaps not related to the other two, an Episcopal clergyman, who died in Charleston in 1756, after a service of thirty-four years as the rector of St. Philip's in that city. This man, a native of Scotland, came to South Carolina about the year 1720, being then not far from thirty-five years old; and besides his rectorship in Charleston, he held for the larger part of his life the office of commissary to the Bishop of London, for the Carolinas, Georgia, and the Bahama islands. He was a person of extraordinary influence in his day. All his opinions were sharply defined; and in the expression of them he was absolutely without fear. He stood for the authority of his church in all things; he was an austere disciplinarian, orderly, energetic, neither taking nor granting any relaxation from the letter of ecclesiastical law. For example, he would never perform the ceremony of marriage in Lent, or on any fast day, or in any manner deviating in the smallest particular from that prescribed in the Prayer-book; for marriage-fees, he would receive not one penny less or more than the law allowed; and exactly one-tenth of his income was measured out with arithmetical precision as charity to the poor.[87]

In the year 1740, alarmed and disgusted by the proceedings of the great preacher, George Whitefield, who was a clergyman of the Church of England, Garden not only prosecuted him vigorously in

---

[86] Reprinted, Raleigh, N. C., 1860. A physician named John Brickell, apparently an Irishman, and settled in the practice of his profession in N. C., published at Dublin, in 1737, "The Natural History of North Carolina;" but this book is an extensive and very impudent plagiarism from John Lawson.

[87] David Ramsay, "Hist. S. C." II. 466–469.

the ecclesiastical court, but pursued him with energy and wit in the wider court of public opinion. He preached, and then published, two sermons entitled "Regeneration and the Testimony of the Spirit," based upon the text, "They who have turned the world upside down have come hither also;" and referring caustically to Whitefield as a preacher whose sermons are "a medley of truth and falsehood, sense and nonsense, served up with pride and virulence, and other like saucy ingredients." [88] He likewise published a series of six letters to Whitefield, which are sprightly and pungent, and which the New England divine, Thomas Prince, described as "full of mistake, misconstruction, misrepresentation, cavil, ill nature, ill manners, scorn, and virulence." [89] Three years afterward, in the year 1743, Garden himself reviewed the tremendous controversy, and justified his own course in it, doing this in a letter [90] to a friend, some sentences of which may sufficiently represent to us the rather tart and spicular quality of his style. All his efforts, he says, have been directed solely in defence of "the cause of truth against the frantics gone forth amongst us. . . . I could now indeed wish that my pen against Whitefield had run in somewhat smoother a style. But had you been here on the spot to have seen the frenzy he excited among the people, the bitterness and virulence wherewith he raved against the clergy of the Church of England in general, and how artfully he labored to set the mob upon me in particular, I dare say you would have thought the provocation enough to ruffle any temper, and a sufficient apology for the keenest expressions I have used against him. . . . As to the state of religion in this province, it is bad enough, God knows. Rome and the Devil have contrived to crucify her 'twixt two thieves, —Infidelity and Enthusiasm. The former, alas, too much still prevails; but as to the latter, thanks to God, it is greatly subsided, and even at the point of vanishing away. We had here trances, visions, and revelations both 'mong blacks and whites, in abundance. But ever since the famous Hugh Brian, sousing himself into the River Jordan, in order to smite and divide its waters, had his eyes opened, and saw himself under the delusion of the Devil, those things have dwindled into disgrace, and are now no more. Bad also is the pres-

[88] Pref. to sermons.   [89] Catalogue of Prince Library, 26.
[90] First printed in N. E. Hist. and Geneal. Reg. XXIV. 117–118.

ent state of the poor orphan-house in Georgia,—that land of lies, and from which we have no truth but what they can neither disguise nor conceal. The whole colony is accounted here one great lie, from the beginning to this day; and the orphan-house, you know, is a part of the whole—a scandalous bubble."

5. GEORGIA

I

The story usually given concerning the original settlement, in 1733, of the youngest of the American colonies, reads like a chapter from some political romance, in which the hero, General James Oglethorpe, appears to be a compound of Solon, Achilles, Don Quixote, and the Man of Ross. The commonwealth of Georgia makes a prompt and rather brilliant entrance into American literature, by virtue of a little book written just seven years after the colony was founded,—the joint production of Patrick Tailfer, Hugh Anderson, David Douglass, and other primitive inhabitants of the colony. These men, apparently of considerable literary culture, had quarrelled with Oglethorpe, and had been worsted; and having escaped to Charleston in 1740, they continued the fight by publishing in that year, both there and in London, an artful and powerful book against Oglethorpe, called "A True and Historical Narrative of the Colony of Georgia."

Within a volume of only one hundred and twelve pages, is compressed a masterly statement of the authors' alleged grievances at the hands of Oglethorpe. The book gives a detailed and even documentary account of the rise of the colony, and of its quick immersion in suffering and disaster, through Oglethorpe's selfishness, greed, despotism, and fanatic pursuit of social chimeras. It charges his deputy, Thomas Causton, with a long course of brutal tyranny and cruelty, in which he was sustained by his master. Its summary of "the causes of the ruin and desolation of the colony," contains these seven particulars,—delusive reports in England of the natural advantages of Georgia, restrictions upon the tenure and use of its lands, enormous quit-rents, paralysis of agriculture through Oglethorpe's refusal to admit negro-labor, the cruel abuse of authority by Oglethorpe and his subordinates, their neglect of manufactures, finally, Oglethorpe's perversion of moneys entrusted to him in Christian charity for the erection of churches and schools.

Whatever may be the truth or the justice of this book, it is abundantly interesting; and if any one has chanced to find the prevailing rumor of Oglethorpe somewhat nauseating in its sweetness, he may here easily allay that unpleasant effect. Certainly, as a polemic, it is one of the most expert pieces of writing to be met with in our early literature. Its mastery of the situation is everywhere maintained, through the perfect mastery on the part of the authors, of their own temper. It never blusters or scolds. It is always cool, poised, polite, and merciless; and it passes back and forth, with fatal ease, between dreadful fact and equally dreadful invective and raillery. For example, it accuses Oglethorpe of caring more for the prosperity of his political hobbies, than for the happiness of his colonists: "Alas, our miseries could not alter his views of things." [91] It contrasts the brave and beautiful fictions about Georgia that were sown broadcast over England, with the sorrowful and terrible realities: "Thus, while the nation at home was amused with the fame of the happiness and flourishing of the colony, . . . the poor miserable settlers and inhabitants were exposed to as arbitrary a government as Turkey or Muscovy ever felt. Very looks were criminal; and the grand sin of withstanding . . . authority . . . was punished without mercy." [92] After spreading before the world the whole horrible story, the book concludes with this powerful and pathetic sentence: "By these and many other such hardships, the poor inhabitants of Georgia are scattered over the face of the earth,—her plantations a wild, her towns a desert, her villages in rubbish, her improvements a byword, and her liberties a jest, an object of pity to friends, and of insult, contempt, and ridicule to enemies."

The above description of the contents of the book may prepare the reader to appreciate the most artistic and amusing part of it,—the dedication. With exquisite mockery, the book is inscribed to Oglethorpe himself. It places his name in full at the head of the address, prefixing and affixing all his sonorous titles, military, political, literary, and feudalistic; it addresses him always, with feigned reverence,

[91] "Narrative," etc. Pref. viii.   [92] Ibid. 36.

as "your Excellency;" and it forms altogether a most laughable burlesque upon laudatory dedications in general, and an elegant and most caustic satire upon what the authors call the vanity and hypocrisy of Oglethorpe in particular. Referring to the confusion, the poverty and wretchedness into which the colony had fallen, and veiling this deadly meaning under the forms of utmost urbanity and compliment, it thus salutes him: "May it please your Excellency, As the few surviving remains of the colony of Georgia find it necessary to present the world, and in particular Great Britain, with a true state of that province, from its first rise to its present period, your Excellency, of all mankind, is best entitled to the dedication, as the principal author of its present strength and affluence, freedom and prosperity. And though incontestable truths will recommend the following narrative to the patient and attentive reader, yet your name, Sir, will be no little ornament to the frontispiece, and may possibly engage some courteous reader a little beyond it."

It then delicately taunts Oglethorpe with the elaborate and nauseous flattery in prose and verse to which he was accustomed, and which he seemed to encourage: "That dedication and flattery are synonymous, is the complaint of every dedicator, who concludes himself ingenious and fortunate, if he can discover a less trite and direct method of flattering than is usually practised; but we are happily prevented from the least intention of this kind, by the repeated offerings of the muses and news-writers to your Excellency, in the public papers. 'Twere presumptuous even to dream of equalling or increasing them. We therefore flatter ourselves that nothing we can advance will in the least shock your Excellency's modesty, not doubting but your goodness will pardon any deficiency of elegance and politeness, on account of our sincerity, and the serious truths we have the honor to approach you with."

With the most deferential tones they then proceed to compliment him on the principal traits of novelty in his arrangements for Georgia, every item mentioned as an encomium being, in fact, a thrust of deadly sarcasm: "We have seen the ancient custom of sending forth colonies, for the improvement of any distant territory or new acquisition, continued down to ourselves; but to your Excellency alone it is owing that the world is made acquainted with a plan highly refined from those of all former projectors. They fondly imagined it necessary to communicate to such young settlements the fullest rights and properties, all the immunities of their mother-countries, and privileges rather more extensive. By such means, indeed, these colonies flourished with early trade and affluence. But your Excellency's concern for our perpetual welfare could never permit you to propose such transitory advantages for us. You considered riches, like a divine and a philosopher, as the 'irritamenta malorum,' and knew that they were disposed to inflate weak minds with pride, to hamper the body with luxury, and introduce a long variety of evils. Thus have you 'protected us from ourselves,' as Mr. Waller says, by keeping all earthly comforts from us. You have afforded us the opportunity of arriving at the integrity of the primitive times, by entailing a more than primitive poverty on us. The toil that is necessary to our bare subsistence, must effectually defend us from the anxieties of any further ambition. As we have no properties to feed vainglory and beget contention, so we are not puzzled with any system of laws to ascertain and establish them. The valuable virtue of humility is secured to us by your care to prevent our procuring, or so much as seeing, any negroes, . . . lest our simplicity might mistake the poor Africans for greater slaves than ourselves. And that we might fully receive the spiritual benefit of those wholesome austerities, you have wisely denied us the use of such spirituous liquors as might in the least divert our minds from the contemplation of our happy circumstances.

"Be pleased, . . . Great Sir, to accompany our heated imaginations in taking a view of this colony of Georgia,—this child of your auspicious politics,—arrived at the utmost vigor of its constitution at a term when most former states have been struggling through the convulsions of their infancy. This early maturity, however, lessens our admiration that your Excellency lives to see (what few Founders ever aspired after) the great decline and almost final termination of it. So many have finished their course during the progress of the experiment, and such numbers have retreated from the phantoms of poverty and slavery which their cowardly imaginations pictured to them, that you may justly vaunt with the boldest hero of them all,

Literature in the South

'Like Death you reign
O'er silent subjects and a desert plain.'

"Yet must your enemies (if you have any) be ready to confess that no ordinary statesman could have digested, in the like manner, so capacious a scheme, such a copious jumble of power and politics. We shall content ourselves with observing that all those beauteous models of government which the little states of Germany exercise, and those extensive liberties which the boors of Poland enjoy, were designed to concentre in your system; and were we to regard the modes of government, we must have been strangely unlucky to have missed of the best, where there was an appearance of so great a variety. For, under the influence of our Perpetual Dictator, we have seen something like aristocracy, oligarchy, as well as the triumvirate, decemvirate, and consular authority of famous republics, which have expired many ages before us. What wonder, then, we share the same fate? Do their towns and villages exist but in story and rubbish? We are all over ruins; our public-works, forts, wells, highways, light-houses, stores, and water-mills, and so forth, are dignified like theirs with the same venerable desolation. The log-house, indeed, is like to be the last forsaken spot of your empire; yet even this, through the death or desertion of those who should continue to inhabit it, must suddenly decay; the bankrupt jailor himself shall soon be denied the privilege of human conversation; and when this last moment of the spell expires, the whole shall vanish like the illusion of some eastern magician.

"But let not this solitary prospect impress your Excellency with any fears of having your services to mankind, and to the settlers of Georgia in particular, buried in oblivion; for if we diminutive authors are allowed to prophesy,—as you know poets in those cases formerly did,—we may confidently presage, that while the memoirs of America continue to be read in English, Spanish, or the language of the Scots Highlanders, your Excellency's exploits and epocha will be transmitted to posterity.

"Should your Excellency apprehend the least tincture of flattery in anything already hinted, we may sincerely assure you, we intended nothing that our sentiments did not very strictly attribute to your merit; and in such sentiments we have the satisfaction of being fortified by all persons of impartiality and discernment.

"But not to trespass on those minutes which your Excellency may suppose more significantly employed on the sequel, let it suffice at present to assure you that we are deeply affected by your favors; and though unable of ourselves properly to acknowledge them, we shall embrace every opportunity of recommending you to higher powers, who, we are hopeful, will reward your Excellency according to your Merit!"

Chapter XVIII

General Literary Forces in the Colonial Time

I. Tendency in each colony toward isolation—Local peculiarities in thought and language—Distribution of personal and literary types.

II. General tendencies toward colonial fellowship, founded on kinship, religion, commerce, subjection to the same sovereign, peril from the same enemies—Special intellectual tendencies toward colonial fellowship, founded on the rise of journalism, the establishment of colleges, and the study of physical science.

III. The rise of American journalism—"Public Occurrences," in 1690—"The Boston News-Letter," in 1704—Dates of the founding of the first newspapers in the several colonies—Whole number founded in each colony before 1765—Description of the colonial newspapers—Their effect on intercolonial acquaintance—The growth of literary skill in them—Early literary magazines—First one founded by Franklin, in 1741—"The American Magazine," at Boston—"The Independent Reflector," at New York—"The American Magazine," at Philadelphia.

IV. Early American colleges—Seven founded before 1765—Harvard, William and Mary, Yale, New Jersey, King's, Philadelphia, Rhode Island—Grade and extent of instruction in them—Predominant study of the ancient classics—Requirements for admission at Harvard and Yale—Latin in ordinary use in the colleges—Range of studies—Expertness in the use of the ancient languages—How the early colleges led to colonial union—Their vast influence on literary culture—Their promotion of the spiritual conditions on which the growth of literature depends—One effect of their work seen in the state papers of the Revolutionary period—Lord Chatham's tribute.

V. Study of physical science in America—Begun by the earliest Amer-

History of American Literature

icans—Eminence of John Winthrop of Connecticut—His connections with the Royal Society—Fitz John Winthrop—Stimulus given to study of nature in New England—Increase Mather—John Williams—Cotton Mather—Jared Eliot—Joseph Dudley—Paul Dudley—Study of science in Virginia—John Banister—William Byrd—Mark Catesby—John Clayton—John Mitchell—John Bartram of Pennsylvania—John Winthrop of Harvard College—The intercolonial correspondence of scientific men—Culmination of scientific research between 1740 and 1765—The brilliant services of Franklin—America instructing Europe in electricity—Leading scientific men in the several colonies—Scientific fellowship a preparation for political fellowship—Impulse given by science to literature.

VI. Great change in the character of American literature after 1765.

I

THE study of American literature in the colonial time, is the study of a literature produced, in isolated portions, at the several local seats of English civilization in America. Before the year 1765, we find in this country, not one American people, but many American peoples. At the various centres of our colonial life,—Georgia, the Carolinas, Virginia, Maryland, Pennsylvania, New York, Connecticut, Rhode Island, Massachusetts,—there were, indeed, populations of the same English stock; but these populations differed widely in personal and social peculiarities—in spirit, in opinion, in custom. The germs of a future nation were here, only they were far apart, unsympathetic, at times even unfriendly. No cohesive principle prevailed, no centralizing life; each little nation was working out its own destiny in its own fashion. The Swedish scholar, Peter Kalm, travelling through the colonies from 1748 to 1751, was astonished at the isolation of each in laws, in moneys, in military plans, in social usages.[1] In 1765, on the assembling at New York of the first continental congress, the delegates from the several colonies, like ambassadors from remote nations, could at first only stare at one another as utter strangers in face, in character, even in name.

This notable fact of the isolation of each colony or of each small group of colonies, reflects itself both in the form and in the spirit of

[1] "Travels," I. 262-263.

General Literary Forces

our early literature,—giving to each colony or to each group its own literary accent.

The English language that prevailed in all the colonies was, of course, the English language that had been brought from England in the seventeenth century; but, according to a well-established linguistic law, it had at once suffered here an arrest of development, remaining for some time in the stage in which it was at the period of the emigration; and when it began to alter, it altered more slowly than it had done, in the meantime, in the mother-country, and it altered in a different direction. Indeed, even in the nineteenth century, "the speech of the American English is archaic with respect to that of the British English," [2]—its peculiarities consisting, in the main, of "seventeenth century survivals as modified by environment." [3]

Moreover, just as environment led to many modifications of the English language as between the several colonies and the mother-country, so did it lead to many modifications of the English language as between the several colonies themselves; and by the year 1752, it was possible for Benjamin Franklin to say that every colony had "some peculiar expressions, familiar to its own people, but strange and unintelligible to others." [4]

But the separate literary accent of each colony was derived, also, from dissimilarities deeper than those relating to verbal forms and verbal combinations, namely, dissimilarities in personal character. Thus, the literature of the Churchmen and Cavaliers of Virginia differed from the literature of the Calvinists and Roundheads of New England, just as their natures differed: the former being merry, sparkling, with a sensual and a worldly vein, having some echoes from the lyric poets and the dramatists of the seventeenth century, and from the wits of the time of Queen Anne; the latter, sad, devout, theological, analytic, with a constant effort toward the austerities of the spirit, looking joylessly upon this material world as upon a sphere blighted by sin, giving back plaintive reverberations from the diction of the Bible, of the sermon-writers, and of the makers of grim and

---

[2] A. J. Ellis, "Early Eng. Pron." Part I. 19–20, whose language in stating the general law, I closely follow above in my statement of a special illustration of it.
[3] Ibid. Part IV. xvii.   [4] Works, VII. 56.

sorrowful verse. Between these two extremes,—Virginia and New England,—there lay the middle regions of spiritual and literary compromise, New York and Pennsylvania; and there the gravity and immobility of the Dutch Presbyterians, the primness, the literalness, the art-scorning mysticism of the Pennsylvania Quakers, were soon tempered and diversified by an infusion of personal influences that were strongly stimulating and expanding,—many of them being, indeed, free-minded, light-hearted, and moved by a conscious attraction toward the catholic and the beautiful. In general, the characteristic note of American literature in the colonial time, is, for New England, scholarly, logical, speculative, unworldly, rugged, sombre; and as one passes southward along the coast, across other spiritual zones, this literary note changes rapidly toward lightness and brightness, until it reaches the sensuous mirth, the frank and jovial worldliness, the satire, the persiflage, the gentlemanly grace, the amenity, the jocular coarseness, of literature in Maryland, Virginia, and the farther south.

II

On the other hand, the fact must not be overlooked that, while the tendency toward colonial isolation had its way, throughout the entire colonial age, there was also an opposite tendency—a tendency toward colonial fellowship—that asserted itself even from the first, and yet at the first faintly, but afterward with steadily increasing power as time went on; until at last, in 1765, aided by a fortunate blunder in the statesmanship of England, this tendency became suddenly dominant, and led to that united and great national life, without which a united and great national literature here would have been forever impossible. This august fact of fellowship between the several English populations in America,—a fellowship maintained and even strengthened after the original occasion of it had ceased,—has perhaps saved the English language in America from finally breaking up into a multitude of mutually repellent dialects; it has certainly saved American literature from the pettiness of permanent local distinctions, from fitfulness in its development, and from disheartening limitations in its audience.

General Literary Forces

Of the causes that were at work during our colonial age to produce and strengthen this benign tendency toward colonial fellowship, and to ripen it for the illustrious opportunity that came in the year 1765, several belong especially to the domain of general history; and it will be enough for our present purposes merely to name them here. First, it is evident that, between the English residents in America, blood told; for, whatever partisan distinctions, religious or political, separated the primitive colonists on their departure from England and during their earlier years here, these distinctions, after a while, grew dim, especially under the consciousness that they who cherished them were, after all, members of the same great English family, and that the contrasts between themselves were far less than the contrasts between themselves and all other persons on this side of the Atlantic,—Frenchmen, Spaniards, and Indians. Secondly, there were certain religious sympathies that led to intercolonial acquaintance,—Churchmen in one colony reaching out the hand of brotherhood to Churchmen in another colony, Quakers in Pennsylvania greeting Quakers in New Jersey or Rhode Island, the Congregational Calvinists of New England reciprocating kind words with the Presbyterian Calvinists of the middle colonies and the south. Thirdly, in the interchange of commodities between the several colonies, commerce played its usual part as a missionary of genial acquaintance and coöperation. Fourthly, there were in all the colonies certain problems common to all, growing out of their relation to the supreme authority of England; and the method of dealing with these problems in any one colony was of interest to all the others. Finally, all were aware of a common peril from the American ambition of France, and from the savage allies of France on this continent.

Besides these general causes leading toward colonial union,—kinship, religion, commerce, dependence upon the same sovereign, peril from the same enemies,—there were three other causes that may be described as purely intellectual—the rise of journalism, the founding of colleges, and the study of physical science. To these we now need to pay some attention, for the double reason that they worked strongly for the development of that intercolonial fellowship, without which no national literature would ever have been born here, and, also, that they were in themselves literary forces of extraordinary importance.

III

The first newspaper ever published in America appeared in Boston in 1690, and was named "Public Occurrences." For the crime of uttering "reflections of a very high nature," it was immediately extinguished by the authorities of Massachusetts,—not even attaining the dignity of a second number.[5] Under this rough blow, the real birth of American journalism hesitated for fourteen years. On the fourth of April, 1704, was published in Boston the first number of an American newspaper that lived. It was called "The Boston News-Letter." For fifteen years, it continued to be the only newspaper in America. At last, on the twenty-first of December, 1719, a rival newspaper was started, named "The Boston Gazette;" and on the twenty-second day of the same month, in the same year, there appeared in Philadelphia the first newspaper published in this country outside of Boston. This was called "The American Weekly Mercury." From that time onward, the fashion of having newspapers spread rapidly. In 1721, James Franklin began in Boston "The New England Courant," in which his renowned apprentice got his first training as a writer for the press. In 1725, William Bradford founded in New York the first newspaper there. Maryland followed with its first newspaper, in 1727; next came South Carolina and Rhode Island, both in 1732; then Virginia, in 1736; then North Carolina and Connecticut, both in 1755; then New Hampshire, in 1756; finally, Georgia, in 1763. Before the close of the year 1765, there had been established in the American colonies at least forty-three newspapers,—one in Georgia, four in South Carolina, two in North Carolina, one in Virginia, two in Maryland, five in Pennsylvania, eight in New York, four in Connecticut, three in Rhode Island, two in New Hampshire, and eleven in Massachusetts.[6]

[5] F. Hudson, "Journalism in the U. S." 44-49.
[6] For the above titles and dates, I depend chiefly on I. Thomas, "Hist. Printing in Am." II. 1-174.

General Literary Forces

Nearly all of these newspapers were issued once each week; many of them were on diminutive sheets; and for a long time, all of them clung to the prudent plan of publishing only news and advertisements, abstaining entirely from the audacity of an editorial opinion, or disguising that dangerous luxury under pretended letters from correspondents. News from Europe,—when it was to be had,—and especially news from England, occupied a prominent place in these little papers; but, necessarily, for each one, the affairs of its own colony, and next, the affairs of the other colonies furnished the principal items of interest. Thus it was that early American journalism, even though feeble, sluggish, and timid, began to lift the people of each colony to a plane somewhat higher than its own boundaries, and to enable them, by looking abroad, this way and that, upon the proceedings of other people in this country, and upon other interests as precious as their own, to correct the pettiness and the selfishness of mere localism in thought. Colonial journalism was a necessary and a great factor in the slow process of colonial union.

Besides this, our colonial journalism soon became, in itself, a really important literary force. It could not remain forever a mere disseminator of public gossip, or a placard for the display of advertisements. The instinct of critical and brave debate was strong even among those puny editors, and it kept struggling for expression. Moreover, each editor was surrounded by a coterie of friends, with active brains and a propensity to utterance; and these constituted a sort of unpaid staff of editorial contributors, who, in various forms, —letters, essays, anecdotes, epigrams, poems, lampoons,—helped to give vivacity and even literary value to the paper.

Our early journalism, likewise, included publications of a more explicit literary intention than the newspapers; publications in which the original work was done with far greater care, and in which far more space was surrendered to literary news and literary criticism, and to the exercise of many sorts of literary talent. The generic name for these publications is the magazine; and the first one issued in this country was by Benjamin Franklin, at Philadelphia, in 1741, and was called "The General Magazine and Historical Chronicle, for all the British Plantations in America." It contained, besides general news, copious extracts from new books, and original poems and prose essays. Two years afterward, was started in Boston "The American Magazine and Historical Chronicle," closely modelled after "The London Magazine," and edited by an eminent lawyer of literary proclivities, Jeremiah Gridley. It was published once a month; and it undertook to give in each number reprints of the best essays from the journals of London and the colonies, the proceedings of the Royal Society, a list of new books, abundant extracts from new books, "select pieces relating to the arts and sciences," "essays, moral, civil, political, humorous, and polemical," and "poetical essays on various subjects."[7] The next notable publication of this kind was "The Independent Reflector," begun at New York in 1752, and particularly devoted to ethical, political, and humorous essays, in prose and verse, which were contributed by a club of literary men in New York and its neighborhood, including William Livingston, President Aaron Burr, John Morin Scott, and the historian, William Smith.[8]

By far the most admirable example of our literary periodicals in the colonial time, was "The American Magazine," published at Philadelphia from October, 1757, to October, 1758, and conducted, according to its own announcement, "by a society of gentlemen." In the first number, these gentlemen gave a rather lively description of themselves "as persons whose talents and views in life are very different. . . . Some are, accordingly, of one temper and disposition, and some of another. Some are grave and serious, while others are gay and facetious. . . . Some indulge themselves in the belles-lettres and in productions of wit and fancy, while others are wrapt up in speculation and wholly bent on the abstruser parts of philosophy and science."[9] The magazine contains a summary of the world's news, philosophical and political discussions, æsthetic and playful essays, poems grave and gay,—all indicating literary feeling, if not literary power. William Smith, the clergyman and president of the young college at Philadelphia, was its principal contributor, and indeed the leading spirit in its management.

[7] Part of prospectus, in I. Thomas, "Hist. Printing in Am." II. 68.
[8] I. Thomas, "Hist. Printing in Am." II. 125.
[9] "The Am. Mag." Oct. 1757, Pref. 4-5.

General Literary Forces

IV

No other facts in American history are more creditable to the American people, than those which relate to their early and steady esteem for higher education, and especially to their efforts and their sacrifices in the founding of colleges. Before the year 1765, seven colleges were established here, all of which, excepting the one of latest birth, have been mentioned already in the progress of this history: Harvard, in 1636; William and Mary, in 1693; Yale, in 1700; New Jersey, in 1746; King's,[10] in 1754; Philadelphia,[11] in 1755; Rhode Island,[12] in 1764.

Though all these little establishments bore the name of colleges, there were considerable differences among them with respect to the grade and extent of the instruction they furnished,—those founded latest being, in that particular, the most rudimental. Nevertheless, at them all one noble purpose prevailed,—the study of the ancient classics. Thus, at Harvard, so early as 1643, the requirements for entrance were stated as follows: "When any scholar is able to understand Tully or such like classical Latin author extempore, and make and speak true Latin in verse and prose; . . . and decline perfectly the paradigms of nouns and verbs in the Greek tongue, let him then, and not before, be capable of admission into the college."[13] In 1719, when Jonathan Edwards was a Junior at Yale College, he sent to his father this account of the entrance examination at that college of a lad named Stiles, in whom both were interested: "He was examined in Tully's Orations, in which, though he had never construed before he came to New Haven, yet he committed no error,—in that or any other book, whether Latin, Greek, or Hebrew,—except in Virgil, wherein he could not tell the 'præteritum' of 'requiesco.' "[14] Once within the college, the student was required to drop the English language, and to use Latin as the usual medium of intercourse: "Scholares vernaculâ linguâ, intra collegii limites, nullo praetextu utuntor."[15] The course of study "embraced the contemporaneous learning of the colleges in England;"[16] and as far as possible, every-

[10] Now Columbia College.   [11] Now the University of Pennsylvania.
[12] Now Brown University.   [13] B. Peirce, "Hist. Harv. Univ." Appendix, 4–5.
[14] Works of J. Edwards, I. 31.   [15] J. Quincy, "Hist. Harv. Univ." I. 578.
[16] B. Peirce, "Hist. Harv. Univ." 7.

thing was done here "pro more Academiarum in Anglia." At Harvard College, the studies included grammar, rhetoric, logic, arithmetic, geometry, physics, astronomy, ethics, politics, divinity; "exercises in style, composition, epitome, both in prose and verse;" Greek, Latin, Hebrew, Syriac, and Chaldee. No one was deemed "fit to be dignified with his first degree," until he was "found able to read the originals of the Old and New Testament into the Latin tongue, and to resolve them logically." [17]

This extraordinary training in the ancient languages led to forms of proficiency that have no parallel now in American colleges. So early as 1649, President Dunster wrote to Ravius, the famous orientalist, that some of the students at Harvard could "with ease dexterously translate Hebrew and Chaldee into Greek." [18] In 1678, there was in that college even an Indian student who wrote Latin and Greek poetry; and this accomplishment continued to be an ordinary one there as late [as] the Revolutionary War; while the facile use of Latin, whether for conversation or for oratory, was so common among the scholars of Harvard and of Yale as to excite no remark. It is a token of the learning of those days that a graduate of Yale, of the class of 1746, who rose to be the president of his college, delivered on a certain Commencement-day two elaborate orations,—one being in Latin and the other in Hebrew. Finally, nearly all the superior men in public life, after the immigrant generation, were educated at these little colleges; and in all the studies that then engaged the attention of scholars in the old world, these men, particularly if clergymen, had a scholarship that was, in compass and variety, fully abreast of the learning of the time.

The existence here of these early colleges was in many ways a means of colonial fellowship. Each college was itself, in all portions of the country, a point of distinction for its own colony; at each college were gathered some students from other colonies; between all the colleges there grew a sense of fraternity in learning and letters, and this reënforced the general sense of fraternity in civic destinies; finally, at these colleges was trained no little of that masterly statesmanship of our later colonial time, which, at a glance, interpreted the danger that hung upon the horizon in 1765, proclaimed the

[17] B. Peirce, "Hist. Harv. Univ." Appendix 7; also J. Quincy, "Hist. Harv. Univ." I. 190–191.   [18] J. B. Felt, "Eccl. Hist. N. E." II. 10.

General Literary Forces

imminent need of colonial union, and quickly brought it about.

But the vast influence that our early colleges exerted upon literary culture, can hardly be overstated. Among all the people, they nourished those spiritual conditions out of which, alone, every wholesome and genuine literature must grow; and in their special devotion to classical studies, they imparted to a considerable body of men the finest training for literary work, that the world is yet possessed of. It was of incalculable service to American literature that, even in these wild regions of the earth, the accents of Homer, of Thucydides, of Cicero, were made familiar to us from the beginning; that a consciousness of the æsthetic principle in verbal expression was kept alive here, and developed, by constant and ardent study of the supreme masters of literary form; and that the great, immemorial traditions of literature were borne hither across the Atlantic from their ancient seats, and were here housed in perpetual temples, for the rearing of which the people gladly went to great cost.

The worst disasters to which young commonwealths are liable, and on which all noble literary growth is the most surely wrecked, are certain base spiritual conditions,—particularly, a loss of deference to what is ancient and permanent, hatred of discipline, impatience with slow and careful work, and by consequence, vulgarity of tone, superficiality, and barbarism. Against these disasters, our early colleges were in some measure a barrier, as they were in every respect a protest. They stood, in their quietness, year by year, generation after generation, inculcating respect for what is most ancient and most permanent, in thought, in speech, in conduct; they abashed modern egotism by the study of sublime antique models of virtue and greatness; they taught that the worship of wisdom is nobler than the worship of gold, that substance is better than show, that every true man will be simple, and modest, and patient, and faithful, and will hate all shirking and all lies; they testified that even in this world, in the long run, the sovereign power is the power of simple rectitude in all matters of state and church and commerce and personal behavior; they did their best to breed up, for the service of this new land, scholars of catholic learning, preachers who would not part with the ownership of their own souls, and statesmen who would neither serve tyrants nor flatter mobs. By their nourishment of these pure and sound spiritual conditions of a national life, and by their steady discouragement of all spiritual conditions opposite to these, the early American colleges stood for the things without which great thoughts and noble words cannot come. And some fruitage from all that brave work of theirs was gathered sooner, perhaps, than men expected. For example, the tribute of most eloquent homage, which, in 1775, in the House of Lords, the Earl of Chatham paid to the intellectual force, the literary symmetry, and the decorum of the state-papers then recently transmitted from America, and then lying upon the table of that House, was virtually an announcement to Europe of the astonishing news,—that, by means of an intellectual cultivation formed in America, in its own little colleges, on the best models of ancient and modern learning, America had already become not only an integral part of the civilized world, but even a member of the republic of letters.

V

The study of physical science in this country began with the very settlement of the country. It is not strange that the men who came to the new world should have inspected it inquisitively, either from love of novelty or from love of gain; and the writings of the first Americans are strewn with sharp observations on the geography of America; on its minerals, soils, waters, plants, animals; on its climates, storms, earthquakes; on its savage inhabitants, its diseases, its medicines; and on the phenomena of the heavens as they appeared to this part of the earth. There were here, even in our earliest age, several men of special scientific inclination, such as William Wood, John Josselyn, John Sherman, John Winthrop of Massachusetts, and John Winthrop of Connecticut. Indeed, the latter was recognized as an eminent physicist even among the contemporaneous physicists of England; and in Connecticut, where he founded the city of New London, and where he was for many years governor, he pursued with great zeal his scientific researches, carrying them even into the fatal chase for the philosopher's stone.[19] He was on terms of endearing intimacy with Watkins, Robert Boyle, and other great leaders of sci-

---

[19] "The Winthrop Papers," in 3 Mass. Hist. Soc. Coll. IX. 226–301; X. 1–126; also VI–VII. of the 4th series; and J. R. Lowell, "Among my Books," 1st series, 265–273.

ence in England; and it is said that under the menace of public calamities there, and drawn, likewise, by their friendship for Winthrop, these men had proposed to leave England, and to establish in the American colony over which Winthrop presided "a society for promoting natural knowledge." [20] They were, however, induced by Charles the Second to remain in England; and accordingly, with the coöperation of Winthrop, who happened to be in London at the time, they founded there, instead of in New London, the association that soon became renowned throughout the world as the Royal Society. Of that society, Winthrop "was in a particular manner invited to take upon himself the charge of being the chief correspondent in the West, as Sir Philiberto Vernatti was in the East Indies; [21] and as long as he lived, he was a diligent contributor to it both of scientific specimens from America and of papers on science. Happily, also, in the eager prosecution of such studies, he was succeeded by his son, Fitz John Winthrop, who was also a governor of Connecticut and a Fellow of the Royal Society.

The formation of the Royal Society gave an impulse to the study of physical science, that was felt in every part of the earth, and was especially felt in America. One of the first tokens of its influence here was seen in New England, where the clergy and other learned men turned with uncommon zest from metaphysical subjects to the investigation of natural history. Increase Mather formed in Boston a society of scholars for that purpose; and his writings show that he was alert in observing the world's progress in physical science. John Williams, the minister of Deerfield, was a zealous student of nature, and among his writings are papers treating of matter, wind, fire, water, the earth, beasts, birds, fishes, insects, of the method of drawing a meridian line upon a horizontal plane, of Mars, Mercury, Vulcan, and so forth.[22] In 1721, Cotton Mather published "The Christian Philosopher; a Collection of the best Discoveries in Nature, with religious Improvements;" in which he explains the latest theories in astronomy, meteorology, physics, zoölogy, and ethnography, and shows a large and minute acquaintance with these subjects. In

[20] John Eliot, "Biograph. Dict." 505.
[21] Dr. Cromwell Mortimer, "Phil. Trans." XL. Dedication.
[22] S. W. Williams, "A Biographical Memoir" of J. Williams, 131.

1748, was published "An Essay on Field Husbandry in New England,"—one of the earliest attempts ever made in this country to reenforce by science the empiricism of agriculture. The author was Jared Eliot, a graduate of Yale College, a preacher, physician, naturalist, and farmer; a man whose brain, eye, and hand conspired together through a long life, for the glory of God in the relief of man's estate. Governor Joseph Dudley, who died in Massachusetts in 1720, added to his great learning in law, divinity, and literature, a large acquaintance with science; and his son, Paul Dudley, who died in 1752, and who resembled his father in variety of learning, was specially devoted to natural history; and several papers of his upon that subject appeared in the "Philosophical Transactions."

During the latter part of the seventeenth century, John Banister, a correspondent of the English naturalist, John Ray, was settled in Virginia, and was eagerly engaged in the preparation of a work on the natural history of that colony; and, besides a catalogue of the plants of Virginia, papers of his were published on "The Insects of Virginia," "Curiosities in Virginia," "The Unseen Lupus," and "The Pistolochia, or Serpentaria Virginiana." [23] William Byrd of Westover made many careful notes on the plants and animals of Virginia. Between the years 1710 and 1726, Mark Catesby, a friend of Sir Hans Sloane, pursued a systematic investigation of natural objects in Virginia, the Carolinas, Georgia, and even in Florida and the Bahama islands, and afterward published a large work upon that subject. John Clayton, a physician and botanist, who lived in Virginia from 1706 to 1773, was a tireless student of the plants of that region, greatly enlarged the botanical catalogue, corresponded with Linnæus and Gronovius, and contributed many papers to the "Philosophical Transactions." During the larger part of the same period, John Mitchell, likewise a physician and a Fellow of the Royal Society, pursued in Virginia the study of botany, publishing a treatise on the subject, and sending abroad to learned men and learned societies many botanical specimens and many scientific papers.

Perhaps there was no one of these early American students of nature whom it is now pleasanter to recall than the Quaker naturalist,

---

[23] F. S. Drake, "Dict. Am. Biog." 59; also, E. Tuckerman, in "New England's Rarities," Introd. 15.

General Literary Forces

John Bartram. Born in Pennsylvania, in 1701, and left an orphan at thirteen, he had little help from schools, and only such leisure as he could create after his daily work was done; but having, also, a sincere love of nature, a thirst for all sorts of truth, and an aptitude for all sorts of mechanic performance, he throve in various ways. He built with his own hands a house, on his own grounds near Philadelphia, and founded there the first botanic garden in America. In that garden he labored every day, reared a large family, made himself proficient in medicine and surgery, sent botanic specimens to the gardeners of Europe, wrote papers on botany for European scientific societies, was appointed American botanist to George the Third, and won from Linnæus the praise of being "the greatest natural botanist in the world." [24] He had the naturalist's passion for discovery, his friend Peter Collinson saying that he would go fifty or a hundred miles to see a new plant. Twice he made long tours of scientific exploration, first in 1743 through Pennsylvania and New York to Lake Ontario, and again in 1765 and 1766 through the Floridas. Each of these expeditions resulted in a book of narration and description, having indeed no literary merit besides simplicity and directness of statement, but interesting and good as the jottings of an eager naturalist while passing through a new world.

As John Bartram represents high attainments in science reached under all outward disadvantages, so John Winthrop of Harvard College represents still higher attainments in science reached under all outward advantages. A descendant of the first governor of Massachusetts, and thus belonging to a race in which the study of nature was an hereditary passion, he was graduated at Harvard in 1732, at the age of seventeen; and from 1738 until his death in 1779, he served his Alma Mater with great distinction as professor of mathematics and natural philosophy. For extent and depth of learning in his special departments, he was probably the foremost American of his day; and in other departments—history, literature, theology, languages, politics—he had made great acquisitions. During his long career at the college, he was the inspirer of his pupils, as well as their guide. His aspect was very noble, having in it both dignity and tenderness; and those who looked upon him saw realized their high-

[24] J. A. Allibone, "Dictionary of Authors," art. J. Bartram.

est conceptions of the sage and the gentleman. He had an exquisite faculty of giving instruction; one who was both his pupil and associate said of him that "each new lecture was a new revelation."[25] His life was given to research and to oral instruction rather than to the writing of books; yet he published several small works, all upon scientific subjects, and all occasioned by events that then occurred in the earth or the heavens—earthquakes, comets, meteors, and the transits of Venus. These writings are models of scientific exposition, —thorough, simple, terse, lucid, graceful, having an occasional stroke of poetic beauty in epithet, often rising into an effortless and serene eloquence. His manner of reasoning is as noble as his manner of utterance; modest, judicial, never heedless or dictatorial in statement, never exaggerating scientific conjectures into scientific facts, never insisting upon immoderate inferences from his scientific facts. All things considered, he was probably the most symmetrical example both of scientific and of literary culture produced in America during the colonial time; representing what was highest and broadest in it, what was most robust and most delicate; a thinker and a writer born and bred in a province, but neither in thought nor in speech provincial; an American student of nature and of human nature, who stayed at home, and bringing Europe and the universe to his own door, made himself cosmopolitan.

Thus, from the earliest moment of American civilization, there were, here and there in this country, eager and keen students of nature,—their number greatly multiplying with the passing of the years. But it belongs to the essence of such studies that they who pursue them should seek the fellowship of their own brethren, either for help in solving difficulties or for delight in announcing discoveries; and it is, beyond question, true, that the union of the American colonies was first laid in the friendly correspondence and intellectual sympathies of students of physical science, who from an early day were dispersed through these colonies, and who, even before commerce, or politics, or religion had overstepped the barriers between them, had sought one another out in their scattered homes, and had begun those generous interchanges of scientific information, which

[25] Professor Stephen Sewall, Funeral Oration, 4.

General Literary Forces

were a joy in themselves, and which led to many other beneficent forms of intercolonial acquaintance.

By the year 1740, the American students of nature had become a multitude; and from that year to the year 1765, the glory of physical research among us culminated in the brilliant achievements of Benjamin Franklin, whose good fortune it then was to enable his country to step at once to the van of scientific discovery, and for a few years to be the teacher of the world on the one topic of physical inquiry then uppermost in men's thoughts. In 1754, the leading physicists of France—Buffon, Marty, Dubourg, Fonferrière, Dalibard—paused in their studies, and sent across the ocean this reverent word to the great physicist of America: "We are all waiting with the greatest eagerness to hear from you." [26] Nine years before that, in proposing the formation of "The American Philosophical Society," this wonderful man had announced to his own countrymen that the time had come for them to make new and greater exertions for the enlargement of human knowledge: "The first drudgery of settling new colonies . . . is now pretty well over; and there are many in every province in circumstances that set them at ease, and afford leisure to cultivate the finer arts, and improve the common stock of knowledge." [27] Inspired by the noble enthusiasm of Franklin, whose position brought him into large personal acquaintance in all the colonies, the activity and the range of scientific studies in America were then greatly increased. Alexander Garden, James Logan, Thomas Bond, John Bard, John Bartram, Ebenezer Kinnersley, Lewis Evans, Thomas Godfrey, James Alexander, Cadwallader Colden, Samuel Johnson, Thomas Clap, Jared Eliot, Paul Dudley, John Winthrop, were, in those years, with Franklin, the leading students of nature in this country, who, in colonies the most remote from one another, were pushing forward similar researches, and who found in these researches a bond of scientific communion that helped to prepare the way for political communion—whenever the hour for that should come.

The direct impulse given by all this eager study of physical science to the development of American literature is to be seen not only in

[26] Works of Franklin, VI. 194.   [27] Works, VI. 14.

scientific writings like those of Winthrop and of Franklin, which have high and peculiar literary merit, but in the general invigoration of American thought, in the development of a sturdy rational spirit, and in a broadening of the field of our intellectual vision.

VI

In spite of all these influences working toward colonial fellowship, the prevailing fact in American life, down to the year 1765, was colonial isolation. With that year came the immense event that suddenly swept nearly all minds in the several colonies into the same great current of absorbing thought, and that held them there for nearly twenty years. From the date of that event, we cease to concern ourselves with an American literature in the east or the south, in this colony or in that. Henceforward American literature flows in one great, common stream, and not in petty rills of geographical discrimination. Our future studies will deal with the literature of one multitudinous people, variegated, indeed, in personal traits, but single in its commanding ideas and in its national destinies.

Index

[The entries in this index are essentially the same as those in the first edition. A few corrections have been made and some new entries added to cover material in the publisher's notes.]

Adams, John, his receipt for making a New England in Virginia, 96; on Jonathan Mayhew, 433

Adams, John, the poet, 257; his life, 307-309; his Poems on Several Occasions, 307; his contribution to Poems by Several Hands, 307-308

Addison, Joseph, 366

Alexander, James, 537

Allibone, J. Austin, his Dictionary of Authors cited in notes, 465, 535

Almanac, its place in literature, 363; its early prominence and character in America, 363-364; Poor Richard's, 364-365; Nathaniel Ames's, 365-372

Alsop, George, 3; his life, 57-58; his Character of the Province of Maryland, 57-61; his description of his voyage, 60

American Apologetics, writers of, 3, 9

American colonies, order of settlement, 6; tendencies toward isolation, 522-524; a separate literary accent in each, 523-524; tendencies toward union, founded on race, religion, commerce, common dependence, common perils, 524; founded on journalism, 526-528; on colleges, 529-532; on study of science, 523-538; their union rapidly developed from 1765, 538

American colonists, traits of, in first period, 7, 17, 54-55, 71-80, 81-99, 107-109, 112; in second period, 439-440, 456-458

American Journal of Numismatics, cited, 303 note

American literature, its beginning, 5-14; its Founders immigrant authors, 7; England and America joint proprietors of our earliest literature, 7; early American writings classified, 8-10; first group, news sent back, 8; second group, controversial appeals, 8; third group, American Apologetics, 8-9; fourth group, accounts of the Indians, 9; fifth group, descriptions of nature, 10; sixth group, accounts of the altered conditions of life in the new world, 10; seventh group, books written with special reference to Americans themselves, 10; American literature dates from our first colony, 10; its birth-epoch a fortunate one, 11; changes in style, 63-64; during first period confined to two localities, Virginia and New England, 70; comparative literary barrenness of the former, and the causes, 70-80; two periods of, in colonial time, 259-263; with second period begin writers of American birth, 263; range of its topics in New England in second period, 340-341; its early condition in New York, 440; in Pennsylvania, 457-458; its isolated character in colonial times, 522; its separate character in each colony, 523-524; its development toward uniformity dependent on colonial union, 524-

Index

American literature (*continued*) 525, 537-538; stimulated by journalism, 526-527; by early colleges, 530-532; by study of physical science, 537-538

Americans, a new race, 260-261

Ames, Nathaniel, 257; his Almanac, 365-372

Andros Tracts, 401 note

Archæologia Americana, cited, in notes, 37, 133, 135, 136, 328

Aristotle, denounced by Cotton Mather, 334-335

Armstrong, Edward, his edition of Leeds's News, etc., 442 note

Arnold, Thomas, on the Fantastic writers, 244 note

Aspinwall Papers, cited, 72 note

Bacon, Francis, 6, 18, 197, 365, 371

Bacon, Nathaniel, his rebellion, 61-63, 70, 260, 488 note, 491; anonymous papers concerning his rebellion, 63-70; poem on his death, 68-70

Ballads, early American, 304

Baltimore, Lord, founds Maryland, 53; Alsop's book dedicated to, 58-59

Bancroft, George, cited, in notes, 37, 82; his description of Virginia, 73, 75; on early religious intolerance in Virginia, 79 note

Banister, John, 257; as a student of science, 534

Bard, John, 537

Barnard, John, 256, 336, 376 note; his life and traits, 412-413; his sermons, 413-414

Barnes, Albert, 471 note

Bartram, John, 257, 537; his life, 534-535; as a student of science, 535

Bay Psalm Book, its origin and peculiarities, 236-238

Beaumont and Fletcher, 243

Belknap Papers, cited, in notes, 303, 428

Berkeley, George, Bishop of Cloyne, denunciation of, by William Douglass, 395-396; his influence on American thought, 419 note

Berkeley, Sir William, his treatment of Bacon and his followers, 62, 63, 67; his opposition to schools and printing in Virginia, 77-78; his connection with the elder Beverley, 491

Bermudas, described by William Strachey, 40

Beverley, Robert, 61, 257; his arraignment of the Virginians, 75, 76, 493; on religious intolerance in Virginia, 79 note; his life, 491-492; his History of Virginia, 491-494; his description of the climate of Virginia, 494

Bigelow, John, his life of Franklin, etc., cited, in notes, 466, 468, 473, 481

Blackmore, Sir Richard, 296

Blair, James, 256; his life, 488; founds William and Mary College, 488-489; his Present State of Virginia, 489-490; his Sermons, 490-491

Bond, Thomas, 537

Boston News-Letter, 296 note, 526

Boyle, Robert, 133, 134, 532

Bradford, William, 3, 91 note, 109; his learning, 86, 102-103 note; his life, 101-102; his History of Plymouth Plantation, 102-106; his mind and style, 106-109; his Journal, 138-141

Bradford, William, the printer, 442; founds first newspaper in New York, 526

Bradstreet, Anne, 3, 265, 278; her life and writings, 239-252; as a prose-writer, 241-242; as a poet, 239-240, 242-243; her Four Elements, 244-248; her Four Monarchies, 248; her Contemplations, 248-251; her hymns, 251; her defence of women, 251-252; concluding estimate of, 252-253; only professional poet in New England in first period, 263; her influence on subsequent writers, 263; John Norton's elegy on, 263-265; John Rogers's poem to, 266-268

Bradstreet, Simon, 86, 123, 342; his early life, 240; his career in New England, 240

Breintnal, Joseph, 257; his part in The Busy Body, 468

Brewster, William, 86

Brickell, John, his plagiarism from John Lawson, 513 note

Brodhead, John Romeyn, his History of New York, cited, 439 note, 455

Brooke, Henry, 257; his life and writings, 464

Brown, John Nicholas, 275 note

Browne, Sir Thomas, 347

Index

Buckingham, Joseph T., in notes, 288, 364

Budd, Thomas, 256; his Good Order Established, 442

Bulkley, Peter, 3, 186, 232 note; his scholarship, 86; his elegy on Thomas Hooker, 171; his life and writings, 187-188; as a verse-writer, 230

Bunyan, John, 277

Burk, John D., on schools in Virginia, 76; on early religious persecution in Virginia, 79

Burr, Aaron, president, 528

Burwell Papers, 3, 61-70, 63 note, 70 note

Butler, Samuel, 366

Byles, Mather, 256, 257, 296, 303, 336, 376 note; his part in Poems by Several Hands, 307-309; his rupture with Hollis Street Church, 426-428; his versatility and wit, 428; his traits as a preacher, 428-432

Byrd, William, 256; his life and character, 497-498; his History of the Dividing Line, 498-503; his Progress to the Mines, and his Journey to the Land of Eden, 503-504; his account of John Lawson's death, 512 note; as a student of science, 534

Calef, Robert, 257; his More Wonders of the Invisible World, 342-343

Callender, John, 256; his historical discourse on Rhode Island, 390

Campbell, Charles, cited, in notes, 61, 74, 76, 77, 489; his description of early Virginia colonists, 76; on religious intolerance in Virginia, 79; his edition of Beverley, 492 note

Catesby, Mark, as a student of science, 534

Chalkley, Thomas, 457

Chalmers, George, in note, 78

Chaplin, J., 94 note

Chatham, Lord, on American state-papers, 532

Chaucer, 349, 474

Chauncey, Charles, of Harvard College, 3, 186, 318; his scholarship, 86; his life, 191-193; his writings, 193-195; fate of his unpublished writings, 194-195

Chauncey, Charles, of Boston, 256, 336; his estimate of Jeremiah Dummer, 360; his career and influence before the Revolution, 432-434; his hostility to religious enthusiasm, 433-436

Chauncey Memorials, cited, in notes, 192, 433, 434

Church, Benjamin, 256; his life, 381; his History of Indian Wars, 381-382

Clap, Roger, 83 note

Clap, Thomas, 257, 537

Clarendon, Lord, his History of the Rebellion denounced by Cotton Mather, 334

Clayton, John, 257; as a student of science, 534

Clergy of New England, 161-195; their supremacy, 161-164; their prolixity, 163-166; their ability, 166-167; their literary prominence, 340, 398-399; their influence divided with the laity, 340-341

Cleveland, John, 243

Colden, Cadwallader, 256, 257, 537; his life, 445-446; his History of the Five Indian Nations, 446-447; his censure on Smith's History of New York, 455

Colleges (see Education)

Colman, Benjamin, 256, 257, 296, 336, 376 note; biography of, by E. Turell, 375; on Solomon Stoddard, 407 note; his life and character, 408-412; his Sermons, 411-412

Connecticut, the order of its colonization, 6

Cook, Ebenezer, 257; his Sot-Weed Factor, 483-487; his Sot-Weed Redivivus, 488

Corlet, Elijah, 171 note

Cotton, John, 3, 123, 156, 167, 168, 179, 189, 216, 220, 223, 324, 364, 374; his scholarship, 86; his elegy on Thomas Hooker, 171-172; his life, 181-185; his writings, 185-186; his traits, 186-187; Thomas Carlyle's estimate of him, 184 note; his controversy with Roger Williams, 215-220; as a versifier, 230

Cotton, John, of Plymouth, 377 note

Cowley, Abraham, 243

Coxe, Daniel, 256; his Description of Carolana, 447-448; his plan of colonial union, 448

Crashaw, Richard, 243, 292 note

Crashawe, William, 292 note; describes early opponents of American coloni-

541

Index

Crashawe, William (*continued*) zation, 9; his references to William Whitaker, 41 note, 42

Cromwell, Oliver, 58, 72, 132, 189, 239; his letter to John Cotton, 184

Cushman, Robert, 138 note; his complaint concerning the Pilgrims, 108

Dana, Richard H., the first, 253 note

Dana, Richard H., the second, 253 note

Danforth, Samuel, extract from his epitaph, 232

Davenport, John, his scholarship, 86

Davies, Sir John, 158

Davies, Samuel, 256; his life, 470; his prophetic allusion to Washington, 470-471; as a pulpit-orator, 471; his sermon on the resurrection, 471-473

Dean, John Ward, in notes, 184, 197, 278

Deane, Charles, his edition of Smith's True Relation, 19 notes; his edition of Bradford's Dialogue, 103 note, 308 note; his paper on the Magnalia, 329 note

De Foe, Daniel, 365, 382

Denton, Daniel, 256, 442; his Brief Description of New York, 441-442

Description and Narration, writers of, 3, 10, 27-31, 35-45, 137-160, 256, 343-345, 379-381, 441-442, 447-448, 458-461, 495-504, 505-513, 515-520

Dexter, Henry Martyn, 109 note; his monograph on Roger Williams, 95 note, 107 note, 215 note, 226 note; his edition of Church's Indian Wars, 381 note

Diary, its place in literature, 343

Dickenson, Jonathan, of Pennsylvania, 256; his Protecting Providence, 460-461

Dickinson, Jonathan, of New Jersey, 256; his life, 448-449; his skill as a logician, 449; his Familiar Letters, 449

Dixon, W. Hepworth, cited, in notes, 457, 458

Donne, John, 33, 243, 244 note, 292

Douglass, William, 256; on Salem, 291; his life and character, 390-393; his Summary, 393-396

Drake, Francis S., 534 note

Drake, Samuel G., in notes, 276, 338; his edition of Hubbard's Indian Wars, 377 note; his edition of Prince, 388 note

Drayton, Michael, 158, 248 note; his farewell ode to the Virginia colonists, 12-15; his exhortation to George Sandys, 46-47

Dryden, John, 243, 378, 451; his estimate of Sandys, 51; his influence on American verse, 275, 292, 296, 366

Dudley, Joseph, as a student of science, 534

Dudley, Paul, as a student of science, 534, 537

Dudley, Thomas, his learning, 86; on toleration, 93; his trouble with John Winthrop, 163; as a verse-maker, 230

Dummer, Jeremiah, 257, 336, 406; his life and character, 360-362; his Letter to a Noble Lord, 362; his Defence of the New England Charters, 362-363

Dunster, Henry, his scholarship, 86; his presidency of Harvard College, 192; on oriental studies at Harvard, 530

Dunton, John, of London, his account of William Hubbard, 376; of John Higginson, 399

Duyckinck's Cyclopædia of American Literature, Simons's edition, cited, in notes, 273, 274-275, 296

Dwight, Sereno E., his edition of Works of Jonathan Edwards, cited, in notes, 415, 416, 417, 418, 419, 420, 421, 422, 423, 424, 425, 426

Dwight, Theodore, 344 note

Education, in Virginia in seventeenth century, 76-79; in New England during same period, 86-87; in New York, 440; in Pennsylvania, 457-458, 463-464; rise of Colleges, 529-532

Edwards, Jonathan, 179, 256, 323, 449, 470; his life, 414-415; his precocity, 415-420; his studies in physical science, 421; his habits as a student, 421-423; his sorrows, 422; his power as a preacher, 423-426; his Sinners in the Hands of an Angry God, 424-426; concluding estimate of, 426; describes entrance examinations at Yale, 529

Eliot, Jared, 257; as a student of science, 534, 537

Eliot, John, 132, 133, 211; his scholar-

Index

ship, 86; his part in the Bay Psalm Book, 237

Eliot, John, of Boston, cited, in notes, 162, 317, 376, 533

Ellis, Alexander J., his Early English Pronunciation, cited, 523 note

Ellis, John Harvard, his edition of Anne Bradstreet's works, 239, 265, 268, notes

Endicott, John, 91, 94, 122, 123, 125

English Language, as modified in America, 523

Evans, Lewis, 256, 537; his Analysis of the Middle Colonies, 469-470

Fantastic writers, 243-244, 292, 335-336

Felt, J. B., cited, 530 note

Fisher, Joshua F., cited, in notes, 462, 464

Fleet, Henry, his Journal, 53 note

Folger, Peter, 257, 274; his Looking-Glass for the Times, 274; Franklin's reference to, 274

Fontaine, James, cited, 492 note

Force, Peter, his Historical Tracts, cited in notes, 38, 53, 54, 70, 74, 76

Ford, John, 243

Frame, Richard, 256; his Short Description of Pennsylvania, 460

Franklin, Benjamin, 257, 323, 448, 458, 463, 465, 466, 473, 537; his father's family, 83 note; his reference to Peter Folger, 274; his tribute to Cotton Mather's Bonifacius, 332; his Poor Richard's Almanac, 364-365; on Breintnal, 468; his literary and scientific eminence prior to 1765, 479-481; appreciation of, by Hume, 479; by French savans, 479, 537; on American provincialisms, 523; founds first magazine in America, 527-528

Franklin, James, his Almanac, 365; founds the New England Courant, 526

Fraser, Professor A. C., his edition of Works of Bishop Berkeley, 419 note

Fuller, Thomas, his estimate of Capt. John Smith, 32; of Sandys's Ovid, 51

Furman, Gabriel, his edition of Denton's Brief Description, 441 note

Garden, Alexander, the clergyman, 256; his life and character, 513; his sermons, 513; his hostility to Whitefield, 513-515

Garden, Alexander, the physician, 257, 513, 537

Gardener, Lion, 130 note

Gee, Joshua, cited, 328 note

Georgia, colonization of, 6 note; its part in colonial literature, 515-520

Godfrey, Thomas, the mathematician, 473, 537

Godfrey, Thomas, the poet, 257; his life, 473; his Juvenile Poems, 473-475; his Prince of Parthia, 474-479

Gookin, Daniel, 3; his learning, 86; his life and character, 130-133; his Historical Collections of the Indians in New England, 133-136; his Account of the Christian Indians in New England, 135; his History of New England, 136

Gorton, Samuel, 91, 111

Gosnold, Bartholomew, 17, 33

Grahame, James, his History of United States, cited, 457 note

Green, John Richard, 71 note

Green, Joseph, 257; his life, 301; his facetiousness, 301; his impromptu verses, 301-303; his Entertainment for a Winter Evening, and other satires, 302-304

Green, Samuel A., 274 note

Gridley, Jeremiah, edits American Magazine, 528

Griswold, Rufus W., his Curiosities of American Literature, cited, 304 note; his Poets and Poetry of America, cited, in notes, 464, 469

Hale, Edward Everett, 37 note

Hammond, John, 3, 53-54, 57; his Leah and Rachel, 54-57

Harris, Thaddeus Mason, 376 note

Hartlib, Samuel, 322

Harvard College, founded, 86-87, 529; early requirements for admission to, 529; early course of study in, 530

Haven, Samuel F., 328 note

Hawks, Francis L., 41 note

Hawthorne, Nathaniel, on our New England ancestors, 95; on early New England, 97

Haynes, John, 86

Hening, W. W., 78 note

543

Index

Herbert, George, 243, 292
Herrick, Robert, 243
Higginson, Francis, 3, 399; his life, 144; his True Relation and his New England's Plantation, 144-147
Higginson, John, 168, 179, 256, 291; lines on, by Nicholas Noyes, 293-294; his life and writings, 399-400
Higginson, Thomas Wentworth, cited, in notes, 147, 164
Hildreth, Richard, 82 note, 448 note; on early religious intolerance in Virginia, 79 note; on education in early New England, 86
Historical Magazine, 469 note
Historical writers, 3, 61-70, 100-136, 256, 374-396, 445-447, 455-456, 491-494, 504-506
Holme, John, his True Relation of Pennsylvania, 460
Holmes, Oliver Wendell, 253 note
Hooke, William, 3, 186; his life and writings, 189-191; his graphic description of a battle scene, 190
Hooker, E. W., in notes, 172, 174
Hooker, Thomas, 3, 123, 164, 179, 186, 231; his scholarship, 86; his life and character, 167-172; his writings, 172-177; on Richard Mather, 316
Hopkins, Edward, extract from his epitaph, 232
Hopkins, Stephen, 123
Howison, R. R., on early religious intolerance in Virginia, 79 note
Hubbard, William, 184 note, 187 note, 256, 276, 374; on President Dunster, 192 note; his life and character, 375-376; his General History of New England, 376; his Indian Wars, 377-379
Hudson, Frederic, his Journalism in the United States, cited, 526 note
Hume, David, his appreciation of Franklin, 479
Hutchinson, Anne, 123
Hutchinson, Thomas, 102, 338, 374; in notes, 82, 92, 163, 361; on William Hubbard, 375

Indians, the subject of a large class of early American writings, 9; descriptions of, 29, 30, 31, 140-141, 142, 147, 153-156; Whitaker's appeal in behalf of, 42-43; massacres by, 47, 62; wars with, 64-68, 124, 127-130, 130 note, 132, 135-136, 211-212, 377-384; Morrell's appeal in behalf of, 236; described by John Lawson, 510-512
Intolerance (see Religious Persecutions)
Irving, Washington, 493

Jamestown, 16, 25, 47, 75
Jefferson, Thomas, 359; on early religious intolerance in Virginia, 79 note; his criticism on Stith's style, 505
Johnson, Edward, 3, 162 note; his life, 118-119; his Wonder-Working Providence, 118-126; as a versifier, 125-126
Johnson, Samuel, of Stratford, 257, 537
Jones, Hugh, 256; his career in Virginia, 495; his Present State of Virginia, 495-496
Jonson, Ben, 18, 32, 68, 158, 243
Josselyn, John, 3, 532; his life, 156-158; his New England's Rarities, and his Two Voyages to New England, 158-160; his credulity illustrated, 158-160
Journalism in America, first attempts in, 340-341, 525-528; its influence on colonial union, 527; on literature, 527-528

Kalm, Peter, on colonial isolation, 522
Keimer, Samuel, 465, 466
Kettell, Samuel, his Specimens of American Poetry, cited, in notes, 274-275, 302, 303, 304
King Philip's War, 127, 132, 135-136, 260, 272, 378-379, 381-382
King's College, founded, 529
Kinnersley, Ebenezer, 537
Knapp, Francis, his life, 296; a disciple of Pope, 296
Knapp, Samuel L., cited, in notes, 296, 302
Knight, Sarah Kemble, 256; her Journal, 343-345
Knowles, J. D., cited, 211 note

Laud, William, his persecutions of the Puritans, 167, 177, 178-179, 183, 192, 196, 197
Lawson, John, 256; his coming to America, 507; his description of Charleston and the South Carolinians, 507-508; his History of North Carolina, 508-513; his tragic death, 512

544

Index

Lechford, Thomas, his Plain Dealing, 165 note
Lee, Eliza B., 253 note
Leeds, Daniel, 257; his News of a Trumpet, etc., 442
Leeds, Josiah W., his History of the United States, 457 note
Literary Periods, two in our colonial time, 260-263
Livingston, William, 257, 528; his life, 450; his character, 452; his Philosophic Solitude, 450-452; his travesty on the Thirty-Nine Articles, 452-453; his Review of Military Operations in America, 453; his poem to Eliza, 454
Locke, John, 117, 415, 451
Logan, James, 257, 463, 464, 537; his life, 461-462; his scholarship, 462; his writings, 462-463
Longfellow, Henry Wadsworth, 94 note, 97, 158, 183 note, 189
Lounsbury, Thomas R., 243 note
Lowell, James Russell, in notes, 7, 82, 532; on Wigglesworth's Day of Doom, 288
Lyford, John, satirical description of, 107

Magazines, early examples of in America, 527-528
Marston, John, 12 note
Maryland, the order of its colonization, 6; founded by Lord Baltimore, 53; its earliest literature blended with Virginia's, 53; John Hammond's defence of, 53-57; George Alsop's Character of, 57-61; its part in later colonial literature, 483-488
Mason, Captain John, 3, 381; his history of Pequot War, 127-130
Massachusetts Bay, 112, 213; the order of its colonization, 6; its conservative character, 81
Massachusetts Historical Society Collections, cited, in notes, 45, 63, 70-71, 72, 92, 102, 128, 130, 134, 147, 156, 160, 162, 234, 298, 303, 341, 342, 377, 384, 388, 428, 505, 532
Massachusetts Historical Society Proceedings, cited, in notes, 70, 278, 329, 346, 349
Massinger, Philip, 243

Mather, Cotton, 256, 266, 276, 292, 293, 350, 351, 374; in notes, 82, 83, 87, 90, 91, 93, 162, 169, 170, 171, 183, 184, 185, 186, 187, 191, 192, 193, 232, 233, 237, 316, 317, 318, 320, 327, 328, 343; on Michael Wigglesworth, 277; his preeminence among the Mathers, 323; a victim of adulation, 324; his intellectual endowments, 324; his moral affectations, 325; his asceticism, 326; his industry and attainments, 327-328; the multitude of his writings, 328-329; his Magnalia, 329-332; his anxieties respecting its publication, 330-331; its scope, 331; his qualifications for writing it, 331-332; estimate of its historical character, 332; his Bonifacius, 332; his Psalterium Americanum, 332-333; his Manuductio ad Ministerium, 333-335; its advice on study of Hebrew, 333; of history, 333-334; of natural philosophy, 334; its assault on Aristotle, 334-335; his place in American literature, 335; his Fantastic style, 335-336; his style not agreeable to his later contemporaries, 336; his theory of style, 336-337; his biography, by Samuel Mather, 375; his reference to Urian Oakes, 402; as a student of science, 533
Mather, Increase, 256, 350, 351, 361, 374, 405; in notes, 128, 338; on Urian Oakes, 269; his life, 318-319; his learning, 319-320; as a student, 320; as a pulpit-orator, 320-321; his writings, 321-323; their literary merit, 321; his Illustrious Providences, 322-323; as a student of science, 533
Mather, Richard, 318, 374; his scholarship, 86; his part in the Bay Psalm Book, 237; his life, 316-318; traits of the Mather family, 317; his writings, 317; as a student, 317; his epitaph, 323
Mather, Samuel, 256; his biography of Cotton Mather, cited, in notes, 325, 326, 327, 328, 336; its faults, 375; his life and writings, 337-338
May, Samuel J., his account of Mather Byles in Hollis Street Church, 427
Mayer, Brantz, his edition of the Sot-Weed Factor, 488 note
Mayhew, Jonathan, 256, 336, 376 note;

545

Index

Mayhew, Jonathan (*continued*) his great political and religious influence, 432-433
Maylem, John, 257; his life, 306-307 note; his Conquest of Louisburg, 305; his Gallic Perfidy, 305-306
McClure, A. W., cited, 185 note
Milton, John, 19, 126, 209, 223 note, 229, 243-244 note, 308, 322, 366, 443, 451; quoted, 88; his views on toleration less liberal than those of Roger Williams, 216-217
Miscellaneous prose-writers, 3, 196-226, 257, 339-372, 444, 450-454
Mitchell, John, 257; as a student of science, 534
Mitchell, Jonathan, 318; his epitaph, 232
Montagu, Lady Mary, on prevalence of verse-making in her time, 229
Morley, Henry, on Fantastic Writers, 244 note
Morrell, William, 3; his life, 334; his Nova Anglia, 334-336
Morris, Lewis, 257; his life, 442-443; his writings, 444-445
Morton, Nathaniel, 3, 102; in notes, 91, 171, 184, 232, 233; his life, 109-110; his New England's Memorial, 110-111; his lack of originality, 111; on death of John Cotton, 185; Hubbard's indebtedness to New England's Memorial, 377
Mourt's Relation, 138 note
Murphy, Henry C., his Anthology of New Netherland, cited, 439 note

Narragansett Club Publications, cited, in notes, 93, 95, 111, 184, 210, 212, 213, 215, 216, 217, 218, 219, 220, 222, 223, 224, 225, 226
Narration, writers of (see Description)
Neill, Edward D., his History of the Virginia Company of London, cited, in notes, 12, 16; his Founders of Maryland, cited, 53 note; his Notes on the Virginia Colonial Clergy, cited, 488 note
New England, contrasted with Virginia, 72-74; its colonization, 81-82
New-England Historical and Genealogical Register, cited, in notes, 268, 291, 342, 514

New-Englanders, character of early, 81-99, 107-108, 112; their large families, 82-83; a race of thinkers, 83-85; their esteem for learning, 86-87; their earnestness and faith in prayer, 87-90; their asceticism, 91-92; their severity and intolerance, 91-95; their literary environment, 95-99; their faith in Providence, 124-125; their attitude toward poetry and art, 227-231
New Hampshire, order of its colonization, 6
New Hampshire Historical Society Collections, cited, 382 note
New Jersey, order of its colonization, 6; its part in colonial literature, 439-456
New Jersey, College of, founded, 529
New York, order of its colonization, 6; its characteristics under Dutch rule, 439-440; under English rule, 440; its part in colonial literature, 439-456
New York Historical Society Collections, cited, 455 note
Nichol, Professor John, on the Bay Psalm Book, 237
Niles, Samuel, 256; his History of the Indian and French Wars, 384
North Carolina, order of its colonization, 6; sarcasms on, by William Byrd, 500-502; its part in colonial literature, 507-513; described by John Lawson, 507-510
Norton, John, of Boston, 3; his scholarship, 86; on toleration, 94; his life and writings, 188-189
Norton, John, of Hingham, 253 note, 257, 265; his life, 263; his elegy on Anne Bradstreet, 264-265
Noyes, Nicholas, 257, 296; his life and character, 291-292; the greatest of our Fantastic poets, 292, 293, 335; his prefatory poem on the Magnalia, 292-293; his lines on John Higginson, 294; on Joseph Green, 294; on the malady of James Brayley, 294-295

Oakes, Urian, 256, 257, 376 note; his life and character, 268-269; his high literary capacity, 269; his elegy on Thomas Shepard, 270-272; as a prose-writer, 402; his sermons, 402-405
Oglethorpe, General James, Tailfer's denunciation of, 515-520

Index

Oldmixon, John, blunders in his British Empire in America, 492

Oliver, Peter, 257; his life, 309; his poem on Josiah Willard, 309

Osborn, John, 257; his life and writings, 304 note

Palfrey, John Gorham, cited, 83 note

Parton, James, his Life of Franklin, cited, 365 note

Peabody, A. P., 278 note

Peabody, W. B. O., 325 note

Peirce, Benjamin, his History of Harvard University cited, in notes, 529, 530

Pemberton, Ebenezer, on Samuel Willard, 405

Penhallow, Samuel, 256, 304 note; his life, 382; his History of Indian Wars, 382-384

Penn, William, 459, 461, 464; suggests colonial union, 448 note; his character, 457

Pennsylvania, order of its colonization, 6; its part in colonial literature, 457-481; character of its founders, 456-458; anonymous poem in praise of, 468-469

Pennsylvania Historical Society Memoirs, cited, in notes, 458, 460, 461, 462, 463, 464

Pequot War, 124, 127-130, 211-212

Percy, George, 3, 17; in notes, 15, 16, 37; one of the first settlers of Virginia, 35; his Discourse of Virginia, 36-37

Peters, Hugh, 125-126

Philadelphia, College of, founded, 529

Phillips, Wendell, 253 note

Pietas et Gratulatio, 257, 309-314; its occasion, 309-310; its authors, 311 note

Pilgrim Fathers (see Plymouth Colony)

Pinkerton, John, in notes, 18, 72

Plymouth Colony, 213; order of its colonization, 6; character of its people, 85, 107-109

Poems by Several Hands, its occasion and character, 307-309

Poets (see Verse-Writers)

Pond, Enoch, 319 note

Poole, William Frederick, his edition of Johnson's Wonder-Working Providence, cited, in notes, 120, 162

Pope, Alexander, 465; his estimate of Sandys's Ovid, 51; his influence on American poetry, 292, 296, 307, 366, 450, 451, 474

Pory, John, 3, 46, 48; his life, character, and writings, 43-45; his sketch of the Indians, 44; of the country and of pioneer life in Virginia, 44-45

Prince, Thomas, 102, 111, 256, 364, 389; in notes, 128, 177, 238, 327, 328; on Cotton Mather's style, 336; his life and character, 384-386; his special fitness for historical writing, 386; his Chronological History of New England, 386-389; on Alexander Garden, 514

Prince Society, 148 note

Printing, restrictions on, in Virginia, 78; in New England, 97-98; first use of, in the colonies, 237, 363

Prior, Matthew, 410

Proud, Robert, his History of Pennsylvania, cited, 456 note

Purchas, Samuel, 33, 36; in notes, 15, 16, 37, 38

Pynchon, William, 86

Quarles, Francis, 156, 243, 292

Quincy, Josiah, his History of Harvard University, cited, in notes, 87, 92, 529, 530

Raleigh, Sir Walter, 18, 248, 451

Ralph, James, his career, 465

Ramsay, David, his History of South Carolina, cited, 513 note

Religious Persecutions, in Virginia, 78-79, 131; in New England, 93-95, 121-122; Roger Williams on, 216, 217, 218-222, 226

Religious Writers (see Theological Writers)

Rhode Island, order of its colonization, 6; character of its first inhabitants, 85; excluded from first New England Union, 213; Callender's discourse on, 390

Rhode Island College, founded, 529

Rhode Island Historical Society Collections, cited, in notes, 390

Rives, William C., on early religious intolerance in Virginia, 79 note

Rogers, John, 257, 268; his life and character, 265-266; incident during

547

Index

Rogers, John (*continued*) his presidency of Harvard, 266; his poem to Anne Bradstreet, 267-268

Rogers, Nathaniel, 123

Rose, Aquila, 257; his Poems on Several Occasions, 465

Rowe, Elizabeth, her friendship with Benjamin Colman, 410

Rowlandson, Mary, 256; her narrative of Indian Captivity, 379-380

Rupert, Prince, characterized, by Nathaniel Ward, 198; by Roger Williams, 224

Sandys, George, 3, 52, 53, 158; his life and character, 45-48; Drayton's exhortation to him, 46-47; his translation of Ovid's Metamorphoses, 46-51; story of Philomela and Procne, 49-51; estimates of him as a versifier, by Thomas Fuller, Dryden, and Pope, 51

Savage, James, cited, in notes, 86, 89, 332, 376

Science, writers on, 147-160, 419-421, 461-463, 479-481, 532-537; its influence on colonial union, 536-537; on American literature, 537-538

Scott, John Morin, 528

Scottow, Joshua, 233 note, 257; his Old Men's Tears for their own Declensions, 341; his Narrative of the Planting of Massachusetts, 342

Seccomb, John, 257; his life, 299; his literary character, 300; his Father Abbey's Will, 299-301

Sedgwick, Theodore, his Life of William Livingston, cited, in notes, 453, 454

Sewall, Samuel, 257; his life and character, 345-346; his Selling of Joseph, 346-347; his Description of the New Heaven, 347-348; his championship of women, 348; other writings, 349 note

Sewall, Professor Stephen, his oration on John Winthrop of Harvard, cited, 536 note

Shakespeare, 18, 242-243; germs of the Tempest, 37-38

Shea, John Gilmary, his edition of Alsop's Character of Maryland, 57 note; his edition of Colden's History, 446 note

Shepard, Thomas, of Cambridge, 3, 123, 167, 186; his scholarship, 86; his prayer for proficiency in note-taking, 90; on toleration, 94; his life and writings, 177-181; his interview with Laud, 177-178; his peculiarities, 179; his theology illustrated, 179-181

Shepard, Thomas, of Charlestown, elegy on, by Urian Oakes, 270-272, 402

Sherman, John, 233 note, 269 note, 532

Shippen, Joseph, 257; his verses, 469

Shirley, James, 243

Sibley, John Langdon, his Harvard Graduates, cited, in notes, 164, 322; his edition of Father Abbey's Will, cited, 299 note

Sidney, Algernon, 117

Sidney, Sir Philip, 18, 77

Smith, Goldwin, on the colony of Pennsylvania, 456

Smith, Captain John, 3, 48, 72 note, 158; his character, 17-19; the first American writer, 17; as a story-teller, 17, 33; his services in colonizing both Virginia and New England, 18; a prolific author, 19; his True Relation, 19-24; his tour up the Chickahominy, 21; his story of Pocahontas, 21, 23; his interviews with Powhatan, 22-23; circumstances under which the book was written, and its style, 23-24; his letter to his London patrons, 25-27; his Map of Virginia, 27-31; vivid pictures of the country, climate, and productions, 27-28; of the Indians, 29-30; of his companions, 30; of Powhatan, 30; of the Susquehannocks, 30; his return to London, and voyage to New England, 31-32; subsequent career, 32; Thomas Fuller's estimate of him, 32; his defenders and eulogists, 33; final estimate, 33-34; his historical veracity attested by William Stith, 504, 505

Smith, Samuel, 256; his History of New Jersey, 456

Smith, William, of New York, 256, 528; on neglect of education in New York, 446; his History of New York, cited, in notes, 443; his life and writings, 455-456

Smith, William, of Pennsylvania, 256; his life, 463; his General Idea of the College of Mirania, 463-464; as an educator, 464; his Discourses, 464

548

Index

note; edits American Magazine, 528
South Carolina, order of its colonization, 6; described by John Lawson, 507-508; its part in colonial literature, 513-515
Sparks, Jared, his edition of Franklin's Works, cited, in notes, 462, 479, 523, 537
Spence, Joseph, cited, 51 note
Spofford, Ainsworth R., his American Almanac, cited, 364 note
Sprague, William B., his Annals of the American Pulpit, cited, in notes, 172, 190, 192, 231, 317, 322, 407, 412, 427, 428, 449; his edition of Davies's Sermons, cited, in notes, 471, 473
Standish, Captain Miles, 127-128
Stedman, Edmund Clarence, cited, 228 note
Stiles, Ezra, 360; his orations in Latin and in Hebrew, 530
Stith, William, 256, 497 note; his life, 504-505; his History of Virginia, 504-506; on James the First, 506
Stoddard, Solomon, 256; his life, 407; his Answer to Some Cases of Conscience, 407-408
Stone, Samuel, his scholarship, 86; threnody on, 231
Stoughton, William, 256; his life, 400-401; his Narration of the Proceedings of Andros, 401; his New England's True Interest, not to Lie, 401-402
Strachey, William, 3, 46, 48; his voyage to Virginia, 37-38; his True Reportory, 38-40; his description of a storm at sea, 39-40
Straus, Oscar S., his Roger Williams the Pioneer of Religious Liberty, 226 note
Sylvester, Joshua, 243

Tailfer, Patrick, 256; his Historical Narrative of Georgia, 515-520
Taine, H. A., on Paradise Lost, 229; on the Fantastic writers, 244 note
Taylor, Jacob, 257; his life and writings, 464
Thacher, James, his American Medical Biography, cited, 392 note
Theological and Religious Writers, 3, 161-195, 256, 397-436, 448-449, 463-464, 470-473, 488-491
Thomas, Gabriel, 256; his Account of Pennsylvania, and of West New Jersey, 458-460
Thomas, Isaiah, his History of Printing in America, cited, in notes, 78, 97, 98, 237, 363, 526, 528
Thomson, James, 309, 366
Ticknor, George, 231 note, 308 note
Tilden's Miscellaneous Poems, 304-306
Tompson, Benjamin, 257, 328 note; his life, 274; his New England's Crisis, 274-276; his New England's Tears for her Present Miseries, 275 note; his minor poems, 276
Trumbull, J. Hammond, his edition of Roger Williams's Key, in notes, 211, 213
Tuckerman, Professor Edward, 159, 160 note, 534 note
Tudor, William, his Life of James Otis, cited, 428 note
Turell, Ebenezer, 256, 297 note; his Life of Benjamin Colman, 375; his Life of Jane Turell, 375 note
Turell, Jane, 257, 297; as a verse-writer, 375 note
Tyson, Job R., 457 note

Underhill, Captain John, 129, 130 note

Vane, Sir Henry, the younger, 123, 209
Veazie, William, edition of New England's Rarities, 157 note
Verse-Writers, 3, 45-51, 228-253, 257, 259-314, 450-453, 464-469, 473-479, 483-488
Vincent, Philip, 130
Virginia, the first of the American colonies, 5, 6, 16, 81-82; described by John Pory, 44-45; defended by John Hammond, 53-57; rebellion in, 61-67; its literary barrenness, and the causes, 70-80; contrasted with New England, 72-75; its dispersed social organization, 74-76; neglect of education, 76-78; religious intolerance, 78-79; its part in later colonial literature, 488-506
Virginians, character of early, 17, 55, 71-80, 498-499

Waller, Edmund, 243 note
Walker, Francis A., on the population of early New England, 82 note

549

Index

Walton, Izaak, 148

Ward, Nathaniel, 3, 184 note; his scholarship, 86; on toleration, 94; on long sermons, 164; his life, 196-198; his Simple Cobbler of Agawam, 198-208; on Prince Rupert, 198; mental traits of Ward, 200; satire on fashionable women, 203-204; his discussion of the troubles in England, 205-206

Washington, George, on early religious intolerance in Virginia, 79 note; prophetic allusions to, by Samuel Davies, 470

Waterland, Daniel, edits and commends Sermons of James Blair, 490

Watson, John F., his Annals of Philadelphia, cited, in notes, 462, 466

Watts, Isaac, 297, 451

Webb, George, 257; his career, 466; his Bachelors' Hall, 466-468

Webbe, John, 257; his Discourse on Paper-Money, 469

Webster, John, 243

Welde, Thomas, his part in the Bay Psalm Book, 237

Westcott, Thompson, his History of Philadelphia, cited, 468 note

Wharton, Thomas I., his Provincial Literature of Pennsylvania, cited, in notes, 458

Whitaker, Alexander, 3, 48, 70; his life and character, 41; his Good News from Virginia, 42-43

White, Father Andrew, his Relatio Itineris in Marylandum, 53

Whittier, John Greenleaf, 156; his Prophecy of Samuel Sewall, 346, 348

Whitwell, William, on John Barnard, 412

Wigglesworth, Michael, 257, 288; his life and character, 276-278; as a poet, 278; his God's Controversy with New England, 278-280; his Meat out of the Eater, 280; his Day of Doom, 280-288

Wigglesworth, Samuel, 257; his life, 288; his elegy on Nathaniel Clarke, 288-291

Willard, Samuel, 256; his life, 405; his Body of Divinity, 405-407

William and Mary College, founded, 77, 488, 529; Commencement at in 1700, 489; its poverty lamented by Hugh Jones, 496

Williams, John, 256; his Redeemed Captive, 380-381; as a student of science, 533

Williams, Roger, 3, 111; his scholarship, 86; his reference to Morton's Memorial, 111 note; on John Cotton, 184; his life and character, 208-212; his writings, 213-216; his Key, 213-214; his answer to John Cotton, 215-216; his book against a national church, 216-217; his Bloody Tenet of Persecution, 218-219; Cotton's reply and Williams's rejoinder, 219-222; his book against George Fox, 223; his letters, 223-226; his celebrated letter to the people of Providence on the limits of personal liberty, 225-226; his Christenings Make Not Christians, 226 note

Williamson, H., his History of North Carolina, cited, 63 note

Wilson, John, 162, 163; as a versifier, 233

Winslow, Edward, 3, 110, 111; his Journal, 138-142; his letter appended thereto, 141-142; his Good News from New England, 142-144; on Roger Williams, 209

Winsor, Justin, 160 note, 312 note; his Catalogue of the Prince Library, 186 note, 385 note

Winthrop, Fitz John, 276 note; as a student of science, 533

Winthrop, John, of Connecticut, 89, 111 note, 209, 224, 276 note, 297; his learning, 86; story concerning his Prayer-Book, 89-90; as a student of science, 533

Winthrop, John, of Harvard College, 257, 537; his life and character, 535-536; his eminence in science, 536-537

Winthrop, John, of Massachusetts, 3, 123, 156, 163, 209, 533; in notes, 89, 90, 93, 332; his learning, 86; his life and writings, 112-118; his Model of Christian Charity, 112-113; his History of New England, 113-118; his famous speech on human liberty, 117-118; Hubbard's indebtedness to, 377

Winthrop, Robert C., 276 note, 298 note; his Life and Letters of John Winthrop, cited, 117 note

Wise, John, 257; his life and character, 349-350; his Churches' Quarrel

550

Index

Espoused, 350-360; his Vindication, 355-358; his style, 358-360, 376 note

Wither, George, 33, 243, 292

Wolcott, Roger, 257; his life and character, 297; his Connecticut epic, 297; his Poetical Meditations, 298-299

Wood, William, 3, 532; his New England's Prospect, 147-156; his powers of description illustrated, 150-151; playful sketches of the Indians, 153-155

Wynne, Thomas H., his edition of Byrd Manuscripts, 498 note

Yale College, founded, 529; early requirements for admission to, 529

Yeardly, Sir George, 43, 44

Young, Alexander, his Chronicles, cited, in notes, 89, 90, 91, 95, 138, 139, 140, 141, 142, 143, 144, 145, 146, 147, 177, 178, 316, 317, 377

Young, Edward, 309